SEQUELS

*An Annotated Guide to
Novels in Series*

2nd edition

SEQUELS

An Annotated Guide to Novels in Series

2nd edition

JANET HUSBAND
and
JONATHAN F. HUSBAND

CHICAGO AND LONDON
American Library Association
1990

Designed by Harvey Retzloff
Composed by Ampersand Publisher Services
in Caledonia on a Digitek typesetting system

Printed on 50-pound Glatfelter,
a pH-neutral stock, and bound
in B-grade Holliston linen cloth
by Edwards Brothers, Inc.

The paper used in this publication meets the minimum requirements
of American National Standard for Information Sciences—
Permanence of Paper for Printed Library Materials,
ANSI Z39.48-1984. ∞

Library of Congress Cataloging-in-Publication Data

Husband, Janet, 1942–
　　Sequels, an annotated guide to novels in series / by Janet Husband
and Jonathan F. Husband. — 2nd ed.
　　　　p.　cm.
　　ISBN 0-8389-0533-1 (alk. paper)
　　　　1. Fiction—Bibliography.　2. Sequel (Literature)—Bibliography.
I. Husband, Jonathan F.　II. Title.
Z5917.S44H87　1990
[PN3448.S47]
016.80883—dc20　　　　　　　　　　　　　　　　　　　　　　　　90-180

Printed in the United States of America.

94　93 92 91 90　　5 4 3 2 1

Contents

Preface

The warm reception given the first edition of *Sequels*, and a continuing demand to update and expand it, made *Sequels II* an inevitability.

This second edition includes new series created since 1982, and expands coverage of genre fiction, especially detective series. Titles in continuing series have been updated through 1989. We have retained all of the series from the first edition, except two paperback series (by Peter Danielson and Douglas Elliot), which seemed not to have stood the test of time.

In its basic format and philosophy, this second edition remains unchanged from the first edition. It lists series which might be found in a medium-sized public library collection. No claims of comprehensiveness are made.

This edition has been a joint effort with my husband Jonathan. Like most librarian couples, we enjoy sharing our profession and collaboration in bibliography has been mutually enriching.

As director of the Rockland Memorial Library, a small public library, access to materials has narrowed. Jonathan's position as head of reader services at the Framingham State College library, gave him access to the holdings of the 22 public libraries in the Minuteman Library Network for which we are grateful.

In selecting titles for inclusion, we have used the following criteria for defining a series:

1. Primarily, a series shows development of plot or character from book to book. Most works listed here fit this requirement; even some of the mysteries—e.g., Sayers's Lord Peter books—have a chronology.
2. Books that share a cast of characters or location, where chronology is minimal or debatable. Guareschi's Don Camillo books fit this de-

scription, as do Gallico's Mrs. 'Arris books, and many mystery series.

3. Books that were conceived as a series by the author, such as Durrell's Alexandria Quartet and Mishima's Sea of Tranquility.

Only novels in series are listed. Nonfiction is excluded. Tempting though it was to list James Herriot's best-sellers about the Yorkshire veterinarian, they are always classed as nonfiction. Short stories are also excluded except in instances for clarity and completion of other works. For example, G. K. Chesterton's Father Brown mysteries, which are all short stories collected into book form, are not listed. But see the entry under Raymond Chandler for inclusion of a volume of short stories featuring Philip Marlowe, the hero of Chandler's novel series.

This bibliography does not include children's books except for a few borderline cases: Louisa May Alcott and L. M. Montgomery, read by adults primarily for their nostalgia value, are included.

This list does include some books only published in paperback or only available in this country in large-print editions. It also includes many out-of-print titles.

In considering the question of literary merit, we sought to balance considerations of artistic quality with those of popularity. Hence, when in doubt about the inclusion of a work, we tried to gauge its general availability in medium-sized public library collections. This criterion has eliminated many obscure and esoteric works, as well as some series generally considered too ephemeral for library collections.

These guidelines still leave a great deal of latitude for the compiler of such a work. The decision to include one author and not another was in the end a pragmatic one, based on the likelihood of which author is more likely to be read.

Editions listed are the first American hardcover edition unless otherwise noted. For works in many different editions, we have listed what seemed the best current edition. Except where indicated, the numbering represents the *preferred order for reading.* Thus, dates of first publication will not necessarily correspond to the numbered order. In some cases, especially with mystery series where reading sequence is unimportant, numbering follows the order of publication.

We would like to thank the interlibrary loan staff at Framingham State College, Ronnie Klein and Madelyn Good, for their work in tracking down elusive titles. We also thank our colleagues near and far who took the time to write to suggest an author or a series for inclusion.

JANET HUSBAND

ANNOTATED
SERIES

Adams, Douglas

I. The Hitchhiker series is a blend of science fiction and contemporary zaniness that fans of Monty Python will love. In fact, Adams has written scripts, for two BBC television imports—"Monty Python" and "Dr. Who"—and his Hitchhiker novels began as a BBC radio, then TV, series. The hero of his episodic space adventure is a 30-year-old Englishman, Arthur Dent. When the earth is destroyed to make room for an intergalactic highway, Arthur is saved by his friend Ford Prefect, who is really an alien traveling through the universe as a researcher for the compendious *Hitchhiker's Guide to the Galaxy* (a hip electronic intergalactic Baedeker). *The Hitchhiker's Trilogy* (Harmony, 1984) is an omnibus containing the first three volumes of the series.

1. *The Hitchhiker's Guide to the Galaxy* (Harmony, 1980)
   Arthur and his odd friend Ford Prefect begin their journey as stowaways on a Vogon spaceship and soon meet up with Zaphod Beeblebrox and his girlfriend Trillian.
2. *The Restaurant at the End of the Universe* (Harmony, 1981)
   In search of the ultimate question, Arthur and Ford visit the restaurant at the end of time where each evening's entertainment features the destruction of the universe.
3. *Life, the Universe and Everything* (Harmony, 1982)
   Arthur and Ford fight to keep the evil rulers of the planet Krikkit from destroying the universe.
4. *So Long, and Thanks for All the Fish* (Crown, 1984)
   After eight years of space travel, Arthur returns to a dolphinless earth and the girl he left behind.

II. Adams's new series stars Dirk Gently, a "holistic" private eye, brilliant but rather seedy, who uses his psychic powers to find lost cats, or to save the human race. Like the "Hitchhiker" series, the "holistic" detective series is a blend of science fiction, humor, and action, entertainingly presenting some mind-boggling ideas.

1. *Dirk Gently's Holistic Detective Agency* (Simon & Schuster, 1987)
   Samuel Taylor Coleridge, King George III, an Electric Monk, a

3

four-billion-year-old ghost, a computer programmer, an absent-minded Cambridge Professor of Chronology, and a horse in the bathroom are somehow all part of the solution to Dirk Gently's case.

2. *The Long Dark Tea-Time of the Soul* (Simon & Schuster, 1989)
The explosion of a check-in desk at Heathrow Airport and a severed head on a stereo turntable lead to Dirk's encounter with some Norse Gods (still alive and living in London).

Aird, Catherine (pseud. of Kinn McIntosh)

Detective Inspector C. D. Sloan, head of the small criminal investigation department in the town of Berebury, West Calleshire, belongs to the growing fictional fraternity of local Criminal Investigation Department (CID) men who patrol England's smaller towns (see also Rendell's Wexford and Thomson's Rudd). Sloan is competent, mild mannered, and likable. He suffers the callow youth of his assistant, Constable Crosby, and the superfluous advice of Superintendent Leeyes with admirable tolerance and humor. Sloan is happily married and his hobby is his rose garden.

1. *The Religious Body* (Doubleday, 1966)
A nun is murdered in a convent, and an effigy burnt on Guy Fawkes Day at a neighboring school is wearing her glasses.
2. *Henrietta Who?* (Doubleday, 1968)
Henrietta Jenkins comes home from the university to identify the dead body of her mother, but Inspector Sloan must identify Henrietta.
3. *The Stately Home Murder* (Doubleday, 1970)
A dead body is discovered inside a suit of armor at Ornum House. English title: *The Complete Steel.*
4. *A Late Phoenix* (Doubleday, 1971)
Workmen find a corpse buried in the wreckage of a war-bombed house, and Sloan must investigate a murder three decades old.
5. *His Burial Too* (Doubleday, 1973)
A dead body is discovered amidst the rubble of a fallen marble statue inside a church tower.
6. *Slight Mourning* (Doubleday, 1976)
Could one of the eight guests at a dinner party have slipped the host, Bill Fent, a lethal dose of barbiturates?

4

7. *Parting Breath* (Doubleday, 1978)
   A murdered student brings Sloan to a university troubled by plotting student activists.
8. *Some Die Eloquent* (Doubleday, 1980)
   Miss Wansdyke's death, apparently of natural causes, begins to look suspicious when Sloan discovers her little dog missing.
9. *Passing Strange* (Doubleday, 1981)
   Nurse Joyce Cooper is found strangled to death behind her fortune-telling tent at the annual Almstone Horticultural Fair.
10. *Last Respects* (Doubleday, 1982)
    Local fisherman Horace Boller finds a dead man in the river and suspicions run to murder.
11. *A Dead Liberty* (Doubleday, 1987)
    Lucy Durmast is accused of serving some deadly chili, but she refuses to speak a word in her own defense.

Note: *A Most Contagious Crime* (Doubleday, 1967) is not one of the series.

Alcott, Louisa May

I. Alcott's Victorian period pieces, sticky with sentiment and old-fashioned virtues, still appeal to many young readers today. Their direct, easy-to-read prose and the timelessness of childhood interests may account for their enduring charm. Adults who read them for their nostalgia value will find that certain scenes still bring a tear to the eye. The characters of *Little Women* were drawn from Alcott's family—she had three sisters. Jo is thought to be the autobiographical figure.

1. *Little Women; or Meg, Jo, Beth and Amy* (Roberts, 1868)
   This book introduces the March girls and their mother, Marmee. The Civil War keeps Mr. March from his family until the end of the book. Note: *Good Wives*, also called *Little Women Married*, was published separately in 1869 but is now incorporated as the second half of *Little Women* in almost all editions.
2. *Little Men; Life at Plumfield with Jo's Boys* (Roberts, 1871)
   A grown-up Jo and her husband, Professor Bhaer, run a boarding school called Plumfield.

3. *Jo's Boys, and How They Turned Out* (Roberts, 1886)
   The children of Plumfield have grown up to face life's trials.

II. Alcott fans won't want to miss these two books about a lonely young girl surrounded by her boy cousins, and her handsome guardian who has unusual views about child rearing.

1. *Eight Cousins* (Roberts, 1874)
   Thirteen-year-old Rose Campbell, an orphan, comes to live with her Uncle Alec; her seven lively cousins live nearby.
2. *Rose in Bloom* (Roberts, 1876)
   Continues the story of Rose, her cousins, and friend Phoebe, now grown up.

Aldiss, Brian

Helliconia is a distant planet where each season lasts for hundreds of years. It is inhabited by humans, various humanoid species, and some malevolent horned furry creatures called phagors. Each book in the trilogy weaves the lives of many characters and multiple viewpoints into a dense fabric. Aldiss is a prolific British writer of sophisticated and thoughtful science fiction. The verbal inventiveness and broad scope evident in the Helliconia trilogy are characteristic of his work.

1. *Helliconia Spring* (Atheneum, 1982)
   The series begins with the story of the young hunter Yuli who loses his father and must find shelter or die.
2. *Helliconia Summer* (Atheneum, 1983)
   War rages between humans and phagors while the King of Borlien seeks a new queen.
3. *Helliconia Winter* (Atheneum, 1985)
   As winter's long night draws closer, the phagors' ultimate triumph seems inevitable.

Aldrich, Bess Streeter

A Lantern in Her Hand is an unpretentious story of pioneer life in Nebraska after the Civil War. It is narrated by Abbie Deal, who leaves her log cabin home in Iowa in 1868 with her young husband and baby. The hardships and trials of making a home in unsettled territory and raising a family toughen Abbie into a strong pioneer woman. Aldrich's hymn to womanly self-sacrifice grows a bit less palatable in the sequel.

1. *A Lantern in Her Hand* (Appleton, 1928)
   Will and Abbie Deal set out for Nebraska in 1868 and brave frontier hardships to build a home for their growing family.
2. *A White Bird Flying* (Appleton, 1931)
   Abbie's granddaughter, young Laura Deal, is torn between her hopes for a literary career and her love for Allen Rinemiller.

Allen, Hervey

In addition to his most famous work, the best-seller *Anthony Adverse*, Allen wrote this series of colonial novels, The Disinherited, about Salathiel Albine, who was raised by Indians in New York State and then returned to white society. Though the series was never completed, the omnibus volume, *The City in the Dawn* (Rinehart, 1950), contains a-bridgments of the first three books plus sections of the fourth.

1. *The Fort and the Forest* (Rinehart, 1943)
   After being raised as an Indian chieftain's son, Albine returns to white society at Fort Pitt.
2. *Bedford Village* (Rinehart, 1944)
   Young Albine helps refugees from the Indian wars and falls in love.
3. *Toward the Morning* (Rinehart, 1948)
   Albine travels to Philadelphia.

Allingham, Margery

Allingham, who came from a family of writers, took naturally to the pen and produced her first Albert Campion detective novel at the age of twenty-three. In that book, *The Black Dudley Murder*, Campion appears as an upper-class buffoon—a silly, pale, bucktoothed fellow, obviously royalty in disguise—who has insinuated himself into a weekend house party for reasons of his own. In later novels, Allingham replaced Campion's foolishness with a avuncular appeal. Magersfontein Lugg, the reformed Cockney burglar who serves Campion as valet and brave assistant, is introduced in the second book, *Mystery Mile*. And a romantic interest is added with the introduction of the red-haired Lady Amanda Fitton in *Kingdom of Death*. Nevertheless Allingham seems to have grown weary of Campion, since she gave him only small roles in some of her later books and completely omitted him from her 1940 mystery novel *Black Plumes*. There have been two omnibus editions of Campion stories. *Crime and Mr. Campion* (Doubleday, 1959) contains numbers 6, 7, and 9 listed below. *Three Cases for Mr. Campion* (Doubleday, 1961) contains numbers 3, 10, and 11.

1. *The Black Dudley Murder* (Doubleday, 1930)
   Campion, a rather fatuous and effete young man, emerges as a natural leader when sinister forces imprison the weekend guests following a murder at the Black Dudley mansion. English title: *The Crime at Black Dudley*.
2. *Mystery Mile* (Doubleday, 1930)
   Campion must protect an American judge from a master criminal and his gang.
3. *The Gyrth Chalice Mystery* (Doubleday, 1931)
   Concerns robbery in the quiet Suffolk village of Sanctuary. English title: *Look to the Lady*.
4. *Police at the Funeral* (Doubleday, 1932)
   Campion is hired by strong-willed Great Aunt Caroline Faraday to discover who killed Uncle Andrew and to protect the family.
5. *Kingdom of Death* (Doubleday, 1933)
   Introduces Lady Amanda Fitton, an awkward adolescent in danger of losing her royal inheritance to a master criminal. English title: *Sweet Danger*; variant title: *The Fear Sign*.
6. *Death of a Ghost* (Doubleday, 1934)
   Murder occurs at a posthumous unveiling of the work of a famous British painter.
7. *Flowers for the Judge* (Doubleday, 1936)
   The murder of a publisher occupies Campion. Variant title: *Legacy in Blood*.
8. *Mr. Campion, Criminologist* (Doubleday, 1937)
   Contains seven short stories and the novelette "The Case of the Late Pig," which was published separately in England and concerns the strange death of an old schoolfellow of Campion's. English title: *Mr. Campion and Others*.

9. *Dancers in Mourning* (Doubleday, 1937)
   A musical-theater background is the setting for this mystery in which Campion loses his heart. Variant title: *Who Killed Chloe?*
10. *The Fashion in Shrouds* (Doubleday, 1938)
    Amanda Fitton reappears in this strange case, in which sixty cages of canaries are stolen. Set in the world of *haute couture.*
11. *Traitor's Purse* (Doubleday, 1941)
    Campion has amnesia, and Amanda seems to be drifting away. More adventure than mystery. Variant title: *The Sabotage Murder Mystery.*
12. *Pearls before Swine* (Doubleday, 1945)
    Albert, newly married, is in no mood to investigate a murder, but Lady Carados and the faithful Lugg conspire to involve him. English title: *Coroner's Pidgin.*
13. *The Case Book of Mr. Campion* (American Mercury, 1947)
    Short stories.
14. *More Work for the Undertaker* (Doubleday, 1949)
    Campion aids Scotland Yard's inquiry into the death of two members of the eccentric Palinode family.
15. *The Tiger in the Smoke* (Doubleday, 1952)
    "The Tiger," evil Jack Havoc, follows the trial of some hidden treasure through "the Smoke" of London.
16. *The Estate of the Beckoning Lady* (Doubleday, 1955)
    Concerns the murder of an income tax collector. English title: *The Beckoning Lady.*
17. *Tether's End* (Doubleday, 1958)
    Campion plays only a small role in this novel about how events conspire to defeat a murderer's plans. English title: *Hide My Eyes;* variant title: *Ten Were Missing.*
18. *The China Governess* (Doubleday, 1962)
    This case revolves around a statuette of a governess charged with murder many years earlier.
19. *The Mind Readers* (Morrow, 1965)
    Campion gets involved in a strange case complicated by a research team that has perfected a workable ESP method.
20. *Cargo of Eagles* (Morrow, 1968)
    This book was completed by Philip Youngman Carter, Margery Allingham's husband, after her death. It concerns poison-pen letters, a pretty woman doctor, and a hunt for buried treasure.
21. *Mr. Campion's Farthing* (Morrow, 1969)
    Written by Philip Youngman Carter, this book shows Campion following the trial of a missing Russian scientist to a monastery in the English countryside.

22. *Mr. Campion's Quarry* (Morrow, 1971)
    Murder, double agents, and an archaeological dig occupy Campion in his second case by Philip Youngman Carter. English title: *Mr. Campion's Falcon.*

Anderson, John R. L.

Peter Blair, the star of this international espionage series, was educated at Sandhurst, reached the rank of major in the army, and moved easily into commerce. Then, at mid-life, after dropping out of a successful career (and first marriage), Peter accidentally becomes the target of a murderous conspiracy, and finds his true vocation as an agent of the British Home Office Liaison Group. It is no accident that Peter almost always finds himself on board a boat of some kind—author Anderson is himself an avid sailor.

1. *Death on the Rocks* (Stein & Day, 1975)
   A pleasant day out in his sailboat is interrrupted when Peter finds a dead woman on some rocks off shore.
2. *Death in the Thames* (Stein & Day, 1975)
   Peter turns up poisoned darts in this tale of industrial espionage.
3. *Death in the North Sea* (Stein & Day, 1976)
   Now Colonel Blair, Peter's assignment takes him aboard some highly explosive cargo ships in the North Sea.
4. *Death in the Desert* (Stein & Day, 1977)
   Colonel Blair flies to Africa to investigate the deaths of an American geologist and two mining company workers.
5. *Death in the City* (Scribner, 1982)
   This search for a missing shipping magnate leads Peter into the murky waters of international finance. First published in 1977.
6. *Death in the Caribbean* (Stein & Day, 1977)
   Peter braves the dangers of a Caribbean dictatorship.
7. *Death in the Greenhouse* (Scribner, 1983)
   A quiet village is disturbed when a retired English horticulturalist is murdered.
8. *Death in a High Latitude* (Scribner, 1984)
   When a seventeenth-century map is stolen from a Cambridge museum, Peter and his new wife follow the trail north to the Arctic.

Andrews, V. C.

I. Current interest in the subject of child abuse and neglect is no doubt responsible for these nasty and sensationalized popular fictions. Andrews updates the Hansel and Gretel theme with incest and a dollop of Stephen-King–sinister in this series about the four Dollanganger children. Read instead a moving true story. Torey Hayden's *One Child* (Putnam, 1980), or Eleanor Craig's *One, Two, Three . . . The Story of Matt* (McGraw-Hill, 1978).

1. *Garden of Shadows* (Poseidon, 1987)
   Though published last, this novel relates the earliest events, beginning with the wedding of Malcolm and Olivia Foxworth, when all the troubles started.
2. *Flowers in the Attic* (Simon & Schuster, 1980)
   A miserly and sex-phobic old grandmother keeps her four grandchildren locked up in the attic.
3. *Petals on the Wind* (Simon & Schuster, 1981)
   Follows Chris, Cathy, and Carrie as they escape and grow up.
4. *If There Be Thorns* (Simon & Schuster, 1981)
   Young Bart, Cathy's son, drifts from his happy home to mysterious next-door neighbors, a shrouded old woman and her strange butler.
5. *Seeds of Yesterday* (Poseidon, 1984)
   In the concluding volume, Young Bart brings his tormented family together for a reunion at Foxworth Hall.

II. Before she died in 1986 Andrews wrote a trilogy about another family of abused children: the Casteels, a poor West Virginia hillbilly family. Heaven Leigh, the principal character, is ten years old when the trilogy starts. She goes through the whole gamut of bad experiences Andrews children must endure before finding married happiness at the end.

1. *Heaven* (Poseidon, 1985)
   The Casteel family is broken up when their shiftless father sells the children to different families.
2. *Dark Angel* (Poseidon, 1986)
   Heaven moves to Boston to live with her wealthy grandmother.
3. *Fallen Hearts* (Poseidon, 1988)
   Now a teacher and engaged to Logan, Heaven hopes to shake the traumas of her past life.

Andrić, Ivo

After he won the Nobel Prize in 1961, Andrić's work became more accessible in this country. The Yugoslavia described in both his historical and his contemporary fiction is a land of contrasts: austere mountains and bustling blue coast; an ethnicly and religously diverse population composed of Orthodox Catholics, Roman Catholics, Jews, and Moslems. These three volumes, called the Bosnian Trilogy, are a good introduction to Andrić.

1. *The Bridge on the Drina* (Macmillan, 1959)
   By documenting the effect of a bridge—telling of the people and goods that cross it and of the towns that grow up around it—Andrić recaps three and a half centuries of Yugoslavian history. Translated from the Serbo-Croatian by Lovett Edwards. First published in 1945.
2. *Bosnian Chronicle* (Knopf, 1963)
   Concentrates on the seven years before the fall of Napoleon and on the person of Daville, Napoleon's consul. Translated from the Serbo-Croatian by Joseph Hitrec. First published in 1945.
3. *The Woman from Sarajevo* (Knopf, 1965)
   The sad story of Miss Raika, a miser, takes place in the Sarajevo locale of the assassination that triggered World War I. Translated from the Serbo-Croatian by Joseph Hitrec. First published in 1945.

Angoff, Charles

These eleven volumes are a chronicle of the Jewish experience in America. The narrator, David Polonsky, is also the chief protagonist, but the cast of supporting characters is large and drawn with loving detail. In the first volume, David tells of his parents and grandparents and of their emigration to the United States to escape czarist oppression. In later volumes, his own life takes the forefront.

1. *Journey to the Dawn* (Beechhurst, 1951)
   David Polonsky recalls his childhood and his family's flight from Russia.
2. *In the Morning Light* (Beechhurst, 1952)
   David spends his school years in Boston.

3. *The Sun at Noon* (Beechhurst, 1955)
   In 1919, David goes to Harvard.
4. *Between Day and Dark* (Yoseloff, 1959)
   After graduation, David toils on a suburban weekly, then gets his big break.
5. *The Bitter Spring* (Yoseloff, 1961)
   David enters the literary life in New York City in 1928.
6. *Summer Storm* (Yoseloff, 1963)
   David endures the years 1933–35, the low point of the Great Depression.
7. *Memory of Autumn* (Yoseloff, 1968)
   By the early 1940s, David is editor of the liberal Globe magazine in New York City.
8. *Winter Twilight* (Yoseloff, 1969)
   This volume covers the years 1945–47, ending with a celebration on the eve of the establishment of Israel.
9. *Season of Mists* (Yoseloff, 1971)
   David's relationship with Helen and his mother's illness are the central issues in this volume set in the early fifties.
10. *Mid-Century* (Barnes, 1973)
    The political turmoil of the early fifties impinges on David.
11. *Toward the Horizon* (Barnes, 1978)
    Contemporary academic life is featured in this volume.

Anthony, Evelyn (pseud. of Evelyn Stephens Ward-Thomas)

This prolific British author began by writing historical fiction and period romances, but has found her greatest popular success writing contemporary thrillers with a strong romantic element. One of these, *The Tamarind Seed* (Coward, 1971), was made into a film starring Julie Andrews and Omar Sharif. Four of her thrillers feature agent Davina Graham, who is young and rather plain when first met, though already known as a brilliant investigator and "tough as nails."

1. *The Defector* (Coward, 1981)
   Davina is assigned to debrief a Russian defector, Ivan Sasanov, but finds herself falling in love.

2. *The Avenue of the Dead* (Coward, 1982)
   Widowed Davina comes out of retirement to take on a case of special personal significance.
3. *Albatross* (Putnam, 1983)
   A job in advertising is a cover for Davina's unauthorized investigation of a Russian counter-spy whose code name is "*Albatross.*"
4. *Company of Saints* (Putnam, 1984)
   Davina, now chief of the agency, and her lover are on vacation in Venice when the U.S. Secretary of Defense is killed.

Archer, Jeffrey

Archer served as a Conservative member of the British Parliament from 1969–74. He also owns an art gallery and has been a commercially successful author since the publication of his first novel in 1976. That book, the thriller *Not a Penny More, Not a Penny Less*, is supposedly based on Archer's own nasty experience with a con man. The two novels below are undemanding family/business sagas set in America. Both achieved best-seller status.

1. *Kane and Abel* (Simon & Schuster, 1980)
   Tells of the rise to fame and fortune of two men born on the same day in 1906—Bostonian William Kane and Polish-born Abel Rosnovski—and of the rivalry that develops between them.
2. *The Prodigal Daughter* (Simon & Schuster, 1982)
   The family saga continues as the focus shifts to the trials and successes of Florentyna, the only daughter of Abel Rosnovski.

Argo, Ellen (pseud. of Ellen Argo Johnson)

Julia Howard is the strong central figure of this trilogy set on Cape Cod from 1827 to 1860. Born at sea aboard one of her father's ships, young Julia acquires a love of the sea and knowledge of shipbuilding at an early age. Not content to stay at home and run the shipyard, she eventually sees her share of adventure.

1. *Jewel of the Seas* (Putnam, 1977)
   Julia, a happy child who putters about her father's shipyard, grows

14

into a beautiful and headstrong young woman determined to go to sea.

2. *The Crystal Star* (Putnam, 1979)
   Julia accompanies her husband Stephen Logan on the ship she helped to build, and shares in the dangers and pleasures of a South Seas voyage.

3. *The Yankee Girl* (Putnam, 1980)
   Julia's story continues through rough weather: personal storms, losses, and triumphs.

Arlen, Leslie (pseud. of Christopher Nicole)

The Borodins is a series of smoldering paperback romances set in Russia. General Borodin, a liberal-minded aristocrat who has given his daughters a dangerous taste for freedom, is killed as the Japanese take Port Arthur in 1904. His daughers, Ilona and Tatania, and son, Peter, wend their passionate way through the Russian Revolution and beyond. George Hayman, a handsome American war correspondent, comes under Ilona's spell, as does her young servant, Michael Ivanovich. Peter falls in love with a young Jewish girl. While battle scenes and guest appearances by the likes of Rasputin give the narrative some historical framework, this is basically escapist fantasy.

1. *Love and Honor* (Jove, 1980)
   Beautiful young Princess Ilona Borodin is awakened to love when she meets American George Hayman, but she is betrothed to the cold Prince Roditchev.

2. *War and Passion* (Jove, 1981)
   The Revolution sweeps through Russia, touching all the Borodins, especially Peter, the last Borodin prince, and his friend Judith.

3. *Fate and Dreams* (Jove, 1981)
   Tattie, now the famous star of a Russian dance troup, disappears while on tour in London.

4. *Hope and Glory* (Jove, 1982)
   Young American John Hayman and ballerina Natasha Brusilow fight the Nazi invaders of Russia in World War II.

5. *Rage and Desire* (Jove, 1982)
   Soviet intelligence agent Grigori is sent to the United States to steal the secret of the atomic bomb.

6. *Fortune and Fury* (Jove, 1984)
   The series conclusion is set in 1952 at the peak of the Cold War

years. Nothing will deter Prince Peter Borodin's determination to destroy Stalin.

Asimov, Isaac

I. The Foundation books have long been regarded as Asimov's best contribution to science fiction. The work was conceived by Asimov as the science fiction equivalent of Gibbon's *Decline and Fall of the Roman Empire*. The first stories began appearing in *Astounding Science Fiction* in 1942 and continued regularly. In the early 1950s they were published as three novels (numbers 2, 3, and 4 below) and became known as the Foundation trilogy. A three-volume omnibus edition was published by Doubleday in 1964.

The connecting thread in the series is Hari Seldon's invention of the science of "psychohistory" which enables the founders of the First and Second Foundations to predict and manipulate the future.

Asimov lost interest in the series but, after a hiatus of thirty years, was persuaded to return to it in 1982 because his publisher, Doubleday, "got tired of waiting and offered me five-figure (and then six-figure) advances to write more" (personal communication).

The new Foundation volumes have been best-sellers and have won Asimov a new generation of fans. In his recent work, Asimov has created connecting links which tie together his science fiction output in one large Galactic Empire scheme. The later volumes of the Robot series (see Section II) are linked to the Foundation novels. There are also three novels published by Doubleday in the 1950s which are set in the same universe, when the Empire was at its height (*Pebble in the Sky*, 1950; *The Stars Like Dust*, 1951; *The Currents of Space*, 1952).

1. *Prelude to Foundation* (Doubleday, 1988)
   This prequel relates the adventures of Hari Seldon, inventor of "psychohistory" and the Seldon Plan, during the reign of Galactic Emperor Cleon.
2. *Foundation* (Gnome, 1951)
   The First Foundation of physical scientists is set up on Terminus, a planet on the outer fringes of a decaying Galactic Empire. (Abridged variant: *The Thousand Year Plan*.)
3. *Foundation and Empire* (Gnome, 1952)
   A threat to the Seldon Plan arrives in the person of the Mule, a mutant not predicted by "psychohistory." (Variant title: *The Man Who Upset the Universe*.)

4. *Second Foundation* (Gnome, 1953)
   The First Foundation and the Mule search for the secret Second Foundation, which is composed of psychologists who can mentally tamper with, and "adjust" individuals.
5. *Foundation's Edge* (Doubleday, 1982)
   Several hundred years later, the First and Second Foundations are jockeying for power as facilitators of the Seldon Plan.
6. *Foundation and Earth* (Doubleday, 1986)
   Having second thoughts about the momentous decision he made in *Foundation's Edge*, Golan Trevize goes in search of the legendary mother-planet "Earth."

II. Asimov is also the creator of the Positronic Robot and a series of more than thirty robot short stories published over a span of nearly forty years. They are collected in *The Complete Robot* (Doubleday, 1982). He has also written a series of novels about an interstellar police detective named Elijah Baley and his robot partner Daneel Olivaw. The first three novels are a very successful hybrid of the science fiction and detective story genres. In the fourth novel, *Robots and Empire*, Asimov explicitly links this series with the Foundation series.

1. *The Caves of Steel* (Doubleday, 1954)
   Human detective Elijah Baley, a resident of the despised planet Earth, is linked up with robot detective R. Daneel Olivaw to solve the murder of Dr. Sarton.
2. *The Naked Sun* (Doubleday, 1957)
   Baley and Olivaw are sent to the planet Solaria to solve another murder.
3. *The Robots of Dawn* (Doubleday, 1983)
   The detective pair travel to Daneel's home planet, Aurora, in order to help clear the name of his creator, Dr. Fastolfe.
4. *Robots and Empire* (Doubleday, 1985)
   Daneel aids the Settler descendants of Elijah Baley in thwarting the Spacer's plan to burn up the Earth's crust.

Asturias, Miguel

The "volcanic vehemence" of Asturia's fiction won him the Nobel Prize in 1967. His novels are long and kaleidoscopic in range, rich in fantasy, robust humor, and lyric prose. The Banana Republic trilogy, representative of his best work, is set in the vast stretch of banana plantations in a Central American republic very much like his native Guatemala. Dominated and exploited by a powerful North American fruit company, the land and people rebel.

1. *Strong Wind* (Delacorte, 1968)
   American Lester Mead and his wife try to bring harmony to the plantation, but nature's "strong winds" defeat them. Translated from the Spanish by Gregory Rabassa. First published in 1962.
2. *The Green Pope* (Delacorte, 1971)
   Ruthless George Maker Thompson of the United States founds the plantations. Translated from the Spanish by Gregory Rabassa. First published in 1954.
3. *The Eyes of the Interred* (Delacorte, 1973)
   Thompson has a violent downfall. Translated from the Spanish by Gregory Rabassa. First published in 1960.

Auel, Jean

Earth's Children is the title of a projected six-volume series set in a time, dated at 35,000 years ago, when two species of early man—Cro-Magnon and Neanderthal—inhabited the earth. Jean Auel has researched the subject thoroughly, then let her imagination create a convincing and dramatic portrait of what might have happened when the two species encountered each other. Some of her prehistoric people communicate with hand signals and a sort of racial telepathy rather than words, but in other ways they are wonderfully human, and their story is as engaging as any other family saga.

1. *The Clan of the Cave Bear* (Crown, 1980)
   This begins when Ayla, a weak, hairless, and babbling orphan is adopted by a group of darker hunting people. She learns their ways, yet remains strangely different.
2. *The Valley of Horses* (Crown, 1982)
   Ayla shares a lonely valley with a herd of steppe horses and with a man who teaches her the meaning of companionship and love.
3. *The Mammoth Hunters* (Crown, 1985)
   At last among her own kind at Lion Camp, Ayla learns the ways

of her people and shares with them her innovations, the domestication of the horse and the wolf.

Baldwin, Faith

Little Oxford, Connecticut, is a fictitious town—typically New England—in which Baldwin set her 1938 novel *Station Wagon Set*. In 1970 she used the locale again, updated, in *Any Village*, and her more recent romances were set there almost exclusively. This is a series only in the geographical sense; after the first two novels, there is no chronological order.

1. *Station Wagon Set* (Farrar, 1938)
   Six connected stories sketch the residents of Little Oxford. The young Dr. Bing Irvington is featured in the story entitled "Mixed Doubles."
2. *Any Village* (Holt, 1971)
   Dr. Bing Irvington is now the older doctor in town, and his son Ben has joined his practice. Ben falls in love in this installment.
3. *No Bed of Roses* (Holt, 1973)
   This is about a young married couple in Little Oxford: Katie Palmer, a real estate agent, and her husband, Jeremy, owner of a bookstore.
4. *Time and the Hour* (Holt, 1974)
   Stacy Armitage, recently divorced, meets architect Lee Osborne.
5. *New Girl in Town* (Holt, 1975)
   Maggie Knox faces her growing interest in a married man.
6. *Thursday's Child* (Holt, 1976)
   Aristocratic Abby Morrison Allen returns to her New England home with Sara Foster, her twenty-four-year-old granddaughter.
7. *Adam's Eden* (Holt, 1977)
   Cosmopolitan bachelor Adam, Vanessa Steele's grandson, settles in Little Oxford.

Ball, John

Virgil Tibbs, a young black man waiting for a train in the small southern city of Wells, is picked up as a murder suspect. But much to the embarrassment of local police chief Gillespie, he turns out to be a homicide detective from the Pasadena police force who is in the area to visit relatives. So begins the fictional life of Ball's clever and sophisticated detective, elegantly played by Sidney Poitier in the excellent 1965 film *In the Heat of the Night*. Tibb's further cases have continued to delight mystery readers.

1. *In the Heat of the Night* (Harper, 1965)
   Tibbs stays in Wells to help catch the murderer and teach the bigoted Chief Gillespie a lesson.
2. *The Cool Cottontail* (Harper, 1966)
   An unidentified dead man found in the swimming pool of a nudist camp is Tibb's next assignment.
3. *Johnny Get Your Gun* (Little, 1969)
   An obsessed nine-year-old bent on revenge makes a different kind of case for Sergeant Tibbs. (Variant title: *Death for a Playmate*.)
4. *Five Pieces of Jade* (Little, 1972)
   When the owner of a valuable jade collection is murdered, drugs and other tangles complicate Tibb's search for a solution.
5. *The Eyes of Buddha* (Little, 1976)
   The trail of a dead woman in Pasadena and a missing heiress leads Tibbs halfway around the world to the Monkey Temple in Tibet.
6. *Then Came Violence* (Doubleday, 1980)
   Bachelor Tibbs comes home from work one day to find that he has mysteriously acquired a wife and two children.
7. *Singapore* (Dodd, 1986)
   Miriam Motambori, who appeared in *Then Came Violence*, is being held for murder in a Singapore prison when Tibbs comes to her aid.

Balzac, Honoré de

No current trend is likely to send modern readers through all ninety-two novels and stories of Balzac's The Human Comedy, an inventory of the vices and virtues of nineteenty-century French society. But the recent Masterpiece Theatre productions "Cousin Bette" and "Père Goriot" may well revive interest in some of the masterpieces of this early French Realist. Balzac altered the titles and categories of The Human Comedy as the series developed. Many projected volumes were never written. Its three major groups are Studies of Manners, the largest and most important group; Philosophical Studies, consisting mainly of less interesting occult works; and Analytical Studies, containing only two treatises on marriage. The list below of titles actually written follows Balzac's own 1845 classification. Note: *Droll Stories*, the 1832 collection of thirty Rabelaisian short stories, is not a part of The Human Comedy.

For an authoritative bibliography, see W. H. Royce's *A Balzac Bibliography* (Univ. of Chicago Pr., 1929). Herbert Hunt's *Balzac's Comedie Humaine* (Univ. of London Pr., 1959) is a useful guide to the series. Dates listed are of the original French publications. Many English editions of Balzac's works are available, the most complete being the forty-volume Dutton edition of 1895–99. Annotations are given for only the most accessible and highly regarded titles.

I. STUDIES OF MANNERS

    A.   Scenes of Private Life
1. *At the Sign of the Cat and the Racket* (1830)
   The heroine of this novelette is a draper's daughter unhappily married above her station.
2. *The Dance of Sceaux* (1830)
   Balzac satirizes people who affect to despise business.
3. *Recollections of Two Young Brides* (1842)
   The very different marriages of two young girls are contrasted.
4. *The Purse* (1832)
   This is a charming story of love and innocence.
5. *Modeste Mignon* (1844)
   This comic story deals with the romantic Modeste, who falls in love with the portrait of a famous poet and begins writing him letters.
6. *A Start in Life* (1844)
   In this humorous story, a young man is cured of his vanity.
7. *Albert Savarus* (1842)
   An unscrupulous girl destroys the life of the man she loves.
8. *The Vendetta* (1830)
9. *A Double Family* (1830)
10. *The Peace of the Household* (1842)
11. *Madame Firmiani* (1832)
12. *A Study of Woman* (1831)

13. *The Pretended Mistress* (1842)
14. *The Daughter of Eve* (1839)
15. *Colonel Chabert* (1832)
    In this tragic tale, a man renounces wealth, fame, and even
    his own identity rather than punish his odious wife.
16. *The Message* (1832)
17. *La grenadière* (1832)
18. *The Forsaken Woman* (1839)
19. *Honorine* (1844)
20. *Béatrix* (1839)
    This story of a young man in love with a heartless coquette is
    set in a quaint, old-fashioned town in Brittany.
21. *Gobseck* (1830)
22. *A Woman of Thirty* (1831)
    An attractive young woman is married to a dull man.
23. *Père Goriot* (1835)
    One of Balzac's masterpieces, this shows old Goriot sacrific-
    ing to give his daughters dowries and then further ruining
    himself to save them from their own follies.
24. *Pierre Grassou* (1841)
25. *The Atheist's Mass* (1836)
26. *The Interdiction* (1836)
27. *The Marriage Contract* (1835)
    In the negotiation of a marriage settlement, a spendthrift
    mother is determined to get the better of her future son-in-
    law.
28. *Another Study of Women* (1831)

B. Scenes of Provincial Life
    1. *Lily of the Valley* (1835)
       Here a good woman is married to a bad man.
    2. *Ursule Mirouet* (1841)
       Balzac injects the occult into this story of a pious young girl
       who converts her atheist guardian.
    3. *Eugenie Grandet* (1833)
       Regarded as Balzac's most perfect book, this tells the sad
       tale of Eugenie Grandet, the good and beautiful daughter of
       a miser.
    4. *The Celibates*
       This volume contains three parts, originally published sep-
       arately. They are:
       a. Part 1. *Pierrette* (1840)
       b. Part 2. *The Vicar of Tours* (1832)

c. Part 3. *A Bachelor's Establishment* (1842)
5. *The Parisians in Provincial France*
   This volume has four parts that were originally published separately. They are:
   a. Part 1. *Gaudissart the Great* (1833)
   b. Part 2. *Wrinkled People* (1833)
   c. Part 3. *The Muse of the Department* (1843)
   d. Part 4. *An Actress Abroad* (1843)
6. *The Superior Woman* (1833)
7. *The Rivalries* (1836)
   Part 3 is *The Old Maid*. Parts 1 and 2 were never written.
8. *The Provincials in Paris* (1839)
   Part 1 is *The Cabinet of Antiques*. Part 2 was never written.
9. *Lost Illusions* (1837)
   Lucien Chardon, a young provincial, comes to Paris with literary aspirations but finds disaster. The story has three parts:
   a. Part 1. *The Two Poets*
   b. Part 2. *A Provincial Great Man in Paris*
   c. Part 3. *An Investor's Suffering*. Variant title: *An Inventor's Tribulations*.

C. Scenes of Parisian Life
   1. *History of the Thirteen*
      This volume contains three parts, originally published separately. They are:
      a. Part 1. *Ferragus* (1833)
      b. Part 2. *The Duchess of Langeais* (1834)
      c. Part 3. *The Girl with the Golden Eyes* (1835)
   2. *The Employees* (1838)
   3. *Sarrasine* (1838)
   4. *The Rise and Fall of César Birotteau* (1837)
      A perfumer with social ambitions speculates unwisely and goes bankrupt.
   5. *The House of Nucingen* (1846)
   6. *Facino Cane* (1846)
   7. *The Secrets of the Princess of Cadignan* (1838)
   8. *The Harlot's Progress*
      This volume has four parts, originally published separately. They are:
      a. Part 1. *How Harlots Love* (1843)
      b. Part 2. *What Love Costs an Old Man* (1847)

    c. Part 3. *The End of Evil Ways* (1847)

    d. Part 4. *The Last Incarnation of Vautrin* (1847)

9. *The Prince of Bohemia* (1845)
10. *The Involuntary Comedians* (1846)
11. *A Sample of French Familiar Conversation* (1845)
12. *A Petty Bourgeois* (1856)
13. *The Seamy Side of History* (1848)
14. *Cousin Pons* (1847)

> This story of two old musicians, the sentimental Schmucke and Cousin Pons, is set against the sordid and corrupt life of the Parisian artistic and theatrical world.

15. *Cousin Bette* (1846)

> Poor country cousin Bette plots and watches with glee as her envied cousin Adeline Hulot's family is destroyed by her husband's greedy mistress.

D. Scenes of Political Life
1. *An Episode under the Terror* (1831)
2. *A Dark Affair* (1841)
3. *The Deputy of Arcis* (1847)
4. *Z. Marcas* (1840)

E. Scenes of Military Life
1. *The Chouans* (1829)

> This historical romance of the Royalist struggle in Brittany in 1799 was modeled after Scott. It was Balzac's first successful novel.

2. *A Passion in the Desert* (1830)

F. Scenes of Country Life
1. *The Peasants* (1844)
2. *The Country Doctor* (1833)
3. *The Village Curé* (1839)

II. PHILOSOPHICAL STUDIES
1. *The Wild Ass's Skin* (1831)

> The best-known of this group, this novel explores the function of the human will in an allegorical tale about a magical scrap of leather.

2. *Jesus Christ in Flanders* (1831)
3. *Melmouth Reconciled* (1835)
4. *Massimilla Doni* (1839)

5. *The Unknown Masterpiece* (1831)
6. *Gambara* (1831)
7. *The Quest of the Absolute* (1834)
8. *A Child Accursed* (1834)
9. *Adieu* (1830)
10. *The Maranas* (1832)
11. *The Conscript* (1831)
12. *The Executioner* (1834)
13. *The Seashore Tragedy* (1834)
14. *Master Cornelius* (1832)
15. *The Red Inn* (1831)
16. *About Catherine de Medici* (1843)
17. *The Elixir of Long Life* (1831)
18. *The Exiles* (1831)
19. *Louis Lambert* (1832)
20. *Séraphita* (1834)

III. ANALYTICAL STUDIES
1. *Physiology of Marriage* (1829)
2. *The Pinpricks of Married Life* (1843)

Bangs, John Kendrick

Imagine the world's immortals smoking, dining, and playing billiards at their big club in the sky or, in this case, on their commodious yacht on the River Styx. Naturally all their human foibles show as they debate their achievements, rehash history, and vie for recognition. "How's our little Swanlet of Avon?" asks Dr. Johnson at the billiard table as Shakespeare enters the lounge. Among other things, the question of who wrote Hamlet is definitively answered.

1. *A House-Boat on the Styx* (Harper, 1896)
   Amidst much clever dialogue, Captain Kidd, barred from membership, pirates the houseboat away.
2. *The Pursuit of the House-Boat* (Harper, 1897)
   Sherlock Holmes tracks down Captain Kidd and the houseboat, and a contingent of lady notables succeeds in joining the club.

Banks, Lynne Reid

Jane Graham, unmarried and pregnant, intends to have an abortion, but after making friends with her fellow roomers at a dingy London board-inghouse, she decides to have her baby. This bittersweet look at a young girl's search for love is well written. Its odd characters are plausible and poignant. Leslie Caron played Jane in the 1962 British movie version of *The L-Shaped Room*. Two sequels continue Jane's story.

1. *The L-Shaped Room* (Simon & Schuster, 1961)
   Life looks bleak from Jane's tiny boardinghouse room, but the new friends she makes give her hope.
2. *The Backward Shadow* (Simon & Schuster, 1970)
   Jane lives with baby David in a cottage in the country, but a new restlessness afflicts her.
3. *Two Is Lonely* (Simon & Schuster, 1974)
   Jane marries a loving man who brings security and happiness to herself and to her seven-year-old son David.

Barnard, Robert

Readers who enjoy humorous and somewhat literary mysteries will welcome the appearance of Detective Inspector Perry Trethowen of Scotland Yard. Trethowen's witty narration adds to the pleasure of his cases, though their primary humor comes from the eccentric characters and situations which inevitably figure large.

1. *Death by Sheer Torture* (Scribner, 1982)
   The old English gent discovered dead in spangled tights in a reconstructed Inquisition device turns out to be Perry's estranged father. English title: *Sheer Torture*.
2. *Death and the Princess* (Scribner, 1982)
   Perry is assigned to guard Princess Helena, a minor but notorious British royal figure.
3. *The Case of the Missing* Brontë (Scribner, 1983)
   A manuscript, possibly by Emily Brontë, sets Perry and all the collectors in Yorkshire on a merry chase. English title: *The Missing Brontë*.
4. *Bodies* (Scribner, 1986)
   This installment takes Perry into the world of London's gyms and body-building cults.

5. *The Cherry Blossom Corpse* (Scribner, 1987)
   Perry is on hand to investigate when death interrupts a romance
   writers' conference in Norway.

Barrie, Sir James M.

Barrie's novels of Scottish life and manners are thick with dialect, but
they make engaging and nostalgic reading. Most of his novels, including
his best-known *The Little Minister*, are set in the town of Thrums, but the
two listed below should be read sequentially. They follow the career of
Tommy from the age of five to his death. Tommy epitomizes the man of
feeling; he is nicknamed "sentimental" because his "sympathy was so
easily aroused that he sometimes cried without knowing why."

1. *Sentimental Tommy* (Scribner, 1896)
   Little Tommy leaves his London slum for Thrums, the town of his
   mother's origin.
2. *Tommy and Grizel* (Scribner, 1898)
   Tommy's talents are put to good use in his career as a writer, and
   the virtuous and patient Grizel is devoted to him.

Bates, Herbert Ernest

These books show H. E. Bates in a light mood that may surprise those
who saw his *Love for Lydia* dramatized on "Masterpiece Theatre." They
feature the happy-go-lucky Larkin family, an English variety of hillbilly.
In fact the first novel was translated into an American setting for use as
the basis for the movie *The Mating Game* (1959), starring Debbie
Reynolds as the farm girl and Tony Randall as the tax collector who falls
in love with her.

1. *The Darling Buds of May* (Little, 1958)
   The tax collector comes to the Larkin's junkyard of a farm.
2. *A Breath of French Air* (Little, 1959)
   The Larkins descend on a shabby hotel in Brittany like a hurricane.
3. *Hark, Hark, the Lark!* (Little, 1960)
   Pop Larkin sells a huge white elephant of a manor house to some

city folk who become his neighbors. English title: *When the Green Woods Laugh*.

4. *Oh! To Be in England* (Farrar, 1963)
   The Larkin family has further adventures, including a belated baptism all together.

Beach, Edward L.

Beach graduated from the United States Naval Academy in 1939, saw duty aboard three submarines during World War II, and commanded the nuclear-powered U.S.S. *Triton* in her 1960 underwater circumnavigation of the world. His naval adventures have the authenticity that such a background guarantees plus the action and excitement inherent to the genre. Clark Gable and Burt Lancaster starred in the 1958 film *Run Silent, Run Deep*.

1. *Run Silent, Run Deep* (Holt, 1955)
   The submarine *Walrus* patrols Tokyo Bay during World War II with "Rich" Richardson, Keith Leone, and Jim Bledsoe aboard.
2. *Dust on the Sea* (Holt, 1972)
   "Rich" Richardson and his faithful crew take the submarine *Eel* to the Yellow Sea, as World War II draws to an end.
3. *Cold Is the Sea* (Holt, 1978)
   In 1960, Rich and two of his former officers find themselves together again when the nuclear sub *Cushing* is threatened by the Russians.

Bedford, Sybille

Suggest this pair of novels by an English author to readers who like thoughtful women's stories. Bedford's books are well-written and wonderfully evocative of Europe in the 1920s and 1930s. They concern Anna Howland, an American heiress who marries an Italian prince, her daughter Constanza, and her granddaughter Flavia. How each of these women meet the crises in their lives profoundly affects the others.

1. *A Favorite of the Gods* (Simon & Schuster, 1963)
   Anna's New England girlhood is a curious preparation for her

married life in Italy, and Constanza must make her own bargain with life.

2. *A Compass Error* (Knopf, 1969)
   Constanza, now settled in a French coastal town, is painfully affected by Flavia's coming of age.

Bellamann, Henry

The midwestern town of Kings Row, thought to be based on Fulton, Missouri, is more the subject than the setting of these readable melodramas. Seen through the eyes of Parris Mitchell from his school days in the 1890s through World War I, the town's pioneer ideals seem to have degenerated into cynicism, greed, and incompetence. Parris, a sensitive young man who becomes a psychiatrist, hates the cruelty and pettiness of the town's residents but is too loyal to leave. A third planned volume was never written.

1. *Kings Row* (Simon & Schuster, 1940)
   Parris grows up and goes off to study medicine as tragedy befalls his childhood friend Drake McHugh.
2. *Parris Mitchell of Kings Row* (Simon & Schuster, 1948)
   This begins in 1916 and tells how young Dr. Mitchell, now established as a psychiatrist at the State Hospital for the Insane, is almost destroyed by his childhood enemy Fulmer Green. Completed by the author's wife, Katherine, after his death.

Bennett, Arnold

Like Hardy, Bennett set most of his novels in a fictitious locale heavily based on a real district of England. His Five Towns (the industrial Midlands), which he immortalized in *The Old Wives' Tale*, also provided the setting for many other works, including the Clayhanger series. The figure of Edwin Clayhanger is thought to be highly autobiographical, and it is the conflict between the young man and his overbearing father that makes the first book in the series so powerful.

1. *Clayhanger* (Dutton, 1910)
   Covers the youth of Edwin Clayhanger and his relationship to his father Darius.

2. *Hilda Lessways* (Dutton, 1911)
   Concerns young Hilda Lessway's girlhood and disastrous first marriage.
3. *These Twain* (Doran, 1916)
   Hilda and Edwin finally marry, but wedded bliss eludes them.
4. *The Roll Call* (Doran, 1919)
   In this addendum to what was originally conceived as a trilogy of novels, Hilda's son George wins recognition as an architect and falls in love.

Benson, E. F. (Edward Frederic)

Mrs. Emmeline Lucas, or Lucia (pronounced in the Italian manner that she affects), is equal parts snob and busybody, and the leading light of the small town of Riseholme. Two generations of readers have found her pretensions delightful and the misadventures of her set captivating. *Make Way for Lucia* (Crowell, 1977) is an omnibus volume containing all six novels as well as a short story, "The Male Impersonator," published here for the first time.

1. *Queen Lucia* (Doran, 1920)
   Introduces Lucia, her husband, Philip (Peppino), her friend Georgie Pillson, and her archrival, Daisy Quantock.
2. *Lucia in London* (Doubleday, 1928)
   Lucia crashes London society and is taken up as a sort of amusement but eventually returns to Riseholme and an ailing husband.
3. *Miss Mapp* (Doran, 1923)
   Lucia is absent from this volume, which introduces Miss Elizabeth Mapp of the seaside town of Tilling and her bachelor neighbors Major Benjy Flint and Captain Puffin.
4. *Mapp and Lucia* (Doubleday, 1931)
   Now widowed, Lucia rents Miss Mapp's house for the summer and proceeds to take over Tilling society. This volume contains the episode where Lucia and Elizabeth Mapp are carried out to sea on the kitchen table.
5. *The Worshipful Lucia* (Doubleday, 1935)
   In her search for new fields to conquer, Lucia enters politics. Elizabeth Mapp is now married to Major Benjy. Lucia eventually marries Georgie. Original English title: *Lucia's Progress*.

6. *Trouble for Lucia* (Doubleday, 1939)
   Lucia is agile as always at getting out of scrapes; her exploits as mayor of Tilling fill this final volume.

Bentley, E. C. (Edmund Clerihew)

Agatha Christie regarded *Trent's Last Case* as one of the three best detective stories ever written. Bentley, an English newspaperman, is supposed to have written the mystery, his first, on a bet from his friend G. K. Chesterton, as a demonstration of the fallibility of the deductive method favored by fictional sleuths of that day. His detective, Philip Trent, age thirty-two, is a successful painter whose imaginative and inquisitive mind makes him a brilliant natural detective. He accepts occasional assignments as a special murder correspondent from Sir James Molloy's newspaper, the *Record*. *Trent's Last Case* makes tantalizing reference to Trent's earlier cases, but unfortunately his creator let those go unrecorded. *Trent's Case Book* (Knopf, 1953) is an omnibus containing all three volumes listed below.

1. *Trent's Last Case* (Knopf, 1929)
   When millionaire financier Sigsbee Manderson is murdered, Trent matches wits with Inspector Murch of Scotland Yard and comes up with a brilliant solution that is almost correct.
2. *Trent's Own Case* (Knopf, 1936)
   Trent himself is Inspector Gideon Bligh's chief suspect in the murder of philanthropist James Randolph. Written with H. Warner Allen.
3. *Trent Intervenes* (Knopf, 1938)
   This is a book of short stories.

Berger, Thomas

The Reinhart Saga is a series of comic novels following the career of Carlo Reinhart, a good-natured and guileless fellow who is victimized by all who meet him. Reinhart embodies the average middle-class American's optimism and good intentions, and his disillusionment with the absurdity and fraud of modern life is just as inevitable as it is hilarious. The story takes him from a fumbling adolescence to a paunchy middle age.

1. *Crazy in Berlin* (Scribner, 1958)
   As a soldier in occupied Germany, Reinhart finds himself in a maze of spies and corruption that eventually drives him over the edge.
2. *Reinhart in Love* (Scribner, 1962)
   Now home and going to college on the GI bill, Carlo is again ill-used by all; he is married to a shrew and even a failure at suicide.
3. *Vital Parts* (Scribner, 1970)
   Reinhart in the bewildering seventies copes with a fat daughter and a nasty son; he pins his hopes on a cryogenics scheme.
4. *Reinhart's Women* (Delacorte, 1981)
   Women mean trouble to Reinhart, from his daughter Winona and her lesbian lover to a neighborhood girlfriend, his ex-wife Genevieve, and an amorous co-worker.

Bjarnhof, Karl

Born in 1898 to a poor family in a provincial Danish town, Bjarnhof, like the narrator of these two books, began to go blind at an early age. That experience is movingly portrayed in these fictionalized accounts. As the young boy's decreasing vision gradually cuts him off from the world of his peers and schoolmates, he makes friends at a local home for blind girls and turns to music for satisfaction. His strange, brooding father and the poverty of his family make the story even more poignant.

1. *The Stars Grow Pale* (Knopf, 1958)
   Though reluctant to admit it, the young boy can no longer see the blackboard or the red ball of his playmates.
2. *The Good Light* (Knopf, 1960)
   At fourteen, the nearly sightless hero enters the institute for the blind in Copenhagen.

Bjorn, Thyra Ferré

Heartwarming and homespun are the usual adjectives applied to Thyra Bjorn's books about a Swedish minister, Pastor Franzon, his wife, Maria, and their eight children. Mama is the benevolent but firm ruler of the family, and it is her determination that finally gets them moved to America. Bjorn admitted her stories were drawn from her own family; Button, the oldest daughter, is the autobiographical figure. Numbers 1, 2, and 3 below were published in an omnibus volume (Rinehart, 1960).

1. *Papa's Wife* (Rinehart, 1955)
   Housemaid Maria marries Pastor Franzon, raises eight children, and eventually settles the family into the new country.
2. *Papa's Daughter* (Rinehart, 1959)
   The story of Charlotta Maria, nicknamed Button, the second child of the Franzons.
3. *Mama's Way* (Rinehart, 1959)
   A collection of little sermons woven into story form—only loosely connected to the first two books.
4. *Dear Papa* (Holt, 1963)
   An addendum of letters written by Mama to her deceased husband—full of humorous anecdotes about their large family.

Blake, Nicholas (pseud. of Cecil Day-Lewis)

Needless to say, these mysteries written under a pseudonym by Britain's late poet laureate are beautifully crafted, literate, and sophisticated entertainments. Nigel Strangeways is a tall, sandy-haired private investigator who solves good old-fashioned jigsaw puzzlers with urbanity and wit. There is a definite chronology to Strangeway's adventures. The books chronicle his courtship and marriage to Georgia Cavendish, their early married years in London, the war years, and, after Georgia's death, Nigel's relationship with sculptress Clare Massinger. Strangeways is the name of a prison in Manchester. Not all of Blake's mysteries feature Strangeways.

1. *A Question of Proof* (Harper, 1935)
   Nigel investigates a murder in Sudeley Hall, a boys' prep school, during the 1930s.
2. *Shell of Death* (Harper, 1936)
   Nigel goes to rural Somerset to protect the life of Britain's legendary air hero, Fergus O'Brien. He meets Georgia. English title: *Thou Shell of Death.*

3. *There's Trouble Brewing* (Harper, 1937)
   Nigel and Georgia are married as this case begins with an invitation to a literary society and the death of a dog.
4. *The Beast Must Die* (Harper, 1938)
   A grief-stricken father forces himself to live with a murderer so that he can avenge his son's death.
5. *The Smiler with the Knife* (Harper, 1939)
   Nigel and his wife fight a master criminal who has a sinister plot to take over England. This book is more thriller than mystery.
6. *The Summer Camp Mystery* (Harper, 1940)
   Someone calling himself the "Mad Hatter" is playing pranks on vacationers in a British holiday camp. English title: *Malice in Wonderland*. Variant title: *Malice with Murder*.
7. *The Corpse in the Snowman* (Harper, 1941)
   In wintry Essex, Nigel investigates the strange behavior of a cat until more grisly matters turn up. English title: *The Case of the Abominable Snowman*.
8. *Minute for Murder* (Harper, 1947)
   In wartime Britain, someone has given beautiful blond Nita Prince a poisoned cup of coffee.
9. *Head of a Traveler* (Harper, 1949)
   Who was the headless corpse? And why was his head hidden on Robert Seaton's estate?
10. *The Dreadful Hollow* (Harper, 1953)
    Involves poison-pen letters and a dead body at the bottom of the dreadful hollow in the little village of Prior's Umborne.
11. *The Whisper in the Gloom* (Harper, 1954)
    A dying stranger hands a crumpled message to a small boy in a park.
12. *End of a Chapter* (Harper, 1957)
    Somebody slips libelous passages into General Thoresby's autobiography. Introduces Clare Massinger, who will become the new woman in widower Nigel's life.
13. *The Widow's Cruise* (Harper, 1959)
    Nigel, on a cruise of the Greek islands with Clare Massinger, investigates the murder of a fellow passenger.
14. *The Worm of Death* (Harper, 1961)
    Dr. Piers Loudon, the new neighbor of Nigel and Clare, disappears and is found dead.
15. *The Sad Variety* (Harper, 1964)
    Russians have kidnapped Professor Wragby's daughter, and Nigel must keep him from trading secrets for her return.

16. *The Morning after Death* (Harper, 1966)
    The local police enlist Nigel's help in solving the murder of a classics professor. Nigel is spending a year at an Ivy League college near Boston.

Blatty, William Peter

The Exorcist spawned so many imitations that, for a while, the "possession" novel threatened to become a genre of its own. Blatty's screenplay for the movie version (1973) won him an Oscar. *Exorcist II: The Heretic* (1977), the inevitable movie sequel, seems to have no relation to the print sequel.

1. *The Exorcist* (Harper, 1971)
   A graphic horror story of the possession and eventual exorcism of sweet young Regan MacNeil.
2. *Legion* (Simon & Schuster, 1983)
   Detective Bill Kinderman reappears in this case which starts with a series of gruesome murders and leads to a madman.

Block, Lawrence

I. This prolific American has written two series that are generally available in libraries. One set stars Matthew Scudder, an alcoholic ex-police detective who cannot escape the pain and guilt he feels after having accidentally shot and killed a seven-year-old girl. Matt occasionally rouses himself out of his alcoholic haze long enough to use his old police skills and connections to help a friend solve a problem. Jeff Bridges played Scudder in the movie *Eight Million Ways to Die* (1986), rather loosely based on several novels in the series.

1. *When the Sacred Ginmill Closes* (Arbor House, 1986)
   Scudder is one of a roomful of customers who witness the robbery of an after-hours Irish pub. Though published after number 6, this is told as a flashback to the summer of 1975.
2. *In the Midst of Death* (Dell, 1976)
   Venal cop Jerry Broadhurst is blowing the whistle on his fellow policemen by testifying to a special prosecutor investigating police corruption.

3. *The Sins of the Fathers* (Dell, 1977)
   Cale Hannaford, a prosperous businessman, asks Matt to find out more about the circumstances of his estranged daughter's murder.
4. *Time to Murder and Create* (Dell, 1977)
   Spinner, a prosperous but doomed blackmailer, pre-pays Scudder to investigate his murder.
5. *A Stab in the Dark* (Arbor House, 1981)
   Nine years after her death, Scudder tries to discover who killed Barbara Ettinger.
6. *Eight Million Ways to Die* (Arbor House, 1982)
   Prostitute Kim Dakkinen wants to get out of "the life," and asks Scudder to speak to Chance, her pimp.
7. *Out on the Cutting Edge* (Morrow, 1989)
   Scudder, trying to stay off alcohol with the help of Alcoholics Anonymous, is investigating the disappearance of a girl from Muncie, Indiana, and the alleged suicide of a fellow AA member.

II. Bernie Rhodenbarr is a gentlemanly New York cat burglar who turns detective from time to time, mostly to clear himself of false charges. His lock-picking skills and street smarts give him an edge over most police detectives. Readers who can tolerate Bernie's incessant wisecracking will enjoy these breezy tales of a modern Robin Hood. Bernie was transmogrified into "Bernice" Rhodenbarr in the Whoopi Goldberg movie *Burglar* (1987), loosely based on this series.

1. *Burglars Can't Be Choosers* (Random, 1977)
   Bernie is employed to steal a mysterious blue leather box, but his mission is interrupted by the arrival of the police who find a corpse in the bedroom.
2. *The Burglar in the Closet* (Random, 1978)
   Hiding in a bedroom closet, Bernie becomes an inadvertent witness to a murder.
3. *The Burglar Who Liked to Quote Kipling* (Random, 1979)
   A rare Kipling volume is Bernie's objective, but he has lots of competition.
4. *The Burglar Who Studied Spinoza* (Random, 1981)
   Bernie is running a used book store in the Village in this episode which centers on the theft of some rare coins.
5. *The Burglar Who Painted like Mondrian* (Arbor House, 1983)
   Somebody else stole the Mondrian masterpiece, but unless Bernie finds it, he'll take the rap.

Boissard, Janine

There is a decided "young adult" tone to these pleasant books about a prosperous French family living in a small town near Paris. Dr. Moreau and his wife have four teenage daughters: Claire, Bernadette, Pauline, and Cecile. Pauline, the narrator and main character, is presumably somewhat autobiographical. J. G. Murray characterized the first book in this series as a "Gallic *Little Women*" (*The Critic*, May 1980). All are translated from the original French.

1. *A Matter of Feeling* (Little, 1980)
   The bittersweet story of Pauline's first love affair with an older man who is an artist.
2. *Christmas Lessons* (Little, 1984)
   Pauline relates events as the family gathers for a traditional Christmas holiday at Grandmother Moreau's.
3. *A Time to Choose* (Little, 1985)
   With her two older sisters now married, Pauline enrolls in journalism school and falls in love again.
4. *Cecile* (Little, 1988)
   Dr. Moreau's death saddens the family, but Cecile and her mother, now alone in the big house, suffer most.

Borrow, George

If only to meet the original "Borrovian gentleman," readers should dip into these strange and charming works by the nineteenth-century English poet of the open road. There is some speculation that George Borrow was himself a Gypsy, his knowledge of the ways of those wandering folk is so detailed. It is certain that much of *Lavengro* is autobiographical, though its author denied it. Borrow was much admired by the American transcendentalist writers, especially Emerson.

1. *Lavengro* (Harper, 1851)
   Introduces the remarkable young George, who teaches himself many languages, goes to London to become a writer, and wonders, What is truth?
2. *Romany Rye* (Harper, 1857)
   Further adventures of George, now called Romany Rye, his Gypsy friend Jasper Petulengro, Isopel, and others. A defense of *Lavengro* is appended.

Box, Edgar (pseud. of Gore Vidal, q.v.)

As one might expect, Vidal's amateur sleuth rivals Lord Peter Wimsey in wit and social polish. With his well-bred, Ivy League manners, Peter Cutler Sargeant III moves with ease in Long Island's social world as well as in political and artistic circles. His occupation as a self-employed public relations man is what gets him involved in two of his three cases. Fans wish Vidal would add to this short opus and give his bright young detective a chance, at least, to find his Harriet Vane. *Three by Box* (Random, 1978) contains all three of Peter Sargeant's cases.

1. *Death in the Fifth Position* (Dutton, 1952)
   When a Russian ballet troupe retains Peter to keep an eye on things, he doesn't expect murder onstage.
2. *Death before Bedtime* (Dutton, 1953)
   Peter goes to Washington to handle publicity for Senator Leander Rhodes, only to find his client has been killed by a bomb.
3. *Death Likes It Hot* (Dutton, 1954)
   Peter spends a long weekend in East Hampton, where a society party leads to sex, murder, and mystery.

Bradford, Barbara Taylor

This trilogy of novels chronicles the rise of Emma Harte from poverty to great wealth and the struggle for control of her legacy among her children and grandchildren. The story is familiar but well-told, with strong female characters, authentic historical background, and a glamorous backdrop of money and success. Bradford, a native of Emma Harte's Yorkshire, was a fashion editor, syndicated columnist, and author of books on decorating and etiquette before she struck real paydirt with the best-selling *A Woman of Substance*, which was produced as a television mini-series featuring Deborah Kerr as the mature Emma.

1. *A Woman of Substance* (Doubleday, 1979)
   Emma Harte remembers her rise from a poor Yorkshire servant girl to a rich and powerful department store magnate.
2. *Hold the Dream* (Doubleday, 1985)
   Emma hands the business over to three of her grandchildren: Paula, Emily, and Alexander.

3. *To Be the Best* (Doubleday, 1988)
   Paula, the granddaughter who most resembles Emma, fights her treacherous cousin Jonathan for control of the family empire.

Bradley, Marion Zimmer

In the very popular Darkover series, Marion Zimmer Bradley combines sword-and-sorcery adventure with a science fiction setting. Darkover is a distant planet illuminated by a dim, red sun and four multicolored moons. Many intelligent beings roam this cold and mountainous planet, some in the form of cats, small apes, or birds. Early human settlers from a crashed spaceship have mixed with the planet's psi-gifted natives to form a culture where mental powers have replaced machines. When technologically advanced Terrans try to dominate the planet, conflict is inevitable. Gregg Press, a division of G. K. Hall, has done libraries a service by reprinting in hardcover all but the most recent titles of this series that was originally published in paperback.

1. *Stormqueen!* (DAW Bks., 1978)
   This story is set in Darkover's Age of Chaos, before the Seven Great Houses were established or the force of the matrix was fully understood.
2. *Two to Conquer* (DAW Bks., 1980)
   During the Hundred Kingdoms, Varzil dreams of uniting Darkover and Bard Di Asturien is exiled for murder.
3. *Hawkmistress!* (DAW, Bks., 1982)
   The story of young Romilly MacAran, who leaves home rather than marry, and her unusual ability to communicate with hawks.
4. *Darkover Landfall* (DAW Bks., 1972)
   Humans crash-land into the alien world of Darkover and adapt to its harsh climate and strange winds.
5. *The Spell Sword* (DAW Bks., 1974)
   Damon Ridenow and Andrew Carr rescue the sorceress Callista from imprisonment and destroy the threat of the cat people.
6. *The Forbidden Tower* (DAW Bks., 1977)
   Powerful physical and psychological forces separate Terran Andrew Carr and Darkovan Callista.

7. *The Shattered Chain* (DAW Bks., 1976)
   Lady Rohana, Free Amazon Jaelle, and the Terran agent Magda break the chains of their female roles.
8. *Thendara House* (DAW Bks., 1983)
   This continues the stories of Magda and Jaelle as their roles are somewhat reversed.
9. *City of Sorcery* (DAW Bks., 1984)
   This third book about Magda and Jaelle forms a sort of feminist trilogy within the series. It tells of their journey out to the arctic land beyond the Domains.
10. *Star of Danger* (Ace, 1965)
    Terran Larry Montray and Darkovan Kennard Alton become friends despite their cultural differences.
11. *The Winds of Darkover* (Ace, 1970)
    Barran falls in love with Melitta, and together they evoke the power of the dangerous Darkovan fire goddess to rid Storn Castle of its bandit captors.
12. *The Bloody Sun* (Ace, 1964)
    Jeff Kerwin returns to Darkover after many years to find that there is no record of his birth on the planet.
13. *The Heritage of Hastur* (DAW Bks., 1975)
    The story of the Sharra uprising is seen through the eyes of Lew Alton, who is of mixed Darkovan and Terran lineage.
14. *Sharra's Exile* (DAW Bks., 1981)
    Lew Alton returns to Darkover prepared to fight for his inheritance, when other conflicts intervene in this reworking of number 15.
15. *The Sword of Aldones* (Ace, 1962)
    Lew Alton returns armed with a sword of the Sharra matrix to battle for the future of Darkover.
16. *The Planet Savers* (Ace, 1962)
    When Darkover is threatened by an epidemic, Dr. Jason Allison appeals to the nonhuman Trailmen for help. Bound with *The Sword of Aldones.*
17. *The World Wreckers* (Ace, 1971)
    Darkover is threatened by a clandestine organization determined to pave the way for industrial exploitation.

Note: The following titles are collections of Darkover short stories written by Bradley and other "Friends of Darkover," whose love for the series has prompted them to contribute an episode or two. Each contains information on how to join the Friends. *The Keeper's Price* (DAW

Bks., 1980); *Sword of Chaos and Other Stories* (DAW Bks., 1982); *Free Amazons of Darkover* (DAW Bks., 1985); *The Other Side of the Mirror and Other Darkover Stories* (DAW Bks., 1987); *The Red Sun of Darkover* (DAW Bks., 1987); and *Four Moons of Darkover* (NAL/DAW Bks., 1988).

Braine, John

Perhaps the best known of the Angry Young Man school of working-class British novels, *Room at the Top* shows young Joe Lampton rising above his mining-town origins at the cost of many around him. The 1958 film was nominated for an Academy Award for best picture. Critics regarded it as the first British movie to take sex seriously. Simone Signoret won an Academy Award for her portrayal of Alice, the older woman whose love for Joe destroys her. Laurence Harvey played the role of Joe.

1. *Room at the Top* (Houghton, 1957)
   Joe Lampton comes to Warley to take a job in the city council treasurer's office, and eventually marries the wealth and position he seeks.
2. *Life at the Top* (Houghton, 1962)
   Now rich and powerful, Joe realizes how much of his personal freedom he has traded for success.

Brett, Simon

I. This mystery series features amateur sleuth Charles Paris, a middle-aged, under-employed London actor whose predilection for ladies and drink have estranged his long-suffering wife Frances. Charles's foibles and his satirical insider's view of England's theatrical and television world give these books their considerable appeal. Author Brett writes from first-hand knowledge, having been a producer for the BBC.

1. *Cast, in Order of Disappearance* (Scribner, 1976)
   Charles's first attempt at sleuthing begins when Jacquie Mitchell, an old girlfriend, asks him to deliver some compromising photos to her lover.

2. *So Much Blood* (Scribner, 1977)
   In Edinburgh to perform a one-man play based on the life of the poet Thomas Hood, Charles investigates the murder of a young actor.
3. *Star Trap* (Scribner, 1978)
   Ill luck seems to be plaguing the production of a musical version of Goldsmith's *She Stoops to Conquer.*
4. *An Amateur Corpse* (Scribner, 1978)
   Charles gets no thanks for critiquing an amateur theatrical performance, but murder gives him a reason to stay on.
5. *A Comedian Dies* (Scribner, 1979)
   On vacation at a seaside town, Charles goes to see a vaudeville show and witnesses a public execution.
6. *The Dead Side of the Mike* (Scribner, 1980)
   When a woman is found with her wrists slashed in a BBC studio, only Charles suspects foul play.
7. *Situation Tragedy* (Scribner, 1981)
   A series of accidents cast a pall on the set of a TV situation comedy, until Charles uncovers the mystery.
8. *Murder Unprompted* (Scribner, 1982)
   Charles's friend Alex had motive and opportunity for shooting actor Michael Banks, but Charles is determined to prove him innocent.
9. *Murder in the Title* (Scribner, 1983)
   A third-rate regional theatre proves the death of an artistic director. Was it murder or suicide?
10. *Not Dead, Only Resting* (Scribner, 1984)
    Somebody kills the chef after a posh celebrity dinner party at the famous Tryst restaurant.
11. *Dead Giveaway* (Scribner, 1986)
    A bit part in the pilot of a new TV game show puts Charles at the scene of a murder.
12. *What Bloody Man Is That?* (Scribner, 1987)
    Charles plays multiple roles in a production of *Macbeth*, but he is miscast as a murderer.
13. *A Series of Murders* (Scribner, 1989)
    A British TV series which has Charles playing a police sergeant opposite an aristocratic amateur detective becomes the scene for two real murders.

II. Brett's new series stars Mrs. Melita Pargeter, a likable busybody, beneficiary of the late Mr. Pargeter, whose business dealings seem to have been lucrative but mysterious and perhaps not entirely on the up-and-up. Mrs. Pargeter has acquired some unusual skills from associates of her late husband, such as "Rewind" Wilson and "Keyhole" Crabbe, which she puts to good use in solving mysteries.

1. *A Nice Class of Corpse* (Scribner, 1987)
   An old lady is killed by a fall at the stuffy Devereux residential hotel in Littlehampton, and the interest of Mrs. Pargeter, the latest resident, is piqued.
2. *Mrs. Presumed Dead* (Scribner, 1989)
   Mrs. Pargeter moves to a new home in Surrey, and soon decides that Theresa Cotton, its former mistress, had come to an unnatural end.

Bristow, Gwen

Seven generations of the Sheramy and Larne families of Louisiana are traced in the Plantation trilogy, from the pioneers who changed the eighteenth-century Louisiana jungles into a society founded on luxury and injustice, through the conflicts of the Civil War and the birth of a new way of life, and finally to the twentieth-century southerners torn between tradition and modernity. Historical background material for each book was supplied in the omnibus volume, *The Plantation Trilogy* (Cromwell, 1962).

1. *Deep Summer* (Crowell, 1937)
   Northerner Judith Sheramy meets Philip Larne, an aristocratic southerner.
2. *The Handsome Road* (Crowell, 1938)
   The lives of housemaid Corrie May and the aristocratic Mrs. Denis Larne are contrasted.
3. *This Side of Glory* (Crowell, 1940)
   The saga of the Larnes and the old plantation is continued through World War II.

Brooks, Terry

I. The Shannara trilogy will probably be enjoyed by most *Lord of the Rings* fans, though its American author, greatly influenced by Tolkien, is a somewhat less sophisticated writer. Brooks's epic fantasies are set in the time following the "War of Ancient Evil" when the earth is peopled by many races—humans, elves, trolls, etc.—and the Power of Darkness threatens all.

1. *The Sword of Shannara* (Random, 1977)
   Half-elf Shea Ohmsford of Shady Vale sets out in search of the mysterious Sword of Shannara which is the only weapon effective against the evil Warlock Lord.
2. *The Elfstones of Shannara* (Ballantine, 1982)
   Will Ohmsford and Amberle must save the precious seed from the dying Ellcrys tree.
3. *The Wishsong of Shannara* (Ballantine, 1985)
   Brin Ohmsford's quest, like that of her father and grandfather, takes her far from the safe world of Shady Vale.

II. Brooks followed his best-selling Shannara books with this series of fantasies about the magic kingdom of Landover.

1. *Magic Kingdom for Sale—Sold!* (Ballantine, 1987)
   Discontented Chicago lawyer Ben Holiday discovers Landover, a less than idyllic magic kingdom.
2. *The Black Unicorn* (Ballantine, 1987)
   The evil wizard Meeks challenges Ben's domain.
3. *Wizard at Large* (Ballantine, 1988)
   Bumbling wizard Questor Thews botches his attempt at restoring court scribe Abernathy's dog body to its original human shape.

Buchan, John

I. Scottish author John Buchan is primarily remembered now for his adventure novels, though it was his government service and more serious writings which doubtless won him the title of Baron Tweedsmuir in 1935. Richard Hannay is featured in five of his books. Hannay pursues rather than detects; his cases are properly classed in the adventure genre, though they have an espionage element. *Four Adventures of Richard Hannay* (Hodder, London, 1930) contains numbers 1 through 4 below; *Adventures of Richard Hannay* (Houghton, 1939) contains 1 through 3.

44

1. *The Thirty-Nine Steps* (Doran, 1915)
   Young Richard Hannay is accidentally caught in a spy plot and finds himself pursued through England and Scotland by police and German agents. Fans of Alfred Hitchcock's 1935 movie version will be surprised to discover that it differs significantly from the novel.
2. *Greenmantle* (Doran, 1916)
   Major Hannay of the New Army is sent on special assignment to track down a secret in Turkey.
3. *Mr. Standfast* (Doran, 1919)
   Hannay pursues the mysterious Mr. Ivery in England, Scotland, and France. Mary Lamington wins Hannay's heart in this volume.
4. *The Three Hostages* (Houghton, 1924)
   Hannay, now Sir Richard, married to Mary, and living at Fosse Manor, takes on a group of postwar fanatics set on revolution.
5. *The Man from Norlands* (Houghton, 1936)
   Sir Richard's young son Peter John helps out with a case that takes them to an island fortress in Scotland. English title: *Island of Sheep*.

II. Buchan fans will also want to read the four books featuring Sir Edward Leithen, a more thoughtful detective, less given to hot pursuits over desolate moors than Hannay. Sir Edward is a lawyer and a bachelor. He is assumed to be a somewhat autobiographical character.

1. *The Power-house* (Doran, 1916)
   Was the mysterious disappearance of Mr. Pitt-Heron connected with a secret society?
2. *John MacNab* (Houghton, 1925)
   Sir Edward and two of his friends plot a caper to impersonate, but elude capture as the poacher, John MacNab.
3. *The Dancing Floor* (Houghton, 1926)
   Sir Edward helps a desperate young Greek girl to escape a tragic death, mysteriously foretold in dreams.
4. *Mountain Meadow* (Houghton, 1941)
   Fighting a losing battle with TB, Sir Edward takes on one last adventure, the search for an American millionaire lost in northern Canada. English title: *Sick Heart River*.

Buck, Pearl

The Good Earth, a masterful portrait of prewar Chinese peasant life, won Buck a Pulitzer Prize in 1932. And for her memorable performance as the long-suffering O-lan in the 1938 movie version, Luise Rainer won an Oscar. Two sequels carrying the story forward to the Revolution complete the House of Earth trilogy, which follows the House of Wang through half a century and three generations of farmers, warlords, merchants, and students.

1. *The Good Earth* (Day, 1931)
   The story of Wang Lung and his family is told.
2. *Sons* (Day, 1932)
   Wang Lung's three sons build their own lives.
3. *A House Divided* (Reynal, 1935)
   Yuan, grandson of Wang Lung, sees China into the modern age.

Buckley, William F., Jr.

America's leading conservative columnist, editor of the *National Review*, and television host of "Firing Line," Buckley added writing spy novels to his list of credits rather late in his career. *Saving the Queen* was an immediate best-seller and each new installment wins more fans to the adventures of his suave and daring CIA agent, Blackford Oakes. Blackie, a wealthy Ivy League type, is only twenty-six when first met, and ages gracefully with the series.

1. *Saving the Queen* (Doubleday, 1976)
   This must be read first, as it tells of Blackie's awful boyhood in an English boarding school. Finding an atomic spy in the Queen's court is his first CIA assignment.
2. *Stained Glass* (Doubleday, 1978)
   In 1952, Blackie is assigned to assassinate Count Wintergrin, a young politician determined to reunite Germany even at the risk of war.
3. *High Jinx* (Doubleday, 1986)
   This is set in 1954 as President Eisenhower worries that the U.S.S.R. has broken the top secret code used between England and the United States.

4. *Who's on First?* (Doubleday, 1980)
   Blackie plays a leading role in the race between the U.S. and the
   U.S.S.R. to put the first satellite into orbit.
5. *Marco Polo, If You Can* (Doubleday, 1982)
   What if Blackie was flying that U-2 spy plane in 1960 and was
   deliberately planning to get caught by the Soviets?
6. *The Story of Henri Tod* (Doubleday, 1984)
   Not even Blackie can stop the Berlin wall from going up in
   1962.
7. *See You Later, Alligator* (Doubleday, 1985)
   Blackie goes to Havana to talk with Che Guevara on the eve of the
   Cuban missile crisis.
8. *Mongoose, R.I.P.* (Random, 1987)
   In 1963 Blackie is sent to Cuba to assassinate Castro.

Buechner, Frederick

The Bebb Chronicles are an unusual mix of high comedy and underlying
seriousness by a writer who is also an ordained Presbyterian minister.
Leo Bebb, ex-convict and evangelist head of the Holy Love church and
diploma mill in Armadillo, Florida, dominates the series and provides
most of its hilarity. Antonio Parr is the narrator. All four books were
collected in the omnibus edition, *The Book of Bebb* (Atheneum, 1979).

1. *Lion Country* (Atheneum, 1971)
   Thirty-four-year-old Antonio Parr gets his ordination through the
   mail, goes to visit Leo Bebb's unorthodox religious school, and falls
   in love with Bebb's daughter.
2. *Open Heart* (Atheneum, 1972)
   Antonio Parr, now married to Sharon and living in Connecticut,
   tells of Bebb's move north to launch another dubious venture in
   evangelism.
3. *Love Feast* (Atheneum, 1974)
   As trouble comes to Antonio's marriage, his father-in-law takes up
   with Gertrude Conover, a seventy-year-old Theosophist, and starts
   the Love Feast movement to evangelize the Pepsi generation.
4. *Treasure Hunt* (Atheneum, 1977)
   Antonio and Sharon travel to the old house in South Carolina left to
   them by Leo Bebb and find it occupied.

Burgess, Anthony

I. The Malayan trilogy seems to have been published in the United States only as an omnibus volume entitled *The Long Day Wanes* (Norton, 1964). The series depicts the "long day" of waning British rule in Malaya as seen through the eyes of Victor Crabbe, a young Englishman who enjoys the colorful polyglot country and its relaxed life-style. Unperturbed by the corruption of both town and school officials, Crabbe cares deeply for the young Malayans he teaches and sympathizes with their desire to oust the British.

1. *Time for a Tiger* (Heineman, London, 1956)
   Victor Crabbe teaches history in an English school in Malaya. His wife, Fenella, dislikes the dangerous and primitive country.
2. *Enemy in the Blanket* (Heineman, London, 1958)
   As headmaster at the Haji Ali College, Victor runs into trouble caused by Robert Hardman, a figure from the past.
3. *Beds in the East* (Heineman, London, 1959)
   Now chief education officer and alone—his wife left to go back to England—Victor tries to help a promising young Chinese musician.

II. The other series by this prolific British author concerns the quirky bard F. X. Enderby who writes all his best poetry in the bathroom. Bawdy and hilarious, these books are quite different from the Malayan trilogy.

1. *Inside Mr. Enderby* (McGraw-Hill, 1984)
   Enderby meets and marries the glamorous Vesta Bainbridge and takes a honeymoon trip to Rome. First published pseudonymously in England in 1963.
2. *Enderby Outside* (McGraw-Hill, 1984)
   Having lost Vesta, Enderby renounces poetry and tries out an alter ego (as Hogg the bartender), but his muse reclaims him in Tangiers. Published in England in 1968.
3. *The Clockwork Testament; or Enderby's End* (Knopf, 1974)
   Now famous and living in New York, Enderby teaches and appears on TV talk shows, valiant to his sudden end.
4. *Enderby's Dark Lady; or No End to Enderby* (McGraw-Hill, 1984)
   Burgess revives Enderby and takes him to Indiana to work on the script of a muscial life of Shakespeare.

Note: *Enderby* (Norton, 1968), containing numbers 1 and 2 above, first introduced the poet to American readers.

Butler, Samuel

Although Butler used the New Zealand terrain as the basis for his scenic descriptions, the civilization he wrote about is what its name read backwards implies: Nowhere. By creating a mock civilization to criticize a real one, Butler was able to expose the hypocrisy of his day and attack humbug of all sorts. Erewhon has Musical Banks and a College of Unreason. Its people are punished for getting sick and treated to cures for crime. Butler's satires are still surprisingly sharp and enjoyable and not at all difficult to read, though originally published in 1872 and 1901. The two selections listed below are bound together.

1. *Erewhon; or, Over the Range* (Dutton, 1910)
   Young George Higgs discovers a strange civilization where everything is backwards, including its name. First published in England in 1872.
2. *Erewhon Revisited* (Dutton, 1910)
   George Higgs's young son John tells of his father's return to Erewhon after a twenty-year absence and of the significant changes the older man finds. First published in England in 1901.

Cadell, Elizabeth

Twenty-four-year-old Lucille is the oldest of the six Wayne children, who seem to be happily going their own way. But when Lucille decides to sell the family home, Wood Mount, they all come back to object: Nicholas from the National Service, Roselle from her job in London, Julia from boarding school, and young Simon and Dominic from their home with an aunt and uncle in Shropshire. The first story about this likeable family and their friends was so successful that the author wrote two further books about them.

1. *The Lark Shall Sing* (Morrow, 1955)
   All six Wayne children converge on their family home in Greenhurst, England, when Lucille decides to sell it.

49

2. *The Blue Sky of Spring* (Hodder, London, 1956)
   All is peaceful at Wood Mount, now divided into flats, until American playwright Cliff Herman arrives on the scene.
3. *Six Impossible Things* (Morrow, 1961)
   Nicholas finds a wife, and little Julia returns from Rome, grown-up and beautiful.

Caldwell, Taylor

Caldwell dissects the affairs of the Barbour and Bouchard families of munitions makers from 1837 to the beginning of World War II in these three hefty novels. Ernest Barbour dominates the family and builds the Barbour-Bouchard business and fortune with his ruthless energy. But Caldwell's inclusion of the lives, loves, conflicts, and hatreds of even minor family members gives her work epic proportions.

1. *Dynasty of Death* (Scribner, 1938)
   This book introduces the Barbour and Bouchard families, telling of their emigration to Pennsylvania and of the founding and early years of their arms factory.
2. *The Eagles Gather* (Scribner, 1940)
   The Barbour-Bouchard story continues through the twenties as the company grows in wealth and power amid internal power struggles.
3. *The Final Hour* (Scribner, 1944)
   Covers the period 1939–42, showing the Bouchard family divided between supporting Hitler and the United States.

Calisher, Hortense

Calisher's unique fiction is an imaginative blend of southern gothic and Jamesian introspection, amply leavened with contemporary angst. *False Entry* was well-received as a remarkably accomplished first novel. Those who have read it will want to know more about what happens to Ruth.

1. *False Entry* (Little, 1961)
   In a journal of self-discovery, "Pierre Goodman" recalls his youth in Alabama and the key role he played in a murder trial.

2. *The New Yorkers* (Little, 1969)
   In this exploration of the lives of Ruth and her father, other versions of the murder emerge.

Canning, Victor

These three novels about Samuel Miles, better known as "Smiler," will have special appeal for young adults and animal lovers. Though young Smiler at fifteen has already run afoul of the law, he is a sensitive and observant friend to the animals who share his adventures. Canning writes touchingly but without sentimentalizing or anthropomorphizing his subject.

1. *The Runaways* (Morrow, 1972)
   Smiler finds that his hideout is shared by a cheetah escaped from its enclosure at Longleat Park.
2. *Flight of the Grey Goose* (Morrow, 1973)
   Smiler and a wounded greylag goose take shelter at a beautiful island castle in Scotland.
3. *The Painted Tent* (Morrow, 1974)
   A peregrine falcon is Smiler's companion at the Gypsy farm where Smiler makes his home.

Carr, Phillipa (pseud. of Eleanor Hibbert)

Carr's novels are a blend of gothic and historical, sometimes called costume gothics. They feature the traditional gothic plot of a woman caught in a vaguely menacing mystery and torn between two men—one a passionate or dangerous rogue, and the other a mild-mannered gentleman. The author has fit her main characters into a tenuous family tree covering many generations and called the series the Daughters of England. Victoria Holt (q.v.) and Jean Plaidy (q.v.) are the author's other pseudonyms.

1. *The Miracle at St. Bruno's* (Putnam, 1972)
   Set during the English Reformation, this follows the story of young Damask Farland, whose father was beheaded for helping a monk.

2. *The Lion Triumphant* (Putnam, 1974)
   The early Elizabethan time, with its religious clashes and strife with Spain, gives flavor to Catherine's story.

3. *The Witch from the Sea* (Putnam, 1975)
   The defeat of the Spanish Armada (1588) figures in Linnet Pennylon's journal, as does her traumatic encounter with the evil Squire of Castle Paling.

4. *Saraband for Two Sisters* (Putnam, 1976)
   The story of identical twins, Angelet and Bersaba Landor, is set against the Royalist/Puritan struggles of England in the 1640s.

5. *Lament for a Lost Lover* (Putnam, 1977)
   This tells Arabella Tolworthy's story from her exile in France in 1658 to her marriage with Cavalier Edward Eversleigh and her return to England.

6. *The Love-Child* (Putnam, 1978)
   Young Priscilla Eversleigh's quiet life at Eversleigh Court is abruptly changed with the arrival of Harriet Main and a troubled religious fugitive, Jocelyn Frinton.

7. *The Song of the Siren* (Putnam, 1980)
   Set at the time of the Jacobite uprising (1688), this concerns two half-sisters, the placid Damaris and the fiery Carlotta.

8. *Will You Love Me in September?* (Putnam, 1981)
   This takes up the story of Clarissa Hessenfield, the orphaned love-child of Carlotta, beginning in 1715. English title: *The Drop of the Dice*.

9. *The Adulteress* (Putnam, 1982)
   Zipporah goes to Eversleigh Court to try to uncover a family secret.

10. *Knave of Hearts* (Putnam, 1983)
    Lottie, a young English girl, travels to France during the reign of Louis XV to solve the mystery surrounding her true parentage.

11. *Voices in a Haunted Room* (Putnam, 1984)
    Claudine de Tournville marries one twin, but is in love with the other.

12. *The Return of the Gypsy* (Putnam, 1985)
    A young English girl loses her heart to a gypsy.

13. *Midsummer's Eve* (Putnam, 1986)
    One Midsummer's night, young Annora learns of an evil secret that destroys her happiness. Set early in Victoria's reign.

14. *The Pool of St. Branok* (Putnam, 1987)
    Angelet travels to Australia and meets Ben, with whom she shares a guilty secret.

15. *The Changeling* (Putnam, 1989)
    Victorian London and Cornwall are the scenes for this tale of sibling rivalry between Rebecca, her half-sister Belinda, and Lucie, who has been "adopted" by Rebecca's stepfather.

Carvic, Heron

Miss Emily Seeton is a retired English art teacher whose happy involvement in a series of mysteries has delighted her many fans. As a sleuth armed with an umbrella—her "brolly"—and sometimes in disguise, she is always comic and suspenseful. Her protector and supporter, Superintendent Delphick of Scotland Yard (nicknamed "the Oracle," naturally) supervises Miss Seeton's always chaotic cases.

1. *Picture Miss Seeton* (Harper, 1968)
   Miss Seeton makes her debut as a murder witness in need of protection. But her success in nabbing the mastermind of a dope ring guarantees an encore.
2. *Miss Seeton Draws the Line* (Harper, 1970)
   On vacation in the quiet village of Plummergen, Miss Seeton spies out the nefarious activities of a murderer, an embezzler, and two bicycle bandits.
3. *Witch Miss Seeton* (Harper, 1971)
   When devils and witchcraft seem to be taking over the village of Plummergen, Miss Seeton is on the scene to investigate.
4. *Miss Seeton Sings* (Harper, 1973)
   Forged bank notes and a Greek millionare lead Miss Seeton a merry chase all over Europe.
5. *Odds on Miss Seeton* (Harper, 1975)
   Miss Seeton in jewels and a mauve wig takes up gambling to help break up an organized-crime syndicate.

Cary, Joyce

I. Moviegoers will remember Alec Guinness's portrayal of the irrepressible Gully Jimson in the 1959 film *The Horse's Mouth*. The two earlier novels of that trilogy are filled with an equally memorable cast, including Sara the housekeeper and thoughtful Tom Wilcher. Cary is a novelist of character rather than action; he dissects the entanglements of human relationships with humor, wisdom, and style.

1. *Herself Surprised* (Harper, 1948)
   This book introduces Sara Monday, amiable cook and housekeeper, whose casual view of property finally lands her in jail.
2. *To Be a Pilgrim* (Harper, 1949)
   Tom Wilcher, retired English lawyer, narrates this memoir as he awaits Sara's release from jail.
3. *The Horse's Mouth* (Harper, 1950)
   Gully Jimson, sixty-seven-year-old artist recently released from jail, has the inspiration for his life's masterpiece.

II. This trilogy shows Cary in a somewhat more serious, though no less perceptive, mood. The three books do not fit together chronologically but rather show events from three different points of view. They are best read in order as written.

1. *Prisoner of Grace* (Harper, 1952)
   Nina, the narrator of this volume, is unhappily married to Chester Nimmo.
2. *Except the Lord* (Harper, 1953)
   Chester Nimmo, politician and labor leader, tells of his childhood.
3. *Not Honour More* (Harper, 1955)
   Nina's second husband relates the final dramatic conclusion.

Chandler, Raymond

The tawdry neon wilderness of southern California lends a distinctive atmosphere to Chandler's hard-boiled detective stories. Private eye Philip Marlowe is cold and cynical, yet gruffly compassionate toward the victims of evil. Many of the novels have been filmed: Robert Mitchum, Humphrey Bogart, James Garner, Robert Montgomery, Elliott Gould, and Dick Powell have all played Marlowe. One of the best Marlowe films was Howard Hawkes's 1946 version of *The Big Sleep*, starring Bogart and Lauren Bacall, which was adapted for the screen by William Faulkner. And perhaps one of the worst was the 1977 remake of that title that was set in London, thereby losing all credibility. *The Raymond*

Chandler Omnibus (Knopf, 1964) contains numbers 1, 2, 3, and 4 listed below. The books are listed in order of their publication since there is no real chronology. Chandler published eight volumes in the Marlowe series during his lifetime, and left the first four chapters of a ninth book at his death. Mystery fans had to wait thirty years for *Poodle Springs* to be finished by Robert B. Parker (q.v.). In *Raymond Chandler's Philip Marlowe: A Centennial Celebration* (Knopf, 1988) twenty-three current mystery writers have each written a short story featuring Philip Marlowe.

1. *The Big Sleep* (Knopf, 1939)
   A paralyzed California millionaire and his psychotic daughters are featured in this case of blackmail that turns into murder.
2. *Farewell, My Lovely* (Knopf, 1940)
   Marlowe is hired to hunt down an ex-convict's girlfriend.
3. *The High Window* (Knopf, 1942)
   A stolen coin, a secretive old lady, and her frightened secretary lead Marlowe into the mind of a murderer.
4. *The Lady in the Lake* (Knopf, 1943)
   The corpse in the lake is not the missing lady Marlowe seeks.
5. *The Little Sister* (Houghton, 1949)
   A mousy girl from Kansas hires Marlowe to find her brother. Variant title: *Marlowe*.
6. *The Simple Art of Murder* (Houghton, 1950)
   This is a collection of Chandler short stories, some of which feature Marlowe.
7. *The Long Goodbye* (Houghton, 1953)
   Terry Lennox thinks he has committed a murder, and Marlowe helps him run away to Mexico.
8. *Playback* (Houghton, 1958)
   Marlowe helps a young girl who may be imagining danger.
9. *Poodle Springs* (Putnam, 1989)
   Married to his true love Linda Loring, but ill-at-ease in posh Poodle (i.e., Palm) Springs, Marlowe takes on a missing persons case. Co-authored with Robert B. Parker.

Charteris, Leslie (pseud. of Leslie Charles Bower Yin)

The dashing and elegant Simon Templar, a.k.a. the Saint, is known as the Robin Hood of modern crime for his habit of generously redistributing his profits and for his total callousness about "blipping the ungodly over the beezer." His decidedly free-lance exploits include a full measure of danger as well as "plenty of good beer and damsels in distress." George Sanders starred as the Saint in a series of films made by RKO beginning in 1938. Roger Moore and Ian Ogilvie played the Saint in two different British television series. Some later titles were apparently novelizations of television scripts: *The Saint and the Templar Treasure* (Doubleday, 1979); *Leslie Charteris' Count on the Saint* (Doubleday, 1980); *Leslie Charteris' Salvage for the Saint* (Doubleday, 1983).

1. *Meet the Tiger* (Doubleday, 1928)
   The Saint, in pursuit of the Tiger's hidden treasure, is helped by lovely young Patricia Holm, who is established in this first Saint volume and reappears throughout the series as Templar's steady. Variant title: *The Saint Meets the Tiger.*
2. *The Last Hero* (Doubleday, 1930)
   The Saint succeeds where Scotland Yard failed to rid London of some of its worst underworld figures, including Dr. Marius. Variant title: *The Saint Closes the Case.*
3. *Enter the Saint* (Doubleday, 1930)
   Three stories.
4. *The Avenging Saint* (Doubleday, 1931)
   Simon Templar enters the world of international intrigue to prevent another world war. English title: *Knight Templar.*
5. *Wanted for Murder* (Doubleday, 1931)
   This book includes two titles published separately in England, *Featuring the Saint* and *Alias the Saint*, each of which contains three stories.
6. *Angels of Doom* (Doubleday, 1932)
   The Saint meets the beautiful gangster Jill Trelawney and plots a "coup that was to rock England." Variant titles: *She Was a Lady* and *The Saint Meets His Match.*
7. *The Saint v. Scotland Yard* (Doubleday, 1932)
   The duel between the Saint and Inspector Teal of Scotland Yard continues through these three novelettes. Variant title: *The Holy Terror.*
8. *Getaway* (Doubleday, 1932)
   An assortment of crown jewels is stolen several times over. Variant title: *The Saint's Getaway.*
9. *The Saint and Mr. Teal* (Doubleday, 1933)
   Three long stories: "The Gold Standard," "The Man from St.

Louis," and "The Death Penalty." Variant title: *Once More the Saint.*

10. *The Brighter Buccaneer* (Doubleday, 1933)
    This is a collection of short stories starring the Saint.

11. *The Misfortunes of Mr. Teal* (Doubleday, 1934)
    In these three novelettes, Inspector Teal tries unsuccessfully to prove that the Saint is a crook. Variant title: *The Saint in London* and *The Saint in England.*

12. *The Saint Intervenes* (Doubleday, 1934)
    Here are more short stories featuring the Saint. Variant title: *Boodle.*

13. *The Saint Goes On* (Doubleday, 1935)
    This book comprises three novelettes: "The High Fence," "The Ellusive Ellshaw," and "The Case of the Frightened Innkeeper."

14. *The Saint in New York* (Doubleday, 1935)
    Simon Templar bedevils New York City's police commissioner.

15. *The Saint Overboard* (Doubleday, 1936)
    The Saint takes on racketeer "Birdie" Vogel and falls in love with Loretta Page. Variant title: *The Pirate Saint.*

16. *The Ace of Knaves* (Doubleday, 1937)
    The Saint stars in three more novelettes. Variant title: *The Saint in Action.*

17. *Thieves' Picnic* (Doubleday, 1937)
    The Saint rescues a lovely damsel in the Canary Islands, and comes across a fortune in stolen jewels and a winning lottery ticket. Variant titles: *The Saint Bids Diamonds* and *The Saint at the Thieves' Picnic.*

18. *Prelude for War* (Doubleday, 1938)
    The Saint prevents a war that would have ended civilization. Variant title: *The Saint Plays with Fire.*

19. *Follow the Saint* (Doubleday, 1938)
    Three novelettes are included here.

20. *The Happy Highwayman* (Doubleday, 1939)
    Nine short stories feature the Saint.

21. *The Saint in Miami* (Doubleday, 1940)
    The Saint pursues some fifth columnists through Florida.

22. *The Saint Goes West* (Doubleday, 1942)
    These three novelettes are set in Arizona, Palm Springs, and Hollywood.

23. *The Saint Steps In* (Doubleday, 1943)
    The Saint takes on a special assignment for the FBI.

24. *The Saint on Guard* (Doubleday, 1944)
Saboteurs in Galveston and black-market metals occupy the Saint, still aiding the FBI, in these two novelettes. Variant title: *The Saint and the Sizzling Saboteur.*

25. *The Saint Sees It Through* (Doubleday, 1946)
The Saint adapts his ways to the New World in this tough, Raymond Chandler–type adventure.

26. *Call for the Saint* (Doubleday, 1948)
Two novelettes provide more adventures of the Saint.

27. *Saint Errant* (Doubleday, 1948)
Nine short stories follow the Saint.

28. *The Saint in Europe* (Doubleday, 1953)
This is a grand tour of seven stories.

29. *The Saint on the Spanish Main* (Doubleday, 1955)
These six stories are set in the Caribbean.

30. *The Saint Around the World* (Doubleday, 1956)
These six stories include a reappearance of the long-suffering Scotland Yard Inspector, Claud Eustace Teal.

31. *Thanks to the Saint* (Doubleday, 1957)
Six more short stories continue the Saint's adventures.

32. *Senor Saint* (Doubleday, 1958)
More short stories involve the Saint.

33. *The Saint to the Rescue* (Doubleday, 1959)
These six stories are set in Georgia, California, and Florida.

34. *Trust the Saint* (Doubleday, 1962)
More short stories concern the Saint.

35. *The Saint in the Sun* (Doubleday, 1963)
Charteris provides still more short stories.

36. *Vendetta for the Saint* (Doubleday, 1964)
The Saint takes on the Mafia in Sicily.

37. *The Saint on TV* (Doubleday, 1967)
Beginning with this volume, the Saint books have been adaptations of TV programs written by others and only revised or reviewed by Charteris. This books contains two stories: "The Death Game" and "The Power Artist."

38. *The Saint Returns* (Doubleday, 1968)
"The Dizzy Daughter" and "The Gadget Lovers" are included here.

39. *The Saint and the Fiction Makers* (Doubleday, 1968)
The evil Warlock plots to bring to life a series of spy novels.

40. *The Saint Abroad* (Doubleday, 1969)
Two novelettes follow the Saint's adventures.

41. *The Saint in Pursuit* (Doubleday, 1970)
    A young woman receives a letter on her twenty-fifth birthday giving her a huge treasure, but she must outwit Russian and U.S. intelligence agents to get it.
42. *The Saint and the People Importers* (Doubleday, 1970)
    The Saint gets involved in some illegal immigration from Pakistan to Britain.
43. *Catch the Saint* (Doubleday, 1975)
    "The Masterpiece Merchant" and "The Adoring Socialite" make up this book.
44. *The Saint and the Hapsburg Necklace* (Doubleday, 1976)
    On the eve of World War II, Simon Templar helps a beautiful countess retrieve a valuable necklace from Gestapo hands.
45. *The Saint in Trouble* (Doubleday, 1978)
    Two stories, "The Imprudent Professor," and "The Red Sabbath," are included here.

Cheever, John

Set in St. Botolph's, an imaginary shore town in Massachusetts with a striking resemblance to Quincy, Cheever's hometown, these gently satirical novels about the Wapshot family are alternately hilarious and poignant. Although the noble Yankee blood is running thin in young Moses and Coverly, their eccentric and lovable father Leander honors his seafaring ancestors as the crusty captain of the local ferry—until he sinks it. Some still regard these two novels as Cheever's best work.

1. *The Wapshot Chronicle* (Harper, 1957)
   This books introduces old Captain Leander Wapshot, his wife, two sons, and sister Honoria.
2. *The Wapshot Scandal* (Harper, 1964)
   The two young Wapshot boys are the focus here. The "scandal" is that Aunt Honoria neglected to pay her income tax.

Chesney, Marion

Scottish-born Chesney has brought a new vigor to the Regency novel and won many American fans to the genre. Her portrait of the inevitable debs and rakes of London society goes beyond stereotype. She gives inventive twists to the standard plots and describes the dress and manners of the period with authority and wit. In a word, larky.

I. Each novel in the Six Sisters series focuses on one of the daughters of the Reverend Charles Armitage, an amiable but impoverished country vicar with a passion for fox hunting. Faced with the fearsome task of educating two sons and marrying off six daughters with no fortune, the vicar does his plucky best.

1. *Minerva* (St. Martins, 1983)
   Minerva, the oldest daughter, is sent off to London to rescue the family fortune by finding a rich husband.
2. *The Taming of Annabelle* (St. Martins, 1984)
   At 16, Annabelle is beautiful, wildly romantic, and jealous of Minerva.
3. *Deirdre and Desire* (St. Martins, 1984)
   The vicar despairs of ever finding a suitable husband for his intellectual daughter Deirdre.
4. *Daphne* (St. Martins, 1984)
   When Simon Garfield falls into a trap set by the Reverend Armitage for a meddling bishop, he distracts Daphne from her plans to marry vapid Cyril Archer.
5. *Diana the Huntress* (St. Martins, 1985)
   Diana would rather hunt foxes with her father than hunt for a suitable husband.
6. *Frederica in Fashion* (St. Martins, 1985)
   Frederica, the plain sister, leaves school and takes a job as a housemaid for the wicked Duke of Pembury.

II. A House for the Season is the title of this ingenious series of six Regency novels which all take place in the same house: 76 Clarges Street, in the fashionable Mayfair section of London. Each season brings a new tenant with a new story, while the unchanging domestic staff, ruled by the resourceful butler Rainbird, gives continuity.

1. *The Miser of Mayfair* (St. Martins, 1986)
   Beautiful Fiona Sinclair teaches Mayfair some new card tricks and catches the beau of her choice.
2. *Plain Jane* (St. Martins, 1986)
   When Mrs. Rawley comes to Mayfair to launch her two daughters into society, she expects to have the most trouble with her younger daughter, Jane.

3. *The Wicked Godmother* (St. Martins, 1987)
   Sweet and dutiful Harriet Metcalf brings her two wealthy young charges to London for the season, and finds herself eclipsing their success.
4. *Rake's Progress* (St. Martins, 1987)
   Lord Guy Carlton, wounded in the Napoleonic Wars, cuts a dashing figure in Mayfair until he meets his neighbor, the severe Miss Jones.
5. *The Adventuress* (St. Martins, 1987)
   There is something mysterious about the reserved Mr. Goodenough and his beautiful daughter that puzzles the staff.
6. *Rainbird's Revenge* (St. Martins, 1988)
   Rainbird the butler sets everything to rights, exposing the embezzlements of Parker, the real estate agent, and helping Lord Pelham, the house's owner, find a wife.

III. Chesney's newest Regency series, The School of Manners, features Amy and Effie Tribble, resourceful elderly sisters who fend off poverty by going into the chaperoning business. Each of the six scheduled installments will tell the story of a different client.

1. *Refining Felicity* (St. Martins, 1988)
   Amy and Effie take on the unenviable task of preparing horsey Felicity Baronsheath for the marriage market.
2. *Perfecting Fiona* (St. Martins, 1989)
   Beautiful Fiona McCloud skillfully avoids marriage until the rakish Lord Harvard crosses her horizon.
3. *Enlightening Delilah* (St. Martins, 1989)
   No one can understand why beautiful Delilah Wraxall is unmarried at twenty-three.
4. *Finessing Clarissa* (St. Martins, 1989)
   Accomplishing the marriage of the large and clumsy, freckle-faced and red-haired Clarissa Vevian is a tall order even for the redoubtable Tribbles.

Christie, Agatha

I. Agatha Christie's position as the world's most famous modern mystery writer is likely to remain unchallenged for some time. *The Mysterious Affair at Styles*, surely one of the most polished first mystery novels ever written, won her immediate recognition. Though she was capable of writing an inferior book from time to time, the inventiveness and productivity that she sustained over the next fifty-six years were truly remarkable. Not all of Christie's books feature one of her famous detectives: among these are her less successful international espionage thrillers, but also one of her best known, *Ten Little Indians* (also known as *And Then There Were None*). For convenience, these miscellaneous works are listed but not annotated in Section VI below. More information about them, and about many other aspects of Christie's work, including films based on her books, is available in the delightful compendium edited by Dick Riley and Pam McAllister entitled *The Bedside, Bathtub and Armchair Companion to Agatha Christie* (Ungar, 1979).

The retired Belgian police detective Hercule Poirot is the most famous of Christie's detectives. This fastidious little man with the waxed moustache and a fondness for growing vegetable marrows used his remarkable "gray cells" to reason his way to the bottom of the most complicated cases. Sprung fully developed into the world with Christie's first book, Poirot changed little through the years and must have been, by ordinary reckoning, well over 100 years old at the end of his career. Connoisseurs consider the Poirot books the best of Christie's output. The stories are listed here in the order of their publication, which except for a few flashback cases is the correct sequence.

1. *The Mysterious Affair at Styles* (Grosset, 1920)
   Hastings narrates this accomplished first novel, the story of the strychnine poisoning of the imperious Emily Inglethorpe of Styles Court in Essex. Poirot, who lives in the neighborhood, comes to investigate.
2. *Murder on the Links* (Dodd, 1923)
   Poirot arrives too late to save Paul Renaud from being murdered and buried in a shallow grave in his own golf course.
3. *Poirot Investigates* (Dodd, 1925)
   These fourteen stories show Captain Hastings at his most dense. Several flashback stories are included.
4. *The Murder of Roger Ackroyd* (Dodd, 1926)
   This landmark case concerns three deaths and a blackmail. The solution has been thought a stroke of genius by some and a dirty trick by others.
5. *The Big Four* (Dodd, 1927)
   Hastings, Poirot, and Inspector Japp pursue an international gang of criminals bent on the "disintegration of civilization." Not Poirot's metier.

6. *The Mystery of the Blue Train* (Dodd, 1928)
   When murder occurs on the Blue Train to Nice, Poirot is on the spot to help solve the case.

7. *Peril at End House* (Dodd, 1932)
   Hastings and Poirot, while on vacation on the Cornish Riviera, try to protect the young heiress, Nick Buckley, whose life is in danger.

8. *Thirteen at Dinner* (Dodd, 1933)
   Lord Edgware is found dead in his library of a small stab wound at the base of his neck. Variant title: *Lord Edgware Dies*.

9. *Murder on the Orient Express* (Dodd, 1934)
   Stuck on board a train in a snowbank in Yugoslavia, Poirot knows that Ratchett's murderer must be among the passengers. Original title: *Murder in the Calais Coach*.

10. *Murder in Three Acts* (Dodd, 1934)
    Two murders by nicotine poisoning are unrelated except for the suspicious presence of Ellis the butler. Poirot stages another temptation for the murderer. English title: *Three-Act Tragedy*.

11. *Death in the Air* (Dodd, 1935)
    Could Madame Giselle have been murdered by a poison dart with Poirot in a nearby seat on the noon flight from Paris to London? Variant title: *Death in the Clouds*.

12. *The A.B.C. Murders* (Dodd, 1935)
    A mad murderer warns Poirot by letter before committing each of a series of murders.

13. *Murder in Mesopotamia* (Dodd, 1936)
    Poirot happens to be passing through when the murder of a woman on an archaeological expedition on the banks of the Tigris attracts his attention.

14. *Cards on the Table* (Dodd, 1936)
    Poirot shares the spotlight with Ariadne Oliver (see Section III), Superintendent Battle (see Section V), and Colonel Race, a secret-service man, as guest at an unusual dinner party given by socialite and murder authority Dr. Shaitana.

15. *Poirot Loses a Client* (Dodd, 1937)
    A letter draws Hastings and Poirot to the little town of Market Basing, but they find that their correspondent, old Emily Arundell, has been dead for over a month. Variant titles: *Dumb Witness; Murder at Littlegreen House;* and *Mystery at Littlegreen House*.

16. *Dead Man's Mirror* (Dodd, 1937)
    Three stories are included here: "Dead Man's Mirror," "Murder in the Mews," and "Triangle at Rhodes."

17. *Death on the Nile* (Dodd, 1938)
    A rich and beautiful young bride is being driven to distraction by an old friend, her husband's former fiancée. Among the vacationers on the Nile cruise is Hercule Poirot.

18. *Appointment with Death* (Dodd, 1938)
    The murder of fat, obnoxious Mrs. Boynton finds Poirot on vacation in Jerusalem.

19. *Murder for Christmas* (Dodd, 1938)
    Simon Lee, who made his millions in the South African diamond mines, has his throat slit on Christmas Eve at his country estate. Variant titles: *Holiday for Murder* and *Hercule Poirot's Christmas*.

20. *The Regatta Mystery* (Dodd, 1939)
    These nine stories feature Poirot, Miss Marple, and Parker Pyne. Variant title: *Poirot and the Regatta Mystery*.

21. *Sad Cypress* (Dodd, 1940)
    Elinor Carlisle gains a fortune when her Aunt Laura dies, but she loses her only love, Roddy Welman, and finds herself accused of murdering Roddy's new bride.

22. *The Patriotic Murders* (Dodd, 1940)
    Could Dr. Morley, Poirot's dentist, have committed suicide in his office while patients waited? Variant titles: *An Overdose of Death* and *One, Two, Buckle My Shoe*.

23. *Evil under the Sun* (Dodd, 1941)
    At the Jolly Roger Hotel in an English seaside resort, an aging actress is murdered, and Poirot finds no shortage of suspects.

24. *Murder in Retrospect* (Dodd, 1943)
    Carla Crale hires Poirot to find out the truth about her mother, who was convicted of murdering her husband, Carla's father. Variant title: *Five Little Pigs*.

25. *Murder after Hours* (Dodd, 1946)
    A weekend house party at the Angkatells' house, The Hollow, proves fatal for Dr. John Christow, who is shot just as Poirot arrives for lunch. Variant title: *The Hollow*.

26. *The Labours of Hercules* (Dodd, 1947)
    Poirot vows that the cases detailed in these twelve stories will be the last before his retirement; they correspond to the famous labors of the classical Hercules.

27. *There Is a Tide* (Dodd, 1948)
    Poirot lingers in the town of Warmsley Vale after the curious murder of an unidentified man. Variant title: *Taken at the Flood*.

28. *Witness for the Prosecution* (Dodd, 1948)
Only one of the ten stories in this collection features Poirot.

29. *The Mousetrap and Other Stories* (Dodd, 1950)
Three of the nine stories collected here star Poirot. Variant title: *Three Blind Mice.*

30. *The Underdog and Other Stories* (Dodd, 1951)
Nine Poirot stories comprise this book.

31. *Mrs. McGinty's Dead* (Dodd, 1952)
Poirot and Ariadne renew their acquaintance in the village of Broadhinny as Poirot investigates the death of Mrs. McGinty, a domestic whom nobody seems to care about. Variant title: *Blood Will Tell.*

32. *Funerals Are Fatal* (Dodd, 1953)
After three suspicious deaths and a fourth murder attempt, Poirot calls the Abernethie family back to Enderby Hall for a fatal gathering. Variant title: *After the Funeral.*

33. *Hickory, Dickory Death* (Dodd, 1955)
When Poirot's secretary, Felicity Lemon, is worried about some mysterious thefts at the student hotel that her sister runs, Poirot offers to help. Variant title: *Hickory Dickory Dock.*

34. *Dead Man's Folly* (Dodd, 1956)
Ariadne Oliver, who is arranging a murder-hunt game for a charity fete, requests Poirot's help when she feels very uneasy about things.

35. *Cat among the Pigeons* (Dodd, 1959)
Meadowbank School for girls is the scene of this case involving smuggled jewels and a Turkish princess.

36. *The Adventure of the Christmas Pudding* (Collins, London, 1960)
Five Poirots and one Marple story make up this confection.

37. *Double Sin and Other Stories* (Dodd, 1961)
Poirot stories account for four out of nine in this collection.

38. *The Clocks* (Dodd, 1963)
Elements in this curious case are: four clocks frozen at 4:13, a blind murder suspect, and an unidentified victim.

39. *Third Girl* (Dodd, 1966)
Ariadne Oliver helps the aging Poirot with this case of a young girl who thinks she might have committed a murder.

40. *Halloween Party* (Dodd, 1969)
Mrs. Oliver is cured of her apple addiction when a child drowns bobbing for apples, but Poirot solves the murder.

41. *Elephants Can Remember* (Dodd, 1972)
Mrs. Oliver and Poirot work together to solve an old murder case.

42. *Poirot's Early Cases* (Dodd, 1974)
   These stories are all available in other collections as well. Variant title: *Hercule Poirot's Early Cases*.
43. *Curtain* (Dodd, 1975)
   Poirot calls Hastings back to Styles for the case he knows will be his last.
44. *Hercule Poirot's Casebook* (Dodd, 1984)
   This book contains 50 Poirot stories.

II. While Christie grew to hate Poirot, she was always fond of Jane Marple, her white-haired spinster whose knowledge of human nature gained as a lifelong busybody in the little village of St. Mary Mead made her an excellent detective. The character was based somewhat on Christie's grandmother, who, though cheerful, always expected the worst of everybody and was usually right. Margaret Rutherford was all wrong for the part, really, but her movie portraits are delightful anyway. Anne Hart pieced together Miss Marple's "biography" in *The Life and Times of Miss Jane Marple* (Dodd, 1985).

1. *Murder at the Vicarage* (Dodd, 1930)
   When the universally disliked Colonel Protheroe is found murdered in the vicar's study, two people confess, and Miss Marple's curiosity is aroused.
2. *The Tuesday Club Murders* (Dodd, 1933)
   Miss Marple solves thirteen different mysteries while knitting by her fireplace. Variant title: *Thirteen Problems*.
3. *The Regatta Mystery* (Dodd, 1939)
   This collection includes some Marple stories along with Poirots and Parker Pynes. Variant title: *Poirot and the Regatta Mystery*.
4. *The Body in the Library* (Dodd, 1942)
   An unidentified woman in evening clothes appears as if by magic in the library in Gossington Hall.
5. *The Moving Finger* (Dodd, 1942)
   When anonymous obscene letters cause a suicide in the quiet little town of Lymstock, Miss Marple, who is visiting at the vicarage, helps find the guilty party.
6. *The Mousetrap and Other Stories* (Dodd, 1950)
   There are four Marple stories out of nine in this collection. Variant title: *Three Blind Mice*.
7. *A Murder Is Announced* (Dodd, 1950)
   A murder is announced in the "personal" column of the news-

paper, and everybody assumes it to be a new kind of parlor game.

8. *Murder with Mirrors* (Dodd, 1952)
A confusing case for Miss Marple involves the alleged slow poisoning of the lady of the house and a houseful of supposedly reformed delinquent boys. Variant title: *They Do It with Mirrors.*

9. *A Pocket Full of Rye* (Dodd, 1954)
Miss Marple, who knew the murdered servant girl as a child, thinks that a nursery rhyme may yield important information.

10. *What Mrs. McGillicuddy Saw* (Dodd, 1957)
From her window seat, Elspeth McGillicuddy sees a murder taking place in a train running parallel. Fortunately she is on her way to visit Miss Marple. Variant titles: *4:50 from Paddington* and *Murder, She Said.*

11. *The Adventure of the Christmas Pudding* (Collins, London, 1960)
Here is one Marple in a package with five Poirots.

12. *Double Sin and Other Stories* (Dodd, 1961)
This collection has two Marples out of nine stories.

13. *The Mirror Crack'd* (Dodd, 1962)
When American movie actress Marina Gregory and her director-husband move to St. Mary Mead, the little town sizzles with glamour and mystery. Variant title: *The Mirror Crack'd from Side to Side.*

14. *A Caribbean Mystery* (Dodd, 1964)
Thanks to her rich nephew Raymond, Miss Marple is transported to a carefree Caribbean resort, which she finds rather boring until a murder enlivens things.

15. *At Bertrams Hotel* (Dodd, 1965)
Bertrams, a bastion of old London hospitality, provides commodious fireplace chairs where Miss Marple overhears some very curious goings on.

16. *Nemesis* (Dodd, 1971)
Miss Marple will receive a bequest if she can solve a problem that is only vaguely defined and starts with a bus tour of famous English houses.

17. *Sleeping Murder* (Dodd, 1976)
An old murder is recalled by a young woman having a curious case of déjà vu as she renovates a cozy little home in the village of Dillmouth.

18. *Miss Marple: The Complete Short Stories* (Dodd, 1985)
A collection of all 20 Marple short stories.

III. Just as Captain Hastings acted as an early Watson figure for Poirot, Mrs. Ariadne Oliver serves this purpose in the later works, and she adds considerable comic interest as well. There can be little doubt that Ariadne Oliver is an autobiographical figure; she is the best-selling author of mysteries starring the famous vegetarian Finnish detective. Oliver even resembles her creator physically, with her wiry gray hair, tendency to plumpness, and habit of eating apples while writing. Through Mrs. Oliver, who claims to hate the eccentric little detective she has immortalized, Christie indulges in some delicious self-parody.

1. *Mr. Parker Pyne, Detective* (Dodd, 1934)
   Mrs. Oliver first appears as a mystery writer who devises plots for the unusual detection practiced by Parker Pyne, as shown in this collection of cases.
2. *The Pale Horse* (Dodd, 1961)
   Mrs. Oliver plays only a small role in this case, which begins with the murder of a Catholic priest. Narrator-historian Mark Easterbrook is the central figure and detective.

Note: Mrs. Oliver also appears as Poirot's helper or chronicler in the following titles, listed fully above with Poirot's books: *Cards on the Table; Mrs. McGinty's Dead; Dead Man's Folly; Third Girl; Halloween Party;* and *Elephants Can Remember.*

IV. Miss Prudence Cowley, known as Tuppence, and her old friend Tommy Beresford are bored after seeing exciting World War I service— she as a nurse and he as an intelligence agent. For a lark they hire themselves out as adventurers and get involved in their first mystery case. They eventually marry and have children, but Tuppence never learns not to take foolish chances when sleuthing.

1. *The Secret Adversary* (Dodd, 1922)
   A secret message carried from the sinking *Lusitania* by a young girl is at the bottom of the mystery that Tommy and Tuppence bungle into.
2. *Partners in Crime* (Dodd, 1929)
   This collection shows Tommy and Tuppence, now married, using, and parodying, different methods of detection for each case that is brought to them.
3. *N or M?* (Dodd, 1941)
   Doing their part in the World War II effort, Tommy and Tuppence

in disguise try to spot a mysterious Nazi agent at an English hotel.

4. *By the Pricking of My Thumbs* (Dodd, 1968)
   Now graying, but no more cautious, Tuppence pokes into a mystery that involves some dotty old ladies in a nursing home, a painting, and a doll found in a fireplace.

5. *Postern of Fate* (Dodd, 1974)
   Tommy and Tuppence retire to a cottage in the country, where a mysterious message of underlined words in a children's book entices Tuppence to investigate.

V. Superintendent Battle of Scotland Yard appears in four of Christie's complicated country-home murders. Battle is a methodical professional, reputed to be the Yard's best. He is also one of the characters in *Cards on the Table*, listed in Section I.

1. *The Secret of Chimneys* (Dodd, 1925)
   Battle is called to investigate the murder of Count Stanislas of Herzoslovakia at the country estate of Chimneys.

2. *The Seven Dials Mystery* (Dodd, 1929)
   Chimneys is again the setting for this lighthearted thriller featuring Lady Eileen "Bundle" Brent sleuthing into the death of a houseguest at her rented-out family estate. Battle appears, very ineptly disguised.

3. *Easy to Kill* (Dodd, 1939)
   Miss Fullerton is killed in a hit-and-run accident while on her way to inform Scotland Yard of her suspicions. Retired police officer Luke Fitzwilliams does most of the investigating, but Superintendent Battle also appears. This book was recently adapted for television. Variant title: *Murder Is Easy*.

4. *Towards Zero* (Dodd, 1944)
   A clever murder is planned seven months before it takes place, and Superintendent Battle is called in to investigate the murder of Lady Camilla Tressilian at her seaside estate, Gull's Point. Variant title: *Come and Be Hanged*.

VI. Christie also produced a number of mystery novels and short-story collections not featuring one of the above detectives.

1. *The Man in the Brown Suit* (Dodd, 1924)
2. *The Mysterious Mr. Quin* (Dodd, 1930)
   This is a collection of stories.

3. *Murder at Hazelmoor* (Dodd, 1931)
   Variant title: *Sittaford Mystery.*
4. *Why Didn't They Ask Evans?* (Dodd, 1934)
   Variant title: *The Boomerang Clue.*
5. *Ten Little Indians* (Dodd, 1940)
   Variant title: *And Then There Were None.*
6. *Sparkling Cyanide* (Dodd, 1945)
   Variant title: *Remembered Death.*
7. *Death Comes as the End* (Dodd, 1945)
8. *Crooked House* (Dodd, 1949)
9. *They Came to Baghdad* (Dodd, 1951)
10. *So Many Steps to Death* (Dodd, 1954)
    Variant title: *Destination Unknown.*
11. *Ordeal by Innocence* (Dodd, 1958)
12. *Endless Night* (Dodd, 1967)
13. *Passenger to Frankfurt* (Dodd, 1970)
14. *The Golden Ball and Other Stories* (Dodd, 1971)

Churchill, Winston

These solid, leisurely historical novels written by the St. Louis-born American were best-sellers in their day. Naturally there was some confusion in readers' minds between him and the British statesman. It is said that the Englishman wrote to the American, suggesting that one of them should change his name. The American agreed but said that, since the Englishman was younger by three years, the change was his to make. Thereafter the English Churchill's signature read "Winston S. Churchill."

1. *Richard Carvel* (Macmillan, 1899)
   The adventures of young Richard, from his childhood in colonial Maryland to action with John Paul Jones.
2. *The Crisis* (Macmillan, 1901)
   Centers on young Virginia Carvel, descendant of Richard, at the time of the Civil War.

Chute, Carolyn

The dirt poor characters of Faulkner's Yoknapatawpha County, Mississippi, now have some new literary cousins in Maine, thanks to Carolyn Chute. The small and impoverished backwoods town of Egypt is inhabited by people accustomed to privation and violence. Mrs. Chute herself lives in rural Maine, close enough to her prototypes to write with authority, yet with sufficient distance for artfulness.

1. *The Beans of Egypt, Maine* (Ticknor, 1985)
   Young Earlene flees her own family to marry Beal Bean.
2. *Letourneau's Used Auto Parts* (Ticknor, 1988)
   This focuses on the Letourneau clan living in a trailer park outside of Egypt.

Clancy, Tom

Jack Ryan is the indomitable hero of three of Clancy's action suspense stories. Jack lives in Annapolis and teaches history at the Naval Academy—more for love than money, because he has already made enough money as a stock broker to retire. He is also an ex-marine who takes on occasional special assignments for the CIA. The books can be read in any order, though Clancy incorporates a thread of chronology based on Ryan's daughter's age.

1. *Patriot Games* (Putnam, 1987)
   On vacation in London with his wife and daughter, Jack stops a terrorist attack on the Prince and Princess of Wales, and becomes a target for revenge.
2. *The Hunt for Red October* (Naval Institute Press, 1984)
   Both the U.S. and Russian navies are in hot pursuit of a defecting Soviet submarine loaded with deadly missiles.
3. *The Cardinal of the Kremlin* (Putnam, 1988)
   Jack must save Colonel Filtrov, an American agent in the Kremlin.
4. *Clear and Present Danger* (Putnam, 1989)
   Sergeant Chavet and his U.S. Army infantrymen must be extradited from Colombia after a misfired attempt to sabotage the illegal drug trade.

Note: Ryan does not appear in the author's 1986 thriller *Red Storm Rising*.

Clarke, Arthur C.

Although he has won awards and a large following for his science fiction and his science fact writings, Arthur Clarke's greatest claim to fame is his co-authorship (with Stanley Kubrick) of the screenplay to *2001: A Space Odyssey*, which has mesmerized a generation of movie viewers with its special effects, its insane computer HAL, and its hallucinatory ending. The germ of *2001* was Clarke's short story "The Sentinel" (anthologized in his *Expedition to Earth*, Ballantine, 1953). Clarke's novelization of *2001*, which ends differently than the movie, was followed by two "variations on the same theme, involving many of the same characters and situations, but not necessarily happening in the same universe" (preface to *2001*).

1. *2001: A Space Odyssey* (New American Lib., 1968)
   Dave Bowman, his fellow astronauts, and the computer HAL set off with the spaceship *Discovery* in search of proof that extraterrestrials sparked the development of intelligent life on Earth.
2. *2010: Odyssey Two* (Ballantine, 1982)
   In this sequel to the movie version of *2001*, Heywood Floyd is sent on a joint Soviet/American space mission to find out what happened to the *Discovery* and its crew.
3. *2061: Odyssey Three* (Ballantine, 1988)
   Now the oldest man alive, Heywood Floyd embarks on a journey that will culminate in a manned landing on Halley's Comet, while his grandson Chris is stranded on the moon Europa.

Coleman, Lonnie

Readers who enjoyed *Gone with the Wind* will sink happily into Coleman's Beulah Land trilogy. The story of the Kendrick family and the development of their Georgia plantation begins in 1800. Lots of action and lusty characters keep the saga sizzling along.

1. *Beulah Land* (Doubleday, 1973)
   Details the founding of Beulah Land and its flowering during pre-Civil War days.
2. *Look Away, Beulah Land* (Doubleday, 1977)
   The end of the war and the period of reconstruction are hard times for the Kendricks and their land.
3. *The Legacy of Beulah Land* (Doubleday, 1980)
   Hard won stability returns to the Georgia plantation, but social progress brings new challenges.

Colette, Sidonie-Gabrielle

I. *Claudine at School* was an immediate best-seller in France when it was first published in 1900. The story of the intelligent and vivacious Claudine has important parallels to Colette's life. All four Claudine books were written in collaboration with her husband "Willy," Henri Gauthier-Villars. They are collected in *The Complete Claudine* (Farrar, 1976), translated by Antonia White.

1. *Claudine at School* (Boni, 1930)
   Fifteen-year-old Claudine records the events of her last year at school in a journal full of schoolgirl gushing and innuendo. First published in 1900 as *Claudine à l'ecole.*
2. *Claudine in Paris* (Farrar, 1958)
   Now seventeen, Claudine has come to Paris to live with her father; she moves into society and falls in love. Published in 1901 as *Claudine à Paris.*
3. *Claudine Married* (Farrar, 1953)
   Though Claudine and Renaud love each other, their marriage leaves her dissatisfied, and she has a brief lesbian affair. First published in 1902 as *Claudine en manage.* Original English title: *The Indulgent Husband.*
4. *Claudine and Annie* (Farrar, 1934)
   Claudine, reunited with her husband, plays a secondary role in this book, which is the journal of her friend Annie. First published in 1903 as *Claudine s'en va.* Original English title: *The Innocent Wife.*

Note: *La maison de Claudine*, published in France in 1922 and later in English with the title *My Mother's House*, has nothing to do with the early Claudine books. It is thought that Colette used the name Claudine in the title for its commercial advantage.

II. The two books in which Chéri figure are considered among the finest of Colette's mature works. They concern Léa, an aging courtesan, and her handsome young lover, Chéri. Edmée, the rich, young woman Chéri marries, plays a minor role. They were published in the United States in a one-volume edition, *Chéri and the Last of Chéri* (Farrar, 1951).

1. *Chéri* (Boni, 1929)
   Their separation proves devastating for both Léa and Chéri. Paris in 1912 is the setting. First published in 1920. Translated by Janet Flanner.
2. *The Last of Chéri* (Putnam, 1932)
   Chéri, six years later and a war hero, is still unable to adapt to life without Léa. First published in 1926 as *La fin de Chéri*. Translated by Roger Senhouse.

Collins, Jackie

Jackie Collins writes the kind of story her actress sister stars in—Joan is Alexis in "Dynasty." So it's not surprising that her turbulent tales about glamorous, rich, and sexy people have been made into television mini-series ("The World Is Full of Married Women" and "Hollywood Wives"). In *Chances*, Collins stirred crime and the Mafia into her usual spicy brew. What more could her avaricious readers want? A series, naturally. The pair below trace the fortunes of the Santangelo family from humble beginnings to discontented affluence.

1. *Chances* (Warner, 1981)
   The rise of Carrie from prostitution in Harlem, drug addiction, and a stretch in an insane asylum to the position of millionaire society hostess is paralleled by Gino Santangelo's climb up the organized crime career ladder.
2. *Lucky* (Simon & Schuster, 1985)
   Lucky Santangelo, Gino's daughter, is the successful manager of a Las Vegas hotel, but unhappy in her personal life until she falls in love with young comedian Lennie Golden.

Collins, Max Allan

I. Collins has written the comic strip *Dick Tracy* as well as a variety of detective novels. His Nate Heller books are historical detective stories set in Chicago beginning in the 1930s. Private-eye Nate Heller's sleuthing among the likes of Al Capone, Eliot Ness, and Pretty Boy Floyd is a satisfying mix of fact and fiction complete with period photographs and explanatory "afterwords." This series has won critical acclaim as an action-packed, well-characterized, accurate evocation of the past.

1. *True Detective* (St. Martin's, 1983)
   Young Nathan Heller, disgusted by the corruption in the Chicago police force of the 1930s, turns in his badge and goes private. Frank Nitti, Capone's successor as head of the Chicago mob, is one of the leading characters.
2. *True Crime* (St. Martin's, 1985)
   In 1934 Nate finds himself the patsy in a scheme to locate and kill Public Enemy Number One John Dillinger.
3. *The Million Dollar Wound* (St. Martin's, 1986)
   Hearst columnist Westbrook Pegler and movie star Robert Montgomery ask Nate to get the goods on Willy Bioff, corrupt head of the movie technicians' union.
4. *Neon Mirage* (St. Martin's, 1988)
   In 1946, Nate falls in love and gets caught up in the Las Vegas underworld of "Bugsy" Siegel and others.

II. Collins is also the author of three series featuring protagonists known only by their patronomics. Nolan (a thief) and Quarry (a professional killer) are criminals whose adventures have been pretty much confined to paperback originals. Mallory, an aspiring mystery writer who lives in a small town in Iowa, is based on the author, who is Iowa-born and bred. He is a likeable young man who gets personally involved as an amateur investigator when crime crosses his path.

1. *The Baby Blue Rip-off* (Walker, 1983)
   While delivering hot meals to shut-ins, Mallory discovers a murder.
2. *No Cure for Death* (Walker, 1983)
   Mallory defends a woman from an apparent attack and finds himself involved in murder.
3. *Kill Your Darlings* (Walker, 1984)
   In Chicago for a convention of mystery lovers, Mallory finds his idol, best-selling author Roscoe Kane, the victim of sudden death in a mystery involving an unpublished Dashiell Hammett manuscript.
4. *A Shroud for Aquarius* (Walker, 1984)
   Troubled by the apparent suicide of his high school friend, Ginnie Mullins, Mallory turns up an unsavory past.

Condon, Richard

The Prizzi trilogy is a satirical look at an American Mafia family rather than a family saga like *The Godfather*. As portrayed by Richard Condon the Prizzis' operations are legitimate business enterprises catering to public demand rather than criminal activities. Professional killers like Charley Partanna and Irene Walker seem quite ordinary and even likeable, a view reinforced by the movie version of *Prizzi's Honor* starring Jack Nicholson as Charley and Kathleen Turner as Irene. Richard Condon's pessimistic, cynical view of human nature and institutions is displayed in such best-sellers as *The Manchurian Candidate* and *Winter Kills* as well as in the Prizzi trilogy.

1. *Prizzi's Family* (Putnam, 1986)
   Charley Partanna, hitman for the Prizzi crime empire, is torn between his love for showgirl-heiress Mardell La Tour and his duty to marry Maerose Prizzi, the Don's granddaughter.
2. *Prizzi's Honor* (Coward, 1982)
   Ten years later Charley must choose between love and duty again when he falls for Irene Walker, a free-lance professional killer who has stolen money from a Prizzi operation in Las Vegas.
3. *Prizzi's Glory* (Dutton, 1988)
   The Prizzis try to transform Charley into America's most respected businessman in order to capture the White House in the 1992 presidential election.

Connell, Evan

These companion pieces are understanding portraits of the typical middle-class American family of the 1930s. The Bridges of Kansas City live in a good residential neighborhood, attend the local Congregational church, and worry about properly raising their three children. Walter is a lawyer who looks as though he was born wearing a suit and tie. India is competent, selfless, and always gracious. The stories are not altogether as dull as they sound.

1. *Mrs. Bridge* (Viking, 1959)
   This series of vignettes shows India running an efficient home, negotiating the small dramas of family life with skill and kindness, and facing the approach of middle age with quiet resignation.

2. *Mr. Bridge* (Knopf, 1969)
   A good, though undemonstrative, husband and father, Walter Bridge is shown interacting with friends and family, deciding to buy a new car, explaining Prohibition to his daughter, etc.

Conrad, Joseph

The characteristics of Conrad's later work were already present in his remarkable first novel, *Almayer's Folly*—the brooding tropical setting, the European protagonist slowly degenerating in a savage culture, the suspense and violence inherent to the story, and the beautiful prose style. Conrad didn't begin writing until 1889, after sixteen years at sea aboard French and English merchant ships. He wrote in self-taught English rather than his native Polish, and is known to have carried the manuscript of *Almayer's Folly* with him on many voyages.

1. *The Rescue* (Doubleday, 1920)
   Captain Lingard, who appears as the trader Rajah Laut in numbers 2 and 3, falls in love as a young man with the dangerous Edith Travers.
2. *An Outcast of the Islands* (Appleton, 1896)
   The story of Willems, a shady European, and his obsession with the Malayan woman Aissa. Almayer plays a subordinate part in this novel; his daughter Nina is seen as a little girl.
3. *Almayer's Folly: A Story of an Eastern River* (Macmillan, 1895)
   Doom pursues European Kaspar Almayer's decision to marry a native girl and to live and raise his beloved daughter in Malaya. Although this was Conrad's first novel, it follows *An Outcast of the Islands* chronologically.

Constantine, K. C. (pseud.)

Rocksburg, Pennsylvania, is a depressed and grimy coal-mining town near Pittsburgh. Its police chief, Mario Balzic, is overweight, irascible, and inclined to drink too much, but he is a conscientious public servant with compassion for the people of his community and an unusual sensitivity to what motivates them. The Rocksburg novels have become, as the series has progressed, studies of character and evocations of a region rather than conventional mysteries or police procedurals. The pseudonymous K. C. Constantine, who jealously protects his anonymity, lives in the region he describes so well.

1. *The Rocksburg Railroad Murders* (Saturday Review, 1972)
   The reader is introduced to Mario Balzic and the town of Rocksburg. Balzic investigates the murder of a former schoolmate.
2. *The Man Who Liked to Look at Himself* (Saturday Review, 1973)
   Balzic has to work with a racist, incompetent state police lieutenant while solving the mystery of a dismembered corpse.
3. *The Blank Page* (Saturday Review, 1974)
   Janet Pisula, a shy college student, is slain.
4. *A Fix like This* (Saturday Review, 1975)
   A stabbing and two beating deaths lead Balzic into an investigation of the local numbers racket.
5. *The Man Who Liked Slow Tomatoes* (Godine, 1982)
   A missing person, very early tomatoes, and exasperating contract negotiations with the local bureaucracy engage Balzic.
6. *Always a Body to Trade* (Godine, 1983)
   Balzic copes with murder, robbery, drug dealers, crooked narcotics agents, and a new mayor who is inclined to meddle.
7. *Upon Some Midnight's Clear* (Godine, 1985)
   Balzic's troubles with meddling Mayor Strohn continue as he contends with an alleged mugging, a nude protest by Vietnam veterans, and a pre-Christmas attack of post-holiday depression.
8. *Joey's Case* (Mysterious, 1988)
   Former coal miner Albert Castelucci persuades Balzic to conduct an unofficial investigation into the homicide of his son Joey.

Cook, David

This pair of novels traces the life of severely retarded Walter from his birth in 1930 through his parents' deaths, his institutionalization, and his eventual escape to an impoverished existence in London. Walter is treated sympathetically but unsentimentally by the author, who reserves his anger for the society that dooms its mentally handicapped to such misery. *Walter* won the prestigious Hawthornden Prize for Literature in

1978, and was the basis for a television drama written by Cook, a British writer and actor.

1. *Walter* (Overlook, 1985)
   Walter is so severely retarded, unteachable, and incontinent that his mother seriously considers killing "God's mistake."
2. *Winter Doves* (Overlook, 1985)
   Twenty years after he has been committed to a mental hospital, Walter feels that he "belongs," until the arrival of the violent, suicidal June.

Cookson, Catherine

I. Cookson's melodramas have caught on with American readers. The historical Mallen trilogy was her first big success. The callous and high-living Mallens of High Banks Hall had fathered illegitimate sons all across the Northumberland countryside for the better part of a hundred years. The family trait, a distinctive shock of white hair running down to the left temple, known as the Mallen Streak, marked their parentage. It was said that those who bore the Mallen Streak did not die old or in their beds. The series covers the years from 1851 to World War I.

1. *The Mallen Streak* (Dutton, 1973)
   This first novel in the Mallen trilogy begins with old Thomas Mallen's losing his estate to creditors and retiring to a small cottage with his two wards and their governess.
2. *The Mallen Girl* (Dutton, 1973)
   This book follows the childhood and stormy courtship of head-strong young Barbara, old Thomas's daughter.
3. *The Mallen Lot* (Dutton, 1974)
   The final volume goes up to World War I and shows Barbara, will-ful and unhappy, making life difficult for everyone around her. English title: *The Mallen Litter*.

II. The industrial Tyneside region of northern England is the setting for these contemporary novels with a working-class background. The series follows the plucky and captivating Mary Ann Shaunessy from the age of eight through her school days, first romance, marriage, and motherhood. Cookson paints the Tyneside region with the authenticity of a native;

her autobiography, *Our Kate* (Bobbs-Merrill, 1969), shows that there is a little of herself in Mary Ann.

1. *A Grand Man* (Morrow, 1975)
   Mary Ann is instrumental in getting her parents to leave their dockside tenement for a farm outside the city.
2. *The Lord and Mary Ann* (Morrow, 1975)
   Mary Ann learns that the move to the farm isn't all that's needed to cure her dad's drinking problem.
3. *The Devil and Mary Ann* (Morrow, 1976)
   Mary Ann, aged nine, goes off to convent school.
4. *Love and Mary Ann* (Morrow, 1976)
   Mary Ann, aged thirteen, has a sweetheart in Corny Boyle.
5. *Life and Mary Ann* (Morrow, 1977)
   Mary Ann, now seventeen, is still in love with Corny, but the course of true love never runs smooth.
6. *Marriage and Mary Ann* (Morrow, 1978)
   The wedding bells ring at last for Mary Ann.
7. *Mary Ann's Angels* (Morrow, 1978)
   Rose Mary and David, twins, are now six years old.
8. *Mary Ann and Bill* (Morrow, 1979)
   Bill, the dog, provides some of the chuckles in this installment.

III. Cookson's latest work is a trilogy that begins in the English mining country during the late nineteenth century and follows Tilly Trotter to the New World and back.

1. *Tilly* (Morrow, 1980)
   Orphaned in her teens, Tilly finds a job as nursemaid to the children of a rich mine owner, but her troubles are not over. English title: *Tilly Trotter*.
2. *Tilly Wed* (Morrow, 1981)
   Tilly goes to Texas with her new husband. English title: *Tilly Trotter Wed*.
3. *Tilly Alone* (Morrow, 1982)
   Tilly returns from Texas to take over the estate and the mines, trapped by the promise she made to her dying husband. English title: *Tilly Widowed*.

Cooper, James Fenimore

The adventures of frontiersman Natty Bumppo, a man of many nicknames—Hawkeye, Leatherstocking, Pathfinder, Deerslayer, La Longue Carabine, and The Trapper—are told in five volumes known collectively as The Leatherstocking Tales. Although Masterpiece Theatre's version of *The Last of the Mohicans* was marred by the English actors' funny attempts at American accents, the old 1936 film was a real spine-tingler. *The Leatherstocking Saga* (Pantheon, 1954) is a pastiche of all the adventures of Natty Bumppo, not strictly an omnibus.

1. *The Deerslayer; or, The First War-Path* (Lea & Blanchard, 1841)
   Hawkeye, Uncas, and the two sisters Judith and Hetty are caught up in the war between the Iroquois and the white settlers at Lake Otsego.
2. *The Last of the Mohicans* (Lea & Carey, 1826)
   Uncas meets the treacherous Magua in this, the most popular book of the series.
3. *The Pathfinder; or, The Inland Sea* (Lea & Blanchard, 1840)
   Chingachgook, father of Uncas, helps Natty lead Mabel Dunham to safety during the French and Indian War.
4. *The Pioneers; or, The Sources of the Susquehanna* (Charles Wiley, 1823)
   Chingachgook, now called John Monhegan or old Indian John, helps again in the rescue of Elizabeth Temple.
5. *The Prairie* (Lea & Carey, 1827)
   Encroaching civilization has driven Natty Bumppo, now an old trapper, west to end his life beyond the Mississippi.

Cooper, William (pseud. of Harry Summerfield Hoff)

Scenes from Provincial Life inspired a generation of post-war British writers. Its good-humored and realistic story about a young science master at a provincial grammar school pointed the way back to traditional narrative and away from the experimentalism of Joyce and Woolf. Like Joe Lunn, the principal character of this semiautobiographical series, Cooper was a teacher, a civil servant, and a novelist. The other major characters are based upon significant people in Cooper's life: C. P. Snow (q.v.) is the original of Robert, Joe Lunn's friend and fellow writer. *Scenes from Metropolitan Life*, the second volume, was postponed for nearly thirty years to avoid possible lawsuit by the original of Myrtle, Joe's girlfriend. *Scenes from Later Life*, written twenty years after the first novels, brings Joe into the late 1970s. Numbers 1 and 3 were published in the United States as *Scenes from Life* (Scribner, 1961). The tetralogy was published in two volumes by Dutton (1983, 1984).

1. *Scenes from Provincial Life* (Cape, London, 1950)
   In 1939 28-year-old Joe Lunn is teaching science, writing his fourth novel, worrying about war, and avoiding marriage with Mildred.
2. *Scenes from Metropolitan Life* (Macmillan, London, 1982)
   In 1946 Joe is working in the same Whitehall office as his provincial friend Robert, and pursuing Myrtle, who is married to someone else.
3. *Scenes from Married Life* (Macmillan, London, 1961)
   Almost 40, Joe marries and has a daughter. His writing, his job, and his marriage are all going well.
4. *Scenes from Later Life* (Macmillan, London, 1983)
   Joe is 67, retired, and facing diminished means, ill health, and his mother's impending death.

Cornwell, Bernard

Richard Sharpe, the dauntless hero of this military adventure series set during the Napoleonic Wars, is an infantryman who has risen from the ranks in Lord Wellington's Peninsular Army. Sergeant Harper, a genial Irish giant, shares many of his adventures. The stories offer both exciting narrative and historical accuracy, including some fairly gruesome battlefield scenes. Fans of C. S. Forester's Hornblower novels, acknowledged as a model by British author Cornwell, should enjoy these tales.

1. *Sharpe's Rifles; Richard Sharpe and the French Invasion of Galicia, January 1809* (Viking, 1988)
   Sharpe begins this novel as a quarter-master, but soon rises to lieutenant and receives his first command in French-occupied Spain.

2. *Sharpe's Eagle; Richard Sharpe and the Talavera Campaign, July 1809* (Viking, 1981)
   Lieutenant Sharpe and a small detachment of men are separated from their battallion in Portugal.
3. *Sharpe's Gold; Richard Sharpe and the Destruction of the Almeida, August 1810* (Viking, 1982)
   Wellington, in desperate need of funds, sends Captain Sharpe to search for gold hidden in the Portuguese hills.
4. *Sharpe's Company; Richard Sharpe and the Siege of Badajoz, January to April 1812* (Viking, 1982)
   Sharpe joins the bitter fighting to capture the ancient fortress city of Badajoz.
5. *Sharpe's Sword; Richard Sharpe and the Salamanca Campaign, June and July 1812* (Viking, 1983)
   Sharpe tracks down the infamous French spy Captain Leroux.
6. *Sharpe's Enemy; Richard Sharpe and the Defense of Portugal, Christmas 1812* (Viking, 1984)
   Major Sharpe must rescue Lady Farthingdale from a dangerous band of deserters.
7. *Sharpe's Honour; Richard Sharpe and the Vitoria Campaign, February to June 1813* (Viking, 1985)
   Framed by Napoleon's cunning spy Major Ducos, Sharpe is court-martialed, but eludes his death sentence.
8. *Sharpe's Regiment; Richard Sharpe and the Invasion of France, June to November 1813* (Viking, 1986)
   Sharpe grows impatient waiting for replacements and sails to England to investigate the delay.
9. *Sharpe's Siege; Richard Sharpe and the Winter Campaign, 1814* (Viking, 1987)
   Sharpe is betrayed and trapped in a French fort, but manages a harrowing escape.
10. *Sharpe's Revenge; Richard Sharpe and the Peace of 1814* (Viking, 1989)
    Major Ducos has stolen Napoleon's treasure and shifted the blame to Sharpe.

Creasey, John

I. When John Creasey died in 1973 at the age of sixty-four, he had published nearly 600 books under some twenty-five pseudonyms, including western, romance, sports, and juvenile titles as well as thrillers and mysteries. For the best record of his work to 1968, see the October, 1968, issue of *The Armchair Detective*, a quarterly edited and published by Allen Hubin which contains an article by Creasey and a seventeen-page bibliography. The sheer volume of work and the unavailability of many titles never published in the United States make annotation for each title impossible. Listed below are the two most popular series written under the Creasey name. See the entries under J. J. Marric for the Gideon Books and under Anthony Morton for the Baron Series. Titles are arranged by their British publication date, which is usually the correct chronological sequence as well, though development through time is of minor importance.

Roger West, known as "Handsome" West for his tall, blond good looks, is introduced in 1942 as an inspector and gradually works his way up to chief superintendent of Scotland Yard. West has a talent for correctly anticipating his quarry's every step. Happily married—though they once came close to divorce—Roger and Janet West have two sons whose development from birth to college is chronicled in the books.

1. *Inspector West Takes Charge* (Scribner, 1972)
2. *Getaway for Inspector West* (Scribner, 1972)
   English title: *Inspector West Leaves Town.*
3. *Inspector West at Home* (Scribner, 1973)
4. *Inspector West Regrets* (Paul, London, 1946)
5. *Holiday for Inspector West* (Paul, London, 1946)
6. *The Case against Paul Raeburn* (Harper, 1958)
   English title: *Triumph for Inspector West.*
7. *Battle for Inspector West* (Paul, London, 1948)
8. *Sport for Inspector West* (Harper, 1958)
   English title: *Inspector West Kicks Off.*
9. *The Creepers* (Harper, 1952)
   English title: *Inspector West Cries Wolf.*
10. *Inspector West Alone* (Scribner, 1975)
11. *The Dissemblers* (Scribner, 1967)
    English title: *Puzzle for Inspector West.*
12. *The Figure in the Dusk* (Harper, 1953)
    English title: *A Case for Inspector West.*
13. *The Case of the Acid Thrower* (Harper, 1954)
    English title: *Inspector West at Bay.* Variant title: *The Blind Spot.*

14. *Send Inspector West* (Scribner, 1976)
 English title: *Send Superintendent West.*
15. *Give a Man a Gun* (Harper, 1954)
 English title: *A Gun for Inspector West.*
16. *The Beauty Queen Killer* (Harper, 1954)
 English title: *A Beauty for Inspector West.*
17. *The Gelignite Gang* (Harper, 1955)
 English title: *Inspector West Makes Haste.* Variant titles: *Night of the Watchman* and *Murder Makes Haste.*
18. *Murder 1, 2, 3* (Harper, 1955)
 English title: *Two for Inspector West.* Variant title: *Murder Tips the Scales.*
19. *Death of an Assassin* (Scribner, 1960)
 English title: *A Prince for Inspector West.*
20. *Death of a Postman* (Harper, 1957)
 English title: *Parcels for Inspector West.*
21. *Hit and Run* (Scribner, 1959)
 English title: *Accident for Inspector West.*
22. *Trouble at Saxby's* (Harper, 1959)
 English title: *Find Inspector West.* Variant title: *Doorway to Death.*
23. *The Killing Strike* (Scribner, 1961)
 English title: *Strike for Death.*
24. *Murder London–New York* (Scribner, 1961)
25. *Death of a Racehorse* (Scribner, 1962)
26. *The Case of the Innocent Victims* (Scribner, 1966)
27. *Murder on the Line* (Scribner, 1963)
28. *The Scene of the Crime* (Scribner, 1963)
29. *Death in Cold Print* (Scribner, 1962)
30. *Policeman's Dread* (Scribner, 1964)
31. *Hang the Little Man* (Scribner, 1964)
32. *Look Three Ways at Murder* (Scribner, 1965)
33. *Murder London–Australia* (Scribner, 1965)
34. *Murder London–South Africa* (Scribner, 1966)
35. *The Executioners* (Scribner, 1967)
36. *So Young to Burn* (Scribner, 1968)
37. *Murder London–Miami* (Scribner, 1969)
38. *A Part for a Policeman* (Scribner, 1970)
39. *Alibi?* (Scribner, 1971)
40. *A Splinter of Glass* (Scribner, 1972)
41. *The Theft of Magna Carta* (Scribner, 1973)
42. *The Extortioners* (Scribner, 1974)

43. *A Sharp Rise in Crime* (Scribner, 1979)

II. The Toff is the Honorable Richard Rollison, a handsome gentleman-adventurer whose exploits and amours are serviceable escapist fare. Jolly, the Toff's funereally correct valet-secretary, is a loyal and resourceful assistant. Numbers 17, 25, 34, 36, 42, and 45 were published in the United States in paperback (Pyramid, 1964–65).

1. *Introducing the Toff* (Long, London, 1938)
2. *The Toff Steps Out* (Long, London, 1939)
3. *The Toff Goes On* (Long, London, 1939)
4. *The Toff Breaks In* (Long, London, 1940)
5. *Here Comes the Toff* (Walker, 1967)
6. *Salute the Toff* (Walker, 1971)
7. *The Toff Proceeds* (Walker, 1968)
8. *The Toff is Back* (Walker, 1974)
9. *The Toff Goes to Market* (Walker, 1967)
10. *Accuse the Toff* (Walker, 1972)
11. *The Toff among the Millions* (Walker, 1976)
12. *The Toff and the Great Illusion* (Walker, 1967)
13. *The Toff and the Curate* (Walker, 1969)
    Variant title: *The Toff and the Deadly Parson.*
14. *Feathers for the Toff* (Walker, 1970)
15. *The Toff and the Lady* (Walker, 1970)
16. *Hammer the Toff* (Long, London, 1947)
17. *The Toff on Ice* (Long, London, 1947)
    Variant title: *Poison for the Toff.*
18. *The Toff in Town* (Walker, 1971)
19. *The Toff Takes Shares* (Walker, 1972)
20. *The Toff and Old Harry* (Walker, 1970)
21. *The Toff on Board* (Walker, 1973)
22. *Kill the Toff* (Walker, 1966)
23. *Foul Play Suspected* (Walker, 1966)
    English title: *Fool the Toff.*
24. *A Mask for the Toff* (Walker, 1966)
    English title: *The Toff Goes Gay.*
25. *A Knife for the Toff* (M. Evans, London, 1951)
26. *Hunt the Toff* (Walker, 1969)
27. *Call the Toff* (Walker, 1969)
28. *The Toff Down Under* (Walker, 1969)

29. *The Toff at Butlins* (Walker, 1976)
30. *The Toff at the Fair* (Walker, 1968)
31. *A Six for the Toff* (Walker, 1969)
32. *The Toff and the Deep Blue Sea* (Walker, 1967)
33. *Make Up for the Toff* (Walker, 1967)
34. *The Toff in New York* (Hodder, London, 1956)
35. *The Toff on Fire* (Walker, 1966)
36. *Model for the Toff* (Hodder, London, 1957)
37. *The Toff and the Stolen Tresses* (Walker, 1965)
38. *The Toff on the Farm* (Walker, 1964)
39. *The Toff and the Runaway Bride* (Walker, 1964)
40. *Double for the Toff* (Walker, 1965)
41. *The Toff and the Kidnapped Child* (Walker, 1960)
42. *A Rocket for the Toff* (Hodder, London, 1960)
43. *Follow the Toff* (Walker, 1967)
44. *The Toff and the Toughs* (Walker, 1968)
    English title: *The Toff and the Teds.*
45. *Leave It to the Toff* (Hodder, London, 1962)
46. *A Doll for the Toff* (Walker, 1965)
47. *The Toff and the Spider* (Walker, 1966)
48. *The Toff in Wax* (Walker, 1966)
49. *A Bundle for the Toff* (Walker, 1968)
50. *Stars for the Toff* (Walker, 1968)
51. *The Toff and the Golden Boy* (Walker, 1969)
52. *The Toff and the Fallen Angels* (Walker, 1970)
53. *Vote for the Toff* (Walker, 1971)
54. *The Toff and the Trip-Trip Triplets* (Walker, 1972)
55. *The Toff and the Terrified Taxman* (Walker, 1973)
56. *The Toff and the Sleepy Cowboy* (Walker, 1974)
57. *The Toff and the Crooked Copper* (Walker, 1977)
58. *The Toff and the Dead Man's Finger* (Hodder, London, 1978)

Crispin, Edmund (pseud. of Robert Bruce Montgomery)

Oxford don Gervase Fen wears his erudition lightly when he forays beyond those ivied halls as an amateur sleuth. At forty-two, he is tall and lean, with a cheerfully ruddy complexion and a mischievous glint in his eyes as he drives his disreputable old roadster into one sophisticated and literate case after another. In an article in *Murder Ink* (Workman, 1977), Catherine Aird (q.v.) characterizes Crispin's mysteries as belonging to the "teacake" school of English detective stories, where everything stops at four o'clock for a civilized repast.

1. *Obsequies at Oxford* (Lippincott, 1945)
   Fen is on the scene to investigate the mysterious death of an actress engaged for the Oxford performance of a new experimental drama. English title: *The Case of the Gilded Fly.*
2. *Holy Disorders* (Lippincott, 1946)
   While vacationing in the cathedral town of Tolnbridge, Fen investigates a case involving a haunted church, Nazi spies, and a mugged organist.
3. *The Moving Toyshop* (Lippincott, 1946)
   In this very mysterious case, a toy shop changes magically into a grocery store, and a murdered corpse vanishes.
4. *Dead and Dumb* (Lippincott, 1947)
   This case of murder at the opera gets very complicated when the suspected murderer is himself done in. English title: *Swan Song.*
5. *Love Lies Bleeding* (Lippincott, 1948)
   A lost Shakespeare play, a burglary, and two murders are neatly wrapped into this amusing case with an English public school background.
6. *Buried for Pleasure* (Lippincott, 1948)
   Fen stands for Parliament and meets Inspector Humbleby for the first time on this case of the murder of an old classmate and the poisoning of a respectable ex-prostitute.
7. *Sudden Vengeance* (Dodd, 1950)
   Fen assists Inspector Humbleby in his investigation of the suicide of a young film actress and some murdered movie moguls. English title: *Frequent Hearses.*
8. *The Long Divorce* (Dodd, 1951)
   Murder following a rash of anonymous letters in a small English village is the subject of this highly polished puzzle. Variant title: *A Noose for Her.*
9. *Beware of the Trains* (Walker, 1962)
   This is a collection of short stories.
10. *The Glimpses of the Moon* (Walker, 1978)
    On sabbatical in a small Devonshire village, Fen helps the very

dull-witted local constabulary solve a case of three particularly messy murders.

11. *Fen Country* (Walker, 1980)
Twenty-six short stories are collected here.

Crofts, Freeman Wills

Crofts's classic early mystery *The Cask* (Collins, 1920), starring an Inspector French precursor named Burnley, was written while he was still employed as a railway engineer. Though he eventually retired to devote more time to writing, his best books, with a few wartime exceptions, were written before 1940. After that, his portrayal of Scotland Yard's Inspector Joseph French, a tweedy alibi-buster who never misses a chance to follow a clue abroad, became too slow-moving for most readers.

1. *Inspector French's Greatest Case* (Seltzer, 1925)
A murdered clerk is found next to the empty safe in a diamond merchant's Hatton Street office.
2. *The Cheyne Mystery* (Boni, 1926)
When young Maxwell Cheyne is drugged and his home ransacked, Inspector French's only clue is a scrap of a hotel bill. English title: *Inspector French and the Cheyne Mystery*.
3. *The Starvel Hollow Tragedy* (Harper, 1927)
A love story is woven into this case of a miser's missing money. English title: *Inspector French and the Starvel Tragedy*.
4. *The Sea Mystery* (Harper, 1928)
A mysterious wooden chest found floating off the coast of Wales contains the corpse of a murdered man.
5. *The Purple Sickle Murders* (Harper, 1929)
Young women who work in London movie box offices are being murdered. English title: *The Box Office Murders*.
6. *Sir John Magill's Last Journey* (Harper, 1930)
Plenty of railway details pack this leisurely case about the disappearance of a wealthy Belfast linen manufacturer.
7. *Mystery in the English Channel* (Harper, 1931)
Two dead English businessmen are found aboard a yacht in midchannel. English title: *Mystery in the Channel*.

8. *Sudden Death* (Harper, 1932)
Death at a country house occupies French in this somewhat atypical case seen through the eyes of the housemaid.
9. *Double Death* (Harper, 1932)
Two young construction engineers working on a railway project near the English Channel coast are murdered. English title: *Death on the Way.*
10. *The Strange Case of Dr. Earle* (Dodd, 1933)
The disappearance of a golfing doctor from his home in Surrey forms the beginning of this diabolical case. English title: *The Hog's Back Mystery.*
11. *Wilful and Premeditated* (Dodd, 1934)
Charles Swinburn waits and watches to see if he can get away with the carefully planned murder of a rich uncle. English title: *The 12:30 from Croydon.*
12. *Crime at Guildford* (Dodd, 1935)
The senior accountant for a firm of jewelers is murdered while attending a business conference near Guildford. Variant title: *The Crime at Nornes.*
13. *Crime on the Solent* (Dodd, 1935)
Industrial spying between two rival cement firms leads to the murder of a night watchman. English title: *Mystery on Southampton Water.*
14. *The Loss of the Jane Vosper* (Dodd, 1936)
An insurance investigator checking into the sinking of a loaded freighter disappears.
15. *Man Overboard!* (Dodd, 1936)
Inspector French goes to Ireland to investigate the death of a man working on a secret chemical process. Variant title: *Cold-blooded Murder.*
16. *Found Floating* (Dodd, 1937)
Involves poison at a family dinner and a disappearing passenger on a Mediterranean cruise ship.
17. *Futile Alibi* (Dodd, 1938)
Everybody hated unscrupulous financier Andrew Harrison, but the manner of his death seems to rule out both murder and suicide. English title: *The End of Andrew Harrison.*
18. *Antidote to Venom* (Dodd, 1939)
George Sturridge, a kindly, well-meaning zoo director, becomes an accomplice to murder.
19. *Tragedy in the Hollow* (Dodd, 1939)
Harry Morrison leaves his post at a London travel agency for a job

on a casino cruise ship, where murder occurs. English title: *Fatal Venture.*

20. *Golden Ashes* (Dodd, 1940)

    An art expert is murdered, and his huge collection of old masters is lost in a house fire.

21. *Circumstantial Evidence* (Dodd, 1941)

    Crofts gives his readers plenty of evidence and time in which to deduce the murderer of James Tarrant along with Inspector French. English title: *James Tarrant, Adventurer.*

22. *A Losing Game* (Dodd, 1941)

    When detective-story writer Tony Meadows is charged with the murder of a blackmailer, Inspector French comes to his rescue.

23. *Fear Comes to Chalfont* (Dodd, 1942)

    When an amateur chemist is murdered, his wife comes under suspicion.

24. *The Affair at Little Wokeham* (Dodd, 1943)

    This unusual case is a detective story without a mystery. Crofts tells his readers how and by whom the murder has been committed and how the murderer has planned to escape the consequences. Variant title: *Double Tragedy.*

25. *Enemy Unseen* (Dodd, 1945)

    This ingenious story of wartime Britain is one of Crofts's better later efforts.

26. *Death of a Train* (Dodd, 1946)

    Saboteurs plot to derail a train full of radio valves.

27. *Murderers Make Mistakes* (Hodder, London, 1947)

    This is a collection of short stories.

28. *Silence for the Murderer* (Dodd, 1948)

    Dulcie Heath and Frank Roscoe plan to defraud the patients of a Harley Street doctor.

29. *Dark Journey* (Dodd, 1951)

    A family feud and guilty parties everywhere keep French, now superintendent, busy. English title: *French Strikes Oil.*

30. *Many a Slip* (Hodder, London, 1955)

    More short stories are collected here.

31. *The Mystery of the Sleeping Car Express* (Hodder, London, 1956)

    This is a third short-story collection.

32. *Anything to Declare?* (Hodder, London, 1957)

    An ingenious gang smuggles Swiss watches into England.

Cronin, A. J. (Archibald Joseph)

I. A. J. Cronin, a Scottish physician, took up writing while recuperating from an illness. He drew on his experiences in medicine for his fiction, scandalizing many by his unromanticized view of the medical profession. The ambitious doctor portrayed in his best-known novel, *The Citadel* (Little, 1937), created quite a furor. The two books listed below feature Robert Shannon from early youth to his career as a dedicated medical researcher.

1. *The Green Years* (Little, 1944)
   The story begins as eight-year-old Robert Shannon comes to live with his grandparents in Scotland.
2. *Shannon's Way* (Little, 1948)
   Shannon is a young doctor doing medical research.

II. This set also features a young boy who grows up to enter medicine, but Laurence Carroll's career heads in a different direction, and he meets with different problems.

1. *A Song of Sixpence* (Little, 1964)
   Laurence Carroll experiences the trials and joys of growing up Catholic in a Scottish Presbyterian town. He is six when the story begins.
2. *A Pocketful of Rye* (Little, 1969)
   Carroll, now head of a Swiss clinic, meets a figure from his past.

Cross, Amanda (pseud. of Carolyn Heilbrun)

Kate Fansler, professor of English, is the detective in these very literate mysteries which feature clues from the likes of James Joyce and Lionel Trilling along with plenty of highbrow patter and wit. Carolyn Heilbrun—herself a critic, author, and teacher—catches the academic atmosphere with a deliciously droll eye. Reed Amhearst is the lawyer whose aid and district attorney connections Kate calls upon from time to time. Their relationship progresses from book to book.

1. *In the Last Analysis* (Macmillan, 1964)
   Kate's first case has to do with the murder of a student. Reed's help comes in handy.
2. *The James Joyce Murder* (Macmillan, 1967)
   This installment finds Kate summering in the Berkshires when a mystery calls. Reed comes to visit.
3. *Poetic Justice* (Knopf, 1970)
   Campus unrest sets the tone here. Reed holds out for marriage.
4. *The Theban Mysteries* (Knopf, 1971)
   Kate now answers somewhat reluctantly to the name of Mrs. Reed Amhearst.
5. *The Question of Max* (Knopf, 1976)
   Kate travels to Maine to find a dead body.
6. *Death in a Tenured Position* (Dutton, 1981)
   Kate goes to Harvard to help an old classmate combat the anti-feminists plaguing her. English title: *A Death in the Faculty.*
7. *Sweet Death, Kind Death* (Dutton, 1984)
   Did Patrice Umphelby, history professor at a small New England women's college, commit suicide or was she pushed into the lake?
8. *No Word from Winifred* (Dutton, 1986)
   The elusive connection between the missing Winifred Ashby and famous English author Charlotte Stanton is the key to this mystery.
9. *A Trap for Fools* (Dutton, 1989)
   Black political activist Humphrey Edgerton, suspected of the murder of Middle Eastern studies professor Canfield Adams, has no alibi for the night Adams was pushed or fell from his seventh-story office window.

Cunningham, E. V. (pseud. of Howard Fast, q.v.)

Masao Masuto, Beverly Hills's American-born Japanese detective, is a Zen Buddhist. His wily and tenacious cast of mind helps him sort out some complicated cases, and his knowledge of karate comes in very handy at times. Beverly Hills is too small and peaceful a town to have a permanent homicide squad, but when a case involves possible murder, Masuto and his partner Sy Beckman take over. Reviews indicate this series is getting better as it continues.

1. *Samantha* (Morrow, 1967)
   Masuto must identify and stop the mysterious "Samantha" as, one by one, a series of film stars and executives are murdered.
2. *The Case of the One Penny Orange* (Holt, 1977)
   Involves the murder of a stamp collector, an ex-SS man, and the theft of a valuable stamp.
3. *The Case of the Russian Diplomat* (Holt, 1978)
   Masuto's investigation into the drowning of a Russian diplomat is complicated when his own daughter, Ana, is kidnapped.
4. *The Case of the Poisoned Eclairs* (Holt, 1979)
   A Chicano maid eats eclairs intended for her Beverly Hills employer and dies of botulism.
5. *The Case of the Sliding Pool* (Delacorte, 1981)
   When a canyon mudslide reveals a skeleton, Masuto must reconstruct a crime committed twenty-five years earlier.
6. *The Case of the Kidnapped Angel* (Delacorte, 1982)
   The kidnapping of Angel Barton eventually leads to three murders.
7. *The Case of the Murdered Mackenzie* (Delacorte, 1984)
   The trial of actress Eva Mackenzie, accused of murdering her husband in the bathtub, strikes a false note with Masuto.

Cussler, Clive

Dirk Pitt, an expert in underwater salvage, uses his talents to retrieve all kinds of sunken treasure—rare metals, secret treaties—you name it, he can dredge it up. The three novels in which he stars are exciting and suspenseful enough to keep any reader on the edge of his chair. They are a wonderful find for fans of the old Lloyd Bridges TV show "Sea Hunt."

1. *Raise the Titanic!* (Viking, 1976)
   Both the Russians and the United States are after the rare element byzanium thought to be in the hold of the sunken *Titanic.*
2. *Night Probe!* (Bantam, 1981)
   Pitt's search for a 1914 Canadian-American treaty involves underwater excavations of a ship and a train.
3. *Deep Six* (Simon & Schuster, 1984)
   Pitt helps the Environmental Protection Agency locate the source of some deadly nerve gas contaminating Alaskan waters.

Daudet, Alphonse

Tartarin has been called the "French Pickwick." Daudet, an admirer of Dickens, worked from the same palette in satirizing the southern French temperament. His Tartarin is an irrepressible braggart whose adventures are riotous exaggerations embroidered around a few bare threads of fact. The lion he fights, for instance, is a tame and toothless old feline. Tartarin naturally sees himself as a tragic figure who has the heroic and chivalrous soul of a Don Quixote trapped in a fat and lazy little Sancho Panza body. The first two Tartarin books were bound together in the Everyman's Library edition (Dent/Dutton, 1910).

1. *Tartarin of Tarascon, Traveller, "Turk," and Lion-Hunter* (Crowell, 1895)
   Tartarin proves his reputation for valor and resourcefulness on an expedition to Algeria. First published in 1872 as *Adventures prodigieuses de Tartarin.* Translated from the French by Henry Firth.
2. *Tartarin on the Alps* (Crowell, 1894)
   Tartarin the mountain climber defies death. First published in 1885 as *Tartarin sur les Alpes.* Translated from the French by Henry Firth.
3. *Port Tarascon* (Harper, 1890)
   The intrepid Tartarin leads a colony to the South Pacific. First published in 1862 under the same name. Translated from the French by Henry James.

Davies, Robertson

I. Robertson Davies is Canada's leading man of letters. In addition to writing novels, he is a playwright, critic, and professor at the University of Toronto; for twenty years he was the editor of the *Peterborough* (Ontario) *Examiner*. As a young man he studied acting at the Old Vic. Davies draws on these experiences in his Salterton trilogy, which has been treasured loyally by fans for years. *The Salterton Trilogy* (Penguin, 1985) includes numbers 1, 2, and 3.

   1. *Tempest-Tost* (Rinehart, 1952)
     A production of *The Tempest* occupies the leading citizens of the provincial Canadian town of Salterton. Eccentric organist Humphrey Cobbler and censorious old Miss Puss are among the memorable characters in this, the most humorous of all Davies's novels.

   2. *Leaven of Malice* (Scribner, 1955)
     A malicious joke—the false engagement announcement of Pearl Vambrace and Solly Bridgetower—starts the action.

   3. *A Mixture of Frailties* (Scribner, 1958)
     Monica Gall seizes her chance to study voice in London and achieves success and maturity in integrating her new life and her old.

II. The Deptford novels, named for the small town in Canada where the story starts, have achieved a wider recognition than the earlier trilogy. This series lacks the humor of the first, but is more ambitious in presenting a Jungian view of history and personality. *The Deptford Trilogy* (Penguin, 1985) includes numbers 1, 2, and 3.

   1. *Fifth Business* (Viking, 1970)
     Dunstan Ramsay, a retired history teacher, remembers his Canadian boyhood and the fateful misaimed snowball that reverberated through the years in the lives of his friends.

   2. *The Manticore* (Viking, 1972)
     Rich and successful lawyer David Staunton relates the course of the Jungian analysis he undertakes after the mysterious death of his father.

3. *World of Wonders* (Viking, 1970)
   World-famous magician Magnus Eisengrim (alias Paul Dempster) tells his life story.

III. Davies has followed the Deptford trilogy with a trilogy of novels in which the connecting link is Francis Cornish: painter, art forger, and art collector.

1. *The Rebel Angels* (Viking, 1982)
   Maria Theotoky, a beautiful scholarly half-Gypsy, Dr. Parlabane, renegade monk, and other scholars at the College of St. John and the Holy Ghost in Toronto are thrown into turmoil by the legacy of the late Francis Cornish.
2. *What's Bred in the Bone* (Viking, 1985)
   Two *daimons* discourse on the life of Francis Cornish from his origins in the provincial Canadian town of Blairlogie to his death.
3. *The Lyre of Orpheus* (Viking, 1988)
   The Cornish Foundation sponsors the completion of an unfinished opera by E. T. A. Hoffmann called *Arthur of Britain, or The Magnanimous Cuckold*.

De Andrea, William L.

Matt Cobb, chief troubleshooter for The Network, a major commercial television network, is the investigator in this series of puzzle mysteries in the classic mode. These quietly humorous tales feature intimate views of the inner workings of television broadcasting, excellent plotting, and realistic characters and dialogue. De Andrea, frustrated in his ambition to become a television director, turned to mystery writing and won the Edgar Allan Poe Award for his first two novels: *Killed in the Ratings* and *The Hog Murders* (not one of the Cobb series).

1. *Killed in the Ratings* (Harcourt, 1978)
   A scheme to rig the ratings creates panic at The Network and produces homicide.
2. *Killed in the Act* (Doubleday, 1981)
   The Network is celebrating its fiftieth anniversary with a giant spectacular. A souvenir bowling ball is stolen, and a kinescope technician is killed.

3. *Killed with a Passion* (Doubleday, 1983)
   Matt Cobb returns to his alma mater for the wedding of former classmate Debbie Whitney, who winds up dead.
4. *Killed on the Ice* (Doubleday, 1984)
   While preparing a taping of figure skater Wendy Ichimi, Matt finds the corpse of Paul Dinkover, psychiatrist and left-wing activist.
5. *Killed in Paradise* (Mysterious, 1988)
   Matt escorts the two winners of a Network contest on a mystery cruise in the Caribbean, and becomes involved with a group of mystery writers.

Deforges, Régine

This trilogy of French best-sellers set during World War II tells the story of beautiful and passionate young Léa Delmas, daughter of a rich Bordeaux wine grower. The novels combine high romance with a historically accurate description of these interesting and dramatic times. The work was originally commissioned as a remake of *Gone with the Wind*, and parallels between the major characters in the two sagas are easy to spot.

1. *The Blue Bicycle* (Lyle Stuart, 1986)
   As the Germans overrun France, Léa is determined to save her family estate, Montillac, and hide her disappointment in love. Covers 1939–42. Translation by Ros Schwartz of *La bicyclette bleue* (1981).
2. *Léa* (Lyle Stuart, 1987)
   Léa delivers messages to the Resistance on her blue bicycle and has an affair with the treacherous Francois Tavernier. Covers 1942–44. Translation by Elizabeth Fairley Mueller of *101, avenue Henri-Martin* (1983).
3. *The Devil Laughs Again* (Lyle Stuart, 1988)
   Léa is besieged by destruction and the violent deaths of friends and relatives as the liberation of France enters its final stages. Covers 1944–45. Translation by Elizabeth Fairley Mueller of *La diable en rit encore* (1985).

Deighton, Len

I. Deighton's spy thrillers differ from those of John Le Carré (q.v.), Graham Greene, and others in that his spy is not upper middle class. His anonymous spy/narrator, who sometimes uses the name Harry Palmer, is working class and rather snide about the public school types he works for. Michael Caine used a Cockney accent in his portrayal of Deighton's spy in the 1965 film *The Ipcress File*, which was so successful that two other Deighton films quickly followed: *Funeral in Berlin* in 1966 and *Billion Dollar Brain* in 1967. In other respects, Deighton runs true to the genre: his plots are easily as convoluted as Le Carré's; his climaxes are perhaps a little more grisly.

1. *The Ipcress File* (Simon & Schuster, 1962)
   A British agent's assignment to recover a kidnapped biochemist involves him in a maze of spies and counterspies from London to the Far East.
2. *Horse under Water* (Putnam, 1963)
   An unnamed spy/narrator is after sunken treasure in the form of canisters of heroin.
3. *Funeral in Berlin* (Putnam, 1964)
   This chilling tale of revenge is set in the divided city haunted by the still-murderous memories of the recent Nazi past.
4. *The Billion Dollar Brain* (Putnam, 1966)
   This story about a computer programmed by an evil and murderous genius ranges across the globe from Helsinki to San Antonio.
5. *An Expensive Place to Die* (Putnam, 1967)
   Paris, the city of light, seems a dark and sinister place of violent death, nuclear rumors, and sleazy underworld types.

II. British undercover agent Bernard Samson relates his moves in the deadly game of espionage in the Game/Set/Match trilogy. Samson must match wits with the KGB, guard against London Central's intrigues, and cope with his wife's defection to the enemy. Deighton plans to extend the series with a second trilogy, two of which have been published so far. Suspense readers will be patiently waiting for the Sinker installment. *Game, Set and Match* (Knopf, 1989) is an omnibus volume containing numbers 1, 2, and 3, published to coincide with the PBS series starring Ian Holm as Samson.

1. *Berlin Game* (Knopf, 1984)
   Bernard Samson must help an undercover agent known as Brahms
   Four escape from East Berlin.
2. *Mexico Set* (Knopf, 1985)
   Fiona, Samson's wife and co-worker, defects to the KGB while
   Samson tries to persuade KGB major Erich Stinnes to defect to
   London.
3. *London Match* (Knopf, 1986)
   Suspicions of KGB moles and plants at London Central exacerbate
   Samson's concern for his motherless children.
4. *Spy Hook* (Knopf, 1988)
   Samson is sent to Washington to locate half a million pounds miss-
   ing from the German desk of London Central.
5. *Spy Line* (Knopf, 1989)
   Samson is a fugitive from England, with London Central, the CIA,
   and the KGB all after him.

Delacorta (pseud. of Daniel Odier)

This series chronicles the escapades of Serge Gorodish, failed classical
pianist, sometime painter, and con artist, and his thirteen-year-old companion, the beautiful kleptomaniac Alba. The novels, translated from the
French by Lowell Bair (1), Victoria Reiter (2, 3, 4, and 5) and Catherine
Texier (6) are sophisticated satirical thrillers not to be taken too seriously. A 1982 French movie entitled *Diva*, loosely based on the novel,
was an international hit. Daniel Odier is a Swiss novelist and poet living
in Paris.

1. *Nana* (Summit, 1984)
   In this prequel to *Diva*, Serge Gorodish leaves Paris for a small
   French town where he first lays eyes upon the beautiful blonde
   nymphet Alba, and has a brush with a motorcycle gang called
   the Vampires.
2. *Diva* (Summit, 1983)
   Gorodish and Alba are pursuing their shady careers in Paris. Jules,
   a teenage messenger, becomes obsessed with Cynthia Hawkins, an
   Afro-American operatic soprano.
3. *Luna* (Summit, 1984)
   Delaborde, a very rich lunatic, on the advice of Alcan, his insane

psychiatrist, abducts Alba in order to act out his fantasy of dragon-fly mating.

4. *Lola* (Summit, 1985)
Gorodish and Alba search for Lola Black, an American heavy metal rock singer, long presumed dead.

5. *Vida* (Summit, 1985)
Gorodish and Alba move to Los Angeles, where Alba is hired as a private investigator by a ten-year-old tycoon in search of his father, the great architect Marlowe Wrightson.

6. *Alba* (Atlantic, 1989)
While Gorodish serves a jail term for littering, Alba drives blind Jason to the Mojave Desert for a rendezvous with The Group.

De La Roche, Mazo

The sixteen Jalna novels, also called the Whiteoak Chronicles, cover the 100-year history of the Whiteoak family of Canada. *Jalna*, the first published volume (they were not written chronologically), quickly became a best-seller, and successive volumes attracted the kind of following more common to television shows today. Fans wrote Miss De La Roche about whom Finch should marry or whether Renny should sell any more land. Although this Canadian author wrote many other books, none matched the success of the Jalna novels. Caution: Un-enlightened attitudes about women and minorities may set some modern teeth on edge.

1. *The Building of Jalna* (Little, 1944)
In 1850 Captain Whiteoak and his young wife Adeline settle on the shore of Lake Ontario.

2. *Morning at Jalna* (Little, 1960)
During the Civil War, a family of Southerners come to stay with Adeline and her four young children.

3. *Mary Wakefield* (Little, 1949)
In 1893, Adeline is in her sixties. Mary Wakefield comes from England to be a governess to Philip's children and becomes his wife.

4. *Young Renny* (Little, 1935)
By 1906, Adeline is eighty. Her unpleasant cousin comes to stay, and young Renny tries to drive him away.

5. *Whiteoak Heritage* (Little, 1940)
   Young Renny returns home from World War I to take his place as head of the family.
6. *The Whiteoak Brothers* (Little, 1953)
   Gold fever spreads through the family in 1923. Adeline is ninety-eight.
7. *Jalna* (Little, 1927)
   Romance takes unexpected turns as the handsome Whiteoak brothers begin to think about marrying. Adeline is the ancient matriarch whose 100th birthday closes the novel. Winner of the Atlantic Monthly Prize of $60,000.
8. *Whiteoaks of Jalna* (Little, 1929)
   This volume centers on Finch, the odd musical brother to whom Adeline has left all her money. English title: *Whiteoaks.*
9. *Finch's Fortune* (Little, 1931)
   Finch again stars, as his inheritance dwindles and his love seems hopeless.
10. *The Master of Jalna* (Little, 1933)
    Hard times come to Jalna in 1932–33, but Renny manages to hold things together.
11. *Whiteoak Harvest* (Little, 1936)
    The years 1934–35 are a time of growth, sometimes painful, for Renny and Alayne and their little daughter Adeline, so much like her grandmother.
12. *Wakefield's Course* (Little, 1941)
    Wakefield, already a successful actor, becomes a war hero in 1939–40, but he is unlucky in love.
13. *Return to Jalna* (Little, 1946)
    Jalna has a special charm for the Whiteoak men returning from World War II in 1943–45.
14. *Renny's Daughter* (Little, 1951)
    Young Adeline, now eighteen, visits Ireland and falls in love, while Renny fights off suburban development at Jalna.
15. *Variable Winds at Jalna* (Little, 1954)
    The younger generation sort out tangled loves, and television comes to Jalna.
16. *Centenary at Jalna* (Little, 1958)
    The final novel draws the family from far and wide to celebrate the centennial with a wedding.

Delderfield, R. F.

I. Delderfield's richly charactered chronicles are satisfying long reads that dramatize a century of social change in England. The Swann family trilogy is perhaps his best known. It tells the story of Adam Swann, a professional soldier who parlays a necklace captured on the field of battle in India into a vast commercial enterprise, a fortune, and a dynasty.

1. *God Is an Englishman* (Simon & Schuster, 1970)
   Adam Swann marries Henrietta and starts his business in freight-hauling coaches during the years 1857–66.
2. *Theirs Was the Kingdom* (Simon & Schuster, 1971)
   The Swann family prospers as the four children grow up. Young George leads the business into motorized cars.
3. *Give Us This Day* (Simon & Schuster, 1973)
   Old Adam's grandchildren and great-grandchildren appear in this last volume, which ends on the eve of World War I.

II. The Craddock family is featured in this pair of novels set in rural England.

1. *A Horseman Riding By* (Simon & Schuster, 1967)
   Young Paul Craddock comes home from the Boer War and purchases a run-down estate in Devonshire. Also issued in two paperbacks (Pocket Bks., 1974): vol. 1, *The Long Summer Day* and vol. 2, *Post of Honor*.
2. *The Green Gauntlet* (Simon & Schuster, 1968)
   Squire Craddock remains dedicated to his land, to his children and grandchildren, to his tenants, and to the vanishing rural life they represent.

III. The Carver family of London provides the focus for *The Avenue* (Simon & Schuster, 1969), originally published in England in two volumes.

1. *The Dreaming Suburb* (Hodder, London, 1958)
   Jim Carver, a widower with seven children, is at the center of this story about all the inhabitants of an ordinary London street from 1918 to the beginning of World War II.

2. *The Avenue Goes to War* (Hodder, London, 1958)
   The wartime experiences of the people of the avenue, covering the years 1940–48.

Dennis, Patrick

Auntie Mame's unconventional charm and hilarious doings have been entertaining people practically nonstop since 1955. She has endured adaptation from the novel to the stage, then to a successful movie version starring Rosalind Russell in 1958. Further metamorphosis into the musical comedy *Mame*, with Angela Lansbury in the title role, won Broadway's approval, though the 1974 movie version starring Lucille Ball was awful. Dennis's books can still make readers laugh out loud. They have the delightfully droll narration of nephew Patrick, which is missing in the dramatizations.

1. *Auntie Mame* (Vanguard, 1955)
   In 1929, orphaned, ten-year-old Patrick goes to live with his zany aunt who lives wholeheartedly in phases, playing to the hilt each new role from showgirl to southern belle to tweedy authoress.
2. *Around the World with Auntie Mame* (Harcourt, 1958)
   In 1934, Mame treats Patrick to a trip around the world before he starts college.

Dexter, Colin

Public television's "Mystery" has aired the marvelous Inspector Morse series originally produced by Central Independent Television of London. Actor John Thaw catches just the right air of eccentric melancholy in his portrayal of Detective Chief Inspector Morse of Oxford. Morse is an opera fan and a crossword puzzle addict. His drinking sometimes gets out of hand, especially when his shy amorous approach to women meets rebuff. Morse is assisted by Sergeant Lewis, a pragmatic and conventional family man who gathers the facts that Morse puzzles together. The interplay between the two partners provides a touch of humor. British author Colin Dexter lives in Oxford and shares his character's interest in crossword puzzles.

1. *Last Bus to Woodstock* (St. Martin's, 1975)
   Two girls are waiting together for the last bus to Woodstock. The one who catches the bus is discovered dead in a pub parking lot.
2. *Last Seen Wearing* (St. Martin's, 1976)
   Morse investigates the disappearance of a schoolgirl and the murder of a teacher.
3. *The Silent World of Nicholas Quinn* (St. Martin's, 1977)
   Partially deaf Nicholas Quinn, a member of the Foreign Examinations Syndicate, is murdered.
4. *Service of All the Dead* (St. Martin's, 1980)
   The Oxford Church of St. Frideswide is rocked by a series of murders.
5. *The Dead of Jericho* (St. Martin's, 1982)
   Morse meets the attractive Anne Scott at a party. She is found dead, an apparent suicide, six months later.
6. *The Riddle of the Third Mile* (St. Martin's, 1983)
   Terminally ill Oxford don Browne-Smith disappears on a trip to London. Then a headless, handless, and partially legless corpse is found.
7. *The Secret of Annexe 3* (St. Martin's, 1987)
   The prize-winner of a fancy dress contest is found dead in his Oxford hotel room after a New Year's Eve party.

Dobyns, Stephen

New York's Saratoga Springs, home of the famous horse-racing track, is also home to detective Charlie Bradshaw and his amusingly sleazy partner, Victor Plotz. Charlie is an unassuming fellow with a 1940s code of honor and a nostalgia for the bygone glory of Saratoga Springs. He begins the series as a policeman, then moves into the private sector. Stephen Dobyns is a poet (*The Balthus Poems; Black Dog, Red Dog*) who writes mysteries as a diversion.

1. *Saratoga Long Shot* (Atheneum, 1976)
   Sergeant Charlie Bradshaw of the Saratoga police force comes to New York City in search of the missing son of an old girl-friend.
2. *Saratoga Swimmer* (Atheneum, 1981)
   Lew Ackerman, owner of Lorelei Stables, hires Charlie to head security, then is shot to death in a YMCA pool.

3. *Saratoga Headhunter* (Viking, 1985)
   Charlie, now a private investigator moonlighting as a milkman, offers sanctuary to McClatchy, a race-throwing jockey-turned-in-
   formant, who proceeds to lose his head.
4. *Saratoga Snapper* (Viking, 1986)
   Victor Plotz photographs a group at the hotel owned by Charlie's
   mother, and is nearly killed by a hit-and-run driver.
5. *Saratoga Bestiary* (Viking, 1988)
   Someone steals a painting of a famous racehorse, and Charlie is
   hired to deliver the ransom money.

Dominic, R. B. (pseud. of Mary J. Latis and Martha Hennissart)

Emma Lathen (q.v.) by another name is still the successful team of Mary
J. Latis and Martha Hennissart. This series is set in Washington, D.C.,
and stars the Democratic congressman from Newburg, Ohio, Benton
Safford. Sixteen years in Congress have given Safford the influence and
contacts to open doors whenever he needs information. He is an amiable man with a gift for making even new suits look rumpled. His shrewd
judgment of people and situations make him a good detective.

1. *Murder, Sunny Side Up* (Abelard-Schuman, 1968)
   A House subcommittee investigating Ova-Cote, a spray-on preser-
   vative for eggs, turns up some rotters.
2. *Murder in High Place* (Doubleday, 1970)
   When fiery Karen Jenks is recalled from the small South American
   country where she was researching her master's thesis, she demands that her congressman help her fight back.
3. *There Is No Justice* (Doubleday, 1971)
   A Supreme Court nominee, Coleman Ives, is murdered. English
   title: *Murder out of Court*.
4. *Epitaph for a Lobbyist* (Doubleday, 1974)
   A woman lobbyist is murdered at National Airport.
5. *Murder out of Commission* (Doubleday, 1976)
   A sleepy Ohio town in Safford's district suddenly explodes into
   violence over the issue of a proposed nuclear power plant.
6. *The Attending Physician* (Harper, 1980)
   A medical scandal in Ben's home district leads to murder.

7. *Unexpected Developments* (St. Martin's, 1984)
Safford uncovers murder and bribery in the aircraft industry. English title: *A Flaw in the System.*

Donaldson, Stephen R.

I. The Chronicles of Thomas Covenant the Unbeliever would be just the thing to recommend to fantasy readers looking for something to follow Tolkien. This imaginative epic fantasy for adults stars Thomas Covenant, who is lonely and shunned in real life because of his leprosy. In the magical world of his dreamlike adventures, however, he is regarded as the reincarnated legendary hero Berek Halfhand, and his white-gold wedding ring is a talisman of great power. Lord Foul the Despiser is the arch villain who threatens the land from its Northern Climbs to the Garroting Deep. Saltheart Foamfollower, Hile Troy, and Caerroil Wildwood are some of the good guys.

1. *Lord Foul's Bane* (Holt, 1977)
Covenant travels to Revelstone and leads the lords to Mount Thunder in pursuit of the magic Staff of Drool, the evil cavewight.
2. *The Illearth War* (Holt, 1977)
After a month in real life, but forty years in the land, Covenant returns to find that his daughter Elena is now the high lord.
3. *The Power That Preserves* (Holt, 1977)
Returned again to the land, Covenant makes his tortuous way to Foul's Creche and meets Lord Foul in final combat.
4. *The Wounded Land* (Ballantine, 1980)
This book begins the Second Chronicles of Thomas Covenant, which picks up ten years after the first. Covenant returns to the land, this time accompanied by a young woman doctor, Linden Avery.
5. *The One Tree* (Ballantine, 1982)
Thomas and Dr. Avery search for the One Tree, with which they must fashion a new staff of life to thwart Lord Foul and Sunbane.
6. *White Gold Wielder* (Ballantine, 1983)
Covenant and Avery return to the land in a last desperate attempt to heal its wounds in this climactic volume of the second trilogy.

II. Donaldson followed his Covenant series with a two-book sequence, "Mordant's Need," another epic in which someone from "our world" is brought to a fantasy world in order to save it. The land of Mordant, located in a sort of Arthurian alternative universe, is threatened by enemies from within and without.

1. *The Mirror of Dreams* (Ballantine, 1986)
   Poor little rich girl Terisa Morgan is lured to Mordant by the Congery of Imagers.
2. *A Man Rides Through* (Ballantine, 1987)
   Lady Terisa and bumbling apprentice Geraden are revealed to possess extraordinary magical powers as monsters, evil wizards, and hostile armies threaten Mordant.

Dos Passos, John

U.S.A. is a trilogy of novels chronicling American life from 1900 to the eve of the Great Depression. The collage technique that Dos Passos perfected in these books gives the work its epic quality. Sprinkled throughout the narrative are "Newsreel" sections composed of news clips, headlines, song lyrics, and other documentary material; "Camera Eye" sections of the interior monologues of various unidentified people; and biographical sections detailing the lives of the famous. A one-volume edition is available: *U.S.A.* (Harcourt, 1937).

1. *The 42nd Parallel* (Harper, 1930)
   The stories of Mac, the I.W.W. typesetter; Joe, the sailor; Ben, the radical leader; Eleanor; Janey; and many others.
2. *1919* (Harcourt, 1932)
   This volume covers the war years.
3. *The Big Money* (Harcourt, 1936)
   This book takes the reader from postwar exuberance to the Great Depression.

Douglas, Lloyd

Medical melodrama, romance, and a secret formula for success in life are the elements that made *Magnificent Obsession* a best-seller during

108

the Depression. It was filmed twice: the 1935 version starred Robert Taylor and Irene Dunne; the 1954 remake featured Rock Hudson and Jane Wyman. In 1939, Douglas followed his success with a second book purporting to be the secret journal that was discovered in *Magnificent Obsession*.

1. *Doctor Hudson's Secret Journal* (Houghton, 1939)
   The famous brain specialist's inspiring journal, which figured so prominently in *Magnificent Obsession*. Though written second, this is an "overture" to the original volume.
2. *Magnificent Obsession* (Houghton, 1929)
   The secret of the famous Dr. Hudson's success inspires young Bobby Merrick and aids in the discovery that enables him to save the life of the woman he loves.

Doyle, Arthur Conan

Barzun and Taylor's *A Catalog of Crime* (Harper, 1971) has a chapter devoted exclusively to the literature of Sherlock Holmes, listing sixty-one books. And the last decade has seen the canon enlarged by at least a score of interesting new works, including Samuel Rosenberg's witty biography *Naked Is the Best Disguise* (Bobbs-Merrill, 1974). For two "newly discovered" memoirs by Dr. Watson, see the entries under Nicholas Meyer. Two Holmes parodies are listed under Robert L. Fish. And two books starring Moriarty are listed under John E. Gardner.

Real Holmes fans know their detective's cases down to the last detail. Listed below is a basic chronology. Note: Only numbers 1, 2, 4, and 7 are novels; the others are collections of stories included here for convenience.

1. *A Study in Scarlet* (Lippincott, 1890)
   A wrong committed in Utah is eventually connected to a mysterious double murder in London in Mr. Holmes's debut.
2. *The Sign of the Four* (Collier, 1891)
   The story of a vendetta. Variant title: *The Sign of Four*.
3. *The Adventures of Sherlock Holmes* (Harper, 1892)
   This is a collection of short stories.
4. *The Hound of the Baskervilles* (McClure, 1902)
   Though written later, this is generally supposed to be a pre-Reichenbach Falls story. It shows Holmes at the peak of his powers

as he solves a sinister case involving some very menacing canines.

5. *The Memoirs of Sherlock Holmes* (Harper, 1893)
   This short-story collection ends with Holmes's encounter with Moriarty at the Reichenbach Falls. Doyle intended to kill off his detective, but popular demand brought him back to life.

6. *The Return of Sherlock Holmes* (McClure, 1905)
   More stories are collected here.

7. *The Valley of Fear* (Doran, 1915)
   A murder engineered by a secret society is solved in the wilds of America.

8. *His Last Bow: Some Reminiscences of Sherlock Holmes* (Doran, 1917)
   From his wartime home in the English countryside, the famous detective solves cases for the government.

9. *The Case-Book of Sherlock Holmes* (Doran, 1927)
   These are the final stories.

Drabble, Margaret

Margaret Drabble must surely rank among the best contemporary writers of serious fiction. Her first novels, published in the early 1960s, established her as a feminist author whose portraits of young motherhood captured the ambivalence of a generation of women. Her recent novels examine a larger cross-section of British society with sharper political and social comment. But she continues to fill each book with a diverse cast of memorable women characters. Readers who met Liz Headland, Alix Bowen, and Esther Breuer in *The Radiant Way* will be delighted to discover a sequel, and a promised third volume on the way.

1. *The Radiant Way* (Knopf, 1987)
   This follows the lives of three women from January 1979 to June 1985, with flashbacks to their student days at Cambridge University in 1952. The large cast of characters includes their husbands, lovers, children, friends, and relatives.

2. *A Natural Curiosity* (Viking, 1989)
   This continues the lives of the three women, now living in different parts of England, as they cope with aging amid the increasing polarization and strife of the Thatcher era.

Dreiser, Theodore

In contrast to *Sister Carrie*, which Dreiser based on the character of his sister, *The Financier* required considerable research into the world of banking, the stock market, the Philadelphia political scene, and the career of Charles T. Yerkes, his model for Frank Cowperwood. Dreiser's novel documents the rags-to-riches story of his ruthless and corrupt protagonist, with all its dramatic reversals, scandals, and passions. Two further novels continue Cowperwood's story to his death and complete the Trilogy of Desire.

1. *The Financier* (Harper, 1912)
   Frank Cowperwood rises to power in Philadelphia; his life is complicated by troublesome passions for women.
2. *The Titan* (John Lane, 1914)
   Chicago in the 1870s is the setting for the second chapter in the career of Frank Cowperwood.
3. *The Stoic* (Doubleday, 1947)
   Posthumously published, this concluding volume shows Frank Cowperwood involved in the transit industry of London and various philanthropic projects.

Druon, Maurice

Druon combines the conscience of the historian with the imagination of the writer in these six novels of medieval France. Known collectively as The Accursed Kings, the series follows the House of Valois, whose members were cursed for thirteen generations by the dying Jean de Molay, who was burned at the stake by Philip IV. Druon catches the color of life in the fourteenth century, with its tournaments, court intrigues, stately dances, and dark underside of witchcraft and murder. Translated from the French by Humphrey Hare.

1. *The Iron King* (Scribner, 1956)
   This book recreates the turbulent reign (1285–1314) of Philip IV of France, with its extremes of violence and reform.
2. *The Strangled Queen* (Scribner, 1957)
   Louis X succeeds to the French throne in 1314 and a power struggle ensues.
3. *The Poisoned Crown* (Scribner, 1957)
   The last months of the reign of Louis X bring violence and intrigue to France in the early fourteenth century.

4. *The Royal Succession* (Scribner, 1958)
   A struggle for the crown of France follows the death of Louis X in 1316 and culminates in the coronation of Philip V.
5. *The She-Wolf of France* (Scribner, 1960)
   In 1327, Queen Isabella of England plots successfully to murder her husband, King Edward II, and place her fifteen-year-old son Edward upon the throne.
6. *The Lily and the Lion* (Scribner, 1961)
   The early reign of Edward III of England (1312–77) is brutal, and Robert Artois and the Countess Mahaut feud ruthlessly in France.

Drury, Allen

I. These six novels on the theme of American politics share many of the same characters. The first and best in the series, *Advise and Consent*, won the Pulitzer Prize for 1960. It presents a fascinating picture of the Washington political world. The all-star cast of the successful 1962 movie version included Charles Laughton, Henry Fonda, and Walter Pidgeon. Though Drury's conservative views color the whole series, his pen weighs especially heavily in the later volumes as his characters lose their three-dimensionality and his plots take on a good-versus-evil configuration that verges on fantasy.

1. *Advise and Consent* (Doubleday, 1959)
   The controversial nomination of Robert Leffingwell as secretary of state sets off reverberations throughout Washington.
2. *A Shade of Difference* (Doubleday, 1962)
   A racial incident in Charleston, South Carolina, touches off this drama on the United Nations.
3. *Capable of Honor* (Doubleday, 1966)
   Liberal Washington columnist Walter Dobius is the villain of this volume.
4. *Preserve and Protect* (Doubleday, 1968)
   President Harley Hudson's death in an airplane crash is just the beginning of the violence in this installment.
5. *Come Nineveh, Come Tyre: The Presidency of Edward M. Jason* (Doubleday, 1973)
   Assassination, kidnapping, and suicide figure in the Armageddon caused by soft liberal policies.

6. *The Promise of Joy* (Doubleday, 1975)
This volume offers an alternative scenario in which Edward M. Jason is only vice-president and Orin Knox must save the country from destruction.

II. The good versus evil confrontation is carried forward to the late 1980s in a pair of geopolitical melodramas where good president Hamilton Delbacher faces off against evil president Yuri Serapin. The Soviets are bent on world conquest, while the Americans are slipping militarily and becoming demoralized by the weak-kneed, traitorous, liberal media. Drury's Russophobia is fairly rabid in these tracts.

1. *The Hill of Summer: A Novel of the Soviet Conquest* (Doubleday, 1981)
Almost simultaneously vice-president Hamilton Delbacher succeeds to the presidency of a weakened United States while Yuri Serapin is "elected" as leader of the U.S.S.R.
2. *The Roads of Earth* (Doubleday, 1984)
After signing a Sino-Soviet pact, the Russians launch a series of attacks on Mexico, South Africa, Saudi Arabia, and Taiwan.

III. Drury's interest in ancient Egypt is evident in this pair of historical novels about the Eighteenth Dynasty told in a series of monologues by observers and participants.

1. *A God against the Gods* (Doubleday, 1976)
Suffering from delusions of grandeur, Akhenaton displaces the old gods, and in so doing alienates his family and subjects.
2. *Return to Thebes* (Doubleday, 1977)
Nefertiti, Akhenaton's cousin-wife, falls into disfavor. Akhenaton is murdered and succeeded by his youngest brother, Tutankhamen.

Dumas, Alexandre

Dumas's trilogy about the three musketeers is a classic swashbuckler; its most recent film version starred Michael York, Racquel Welch, and Richard Chamberlain. At least eight earlier versions have been made, including the 1921 spectacular starring Douglas Fairbanks and a 1939 comedy with Don Ameche as the "Singing Musketeer." Readers will find Dumas's prose a little cumbersome at times, but the adventures of brave D'Artagnan, gallant Athos, large-hearted Porthos, and Aramis the schemer are still as engaging as ever.

1. *The Three Musketeers* (Little, 1888)
   D'Artagnan arrives in Paris and joins Athos, Porthos, and Aramis in a whirlwind of court intrigue and adventures covering the years 1626–28. First published in 1844 as *Les trois mousquetaires.*
2. *Twenty Years After* (Little, 1888)
   This volume covers the period 1648–49, the regency of Anne of Austria, and the uprising against Cardinal Mazarin. First published in 1846 as *Vingt ans après.*
3. *The Vicomte de Bragelonne; or, Ten Years Later* (Little, 1904)
   Set during the reign of Louis XIV, this book contains episodes frequently published separately—i.e., *The Man in the Iron Mask* and *Louise de la Valliere.* First published in 1851 as *Le vicomte de Bragelonne.*

Dunlap, Susan

I. Susan Dunlap has created three very engaging female detectives in the six years that she has been writing mysteries. Two are series characters and perhaps the third will earn a series of her own in time. Jill Smith is Dunlap's police detective. She is a young homicide detective on the Berkeley, California, police force. Her level-headed, tough but sensitive style makes her very good at her job. Jill is a divorced, totally undomestic new woman—her living quarters always sound perfectly awful and she never eats anything but junk food. Her friendship with her office mate Howard, a substance abuse officer, warms as the series progresses.

1. *As a Favor* (St. Martin's, 1984)
   Smith's former husband asks her to investigate the disappearance of Anne Spaulding, an unpopular welfare investigator.
2. *Not Exactly a Brahmin* (St. Martin's, 1985)
   The fatal automobile accident of rich establishment figure Ralph Palmerston looks suspicious to Smith.
3. *Too Close to the Edge* (St. Martin's, 1987)
   Wheelchair-bound Liz Goldenstern is drowned at the site of Marina Vista, an apartment complex she was planning to build.

4. *A Dinner to Die For* (St. Martin's, 1987)
Gourmet restauranteur Mitchell Biekma is poisoned by soup spiked with deadly aconite.

II. Vejay Haskell is Dunlap's contribution to the amateur detective genre. Vejay is a youthful iconoclast who has ditched her high-powered PR job and her husband to live the quiet life in a peaceful resort town north of San Francisco, where she finds herself a job reading gas meters. But Vejay discovers that small-town life is anything but pastoral as she stumbles into one mystery after another.

1. *An Equal Opportunity Death* (St. Martin's, 1984)
Newly transplanted Vejay runs the risk of alienating the townsfolk while trying to clear herself of the murder of a local bartender.
2. *The Bohemian Connection* (St. Martin's, 1985)
The sinister events during the town's Festival Week include the discovery of a dead body in a sewer trench.
3. *The Last Annual Slugfest* (St. Martin's, 1986)
Edwina Hastings, slug-tasting judge at the annual Slugfest celebration, is poisoned.

Note: *Pious Deception* (Villard, 1989) is set in Phoenix, Arizona, and stars Kiernan O'Shaughnessy, a young medical examiner turned private eye. Let's hope we see more of her.

Dunnett, Dorothy

I. These six volumes of swash and buckle star Francis Crawford of Lymond, second son of a noble Scottish family. A strange prophecy has cast a shadow over this haunting and magnetic hero who pursues his destiny across sixteenth-century Europe in various roles—as a galley slave, a foreigner in masquerade at the corrupt French court, an ambassador to a sultan, an outlaw leader, and a commander of the Russian army. The series is compulsively readable.

1. *The Game of Kings* (Putnam, 1961)
Condemned outlaw Francis Crawford of Lymond returns to Scotland in 1547 to try to clear his name and gets swept up in the dramatic events of his war-torn country.

2. *Queen's Play* (Putnam, 1964)
   Lymond is sent to France on a secret mission to protect the seven-year-old future monarch, Mary Stuart, and Scotland's hopes of a French alliance.
3. *The Disorderly Knights* (Putnam, 1966)
   Lymond is fatefully enmeshed in the Turkish attack on Malta in 1551.
4. *Pawn in Frankincense* (Putnam, 1969)
   Lymond carries valuable cargo from France to the sultan of Constantinople and searches for his illegitimate infant son. He finds himself in a deadly game of chess.
5. *The Ringed Castle* (Putnam, 1972)
   Lymond is led to Russia by the beautiful courtesan Guzel and serves Ivan the Terrible.
6. *Checkmate* (Putnam, 1975)
   At the time of Philip II's accession to the Spanish throne, Lymond finally unravels his true ancestry in this concluding episode.

II. "The House of Niccolo," Dunnett's newest historical sequence, chronicles the fortunes of Claes, or Niccolo, a plucky lad of fifteenth-century Flanders, following his adventures through Florence to Byzantium and other points east.

1. *Niccolo Rising* (Knopf, 1986)
   Illegitimate Niccolo is apprenticed at the age of ten to the widowed Marian de Charetty, a wealthy Bruges merchant.
2. *The Spring of the Ram* (Knopf, 1988)
   Nineteen-year-old Niccolo, now married to Marian, flees a bitter foe and journeys east to establish trade with the Emperor of Trebizond.

III. As a change of pace from her historical novels, Dunnett also writes a series of suspense yarns united by the presence of Johnson Johnson, playboy painter and master counterspy, and his yacht *Dolly*. Johnson usually stays in the background, as the heroine ("bird") of each novel occupies center stage and narrates her adventures. This series of humorous thrillers is published in the United Kingdom under the author's maiden name, Dorothy Halliday.

1. *The Photogenic Soprano* (Houghton, 1968)
   We are introduced to Johnson Johnson and *Dolly* in an adventure

featuring coloratura Tina Rossi. Set in the Hebrides. English title: *Dolly and the Singing Bird.*

2. *Murder in the Round* (Houghton, 1970)
   The body of an impoverished English lord turns up on the island of Ibiza. English title: *Dolly and the Cookie Bird.*

3. *Match for a Murderer* (Houghton, 1971)
   Dr. Beltanno Douglas MacRannoch, physician and daughter of a Scottish clan chieftain, is the heroine of this adventure set in the Bahamas. English title: *Dolly and the Doctor Bird.*

4. *Murder in Focus* (Houghton, 1973)
   A girl astronomer and her photographer boyfriend become embroiled in a wild assortment of trouble in Rome. English title: *Dolly and the Starry Bird.*

5. *Dolly and the Nanny Bird* (Knopf, 1982)
   Joanna Emerson, undercover agent, is hired as a nanny by the jet-setting Booker-Readmans to care for their infant Benedict.

6. *Dolly and the Bird of Paradise* (Knopf, 1984)
   Rita Geddes, a young Scottish makeup artist, is hired to "tune up" the face of Natalie Sheridan, a high-society filmmaker.

Durrell, Lawrence

I. Durrell's literary conundrums are an acquired taste. For the persistent reader, the rewards are great. The Alexandria Quartet is the major work on which Durrell's reputation rests secure. It captures the modern Egyptian city in all its enigmatic splendor and decadence. Durrell intended the first three novels as "siblings" showing three sides of space, with the fourth adding the dimension of time. The tetralogy is available in a one-volume omnibus, *Alexandria Quartet* (Dutton, 1962).

1. *Justine* (Dutton, 1957)
   An unidentified narrator tells the story of his affair with the beautiful and complex Justine Hosnani as World War II threatens Alexandria. All the other characters are introduced in this volume.

2. *Balthazar* (Dutton, 1958)
   S. Balthazar, a homosexual physician, has "corrected the errors and omissions" in the account above, now revealed to be the memoir of L. G. Darley, a poor Anglo-Irish schoolteacher.

3. *Mountolive* (Dutton, 1959)
   David Mountolive, who eventually becomes the English ambas-

sador to Egypt, tells his story. His view of the events related in the two preceding volumes adds a political perspective; the Zionist activities of Justine and her husband are revealed.

4. *Clea* (Dutton, 1960)
   After a lapse of several years, Darley resumes his narrative, covering events through his postwar affair with the artist Clea Montis. The tale has a strong conclusion.

II. The titles of this pair of novels refer to the epigraph by Petronius "Aut Tunc Aut Nunquam," which, loosely translated, means "now or never."

1. *Tunc* (Dutton, 1968)
   Felix Charlock, the inventor of a giant computer named Able, has bawdy, fantastic adventures.
2. *Nunquam* (Dutton, 1970)
   Felix Charlock has developed the miraculously lifelike doll Iolanthe for the Merlin Corporation.

III. The Avignon quintet or "quincunx" is Durrell's most complicated concoction yet, featuring exotic settings, improbable characters, Gnostic conspiracies, and buried treasure.

1. *Livia; or, Buried Alive* (Viking, 1979)
   This novel comes first chronologically, but was written after *Monsieur*. It describes a band of friends and lovers gathered near Avignon in the days between the world wars, including British consul Felix Chatto, the novelist Blanford, and Livia, within whose beautiful body a man is "buried alive."
2. *Monsieur; or, The Prince of Darkness* (Viking, 1975)
   A lifelong menage à trois between Piers and Sylvie, brother and sister, and Bruce, their doctor friend, is punctuated by philosophic and amatory quests and a ritual suicide carried out by a cult of Gnostics.
3. *Constance; or, Solitary Practices* (Viking, 1982)
   World War II scatters Avignon's English colony. Psychoanalyst Constance resumes her studies in Geneva, while her husband Sam and novelist Blanford find themselves in the Egyptian campaign.
4. *Sebastian; or, Ruling Passions* (Viking, 1984)
   The Egyptian banker Affad, also known as Sebastian, falls in love

with Constance, and falls afoul of the mysterious Gnostic brother-hood.

5. *Quinx; or, The Ripper's Tale* (Viking, 1985)
Blanford returns to Avignon after the war with his friend Constance, and with Sutcliffe, his fictional creation and alter ego.

Egan, Lesley (pseud. of Elizabeth Linington)

Police detective Vic Varallo and Jewish lawyer Jesse Falkenstein shared top billing in *A Case for Appeal*, the first novel in this series of police procedurals set in Glendale, California. They have alternated as the main character in the (roughly) annual volumes which have appeared since then. The relationship between Falkenstein and his wife Nell and Varallo's domestic problems are continuing threads in the series. Egan also writes police procedurals under her alter egos Dell Shannon and Elizabeth Linington (q.v.). Since each novel deals with a tangle of different cases, annotations are not provided.

1. *A Case for Appeal* (Harper, 1961)
2. *Against the Evidence* (Harper, 1962)
3. *The Borrowed Alibi* (Harper, 1962)
4. *Run to Evil* (Harper, 1963)
5. *My Name Is Death* (Harper, 1965)
6. *Detective's Due* (Harper, 1965)
7. *Some Avenger, Rise!* (Harper, 1966)
8. *The Nameless Ones* (Harper, 1967)
9. *A Serious Investigation* (Harper, 1968)
10. *The Wine of Violence* (Harper, 1969)
11. *In the Death of a Man* (Harper, 1970)
12. *Malicious Mischief* (Harper, 1971)
13. *Paper Chase* (Harper, 1972)
14. *Scenes of Crime* (Doubleday, 1976)
15. *The Blind Search* (Doubleday, 1977)
16. *A Dream Apart* (Doubleday, 1978)
17. *Look Back on Death* (Doubleday, 1978)
18. *The Hunter and the Hunted* (Doubleday, 1979)
19. *Motive in Shadow* (Doubleday, 1980)
20. *A Choice of Crimes* (Doubleday, 1980)
21. *The Miser* (Doubleday, 1981)
22. *Random Death* (Doubleday, 1982)

23. *Little Boy Lost* (Doubleday, 1983)
24. *Crime for Christmas* (Doubleday, 1984)
25. *Chain of Violence* (Doubleday, 1985)
26. *The Wine of Life* (Doubleday, 1985)

Ehle, John

John Ehle (pronounced EE-lee) has written seven novels about the Wright and King families of North Carolina, from the first settlers to come to the wilderness mountain country in the 1770s, through the Civil War with its social discord and increasing settlement, and into twentieth-century growth and economic problems. Ehle writes realistically of the people and their ways while evoking the beauty of their land.

1. *The Land Breakers* (Harper, 1964)
   Mooney Wright is the first man to arrive in the valley; a small community develops around his farm.
2. *The Journey of August King* (Harper, 1971)
   Community and church leader August King helps a young runaway slave girl on her way in about 1810.
3. *Time of Drums* (Harper, 1970)
   The Civil War is seen through the eyes of Colonel Wright, leader of a Confederate mountain regiment.
4. *The Road* (Harper, 1967)
   Weatherby Wright helps bring the railroad to open up the North Carolina mountains during the 1870s.
5. *Last One Home* (Harper, 1984)
   Pinkney Wright moves his family from its mountain farm community to the "big city" of Asheville around the turn of the century.
6. *Lion on the Hearth* (Harper, 1961)
   A prosperous mountain family weathers the Depression of the 1930s.
7. *The Winter People* (Harper, 1982)
   Collie Wright, who lives alone with her baby, befriends Wayland Jackson, a recently widowed clockmaker, and his twelve-year-old daughter.

Elman, Richard

The television production of "Holocaust" by Gerald Greene renewed reader interest in books about the Jewish experience during World War II. Here is a trilogy that sensitively explores the anguish and fear of a Jewish family as they at first deny, then fight, and finally face their doom. The story concerns the Yagodah family of Clig, Hungary. Because each volume tells of the same events, but from different points of view, there is no chronology. They are perhaps best read in sequence as published.

1. *The 28th Day of Elul* (Scribner, 1967)
   In a memoir, Alex, or Shandor, the son of the Yagodah family, tells how the German occupation affected his prosperous family and his love for his cousin Lilo.
2. *Lilo's Diary* (Scribner, 1968)
   The fate of a beautiful and vivacious young Jewish girl in these terrible times is recorded in Lilo's diary, a moving addendum to the first book.
3. *The Reckoning* (Scribner, 1969)
   This diary kept by Newman, the father of the Yagodah family, reveals his refusal to accept the true dangers of the German occupation and his hopes for eluding disaster.

Engel, Howard

Benny Cooperman is a Jewish private detective working out of Grantham, Ontario, a small industrial city near Toronto based in part on the real city of St. Catharines. Benny is a genial plodder who lives in a hotel, eats in luncheonettes, and is a good son to his old mother who reads Proust because she likes "family novels." Howard Engel, a Toronto native, is a producer for the Canadian Broadcasting Corporation.

1. *The Suicide Murders* (St. Martin's, 1984)
   Hired to tail a husband suspected of infidelity, Benny gets involved with a series of suspicious "suicides."
2. *The Ransom Game* (St. Martin's, 1984)
   Benny reopens an old kidnapping case involving half a million dollars in lost ransom money.

3. *Murder on Location* (St. Martin's, 1985)
   In search of a real estate dealer's theatrical wife, Benny travels to Niagara Falls, where a film is being shot.
4. *Murder Sees the Light* (St. Martin's, 1985)
   Benny guards television evangelist Norbert Patten while the U.S. Supreme Court decides on the tax status of the "Ultimate Church."
5. *A City Called July* (St. Martin's, 1986)
   The local Grantham rabbi asks Benny to find Larry Geller, treasurer of the shul, who has disappeared with over two million dollars.
6. *A Victim Must Be Found* (St. Martin's, 1988)
   Benny investigates the murder of an art collector and some missing paintings.

Erdrich, Louise

Love Medicine's engaging story, lyric style and unstereotyped portrayal of Native Americans won Erdrich's first novel both popular and critical success. It received the 1984 National Book Critics Circle Award for Fiction. *The Beet Queen* and *Tracks* are not sequels in the chronological sense, but the three novels share the same North Dakota setting and some of the same characters. *The Beet Queen* focuses on white settlers, while *Tracks* shows Native Americans struggling against great odds to keep their culture alive. Erdrich grew up in Wahpeton, North Dakota, near the reservation where her grandfather headed the Turtle Mountain Chippewa tribe.

1. *Love Medicine* (Holt, 1984)
   The death of June Kashpaw stirs memories among members of the Kashpaw and Lamartine families of the Turtle Mountain band of Chippewas.
2. *The Beet Queen* (Holt, 1986)
   This tells about the lives of Karl and Mary Adare, abandoned in childhood in Argus, North Dakota, the "Sugar-beet Capital of America."
3. *Tracks* (Holt, 1988)
   The story of Fleur Pillager, a Chippewa woman suspected of witchcraft, is told by Nanapush, a tribal elder, and by Pauline, an Indian woman who has become a nun.

Estleman, Loren D.

I. Private eye Amos Walker is as hard-boiled as they come. Shaped by his hometown, Detroit—"the place where the American Dream stalled and sat rusting in the rain"—Walker is weary, tough, and cynical, but still compassionate. His bachelor flat is in the Polish section of the city. Walker deals with the usual inner-city crimes: drug dealing, prostitution, pornography, violence, and venal politicians. Estleman, from Michigan himself, gets the Detroit ambience just right.

1. *Motor City Blue* (Houghton, 1980)
   Amos Walker gets involved with a missing girl, a pornography racket, and some corrupt VIPs.
2. *Angel Eyes* (Houghton, 1981)
   A nightclub dancer gives Walker a diamond ring as a retainer before disappearing.
3. *The Midnight Man* (Houghton, 1982)
   Four young thugs ambush three Detroit policemen, killing two, and paralyzing the third.
4. *The Glass Highway* (Houghton, 1983)
   Walker is hired to find the twenty-year-old son of a television newscaster.
5. *Sugartown* (Houghton, 1984)
   A nineteen-year-old disappearance case becomes intertwined with a case involving a Soviet defector.
6. *Lady Yesterday* (Houghton, 1987)
   Jamaican ex-prostitute Iris hires Walker to find her missing father, an obscure jazz trombonist.
7. *Downriver* (Houghton, 1988)
   Richard DeVries, ex-convict, wants Walker to find the real culprit behind the 1967 arson and armored car robbery for which he was framed.
8. *General Murders* (Houghton, 1988)
   A book of short stories.
9. *Silent Thunder* (Houghton, 1989)
   Arms dealers, a woman suspected of killing her husband, and venal policemen are among the problems facing Walker.

II. Another Detroit-based series features Peter Macklin, a hitman who sometimes finds himself working with terrorists, spies, and other political types outside his usual line of business.

1. *Kill Zone* (Mysterious, 1984)
   The Detroit mob, the FBI, and the Secret Service all want Macklin to handle the negotiations when terrorists take eight-hundred hostages on a Lake Erie steamboat.
2. *Roses Are Dead* (Mysterious, 1985)
   Macklin has his hands full: sharpshooters and flame-throwing giants are trying to kill him; his wife wants a divorce; and his teen-age son wants to take up his line of business.

III. Estleman added two books to the Sherlock Holmes canon with these "lost manuscripts" of Doctor Watson.

1. *Sherlock Holmes vs. Dracula* (Doubleday, 1978)
   Holmes tries to prevent the "sanguinary count" from finding fresh blood in England. Variant title: *Sherlock Holmes and the Sanguinary Count*.
2. *Dr. Jekyll and Mr. Holmes* (Doubleday, 1979)
   Holmes and Watson get involved with a man who has a dual personality problem.

IV. Estleman has also written a series of westerns set in the 1880s featuring Page Murdock, Deputy U.S. Marshal for the Montana Territory. Murdock, almost as "hard-boiled" as Amos Walker, is an interesting hero for a traditional action western. The period detail is especially well done.

1. *The High Rocks* (Doubleday, 1979)
   Bear Anderson, the "Mountain That Walks," terrifies the Flathead Indians who massacred his parents, and everyone else in the Montana Territory.
2. *Stamping Ground* (Doubleday, 1980)
   Murdock escorts renegade Cheyenne Ghost Shirt to his public hanging in Bismarck, Dakota Territory.
3. *Murdock's Law* (Doubleday, 1982)
   Murdock becomes the town marshal of Breen, Montana, and has trouble sorting out friends and enemies.
4. *The Stranglers* (Doubleday, 1984)
   Murdock leads a posse in search of a teenaged killer, and is betrayed by an Indian tracker.

Exley, Frederick

This thinly fictionalized autobiography chronicles the messy life of a character named Frederick Exley as he spirals downward into alcoholism, divorce, random sex, and mental breakdown. *A Fan's Notes* won the William Faulkner Award for best first novel and stirred debate about the "emasculation" of the American male. Some readers find the trilogy funny and moving. Others are repelled by its self-indulgence and blurring of fact and fiction.

1. *A Fan's Notes* (Harper, 1968)
   Frederick Exley tells about his frustrated life and his two idols: his athletic father and Giants halfback Frank Gifford.
2. *Pages from a Cold Island* (Random, 1975)
   The death of literary critic Edmund Wilson preoccupies Exley, who is now burdened with the task of sustaining his initial writing success.
3. *Last Notes from Home* (Random, 1988)
   Exley visits his brother, Colonel Bill Exley, dying of cancer in Hawaii.

Fair, A. A. (pseud. of Erle Stanley Gardner, q.v.)

Bertha Cool does not need a woman's movement to liberate her. Though she looks like a hefty, gray-haired, grandmotherly type, she talks like a sailor and runs her Los Angeles private-detective agency like a shrewd army sergeant. Donald Lam, her partner, is as small as Bertha is big, but he is an ingenious legman. Ably assisted by the shy and efficient Elsie Brand, this unique team has solved twenty-nine enjoyable cases.

1. *The Bigger They Come* (Morrow, 1939)
   Donald Lam, a disbarred attorney, is introduced as he takes his first job with Bertha Cool's detective agency and gets involved in some tricky legalities for getting a murderer off the hook. English title: *Lam to the Slaughter.*
2. *Gold Comes in Bricks* (Morrow, 1940)
   The plot of this story concerns a gold mine, a murdered gambler, and a young girl who has paid a stranger three large checks.

3. *Turn on the Heat* (Morrow, 1940)
   When the case they are investigating proves to have a bearing on the political situation in a nearby city, Donald and Bertha start feeling some heat.

4. *Double or Quits* (Morrow, 1941)
   Missing jewels and a double-indemnity insurance suit occupy Donald and Bertha.

5. *Spill the Jackpot* (Morrow, 1941)
   Donald hits the jackpot on a rigged slot machine and is almost arrested as a swindler while Bertha battles nobly to keep her new svelte shape.

6. *Owls Don't Blink* (Morrow, 1942)
   Cool and Lam are hired to find Roberta Fenn, a New Orleans woman who has been missing for two years. Donald enlists in the navy at the book's end.

7. *Bats Fly at Dusk* (Morrow, 1942)
   Bertha misses Donald, but when he solves this case—involving a blind beggar and a possibly forged will—by telegram, Bertha relaxes.

8. *Cats Prowl at Night* (Morrow, 1984)
   With Donald still off in the navy, Bertha accepts an easy case that turns nasty, and she makes use of a Lam technique for getting out of a tight spot.

9. *Give 'Em the Ax* (Morrow, 1944)
   Lam narrowly escapes being charged as an accessory in his first case after coming home with a medical discharge from the navy. English title: *An Axe To Grind*.

10. *Crows Can't Count* (Morrow, 1946)
    Emeralds and murder mix in this deadly brew.

11. *Fools Die on Friday* (Morrow, 1947)
    Bertha accepts a fat retainer to prevent Daphne Ballwin from poisoning her husband.

12. *Bedrooms Have Windows* (Morrow, 1949)
    A blond lures Donald into an auto tourist court and very close to a murder charge.

13. *Top of the Heap* (Morrow, 1952)
    Bertha plays a very minor role in this case of stock manipulation and income-tax fraud.

14. *Some Women Won't Wait* (Morrow, 1953)
    Cool and Lam venture to Hawaii in this case of nasty doings focusing on a pair of "good time" girls.

15. *Beware the Curves* (Morrow, 1956)
    Donald uses some outrageous legal maneuvers as he masterminds a murderer's defense.
16. *You Can Die Laughing* (Morrow, 1957)
    A loud Texan and some pretty girls figure in this case of a cleverly masked murder.
17. *Some Slips Don't Show* (Morrow, 1957)
    This comedy of errors shows Donald to be a patron of the arts.
18. *Count of Nine* (Morrow, 1958)
    Murder by blowpipe and a flawless income-tax dodge are the seemingly incongruous elements of this case.
19. *Pass the Gravy* (Morrow, 1959)
    Donald takes on a charity case for a pathetic teenager, and it turns out to be highly profitable.
20. *Kept Women Can't Quit* (Morrow, 1960)
    Lam is on the trail of $100,000 taken in an armored-car robbery.
21. *Bachelors Get Lonely* (Morrow, 1961)
    Lam gets himself arrested as a peeping Tom in order to solve this highly unusual case.
22. *Shills Can't Cash Chips* (Morrow, 1961)
    A case of insurance fraud leads Donald into some surprising complications. English title: *Stop at the Red Light.*
23. *Try Anything Once* (Morrow, 1962)
    Lam does a stint as a special investigator for the Los Angeles District Attorney's office.
24. *Fish or Cut Bait* (Morrow, 1963)
    Jarvis Archer, a very big fish, wants his secretary protected round the clock and is willing to pay the hefty fee.
25. *Up for Grabs* (Morrow, 1964)
    Homer Breckinridge hires Donald to investigate an insurance claim.
26. *Cut Thin to Win* (Morrow, 1965)
    A hit-and-run injury claim leads to bigger things.
27. *Widows Wear Weeds* (Morrow, 1966)
    Mrs. Nicholas Baffin hires Donald to pay off a blackmailer.
28. *Traps Need Fresh Bait* (Morrow, 1967)
    Cool and Lam are hired to investigate a suspected insurance swindle.
29. *All Grass Isn't Green* (Morrow, 1970)
    Wealthy young tycoon Milton Calhoun hires Bertha and Donald to find the novelist Colburn Hale.

Farmer, Philip Jose

I. The Riverworld Series of five science fiction novels explores the fascinating question of what would happen if practically the whole human race were reincarnated simultaneously and squashed into a crowded and bewildering new world. Historic figures clash with Neanderthals and even a few aliens from outer space in Farmer's mysterious "after-Earth world," which seems to be one long river valley. For another variation on this theme, see John Bangs's *A House-Boat on the Styx* and its sequel.

1. *To Your Scattered Bodies Go* (Putnam, 1971)
   Adventurer-explorer Richard Burton is among those who find themselves reborn—hairless, naked, and young again—into a baffling new world.
2. *The Fabulous Riverboat* (Putnam, 1971)
   Samuel Clemens builds a boat so that he can sail to the river's source and discover the reason behind this strange "after-Earth world."
3. *The Dark Design* (Berkley/Putnam, 1977)
   Clemens, Burton, and their band drive on toward the river's headwaters and Misty Tower, the home of the Ethicals.
4. *The Magic Labyrinth* (Putnam, 1980)
   The mystery is revealed as Burton and Alice Hargreaves reach the perilous north and its truth.
5. *Gods of Riverworld* (Putnam, 1983)
   Now in command of the Ethicals' polar control center, members of the band can "play God" themselves.

Note: *River of Eternity* (Phantasia, 1983), originally written in 1952 for a contest, but not published until 1983, is the initial version of the Riverworld saga.

II. The World of Tiers series is an action-packed sci-fi adventure series based on the premise of alternative "pocket universes," each smaller than the Solar System, created by immortal, ruthless, humanoid Lords. Published by Ace Books as paperback originals, they have been reprinted in hardcover by Phantasia Press.

1. *The Maker of Universes* (Phantasia, 1980)
   Robert Wolff is transported from Earth to the World of Tiers and

eventually leads an attack on the planet's Lord. First published in 1965.

2. *The Gates of Creation* (Phantasia, 1981)
Wolff's world is invaded by a rival Lord, his own father. First published in 1966.

3. *A Private Cosmos* (Phantasia, 1981)
Earthling Paul Janus Finnegan, or Kickaha, defends Wolff's world from an invasion by Black Bellers. First published in 1968.

4. *Behind the Walls of Terra* (Phantasia, 1982)
Pursuing the last Beller, Kickaha learns that the Solar System is really a pocket universe created by the Lords. First published in 1970.

5. *The Lavalite World* (Phantasia, 1983)
Kickaha goes to a pocket universe centered on a plastic planet in a constant state of change. First published in 1977.

Farrell, James T.

I. Studs Lonigan of Chicago's Irish Catholic South Side is the archetypal working-class boy whose brave youthful dreams turn all too quickly to dissolution and tragedy. Farrell, who wrote with the authority of one who grew up in the same environment, saw Studs as a victim of the spiritual poverty of his time and class. While it was once fashionable to dismiss Farrell as a "merely sociological" writer, the Lonigan trilogy will always demand a place in American literature. It is a powerful and moving work. All three novels are included in the omnibus volume *Studs Lonigan*, published by Vanguard in 1935.

1. *Young Lonigan: A Boyhood in Chicago Streets* (Vanguard, 1932)
This story begins in 1916, as fifteen-year-old Studs graduates from grammar school and dreams of becoming a "great guy."

2. *The Young Manhood of Studs Lonigan* (Vanguard, 1934)
This volume carries Studs into the twenties working with his father as a house painter, hanging out at the local poolroom, and drinking too much Prohibition alcohol.

3. *Judgment Day* (Vanguard, 1935)
Though he is engaged to the gentle Catherine Banahan, hard times and illness plague the doomed Studs. This account covers six months of 1931.

II. The Danny O'Neill pentalogy stars a young man who appeared briefly as a college student in the second Lonigan volume; it is sometimes called the O'Neill-O'Flaherty pentalogy. Danny is more of an autobiographical figure than Studs.

1. *The Face of Time* (Vanguard, 1953)
   Though written last, this book is actually the first of the pentalogy chronologically. It relates how three-year-old Danny came to be brought up by his O'Flaherty grandparents.
2. *A World I Never Made* (Vanguard, 1936)
   Timid and overprotected, Danny at seven becomes interested in baseball.
3. *No Star Is Lost* (Vanguard, 1938)
   Still preadolescent, Danny begins to reckon with a cruel world.
4. *Father and Son* (Vanguard, 1940)
   In high school, Danny realizes that he will never fit into the social life of his neighborhood.
5. *My Days of Anger* (Vanguard, 1943)
   Danny "finds himself" during his college days at the University of Chicago. The series ends with Danny at the threshold of adult life.

Note: Danny O'Neill also figures in two later books: *Boarding House Blues* (Paperback Library, 1961), which was retitled *Slum Street U.S.A.*; and *New Year's Eve/1929* (Smith/Horizon, 1967).

III. In a sense, the Bernard Carr trilogy takes up where the Danny O'Neill books left off.

1. *Bernard Clare* (Vanguard, 1946)
   Clare was changed to *Carr* after this first book was the subject of a libel suit brought by a man named Bernard Clare. In 1927, the fictional Bernard is struggling to be a writer in New York City.
2. *The Road Between* (Vanguard, 1949)
   By 1932–33, Bernard is married; his first novel is a success.
3. *Yet Other Waters* (Vanguard, 1952)
   The year 1935 brings Bernard a third successful novel, a growing family, and disenchantment with the Communist party.

IV. Farrell's later novels are generally conceded to be less successful than the rest, yet the worn bindings of most library copies attest to the countless hours of reading pleasure his solid stories have provided.

Farrell had formulated a master plan for a cycle of thirty novels, tales, and poems to be called the Universe of Time, which was left unfinished at his death. Some of the related titles are as follows:

1. *The Silence of History* (Doubleday, 1963)
   This introduces Eddie Ryan, another autobiographical figure around whom the series revolves.
2. *Lonely for the Future* (Doubleday, 1966)
   Eddie's friends George Raymond and Alec McGonagle are the focus.
3. *What Time Collects* (Doubleday, 1964)
   The story of Anne Duncan and Zeke Daniels.
4. *A Brand New Life* (Doubleday, 1968)
   Anne comes to Chicago and meets Roger and George Raymond.
5. *Judith* (Doubleday, 1969)
   Eddie Ryan gives a retrospective account of his affair with concert pianist Judith.
6. *The Dunne Family* (Doubleday, 1976)
   The life of Grace Hogan Dunne, Eddie's grandmother, is recounted.
7. *The Death of Nora Ryan* (Doubleday, 1978)
   Nora Ryan, Eddie's mother, suffers a massive stroke on New Year's Day, 1946.

Fast, Howard

The dominant figures in this popular quintet are Dan Lavette, the hardworking patriarch of the Lavette family and corporate enterprises; his rich and beautiful but cold wife, Jean; their troubled daughter, Barbara; and the Lavette sons, Tom and Joe. The alluring May Ling and Dan's business partner, Mark Levy, are among the host of characters bustling through the colorful story, which stretches from the San Francisco earthquake to the Vietnam War days. Fast also has written under the name of E. V. Cunningham (q.v.).

1. *The Immigrants* (Houghton, 1977)
   Determined son of French-Italian immigrants, Dan Lavette builds an empire of department stores, commercial airlines, and steamships, but he is torn between two beautiful women.

2. *The Second Generation* (Houghton, 1978)
   In 1934–36, young Barbara takes up the cause of striking dock-
   workers as she matures personally and professionally.
3. *The Establishment* (Houghton, 1979)
   Barbara, now a successful writer, gets caught in Senator Joe
   McCarthy's web as Tom moves ruthlessly toward ever greater success and his brother Joe's dedication to medicine turns his marriage sour.
4. *The Legacy* (Houghton, 1981)
   After Dan Lavette's death, daughter Barbara takes center stage as
   the story continues during the fifties and sixties, through marriage,
   divorce, and activity in the women's movement and the antiwar
   movement.
5. *The Immigrant's Daughter* (Houghton, 1985)
   Barbara Lavette campaigns for Congress and continues her antiwar activities.

Faulkner, William

In a sense, all the novels set in the fictional county of Yoknapatawpha,
Mississippi, are a series—they share not only a time and a place but a
unique world. And because Faulkner did not catch his characters neatly
between book covers but let them ramble with lifelike imprecision from
book to book, unraveling a satisfactory chronology is a major under-
taking—certainly beyond the scope of this bibliography. Readers who
want more than the simple conjugation of Snopses offered below should
refer to *The Reader's Guide to William Faulkner* by Edward Volpe
(Farrar, 1964, reprinted by Octagon, 1974) or *William Faulkner: Bib-
liographical and Reference Guide* edited by Leland H. Cox (Gale, 1982).
Though various members of the Snopes family appear in other novels
(*Satoris; The Unvanquished; Sanctuary*), they take center stage in the
three novels called the Snopes trilogy. Faulkner portrays them as a sub-
human tribe, giving them names such as Mink, Eck, and Lump. They
symbolize modern commerce—avaricious, immoral, and dehumaniz-
ing.

1. *The Hamlet* (Random, 1940)
   The rise of the Snopes family begins when Flem Snopes comes to
   Frenchman's Bend in 1900. This volume is more comic than the
   following two, which were written much later.

2. *The Town* (Random, 1957)
   Flem and his family move to Jefferson, where he rises from restaurant owner to vice-presidency of Colonel Sartoris's bank.
3. *The Mansion* (Random, 1959)
   Flem is now a respectable citizen, and Mink, his cousin, is determined to kill him for failing to come to his aid at a murder trial.

Feuchtwanger, Lion

Robert Graves fans who are looking for a follow-up to the Claudius
books will be pleased to discover this trilogy set in Roman times. It is a
narrative centering on Flavius Josephus, the great Jewish historian. The
series gives a vivid portrait of Rome from A.D. 64 through the rule of
Domitian, and it gives an interesting view of the lives and position of the
Jews at this time.

1. *Josephus* (Viking, 1932)
   Josephus comes to Rome during the last days of Nero to plead at
   the court of the Caesars for three unjustly imprisoned Jews. Translated from the German by Willa and Edwin Muir.
2. *The Jew of Rome* (Viking, 1936)
   Josephus is torn between his high position in the Roman world and
   his Jewish loyalties. Translated from the German by Willa and
   Edwin Muir.
3. *Josephus and the Emperor* (Viking, 1942)
   Josephus has lost the favor of the Emperor Domitian, but his major
   work, the universal history of the Jews, has been completed. Translated from the German by Caroline Oram.

Fielding, Gabriel (pseud. of Alan G. Barnsley)

These three novels about an English family show the Blaydon children
growing up under the influence of a neurotic and domineering mother
and a weak father, a vicar who retires to his study and his prayers when
faced with any unpleasantness. Two tragic deaths—one murder and one
accident—play central parts in the action, but the solitary moments of
insight and compromise involved in growing up are the real pleasures in
these sensitively drawn studies. John, the youngest brother, is the main

character and narrator. The books overlap in time but are perhaps best read in the following order:

1. *In the Time of Greenbloom* (Morrow, 1957)
   After the tragedy that disrupts his life, young John is liberated from his grief and guilt by an eccentric Jewish friend of his brother.
2. *Brotherly Love* (Morrow, 1961)
   The story starts before and ends after the previously listed volume. The central concern is John's brother David, who is not settling into the ministry as well as his mother had hoped.
3. *Through Streets Broad and Narrow* (Morrow, 1960)
   Eighteen-year-old John enters medical school in Dublin in 1935. The story covers five years before and during the war.

Fish, Robert L.

I. Captain José Da Silva—Zé to his friends—is the Brazilian police liaison to Interpol. He is suave and virile and drives like a maniac, though he'll do almost anything to avoid flying. His counterpart from the American embassy is Wilson, a man of such nondescript appearance that nobody ever remembers seeing him. Together they drink a lot of Remy Martin and solve some very puzzling cases against a colorful Brazilian setting, from the posh beaches of Rio to the jungles of the upper Amazon. Fish has also written under the pseudonym Robert L. Pike (q.v.).

1. *The Fugitive* (Simon & Schuster, 1962)
   Sinister ex-Nazis and a briefcase containing $2 million figure in this Edgar-winning novel, which introduced Captain Da Silva and Wilson.
2. *Isle of the Snakes* (Simon & Schuster, 1963)
   A map incised on the skin of a stuffed coral snake leads Da Silva to search for buried treasure on an island crawling with poisonous snakes.
3. *The Shrunken Head* (Simon & Schuster, 1963)
   When an explorer friend returns from the upper Amazon as a shrunken head, Da Silva goes to investigate.
4. *The Diamond Bubble* (Simon & Schuster, 1965)
   Da Silva is on the trail of a clever diamond racket.

5. *Brazilian Sleigh Ride* (Simon & Schuster, 1965)
   Wilson and Da Silva find themselves working against each other in this case involving fraud and an old army pal of Wilson's.
6. *Always Kill a Stranger* (Putnam, 1967)
   An anonymous letter warning of an assassination during a high-level OAS meeting in Rio has everybody jumpy.
7. *The Bridge That Went Nowhere* (Putnam, 1968)
   When a bridge in the middle of the jungle is blown up, the trail seems to lead to a missing young geologist.
8. *The Xavier Affair* (Putnam, 1969)
   Chico Xavier, son of the fourth-richest man in Brazil, is kidnapped.
9. *The Green Hell Treasure* (Putnam, 1971)
   Da Silva follows an ex-convict to his well-hidden loot.
10. *Trouble in Paradise* (Doubleday, 1975)
    After five underworld slayings, Da Silva sets himself up as a decoy.

II. Some think Fish's criminals are even more engaging than his detectives, especially the debonair and high-living Kek Huuygens, the world's greatest smuggler. Huuygens, who is known to have smuggled everything from the original score of a Bach cantata to a two-ton elephant across international borders, has no trouble outwitting the customs authorities who monitor his comings and goings. These delightful volumes feature Kek's adventures.

1. *The Hochman Miniatures* (New Amer. Lib., 1967)
   Kek's debut features Nazi contraband and his plans to avenge the death of his family at the hands of SS Colonel Gruber.
2. *Whirligig* (World, 1970)
   The dashing Kek and his actress wife decide to take $5 million out of Belgium—legally!
3. *The Tricks of the Trade* (Putnam, 1972)
   The oily Señor Sanchez has offered Kek $10,000 plus expenses to transport a suitcase from Buenos Aires to Barcelona.
4. *The Wager* (Putnam, 1974)
   Kek bets that he can smuggle a valuable Chinese carving past U.S. customs.
5. *Kek Huuygens, Smuggler* (Mysterious Pr., 1976)
   Kek fans will want to search out this collection of short stories.

III. Humor and character are more prominent than mystery in these novels. Carruthers, Simpson, and Briggs are three old duffers who used to write mystery stories. Now fallen on sad days, the trio decide to put their still formidable talents to actual use and set up their own bump-off service, executing real murders if the fee is right and the victims sufficiently deserving.

1. *The Murder League* (Simon & Schuster, 1968)
   Carruthers, Simpson, and Briggs form the Murder League and proceed with their first cases until they run into trouble and are rescued by Sir Percival Pugh.
2. *Rub-a-Dub-Dub* (Simon & Schuster, 1971)
   On a cruise ship, Mrs. Mazie Carpenter, an American con-lady and cardsharp, kicks up a bit of trouble. Variant title: *Death Cuts The Deck*.
3. *A Gross Carriage of Justice* (Doubleday, 1979)
   The redoubtable ex-detective writers find themselves captives of two American toughs from Cicero, Illinois, and quickly turn the tables on them.

IV. Sherlock Holmes fans won't want to miss these broad and funny parodies starring Schlock Homes of 221B Bagel St. and his assistant Dr. Watney.

1. *The Incredible Schlock Homes* (Simon & Schuster, 1965)
   Homes has twelve adventures.
2. *The Memoirs of Schlock Homes* (Simon & Schuster, 1974)
   Further stories and parodies continue Homes's adventures.

Fisher, Edward

Scholars may quibble, but this fictionalized biography of Shakespeare is enjoyable light reading that gives a good feeling for Elizabethan times. Naturally Fisher presents his solution to the mystery of the "Dark Lady" of the sonnets. The Silver Falcon is the trilogy title.

1. *Shakespeare & Son* (Abelard-Schuman, 1962)
   William is the son of the title. This volume shows him from ages fifteen to eighteen, a much misunderstood young man.
2. *Love's Labour's Won: A Novel About Shakespeare's Lost Years* (Abelard-Schuman, 1963)

During the years 1583–93, William is on his way to fame with partner Dick Burbage.

3. *The Best House in Stratford* (Abelard-Schuman, 1965)
   The title is ironic, for the Stratford house is old and run-down. Shakespeare finds his London life more compelling.

Fleming, Ian

The enormous appeal of super-agent James Bond—007 of the British Secret Service—is shown in the continuing popularity of the Bond movies. Fleming's own involvement in British intelligence, though extensive and apparently not without drama, cannot have been one-tenth as glamorous and thrilling as the adventures of his fictional hero. Kingsley Amis provides the last word on Fleming's books, and interested readers will not want to miss his authoritative *James Bond Dossier* (New Amer. Lib., 1965). John E. Gardner (q.v.) has attempted to revive Bond. The books listed here have been collected in three omnibus volumes: *Gilt-Edged Bonds* (Macmillan, 1961), containing numbers 1, 5, and 6 listed below; *More Gilt-Edged Bonds* (Macmillan, 1965), containing numbers 2, 3, and 4; and *Bonded Fleming* (Viking, 1965), which includes numbers 8, 9, and 10.

1. *Casino Royale* (Macmillan, 1953)
   At a French casino resort, Bond destroys LeChiffre and the French arm of the Russian espionage ring known as SMERSH. Variant title: *You Asked for It.*
2. *Live and Let Die* (Macmillan, 1954)
   Bond meets Mr. Big of SMERSH in an adventure set in New York, Florida, and Jamaica.
3. *Moonraker* (Macmillan, 1955)
   Bond keeps a villainous millionaire from destroying London with a nuclear rocket. Variant title: *Too Hot to Handle.*
4. *Diamonds Are Forever* (Macmillan, 1956)
   Bond infiltrates the Spang mob of diamond smugglers.
5. *From Russia with Love* (Macmillan, 1957)
   SMERSH makes an all-out effort to assassinate Bond.
6. *Doctor No* (Macmillan, 1958)
   This action is set in the Caribbean, where the maniacal Eurasian Dr. No, who has steel pincers for hands, makes plans to take over the world.

7. *Goldfinger* (Macmillan, 1959)
   Bond must prevent SMERSH from getting all the gold in Fort Knox.
8. *For Your Eyes Only* (Viking, 1960)
   Five stories are included here: "From a View to a Kill"; "For Your Eyes Only"; "Quantum of Solace"; "Risico"; "The Hildebrand Rarity."
9. *Thunderball* (Viking, 1961)
   SPECTRE tries to blackmail the West with hijacked nuclear bombs.
10. *The Spy Who Loved Me* (Viking, 1962)
    This story is told by lovely young Vivienne Michel, who is briefly involved in one of Bond's cases.
11. *On Her Majesty's Secret Service* (New Amer. Lib., 1963)
    Blofeld of SPECTRE is back again with a nasty germ-warfare plot. Bond gives up bachelorhood for Countess Tracy Vincenzo.
12. *You Only Live Twice* (New Amer. Lib., 1964)
    Devastated by Tracy's death, Bond is sent to investigate a strange Japanese death garden.
13. *The Man with the Golden Gun* (New Amer. Lib., 1965)
    A brainwashed Bond is used by the KGB.
14. *Octopussy* (New Amer. Lib., 1966)
    Two novelettes were posthumously published here: "Octopussy," about Maj. Dexter Smyth, a retired British marine officer who is conducting dangerous octopus experiments; and "The Living Daylights," about Bond's assignment to kill a KGB assassin.

Fletcher, Inglis

Adventure, romance, and history in equal parts characterize the Carolina series, sometimes known as the Albemarle series, by this North Carolina novelist. *Raleigh's Eden* was the first published and the first to be set in Albemarle, the fertile coastal district to which its title refers. Thereafter Fletcher produced a new book every two years, moving both forward and backward in time, and eventually covering the period from 1585 to 1789. Some characters reappear in various books, but it is the consistent location that makes this a series. Each novel was designed to stand on its own, and a chronological reading is not really essential, but for those who prefer it, here is the sequence as closely as it can be determined.

1. *Roanoke Hundred* (Bobbs-Merrill, 1948)
   This account is based on the Grenville expedition of 108 Englishmen who settled on Roanoke Island in 1585.
2. *Bennett's Welcome* (Bobbs-Merrill, 1950)
   This story begins in England in 1651, when Richard Monington is banished to Virginia as an indentured servant as punishment for helping King Charles II escape.
3. *Rogue's Harbor* (Bobbs-Merril, 1964)
   Nathan Willoughby joins the settler's rebellion of 1677 as his daughter plans to marry a poor schoolmaster.
4. *Raleigh's Eden* (Bobbs-Merrill, 1940)
   Adam Rutledge and Mary Warden head the cast of characters in this story of plantation life beginning in 1765.
5. *Men of Albemarle* (Bobbs-Merrill, 1942)
   Plantation owner Roger Mainwaring and the mysterious Scottish Lady Mary Tower figure in this installment set from 1710 to 1712.
6. *Lusty Wind for Carolina* (Bobbs-Merrill, 1944)
   Anne Bonney, a beautiful woman pirate, is one of the colorful characters in this tale of Huguenot settlers and the fight for freedom of the seas.
7. *Cormorant's Brood* (Lippincott, 1959)
   The time is 1725–29, and Anthony Granville and Deirdra Treffrey star. The cormorant is greedy British governor George Burrington.
8. *The Wind in the Forest* (Bobbs-Merrill, 1957)
   Set in 1771, this book examines the conflict between the frontier farmers and the wealthy coastal plantation owners.
9. *The Scotswoman* (Bobbs-Merrill, 1954)
   The historical figure Flora MacDonald, savior of Bonny Prince Charlie, is the main character in this book, which focuses on the Scottish settlers in North Carolina in 1773.
10. *Toil of the Brave* (Bobbs-Merrill, 1946)
    Set in 1779–80, this account features Captain Huntley, a liaison officer to General Washington.
11. *Wicked Lady* (Bobbs-Merrill, 1962)
    As the last battles of the Revolution are fought, the town of Edenton, North Carolina, is mesmerized by its newest resident, Lady Anne Stuart.

12. *Queen's Gift* (Bobbs-Merrill, 1952)
    Debate over ratification of the Constitution consumes Albemarle's citizens in 1789.

Ford, Ford Madox

I. In addition to his best-known novel, *The Good Soldier*, Ford Madox Ford (formerly Hueffer) wrote thirty-one other novels, including two series. According to his biographer Arthur Mizener, Ford claimed not to like the Fifth Queen trilogy and did not want to see it republished. But most readers will find it an authentic and gracefully drawn portrait of the court of Henry VIII with all its passion, intrigue, and tragedy. Vanguard issued the trilogy in one volume titled *The Fifth Queen* in 1963.

   1. *The Fifth Queen; and How She Came to Court* (Rivers, London, 1906)
      Katherine Howard is presented as an idealist determined to reestablish the old faith in England.
   2. *The Privy Seal; His Last Venture* (Rivers, London, 1907)
      Katherine's enemy Thomas Cromwell, the Privy Seal, is destroyed.
   3. *The Fifth Queen Crowned* (Nash, London, 1908)
      Katherine meets downfall and death.

II. The four novels that comprise *Parade's End* will appeal to those who enjoyed the BBC's recent dramatization of Vera Brittain's memoir of the war years, *Testament of Youth*. The tetralogy concerns the same time and class and conveys the same sense of the passing of an age. The central character is Christopher Tietjens, son of a good Yorkshire family and the personification of the Edwardian ideals of reason, honor, and integrity. *Parade's End* is the title of the omnibus volume published by Knopf in 1950.

   1. *Some Do Not* (Boni, 1924)
      This story begins in 1912 as Christopher's impossible wife, Sylvia, returns to him after having an affair with another man. He enlists in 1916, is wounded at the front, and is sent home to recover.

2. *No More Parades* (Boni, 1925)
   Sylvia visits Christopher, who has been reassigned to a base near Rouen, and stirs up trouble.
3. *A Man Could Stand Up* (Boni, 1926)
   Discharged after a final traumatic battle, Christopher comes home to England and his friend Valentine.
4. *Last Post* (Boni, 1928)
   In this last volume, Christopher's adjustment to civilian life is seen through the eyes of those who surround him at his country cottage.

Forester, C. S.

Horatio Hornblower, the resourceful and ever valiant British naval hero who has been entertaining readers since 1937, shows no sign of losing his audience. Endowed with a few humanizing flaws—he is shy, tone-deaf, and inclined to self-doubt—Hornblower is otherwise incomparable—good, brave, intelligent, and handsome as well. There are eleven books in the series, one of which was published posthumously, as well as the delightful *Hornblower Companion* (Little, 1964), which contains maps, bits of relevant naval history, and a long essay by Forester on the creation of the Hornblower saga. Forester fans will not want to miss C. Northcote Parkinson's "biography" entitled *The Life and Times of Horatio Hornblower* (Little, 1970) or the series of naval adventures by that author (q.v.) starring Richard Delancey. There are three Hornblower omnibuses: *Young Hornblower* (Little, 1960) contains numbers 1, 2, and 5 below; *Captain Horatio Hornblower* (Little, 1939) comprises numbers 6, 7, and 8; and *The Indomitable Hornblower* (Little, 1963) includes numbers 9, 10, and 11.

1. *Mr. Midshipman Hornblower* (Little, 1950)
   A very young Hornblower fights a duel and is captured by the Spanish during the period June, 1794, to March, 1798.
2. *Lieutenant Hornblower* (Little, 1952)
   Bush narrates this volume which shows how his friend Hornblower gets drawn into marriage to Maria during the period May, 1800, to March, 1803.
3. *Hornblower and the Hotspur* (Little, 1962)
   Between April, 1803 and July, 1805, Hornblower becomes a father and captures Spanish treasure.

4. *Hornblower During the Crisis* (Little, 1967)
   This last Hornblower story was described in a postscript to the *Hornblower Companion*. Forester died before it was completed. It is published here with his notes and two short stories. Forged papers and an espionage plot are the center of the action, which takes place between August and December, 1805.
5. *Hornblower and the Atropos* (Little, 1953)
   Hornblower leads Nelson's funeral barge up the Thames and endures the tragic deaths of his two children between October, 1805, and January, 1808.
6. *Beat to Quarters* (Little, 1937)
   This was the first-written book in the series. It shows Hornblower as captain of the British frigate *Lydia* off the coast of Guatemala. This volume introduces Lady Barbara and covers the period from June to October, 1808. English title: *The Happy Return*.
7. *Ship of the Line* (Little, 1938)
   Hornblower sets out in H.M.S. *Sutherland* to fight against the French squadron and is taken captive. The action takes place between May and October, 1810.
8. *Flying Colors* (Little, 1938)
   Hornblower, Bush, and Brown sail a small boat down the Loire back to freedom and active service. Hornblower and Lady Barbara are finally united. The period is November, 1810, to June, 1811.
9. *Commodore Hornblower* (Little, 1945)
   Hornblower leads a squadron including several bomb vessels to the Baltic between May and October, 1812.
10. *Lord Hornblower* (Little, 1946)
    Stormy weather and personal loss in Normandy afflict Lord Hornblower between October, 1813, and May, 1814.
11. *Admiral Hornblower in the West Indies* (Little, 1958)
    Back in the West Indies and with a tactful and loving Barbara, Hornblower pursues slave traders and contentious fugitives. The period is May, 1821, to October, 1823.

Francis, Dick

I. Though Francis has written many horsey puzzlers, only two of them are about Sid Halley, the ex-jockey whose detecting was featured on public television's "Mystery!" When an accident cripples one of his hands and ends his jockeying days, Halley finds work at the Radnor Agency as a specialist in their racing-investigation section. His first case offers action enough to take his mind off his ruined career and failed marriage.

1. *Odds Against* (Harper, 1965)
   Halley's first case involves stock manipulators who want to sell a racecourse.
2. *Whip Hand* (Harper, 1979)
   With his new battery-powered hand, Halley is hired to guard a friend's racehorse.

II. Kit Fielding, "a knight in racing colors," practices Dick Francis's old profession of steeplechase jockeying. Kit also gets involved in detecting when necessary in order to help friends, relatives, and business associates.

1. *Break In* (Putnam, 1986)
   Kit comes to the aid of his twin sister Holly and her husband, horse trainer Bobby Allardeck, who are victims of a slander campaign.
2. *Bolt* (Putnam, 1987)
   Princess Casilia, Kit's employer, needs help when ruthless Henri Nanterre tries to turn her industrial empire into a munitions works.

Frankau, Pamela

The Clothes of a King's Son trilogy tells of the whole Weston family and their many friends and associates, but the central figure is the son Thomas. He is ten as the story begins and spending the summer of 1926 with his father's theatrical troupe at the English seaside resort of Sawcombe. Thomas has psychic powers and, though all his adventures are capable of rational explanation, they have an element of magic to them. Frankau shares the talent so many English authors have for writing about families and especially children with humor and understanding.

1. *Sing for Your Supper* (Random, 1963)
   Young Thomas, fourteen-year-old Sara, and sixteen-year-old Gerald are the children of widower Philip Weston, impecunious head of a theatrical troupe. Nanny Briggs looks after them all.

143

2. *Slaves of the Lamp* (Random, 1965)
   Tom narrates this installment set against the background of the
   London theater and advertising worlds. Sara is now a writer, and
   Gerald is an actor.
3. *Over the Mountains* (Random, 1967)
   Tom sees service in World War II and capture at Dunkirk, escapes,
   and meets his childhood sweetheart, Rob, again.

Franken, Rose

For a good, old-fashioned wallow in nostalgia, try reading or rereading
the Claudia books that were so popular during the forties. No less a light
than Diana Trilling admitted to enjoying Franken's unpretentious books
more than many more serious novels. Though she criticized Claudia's
"adorably feminine" ignorance of geography, insurance, and wartime
politics (*Nation*, May 22, 1943), she also praised Franken's ability to fill
every page with the "recognizable details of day-to-day living." *The
Book of Claudia* (Farrar, 1950) contains only the first two books in the
series of six.

1. *Claudia: The Story of a Marriage* (Farrar, 1939)
   Claudia at eighteen is the young wife of architect David Naughton.
   In this volume, David and Claudia weather in-law problems and
   budget problems, welcome their first child, and move to an old
   farmhouse in Connecticut.
2. *Claudia and David* (Farrar, 1940)
   Claudia and David now have two boys. They decide to move back
   to New York for the sake of David's career, but Claudia continues
   to suppress her stage ambitions.
3. *Another Claudia* (Farrar, 1943)
   The war years bring Claudia a new maturity.
4. *Young Claudia* (Rinehart, 1946)
   Claudia keeps up the farm till David's return from the war.
5. *The Marriage of Claudia* (Rinehart, 1948)
   The Connecticut farm is sold, the Naughtons move to New York,
   and David contracts tuberculosis.
6. *From Claudia to David* (Harper, 1960)
   David, recovering from TB, Claudia, their three children, and the
   maid Bertha rent a cottage in the Adirondacks.

7. *The Fragile Years* (Doubleday, 1952)
   Claudia faces a series of tragedies including the death of her eldest son and David's illness. English titles: *Those Fragile Years; The Return of Claudia.*
8. *The Antic Years* (Doubleday, 1958)
   Beneficiaries of a legacy, Claudia, David, their two remaining children, and the faithful Bertha take a vacation to Europe.

Franklin, Miles

The success of the superb Australian film *My Brilliant Career* has prompted the reissue of both of Miles Franklin's semiautobiographical novels. Her spunky young heroine, Sybylla, is an early feminist in Victorian Australia, where prim conventions contrast oddly with primitive conditions. In her determination to remain unhobbled by marriage, she must resist society's pressures and the temptations of her own weaker moments.

1. *My Brilliant Career* (St. Martin's, 1980)
   Country girl Sybylla, polished by her sophisticated city relatives, becomes a marriageable young lady, but her writing ambitions and her feminist conscience interfere. First published in 1901.
2. *The End of My Career* (St. Martin's, 1981)
   The success of her book takes Sybylla from Possum Gully to Sydney and further trials and triumphs. First published in 1901.

Fraser, Antonia

English biographer Antonia Fraser, author of *Mary, Queen of Scots* and many other titles, writes mystery stories as a change of pace. Her amateur sleuth, Londoner Jemima Shore, is the star of her own television program, "Jemima Shore—Investigator." Jemima is intelligent, cool-headed, and stylish, living the life of a media celebrity with a married lover. The mysteries are brisk but satisfying, with just the right touch of satire.

1. *Quiet as a Nun* (Viking, 1977)
   Jemima investigates the death of an old schoolmate at Blessed Eleanor's Convent in Sussex.

2. *The Wild Island* (Norton, 1978)
   On holiday in the Scottish Highlands, Jemima gets caught up in a family feud and a zany cabal of neo-Jacobites.
3. *A Splash of Red* (Norton, 1981)
   Jemima agrees to "flat-and-cat sit" for author Chloe Fontaine, but Chloe doesn't leave her building alive.
4. *Cool Repentance* (Norton, 1982)
   Actress Christabel Cartwright returns to her family after an affair with a young rock star, and is scheduled to appear at a local drama festival that Jemima is televising.
5. *Oxford Blood* (Norton, 1985)
   A nursemaid's deathbed confession concerning switched babies starts Jemima on a quest for an heir's true parentage.
6. *Your Royal Hostage* (Atheneum, 1988)
   Jemima covers the impending royal wedding of Princess Amy of Cumberland, while a group of animal rights activists plot to kidnap Princess Amy.

Note: *Jemima Shore's First Case and Other Stories* (Norton, 1987) is a collection of seventeen stories, four of which star Jemima Shore.

Fraser, George MacDonald

I. Harry Flashman, the cad who bullied the younger boys in Thomas Hughes's classic *Tom Brown's School Days*, has been resurrected for these funny and sophisticated picaresque novels. Purporting to be Flashman's own memoirs, they relate his adventures in the most glowing terms and detail his many amorous conquests. Of course, he is a thorough coward and bounder, perhaps the ultimate antihero, but that makes his adventures all the more interesting. Fraser draws in vivid historical backgrounds without ever becoming dull, and his satire has the perfect light touch.

1. *Flashman: From the Flashman Papers, 1839–1842* (World, 1969)
   This book gives a "true" account of Flashman's expulsion from school and of the beginning of his career in the 11th Light Dragoons under the Earl of Cardigan in India.
2. *Royal Flash: From the Flashman Papers, in 1842–3 and 1847–8* (Knopf, 1970)

Flashman poses as Prince Carl Gustav and loses a fortune in jewels in this volume which features Otto von Bismarck and Lola Montez and ties in with Anthony Hope's *Prisoner of Zenda* (q.v.).

3. *Flash for Freedom* (Knopf, 1972)
   At mid-century, Flashman becomes involved in the slave trade, comes to America, and runs into Abraham Lincoln, among others.
4. *Flashman at the Charge* (Knopf, 1973)
   On the scene in the Crimea in 1854, Flashman naturally finds himself leading the charge of the Light Brigade.
5. *Flashman in the Great Game* (Knopf, 1975)
   Flashman spies out the impending India mutiny of 1857. His schoolmate East bites the dust in this installment.
6. *Flashman's Lady* (Knopf, 1978)
   Flashman's wife, the beautiful but dim-witted Elspeth, is kidnapped by a pirate. Extracts from Elspeth's diaries are a new treat.
7. *Flashman and the Redskins* (Knopf, 1982)
   In New Orleans under an alias in 1849, Flashman marries a brothel-keeper, goes west as a wagonmaster, and survives the Battle of Little Big Horn in 1876.
8. *Flashman and the Dragon* (Knopf, 1986)
   Flashman is Britain's semi-official envoy to the rebels in China's Talping Rebellion.

II. In addition to the Flashman books, Fraser has written two books chronicling the wacky adventures of a certain very Scottish Highland Regiment from the end of World War II into peacetime. They might appeal to "M.A.S.H." fans with a tolerance for Scottish dialect.

1. *The General Danced at Dawn* (Knopf, 1973)
   This story begins as Dand MacNeill is commissioned; we meet the battalion characters, including Daft Bob, Sergeant Telfer, and Private McAuslan, the dirtiest soldier in the world.
2. *McAuslan in the Rough* (Knopf, 1974)
   The further adventures of Lieutenant MacNeill and the Highland Regiment feature the top brass on the golf course and McAuslan in love.

Freeling, Nicholas

I. Inspector Van der Valk of the Amsterdam police is a kind of Dutch peasant Maigret. A large-hearted but pragmatic professional, impatient with paperwork and overfond of his French wife's gourmet cooking, Van der Valk plodded stubbornly through ten cases before Freeling felt that his character was going stale. The Dutch setting gives the books a special interest, though Van der Valk usually pursues his investigations in the seamier neighborhoods and in towns where the annual rainfall must be a good deal higher than the average. The last two books listed below are unique addenda to the Van der Valk opus: They star Arlette, the former Mrs. Van der Valk, as their detective.

1. *Love in Amsterdam* (Harper, 1963)
   This account centers on the long interrogation of Martin, who is arrested when his ex-mistress is found shot to death. To write it, Freeling may have drawn on his own experience of having been arrested for a theft he did not commit. Variant title: *Death in Amsterdam.*
2. *Because of the Cats* (Harper, 1964)
   The affluent seaside town of Bloemendael is plagued by a juvenile gang whose activities take a nasty turn into vandalism, rape, and religious cults.
3. *A Question of Loyalty* (Harper, 1964)
   A Dutch girl, Lucienne Englebert, gets mixed up with three Italian boys and lots of trouble. English title: *Guns Before Butter.*
4. *Double Barrel* (Harper, 1965)
   When poison-pen letters cause two suicides, Van der Valk goes to a dreary north Holland town to investigate.
5. *Criminal Conversation* (Harper, 1966)
   Inspector Van der Valk suspects a fashionable nerve specialist of murder.
6. *King of the Rainy Country* (Harper, 1966)
   Van der Valk uncovers some strange doings while tracking down two missing persons, a millionaire and a young girl.
7. *Strike Out Where Not Applicable* (Harper, 1968)
   Recovering from serious injuries, Van der Valk has been made *commissaire* of a small town in the tulip-growing country, where he investigates the suspicious death of a local cafe owner.

8. *Tsing-Boom* (Harper, 1969)

The trail of a woman's death leads back to Vietnam during the French's last stand in Southeast Asia. English title: *Tsing-Boum*.

9. *The Lovely Ladies* (Harper, 1971)

The strange death of an elderly gentleman in the marketplace in Amsterdam leads Van der Valk to Dublin to see the daughter of the deceased. Variant title: *Over the High Side*.

10. *Aupres de ma Blonde* (Harper, 1972)

Van der Valk has been kicked upstairs to a desk job but can't resist the lure of this strange case brought to him by a young jeweler's assistant. English title: *A Long Silence*.

11. *The Widow* (Pantheon, 1979)

Arlette, now remarried and running a counseling service, gets involved in a strange and dangerous affair.

12. *Arlette* (Pantheon, 1981)

Arlette's second case involves a distraught widow and a young man in hiding from the Argentine police. English title: *One Damn Thing after Another*.

II. Freeling's new detective is the French police inspector Henri Castang. A member of a young new breed, Castang holds a university degree and has been known to paraphrase Goethe on the job. He has a gymnast's elasticity of frame, and a tenacious and observant mind. He is still very much in love with his young wife, Vera, a crippled ex-gymnast.

1. *A Dressing of Diamond* (Harper, 1974)

Castang investigates the kidnapping of the eight-year-old daughter of Colette Delavigne, judge in the juvenile courts.

2. *The Bugles Blowing* (Harper, 1975)

Three dead bodies—one of them the naked wife of a high government official—are found shot in the same bed. English title: *What Are Bugles Blowing For?*

3. *Sabine* (Harper, 1976)

A frightened woman is convinced that her son and daughter-in-law are trying to murder her for her money. English title: *Lake Isle*.

4. *The Night Lords* (Harper, 1978)

The daughter of an English high court justice, vacationing in France, finds the corpse of a strange woman in the back seat of the family Rolls Royce.

5. *Castang's City* (Pantheon, 1980)
   When the deputy mayor is murdered in broad daylight, terrorism is suspected, but Castang has other ideas. Mrs. Castang has a baby in this installment.
6. *Wolfnight* (Pantheon, 1982)
   Politician Marc Vibert confesses to Castang that his car plunged off a mountain road with his secretary Viviane Kranitz trapped inside.
7. *The Back of the North Wind* (Viking, 1983)
   Castang gets involved in two grotesque cases: the murder and cannibalization of a young woman, and some bludgeonings with an extremely heavy instrument.
8. *No Part in Your Death* (Viking, 1984)
   Three separate cases are investigated: a distraught woman in Munich, the disappearance of an eccentric Englishwoman, and an apparent double suicide in Dorset.
9. *Cold Iron* (Viking, 1986)
   Newly posted to the provinces, Castang investigates the murder of an aristocratic lady with decidedly paranoid tendencies.
10. *Not as Far as Velma* (Mysterious, 1989)
   A missing person case and the bombing of a convent may both have their roots back in a concentration camp in 1945.

Gainham, Sarah

The Julia Homberg trilogy follows the life of the beautiful leading lady of the Viennese theater from 1938 to the early 1950s. The first volume gives both a panoramic view of Austria during the war years and a close-up of the strain and terror of people living through that cataclysm. The second volume moves on to the fear and political intrigue of the cold war years. The third book movingly examines how survivors restore their shattered lives.

1. *Night Falls on the City* (Holt, 1967)
   Julia's Jewish husband, Franz, thought to have escaped abroad, is really hiding in their apartment.
2. *A Place in the Country* (Holt, 1969)
   The young English officer Robert Inglis rescues Georg Kerenyi and falls in love with Julia's ward, Lali.

3. *Private Worlds* (Holt, 1971)
   Julia, now married to Georg Kerenyi, comes to terms with tragedy and mystery echoing from the past.

Gallico, Paul

Once Mrs. 'Arris, the plucky London charlady, got to Paris, there was no stopping her. Gallico followed that first success with three other adventures, all showing Ada Harris spreading her own inimitable brand of Cockney sweetness and light. "If you wants somefink bad enough, there's always ways," is the motto that buoys her through disappointments and temporary setbacks to the eventual accomplishment of her mission.

1. *Mrs 'Arris Goes to Paris* (Doubleday, 1958)
   Ada Harris goes to Paris to pick out the Dior dress that she has saved and skimped for three years to buy.
2. *Mrs. 'Arris Goes to New York* (Doubleday, 1960)
   Mrs. Harris is off to the New World on a mission of mercy—Little 'Enry Gussett needs a father.
3. *Mrs. 'Arris Goes to Parliament* (Doubleday, 1965)
   Mrs. Harris's slogan "Live and let live" wins her a seat in Parliament and the loyal friendship of John Bayswater.
4. *Mrs. 'Arris Goes to Moscow* (Delacorte, 1974)
   Accompanied this time by her friend Violet Butterfield, Mrs. Harris braves the Kremlin in her search for the lovely Lisabeta.

Galsworthy, John

The Forsyte Saga was the first big American success of a literary work adapted for television—people cancelled other engagements rather than miss an episode of the tortured affairs of Soames, Irene, and the other Forsytes. Of course the polished BBC production deserves some credit, but the main appeal was Galsworthy's compelling story, which, after all, was immensely popular when first published. Soames's death at the end of *Swan Song* was front-page material for London newspapers in 1928. As with most sagas, this one developed from a successful novel, *A*

Man of Property, which featured characters and action that fairly demanded a sequel. The first follow-up was "Indian Summer of a Forsyte"; it is a story, or "interlude," as Galsworthy called it, connecting that first novel with its successor. Still more novels and interludes followed. The television version ended with Soames's death and did not include the last three volumes of the saga (numbers 7, 8, and 9 below), in which Fleur Forsyte plays only a minor role. The series is best grouped into three trilogies with connecting interludes, and the omnibus volumes are organized that way: *The Forsyte Saga* (Scribner, 1922) contains *A Man of Property, In Chancery*, and *To Let; A Modern Comedy* (Scribner, 1929) comprises *The White Monkey, The Silver Spoon*, and *Swan Song*; and *End of the Chapter* (Scribner, 1934) contains *Maid in Waiting, Flowering Wilderness*, and *Over the River*. For convenience, each book is listed here separately.

1. *A Man of Property* (Putnam, 1906)
   Young Soames Forsyte embodies the ideal of his upper-middle-class family—he is industrious, prudent, tenacious, and more than a little self-satisfied. His marriage to the beautiful and romantic Irene proves disastrous. The story begins in 1886 with the engagement of June Forsyte to Philip Bosinney. Soames and Irene are already married. In this volume the older Forsytes are prominent, and they present a fascinating portrait of the Victorian propertied class.

1a. "Indian Summer of a Forsyte" is the interlude inserted here in the first trilogy omnibus. It shows old Jolyon being charmed by Irene in the days just before his death.

2. *In Chancery* (Scribner, 1920)
   Freed by divorce, Irene marries Jolyon and has a son, Jon. Soames marries Annette and has a daughter, Fleur.

2a. "Awakening" is the interlude inserted here. It is about little Jon's childhood.

3. *To Let* (Scribner, 1921)
   This volume begins in 1920 as Jon and Fleur meet, fall in love, and learn of the unbreachable rift that divides their families.

4. *The White Monkey* (Scribner, 1924)
   Fleur's marriage to Michael Mont is threatened by an affair with an artist but strengthened by the birth of a son.

4a. "A Silent Wooing" is the connecting interlude here. It shows young Jon in America meeting the girl who will become his wife.

5. *The Silver Spoon* (Scribner, 1926)
Fleur gets involved in a nasty libel suit, and Soames comes to the rescue.

5a. "Passers By" is the connecting interlude here. It shows Soames and Irene crossing paths.

6. *Swan Song* (Scribner, 1928)
In 1926, Jon Forsyte returns from America with his wife, Ann, and Fleur's revival of their affair ends in tragedy.

7. *Maid in Waiting* (Scribner, 1931)
This episode features young Elizabeth Cherrell, known as Dinny, who is a cousin to Michael Mont. Fleur and Michael are expecting their second child.

8. *Flowering Wilderness* (Scribner, 1932)
Dinny falls in love with the young poet Wilfred Desert, who is haunted by events surrounding his brush with Arab fanatics while traveling in the Middle East.

9. *Over the River* (Scribner, 1937)
In 1932, Dinny worries over dwindling resources, her sister Clair who has left her husband, and the newly elected M. P. Eustace Dornford.

Note: Two volumes of stories by Galsworthy are partially or entirely concerned with the Forsytes, although they are not part of the saga. *On Forsyte 'Change* (Scribner, 1930) contains stories covering various Forsytes from 1821 to 1918, and *Caravan* (Scribner, 1925) begins with "The Salvation of a Forsyte," which is about Swithin.

Gardner, Erle Stanley

To everyone who remembers Perry Mason's long-running success on television, Raymond Burr will always be Erle Stanley Gardner's unflappable lawyer who saves clients with his courtroom wizardry. An earlier radio version was equally popular in the 1940s. Fans will also remember Paul Drake, Mason's fearless and resourceful investigator; Della Street, his faithful secretary; and Hamilton Burger, the Los Angeles D. A. who is Mason's most frequent adversary in court. The earliest Mason novels were crafted in the realistic hard-boiled manner, but by 1937 they had begun to soften somewhat to include more "love interest" for his growing *Saturday Evening Post* audience. Gardner maintained a remarkably consistent and professional standard in the production of all eighty-six of his fast-paced and complex criminal cases. Their colorful titles need no further annotation. See also the entry under Gardner's pseudonym, A. A. Fair.

1. *The Case of the Velvet Claws* (Morrow, 1933)
2. *The Case of the Sulky Girl* (Morrow, 1933)
3. *The Case of the Curious Bride* (Morrow, 1934)
4. *The Case of the Howling Dog* (Morrow, 1934)
5. *The Case of the Lucky Legs* (Morrow, 1934)
6. *The Case of the Caretaker's Cat* (Morrow, 1935)
7. *The Case of the Counterfeit Eye* (Morrow, 1935)
8. *The Case of the Sleepwalker's Niece* (Morrow, 1936)
9. *The Case of the Stuttering Bishop* (Morrow, 1936)
10. *The Case of the Dangerous Dowager* (Morrow, 1937)
11. *The Case of the Lame Canary* (Morrow, 1937)
12. *The Case of the Shoplifter's Shoe* (Morrow, 1938)
13. *The Case of the Substitute Face* (Morrow, 1938)
14. *The Case of the Perjured Parrot* (Morrow, 1939)
15. *The Case of the Rolling Bones* (Morrow, 1939)
16. *The Case of the Baited Hook* (Morrow, 1940)
17. *The Case of the Silent Partner* (Morrow, 1940)
18. *The Case of the Empty Tin* (Morrow, 1941)
19. *The Case of the Haunted Husband* (Morrow, 1941)
20. *The Case of the Careless Kitten* (Morrow, 1942)
21. *The Case of the Drowning Duck* (Morrow, 1942)
22. *The Case of the Buried Clock* (Morrow, 1943)
23. *The Case of the Drowsy Mosquito* (Morrow, 1943)
24. *The Case of the Black-Eyed Blonde* (Morrow, 1944)
25. *The Case of the Crooked Candle* (Morrow, 1944)
26. *The Case of the Golddigger's Purse* (Morrow, 1945)
27. *The Case of the Half-Wakened Wife* (Morrow, 1945)
28. *The Case of the Borrowed Brunette* (Morrow, 1946)
29. *The Case of the Fan-Dancer's Horse* (Morrow, 1947)
30. *The Case of the Lazy Lover* (Morrow, 1947)
31. *The Case of the Lonely Heiress* (Morrow, 1948)
32. *The Case of the Vagabond Virgin* (Morrow, 1948)
33. *The Case of the Cautious Coquette* (Morrow, 1949)
34. *The Case of the Dubious Bridegroom* (Morrow, 1949)
35. *The Case of the Negligent Nymph* (Morrow, 1950)
36. *The Case of the Musical Cow* (Morrow, 1950)

37. *The Case of the One-Eyed Witness* (Morrow, 1950)
38. *The Case of the Angry Mourner* (Morrow, 1951)
39. *The Case of the Fiery Fingers* (Morrow, 1951)
40. *The Case of the Grinning Gorilla* (Morrow, 1952)
41. *The Case of the Moth-Eaten Mink* (Morrow, 1952)
42. *The Case of the Green-Eyed Sister* (Morrow, 1953)
43. *The Case of the Hesitant Hostess* (Morrow, 1953)
44. *The Case of the Fugitive Nurse* (Morrow, 1954)
45. *The Case of the Restless Redhead* (Morrow, 1954)
46. *The Case of the Runaway Corpse* (Morrow, 1954)
47. *The Case of the Glamorous Ghost* (Morrow, 1955)
48. *The Case of the Nervous Accomplice* (Morrow, 1955)
49. *The Case of the Sunbather's Diary* (Morrow, 1955)
50. *The Case of the Demure Defendant* (Morrow, 1956)
    Variant title: *The Case of the Missing Poison.*
51. *The Case of the Gilded Lily* (Morrow, 1956)
52. *The Case of the Terrified Typist* (Morrow, 1956)
53. *The Case of the Daring Decoy* (Morrow, 1957)
54. *The Case of the Lucky Loser* (Morrow, 1957)
55. *The Case of the Screaming Woman* (Morrow, 1957)
56. *The Case of the Calendar Girl* (Morrow, 1958)
57. *The Case of the Footloose Doll* (Morrow, 1958)
58. *The Case of the Long-Legged Models* (Morrow, 1958)
    Variant title: *The Case of the Dead Man's Daughters.*
59. *The Case of the Deadly Toy* (Morrow, 1959)
    Variant title: *The Case of the Greedy Grandpa.*
60. *The Case of the Mythical Monkeys* (Morrow, 1959)
61. *The Case of the Singing Skirt* (Morrow, 1959)
62. *The Case of the Waylaid Wolf* (Morrow, 1959)
63. *The Case of the Duplicate Daughter* (Morrow, 1960)
64. *The Case of the Shapely Shadow* (Morrow, 1960)
65. *The Case of the Bigamous Spouse* (Morrow, 1961)
66. *The Case of the Spurious Spinster* (Morrow, 1961)
67. *The Case of the Blonde Bonanza* (Morrow, 1962)
68. *The Case of the Ice-Cold Hands* (Morrow, 1962)
69. *The Case of the Reluctant Model* (Morrow, 1962)
70. *The Case of the Amorous Aunt* (Morrow, 1963)
71. *The Case of the Mischievous Doll* (Morrow, 1963)
72. *The Case of the Step-Daughter's Secret* (Morrow, 1963)
73. *The Case of the Daring Divorcée* (Morrow, 1964)
74. *The Case of the Horrified Heirs* (Morrow, 1964)
75. *The Case of the Phantom Fortune* (Morrow, 1964)

76. *The Case of the Beautiful Beggar* (Morrow, 1965)
77. *The Case of the Troubled Trustee* (Morrow, 1965)
78. *The Case of the Worried Waitress* (Morrow, 1966)
79. *The Case of the Queenly Contestant* (Morrow, 1967)
80. *The Case of the Careless Cupid* (Morrow, 1968)
81. *The Case of the Fabulous Fake* (Morrow, 1969)
82. *The Case of the Crimson Kiss* (Morrow, 1970)
83. *The Case of the Crying Swallow* (Morrow, 1971)
84. *The Case of the Fenced-In Woman* (Morrow, 1972)
85. *The Case of the Irate Witness* (Morrow, 1972)
86. *The Case of the Postponed Murder* (Morrow, 1973)

Gardner, John E.

I. The English John Gardner is the author of mysteries, World War II suspense stories, and other entertaining volumes. He is perhaps best known for the Boysie Oakes series of comedy-mysteries, which parody the James Bond books. Boysie is luxury-loving, lecherous, and a mass of neuroses. He is afraid of flying and can't stand the sight of blood, and when Britain's Department of Special Security assigns him to "liquidate" anyone, he subcontracts the job to a Soho gangster.

1. *The Liquidator* (Viking, 1964)
   Boysie's first case shows his ingenious way of carrying out an assignment to liquidate some British Secret Service security risks.
2. *Understrike* (Viking, 1965)
   Boysie travels to San Diego to watch some submarine tests, and the Russians send a carefully rehearsed double to take his place.
3. *Amber Nine* (Viking, 1966)
   Boysie's job this time is to liquidate a leftist M.P.
4. *Madrigal* (Viking, 1968)
   Boysie learns about the Chinese the hard way.
5. *Founder Member* (Muller, London, 1969)
   Now working with Griffin and Mostyn in the Grimobo security agency, Boysie gets involved in a rocket romp at Cape Kennedy.
6. *Traitor's Exit* (Muller, London, 1970)
   Boysie helps a detective-story writer get a British defector out of Moscow.

7. *Air Apparent* (Putnam, 1971)
Boysie is in charge of a charter airline, Air Apparent. English title: *The Airline Pirates*.
8. *Killer for a Song* (Muller, London, 1975)
This concerns a revenge plot for an old Secret Service killing in Mexico.

II. In these two Sherlock Holmes spin-offs, Gardner has revived Holmes's archenemy, Moriarty, who, it seems, was not killed at Reichenbach Falls after all but lived on to study London's criminal life in great detail. Gardner, of course, transforms the professor's notebooks into delightful period pieces.

1. *The Return of Moriarty* (Putnam, 1974)
A London gang led by a supercriminal has its troubles with a rival mob.
2. *The Revenge of Moriarty* (Putnam, 1975)
Following a trip to the United States, Moriarty lays an elaborate revenge plot for the destruction of his enemies.

III. There is a touch of the old parodist in Gardner's revival of James Bond, but then Fleming's later work had become almost self-parody. In any case, Gardner's aging 007 now drives a fuel-efficient car and smokes low-tar cigarettes (still specially made for him) but has lost none of his potency otherwise.

1. *License Renewed* (Marek/Putnam, 1981)
Bond tackles the megalomaniac nuclear physicist Anton Murik, who is up to nasty things in his Scottish castle.
2. *For Special Services* (Coward-McCann, 1982)
Bond is sent to the United States to infiltrate a SPECTRE stronghold and prevent their plot to control space satellites.
3. *Icebreaker* (Putnam, 1983)
In order to thwart Count von Gloda's plan to create a Fourth Reich, Bond must travel to the Arctic Circle.
4. *Role of Honor* (Putnam, 1984)
Dr. Jay Autem Holy has designed a computer system for waging war that Bond must destroy.
5. *Nobody Lives Forever* (Putnam, 1986)
The entire criminal population of Europe is competing for the rich prize Tamil Rahani has offered for Bond's head on a silver platter.

6. *No Deals, Mr. Bond* (Putnam, 1987)
   Bond goes to East Germany to investigate a sexual-entrapment operation which has collapsed.
7. *Scorpius* (Putnam, 1988)
   Is Father Valentine a religious guru or the evil arms dealer Vladimir Scorpius in disguise?
8. *Win, Lose or Die* (Putnam, 1989)
   BAST (Brotherhood of Anarchy and Secret Terror) has sinister plans for the leaders of Britain, the Soviet Union, and the United States who are meeting in secret.

IV. The Secret Generations trilogy weds the genres of spy novel and family saga in rather complicated fashion. The English Railtons and the American Farthings are tied together by marriage and by commitment to the espionage trade. The action extends over several generations and decades of this century.

1. *The Secret Generations* (Putnam, 1985)
   Nearly everyone in three generations of the Railton family gets involved in espionage during the years 1909 to 1935.
2. *The Secret Houses* (Putnam, 1987)
   The British investigation of a compromised French Resistance network involves both the Railtons and the Farthings in the late 1940s.
3. *The Secret Families* (Putnam, 1989)
   Donald Railton and Arnold Farthing take part in an undercover operation inside Russia in order to clear the reputations of family members. Starts in 1964.

Gash, Jonathan (pseud. of John Grant)

Lovejoy, an antiques dealer from East Anglia, is an eccentric amateur detective. He is bad-tempered and not overly scrupulous about acquiring his antiques. But his expertise in antiques and ability to squeeze out of tough spots combine to make these books suspenseful, humorous, and instructive as well. John Grant is an English pathologist and micro-biologist. The series has been made into a TV series that has been shown on cable in the United States.

1. *The Judas Pair* (Harper, 1977)
   Lovejoy searches for the thirteenth, or "Judas," pair of dueling pistols made by Durs Egg.
2. *Gold by Gemini* (Harper, 1979)
   Lovejoy gets wind of a treasure trove of early Roman coins some-where on the Isle of Man. English title: *Gold from Gemini.*
3. *The Grail Tree* (Harper, 1980)
   A quest for the Holy Grail turns into a quest for Lovejoy's own survival.
4. *Spend Game* (Ticknor, 1981)
   An old army friend and fellow antiques dealer is murdered after acquiring an item that some very nasty characters are also after.
5. *The Vatican Rip* (Ticknor, 1982)
   Lovejoy is forced into a plan to steal a Chippendale table from the Vatican.
6. *Firefly Gadroon* (St. Martin's, 1984; c.1982)
   Lovejoy sets out to avenge the murder of an old silversmith, and catch a ring of international antiques smugglers.
7. *The Sleepers of Erin* (Doubleday, 1983)
   Mr. and Mrs. Hendricks want Lovejoy to find some "sleepers," valuable antiques that have been deliberately concealed.
8. *The Gondola Scam* (St. Martin's, 1984)
   A quest to uncover an antiques manufacturing scam takes Love-joy from an illegal auction in England to the canals of Venice.
9. *Pearlhanger* (St. Martin's, 1985)
   A colleague named Vernon has disappeared while hot on the trail of a fabulously rare piece of pearl jewelry.
10. *The Tartan Sell* (St. Martin's, 1986)
    A missing bureau and a dead lorry driver bring Lovejoy to a crum-bling manor house in the tiny Scottish town of Tachnadray.
11. *Moonspender* (St. Martin's, 1987)
    Lovejoy appears on a television game show and manages a big wedding in this caper.
12. *Jade Woman* (St. Martin's, 1989)
    Downo and out in Hong Kong, Lovejoy gets involved with that city's criminal gangs and the beautiful but dangerous "jade woman."

Gibbon, Lewis Grassic (pseud. of James Leslie Mitchell)

When *Sunset Song* was dramatized on public television's "Masterpiece Theatre," Alastair Cooke called it *the* great Scottish novel. Two additional volumes complete the trilogy known as A Scots Quair, which tells the story of a Scottish woman, Chris Guthrie, from before the First World War to the Great Depression. Gibbon wrote from a Marxist point of view and described the harshness of peasant life in a poetic language rich in Scottish idiom and cadence. The trilogy is available in a one-volume edition, *A Scots Quair* (Schocken, 1977).

1. *Sunset Song* (Century, 1932)
   Young Chris at fifteen had discovered books and longed to become a teacher. But the land and handsome Ewan Tavendale claim her.
2. *Cloud Howe* (Doubleday, 1934)
   Now Mrs. Colquohoun, wife of an idealistic minister, Chris is considered uppity by the local women.
3. *Grey Granite* (Doubleday, 1935)
   At age thirty-eight, Chris makes yet another new beginning. Her son Ewan, a Communist organizer, plays a large part in this volume.

Gibbons, Stella

Cold Comfort Farm is a wickedly funny parody of the "rustic" novel as written by Mary Webb, author of *Precious Bane*, and by other English novelists. The Starkadders of Cold Comfort Farm are knee-deep in mud and squalor when young Flora Poste comes to visit. But in no time at all, their modern, no-nonsense city cousin has reformed their degenerate ways. Interestingly, this novel won Stella Gibbons the Femina Vie Heureuse, the same prize that had been awarded previously to Mary Webb. The recent TV dramatization of *Cold Comfort Farm* lacked the sparkle of the novel.

1. *Cold Comfort Farm* (Longmans, 1932)
   Flora's sensible rearrangement of life on the farm brings happiness to the Starkadder family and Aunt Ada Doom.

2. *Christmas at Cold Comfort Farm* (Longmans, 1940)
   This is a volume of short stories.
3. *Conference at Cold Comfort Farm* (Longmans, 1949)
   Flora, now the mother of five, returns to Cold Comfort Farm for a postwar conference of the International Thinkers Group. This sequel, which pokes fun at modern artists and pretentious intellectuals, deserves to be better known.

Giles, Janice Holt

I. The pioneers who carved out the first farms in the Great Smoky Mountains of Kentucky were brave and hardy folk. Giles's skillfully woven stories of their trials and hardships, their encounters with hostile Indians, their romances and growing families, and their push further west have brought this period alive for many readers. Most of the novels concern members of the Cooper and Fowler families, and together they cover the years from 1769 to 1869.

1. *The Kentuckians* (Houghton, 1963)
   Young David Cooper sets out for the untouched beauty of the Kentucky frontier he'd heard Daniel Boone describe.
2. *Hannah Fowler* (Houghton, 1956)
   This courageous pioneer woman braves the dangers of wilderness life, including blizzards, wolf attacks, and capture by Indians.
3. *The Land beyond the Mountains* (Houghton, 1958)
   The story of Cass Cartwright from 1783 to his death in 1825 tells of a Spanish conspiracy for control of Kentucky. Not one of the Cooper/Fowler stories.
4. *The Believers* (Houghton, 1957)
   Hannah Fowler's daughter Rebecca marries Richard Cooper and moves with him to a Shaker community during the early 1800s.
5. *Johnny Osage* (Houghton, 1960)
   Hannah Fowler's son Johnny, an Oklahoma trader, is called Johnny Osage because of his friendship with that Indian tribe. The story is set in the 1820s.
6. *Voyage to Santa Fe* (Houghton, 1962)
   Johnny Fowler and his new wife, Judith, set out on the three-month trip to Santa Fe in 1823.

7. *Savannah* (Houghton, 1961)
   Hannah Fowler's granddaughter Savannah is the beautiful and willfully independent central figure in this novel set on a frontier army post in the Arkansas territory.
8. *The Great Adventure* (Houghton, 1966)
   Hannah's grandson Joe leads a group of mountain men on to Oregon.
9. *Six-Horse Hitch* (Houghton, 1969)
   Joe Fowler's son Starr drives the Overland Stage west from Missouri.

II. Giles's first published work was a light romance with comic overtones partly set in the Kentucky hill country of the present. Two sequels followed to form the Piney Ridge trilogy before the author turned to historical novels.

1. *The Enduring Hills* (Westminster, 1950)
   The main character, Hod Pierce, is modeled somewhat on Giles's husband Henry. It shows his youth, service in World War II, and return home with his new wife to Piney Ridge.
2. *Miss Willie* (Westminster, 1951)
   Miss Willie is the new schoolteacher who tries to reform the people of Piney Ridge with little success.
3. *Tata's Healing* (Westminster, 1951)
   A disillusioned doctor comes to Piney Ridge and learns of the healing power of kindness.

Gill, Bartholomew (pseud. of Mark McGarrity)

Shrewd plotting, well-developed characters, and a charming Irish setting are the attractions of this mystery series. Chief Inspector of Detectives Peter McGarr of the Irish Police is a thoughtful, sensitive man with an uncanny ability to break seemingly insoluble cases. His pretty young wife Noreen lends a hand in some of them.

1. *McGarr and the Politician's Wife* (Scribner, 1977)
   An attempted murder aboard an American schooner in Dublin leads McGarr into a case of political intrigue.
2. *McGarr and the Sienese Conspiracy* (Scribner, 1977)
   Three high-ranking agents of the British Secret Service are murdered.

3. *McGarr on the Cliffs of Moher* (Scribner, 1978)
   May Quick is found dead with $27,000 in American currency in her coat pocket.
4. *McGarr at the Dublin Horse Show* (Scribner, 1980)
   A rigged riding accident and the strangling of an old woman blend in this unusual case.
5. *McGarr and the P. M. of Belgrave Square* (Viking, 1983)
   "The Prime Minister of Belgrave Square" is an old bomb-squad dog that helps McGarr investigate a murder and the theft of a French Impressionist masterpiece.
6. *McGarr and the Method of Descartes* (Viking, 1984)
   McGarr traces an assassination plot back to its roots in the "troubles" in Northern Ireland.
7. *McGarr and the Legacy of a Woman Scorned* (Viking, 1986)
   When elderly spinster Fionnuala Watson is murdered, McGarr involves his wife Noreen in the investigation.
8. *The Death of a Joyce Scholar* (Morrow, 1989)
   Kevin Coyle, English professor at Trinity College in Dublin, is murdered after leading the annual Bloomsday tour.

Gilman, Dorothy

Rosalind Russell played Emily Pollifax in the movie made from Gilman's first novel. She is a widowed grandmother from New Brunswick, New Jersey, who resembles a cross between Mrs. 'Arris, and Miss Marple— that is, she ventures indomitably on mysterious missions to exotic lands and always emerges victorious. As there is no real sequence after the first, her adventures are listed here in order of their publication.

1. *The Unexpected Mrs. Pollifax* (Doubleday, 1966)
   At sixty-three, Emily Pollifax is advised that a job would cure her depression, so with characteristic aplomb she applies to the CIA for a position as spy and soon finds herself in Mexico on her first case as a courier. Variant title: *Mrs. Pollifax, Spy.*
2. *The Amazing Mrs. Pollifax* (Doubleday, 1970)
   Emily is off to Istanbul to rescue a beautiful woman spy.
3. *The Elusive Mrs. Pollifax* (Doubleday, 1971)
   Mrs. Pollifax carries forged passports to Bulgaria in her hat.
4. *A Palm for Mrs. Pollifax* (Doubleday, 1973)
   Emily traces some stolen plutonium at a chic health spa in Switzerland.

5. *Mrs. Pollifax on Safari* (Doubleday, 1977)
   In Zambia to take photographs, Mrs. Pollifax falls for the dashing Cyrus Reed.
6. *Mrs. Pollifax on the China Station* (Doubleday, 1983)
   The CIA sends Mrs. Pollifax to China to find and rescue an engineer with secret information.
7. *Mrs. Pollifax and the Hong Kong Buddha* (Doubleday, 1985)
   The recently re-wed Mrs. Reed-Pollifax goes to Hong Kong to find out why a CIA agent is sending worthless reports.
8. *Mrs. Pollifax and the Golden Triangle* (Doubleday, 1988)
   On vacation in Thailand with her husband Cyrus Reed, Mrs. Pollifax seeks out some vital information about a ring of drug smugglers.

Gironella, José Maria

This trilogy about the Alvear family shows how the Spanish Civil War affected the country and its people. The story begins in 1931 and continues through the postwar years. Using the middle-class Alvear family and their hometown of Gerona in Catalonia as a microcosm of Spanish society, Gironella vividly portrays the conflict and tragedy that seared through all facets of Spanish life. The author's sympathies are with the Nationalist rebels (Franco's forces).

1. *The Cypresses Believe in God* (Knopf, 1955)
   The years of political unrest from the beginning of the republic to the war's outbreak are seen primarily through the eyes of Ignacio, the oldest Alvear son. Translated from the Spanish by Harriet de Onís.
2. *One Million Dead* (Doubleday, 1963)
   During the war years, from July, 1936, to April, 1939, Ignacio is a Nationalist. Translated from the Spanish by Joan MacLean.
3. *Peace after War* (Knopf, 1969)
   This novel shows the peacetime problems of rebuilding and reconciliation amidst food shortages and corruption. Translated from the Spanish by Joan MacLean.

Giroux, E. X. (pseud. of Doris Shannon)

Young, urbane London barrister Robert Forsythe and his motherly secretary Abigail "Sandy" Sanderson play sleuth in this series of mysteries. Puzzle mysteries in the classic Agatha Christie tradition, the novels are often set in country homes full of eccentric characters. As the series has progressed, "Sandy" has taken an increasingly active role in detecting. Doris Shannon is a Canadian who started her writing career in her mid-forties.

1. *A Death for Adonis* (St. Martin's, 1984)
   Forsythe is asked to clear the name of English sculptor Sebastian Calvert, who was convicted of the murder of his lover twenty-five years before.
2. *A Death for a Darling* (St. Martin's, 1985)
   Forsythe and Sandy are co-guests in a country house with the cast and crew of a company remaking the film *Wuthering Heights*.
3. *A Death for a Dancer* (St. Martin's, 1985)
   A very dead blackmailer is found in a sarcophagus in the private mausoleum of eccentric Cheshire baronet Amyas Dancer.
4. *A Death for a Doctor* (St. Martin's, 1986)
   Sandy gets directly involved in the investigation of the murders of country town physician Dr. Foster and his family.
5. *A Death for a Dilettante* (St. Martin's, 1987)
   Someone is trying to prevent rich elderly Winslow Maxwell Penndragon from becoming a centenarian.
6. *A Death for a Dietician* (St. Martin's, 1988)
   Sandy plays sleuth on her own when a house party game of pretend murder mystery becomes real.
7. *A Death for a Dreamer* (St. Martin's, 1989)
   The gift of four puppies to the Coralund Home for the elderly leads to murder.

Gold, Herbert

The classic American generation clash between immigrant parents and Americanized children is the subject of Gold's two novels "in the form of a memoir." They are thought to be highly autobiographical. Gold captures his characters' colorful Yiddish-English speech and lovingly evokes their home life in a small town in Ohio. The author has also written *My Last Two Thousand Years* (Random, 1972), which is an impressionistic exploration of Jewish history in relation to his personal history as a Jew.

1. *Fathers* (Random, 1967)
   The story relates the life of Gold's father, who flees persecution in Czarist Russia and becomes a grocer in America.
2. *Family* (Arbor, 1981)
   Gold's mother tries to impose her Old World standards of love on her American-born son.

Golding, William

Nobel laureate William Golding (*Lord of the Flies*, etc.) has published a trilogy describing a sea voyage in the Napoleonic Era (1814–15). An aged ship of the line is carrying an assortment of passengers from England to Australia. Edmund Talbot, a young gentleman, provides a large part of the narrative thread of the novels in a journal he is keeping. Like most of Golding's fiction these novels combine readability and authentic atmosphere with a deeper, allegorical meaning, and a pessimistic view of humanity.

1. *Rites of Passage* (Farrar, 1980)
   Edmund Talbot records the events of the voyage and the fate of young Robert Colley, a clergyman who runs afoul of Captain Anderson.
2. *Close Quarters* (Farrar, 1987)
   The passengers learn of Napoleon's defeat and exile to Elba. Talbot falls in love, and the ship is dismasted in a storm.
3. *Fire Down Below* (Farrar, 1989)
   As the ship becomes increasingly unseaworthy, dissension among the passengers and crew reaches a dangerous level.

Goldman, William

Marathon Man is still Goldman's best-known book. The movie version featured Dustin Hoffman as a brilliant but naive graduate student and aspiring marathon runner; Laurence Olivier's performance as Szell, the sadistic Nazi dentist, was unforgettable. Goldman, an American author who also writes drama, won an Oscar for his screenplay *Butch Cassidy and the Sundance Kid*.

1. *Marathon Man* (Delacorte, 1974)
   Shocked by the murder of his brother, Babe Levy gets entangled in a plot involving Nazi war criminals. Hard to beat for nonstop action and suspense.
2. *Brothers* (Warner, 1987)
   Revived—somewhat incredibly—for this sequel set ten years later, Scylla attempts to alter the balance of world nuclear power.

Goldreich, Gloria

Leah's Journey and *Leah's Children* take artist and philanthropist Leah Goldfeder and her family through the significant historical events of the 1920s through the 1960s. *Leah's Journey* concentrates on Leah's life from post-revolution Russia to the formation of the state of Israel. *Leah's Children* brings the second generation to several trouble spots of the world in the 1950s and 1960s. This is an absorbing and often moving family saga with a strong sense of history.

1. *Leah's Journey* (Harcourt, 1978)
   Fleeing from a pogrom in Russia, Leah marries gentle David, and emigrates with him to New York.
2. *Leah's Children* (Macmillan, 1985)
   Leah's children take on activist roles in Hungary, Mississippi, and Israel.

Goldsborough, Robert

The heirs of Rex Stout (q.v.) have given a "seal of approval" to Robert Goldsborough's re-creations of Nero Wolfe, Stout's obese, orchid-growing detective. *The Bloodied Ivy*, the third in the new series, contains a memoir of Rex Stout by his daughter, Rebecca Stout Bradbury. Wolfe's faithful assistant, Archie Goodwin, continues to narrate the stories of Wolfe's sedentary detecting efforts from the brownstone on 35th Street.

1. *Murder in E Minor* (Bantam, 1986)
   Milan Stevens, controversial new director of the New York Symphony, has been receiving death threats.
2. *Death on Deadline* (Bantam, 1987)
   Wolfe disputes the verdict of suicide when elderly newspaper owner Harriet Haverhill dies.
3. *The Bloodied Ivy* (Bantam, 1988)
   Wolfe leaves his Manhattan brownstone to investigate the fatal "accident" that befell conservative professor Hale Markham at an upstate New York university.
4. *The Last Coincidence* (Bantam, 1989)
   Noreen James's brother Michael has confessed to the murder of Sparky Linville, Noreen's attacker, but Noreen doesn't believe he's guilty.

Goudge, Elizabeth

Goudge writes light fiction of the highest caliber. Her satisfying stories feature fully drawn characters, believable plots, beautiful settings, and highly polished prose. That they almost always have a happy ending requires no apology. Goudge's obvious love of gardening makes her descriptions of the flowering English countryside a real treat for the horticulturally inclined. These novels concern the Eliot family, especially grandmother Lucilla, and cover the years from 1938 to the early 1950s.

1. *The Bird in the Tree* (Coward, 1940)
   Seventy-eight-year-old Lucilla has made her home on the Hampshire coast a special haven for her children and grandchildren, but a romantic storm threatens.
2. *Pilgrim's Inn* (Coward, 1948)
   Lucilla, still charming and lively at eight-six, manipulates the family into becoming innkeepers. English title: *Herb of Grace*.
3. *Heart of the Family* (Coward, 1953)
   Lucilla, now ninety-three, and the Eliot family help an Austrian refugee come to terms with his tragic past.

Grafton, Sue

Produced conveniently in alphabetical order, this engaging detective series features Kinsey Millhone, a private investigator from the town of Santa Teresa, California. An ex-policewoman, Millhone is tough but sensitive, shrewd, and funny. The well-paced and suspenseful novels are filled with a cast of believably eccentric characters. They can be read in any order.

1. *"A" Is for Alibi* (Holt, 1982)
   Millhone is asked to solve the eight-year-old murder of divorce attorney Laurence Fife, for which his wife was wrongfully convicted.
2. *"B" Is for Burglar* (Holt, 1985)
   Wealthy Beverly Danziger asks Millhone to find her missing sister, Elaine Boldt, somewhere in Florida.
3. *"C" Is for Corpse* (Holt, 1986)
   Bobby Callahan, Millhone's gym acquaintance, is convinced that the car crash that injured him was really an attempt on his life.
4. *"D" Is for Deadbeat* (Holt, 1987)
   An alcoholic named Daggett gives Millhone $25,000 in stolen drug money to pass on to a third party.
5. *"E" Is for Evidence* (Holt, 1988)
   Someone tries to make it appear that Millhone is taking bribes while she is investigating a case of industrial arson.
6. *"F" Is for Fugitive* (Holt, 1989)
   Millhone goes to the town of Floral Beach to try to clear Bailey Fowler of a seventeen-year-old murder for which he was wrongfully convicted.

Graham, Winston

"Masterpiece Theatre" viewers will remember the stark beauty of the Cornish coast that gives this historical romance its distinctive flavor. Young Ross Poldark must have been influenced by the Americans he fought against in the colonies, for his fiercely independent and egalitarian spirit is the vital force that sets this series moving. Blending humor, romance and its complications, and action that includes pirates and intrigue in France, the Poldark Saga is hard to beat for pure entertainment. In *Poldark's Cornwall* (Bodley Head, 1985) Winston Graham depicts in word and photograph the real Cornish setting of the Poldark Saga.

1. *Ross Poldark* (Doubleday, 1951)
   Ross comes home from the war in America to find that Elizabeth, the woman he loves, is engaged to another man. This action takes place during 1783–87. Original title: *The Renegade*.
2. *Demelza* (Doubleday, 1953)
   Ross weds the fiery and stubborn Demelza, his former kitchen maid. This volume covers the first years of their marriage, in 1788–90. Original title: *Elizabeth's Story*.
3. *Jeremy Poldark* (Doubleday, 1950)
   During 1790–91, Ross faces imprisonment after being accused of leading a rebellion. Original title: *Venture Once More*.
4. *Warleggan* (Doubleday, 1955)
   In 1792–93, Elizabeth is widowed, and Demelza fears for her marriage. Original title: *The Last Gamble*.
5. *The Black Moon* (Doubleday, 1974)
   Amid the complications of love and war in 1794–95, Elizabeth bears a son, who may be Ross's.
6. *The Four Swans* (Doubleday, 1977)
   Ross wins a seat in Parliament and confronts his old attraction for Elizabeth. The time is 1795–97.
7. *The Angry Tide* (Doubleday, 1978)
   The shock of Elizabeth's death brings Ross to the realization of life's real importance in 1798–99.
8. *The Stranger from the Sea* (Doubleday, 1982)
   This episode begins in 1810, with Captain Ross off fighting under Wellington, and shows young Jeremy and Clowance Poldark growing up, getting into mischief, and falling in love.
9. *The Miller's Dance* (Doubleday, 1983)
   This installment concentrates on the lives and loves of Jeremy and Clowance, the two elder Poldark children. It covers the years 1812–13.
10. *The Loving Cup* (Doubleday, 1985)
    As Napoleon meets his final defeat, the Poldarks are engrossed in marriage settlements for Clowance and young Jeremy.

Granger, Bill

Devereaux, code-named "November," is a spy who works for the shadowy "R Section" set up by President Kennedy to "spy upon the spies." He is a loner so disenchanted with espionage that he has even tried arranging his own "official death." His romance with reporter Rita Macklin gives a chronology of sorts to the series. Granger, an American author, captures that brooding atmosphere reminiscent of LeCarré. His first book, *The November Man*, received a good deal of publicity for its prevision of the motives and methods used by the IRA in its assassination of Lord Mountbatten.

1. *The November Man* (Fawcett, 1979)
   Devereaux investigates an IRA plot to kill Lord Slough, one of England's most important men.
2. *Schism* (Crown, 1981)
   Father Leo Tunney, missing and presumed dead after his capture by the Pathet Lao, turns up again after twenty years, and is taken into CIA custody.
3. *The Shattered Eye* (Crown, 1982)
   Inspired by their war game computer, the Russians plot to overthrow Mitterand's French government and replace it with a Communist one.
4. *The British Cross* (Crown, 1983)
   Devereaux checks on a high KGB official who has offered to defect with a secret potent enough to topple governments.
5. *The Zurich Numbers* (Crown, 1984)
   When his great aunt is threatened by two foreigners, Devereaux returns home to Chicago's South Side.
6. *Hemingway's Notebook* (Crown, 1986)
   Colonel Ready, Caribbean dictator and ex-CIA operative, brings Devereaux out of retirement to find a mysterious notebook.
7. *There Are No Spies* (Crown, 1986)
   Hanley, Devereaux's former boss, is committed to a mental hospital on the orders of his superiors.
8. *The Infant of Prague* (Crown, 1987)
   An attempt to help deliver a Czech defector in Brussels runs into a snag when Anna Jelinak, Czech movie star touring the United States, carries out her own defection.
9. *Henry McGee Is Not Dead* (Warner, 1988)

"Henry McGee," a defected Soviet scientist, disappears from a secret project in Alaska.
   10. *The Man Who Heard Too Much* (Warner, 1989)
       This is about a missing secret tape that could cause a major international crisis.

Grass, Gunter

War and Nazism are the subjects of the grim allegories upon which Grass's international reputation rests secure. *The Tin Drum*, still perhaps his best-known novel, was filmed in 1975 and won an Academy Award as the Best Foreign Film. The first three novels listed below, all set in the Baltic port city of Danzig (now Gdansk, in Poland), are known as the Danzig trilogy. A later work, *The Rat*, brings together the drum-playing dwarf of *The Tin Drum* and the magic fish of *The Flounder*. *The Rat* can be regarded as Grass's pessimistic forecast for the human race. All five novels have been translated into English from the German by Ralph Manheim.

   1. *The Tin Drum* (Pantheon, 1963)
      Oskar Matzerath, who deliberately stopped growing when he was three years old and three feet tall, plays on a tin drum to stimulate his recall of the past. Published in German as *Die Blechtrommel*, 1959.
   2. *Cat and Mouse* (Harcourt, 1963)
      Mahlke, a teenager growing up in Danzig during the War, feels set apart by his huge Adam's apple. Published in German as *Katz und Maus*, 1961.
   3. *Dog Years* (Harcourt, 1965)
      The central relationship in this novel spanning the years from 1917 to 1957 is between athletic Walter Matern and his half-Jewish friend, Eduard Amsel. Published in German as *Hundejahre*, 1963.
   4. *The Flounder* (Harcourt, 1978)
      The magic fish from the fairy tale "The Fisherman and His Wife" is put on trial by a feminist group in a fable spanning centuries of history. Published in German as *Der Butt*, 1977.
   5. *The Rat* (Harcourt, 1987)
      The narrator is troubled by apocalyptic dreams in which a talking

rat documents humanity's demise through ecological and political ignorance. Published in German as *Die Rättin*, 1986.

Graves, Robert

I. The stuttering, timid Claudius portrayed so brilliantly by Derek Jacobi in Masterpiece Theatre's dramatization of these books was a surprisingly admirable Roman in an age of sadistic tyrants. The "autobiography" that Graves has written for him is a fascinating reconstruction of the tumultuous years from 10 B.C. to A.D. 54, covering the reigns of Caesar Augustus, Tiberius, Caligula, and Claudius himself. Needless to say, this poisonous brew of murder and other assorted villanies won't be everybody's cup of tea.

1. *I, Claudius* (Smith & Haas, 1935)
   The machinations of Caesar Augustus and his sinister wife Livia seem mild compared to the cruelty of Tiberius and the outright insanity of Caligula.
2. *Claudius, the God and His Wife Messalina* (Smith & Haas, 1935)
   This book covers the reforms and British conquest of Claudius's reign. Three historical accounts of his death are appended.

II. Perhaps because they were published during the darkest days of World War II, Robert Graves's pair of novels about the American Revolution never received the attention given to his other historical fiction. They are based on the memoirs of Roger Lamb, an Irishman who served with the British Army against the Americans in the Revolutionary War. In his foreword to *Sergeant Lamb's America* Graves stated that he stuck to the historical facts as much as possible, and invented no main characters, yet he was not writing "straight history." The opinions (uncomplimentary for the most part) expressed about Americans are Lamb's, not Graves's.

1. *Sergeant Lamb's America* (Random, 1940)
   Young Gerry Lamb enlists in King George's 9th Foot Regiment and after several years of peacetime service is shipped to Canada to fight the rebellious Americans. English title: *Sergeant Lamb of the Ninth*.
2. *Proceed, Sergeant Lamb* (Methuen, London, 1941)
   As part of Burgoyne's army defeated at Saratoga in 1777, Lamb becomes a prisoner of war, but escapes to fight again with the 23rd Foot, the Royal Welsh Fusiliers.

Greene, Bette

The NBC-TV dramatization of *Summer of My German Soldier*, starring Kristy McNichol, introduced a lot of young readers to author Bette Greene. The poignant and suspenseful story of the friendship between a young Jewish girl and an escaped German prisoner of war may be enjoyed by older readers as well. Its appeal is similar to that of Harper Lee's *To Kill a Mockingbird*.

1. *Summer of My German Soldier* (Dial, 1973)
   Young Patty Bergen, living in Arkansas during World War II, befriends Anton Reiker, an escaped German prisoner of war.
2. *Morning Is a Long Time Coming* (Dial, 1978)
   Four years later, Patty finishes high school and sets out for Europe, where she falls in love and searches for Anton's parents.

Greenleaf, Stephen

Stephen Greenleaf, a lawyer turned mystery writer, writes novels about John Marshall Tanner, a lawyer turned private investigator. San Francisco-based Tanner is in the hard-boiled private eye tradition of Sam Spade and Lew Archer. He hides his sensitive and ethical nature behind a cynical, wisecracking exterior. The complicated plots of the novels usually revolve around a missing person and dark family secrets.

1. *Grave Error* (Dial, 1979)
   The wife of consumer advocate Roland Nelson hires Tanner to find out if her husband is being blackmailed.
2. *Death Bed* (Dial, 1980)
   Dying oil billionaire Max Kottle wants Tanner to find his estranged college activist son.
3. *State's Evidence* (Dial, 1982)
   Tanner is asked to find the missing eyewitness to a fatal hit-and-run accident in the corrupt town of El Gordo.
4. *Fatal Obsession* (Dial, 1983)
   The suicide of his Vietnam veteran nephew brings Tanner to a family reunion in the rural midwest town of Chaldea.
5. *Beyond Blame* (Villard, 1986)
   Berkeley lawyer Lawrence Usser is trying to avoid conviction for

his wife's murder by using the insanity plea he has successfully employed for his criminal clients.

6. *Toll Call* (Villard, 1987)
   Peggy Nettleton, Tanner's secretary, is being harassed by bizarre phone calls.

Greenwood, John (pseud. of John Buxton Hilton)

Detective Inspector Mosley is an elderly, old-fashioned, rural policeman stationed in the north of England. He doesn't go by the book or move in straight lines to his conclusions, which sometimes disturbs his young assistant, Sergeant Beamish, but he always seems to wind up in the right place at the end. These mysteries are notable more for their local color and rural English characters than for the puzzles they present. John Buxton Hilton has written other mystery series under his real name, but most of the titles in these series haven't been published in the United States.

1. *Murder, Mr. Mosley* (Walker, 1983)
   Mr. Mosley is confronted with his first murder case and with a new, scientific-minded, ambitious assistant.
2. *Mosley by Moonlight* (Walker, 1985)
   Mosley's investigation of the disappearance of Lottie Pearson, housekeeper and rumored mistress of Matthew Longden, is complicated by a television crew shooting a commercial.
3. *The Missing Mr. Mosley* (Walker, 1986)
   Superintendent Grimstone sends Sergeant Beamish in search of the vacationing Mosley when villagers at Hempshaw End disappear, and a series of gallows turn up.
4. *Mists over Mosley* (Walker, 1986)
   Nasty old Beatrice Cater is found hanged in her bedroom amid rumors of a coven of witches in Marldale.
5. *The Mind of Mr. Mosley* (Walker, 1987)
   The village of Upper Crudshaw is rocked by the suicide of 74-year-old Reuben Tunicliffe.
6. *What Me, Mr. Mosley?* (Walker, 1988)
   Inspector Mosley identifies stolen property at a second-hand goods market stall in Bagshawe Brooke.

Grimes, Martha

American writer Martha Grimes has taken Christie (q.v.) and Sayers (q.v.) as models for this elegantly written series. Among the continuing characters are: Richard Jury, a dedicated, sensitive Detective Inspector (later Superintendent) of Scotland Yard; Alfred Wiggins, his hypochondriacal professional assistant; Melrose Plant, his aristocratic, dilettantish, unofficial assistant; and Plant's officious American-born Aunt Agatha. Grimes visits England frequently in order to capture authentic atmosphere. Each book is named for the English pub which figures in the story.

1. *The Man with a Load of Mischief* (Little, 1981)
   Five murder victims have been found in or near pubs in the village of Long Piddleton, Northamptonshire, including one corpse in a keg of ale.
2. *The Old Fox Deceiv'd* (Little, 1982)
   A series of deaths and disappearances, including a corpse in Shakespearean costume, bedevil the Yorkshire fishing village of Rackmoor.
3. *The Anodyne Necklace* (Little, 1983)
   Murders in London's East End and in the village of Littlebourne may be connected with a jewelry theft.
4. *The Dirty Duck* (Little, 1984)
   Rich American tourists in Stratford are being murdered and kidnapped while a computer buff is trying to prove that Shakespeare killed Marlowe.
5. *Jerusalem Inn* (Little, 1984)
   The murder of Helen Minton, a chance acquaintance met during the Christmas holidays, brings Jury to a village near Newcastle.
6. *Help the Poor Struggler* (Little, 1985)
   A series of child murders in Devonshire may be linked with a twenty-year-old homicide.
7. *The Deer Leap* (Little, 1985)
   A series of suspicious accidents to people and pets brings Plant to an odd young girl who keeps a sanctuary for abused animals.
8. *I Am the Only Running Footman* (Little, 1986)
   The London strangling of Ivy Childess may be connected to a Devon homicide.
9. *The Five Bells and Bladebone* (Little, 1987)
   The corpse of antique dealer Simon Lean is found in a desk at his shop in Plant's ancestral village.

10. *The Old Silent* (Little, 1989)
    On vacation in Yorkshire, Jury sees Nell Healey shoot her husband, and uncovers an old kidnapping.

Gross, Joel

Two thousand years of Jewish history are related through a succession of heroines named Rachel, the name given to the first female child in each generation of the Cuhena, later called the Cohen, family. Each Rachel must pass a test, whether it be persecution, plague, or love for a Gentile. Readers of this pair of novels will learn much history and acquire a considerable knowledge of the diamond industry.

1. *The Lives of Rachel* (NAL, 1984)
   The crises of five early Rachels are related in a story spanning the time of the Maccabees to the Crusades.
2. *The Books of Rachel* (Seaview, 1979)
   This continues the story of the family of diamond merchants through six centuries and many countries.

Guareschi, Giovanni

If Thurber had written about a little town in Italy's Po Valley, his stories might have been much like these. Don Camillo, the irascible parish priest, talks over all his problems with the Lord, who, of course, replies with calm good sense and a sly humor. Don Camillo's chief antagonist is Mayor Peppone, leader of the local leftists and a prolific writer of party manifestos distinguished by their bad spelling and numerous references to "a certain black-robed reactionary." The passage of time is only faintly discernible in these six episodes.

1. *The Little World of Don Camillo* (Pellegrini, 1950)
   Don Camillo, Peppone, and the other inhabitants of this wayward little parish are introduced.
2. *Don Camillo and His Flock* (Pellegrini, 1952)
   Temporary banishment for Don Camillo, and a flood of the Po River are featured. English title: *Don Camillo and the Prodigal Son.*

3. *Don Camillo's Dilemma* (Farrar, 1954)
   Neri the mason sells his soul, and a headless ghost wanders the village streets at night.
4. *Don Camillo Takes the Devil by the Tail* (Farrar, 1957)
   When Moscow orders the purging of Stalin, Peppone must decide what to do about the enormous fresco at the People's Palace. English title: *Don Camillo and the Devil*.
5. *Comrade Don Camillo* (Farrar, 1964)
   Peppone wins the soccer sweepstakes, and Don Camillo manipulates his way into an official delegation to Moscow.
6. *Don Camillo Meets the Flower Children* (Farrar, 1969)
   The flower child is Don Camillo's niece Flora, whose arrival with a troop of Hell's Angels brings the late sixties to Don Camillo's parish. English title: *Don Camillo Meets Hell's Angels*.

Gulbranssen, Trygve

These two novels are set in the strange and primitive world of Björndal in the far northern woods of Norway. The southern villagers fear their northern neighbors but eventually come to know them. The dominant figure is young Dag, who comes to the town of Broad Leas, wins the heart of Therese, and takes her back north to his prospering estate. The story begins around 1760.

1. *Beyond Sing the Woods* (Putnam, 1936)
   This book covers the period from Dag's arrival in Broad Leas to the engagement of his son young Dag to a village girl. Translated from the Norwegian by Naomi Walford.
2. *The Wind from the Mountains* (Putnam, 1937)
   This sequel continues from young Dag's marriage to Adelaide and old Dag's death. Translated from the Norwegian by Naomi Walford.

Guthrie, A. B. (Alfred Bertram, Jr.)

I. Anyone who thinks westerns are all good-guy-bad-guy shoot-'em-ups should read A. B. Guthrie's intelligent westerns, which combine action, authenticity, and fully realized characters. *The Way West* won him the

Pulitzer Prize for fiction in 1950. This loosely connected series of six novels covers the period from 1830 to the mid-1940s. Some characters appear in more than one book.

1. *The Big Sky* (Houghton, 1947)
   Boone Caudill, a violent man, leaves civilization behind for the life of a fur trapper in the remote Teton Mountains. His Indian wife, Teal Eye, and friends Jim Deakins and Dick Summers play supporting roles in this volume.
2. *The Way West* (Houghton, 1949)
   Dick Summers returns as the guide who leads a wagon train bound for Oregon. Young Brownie Evans meets the beautiful Mercy McBee in this volume.
3. *Fair Land, Fair Land* (Houghton, 1982)
   The later life of Dick Summers is related as he observes the land being despoiled by miners and settlers. Covers 1845 to 1870.
4. *These Thousand Hills* (Houghton, 1956)
   Lat Evans, Brownie's son, trails a herd of Durham cattle into Montana and stakes out a ranch.
5. *Arfive* (Houghton, 1970)
   Benton Collingsworth, the new school principal, comes to the small town of Arfive, Montana, and is greeted by its leading citizen, rancher Mort Ewing.
6. *The Last Valley* (Houghton, 1975)
   Collingsworth and Ewing appear again in this volume, which begins in the mid-1920s when Ben Tate takes over the local newspaper.

II. Guthrie has also written a series of mystery stories set in contemporary Midbury, Montana. They are narrated by young Jase Beard, deputy to Sheriff Chick Charleston. Viewed by Guthrie as "entertainments," they are readable portraits of the life and people of a small western town.

1. *Wild Pitch* (Houghton, 1973)
   Buster Hogue is shot in the head at the town picnic, and his enemy Ben Day is killed soon after.
2. *The Genuine Article* (Houghton, 1977)
   Cattle rustling is followed by the murder of irascible rancher F. Y. Grimsley.
3. *No Second Wind* (Houghton, 1980)
   Mutilated cattle and murder may be linked to a feud between strip miners and locals opposed to strip mining.

4. *Playing Catch-up* (Houghton, 1985)
   A prostitute and a high school girl are strangled, and a sapphire brooch disappears.
5. *Murder in the Cotswolds* (Houghton, 1989)
   While visiting England with his wife Geeta, Chick Charleston assists in a murder investigation in the quaint village of Upper Beechwood.

Haggard, H. Rider

I. *King Solomon's Mines* was consciously modeled after *Treasure Island*. It was an immediate success with readers of all ages—and all walks of life. Having spent his early adult years in Africa, Haggard could give an authentic ring to his books' settings, but his characters are flattened into stereotypes by a heavy romanticism and the prejudices of his day. His English heroes are always noble and brave; his Africans, though sometimes noble, are always bloodthirsty; and his women are, of course, totally unreal. Readers who can accept this as a convention of the genre will find Haggard's tales quite entertaining. Allan Quatermain was so successful as the fictional hero of *King Solomon's Mines* that Haggard revived him again and again, even giving him adventures in previous incarnations, making a chronology next to impossible. The books in which Quatermain appears are listed below in the order of their publication. He also figures in one "She" book and in the Zikali trilogy, both listed separately below. The early life of Umslopagaas, the Zulu warrior who plays a large part in *Allan Quatermain*, and who, like Allan, was resurrected for some of the later novels in the series, is told in the rousing *Nada the Lily* (Longmans, 1892).

1. *King Solomon's Mines* (Harper, 1886)
   Quatermain leads Sir Henry Curtis and Captain Good on a search for the fabulous lost diamond mines of King Solomon. Quatermain is thought to have been based on the hunter F. C. Selous.
2. *Allan Quatermain* (Harper, 1887)
   In this prototypical "lost city" romance, Quatermain follows a subterranean river to a hidden city in the African interior where Curtis finds romance, Allan meets his end, and the great Zulu warrior Umslopagaas fights a spectacular last stand.

3. *Maiwa's Revenge* (Harper, 1888)
   Allan does some fancy shooting and helps an African princess regain her heritage.
4. *Allan's Wife and Other Stories* (Munro, 1889)
   This book consists of four short stories, including "Tale of Three Lions" and "Long Odds."
5. *The Holy Flower* (Ward & Lock, 1915)
   Allan searches for a fabled orchid in the heart of Africa. Variant title: *Allan and the Holy Flower.*
6. *The Ivory Child* (Longmans, 1916)
   Quatermain leads an expedition to Central Africa in search of a lady who has been spirited away.
7. *The Ancient Allan* (Longmans, 1920)
   A drug throws Allan back into a previous existence in ancient Egypt.
8. *Heu-Heu* (Doubleday, 1924)
   Allan and Hans go in search of a lost race troubled by a monstrous, apelike "god."
9. *The Treasure of the Lake* (Doubleday, 1926)
   Allan gets involved with yet another lost race and a white goddess.
10. *Allan and the Ice-Gods* (Doubleday, 1927)
    Features Allan in a previous existence as a prehistoric man.

II. "She" is Ayesha, a strange white goddess who rules a hidden city in deepest Africa. Obviously Haggard caught something of universal allure when he sat down to write his story of "an immortal woman inspired by an immortal love." The 1935 film of *She* inexplicably changed the setting from Africa to the Arctic.

1. *She* (Harper, 1886)
   Leo Vincey and Ludwig Holly search for the mysterious queen of a savage African tribe.
2. *Ayesha: The Return of She* (Doubleday, 1905)
   Leo, in pursuit of his love, Ayesha, is led to a monastery in the forbidding mountains of Central Asia.
3. *She and Allan* (Longmans, 1921)
   Haggard's two leading characters meet, both a little past their prime.
4. *Wisdom's Daughter: The Life and Love Story of She-Who-Must-Be-Obeyed* (Doubleday, 1923)
   Ayesha appears in one of her reincarnations as the daughter of an Arab chief during the fourth century B.C.

III. In the Zikali trilogy and in the earlier novel *Nada the Lily* (Longmans, 1892) Haggard documents the history of the Zulu people and culture. Some feel that he has done for the Zulus what James Fenimore Cooper's Leatherstocking Tales (q.v.) did for the American Indian.

1. *Marie* (Longmans, 1912)
   Allan Quatermain is a young man in 1836 at the time of the Great Trek of the Boers into the African interior and their confrontation with the Zulus.
2. *Child of Storm* (Longmans, 1913)
   The beauty and ambition of Mameena, along with the plotting of the witch doctor Zikali, bring civil war to the Zulus. The story ends at the battle of Tugela in 1856.
3. *Finished* (Longmans, 1917)
   Zikali leads Cetewayo and the Zulus into their fatal clash with the British in the Zulu War during 1877–84.

Hall, Adam (pseud. of Elleston Trevor)

Like Sam Spade, Quiller refuses to carry a gun—he thinks they are for amateurs. And that is one thing nobody would ever consider British agent Quiller. His cold and cynical professionalism never shows a crack as he completes one hazardous mission after another for his bureau, which handles even more sensitive operations than M.I.5. George Segal made a wonderful Quiller in the 1967 film of *The Quiller Memorandum*. English-born Trevor, a former RAF pilot, now lives in the United States. As there is very little chronology to Quiller's cases, they are listed below in the order in which they were published. Numbers 11, 12, and 13 were published as paperbacks only.

1. *The Quiller Memorandum* (Simon & Schuster, 1965)
   In West Berlin to help the Germans flush out dangerous ex-Nazis, Quiller proves his mettle. English title: *The Berlin Memorandum.*
2. *The Ninth Directive* (Simon & Schuster, 1966)
   In Bangkok, Quiller must protect a visiting English dignitary from assassination.
3. *The Striker Portfolio* (Simon & Schuster, 1969)
   Thirty-six Striker planes have crashed, and Quiller must find out what happened.

4. *The Warsaw Document* (Doubleday, 1971)
   In order to stop any disruption of important détente talks in Warsaw, Quiller infiltrates the Polish underground.
5. *The Tango Briefing* (Doubleday, 1973)
   Control sends Quiller to the Sahara, where he must find a crashed and dangerous cargo plane.
6. *The Mandarin Cypher* (Doubleday, 1975)
   Quiller is assigned to Hong Kong and a defecting British engineer.
7. *The Kobra Manifesto* (Doubleday, 1976)
   Quiller follows five international terrorists, known as Kobra, to their unknown target.
8. *The Sinkiang Executive* (Doubleday, 1978)
   After an inexcusable lapse, Quiller is sent on a suicide mission to Russia, but he proves indestructible.
9. *The Scorpion Signal* (Doubleday, 1980)
   Quiller goes to Russia in search of his old colleague Shapiro and gets caught in a tangle of revenge.
10. *The Peking Target* (Playboy, 1982)
    Dispatched to China as a bodyguard, Quiller soon finds himself pursuing the mysterious and deadly Mr. Tung to a monastery in the mountains.
11. *Quiller* (Jove, 1985)
    When an American submarine spying on a Soviet base is torpedoed, Quiller must retrieve a secret tape of the incident.
12. *Quiller's Run* (Jove, 1988)
    Quiller leaves the "Bureau" and goes free-lance to stop Cambodian arms and drug dealer Mariko Shoda.
13. *Quiller KGB* (Berkeley, 1989)
    Quiller joins the KGB in order to foil an assassination plot aimed at Gorbachev.

Hammett, Dashiell

Dorothy Parker wrote that Hammett's detective was so hard-boiled "you could roll him on the White House lawn." Though Sam Spade is without a doubt the most famous of the hard-boiled school of realistic private detectives, he actually figures in only one of Hammett's novels, *The Maltese Falcon*, and in some of the short stories. The unnamed "operative" who works for the San Francisco office of the Continental Agency

stars in several earlier works. He differs from Sam Spade in one important respect: he carries a gun. Hammett based his Continental Op on the
personality of a detective he met and admired during his service with
the Pinkerton Agency. It is surprising to remember that Hammett also
created the effervescent Nick and Nora Charles, the detective couple
featured in *The Thin Man*. Though radio, television, and movie series
eventually stretched these characters very thin indeed, Hammett only
wrote one book about them. Just for the record, *The Glass Key* features
Ned Beaumont as detective.

1. *Red Harvest* (Knopf, 1929)
   The Continental Op cleans up "Poisonville" by playing off the
   gangsters against each other.
2. *The Dain Curse* (Knopf, 1929)
   Perhaps the Op's busiest case, this involves eight murders, one
   seduction, one jewel burglary, and a family curse.
3. *Blood Money* (World, 1943)
   Here are two linked adventures, "The Big Knockover" and
   "$106,000 Blood Money," previously published in *Black Mask*
   magazine.
4. *The Continental Op* (Random, 1974)
   A posthumous collection of stories is published here.

Hamner, Earl, Jr.

Hamner's warm and gently humorous stories of the mountain folk of
Virginia during the depression were the inspiration for the TV series
"The Waltons." These two books are companion pieces covering roughly the same time, 1933. While they focus on fifteen-year-old Clay-Boy,
oldest of the eight Spencer children, the large circle of family and
friends surrounding him at Spencer's Mountain is well-drawn.

1. *Spencer's Mountain* (Dial, 1961)
   The action starts with Clay-Boy's first deer hunt at Thanksgiving
   and continues through the next summer's romance and preparation for departure to college.
2. *The Homecoming: A Novel about Spencer's Mountain* (Random,
   1970)

This short novel covers the dramatic Christmas Eve when Clay fails to return home when expected and young Clay-Boy goes out in search of his father.

Hansen, Joseph

Dave Brandstetter, Los Angeles insurance investigator, is true to the hardboiled private eye model of Hammett (q.v.) and Chandler (q.v.), with one exception: he happens to be a homosexual. Hansen's novels are distinguished by their matter-of-fact, non-apologetic presentation of a homosexual hero and the ambience in which he operates. They display strong characterization, an authentic southern California atmosphere, and an umblinking look at the underside of society.

1. *Fadeout* (Harper, 1970)
   Fox Olsen's wrecked car is found, but his body is missing. Brandstetter, mourning his dead lover, is called in to investigate.
2. *Death Claims* (Harper, 1973)
   Rare book dealer John Oats is the victim of a suspicious drowning.
3. *Troublemaker* (Harper, 1975)
   A young homosexual is the prime suspect in the murder of the co-owner of a gay bar.
4. *The Man Everybody Was Afraid Of* (Holt, 1978)
   When the despotic police chief of La Caleta is murdered, his colleagues instantly arrest a local gay activist leader.
5. *Skinflick* (Holt, 1979)
   Now an independently wealthy free-lance investigator, Dave examines the murder of anti-pornography crusader Gerald Dawson.
6. *Gravedigger* (Holt, 1982)
   A young member of a strange desert cult, who is carrying a large insurance policy on her life, is missing.
7. *Nightwork* (Holt, 1984)
   Independent trucker Paul Myers is killed in a fiery crash shortly after he insured his life for $100,000.
8. *The Little Dog Laughed* (Holt, 1986)
   Blind seventeen-year-old Chrissie finds the body of her father, prominent journalist Adam Streeter.

9. *Early Graves* (Mysterious, 1987)
   A serial killer is murdering young men dying of AIDS.
10. *Obedience* (Mysterious, 1988)
   After Brandstetter is interviewed by *Time* magazine, he is hired to investigate the murder of a prominent Vietnamese businessman.

Note: *Brandstetter and Others* (Countryman, 1984) contains two Brandstetter stories.

Hardwick, Mollie

"The Duchess of Duke Street" was a BBC-TV success before it took book form. Mollie Hardwick has skillfully adapted the story of peppery and indomitable Louisa Trotter. From the Cockney scullery maid who dreams of being the best cook in London, to the honorary "Duchess" of Duke Street where her famed Bentinck Hotel is located, Louisa's story is always engaging. Rosa Lewis, who was the real-life inspiration for the fictional character of Louisa, is also the subject of two biographies that will interest fans of the series: *The Duchess of Jermyn Street* by Daphne Fielding (Little, 1964) and *Rosa Lewis* by Anthony Masters (St. Martin's, 1977). An American edition titled simply *The Duchess of Duke Street* (Holt, 1976) contains numbers 1 and 2 listed below.

Hardwick also wrote two novels in the "Upstairs Downstairs" series, most of which was done by John Hawkesworth. The entire series is listed together under Hawkesworth (q.v.).

1. *The Duchess of Duke Street: The Way Up* (Ulverscroft, London, large print, 1979)
   Louisa rises from apprentice cook in 1900 to proprietor of the Bentinck; she marries, has a liaison with the prince of Wales, and bears a daughter.
2. *The Duchess of Duke Street: The Golden Years* (Ulverscroft, London, 1979)
   With Lord Haslemere in permanent residence and their child with foster parents in the country, propriety and prosperity reign.
3. *The Duchess of Duke Street: The World Keeps Turning* (Ulverscroft, London, 1979)
   This book begins in 1911, takes Louisa through her war years, and ends with her daughter Lottie's coming to stay at the Bentinck.

Harris, Marilyn

The Eden saga won immediate acceptance among readers of historical romance. Harris blends an authentic eighteenth- and nineteenth-century English background into her fast-paced stories, which cover three generations of the stormy Eden family. The tangles begin with the seduction of young Marianne, a fisherman's daughter, and have their bloody resolution with her grandson's return to Eden castle many years later.

1. *This Other Eden* (Putnam, 1977)
   A beautiful young servant girl spurns the advances of lecherous Lord Thomas Eden.
2. *The Prince of Eden* (Putnam, 1978)
   Illegitimate Edward inherits the Eden fortune, but not the title, and goes off to help the poor.
3. *The Eden Passion* (Putnam, 1979)
   Young John, the illegitimate son of Edward Eden, works in the Eden castle scullery until tragedy sends him off to foreign lands.
4. *The Women of Eden* (Putnam, 1980)
   John Murrey Eden casts a blight on all five Eden women surrounding him but especially on young Mary when she falls in love with Burke Stanhope. The action takes place in 1870–71.
5. *Eden Rising* (Putnam, 1982)
   Bereft of his womenfolk, and haunted by the consequences of past financial dealings, John Murrey Eden is nursed back to health by virtuous Susan Mantle.
6. *American Eden* (Doubleday, 1987)
   Lady Mary Eden and her husband Burke Stanhope move to Alabama after the Civil War, where they run afoul of white supremacists.
7. *Eden and Honor* (Doubleday, 1989)
   John Murrey Eden disrupts a family reunion at Eden Castle at the turn of the century. This sees the Eden clan through the Boer War and World War I.

Harris, Mark

I. Henry W. Wiggen, pitcher for the New York Mammoths, tells the story of his life and rise to fame in baseball. His semi-literate prose and exuberant vernacular give the tales a special humor as Wiggen grapples with universal concerns—the price of success, the death of a friend, aging gracefully, etc. Baseball adds suspense to the novels but is no barrier to readers not especially interested in the sport. Harris wrote the screenplay for *Bang the Drug Slowly*, a 1973 film starring Robert De Niro and Michael Moriarty.

1. *The Southpaw* (Bobbs, 1953)
   Pitcher Henry Wiggen moves up the baseball ladder from Perkinsville to the major leagues.
2. *Bang the Drug Slowly* (Knopf, 1956)
   His teammates gradually become aware that catcher Bruce Pearson is dying of Hodgkin's disease.
3. *A Ticket for a Seamstitch* (Knopf, 1957)
   Catcher Piney Woods is being followed around the country by a devoted female fan.
4. *It Looked like For Ever* (McGraw, 1979)
   Henry, now 39 and minus his fastball, is passed over for manager of the Mammoths and released.

II. In this pair of wildly funny novels, college professor and novelist Lee Youngdahl tries to work his way through some personal crises. The stories are told through the letters and other documents written by and to Youngdahl.

1. *Wake Up, Stupid* (Knopf, 1959)
   Lee Youngdahl, professor of English at a San Francisco college, having just mailed a one-act play to his agent, is hit by an identity crisis.
2. *Lying in Bed* (McGraw, 1984)
   Now somewhat older, Youngdahl is smitten with a young student's physical charms and literary ability.

Hartley, Leslie Poles

Those who enjoyed reading Hartley's *The Go-Between* or seeing the exquisite movie made of that novel will want to try other works by this English author. The Eustace and Hilda trilogy is a sensitive and beautifully written exploration of a brother-sister relationship. Some consider it his masterpiece. The omnibus volume *Eustace and Hilda: A*

Trilogy (Putnam, London, 1958) contains a short story entitled "Hilda's Letter" inserted between the first and second books listed below. It concerns a letter of invitation Hilda writes to Dick Stavely.

1. *The Shrimp and the Anemone* (Putnam, London, 1944)
   Eustace Cherrington is a gentle little boy with a weak heart who is dominated by his older sister, Hilda. American title: *The West Window* (Doubleday, 1945)
2. *The Sixth Heaven* (Doubleday, 1947)
   Now an undergraduate at Oxford, Eustace hopes for a romance between Hilda and his aristocratic friend Dick Stavely.
3. *Eustace and Hilda* (Putnam, London, 1947)
   After a holiday in Venice, Eustace attempts a drastic measure to help Hilda.

Hartog, Jan de

Dutch-born Jan de Hartog has made himself a diverse literary reputation. His play *The Four-Poster* won Broadway's Tony Award for 1952 and is often revived by theater groups. *The Hospital* (1962), a non-fiction work describing conditions in a Texas charity hospital, attracted nationwide attention. An early novel *Holland's Glory* (1940) became a symbol of Dutch resistance against the Nazis. Hartog, who ran away to sea at the age of ten, has always been on or near the water. The trio of novels narrated by Martinus Harinxma, Dutch captain of ocean-going tugboats, display Hartog's extensive knowledge of the sea and his ability to write about it.

1. *The Captain* (Atheneum, 1966)
   Captain Harinxma, who has escaped from the Nazis in the Netherlands, takes command of a Dutch tugboat slated for convoy duty on the Iceland-Murmansk run.
2. *The Commodore* (Harper, 1986)
   Now 70 and retired, Harinxma agrees to act as a consultant on board an ultra-modern ocean-going tug that has been sold to a Taiwanese shipper.
3. *The Centurion* (Harper, 1989)
   Harinxma takes up dowsing and gets involved with the life of a Roman centurion from the fourth century A.D.

Hawkesworth, John

"Upstairs Downstairs" seemed to have the widest appeal of any Masterpiece Theatre series, courting many viewers away from commercial television for the first time. The downstairs characters of Rose, Mrs. Bridges, and Mr. Hudson were the compelling figures; the upstairs Bellamy occupants paled by comparison. Fans will relish these competent novelizations almost as much as a summer rerun. Once available in paperback, they will most likely be found in public libraries only in the large-print editions listed below.

1. *Upstairs Downstairs* (Hall, 1980)
   Sarah joins the Bellamy household as houseparlormaid, and young James takes too much of an interest.
2. *In My Lady's Chamber* (Hall, 1980)
   Scandals and indiscretions sweep the decks, and the king comes to dinner.
3. *The Years of Change* (Hall, 1980) (written by Mollie Hardwick)
   War threatens, and Lady Bellamy goes down on the *Titanic*.
4. *The War to End War* (Hall, 1980) (written by Mollie Hardwick)
   Rose becomes a part-time bus conductor, and Mr. Hudson is a special constable.
5. *On with the Dance* (Hall, 1980)
   James's mental scars are slow to heal; Richard remarries, and Mr. Hudson falls in love.
6. *Endings and Beginnings* (Hall, 1980)
   James sets out for the New World; Mr. Hudson has a heart attack; the household is finally dispersed.

Heald, Tim

Heald's unlikely detective, Simon Bognor, is a pudgy, lazy fellow perfectly happy to drift between having meals at his London club and shuffling papers at his desk. But inevitably, his boss orders him off his "fat backside" to investigate some irregularity that has come to the Board of Trade's attention. In the field, Bognor bungles each interview and follows false clues until the mystery seems to solve itself—allowing the reader a nice lead. A romance with girlfriend Monica develops through the series.

1. *Unbecoming Habits* (Stein & Day, 1973)
   Are the friars at Beaubridge sending technological secrets to Russia in their jars of honey?
2. *Blue Blood Will Out* (Stein & Day, 1974)
   Bognor investigates the murder of a flamboyant tycoon at a meeting of owners of England's stateliest homes.
3. *Deadline* (Stein & Day, 1975)
   To find the murderer of a gossip columnist, Bognor poses as a journalist.
4. *Let Sleeping Dogs Die* (Stein & Day, 1976)
   Sent to investigate a possible poisoning of a champion poodle, Bognor uncovers dog smuggling, murder, and other hairy doings.
5. *Just Desserts* (Scribner, 1978)
   Bognor enters the international gourmet scene to investigate gourmet/cook Savarin Smith's strange death.
6. *Murder at Moose Jaw* (Doubleday, 1981)
   Finally wed to Monica-the-blasé and fast getting on to middle age, Bognor goes to Canada to investigate some LSD smuggling.
7. *A Small Masterpiece* (Doubleday, 1982)
   Bognor's class reunion at Oxford is shaken up by the murder of Lord Beckenham, one of his former tutors. English title: *Masterstroke*.
8. *Red Herrings* (Doubleday, 1986)
   The annual Popinjay Clout in the village of Herring St. George takes an unexpected turn when VAT inspector Brian Wilmslow is found shot full of arrows.
9. *Brought to Book* (Doubleday, 1988)
   Bognor becomes a suspect when Vernon Hemlock, publisher and erotica collector, is crushed between the shelves of his library stacks.

Heaven, Constance

I. Ravensley, the home of the Aylsham family, is located in the Fen Country of England. It provides a picturesque setting for this pair of historical romances which chronicle two generations of Aylshams, beginning in the early 1880s. Heaven, an English author, provides a lively mix of love affairs, scandals, natural disasters, and war scenes to keep readers of the genre glued to the page.

1. *Lord of Ravensley* (Coward, 1978)
   A plan to drain the fenlands brings conflict and heartbreak to members of the love-torn Aylsham family.
2. *The Ravensley Touch* (Coward, 1982)
   The star-crossed love of Jethro Aylsham and Laurel Rutland, which begins in Rome, is carried to the battlegrounds of the Crimean War.

II. The Kuragin trilogy also takes place in the first half of the nineteenth century, but in Russia rather than England. Rebellions and revolutions, decadent aristocrats, and exotic scenery form the backdrop for this trio of historical romances.

1. *The House of Kuragin* (Coward, 1972)
   Young Englishwoman Rilla Western travels to Russia to become governess to the aristocratic Kuragin family and to a love affair with Andrei, Count Kuragin's brother.
2. *The Astrov Legacy* (Coward, 1973)
   Sophie Western, visiting her sister Rilla, meets Prince Leonid Astrov and observes the Decembrist Uprising of 1825. English title: *The Astrov Inheritance*.
3. *Heir to Kuragin* (Coward, 1979)
   In 1846 Princess Gadiani, following her missing husband to his ancestral home in the Caucasus, is escorted through dangerous territory by Count Paul Kuragin.

Hebden, Mark (pseud. of John Harris)

Fans of Simenon (q.v.) will enjoy this series starring inspector Evariste Clovis Desire Pel of the French provincial police in Burgundy. Middle-aged and heavy-hearted, Pel often seems to brood his way to the core of each case. Continuing threads in the series include Pel's relationships with several young subordinates to whom he teaches the elements of detection, and his courtship of, and eventual marriage to, the widow Genevieve Faivre-Perret. The books are written in an oddly stilted English that reads like a translation. For another series written by Englishman John Harris, *see* Max Hennessey.

1. *Death Set to Music* (Walker, 1983)
   Mme. Camille-Jeanne Chenandier is found bludgeoned to death in her living room.

2. *Pel and the Faceless Corpse* (Walker, 1982)
A corpse with its face shot away is found at the base of a monument to the French Resistance.
3. *Pel under Pressure* (Walker, 1983)
Pel must deal with drug traffickers and a university prostitution ring.
4. *Pel Is Puzzled* (Hamilton, London, 1981)
Spies, art theft, and a utilities swindle disturb Pel's peace of mind.
5. *Pel and the Staghound* (Walker, 1984)
The disappearance of rich Francois Renssalaer causes more concern to his staghound Archer than to his wife and employees.
6. *Pel and the Bombers* (Walker, 1985)
Terrorists, murder, and a planned assassination get in the way of Pel's courtship of Madame Faivre-Perret.
7. *Pel and the Predators* (Walker, 1985)
Pel must cope with a death threat and three cases of murder, one of them forty years old.
8. *Pel and the Pirates* (Walker, 1987)
The honeymooning Pels find the corpse of a taxi-driver on their doorstep on the Isle of St. Yves.
9. *Pel and the Prowler* (Walker, 1986)
A serial killer of young women leaves a cryptic message near each body and a mark on each victim's cheek.
10. *Pel and the Paris Mob* (Hamilton, London, 1986)
Gangs from Paris and Marseilles are invading Pel's home turf.
11. *Pel among the Pueblos* (Walker, 1988)
The murder of a retired gangster leads Pel to Mexico.
12. *Pel and the Touch of Pitch* (Walker, 1988)
Local deputy Claude Barclay is kidnapped on the eve of national elections.
13. *Pel and the Picture of Innocence* (St. Martin's, 1989)
Pel gets depressed when Maurice Tagliatti and his gang return to town, but Maurice is soon murdered.

Hennessey, Max (pseud. of John Harris)

I. The Lion at Sea trilogy is a story of the British navy in World Wars I and II. The "Lion" is Kelly Maguire ("Ginger" to his shipmates), a young Anglo-Irishman with the courage and resourcefulness of a Hornblower, who is destined to rise to a high rank. His sense of honor, sense of humor, and attractiveness to the ladies guarantee his fictional success.

1. *The Lion at Sea* (Atheneum, 1978)
   The story begins in 1911, when Kelly rescues a drowning man
   and receives a medal even before taking his sublieutenant's exam.
   This volume introduces Kelly's childhood sweetheart, Charlotte
   (Charley) Upford, and continues to the Battle of Jutland, 1916.
2. *The Dangerous Years* (Atheneum, 1979)
   After the war, Lieutenant Maguire rescues refugees in Yalta, is
   sent ashore to help some White Russians escape, and then is off to
   China.
3. *Back to Battle* (Atheneum, 1980)
   Beginning with some run-ins off the coast of Spain during that
   country's civil war and continuing through action in every major
   sea battle of World War II, Ginger Maguire remains indomitable.

II. This prolific British author has also written a trio of British cavalry
books featuring three generations of the Goff family of Yorkshire who
serve with the historic 19th Lancers.

1. *Soldier of the Queen* (Atheneum, 1980)
   Colby Goff joins the 19th Lancers just in time to see action with
   the Light Brigade at Balaclava in 1854. Over the next 25 years he
   serves in India, America during the Civil War, and Africa during
   the Zulu wars.
2. *Blunted Lance* (Atheneum, 1981)
   Colby's son Dabney distinguishes himself in the Boer War and
   World War I.
3. *The Iron Stallions* (Atheneum, 1982)
   Colby's grandson Joshua carries on the family cavalry tradition in
   the "iron stallions" (tanks) of World War II.

III. Another trilogy follows RAF pilot Dicken Quinney from teenage
aerial derring-do in World War I to middle-aged heroics in World War
II. Quinney does have a rather phlegmatic love life, but the novels are
at their best when he is airborne.

1. *The Bright Blue Sky* (Atheneum, 1983)
   Seventeen-year-old Dicken Quinney joins up as a flying wireless
   operator in 1914, but soon finds himself flying combat missions.

2. *The Challenging Heights* (Atheneum, 1983)
Quinney has trouble coping with post-war life in the 1920s and re-joins the RAF.
3. *Once More the Hawks* (Atheneum, 1984)
Near retirement, Quinney is called back into action by the out-break of World War II.

Herbert, Frank

I. Even before *The Last Whole Earth Catalog* recommended *Dune* as an ecological primer, Herbert's novel showed signs of attracting a cult following, and his fans have increased with each new sequel. The series combines the traditional science fiction elements of heroism and peril in an alien world; overtones of religion; and an ecological message—on the desert planet Dune a drop of water is more precious than gold. The long-awaited movie version of *Dune* (1984) unfortunately turned out to be a critical and financial disaster. *The Dune Encyclopedia*, edited by Willis McNelly (Putnam, 1984), is a compendious guide to the first four volumes of the series.

1. *Dune* (Chilton, 1956)
Duke Leto Atreides and his family are exiled to the barren planet of Dune, which is inhabited by ferocious Fremen who ride giant sandworms.
2. *Dune Messiah* (Putnam, 1969)
A mystical sisterhood plots to overthrow Dune's ruler Maud'Dib, who is really Paul Atreides, son of Duke Leto.
3. *Children of Dune* (Berkley/Putnam, 1976)
As power struggles and ecological change rock Maud'Dib's crumbling empire, the twins Leto and Ghanima develop slowly.
4. *God Emperor of Dune* (Berkley/Putnam, 1981)
On the now greening planet of Dune, specimen Fremen are museum attractions for tourists, and the God Emperor Leto Atreides (Paul's son) is turning into a sandworm.
5. *Heretics of Dune* (Putnam, 1984)
The Bene Gesserit, a secret sisterhood, plans to mate Sheeana, who can talk to sandworms, with the latest incarnation of Duncan Idaho.

6. *Chapterhouse Dune* (Putnam, 1985)
   The Bene Gesserit plans to use the sandworms to change Chapterhouse into another desert world.

II. Herbert has also written two books starring saboteur extraordinary Jorj X. McKie of the Bureau of Sabotage in the Confederation of the Sentient Worlds.

1. *Whipping Star* (Putnam, 1970)
   On discovering that some stars are actually intelligent superpowerful beings, Jorj McKie makes a friend of one called Fannie Mae.
2. *Dosadi Experiment* (Putnam, 1977)
   Jorj McKie is assigned to investigate an experiment on extreme overcrowding in progress on the planet Dosadi.

III. *Destination: Void*, an early Herbert novel about a space colonization project and megalomaniac computer, was followed by a trilogy written in collaboration with Bill Ransom. The books continue the story of the transplanted human clone race as it copes with the harsh environment of the planet Pandora.

1. *Destination: Void* (Berkley, 1966)
   Scientists on a spaceship carrying human colonists to a supposedly idyllic planet are forced to create a new supercomputer. Published as a paperback only.
2. *The Jesus Incident* (Berkley, 1979)
   Humans deposited on the planet Pandora try to destroy its native life forms, including a kind of sentient kelp, instead of trying to come to terms with them. Co-authored by Bill Ransom.
3. *The Lazarus Effect* (Putnam, 1983)
   Centuries later Pandoran humanity has split into high-tech Mermen living under the sea and mutant Islanders living on floating islands. Co-authored by Bill Ransom.
4. *The Ascension Factor* (Putnam, 1988)
   The Pandoran humans have learned how to control the intelligent kelp beds which regulate the planet's waterflow, and are wreaking ecological havoc by creating land at an excessive rate. Co-authored by Bill Ransom.

196

Heyer, Georgette

Heyer's admiration of Jane Austen is apparent in her numerous historical romances, which have entertained several generations of readers on both sides of the Atlantic. *Cotillion* (Putnam, 1953) and *Charity Girl* (Dutton, 1970) are among the best of her many novels set in Regency London. The first two titles listed below are uncharacteristic in that they are set in France and England during the reign of Louis XV.

1. *These Old Shades* (Small & Maynard, 1926)
   The duke of Avon takes a Paris guttersnipe for a page—but Leon turns out to be a girl, the disinherited daughter of a French count.
2. *Devil's Cub* (Dutton, 1966)
   The handsome young son of the duke of Avon flees to France after a duel in a London gambling house. First published in England in 1932.
3. *An Infamous Army* (Dutton, 1965)
   The grandchildren of the "Devil's Cub" see action in the Battle of Waterloo. This book is also a sort of sequel to *Regency Buck* (Dutton, 1966) in that Judith Taverner Worth appears in both works. *An Infamous Army* was originally published in England in 1937.

Higgins, George V.

This pair of novels is narrated by Jeremiah Francis (Jerry) Kennedy, a successful Boston criminal lawyer who defends clients of varying degrees of sleaziness. They show the pragmatic world of the criminal lawyer through a series of monologues and dialogues related in the inimitable Boston patois which Higgins has made his own since the success of *The Friends of Eddie Coyle* (Knopf, 1972).

1. *Kennedy for the Defense* (Knopf, 1980)
   Jerry Kennedy tries to balance the demands of his clients against his desire to spend more time with his wife and teenage daughter.
2. *Penance for Jerry Kennedy* (Knopf, 1985)
   Jerry is in trouble with the IRS, a TV commentator, a judge, and his wife's real estate partners.

Higgins, Jack (pseud. of Henry Patterson)

Liam Devlin, former Irish freedom fighter, is the connecting link in this pair of novels by best-selling suspense novelist Jack Higgins. Devlin hates the English but reluctantly finds himself working with them. Higgins' fans know to expect an intricate plot, realistic characters, and plenty of action and suspense. Michael Caine, Donald Sutherland, and Robert Duvall headed the star-studded cast in the 1976 movie versiion of *The Eagle Has Landed*.

1. *The Eagle Has Landed* (Holt, 1975)
   A small, elite force of German paratroopers lands secretly in wartime England in order to carry out a daring plan to capture Winston Churchill.
2. *Touch the Devil* (Stein & Day, 1982)
   Liam Devlin is recruited by British intelligence to stop Frank Barry, a former Irish colleague now working for the Soviet Union.

Highsmith, Patricia

The Ripley novels are suspenseful black comedies starring American ex-patriate Tom Ripley, a charming psychopath who feels most at ease when he is doing something illegal or immoral. The four novels trace his development from callow youth to callous con-man and killer. Ripley was played by Alain Delon in *Purple Noon* (the 1961 film version of *The Talented Mr. Ripley*) and by Dennis Hopper in *The American Friend* (the 1978 film version of *Ripley's Game*).

1. *The Talented Mr. Ripley* (Coward, 1955)
   Young Tom Ripley goes to Italy at the request of Dickie Greenleaf's father in order to bring the young man home.
2. *Ripley under Ground* (Doubleday, 1970)
   Now married to a wealthy woman, and living on a French estate, Ripley is obliged to impersonate an artist whose works Ripley's associates have been forging.
3. *Ripley's Game* (Knopf, 1974)
   To avenge an insult, Ripley involves the offending Englishman in a plot to murder two Mafiosi.
4. *The Boy Who Followed Ripley* (Lippincott, 1980)
   A sixteen-year-old American runaway chooses Ripley as his mentor.

Hill, Reginald

Set in Yorkshire, this series features Superintendent Andy Dalziel and Sergeant (later Inspector) Peter Pascoe. Dalziel is fat, boorish, and irascible while Pascoe is sensitive, introspective, and university-educated. Despite their obvious incompatibility, each has developed a grudging respect for the other, and they work together as a surprisingly effective, if not always harmonious, team.

1. *A Clubbable Woman* (Countryman, 1984)
   Former rugby star Sam Connan awakens to find his wife Mary has been bludgeoned to death while watching television.
2. *An Advancement of Learning* (Countryman, 1983)
   The corpse of the former head of Holm Coultram College is found under a statue on campus.
3. *Ruling Passion* (Harper, 1977)
   Pascoe and his girl, Ellie Soper, find three friends shot to death at a weekend cottage.
4. *April Shroud* (Countryman, 1986)
   Pascoe is on his honeymoon when Dalziel gets caught up in a love affair of his own with a recently widowed woman whose husband met a strange end.
5. *A Pinch of Snuff* (Harper, 1978)
   Pascoe gets involved in an investigation of pornographic films and murder.
6. *A Killing Kindness* (Pantheon, 1981)
   The Yorkshire Choker, a serial killer who quotes Shakespeare, is pursued by Dalziel and Pascoe.
7. *Deadheads* (Macmillan, 1984)
   Patrick Aldermann, accountant and rose grower, is the beneficiary of a series of suspicious accidental deaths.
8. *Exit Lines* (Macmillan, 1985)
   Three old men die of unnatural causes on the same night, and Dalziel is suspected of having a hand in their demise.
9. *Child's Play* (Macmillan, 1987)
   A Yorkshire widow dies, willing money to a son reported missing in action in World War II.
10. *Under World* (Scribner, 1988)
    Young Colin Farr returns to a Yorkshire mining town where he hears disturbing rumors of child-murder and suicide associated with his late father Billy.

Hillerman, Tony

Hillerman's mysteries are a unique blend of detective novel and contemporary western adventure. Lt. Joe Leaphorn and officer Jim Chee of the Navaho Tribal Police confront an extraordinary range of problems, from ancient witchcraft to modern drug traffic. The novels present an authentic, uncondescending picture of the social and religious life of the Navajo, Zuni, and Hopi cultures. Joe Leaphorn is the main protagonist in numbers 1, 2, and 3; Jim Chee in numbers 4, 5, and 6; and they work together in numbers 7, 8, and 9. *The Joe Leaphorn Mysteries* (Harper, 1989) is an omnibus volume containing numbers 1, 2, and 3.

1. *The Blessing Way* (Harper, 1970)
   Anthropologist Bergen McKee goes to the Navajo reservation to pursue his research on witchcraft, and gets involved with murder.
2. *Dance Hall of the Dead* (Harper, 1973)
   When a Zuni youth is killed shortly before a Zuni religious ceremony, suspicion falls on his Navajo friend.
3. *The Listening Woman* (Harper, 1978)
   Searching for the murderers of an old man and a missing helicopter, Leaphorn comes into conflict with the militant Buffalo Society.
4. *People of Darkness* (Harper, 1980)
   Jim Chee searches for a stolen box of keepsakes which may contain the key to a mysterious cult called "The People of Darkness."
5. *The Dark Wind* (Harper, 1982)
   While searching for cocaine missing from a plane crash, Chee gets involved with a Hopi Kachina ceremony.
6. *The Ghostway* (Harper, 1985)
   Chee pursues the men who killed three members of the Navajo Turkey Clan.
7. *Skinwalkers* (Harper, 1987)
   Three murders and an attempt on Chee's life may be the work of a "skinwalker" or Navajo witch.
8. *A Thief of Time* (Harper, 1988)
   Leaphorn and Chee search for an archeologist accused of stealing Anasazi cultural relics.
9. *Talking God* (Harper, 1989)
   The Smithsonian Institution in Washington, D. C., and a Talking God ceremonial mask may hold the answer to two seemingly unrelated crimes.

Himes, Chester

Black American expatriate Chester Himes wrote his first detective novel in Paris for a popular French series of crime fiction. *For Love of Imabelle*, actually published first as a paperback original by Fawcett, became *La reine des pommes* and won the Grand Prix Policier for 1958.

Coffin Ed Johnson and Gravedigger Jones are detectives in the American hardboiled tradition except that they work for the New York Police Department and they are black. As a team they can be quite brutal about enforcing justice as they dash about Harlem in their souped-up black VW. The series is full of violence, sex, absurdist humor, and grimly authentic portraits of life in Harlem in the 1950s and 1960s.

Though Himes felt ambivalent about his detective series, some critics think that it portrays black life in America more effectively than his early serious novels. Movies starring Raymond St. Jacques and Godfrey Cambridge have been made of two of the novels (*Cotton Comes to Harlem* and *Come Back, Charleston Blue*). For a critical study of this series and other works by Himes see Stephen Milliken's *Chester Himes: A Critical Appraisal* (Univ. of Missouri, 1976). Numbers 1–5 were reprinted in hardcover by Chatham Booksellers in 1973.

1. *For Love of Imabelle* (Fawcett, 1957)
   An assortment of sinister characters are after the ore samples, supposedly gold, stolen by Imabelle from her con man husband. Variant title: *A Rage in Harlem.*
2. *The Crazy Kill* (Avon, 1959)
   A guest is killed at the riotous wake of Big Joe Pullen, a dining-car chef and gambler.
3. *The Real Cool Killers* (Avon, 1959)
   Coffin Ed and Gravedigger have to find out which person out of a crowd of strongly motivated people murdered Ulysses Galen, a wealthy white pervert.
4. *All Shot Up* (Avon, 1960)
   An envelope filled with campaign funds disappears when a "robbery" arranged by crooked Harlem politician Casper Holmes gets out of hand.
5. *The Big Gold Dream* (Avon, 1960)
   The search is on for the numbers winnings of a black maid who has apparently cached the money somewhere in the antique hand-me-down furniture that fills her apartment.

6. *Cotton Comes to Harlem* (Putnam, 1965)
   A fanatic white Alabama "colonel" has stuffed $87,000 stolen from the Back-to-Africa movement in a bale of cotton.
7. *The Heat's On* (Putnam, 1966)
   Three million dollars worth of heroin in small plastic sacks has been stuffed into a string of five Hudson River eels. Variant title: *Come Back, Charleston Blue.*
8. *Blind Man with a Pistol* (Morrow, 1969)
   While Harlem is seething with racial unrest, Coffin Ed and Grave-digger are searching for a Gladstone bag containing an old man's life savings. Variant title: *Hot Day, Hot Night.*

Hodge, Jane Aiken

This serviceable saga of family torn by divided loyalties during the American Revolution begins in Savannah in 1774. Hart Purchis, handsome seventeen-year-old heir to Winchelsea Plantation, rescues Mercy Phillips, a young English girl whose Loyalist father has been brutally murdered by an angry revolutionary mob. As they bravely weather the pain, danger, and personal loss of war, their commitment to each other grows.

1. *Judas Flowering* (Coward,1976)
   Orphaned Mercy Phillips is welcomed into the Purchis family and her courage sustains them during the war while young Hart is off fighting.
2. *Wide Is the Water* (Coward, 1981)
   The postwar story begins in 1780 as Hart is in London with his cousin Juliet and Mercy is in Philadelphia.
3. *Savannah Purchase* (Doubleday, 1971)
   Hyde Purchis's French wife Josephine meets her look-alike cousin Juliette in Savannah four years after they had been separated at the Battle of Waterloo.

Hodgins, Eric

Mr. Blandings's trials and tribulations are just as funny now as they were back in 1946. Hodgins's portrait of the city sophisticate helpless in the hands of the local craftsmen who are building his house in the country still delights readers—especially those who are homeowners. Though Cary Grant seemed somewhat miscast as Mr. Blandings, the 1948 movie version was a great success.

1. *Mr. Blandings Builds His Dream House* (Simon & Schuster, 1946)
   When Mr. Blandings, an adman famous for his laxative slogans, is lured out of the city by a lilac-flanked farmhouse, the canny locals regard him as fair game.
2. *Blandings Way* (Simon & Schuster, 1950)
   The Blandings family leaves the countryside for the safety of the big city. Much of the humor of this volume is contributed by the two Blandings daughters.

Hope, Anthony

Hope's cape-and-sword romance, *The Prisoner of Zenda,* has been filmed four times, most successfully by David Selznick, whose 1937 version starred Ronald Colman and Douglas Fairbanks, Jr. The story concerns Rudolf Rassendyll, a vacationing Englishman whose remarkable resemblance to the king of Ruritania enables him to rescue the king from Zenda castle, where he is being held by his evil brother. Princess Flavia provides the love interest in these still very readable adventures.

1. *The Prisoner of Zenda* (Holt, 1894)
   Rassendyll impersonates the king twice and falls in love with Princess Flavia, the kings betrothed.
2. *Rupert of Hentzau* (Holt, 1898)
   Rudolf returns to Ruritania to head off Rupert's evil plot.

Horgan, Paul

Horgan is a seriously underrated author handicapped, like Wright Morris, by the "regional" label. Despite his frequent use of the American Southwest as a setting for his historical and contemporary novels and as a source for his nonfiction, Horgan's themes are the universal ones of moral choice, personal temptation, charity and redemption, and the loss of innocence. His clear prose, expressive yet unmarred by excess, is a model most writers could profit by studying. The Richard trilogy, portraying a sensitive young

203

boy growing through childhood's customary traumas, is written with a grace and perception that are reminiscent of the English author L. P. Hartley (q.v.).

1. *Things as They Are* (Farrar, 1964)
   Richie, aged five in 1908, learns about the world and its peculiar and sometimes cruel ways.
2. *Everything to Live For* (Farrar, 1968)
   Seventeen-year-old Richard tells the story of his cousin Max Chittenden, a Harvard student uneasy about his role as heir to the Chittenden fortune.
3. *Thin Mountain Air* (Farrar, 1977)
   When Richard's father contracts TB in the early 1920s, the family moves to Albuquerque, and Richie leaves college to "toughen up" at the WZL Ranch.

Howatch, Susan

I. Susan Howatch, English author of mysteries and best-selling gothics such as *Penmarric* (1971) and *Cashelmara* (1974), has written a two-volume family saga about the Van Zales, a predacious American banking clan full of odd characters and complicated relationships. According to Howatch *(Contemporary Authors, New Revision Series,* v. 24), the Van Zale saga is a modern dress version of the story of Julius Caesar, Cleopatra, and the Emperor Augustus.

1. *The Rich Are Different* (Simon & Schuster, 1977)
   Dinah Slade, who needs money for the upkeep of her ancestral Norfork manor, meets Paul Van Zale, a rich American banker looking for a mistress. Covers the years 1922 to 1940.
2. *Sins of the Fathers* (Simon & Schuster, 1980)
   In action spanning the years 1949 to 1967, Cornelius Van Zale, grand-nephew and heir of Paul, wreaks havoc on friends and relations, especially his daughter Vicki.

II. With the publication of *Glittering Images,* Ms. Howatch's writing has taken another new turn. These three novels and a fourth on the way, are serious novels about the Church of England in the twentieth century. They are compelling studies of the sometimes tortured inner life of several churchmen from both the psychological and spiritual viewpoints. They also give an insider's look at church politics and the clerical life.

1. *Glittering Images* (Knopf, 1987)
   Canon Charles Ashworth suspects some highly irregular behavior in the domestic life of the charismatic Bishop of Starbridge. Father Jonathan Darrow helps Ashworth sort things out. Set in 1937.
2. *Glamorous Powers* (Knopf, 1988)
   Father Darrow takes center stage in this volume. After 17 years as an Anglican monk, he has a vision which leads him to leave the monastic life. Set in 1940.
3. *Ultimate Prizes* (Knopf, 1989)
   This focuses on Archdeacon Neville Aysgarth's crisis of faith following the death of his child. Set during World War II. Darrow appears briefly.
4. *Scandalous Risks* (forthcoming)

Howells, William Dean

Henry Adams once said that if all reminders of the 1870s were lost, the age could be reconstructed from the novels of William Dean Howells. Though often overlooked by modern readers, Howells's novels were quite popular in his day, perhaps even more highly regarded than those of his contemporary Henry James. He was showered with honors: Columbia, Yale, and Oxford all gave him honorary doctorates, and the Academy of Arts and Letters awarded him its gold medal. Perhaps it is time for a Howells revival. The married couple Basil and Isabel March were favorite characters with Howells; Basil is thought to be an autobiogaphical figure. They appear in all the books listed below, sometimes as main characters, sometimes as peripheral figures.

1. *Their Wedding Journey* (Houghton, 1872)
   The young Bostonian couple Basil and Isabel March travel to Canada for their honeymoon.
2. *A Chance Acquaintance* (Osgood, 1873)
   Kitty Ellison, who appears In *Their Wedding Journey*, has a shipboard romance with Miles Arbuton. The Marches are merely background.

3. *A Hazard of New Fortunes* (Harper, 1890)
   In this novel, generally regarded as one of Howells's best, Basil March accepts the editorship of a literary magazine in New York.
4. *The Shadow of a Dream* (Harper, 1890)
   Basil narrates and plays a small role in this sad tale of how a dying man's dream affects the romance that develops between his widow and his best friend.
5. *An Open-Eyed Conspiracy* (Harper, 1897)
   At the resort of Saratoga, Mr. and Mrs. March are left in charge of a beautiful country girl and facilitate her getting engaged to a young author.
6. *Their Silver Wedding* (Harper, 1899)
   Now middle aged, the Marches tour Germany and see the world in an "evening light."
7. *A Pair of Patient Lovers* (Harper, 1901)
   The Marches play minor roles in two of the short stories in this collection.

Hughes, Richard

The years between the two wars are vividly pictured in these two novels which focus on a young upper-class Englishman named Augustine. Though part of the unfinished series *The Human Predicament,* which Hughes conceived as a history of his own times up to the Second World War, these novels read well separately. They blend the story of Augustine's personal growth, travel, friendships, and romance with the larger events that swirl around him. Incidents of Hitler's rise as reported through the eyes of Augustine's German relatives give the novels their documentary quality.

1. *The Fox in the Attic* (Harper, 1961)
   Augustine visits his Kessen relatives in Germany and falls in love with young Mitzi during the time of Hitler's ill-fated 1923 Munich putsch.
2. *The Wooden Shepherdess* (Harper, 1973)
   Augustine travels in America, Bavaria, and Morocco as social unrest increases. The story ends in 1934 with the "Night of the Long Knives."

Hughes, Thomas

Skimming quickly over the first three chapters will get the reader right into the action that was so splendidly dramatized on "Masterpiece Theatre" and in two previous movie versions. Young Tom is truthful, honest, and loyal—and courageous enough to defend his high principles. Though Hughes denied it, the story is probably autobiographical. The Rugby he depicts is the school as it was after the enlightened educator, Dr. Thomas Arnold, had instituted his reforms there.

1. *Tom Brown's Schooldays* (Houghton, 1857)
   Tom arrives at Rugby and meets his friend East; the two have schoolboy scrapes and a run-in with the bully Flashman. (George MacDonald Fraser (q.v.) recently resurrected Flashman as the antihero of a funny, picaresque series.)
2. *Tom Brown at Oxford* (Burt, 1861)
   Tom attends Oxford as the perfect athlete, scholar, and gentleman, and finally is married.

Hunter, Evan

Last Summer is a chilling little tale of adolescent boredom erupting into violence. The peacefulness of the island resort where Sandy, Peter, and David spend their summer vacation provides an eery contrast to the trio's sadistic bullying of poor Rhoda. Like Golding's *Lord of the Flies*, which it resembles, *Last Summer* made a powerful flim (1969). Both books listed below are narrated by young Peter, whose teenage slang rings true. Hunter also writes police procedurals under the pseudonym of Ed McBain (q.v.).

1. *Last Summer* (Doubleday, 1968)
   Three teenage friends spending their summer at the shore befriend and then abuse the awkward and shy young Rhoda.
2. *Come Winter* (Doubleday, 1973)
   Five years later, on a pre-Christmas ski holiday, the three friends brave dangerous ski trails and deadly human passions.

Innes, Michael (pseud. of. J. I. M. Stewart)

I. John Appleby's erudition and urbanity serve him well in the stately homes and academic settings where his cases usually take him; these qualities have, no doubt, contributed to his rapid rise from uniformed bobby through Scotland Yard to London police commissioner and ultimate knighthood. Oxford professor J. I. M. Stewart, who has written novels, scholarly studies, and biographies under his real name, has endowed Appleby with a formidable command of literature and classics—though not with an Oxford education—and with useful social connections through his wife's family. Readers who like their mysteries solved by quotations will enjoy these literate and witty entertainments.

1. *Seven Suspects* (Dodd, 1937)
   Young Inspector Appleby solves the locked-room murder of Dr. Umbleby, the president of one of Oxford's colleges. English title: *Death at the President's Lodging.*
2. *Hamlet, Revenge!* (Dodd, 1937)
   A murder is perpetrated onstage during an amateur production of *Hamlet* at the duke of Horton's estate.
3. *Lament for a Maker* (Dodd, 1938)
   This case of death and mystery in remotest Scotland begins when a hated laird falls to his death from the top of his ancient, towered home.
4. *The Spider Strikes* (Dodd, 1939)
   Richard Eliot, a mystery writer, is plagued by a series of practical jokes in which his character, "the Spider," seems to come alive. English title: *Stop Press.*
5. *A Comedy of Terrors* (Dodd, 1940)
   Death interrupts a Christmas family gathering when a stray bullet kills one of those present. English title: *There Came Both Mist and Snow.*
6. *The Secret Vanguard* (Dodd, 1941) Nazi spies in Scotland are the focus of this case which involves some lively scenes of pursuit over the lonely Scottish heaths.
7. *Appleby on Ararat* (Dodd, 1941)
   When Appleby's ship is torpedoed in the South Seas, he drifts to an apparently uninhabited island, where he soon gets involved with murder and buried treasure.
8. *The Daffodil Affair* (Dodd, 1942)
   Hannah Metcalfe, the descendant of a witch, leads Appleby on a

lively search through a haunted Bloomsbury house amid London's air raids.

9. *The Weight of the Evidence* (Dodd, 1943)
Inspector Appleby goes to Nesfield University to investigate the mysterious death of Professor Pluckrose.

10. *Appleby's End* (Dodd, 1945)
Sheltered by the unconventional Raven family during a winter storm in the country, Appleby solves some decidedly rustic mysteries and meets his future wife, sculptress Judith Raven.

11. *Night of Errors* (Dodd, 1947)
Though now retired, Appleby is invited to sit in on the puzzling case of the murder of the last surviving member of a set of triplets.

12. *The Paper Thunderbolt* (Dodd, 1951)
Can the disappearance of a number of people from an English village be connected to the doings of a nasty gang of scientist-criminals? English title: *Operation Pax*.

13. *One Man Show* (Dodd, 1952)
Murder and a painting stolen from the Duke of Horton's mansion occupy Appleby in one of his best cases. English title: *A Private View*. Variant Title: *Murder is an Art*.

14. *Dead Man's Shows* (Dodd, 1954)
Appleby stars in twenty-three short stories. English title: *Appleby Talking*.

15. *Appleby Talks Again* (Dodd, 1957)
This book has eighteen more short stories about Appleby.

16. *Death on a Quiet Day* (Dodd, 1957)
More thriller than mystery, this book concerns a young student who finds himself pursued by all sorts of villains. English title: *Appleby Plays Chicken*.

17. *The Long Farewell* (Dodd, 1958)
This short case involves a dead man with two wives and a missing rare book from the Packford library.

18. *Hare Sitting Up* (Dodd, 1959)
Sir John, in search of a bacteriologist missing from his lab, finds himself on a lonely island off the Scottish coast.

19. *Silence Observed* (Dodd, 1961)
Art frauds and some particularly baffling murders occupy Commissioner Appleby's attention.

20. *The Crabtree Affair* (Dodd, 1962)
Sir John and his wife are on holiday when a murder draws them

into an investigation in this exceptionally well-knit case. English title: *A Connoisseur's Case.*

21. *The Bloody Wood* (Dodd, 1966)
Intrigue and murder by one of three possible heirs to a fortune keep Appleby guessing.

22. *Death by Water* (Dodd, 1968)
While exploring a gazebo on a neighboring estate, Sir John discovers a dead body, still warm. English title: *Appleby at Allington.*

23. *Picture of Guilt* (Dodd, 1969)
This story of an art fraud is both mysterious and highly amusing. Appleby's young son Bobby helps in the detecting. English title: *A Family Affair.*

24. *Death at the Chase* (Dodd, 1970)
Young Bobby helps again as Appleby investigates the murder of an eccentric neighbor who believed his former Resistance comrades were trying to kill him.

25. *An Awkward Lie* (Dodd, 1971)
This complicated case involves a mentally straying old man, a large inheritance, and a suddenly illuminated stately home.

26. *The Open House* (Dodd, 1972)
Appleby's problem—an empty house all lit up with dinner waiting and pajamas laid out—has all the classic elements of a first-rate puzzler.

27. *Appleby's Answer* (Dodd, 1973)
Sir John accidentally bumps into this case involving a lady author, a shady military man, and a goat.

28. *Appleby's Other Story* (Dodd, 1974)
Maurice Tytherton, owner of the magnificent Elvedon Court, is murdered.

29. *The Appleby File* (Dodd, 1976)
Eighteen short stories continue Appleby's adventures.

30. *The Gay Phoenix* (Dodd, 1977)
Death aboard a yacht in the South Pacific is the central problem here.

31. *The Ampersand Papers* (Dodd, 1979)
Retired Sir John Appleby is admiring an old Cornish castle when Dr. Sutch, the archivist, plummets to his death from a collapsing staircase.

32. *Sheiks and Adders* (Dodd, 1982)
Sir John investigates the murder of a pseudo sheik at a masquerade ball.

33. *Appleby and Honeybath* (Dodd, 1983)
    Sir John Appleby joins forces with Charles Honeybath, R.A. (see
    section II, below), to solve the mystery of the vanishing body in
    the library of Grinton Hall.
34. *Carson's Conspiracy* (Dodd, 1984)
    Appleby's neighbor Carl Carson must cover up his crazy wife and
    bankrupt business in order to pass himself off as a county
    squire.
35. *Appleby and the Ospreys* (Dodd, 1987)
    Sir John investigates the fatal stabbing of Lord Osprey and the
    disappearance of his coin collection.

II. Charles Honeybath, R. A., is a successful portrait painter who
doubles as an amateur detective. The Honeybath novels are much like
the Appleby novels in structure, style, and ambience. Appleby and Honeybath collaborate in number 4 below (number 33 above).

1. *The Mysterious Commission* (Dodd, 1975)
   Honeybath is offered a nice sum of money if he will agree to
   spend a fortnight at an unspecified country house painting the
   portrait of a client who must remain unidentified.
2. *Honeybath's Haven* (Dodd, 1978)
   Honeybath's attempt to aid old friend and fellow painter Edwin
   Lightfoot draws him into a dangerous mystery.
3. *Lord Mullion's Secret* (Dodd, 1981)
   Honeybath is commissioned to paint the portrait of Lady Mullion,
   but is sidetracked by the theft of a valuable miniature.
4. *Appleby and Honeybath* (Dodd, 1983)
   See number 33 above.

Irwin, Margaret

Anyone who enjoyed Glenda Jackson's portrayal of Queen Elizabeth on
the Masterpiece Theatre production of "Elizabeth R" will find Irwin's trilogy on Elizabeth's early years fascinating. Historical fiction at its best, these
novels are lively, authentic, and gracefully written. Irwin's Elizabeth is a
precocious, witty, cool-headed schemer who has only one aim in life—to
become queen of England. The sixteenth-century court life is vividly re-
created.

1. *Young Bess* (Harcourt, 1945)
   This volume takes Elizabeth from the age of twelve to her brother's death in 1553.
2. *Elizabeth, Captive Princess* (Harcourt, 1948)
   The period here is the reign of Lady Jane Grey, up to the marriage of Queen Mary when Elizabeth was twenty.
3. *Elizabeth and the Prince of Spain* (Harcourt, 1953)
   Here we see Mary's short reign, before Elizabeth's coronation.

Jack, Donald

These volumes, purporting to be the Bandy Papers, star the redoubtable World War I ace Bartholomew Bandy, a Canadian whose stentorian tones and brash disregard for bureaucratic detail invariably set his superior officer's teeth to grinding. Donald Jack, a former RAF man, writes lovingly of the early flying machines his pilot maneuvers through scene after scene of action. The war is a backdrop, not a reality that might impinge on the hero's humorous and daring escapades.

1. *Three Cheers for Me* (Doubleday, 1973)
   Events on the western front get very lively indeed when Bartholomew Bandy arrives on the scene and begins to make his reputation in his Sopwith Camel.
2. *That's Me in the Middle* (Doubleday, 1973)
   Lieutenant-Colonel Bandy lands a liaison job in London, and further misadventures ensue.
3. *It's Me Again* (Doubleday, 1975)
   Bandy takes command of his own squadron of Sopwith Dolphins and gets to see a bit of action in Russia.
4. *Me Bandy, You Cissie* (Doubleday, 1979)
   After the war, Bandy meets a millionaire's daughter, crashes his first commercial airline flight, and gets into the movies.
5. *Me Too* (Doubleday, 1983)
   In the 1920s, Bandy smuggles whiskey, serves in Canada's parliament, and is appointed to the cabinet by Prime Minister Mackenzie King.
6. *This One's on Me* (Doubleday, 1988)
   Bandy gets involved with a beautiful Icelandic doctor and an Indian prince, and tries his hand as a porter at St. Pancreas hospital and as the leader of a maharajah's air force.

7. *Me So Far* (Doubleday, 1989)
   In what is purported to be the final volume of his memoirs, Bandy goes to India to organize the air force of the state of Jhamjarh, and immediately alienates the viceroy.

Jaffe, Rona

Rona Jaffe's first book, *The Best of Everything* (1958), is still her best-known novel. *Class Reunion* and its sequel trace the fortunes of four Radcliffe graduates: golden girl Daphne, clever Chris, beautiful Annabel, and insecure Emily. The changing attitudes of the fifties, sixties, and seventies are chronicled through the lives and trials of the four women and the men with whom they become involved. The characters are recognizable types, even if they lead somewhat implausible lives. The novels are readable portraits of upper-middle-class American women.

1. *Class Reunion* (Delacorte, 1979)
   Four Radcliffe alumnae meet at their twentieth class reunion in 1977, and review their lives from their entrance in college to the present.
2. *After the Reunion* (Delacorte, 1985)
   Their lives not, after all, dramatically improved since their twentieth reunion, Chris, Annabel, Daphne, and Emily face various sexual, family, and career problems.

Jakes, John

I. The Kent Family Chronicles, originally known as the American Bicentennial Series, was conceived as a series of historical novels in commemoration of the U.S. bicentennial. With the appearance of each new volume, its readership increased, and the TV dramatization of part of the series created a second wave of popularity. Jakes attributed the series' success to his readers' need for solid stories about courageous and idealistic men and women who endure life's worst trials without losing faith in America, who are patriotic without being blind to their country's mistakes and flaws. Now complete at eight volumes, the Kent saga begins with Philip Kent in 1770 and continues to the 1880s. Originally published in paperback, the books were eventually issued in hardcover by Doubleday. In addition, Landfall Press has published two omnibus volumes. *The Patriots* contains numbers 1 and 2 listed below; *The Pioneers* comprises numbers 3 and 4. Robert Hawkins has compiled *The Kent Family Chronicles Encyclopedia* (Bantam, 1979), which is a companion to the series and contains condensations of the first seven novels as well as historical essays, background materials, and "kitchen history" of interest.

1. *The Bastard* (Pyramid, 1974)
   Philip Kent, the illegitimate son of an English duke, flees to America. The time is 1770–75.
2. *The Rebels* (Pyramid, 1975)
   In 1775–81 Philip, now a patriot soldier, sees the horrors of battle and finds a new love.
3. *The Seekers* (Pyramid, 1975)
   For twenty years after the war (1794–1814), two generations of Kents struggle to find their place in the new land. Philip's son Abraham falls in love with Amanda.
4. *The Furies* (Pyramid, 1976)
   Amanda Kent progresses from the frontier to New York's high society during the period 1836–52.
5. *The Titans* (Pyramid, 1976)
   The Kent family is torn apart by hatred and greed as the Civil War turns brother against brother. The years are 1860–62.
6. *The Warriors* (Pyramid, 1978)
   The Kents set down new roots after a hard-won peace. In 1864–68, Jeremiah goes west and Gideon moves north.
7. *The Lawless* (Pyramid, 1978)
   Change sweeps the country in 1869–77 as Gideon leads workers in New York and Jeremiah's love of violence leads him to his doom.
8. *The Americans* (Jove, 1980)
   Will Kent, Gideon's youngest son, leaves Theodore Roosevelt's western ranch to practice medicine in the New York slums.

II. Jakes followed the Kent Family Chronicles with a Civil War trilogy covering American history from 1842 through 1876. It traces the fortunes of two families: the Hazards of Pennsylvania and the Mains of South Carolina. The Hazards are industrialists; the Mains are slave-owning proprietors of a rice plantation. Many historical figures cross paths with the fictional Hazards and Mains. The trilogy is excellent popular history: authentic, dramatic, and entertaining. Parts 1 and 2 have been made into mini-series for television.

1. *North and South* (Harcourt, 1982)
   George Hazard and Orry Main, fellow students at West Point, become

friends, and the fortunes of their families become intertwined. Covers 1842 to 1861.

2. *Love and War* (Harcourt, 1984)
Orry Main and George Hazard fight on opposite sides in the Civil War. Covers 1861 to 1865.

3. *Heaven and Hell* (Harcourt, 1987)
George Hazard goes into steel-making, while his brother Stanley goes into politics. Madeleine Main runs the plantation despite threats from the Ku Klux Klan, while young Charles scouts for General Custer. Covers 1865 through 1876.

James, Henry

Christina Light, later the Princess Casamassima, is the one major character in the voluminous output of Henry James who appears in more than one novel. Daughter of an American expatriate, she is beautiful, intelligent, and charming, but given to fads, and destructive to the men who become deeply involved with her.

1. *Roderick Hudson* (Osgood, 1876)
Roderick Hudson's talent for sculpture attracts wealthy Roland Mallet, who takes him to Rome where he meets, among others, the fascinating Christina Light.

2. *The Princess Casamassima* (Macmillan, 1886)
Hyacinth Robinson, an orphan raised in London poverty, is attracted to revolutionary movements, and to the Princess Casamassima who shares his artistic temperament and sympathy for the downtrodden.

James, P. D. (pseud. of Phyllis Dorothy White)

Though regrettably not as prolific as Agatha Christie, P. D. James has the same mastery of pace, suspense, and polished characterization. Her detective, Chief Inspector Adam Dalgliesh, is Scotland Yard's star sleuth. He is tall and handsome, with a secret sorrow—his wife and baby died in childbirth. A skilled, no-nonsense interrogater who modifies his technique to suit the personality of each witness, Dalgliesh always draws out that last salient detail on which the whole case hinges. James is keeping her fans guessing about the romance between Dalgliesh and Cordelia Gray, who was introduced in *An*

Unsuitable Job for a Woman. Three omnibus volumes exist: *Crime Times Three* (Scribner, 1979) contains numbers 1, 2, and 3 listed below; *Murder in Triplicate* (Scribner, 1980) contains numbers 4, 5, and 6; and *Trilogy of Death* (Scribner, 1984) contains numbers 7 and 8 and *Innocent Blood*.

1. *Cover Her Face* (Scribner, 1962)
   Beautiful, scheming Sally Jupp comes to the Maxie house as a maid but plans to move up.
2. *A Mind to Murder* (Scribner, 1963)
   The administrator of a London psychiatric clinic is murdered.
3. *Shroud for a Nightingale* (Scribner, 1971)
   When two student nurses at Nightingale House are murdered, Adam Dalgliesh is called in.
4. *Unnatural Causes* (Scribner, 1967)
   A corpse without hands drifts into Adam's vacation with his aunt in Suffolk.
5. *An Unsuitable Job for a Woman* (Scribner, 1972)
   This book really stars Cordelia Gray, a young private eye investigating the death of a microbiologist's son. She and Adam cross paths and are mutually attracted.
6. *The Black Tower* (Scribner, 1975)
   A minister friend of Adam's is the latest victim in a senseless series of murders that baffles the police.
7. *Death of an Expert Witness* (Scribner, 1977)
   Dalgliesh investigates the murder of Dr. Lorrimer, senior staff member of a forensic science lab.
8. *The Skull Beneath the Skin* (Scribner, 1982)
   Cordelia Gray is hired to protect actress Clarissa Lisle, who has been receiving threatening notes.
9. *A Taste for Death* (Knopf, 1986)
   Sir Paul Berowne, former minister of the Crown and acquaintance of Dalgleish, is found with his throat cut in a London church.

Note: Neither Inspector Dalgliesh nor Cordelia Gray appears in James's novel *Innocent Blood* (Scribner, 1980), a chilling tale about an adopted woman's search for her biological parents.

Jameson, Storm

I. This prolific British author, a feminist and outspoken liberal, has over forty-five novels to her credit. Her early trilogy was a Galsworthian saga following the life of Mary Hervey (née Hansyke) from her birth in 1841 to her death in 1923, tracing her family's shipbuilding business from sail to steam to turbine. Mary, a kind of Woman of Property, has a stormy love life but a sure touch in the business. The books are set in the Yorkshire seaport of Whitby, home of Jameson's own family, also shipbuilders.

1. *The Lovely Ship* (Knopf, 1927)
   After two unsuccessful marriages, Mary, heir to the family ship-building business, meets the love of her life, Gerry.
2. *The Voyage Home* (Knopf, 1930)
   At forty, Mary is the rich and successful head of the shipbuilding business, but family happiness eludes her.
3. *A Richer Dust* (Knopf, 1931)
   Now an old woman living in a world gone slightly mad, Mary sells the business at the height of the war boom.

II. After the success of the above books, Jameson's attention focused for a time on the figure of Hervey Russell, Mary's granddaughter, most likely an autobiographical figure. She wrote several books about Hervey and even planned a series of five novels on contemporary society around her, to be called the Mirror in Darkness, though that was never completed. Hervey Russell is present in the following titles:

1. *The Captain's Wife* (Macmillan, 1939)
   Hervey is just a child in this volume, which is really the story of Sylvia, her mother, who rebels against her family and marries below her station. English title: *Farewell Night; Welcome, Day*.
2. *That Was Yesterday* (Knopf, 1932)
   Hervey survives unhappy early married years during World War I.
3. *Company Parade* (Knopf, 1934)
   Hervey struggles to make a living in postwar London. This book was conceived as the first of a five-volume series, Mirror in Darkness.
4. *Love in Winter* (Knopf, 1935)
   In 1924–25, her marriage a failure, Hervey meets and falls in love with Nicholas Roxby. This book is the second in the Mirror in Darkness series.
5. *None Turn Back* (Cassell, London, 1936)
   The General Strike and the reasons for its failure are at the center of this third installment of the Mirror in Darkness series, after which Jameson abandoned plans for further volumes.

6. *The Journal of Mary Hervey Russell* (Macmillan, 1945)
   This last Hervey Russell book is very thinly disguised autobi-
   ography. The journal shows a sensitive writer and how World
   War II affected her.

Jeffries, Roderic

Prolific English mystery novelist Roderic Jeffries (pseudonyms include
Jeffrey Ashford, Peter Alding, and Roderic Graeme) moved to the
Mediterranean island of Mallorca in 1972, and began a detective series
featuring Spanish policeman Enrique Alvarez. Alvarez is slow-moving
but not slow-witted, overly fond of the pleasures of the table, and easy-
going but tenacious in pursuit of solutions to crimes. Most of the
skulduggery occurs among the tourists and English residents of Mallorca,
and one of the continuous threads is the effect of tourism upon the
natives of this once poor, backward island.

1. *Mistakenly in Mallorca* (Collins, London, 1974)
   John Tatham conceals the ill-timed death of his great-aunt
   Elvina Woods.
2. *Two-Faced Death* (Collins, London, 1976)
   Con man and womanizer John Calvin had good reason to commit
   suicide, but Alvarez suspects murder.
3. *Troubled Deaths* (St. Martin's, 1978)
   An expatriate Englishman loathed by almost everyone dies of
   mushroom poisoning.
4. *Murder Begets Murder* (St. Martin's, 1979)
   Rich, sickly William Heron and his unfaithful mistress are found
   dead of suspected food poisoning.
5. *Just Deserts* (St. Martin's, 1981)
   Frank Finnister, failed novelist in need of money, woos plain,
   middle-aged Miriam Spiller, who takes a fatal spill from her
   balcony. "Jeffrey Ashford" is listed as the author.
6. *Unseemly End* (St. Martin's, 1982)
   Polly Lund, wealthy, nasty, and unpopular, is murdered, and her
   young lover Mark Erington becomes her heir and the prime suspect.
7. *Deadly Petard* (St. Martin's, 1983)
   The apparent suicide of artist Gertrude Deen brings Alvarez
   together in a match of wits with English police officer Cullion.

8. *Three and One Make Five* (St. Martin's, 1984)
Alvarez falls in love with young New Zealander Tracey New-combe while investigating the suspicious death of her lover, Roger Clarke.

9. *Layers of Deceit* (St. Martin's, 1985)
The murder of wealthy Steve Collum produces many suspects including Steve's half-brother Alan.

10. *Almost Murder* (St. Martin's, 1986)
After two Englishmen are blown up in a yacht explosion, an officious bureaucrat is sent from Madrid to bedevil Alvarez.

11. *Relatively Dangerous* (St. Martin's, 1987)
A fatal car crash on a mountain road leads Alvarez to some complicated financial dealings among the British residents.

12. *Death Trick* (St. Martin's, 1988)
There are numerous suspects when Pablo Roig, swindler and womanizer, is murdered.

13. *Dead Clever* (St. Martin's, 1989)
Did heavily-insured Englishman Henry Green really perish in a plane crash off Mallorca?

Jenkins, Dan

Sportswriter Dan Jenkins has written a pair of novels set in the zany and vulgar worlds of professional football and television. The books are somewhat short on plot, but full of hilarious commentary by and about a variety of colorful characters including Billy Clyde Puckett, Giants fullback and television sports "color" man; Barbara Jane Bookman, heiress, model, and television sitcom starlet; her racist oil man father Big Ed Bookman; and Shake Tiller, football player turned best-selling author. There is something here to offend and amuse almost everyone. Burt Reynolds starred in the film version of *Semi-Tough* (1977). Kenny Lee Puckett, Billy Clyde's uncle, is the protagonist in *Dead Solid Perfect* (Atheneum, 1974), a novel about professional golf.

1. *Semi-Tough* (Atheneum, 1972)
The New York Giants are playing the despised Jets for the NFL championship, as Billy Clyde Puckett, the Giants' star fullback, tape-records his impressions of Super Bowl week.

2. *Life Its Ownself* (Simon & Schuster, 1984)
   Billy Clyde, retired from football and working as a television sports commentator, observes the plot of the NFL players' union to deliberately play boring, bad football.

Jerome, Jerome K.

A topographical and historical account of the Thames River was what Jerome intended to write, but fortunately for generations of delighted readers, his sense of humor and knack for telling a good story got in the way. The resulting comic tale of the misadventures of three Englishmen and their dog, Montmorency, on a boat trip up the Thames was a bestseller of its day, both in England and America, though the lack of trans-Atlantic copyright laws lost Jerome any profit from his American sales. The story that begins chapter three is one of the many digressions typical of Jerome. Readers will recognize it as the story of Uncle Podger hanging the picture, adapted for children in *My Uncle Podger* by Wallace Tripp (Little, 1975). The Everyman's Library edition (Dent/ Dutton, 1957) contains both books listed below.

1. *Three Men in a Boat (To Say Nothing of the Dog)* (Holt, 1889)
   The characters of Harris and George were based on Jerome's friends with whom he often spent Sundays on the river. The dog, Montmorency, and many of the book's incidents are also based on fact.
2. *Three Men on Bicycles* (Holt, 1900)
   The same three men, somewhat older and without the dog, take a leisurely cycling tour through Germany. The original English title, *Three Men on the Bummel*, puzzled readers unable to find the word *bummel* in the dictionary. Jerome defines the word, characteristically on the last page, as a rambling holiday without any definite object.

Johnson, Pamela Hansford

I. Readers looking for a good, old-fashioned novel of manners should try anything by Pamela Hansford Johnson: they won't be disappointed. Her solid stories, perceptive characterizations, and satin-smooth prose have won her a loyal public in the United States as well as in England. In private life she was Lady Snow, the wife of writer C. P. Snow (q.v.). The two books featuring Toby Roberts are especially good examples of her art. Toby is one of those attractive and intelligent young men who seem more comfortable observing life than taking part in it. His career languishes, and his love affairs prove almost tragic.

1. *The Good Listener* (Scribner, 1975)
   Young Toby, the good listener, is detached and slow to commit himself as all his Cambridge friends rush madly into life's tangles.
2. *The Good Husband* (Scribner, 1979)
   Toby, now thirty, meets and marries widow Ann Thorold, a much older woman.

II. The Helena trilogy is an older series held together by the figure of Helena, who, even when not present, is a powerful influence on her friends and family. The trilogy was republished in three volumes by Scribner in the early 1970s.

1. *Too Dear for Possessing* (Macmillan, 1940)
   After childhood in Bruges with his author father and stepmother Helena, Claud Pickering goes to England, but he cannot forget the city and Cecil, the English girl he met there.
2. *An Avenue of Stone* (Macmillan, 1948)
   After the war, Helena, now widowed and afraid of her approaching old age, takes a young veteran under her wing.
3. *A Summer to Decide* (Macmillan, 1948)
   Helena's daughter, Charmian, has a new baby and a rapidly deteriorating marriage.

Johnson, Uwe

Uwe Johnson, one of Germany's greatest postwar novelists, was an East German who emigrated to the West. The impact of the split between East and West, the "Free World," and the "People's Democracies" is the dominant theme of his fiction. In *Speculations about Jakob*, Johnson's characters "speculated" about the meaning of the life and enigmatic death of an East German railroad worker. Johnson eventually followed up this novel with the monumental *Anniversaries* (four volumes in German, two volumes in English), which describes one year in the life of

Gesine Cresspahl, Jakob's lover and mother of his child, as she tries to come to terms with her memories of Germany. Johnson's work isn't easy or comforting reading, but it will reward the serious reader.

1. *Speculations about Jakob* (Grove, 1963)
   The mysterious death of Jakob Abs stirs up conflicting recollections of his life by those who knew him. Translation by Ursule Molinaro of *Mutmassungen über Jakob* (1959).
2. *Anniversaries: From the Life of Gesine Cresspahl, August 1967– February 1968* (Harcourt, 1975)
   Six months of the life and recollections of Gesine Cresspahl, who is living in New York with her daughter. Translation by Leila Vennewitz of volume 1 and part of volume 2 of *Jahrestage: Aus dem Leben von Gesine Cresspahl* (1970–72).
3. *Anniversaries II: From the Life of Gesine Cresspahl* (Harcourt, 1987)
   This continues the "journals" of Gesine Cresspahl from February 1968 to August 20, 1968. Translation by Leila Vennewitz and Walter Arndt of part of volume 2 and volumes 3 and 4 of *Jahrestage: Aus dem Leben von Gesine Cresspahl* (1972–83).

Jones, Douglas C.

I. Since his retirement from the U.S. Army, Douglas C. Jones has become a highly regarded author of historical novels about the American West. *The Court-Martial of George Armstrong Custer* examines what might have happened if Custer had survived the Battle of Little Big Horn. The other two novels in this trilogy deal with the history of the events leading up to, and including, the massacre at Wounded Knee. Jones's sympathies are with the Plains Indians. He blames an insensitive, inept government for their tragic defeat.

1. *The Court-Martial of George Armstrong Custer* (Scribner, 1976)
   General Custer, one of the few white survivors of the Battle of Little Big Horn (1876), is put on military trial for insubordination.
2. *Arrest Sitting Bull* (Scribner, 1977)
   In December 1890, Sitting Bull is back on the reservation, and in the middle of the Ghost Dance revolt of the Indians.
3. *A Creek Called Wounded Knee* (Scribner, 1978)
   The story of the 1890 massacre at Wounded Knee, South Dakota,

as seen through the eyes of the Indians, the federal troops, and the press.

II. Jones wrote a trio of novels set in his native Arkansas depicting four generations of a family from the Civil War to the Depression. Numbers 1 and 2 are partially based on his own family history, while number 3 is partly autobiographical.

1. *Elkhorn Tavern* (Holt, 1980)
Ora Hasford and her two teenage children are caught up in the Civil War when their farm becomes part of the battleground of the Battle of Pea Ridge.
2. *Winding Stair* (Holt, 1979)
Young Eben Pay is a lawyer temporarily assigned to the court of "hanging judge" Isaac C. Parker.
3. *Weedy Rough* (Holt, 1981)
Maudie Snowdon is the cause of the breakup of the friendship between Dune Gene Pay and Hoadie Renkin in the town of Weedy Rough, Arkansas, during the Great Depression.

III. In Jones's third trilogy, it is the Comanche Indians of Texas who are forced to come to terms with the ascendancy of the White Man.

1. *Season of Yellow Leaf* (Holt, 1983)
In 1838 ten-year-old Morfanna Perry is captured by Comanches and adopted by their chief under the name "Chosen."
2. *The Barefoot Brigade* (Holt, 1984)
This follows a group of Confederate Army recruits from Arkansas through the Civil War.
3. *Gone the Dreams and Dancing* (Holt, 1984)
In 1875, Comanche chief Kwahadi asks Liverpool Morgan, a survivor of "the Barefoot Brigade," to find out what happened to Chosen, his mother.

Jong, Erica

Fear of Flying was the funniest and most popular of the new wave of women's novels in the seventies which portrayed modern women in the throes—usually graphic and hilarious—of liberation. Jong's heroine Isadora Wing is typical; she is twice married, Barnard educated, under thirty, and fiercely restless. But Jong's crisp and pungent dialogue gives Isadora an edge among the newly liberated and will guarantee her long life as a classic of the genre.

1. *Fear of Flying* (Holt, 1973)
   Isadora leaves her cool psychiatrist husband for a fling with a sexy English Laingian.
2. *How to Save Your Own Life* (Holt, 1977)
   Isadora, now a best-selling author, gets divorced and heads for other loves.
3. *Parachutes and Kisses* (NAL, 1984)
   Isadora at 39, now a successful writer, wife, and mother, is jolted by the desertion of her third husband.

Kallen, Lucille

The continuing subplot in this series of mysteries set in Sloan's Ford, Connecticut, is the relationship between C. B. Greenfield, newspaper editor and amateur detective, and Maggie Rome, reporter and reluctant participant in Greenfield's investigations. Greenfield is crotchety and conservative, a male chauvinist who thinks it is his natural right as the "boss" to order Maggie Rome around. Rome, happily married with grown children, gets involved in Greenfield's cases against her better judgment, but gets a measure of revenge as narrator of the novels and acerbic commentator on Greenfield's foibles. Kallen, a former comedy writer for television, is producing a series of witty and well-plotted mysteries.

1. *Introducing C. B. Greenfield* (Crown, 1979)
   The delivery boy for the *Sloan's Ford Reporter* is badly injured in a hit-and-run accident.
2. *The Tanglewood Murder* (Wyndham, 1980)
   Noel Damaskin, violinist for the Boston Symphony Orchestra, is poisoned at a rehearsal during the Tanglewood Music Festival.
3. *No Lady in the House* (Wyndham, 1982)
   Greenfield's stereo is stolen, and his cleaning lady is murdered.
4. *The Piano Bird* (Random, 1984)
   Maggie Rome is on Sanibel Island, Florida, nursing her invalid mother when thespian Thea Quinn is murdered.
5. *A Little Madness* (Random, 1985)
   After Maggie joins a women's peace group encamped outside a

missile base, Alice Dakin, author of *Why God Gave Us the Bomb,* disappears.

Kaminsky, Stuart M.

I. Like Max Alan Collins (q.v.), Stuart Kaminsky is writing a series of detective novels set in the 1930s and 1940s, which intermingle real and fictional characters. Toby Peters is a typical hardboiled private eye of the era: tough and cynical, but basically honest and good-hearted. His sidekicks include an incompetent dentist, a midget, and a poetic wrestler. Peters works out of Los Angeles. His cases sooner or later involve him with celebrities of the past, many of them from the movie industry. Kaminsky is a film historian and critic. His blend of nostalgia, humor, mysteries, and movie stars is a sure-fire mix.

1. *Bullet for a Star* (St. Martin's, 1977)
   Errol Flynn is Toby's client. The crimes are blackmail and murder. The scenic backdrop is the original set of *The Maltese Falcon.*
2. *Murder on the Yellow Brick Road* (St. Martin's, 1978)
   When a Munchkin from *The Wizard of Oz* is murdered on the MGM lot, Judy Garland and Louis B. Mayer call in Toby Peters.
3. *You Bet Your Life* (St. Martin's, 1979)
   Toby tries to clear Chico Marx of a fake gambling debt. Chicago is the scene of most of the action.
4. *The Howard Hughes Affair* (St. Martin's, 1979)
   Howard Hughes thinks that someone is after the designs of his secret bomber.
5. *Never Cross a Vampire* (St. Martin's, 1980)
   Is the same person threatening Bela Lugosi, and trying to frame William Faulkner for murder?
6. *High Midnight* (St. Martin's, 1981)
   Gary Cooper is being blackmailed into doing a grade "B" cowboy movie called *High Midnight.*
7. *Catch a Falling Clown* (St. Martin's, 1982)
   An elephant is electrocuted at the Rose and Elder Circus, and famous clown Emmett Kelly suspects sabotage.
8. *He Done Her Wrong* (St. Martin's, 1983)
   Mae West's fictionalized autobiography is being held for ransom, while Toby runs into a slew of Mae West impersonators.

9. *The Fala Factor* (St. Martin's, 1984)
   Eleanor Roosevelt suspects that an imposter has been substituted for FDR's beloved Scottie, Fala.

10. *Down for the Count* (St. Martin's, 1985)
    Joe Louis has been set up to take the rap for the murder of Toby's ex-wife's second husband.

11. *The Man Who Shot Lewis Vance* (St. Martin's 1986)
    Someone wants to kill John Wayne, and a man named Lewis Vance does get killed after slipping Toby a drugged Pepsi.

12. *Smart Moves* (St. Martin's, 1987)
    Nazi fifth columnists are trying to discredit, and perhaps assassinate, Albert Einstein. Set mostly in New York.

13. *Think Fast, Mr. Peters* (St. Martin's, 1988)
    Mrs. Sheldon Minck, wife of Toby's dentist officemate, has run off with a Peter Lorre impersonator who is filming a "B" thriller on the roof of a hardware store.

14. *Buried Caesars* (Mysterious, 1989)
    Dashiell Hammett helps Toby look for some papers and money stolen from Gen. Douglas MacArthur.

II. Porfiry Petrovich Rostnikov, Inspector in the Moscow Procurator's Office, is the hero of a series of police procedurals set in the Soviet Union. Porfiry Petrovich is a good cop—dogged, stoic, honest—but his non-ideological competency and his Jewish wife don't make him popular with his superiors or the KGB, who eventually succeed in having him demoted.

1. *Death of a Dissident* (Ace, 1981)
   Dissident Alexander Granovsky is murdered the day before he is due to be put on trial as an "enemy of the people." English title: *Rostnikov's Corpse.*

2. *Black Knight in Red Square* (Berkley, 1983)
   Rostnikov and his associates uncover a plot to bomb Lenin's Tomb at the Moscow Film Festival.

3. *Red Chameleon* (Scribner, 1985)
   A series of crimes such as the theft of the deputy procurator's automobile, the sniper killing of a policeman, and the death of an old man in his bathtub, bedevil Rostnikov.

4. *A Fine Red Rain* (Scribner, 1987)
   Rostnikov must find out who is killing trapeze artists at the Moscow Circus, while his colleague Karpo is trying to find a serial killer of prostitutes.

5. *A Cold Red Sunrise* (Scribner, 1988)
   Rostnikov is assigned to the case of Commissar Illya Rutkin, killed in Siberia while investigating the death of a dissident's daughter.

Kazan, Elia

Kazan is famous as the stage and screen director of *Death of a Salesman, On the Waterfront,* and many other notable successes. It's no accident that his first novel, *America, America,* has a certain cinematic quality. It tells the story of a young Greek man who is determined to leave his home in Anatolia (Turkey) and emigrate to America. The story is based on the experiences of Kazan's uncle. *America, America* was filmed in 1964 with Kazan as writer, director, and producer.

1. *America, America* (Stein & Day, 1962)
   Stavros Topouzoglou is entrusted with his family's wealth in order to establish himself in the rug business in Constantinople, but his deepest desire is to emigrate to America.
2. *The Anatolian* (Knopf, 1982)
   In 1909, Stavros, known to his carpet-selling associates as Joe Arness, is living in New York, and awaiting the arrival of his family from Anatolia.

Keating, H. R. F.

Inspector Ganesh Ghote (pronounced Go'-tay), who works in the crime branch of the Bombay Police Department, is a nice fellow who is pushed about by everyone—by his wife Protima, by his superior officers, and by every sort of rascal and miscreant. But his persistence and wily intelligence enable him to bring all his varied assignments to successful conclusions. Keating's detective is very likeable, and his unusual and colorful Indian setting will seem authentic to Western readers, though the English author admits to only one short visit to India. An additional attraction is that Keating wraps each of his books around a different philosophical theme.

1. *The Perfect Murder* (Dutton, 1965)
   Naturally the newspapers labeled it the "Perfect murder," but the victim, Mr. Perfect, wasn't dead, just bashed into a coma. Inspector

Ghote's delighfully ambiguous first case won the British Crime Writers Association Gold Dagger award for 1964.

2. *Inspector Ghote's Good Crusade* (Dutton, 1966)
   When an American philanthropist and founder of the Masters Foundation for the Care of Juvenile Vagrants is poisoned with arsenic, Inspector Ghote investigates.

3. *Inspector Ghote Caught in Meshes* (Dutton, 1968)
   An American physicist is murdered by highway robbers, but there is more here than meets the eye.

4. *Inspector Ghote Hunts the Peacock* (Dutton, 1968)
   In London for a conference on drug smuggling, Inspector Ghote searches for his missing niece.

5. *Inspector Ghote Plays a Joker* (Dutton, 1969)
   On the trail of a practical joker, Inspector Ghote goes to the Victoria Gardens Zoo to prevent the murder of a flamingo.

6. *Inspector Ghote Breaks an Egg* (Doubleday, 1971)
   Inspector Ghote, disguised as a chicken-feed salesman, investigates a murder that was committed fifteen years earlier.

7. *Inspector Ghote Goes by Train* (Doubleday, 1972)
   Ghote journeys to Calcutta to pick up the con-man art forger Bhattacharya.

8. *Inspector Ghote Trusts the Heart* (Doubleday, 1973)
   This case involves a kidnapping that gets very mixed up.

9. *Bats Fly Up for Inspector Ghote* (Doubleday, 1974)
   Inspector Ghote goes to Los Angeles to find Ranjee Shahani's daughters a disciple of a slick swami in an American ashram.

10. *Filmi, Filmi, Inspector Ghote* (Doubleday, 1976)
    A film star is murdered during the production of an Indian version of *Macbeth*.

11. *Inspector Ghote Draws a Line* (Doubleday, 1979)
    When anonymous letters threaten Judge Asif Ibrahim's life, Ghote is assigned to protect him.

12. *Go West, Inspector Ghote* (Doubleday, 1981)
    Inspector Ghote goes to Los Angeles to find Ranjee Shahani's daughter, a disciple of a slick swami in an American ashram. ·

13. *The Sheriff of Bombay* (Doubleday, 1984)
    The popular sheriff of Bombay comes under suspicion for the "Ripper" murders of two women.

14. *The Body in the Billiard Room* (Viking, 1987)
    The billiards marker at the Ooty Club in the hill station of Ootacamund is murdered, and many of the club's silver trophies are missing.

15. *Dead on Time* (Mysterious, 1989)
    Murder is committed at the Tick Tock Watchworks, and a couple of watches, including Ghote's, are broken in this time-driven mystery.

Kemal, Yashar

I. Kemal is Turkey's greatest living writer. His novels and short stories about the harshness of modern peasant life are eloquent arguments for land reform and have in fact inspired Turkish progessives. Kemal has firsthand experience of the life he writes about, having picked cotton and worked in a factory to earn his way through school. At the age of five, he witnessed the brutal murder of his father. The majestic sweep of his landscape and the near mythic character of his heroes give Kemal's work an epic quality, most apparent in the two books about Ince Memed.

1. *Memed, My Hawk* (Pantheon, 1961)
   A young boy flees his village and the cruel local agha who rules it for the freedom of the hills and life as a brigand. Translated from the Turkish by Edouard Roditi.
2. *They Burn the Thistles* (Morrow, 1977)
   Memed saves the village of Vavray from a greedy agha. Translated from the Turkish by Margaret Platon.

II. Two books set in the village of Yalak show the complexities of village life through the eyes of its many residents. Muhtar Sefer is the village tyrant; Tashbash is the village activist and saint. These novels are more lyrical, less realistic than the earlier pair.

1. *Iron Earth, Copper Sky* (Morrow, 1979)
   A small cotton harvest threatens the villagers of Yalak. Published in Turkey in 1963. Translated from the Turkish by Thilda Kemal.
2. *The Undying Grass* (Morrow, 1978)
   The old woman Meryemdje is like "the undying grass" in her will to survive. Published in Turkey in 1968. Translated from the Turkish by Thilda Kemal.

Kemelman, Harry

Because Rabbi David Small uses talmudic logic to solve mysteries, his cases are simultaneously entertaining and instructive. In his home town of Barnards Crossing, Massachusetts, Police Chief Lanigan often requests the rabbi's help, but even abroad in Israel, Small has a tendency to walk into situations that need his special brand of sorting out. Kemelman ages his characters and shows the rabbi's family and congregation growing throughout the series.

Stuart Margolin played Rabbi Small and Art Carney played police chief Lanigan in *Lanigan's Rabbi,* the television version of *Friday the Rabbi Slept Late,* the pilot for a short-lived series. *Weekend with the Rabbi* (Doubleday, 1969) is an omnibus volume containing numbers 1, 2, and 3.

1. *Friday the Rabbi Slept Late* (Crown, 1964)
   When Rabbi Small is implicated in the murder of a young girl, he helps the town's Catholic police chief find the real murderer.
2. *Saturday the Rabbi Went Hungry* (Crown, 1966)
   A difficult congregational dilemma hangs on whether or not a death was suicide. The rabbi and his wife Miriam are expecting their first child.
3. *Sunday the Rabbi Stayed Home* (Putnam, 1969)
   During Passover, Rabbi Small finds himself deeply involved in the hang-ups of the younger generation who are home from college.
4. *Monday the Rabbi Took Off* (Putnam, 1972)
   In Jerusalem, Rabbi Small gets entangled in the mysterious doings of a TV commentator and some Arab militants.
5. *Tuesday the Rabbi Saw Red* (Fields, 1973)
   A bomb goes off in the dean's office at Windermere Christian College, and Rabbi Small gets to the bottom of it.
6. *Wednesday the Rabbi Got Wet* (Morrow, 1976)
   A young hippie is the suspect in this case of switched pills.
7. *Thursday the Rabbi Walked Out* (Morrow, 1976)
   There are too many suspects in the murder of nasty and anti-Semitic Ellsworth Jordan.
8. *Conversations with Rabbi Small* (Morrow, 1981)
   This book may disappoint mystery fans, but it offers plenty of Rabbi Small's theology as he counsels a young couple on marriage and conversion.

9. *Someday the Rabbi Will Leave* (Morrow, 1985)
   Rabbi Small is concerned about the arrest of a young neighbor for a hit-and-run killing.
10. *One Fine Day the Rabbi Bought a Cross* (Morrow, 1987)
    While on vacation in Jerusalem, Rabbi Small gets involved in a case concerning a Jewish fundamentalist charged with killing an Arab sympathizer.

Kent, Alexander (pseud. of Douglas Reeman)

Just one year after Forester's last Hornblower story was published post-humously, Alexander Kent's hero Richard Bolitho made his debut in *To Glory We Steer* and was immediately accepted by readers of historical naval adventure as a worthy successor to Hornblower. Bolitho's service in the British navy begins earlier than Hornblower's—young Richard is only twelve years old when he goes to sea in 1768—and so he sees action during the American Revolution. But at last count he is still less than fifty years old, though newly promoted to admiral; so fans can anticipate many adventures yet to come. Kent served in the Royal Navy during World War II and is a self-taught naval historian. Under his real name of Douglas Reeman (q.v.), he has written many modern sea stories, usually with a World War II background and a historical series about the Royal Marines.

1. *Richard Bolitho—Midshipman* (Putnam, 1975)
   In 1772, sixteen-year-old Midshipman Bolitho joins the crew of the *Gorgon,* whose mission is to investigate the slave trade off Africa's west coast.
2. *Midshipman Bolitho and the Avenger* (Putnam, 1978)
   Home from the sea on leave in Cornwall in 1773, young Bolitho gets involved with smugglers and murder.
3. *Stand into Danger* (Putnam, 1981)
   Promoted to third lieutenant in 1774, Bolitho boards the frigate *Destiny,* sails to the Caribbean in search of lost gold, and experiences his first love.
4. *In Gallant Company* (Putnam, 1977)
   In 1777 Bolitho's seamanship meets the test of war aboard the *Trojan* as she prevents supplies from reaching Washington's rebel army.

5. *Sloop of War* (Putnam, 1972)

    In 1778 Bolitho gets his first command, the sloop of war *Sparrow,* patroling the busy American coast till Cornwallis's surrender.

6. *To Glory We Steer* (Putnam, 1968)

    In 1782 Bolitho is assigned to the near-mutinous frigate *Phalarope* in the Caribbean and redeems the ship's reputation in battle against pirates.

7. *Command a King's Ship* (Putnam, 1973)

    In 1784 Captain Bolitho protects British interests aboard the frigate *Undine* in the Indian Ocean.

8. *Passage to Mutiny* (Putnam, 1970)

    In 1789 stories of the *Bounty* mutiny reach Bolitho as he faces death and danger in the South Seas.

9. *Form Line of Battle!* (Putnam, 1969)

    Captain Bolitho, in command of the *Hyperion* in 1793, joins Lord Hood's operations against French revolutionary forces. The book ends with Bolitho's marriage to Cheney Seton.

10. *Enemy in Sight!* (Putnam, 1970)

    In 1794, still aboard the *Hyperion* on blockade duty off France, Bolitho copes with a superior officer determined to avoid battle.

11. *The Flag Captain* (Putnam, 1971)

    In 1795 Bolitho serves as flag captain to a stubborn admiral in a squadron attempting to penetrate the Mediterranean.

12. *Signal—Close Action!* (Putnam, 1974)

    Promoted to commodore in 1798, Bolitho is in charge of a squadron assigned to intercept supplies for Napoleon.

13. *The Inshore Squadron* (Putnam, 1979)

    During the battle of Copenhagen in 1800, Lord Nelson leads the British to victory. Now Rear Admiral Bolitho's wounds send him ashore, where he meets and falls in love with a cousin of his long dead wife.

14. *A Tradition of Victory* (Putnam, 1982)

    In 1801, Bolitho and Belinda are separated on the eve of their wedding, and Bolitho is captured by the French.

15. *Success to the Brave* (Putnam, 1983)

    In 1802, Vice-Admiral Bolitho sails on the man-of-war Achates to the Caribbean to return the island of San Felipe to the French.

16. *Colors Aloft!* (Putnam, 1986)

    Admiral Bolitho takes command of a squadron of ships bound for active duty in the Mediterranean.

Keyes, Frances Parkinson

Mrs. Keyes's solid stories, frequently set against an interesting Louisiana background, had quite a large readership in the 1940s and 1950s. Today's readers will find themselves quickly absorbed in her felicitous blend of romance, history, and suspense. *Steamboat Gothic* (Messner, 1952) is perhaps her best-known novel. The pair listed below tell of life in the fertile southwestern area of Louisiana where rice plantations flourished.

1. *Blue Camellia* (Messner, 1957)
   Brent Winslow and his wife and small daughter move from Illinois to Cajun country Louisiana in the 1880s.
2. *Victorine* (Messner, 1958)
   Brent's grandson Prosper is entangled in a murder that threatens his romance with the beautiful Victorine during the mid-1920s. English title: *Gold Slippers.*

Kienzle, William X.

Father Robert Koesler is a priest in the Detroit diocese, editor of a Catholic weekly, reader of mysteries, and keen amateur sleuth. He bears some resemblance to his creator, William X. Kienzle, one-time Detroit parish priest, former editor of a Catholic newspaper, and mystery writer. The Father Koesler stories are in the puzzle mysteries tradition with an urban American setting and an undercurrent of social and religious commentary. Donald Sutherland played Father Koesler in the 1987 movie version of *The Rosary Murders.* For another priest/detective, see Ralph McInerney's Father Dowling (q.v.).

1. *The Rosary Murders* (Andrews, 1979)
   Lieutenant Koznicki of the Detroit police enlists Father Koesler's aid in solving a series of murders of priests and nuns.
2. *Death Wears a Red Hat* (Andrews, 1980)
   A murderer is decapitating his victims, and placing their heads on church statues.
3. *Mind over Murder* (Andrews, 1981)
   Tommy Thompson, head of the Roman Catholic matrimonial court

in Detroit, is missing, but his revealing diary is published in the *Detroit News.*

4. *Assault with Intent* (Andrews, 1982)
   Father Koesler investigates an apparent plot to kill the priests in Detroit-area seminaries.

5. *Shadow of Death* (Andrews, 1983)
   An attempt is made on the life of Archbishop Boyle of Detroit, traveling to Rome for his investiture as Cardinal, as part of a plot to decimate the College of Cardinals.

6. *Kill and Tell* (Andrews, 1984)
   Emma Hoffman drinks a poisoned Rob Roy cocktail intended for her husband Frank, a Detroit automobile executive not universally loved.

7. *Sudden Death* (Andrews, 1985)
   Hank "The Hun" Hunsinger, pro football star, is murdered, and there is no lack of suspects.

8. *Deathbird* (Andrews, 1986)
   Father Koesler believes someone is trying to kill Sister Eileen, chief of a troubled inner-city Catholic hospital.

9. *Marked for Murder* (Andrews, 1988)
   A man in clerical garb is ritually murdering prostitutes in Detroit's inner city.

10. *Eminence* (Andrews, 1989)
    A local monk is attracting media attention through his alleged miraculous cures.

Kirst, Hans Helmut

Gunner Herbert Asch, the engaging hero of these satires on German army life, can charm, bluff and lie his way out of any scrape, while his guileless friend Vierbein gets caught in one snafu after another. "M.A.S.H." fans and others will enjoy the ingenious way the young soldier subverts military discipline and makes fools of his commanding officers. The Nazi German setting seems oddly incongruous with Kirst's essentially comic view-his officers are inept buffoons rather than truly menacing. But the drudgery and mindless routine of military life is portrayed realistically enough, and Gunner Asch's rebellion is a heartening story.

1. *The Revolt of Gunner Asch* (Little, 1955)
   Set in an army post in a small German town just before World

War II, this story concerns Gunner Asch's revolt against the injustices of military life. Originally published in German in 1954 under the title *Zero Eight Fifteen*. Translated by Robert Kee.

2. *Forward Gunner Asch!* (Little, 1956)
   The misadventures of Asch, Vierbein, Schulz, and the others continue on the Russian front. Originally published in Germany under the title *Gunner Asch Goes to War*. Translated by Robert Kee.

3. *The Return of Gunner Asch* (Little, 1957)
   As the war ends, Asch, now a lieutenant, finishes a private war of his own as he tracks down the two Nazi officers who ordered the troop on a last, doomed attack. Translated by Robert Kee.

4. *What Became of Gunner Asch* (Little, 1964)
   The post war years find Asch a hotel owner and mayor of a small West German town, which is the seat of two rival garrisons. Translated by J. Maxwell Brownjohn.

Kita Morio (pseud. of Saito Sukichi)

Since its publication in Japan in 1964, *The House of Nire (Nireke no hitobito)* has been regarded by Japanese critics as a comic masterpiece of Japanese society in the twentieth century. Based to some extent on Kita Morio's own family history, it describes the rise and fall of the Nire family and the family-run Nire mental hospital in Tokyo. Both family and hospital were founded by the eccentric Kiichiro Nire, whose fondness for all things German inspired his unique approach to mental illness. The Nire saga from 1918 to 1946 is very funny, but it has its tragic aspects as well, particularly during World War II and its aftermath.

1. *The House of Nire* (Kodansha, 1984)
   Kiichiro Nire changes his family name, and founds the Nire Mental Hospital, which is really run by his tough-minded wife. Covers 1918 to 1941. Translation from the Japanese by Dennis Keene of Parts 1 and 2 of *Nireke no hitobito* (1964).

2. *The Fall of the House of Nire* (Kodansha, 1985)
   Kiichiro's adopted son Tetsukichi ineptly runs the hospital after Kiichiro's death, while Kiichiro's children and grandchildren are scattered by World II. Covers 1941 to 1946. Translation from the Japanese by Dennis Keene of Part 3 of *Nireke no hitobito* (1964).

Kuniczak, W. S. (Wiselaw Stanislaw)

W. S. Kuniczak, Polish-American journalist and novelist, has written a trilogy about the tragedy of Poland in World War II, when it was invaded and millions of Poles were killed or forced into exile. The novels' epic sweep and large cast of both historical and fictional characters have led some critics to describe them as "Tolstoyan." Some of the characters appear in more than one of the novels; the heroic Polish general Janusz Prus appears in all three. The saga is based on extensive research as well as the personal recollections of the author, who was born in Poland, and lived through many of the events he describes.

1. *The Thousand Hour Day* (Dial, 1967)
   This covers the first thousand hours of World War II, when the German blitzkrieg invaded Poland in September 1939, and the Polish army fought a desperate holding action until their final surrender.
2. *The March* (Doubleday, 1979)
   This volume describes what happened to the Poles when the Soviet Union "liberated" eastern Poland in 1939, massacred thousands, and sent thousands more into exile.
3. *Valedictory* (Doubleday, 1983)
   Polish pilots who escaped to England form the famed 303rd Squadron of the RAF, then shoot down hundreds of German planes during the war.

Kurtz, Katherine

I. The world of the Eleven Kingdoms created by American fantasy writer Katherine Kurtz has expanded into its fourth trilogy. It tells of the struggles between the two, human races that inhabit the Kingdom of Gwynedd, a country that strongly resembles medieval Wales. The Deryni are mutants with magical abilities, who are distrusted and feared by the ordinary folk and their priests. Some Deryni use their powers for the common good, while others are corrupt and seek only self-advancement. *Deryni Archives*, an irregularly issued fanzine, contains articles by Kurtz describing the origins of the series and reprints of some Deryni stories. *The Deryni Archives* (Ballantine, 1986) is a collection of short stories.

The Legends of Camber of Culdi was the second trilogy published, but comes first chronologically. It relates the life of Camber of Culdi, a good Deryni. whose deeds live on in legend after his death.

1. *Camber of Culdi* (Ballantine, 1976)
   Deryni Camber of Culdi helps to overthrow the evil Deryni king
   Imre, and restore the rightful heir, Cinhil Haldane, to the throne of
   Gwynedd.
2. *Saint Camber* (Ballantine, 1978)
   Ariella, sister of the deceased King Imre, plots war against King
   Cinhil, who is nursing a grudge against Camber for removing him
   from his quiet monastery life.
3. *Camber the Heretic* (Ballantine, 1981)
   The period from the death of King Cinhil to Camber's own death sees
   the start of open persecution of the Deryni.

II. *The Heirs of Saint Camber,* the fourth trilogy to be published, is the second chronologically. The one volume written so far deals with the campaign
to destroy the Deryni after the death of Camber.

1. *The Harrowing of Gwynedd* (Ballantine, 1989)
   The Cambrian Council must prevent the regents of young King Airoy
   from killing off all the Deryni leaders.

III. *The Chronicles of the Deryni* take place some two centuries after the
death of Camber. The Deryni have been outlawed, and are living incognito,
but plotting to usurp the throne of Gwynedd. Duke Alaric Morgan, a half-
Deryni, helps teenaged Prince Kelson, the rightful heir, to succeed to the
throne, but Kelson and Morgan must deal with strife within and without the
kingdom through the remainder of the trilogy. Some readers recommend
that this trilogy be read before *The Legends of Camber of Culdi.*

1. *Deryni Rising* (Ballantine, 1970)
   Evil Deryni sorceress Charissa assassinates King Brion and tries to take
   over the kingdom.
2. *Deryni Checkmate* (Ballantine, 1972)
   The clergy of Gwynedd try to frame Alaric Morgan on treason
   charges.
3. *High Deryni* (Ballantine, 1973)
   Civil war almost breaks out before the clergy and the Deryni unite to
   resist the invasion of King Wencit of Torenth.

IV. *The Histories of King Kelson* is the last trilogy chronologically. It shows
King Kelson battling with the anti-Deryni clergy, fighting wars with other
kingdoms, and trying to rehabilitate the memory of Saint Camber.

1. *The Bishop's Heir* (Ballantine, 1984)
   King Kelson is challenged by anti-Deryni fanatic Archbishop Loris and a rival noble family.
2. *The King's Justice* (Ballantine, 1985)
   Kelson continues his war against the pretenders to the throne of Meara and anti-Deryni rebel Edmund Loris.
3. *The Quest for Saint Camber* (Ballantine, 1986)
   The Deryni attain high positions in court and church as King Kelson strives to restore Saint Camber to his rightful place in the Gwynedd pantheon.

L'Amour, Louis

With over eighty novels to his credit, Louis L'Amour has surpassed even Zane Grey in popularity and sales. Though L'Amour preferred to call his novels "stories of the frontier" rather than westerns, they have all the traditional elements of the genre: lots of shoot-outs and hard-riding and good solid storytelling. L'Amour took pride in giving his stories authentic settings and period detail, and his treatment of the American Indian avoided stereotype.

Before his death in 1988, L'Amour wrote *The Sackett Companion* (Bantam, 1988), which helps sort out the various branches of the Sackett family tree as well as the two other families whose members intertwine with the Sacketts: the French Talon family and the Irish Chantry family.

Media adaptations of L'Amour's works include an NBC-TV mini-series based on the Sackett series and the 1953 movie "Hondo," starring John Wayne, which is based on the book of the same name (one of L'Amour's many non-Sackett books). L'Amour also wrote the novelization of the movie *How the West Was Won*, and early in his career produced some of the Hopalong Cassidy series under the pseudonym Tex Burns.

Education of a Wandering Man (Bantam, 1989) is an autobiography that fans will not want to miss. *The Sacketts: Beginning of a Dynasty* (Saturday Review, 1976) is an omnibus volume containing numbers 6, 7, and 8.

1. *Sackett's Land* (Saturday Review, 1974)
   This starts in 1599, and shows Barnabas Sackett on the run in Elizabethan London pursued by the nasty Rupert Genester.
2. *To the Far Blue Mountains* (Saturday Review, 1976)
   Barnabas and Abigail settle on the James River in Virginia, fight off Indians, and raise a family.
3. *The Warrior's Path* (Bantam, 1980)
   Kin-Ring Sackett and his brother Yance make a journey through

treacherous territory to rescue a settler's beautiful daughter. Set in 1630 in what is now Boston.

4. *Jubal Sackett* (Bantam, 1985)
Jubal Sackett, third son of Barnabas, moves west from the Carolinas to what is now New Mexico, where he kills a mastodon and wins a Natchez princess.

5. *Ride the River* (Bantam, 1983)
This tells the story of Echo Sackett, youngest female descendant of Kin-Ring.

6. *The Daybreakers* (Bantam, 1960)
Tye Sackett tells the story of how he and his brother Orrin leave Tennessee for the Great Plains and beyond.

7. *Sackett* (Bantam, 1961)
William Tell Sackett, brother of Orrin and Tye, meets the beautiful Ange in Colorado, and brings her back to become his wife.

8. *Lando* (Bantam, 1962)
In pursuit of buried gold in Mexico, Lando Sackett runs out of luck. Six years in a Mexican prison give him a taste for revenge that nothing will stop.

9. *Mojave Crossing* (Bantam, 1964)
Trouble, in the shape of a black-eyed woman, finds Tell Sackett as he crosses the Colorado with his saddlebags full of gold.

10. *The Sackett Brand* (Bantam, 1965)
In 1877, Tell Sackett and his wife are shot, but his Sackett relatives from high and low come to his aid.

11. *The Lonely Men* (Bantam, 1969)
Tell Sackett is lured into Apache country by the icy beauty of his brother's wife.

12. *Treasure Mountain* (Bantam, 1972)
Orrin Sackett runs into trouble in New Orleans when he tries to investigate his father's disappearance twenty years earlier.

13. *Mustang Man* (Bantam, 1966)
Nolan Sackett, on the run from the law, is slowed down by women—first by the sly Sylvie who tries to poison him, then by Penelope.

14. *Galloway* (Bantam, 1970)
Galloway Sackett goes searching for his brother Flagon, last seen naked and hand-tied by his Indian captors.

15. *The Sky-Liners* (Bantam, 1967)
Black Fletchen is coming for the Sackett boys—Galloway and Flagon—with the most expensive hired guns in the country.

16. *The Man from the Broken Hills* (Bantam, 1975)
Milo Talon tracks a man through the post-Civil War West

17. *Ride the Dark Trail* (Bantam, 1972)
    Old Emily Talon (nee Sackett) of the MT Ranch needs help.
18. *Lonely on the Mountain* (Bantam, 1980)
    Tell, Tyrel, and Orrin Sackett herd cattle across the Dakota plains toward Canada, through trails never crossed before.

Langton, Jane

Fans of Asey Mayo will enjoy meeting Homer Kelly, another Massachusetts sleuth, whose territory includes the affluent suburban towns northwest of Boston—Bedford, Concord, Lincoln, and the fictional "Nashoba." Homer is a "gentleman" detective, just as likely to quote Thoreau as to draw on his past experience as a professional detective in a District Attorney's office. Now retired, Homer co-teaches an American literature class with his wife Mary at Harvard, and leisurely unravels the mysteries that inevitably come his way. Strong on character and local color, the books are illustrated with wonderful line drawings by the author.

1. *The Transcendental Murder* (Harper, 1964)
   This first case shows Homer meeting his future wife Mary as he investigates the murders of some leading authorities on the Transcendentalists. Variant title: *The Minute Man Murder*.
2. *Dark Nantucket Moon* (Harper, 1975)
   A murder occurs on Nantucket during an eclipse of the sun, and Homer comes to the defense of the accused.
3. *Memorial Hall Murder* (Harper, 1978)
   An explosion in Harvard's Memorial Hall disturbs a rehearsal of Handel's *Messiah*, and supplies a headless corpse for Homer to investigate.
4. *Natural Enemy* (Ticknor, 1982)
   Young John Hand is pursuing his study of spiders and working as a summer handyman when he finds a need for his uncle Homer's expert help with some puzzling circumstances.
5. *Emily Dickinson Is Dead* (St. Martin's, 1984)
   Arson and murder shock the academics assembled for a Dickinson symposium in Amherst, but Homer is on hand to set things right.
6. *Good and Dead* (St. Martin's, 1987)
   Too many deaths among the parishioners of Old West Church in Nashoba give Homer an extraordinary case to ponder.

7. *Murder at the Gardner* (St. Martin's, 1988)
   Is the prankster haunting Boston's Isabella Stewart Gardner Museum out for profit or revenge?

Lasswell, Mary

Three old girls who live in a southern California junkyard captured the affection of wartime readers all across America. Toothless Mrs. Feeley, the salty owner of the junkyard named "Noah's Ark," and her friends Mrs. Rasmussen, a marvelously resourceful cook, and Miss Tinkham, a retired music teacher, make the most of reduced circumstances and wartime shortages with high spirits and plenty of cold beer. Readers with a thirst for nostalgia will find the trio's high jinks still hit the spot; others will find pretzels more nutritious. George Price's cartoon illustrations add to the fun.

1. *Suds in Your Eye* (Houghton, 1942)
   In their first adventure, the three ladies play cupid for their Spanish teacher, Miss Kate Logan.
2. *High Time* (Houghton, 1947)
   Further high jinks as the ladies, determined to do their part in the war effort, donate blood, babysit, and take in hungry boarders.
3. *One on the House* (Houghton, 1949)
   The merry trio visits New York and Newark, New Jersey, where they rescue a barroom from the jaws of bankruptcy while the owner is in the hospital.
4. *Wait for the Wagon* (Houghton, 1951)
   This installment follows the ladies on their cross-country drive back to California in their 1926 Cadillac.
5. *Tooner Schooner* (Houghton, 1953)
   While serving as crew of a chartered ex-tuna schooner, the ladies take time to straighten out the captain's love life.
6. *Let's Go for Broke* (Houghton, 1962)
   The beer-loving ladies renovate a dilapidated Victorian house and find their little community much enlarged.

Lathen, Emma (pseud. of Mary J. Latis and Martha Hennissart)

As everybody knows by now, Emma Lathen is really two Boston businesswomen, now retired, Mary J. Latis and Martha Hennissart. Their entertaining mystery series mixes business, banking, and crime with style and wit. John Putnam Thatcher, who is senior vice-president of New York's Sloan Guaranty Trust, the world's third largest bank, is their suave and perceptive amateur detective. They chose a banker because "there is nothing on God's earth a banker can't get into." Not incidentally, Lathen fans will pick up a lot of solid information about the various industries used as settings for each book. *Banking on Murder* (Macmillan, 1984) is an omnibus volume containing numbers 5, 6, and 7. Latis and Hennissart have also written under the name R. B. Dominic (q.v.).

1. *Banking on Death* (Macmillan, 1961)
   Thatcher's first case involves a missing heir, a murder, and some funny business in industrial textiles.
2. *A Place for Murder* (Macmillan, 1963)
   Thatcher solves a murder at a dog show in Connecticut.
3. *Accounting for Murder* (Macmillan, 1964)
   A murder at the National Calculating Corporation is Thatcher's next case.
4. *Murder Makes the Wheels Go Round* (Macmillan, 1966)
   In Detroit to investigate the auto industry as a potential investment for the Sloan Guaranty Trust, Thatcher finds a corpse stashed in a bulletproof car.
5. *Death Shall Overcome* (Macmillan, 1966)
   Trouble on the New York Stock Exchange begins when black millionaire Edward Parry buys a seat.
6. *Murder Against the Grain* (Macmillan, 1967)
   A phony wheat broker collects a check for $985,000, and all hell breaks loose on the big Russian wheat sale.
7. *A Stitch in Time* (Macmillan, 1968)
   The medical industry comes in for some scrutiny in this case involving a possible suicide and $100,000 in insurance.
8. *Come to Dust* (Simon & Schuster, 1968)
   The peculiarties of fund raising by a small New Hampshire college become evident as Thatcher tries to find out who stole a $50,000 bearer bond intended for the college.
9. *When in Greece* (Simon & Schuster, 1969)
   A Greek colonel's revolution spells trouble for the Sloan's investment in a million-dollar hydroelectric project.
10. *Murder to Go* (Simon & Schuster, 1969)
    Trouble in the fast-food industry starts with some very bad eating at a nationwide chain called Chicken Tonight.

11. *Pick Up Sticks* (Simon & Schuster, 1970)
    Hard-sell real estate in New Hampshire comes to grief.
12. *Ashes to Ashes* (Simon & Schuster, 1971)
    The funeral industry and a bankrupt parochial school share the spotlight in this case.
13. *The Longer the Thread* (Simon & Schuster, 1971)
    This look at the ladies' garment industry in Puerto Rico focuses on some very suspicious accidents at Slax Unlimited.
14. *Murder without Icing* (Simon & Schuster, 1972)
    Multiple murder and professional ice hockey are the ingredients.
15. *Sweet and Low* (Simon & Schuster, 1974)
    The cocoa exchange and the candy industry are spotlighted when two high-ranking executives of the Dryer Chocolate Company are murdered.
16. *By Hook or by Crook* (Simon & Schuster, 1975)
    The Oriental rug business gives its exotic flavor to this case.
17. *Double, Double, Oil and Trouble* (Simon & Schuster, 1978)
    Murder and kidnapping trouble the North Sea offshore oil fields.
18. *Going for the Gold* (Simon & Schuster, 1981)
    Phony traveler's checks and a murdered skier take Thatcher to the winter Olympics at Lake Placid, New York.
19. *Green Grow the Dollars* (Simon & Schuster, 1982)
    The research and development of a new super tomato keep Thatcher and Miss Corso busy in this case of dirty dealings in the mail-order nursery business.
20. *Something in the Air* (Simon & Schuster, 1988)
    Sloan Guaranty Trust is concerned that Boston-based commuter airline Sparrow Flyways may be a fly-by-night operation.

Lawrence, D. H. (David Herbert)

The 1970 film *Women in Love,* starring Glenda Jackson, Alan Bates, and Oliver Reed, was as dense and dramatic as the novel it was based upon. Readers turning to the original for clarification found that the author's lush prose lapsed occasionally into impenetrability. But Lawrence's insistence on giving his characters a sexual dimension makes his books come alive for modern readers. What is shocking now is that *The Rainbow* could ever have been condemned as obscene, even in 1915. In 1989 *The Rainbow* was made into a film starring Sammi Davis and Glenda Jackson.

1. *The Rainbow* (Viking, 1915)
   This covers three generations of the Brangwen family of farmers and craftsmen who live in the coal-mining town of Nottinghamshire. Tom Brangwen marries Lydia, whose daughter Anna becomes the mother of Ursula and Gudrun.
2. *Women in Love* (Viking, 1920)
   Ursula and Gudrun, young women of the emancipated twentieth century, seek love and meaning in life. Gudrun is said to have been based on Katherine Mansfield.

Leahy, Syrell Rogovin

This is a family saga covering two generations of the Wolfe family, a rich, distinguished Jewish-American clan that carries a curse: bad genes that sometimes produce defective children. Regina and Judy Wolfe, each in her generation, must come to terms with the "family secret," and eventually realize that family ties and love between family members is more important than individual happiness.

1. *Family Ties* (Putnam, 1982)
   Rich, well-bred Regina Wolfe cannot marry her cousin Jerold because of the dark secret that haunts her family. Set in pre-World War I America.
2. *Family Truths* (Putnam, 1984)
   In 1959, Judy Wolfe drops her law school plans when she learns of her father's long-standing love affair with his cousin Regina.

Le Carré, John (pseud. of David Cornwall)

Alec Guinness made a perfect George Smiley in the British production of "Tinker, Tailor, Soldier, Spy," shown here on public television. Short, stodgy, and bespectacled, he is a man described by his frequently unfaithful wife, Ann, as "breathtakingly ordinary." But Smiley is such a master of espionage that he is always being dragged out of retirement and his study of obscure German poets for one last assignment. Some readers claim that they can actually follow all the convolutions of Le Carré's corkscrew plots, but even readers who miss a turn or two will feel the suspense and excitement that Le Carré spins out so exquisitely. Novels 1 and 2 below are bound together as *The Incongruous Spy* (Walker, 1962).

1. *Call for the Dead* (Walker, 1962)
   Smiley solves a puzzle involving a twisted former hero of the German underground and a once-beautiful woman with a secret. Variant title: *The Deadly Affair.*

2. *A Murder of Quality* (Walker, 1962)
   A baffling, bloody murder of a teacher's wife brings Smiley to an ancient and renowned public school in Dorsetshire.

3. *The Spy Who Came In from the Cold* (Coward, 1964)
   This story of Alec Leamas's last assignment is a classic of the genre. Smiley finds this operation distasteful and is only a shadowy figure throughout. Of particular note to librarians is the nasty stereotype of a librarian, Miss Crail, whom Leamas meets on page 36.

4. *The Looking Glass War* (Coward, 1965)
   Spying seems an extraordinarily pedestrian and seedy business in this novel. Smiley plays a very peripheral part.

5. *Tinker, Tailor, Soldier, Spy* (Knopf, 1974)
   Smiley is shown as a consummate spymaster as he flushes out the mole who has burrowed to the top of British Intelligence.

6. *The Honorable Schoolboy* (Knopf, 1977)
   As head of the Circus, Smiley sends Jerry Westerby, the honorable schoolboy, on a mission to Hong Kong.

7. *Smiley's People* (Knopf, 1979)
   Smiley has a final confrontation with Karla, his mortal enemy and opposite number in the Soviet Union.

Lehmann, Rosamond

These two novels about the Curtis sisters, Kate and Olivia, have the charm of elegant miniatures. In beautiful but spare prose, Lehmann shows the world unfolding for seventeen-year-old Olivia as she enters society. The coltish young girl is awkward and uncomfortable in the flame-colored silk dress that she chose especially for her first ball. At the evening's end, Kate has made a conquest, and Olivia has had a less conventional kind of success.

1. *Invitation to the Waltz* (Holt, 1932)
   In the winter of 1920, Olivia Curtis attends her first dress ball with her sister Kate; her young cousin Reggie is her escort.

2. *The Weather in the Streets* (Reynal, 1936)
   Ten years later, Kate is a happy wife and mother. Olivia and Rollo, who have been less fortunate, meet again.

L'Engle, Madeleine (pseud. of Madeleine L'Engle Camp Franklin)

Madeleine L'Engle is best known for her award-winning science fiction and fantasy for children and young adults. *A Wrinkle in Time* won the 1963 Newbery Award. She has also written several books for adults, including this pair of novels about concert pianist Katherine (Katya) Forrester. The events of these novels are separated by some four decades, but with flashbacks, they portray the transition of a lonely, artistic girl into an accomplished professional artist.

1. *The Small Rain* (Vanguard, 1945)
   The lonely childhood and adolescence of pianist Katherine Forrester is split between Greenwich Village and a French boarding school. Reprinted by Farrar, Straus in 1984.
2. *A Severed Wasp* (Farrar, 1982)
   Decades later, Katherine Forrester Vigueras retires from the concert stage and returns to New York, where she agrees to play one last benefit recital for an old friend who has become an Episcopal priest.

Lessing, Doris

I. Lessing is generally regarded as one of the major postwar women novelists, though it was only after the success of *The Golden Notebook* (Simon & Schuster, 1962) that her work caught on with American readers. The Children of Violence series attracted an immediate following when its first installments appeared in the United States in 1965. This five-volume series takes up the story of Martha Quest in 1938, when she is a rebellious seventeen-year-old living with her middle-class English parents in South Africa. Presumably somewhat autobiographical, the account shows the gradual development of the central character's feminist consciousness and leftist political convictions. The omnibus volume entitled *Children of Violence*, volume 1 (Simon & Schuster, 1965) contains numbers 1 and 2 lis-

246

ted below. *Children of Violence*, volume 2 (Simon & Schuster, 1966) contains numbers 3 and 4.

1. *Martha Quest* (M. Joseph, London, 1952)
Martha leaves her parents for a job in the city, where she falls in with a fast crowd of politically active young people and marries Douglas Knowell.
2. *A Proper Marriage* (M. Joseph, London, 1954)
Martha has a short, unhappy marriage and bears a daughter, Caroline, as World War II begins.
3. *A Ripple from the Storm* (M. Joseph, London, 1958)
As a Communist party member, Martha attends meetings and sells pamphlets while her marriage to Anton Hesse slowly dies.
4. *Landlocked* (MacGibbon & Kee, London, 1965)
As the war ends, Martha has an affair with Thomas Stern; she decides to leave Anton and make a new start in England.
5. *Four-Gated City* (Knopf, 1969)
In London, Martha sinks into madness in a commune of young people as Britain moves ever closer to its disastrous finale.

II. Lessing's Canopus in Argos series is decidedly different from the Martha Quest books. Visionary parables rather than true science fiction, these books provide a forum for her provocative views of the future of Great Britain and civilization in general.

1. *Shikasta: Canopus in Argos—Archives* (Knopf, 1979)
Successful but doomed social experiments are performed by the benevolent Canopean Empire on the colonists of Planet 5, Shikasta (Earth).
2. *The Marriages between Zones Three, Four and Five* (Knopf, 1980)
Sexual politics in Lessing's Canopean world are illustrated by the story of the marriage of arrogant Ben Ata and the radiant queen of the Third Zone.
3. *The Sirian Experiments: Report by Ambien II of the Five* (Knopf, 1981)
The Sirians, rival of the Canopeans, are the focus as narrator Ambien II tells of the dreadful experiments she leads and of her own eventual conversion.
4. *The Making of the Representative for Planet 8* (Knopf, 1982)
Doeg, a Representative on Planet 8, recalls the coming of the Ice Age, the people's hopes for salvation, and their final destruction.

5. *Documents Relating to the Sentimental Agents in the Volyen Empire* (Knopf, 1983)
   The Canopian agent Klorathy reports to his superior Johor about the collapse of the five-world Volyen Empire.

Note: Lessing has published a pair of novels under the pseudonym of Jane Somers (q.v.).

Lewin, Michael Z.

I. Lewin has written in *Murder Ink* (Workman, 1977) that his first detective story was begun as a takeoff to amuse his family. He chose Albert as a particularly undetective-like first name, and set him to work in his hometown of Indianapolis. Like many other fictional private eyes, Albert Samson is a seedy loner who hides his basic decency behind a wisecracking exterior. He is somewhat less inclined to violence than some of his predecessors, and his mid-American locale is a pleasant change from California. Albert has now starred in six books, and appears as a minor character in the three books featuring Leroy Powder.

1. *Ask the Right Question* (Putnam, 1971)
   The search for sixteen-year-old Eloise Crystal's biological father leads Samson into a closetful of family skeletons.
2. *The Way We Die Now* (Putnam, 1973)
   Rosetta Tomerak comes to Samson for help when her Vietnam vet husband is charged with manslaughter.
3. *The Enemies Within* (Knopf, 1974)
   Samson investigates another investigator who is harassing an antiques dealer in a case that involves some very ambiguous relationships.
4. *The Silent Salesman* (Knopf, 1978)
   A frantic woman hires Samson to find out why she isn't allowed to visit her brother in the hospital. Samson's teenaged daughter Sam appears in this volume.
5. *Missing Woman* (Knopf, 1981)
   The search for Priscilla Prynne is the thread that unravels a larger mystery.
6. *Out of Season* (Morrow, 1984)
   Paula Beller, wife of a bank executive, finds that her birth certificate is false when she applies for a passport, so Samson is called in to uncover the real facts of her birth.

II. Leroy Powder is head of the Indianapolis police department's Missing Persons Bureau. Powder is more abrasive and confrontational than the introspective Samson, but he is honest and tenacious in his efforts to get to the bottom of his cases.

1. *Night Cover* (Knopf, 1976)
   Leroy Powder stars in this case of unsolved murders and a bizarre school crime. He crosses Samson's path at times.
2. *Hard Line* (Morrow, 1982)
   Leroy Powder and his new sergeant, wheelchair bound Carollee Fleetwood, work together on cases involving a missing wife, an attempted suicide, some unidentified bodies, and the criminal activities of Powder's son Ricky.
3. *Late Payments* (Morrow, 1986)
   A twelve-year-old boy asks Powder to find his father. Powder is looking for his own son, who has broken his parole.

Lewis, C. S. (Clive Staples)

Not to be confused with Wyndham Lewis's allegorical series (q.v.), this trilogy by the English author and Christian moralist is compulsively readable. Even readers not interested in theological speculation will find his stories inventive, funny, and satisfying adventures that blend fantasy, science fiction, and allegorical elements. C. S. Lewis is also the author of the highly regarded Narnia series of children's books.

1. *Out of the Silent Planet* (Macmillan, 1938)
   Dr. Ransom, a Cambridge philologist, is transported to the planet Malacandra (Mars) and makes some surprising discoveries.
2. *Perelandra* (Macmillan, 1944)
   Dr. Ransom is ordered to Perelandra (Venus) to fight his old enemy Weston again, this time in a reenactment of the Adam-and-Eve struggle.
3. *That Hideous Strength: A Modern Fairy-Tale for Grown-ups* (Macmillan, 1946)
   Ransom and Weston again engage in the struggle between good and evil. Though the setting is an ordinary English village, some extraordinary beings visit and liven things up.

Lewis, Wyndham

The Apes of God, a satire on dilettantism in art and literature in London in the twenties, is the best known work by this English writer and painter. Even his critics will admit that Lewis was a droll satirist and a master of striking imagery. But few will agree with Walter Allen who, in *The Modern Novel* (Dutton, 1964), calls The Human Age, Lewis's unfinished tetralogy, "the most remarkable piece of imaginative writing in English of the past two decades." Most will find the series thoroughly unreadable or worse. Lewis was an early supporter of Hitler. The series had a projected last volume, never published, that was to have been called *The Trial of Man* and to have dealt with the final conflict between the human and the divine.

1. *The Childermass* (Chatto, London, 1928)
   This Judgment Day fantasy starring James Pullman includes parodies of Gertrude Stein and James Joyce.
2. *The Human Age*, volume 2 (Methuen, London, 1955)
   a. *Monstre Gai*
   Pullman and Sutters enter the Magnetic City and find that it is not heaven but a kind of purgatory.
   b. *Malign Fiesta*
   This story is set in Matapolis, which is really Hell; Lord Sammael is the devil.

Linington, Elizabeth

Elizabeth Linington's police procedurals under her own name haven't been as numerous or as popular as those written under the pseudonyms of Dell Shannon and Lesley Egan, although they are just as well written and involving. Sergeant Ivor Maddox of the Los Angeles Police Department (Hollywood branch) and detectives D'Arcy and Rodriguez are the main continuing characters. Love interest is provided by policewoman Sue Carstairs, who becomes Sue Maddox midway through the series. The first three or four volumes in the series were published in England under the pseudonym of Anne Blaisdell. No annotations are provided as each novel pursues several investigations, although it should be noted that Maddox uses an old Agatha Christie novel to solve the main mystery in *Greenmask!*

1. *Greenmask!* (Harper, 1964)
2. *No Evil Angel* (Harper, 1964)
3. *Date with Death* (Harper, 1966)

4. *Something Wrong* (Harper, 1967)
5. *Policeman's Lot* (Harper, 1968)
6. *Practice to Deceive* (Harper, 1971)
7. *Crime by Chance* (Lippincott, 1973)
8. *Perchance of Death* (Doubleday, 1977)
9. *No Villain Need Be* (Doubleday, 1979)
10. *Consequence of Crime* (Doubleday, 1980)
11. *Skeletons in the Closet* (Doubleday, 1982)
12. *Felony Report* (Doubleday, 1984)
13. *Strange Felony* (Doubleday, 1986)

Llewellyn, Richard

How Green Was My Valley, Richard Llewellyn's lyrical novel, won unanimous praise when it was published in 1940. In telling the story of the Morgan family, he gives a vivid picture of a Welsh coal-mining community from the first days of its new prosperity in the nineteenth century to the eventual desolation of both the countryside and its populace. Though their life is hard and often tragic, Llewellyn shows their courage, independence, and lusty humor. The 1941 film version, starring Walter Pidgeon and Maureen O'Hara, won the Academy Award for best picture.

1. *How Green Was My Valley* (Macmillan, 1940)
   Huw Morgan's reminiscences about his boyhood in a Welsh mining town include a loving portrait of his gentle tyrant of a father.
2. *Up, into the Singing Mountain* (Doubleday, 1960)
   Huw, now a skilled cabinetmaker, builds a life for himself in a Welsh community in Patagonia.
3. *Down Where the Moon Is Small* (Doubleday, 1966)
   Huw reminisces about the partnership with Moishe that brought him wealth and the tragic loss of his wife and son.
4. *Green, Green My Valley Now* (Doubleday, 1975)
   Huw, with his second wife, returns to Wales, renovates an ancient house, and finds himself involved with the IRA.

Lodge, David

David Lodge's year as a visiting English professor at the University of California, Berkeley, in 1969 must have been the inspiration for the hilarious

Anglo-American relations depicted in this series of academic novels. Morris Zapp, a manic American super-professor from California's Euphoria University and Philip Sparrow, a mild-mannered English don from Rummidge University in the English Midlands, are the main characters in the first book, and make short appearances in the sequels. Lodge recently retired as professor of English literature at the University of Birmingham and is the author of many novels, non-fiction, and critical works.

1. *Changing Places* (Secker & Warburg, London, 1975)
   Subtitled *A Tale of Two Campuses*, this tells of the eventful year when American Morris Zapp and British Philip Sparrow traded jobs. Published in paperback in the United States by Penguin, 1979.
2. *Small World: An Academic Romance* (Macmillan, 1985)
   Young Irish professor Persse McGarriggle pursues the beautiful but elusive Angelica Pabst around the academic conference circuit.
3. *Nice Work* (Viking, 1989)
   Robin Penrose, youngest teacher in Rummidge University's English Department, is drafted for an industrial exchange program and finds herself attracted to the factory manager with whom she must work one day a week.

Lodi, Maria

Paris in the 1860s is the dramatic setting for this readable three-volume romance. During the dictatorship of Napoleon III the city is a seething mixture of glittering salons and miserable slums. Charlotte Morel is a beautiful and headstrong provincial girl who comes to Paris as a young bride. The dashing journalist Thomas Becque, one of the fearless few who dare to criticize the government, meets Charlotte while protecting her from street rowdies and falls hopelessly in love with her.

1. *Charlotte Morel* (Putnam, 1969)
   From their meeting in the provinces to a final stormy scene, Charlotte resists the passion that Thomas feels for her. Translated from the French by Anne Carter.
2. *Charlotte Morel: The Dream* (Putnam, 1970)
   In 1868, Thomas decides to marry Marie and move his press to the safety of Brussels, but he cannot tear himself away from Charlotte. Translated from the French by Anne Carter.

3. *Charlotte Morel: The Siege* (Putnam, 1970)
   The tragic last act of Thomas's love for Charlotte is set during the privations of the great siege of Paris in 1870. Translated from the French by Anne Carter.

Lofts, Norah

I. What would libraries do without writers like Norah Lofts, whose steady output of consistently interesting historical novels has entertained readers for over thirty years? Lofts can write convincingly of fifteenth-century England, Napoleonic France, or colonial Dutch East India. Her books provide fascinating glimpses into domestic history and the lives of women, and they combine drama, romance, and suspense in just the right proportions. Her first trilogy follows the five-century history of a house in Suffolk, England, beginning with its original builder, Martin Reed, born a serf in 1381.

1. *The Town House* (Doubleday, 1959)
   Martin Reed's rise from serf to prosperous merchant is told in five narrations—by himself, his servant, his daughter Ann, and his two grandchildren, Maude and Nicholas. Maude's story, published separately for young readers as *The Maude Reed Tale* (Nelson, 1971), shows young Maude determined to become a wool merchant rather than a lady of leisure.
2. *The House at Old Vine* (Doubleday, 1961)
   Seven more tales carry the history of the house from 1496 to the end of the seventeenth century.
3. *The House at Sunset* (Doubleday, 1962)
   The story of the house's inhabitants is continued from the eighteenth century to the present.

II. The Godfrey Tallboys trilogy is set in fifteenth-century England. It stars Sir Godfrey, a feckless knight; his understanding wife Sybilla; and their four children. Knight's Acre is the name of the house Godfrey builds for his family in East Anglia; it is the setting for all three novels of the trilogy.

1. *Knight's Acre* (Doubleday, 1975)
   Sir Godfrey leaves his family for a tourney in Spain and is detained for seven years before returning with the lovely young Moorish woman who helped him escape imprisonment.

2. *The Homecoming* (Doubleday, 1976)
   An uneasy peace is established between Sybilla and the fiery young Tana, but Godfrey is soon off to serve in the War of the Roses.
3. *The Lonely Furrow* (Doubleday, 1977)
   Henry, Godfrey's son, now plows the fields at Knight's Acre, and Joanna aims to make herself indispensable to him.

III. These two novels are about the mysteriously haunted English country house purchased by Bob and Jill Spender. What they learn about the nineteenth-century Thorley family and the tragic events that cause them to haunt Gad's Hall forms a story within a story.

1. *Gad's Hall* (Doubleday, 1978)
   When unwed Lavinia Thorley becomes pregnant, Mrs. Thorley keeps her hidden away in Gad's Hall.
2. *The Haunting of Gad's Hall* (Doubleday, 1979)
   The Thorley children grow up, but the sealed room in the attic casts its spell.

Long, William Stuart (pseud. of Vivian Stuart)

The Australians is another of the paperback series produced by book packager Lyle Kenyon Engel after the pattern of the Kent Family Chronicles by John Jakes (q.v.). Eleven volumes of this history of Australia have been published to date, covering the years 1781 to 1900. The reader-tested romance/adventure formula by veteran British author Vivian Stuart writing as "William Stuart Long," plus a renewed interest in things Australian (since Colleen McCullough's best-seller, *The Thorn Birds*), guarantee a continuing audience for this series. Most titles have been reprinted in hardcover by Gregg Press.

1. *The Exiles* (Dell, 1979)
   This follows a group of convicts, including a young woman unjustly accused of theft, as they are shipped out from England in 1781.
2. *The Settlers* (Dell, 1980)
   This focuses on fiery Jenny Taggart.
3. *The Traitors* (Dell, 1981)
   This begins in 1807 as Abigail Tempest comes to Sydney and Jenny Broome struggles alone to raise her children in an alien land.

4. *The Explorers* (Dell, 1981)
   In 1809, Highland lassie Jessica MacLaine travels to New South Wales as lady's maid to the wife of the new governor.
5. *The Adventurers* (Dell, 1983)
   American beauty Katie O'Malley inspires the passion of George DeLancey as Napoleonic War veterans try to adjust to life Down Under.
6. *The Colonists* (Dell, 1984)
   Land speculators exploit exiled English convicts as the settlement of Australia continues in the nineteenth century.
7. *The Goldseekers* (Dell, 1985)
   The fates of Elizabeth Tempest and Captain Red Broome become intertwined during the Australian gold rush of the 1850s.
8. *The Gallant* (Dell, 1986)
   In 1856, heiress Kitty Cadogan travels from Ireland to the Outback.
9. *The Empire Builders* (Dell, 1987)
   Lady Kitty is married to journalist Johnny Broome as the action shifts to New Zealand in 1859.
10. *The Seafarers* (Dell, 1988)
    Jon Fisher, survivor of an 1879 Zulu massacre, and his friend Harry Ryan are both attracted to Jessica Broome, the "most beautiful girl in Sydney."
11. *The Nationalists* (Dell, 1989)
    Java Gordon, daughter of Jessica Broome, gets involved with Slone Shannon, who gets involved with the Boer War.

Longstreet, Stephen

I. Longstreet is an artist and screenwriter as well as a prolific popular novelist. The American Jewish Pedlock family has been the subject of some of his best-known novels. Peter Perry, the narrator of the Pedlock series, is assumed to be an autobiographical figure. He traces the family's colorful history from 1866 to the present, beginning with Confederate army major Joseph Pedlock coming north, marrying Rebecca Manderscheid, and heading west to build a successful mining enterprise. The changing status of Jews in America is shown in the lives of his four children. Later volumes focus on the present-day doings of various branches of the large Pedlock family.

1. *The Pedlocks: The Story of a Family* (Simon & Schuster, 1951)
   This book chronicles eighty years in the history of an American Jewish family, from patriarch Joseph Pedlock to his young grandson Peter Perry.
2. *God and Sarah Pedlock* (McKay, 1976)
   Though written much later, this volume is second chronologically. It shows Judith Pedlock, a rich and salty octogenarian, looking for a husband, while her niece Sarah, a world-famous pianist, suffers a spiritual crisis.
3. *Pedlock & Sons* (Delacorte, 1966)
   Octogenarian Judith Pedlock decides to remarry, and the family takes steps to prevent her from selling her stock in the family department store.
4. *Pedlock Saint, Pedlock Sinner* (Delacorte, 1969)
   Turning to the West Coast branch of the family, this volume focuses on the conflict between two rabbis, the hypocritical Stephen Pedlock and his idealistic young nephew, David Mendoza.
5. *The Pedlock Inheritance* (McKay, 1972)
   San Francisco judge Woodrow Pedlock's appointment to the U.S. Supreme Court is jeopardized by his lawyer son Rufus's championing of unpopular causes.
6. *The Pedlocks in Love* (Avon, 1978)
   At Woodrow's California ranch, two very different Pedlocks—comfortably married Angela and Berkeley professor David—are drawn to each other as a forest fire blazes toward them.

II. The prolific Longstreet is producing another family saga, this time about a rich clan of Italian-American bankers, the Fiores. The story begins with the founder of the clan, George Fiore, in the 1850s.

1. *All or Nothing* (Putnam, 1983)
   George Fiore, a poor Italian immigrant, goes into the money-lending business in San Francisco. Covers the 1850s to 1900.
2. *Our Father's House* (Putnam, 1985)
   In the 1920s, nonagenerian George Fiore and his family continue to expand their banking business, and move into Texas oil and the motion pictures.
3. *Sons and Daughters* (Putnam, 1987)
   Gregory Fiore continues the family banking business, but most of the younger Fiores are more interested in other pursuits. Covers from World War II to the Vietnam War.

Lovell, Marc (pseud. of Mark McShane)

The Appleton Porter novels are entertaining spoofs of the spy genre. Apple is a linguist who speaks six or seven languages fluently and twelve or fifteen competently, a decided asset for a spy in British intelligence. Unfortunately, Apple is also awkwardly tall—a marvelous target for assassins—and a bit of a bumbler. He tries to be hard and ruthless like his cynical, nasty "control," Angus Watkin, but he is incurably gentle and idealistic. McShane has also written many mysteries under his real name, including *Seance on a Wet Afternoon* (Doubleday, 1962).

1. *The Spy Game* (Doubleday, 1980)
   Apple has to find out which members of a visiting Russian ESP team can really read minds, and which ones want to defect.
2. *The Spy with His Head in the Clouds* (Doubleday, 1982)
   Apple goes to a circus in Somerset to discover why the Russians have planted the truth serum Soma-2 in British hands.
3. *Spy on the Run* (Doubleday, 1982)
   Because Russian Olympian Igor Kazov will pass on a secret formula for edible seaweed only on the run, Apple must enter a track meet.
4. *Apple Spy in the Sky* (Doubleday, 1983)
   A KGB plan to spread drugs into British army bases requires Apple's presence on the island of Ibiza.
5. *Apple to the Core* (Doubleday, 1983)
   Apple has to arrange the defection of one of a famous quartet of Russian singers.
6. *How Green Was My Apple* (Doubleday, 1984)
   Apple teams up with a six-foot one-inch female agent to shadow a Russian in London, and loses "Ethel," his beloved converted taxi cab.
7. *The Only Good Apple in a Barrel of Spies* (Doubleday, 1984)
   The death of a Russian cultural attache on a London train platform leads Apple to masquerade as a pickpocket.
8. *The Spy Who Got His Feet Wet* (Doubleday, 1985)
   Apple joins the national basketball team at a tournament in Dublin in order to deal with a Russian player who has information to peddle.
9. *The Spy Who Barked in the Night* (Doubleday, 1986)
   A film crew shooting a movie about Robert Burns in the Scottish Highlands is graced by the presence of Apple posing as an animal trainer.

10. *Good Spies Don't Grow on Trees* (Doubleday, 1986)
    Apple is assigned to the task of "compromising" Russian chess
    champion Alicia Suvov at a tournament in London.
11. *That Great Big Trenchcoat in the Sky* (Doubleday, 1988)
    Apple joins Blushers Anonymous, which may be a front for a
    Communist plot.

Lovesey, Peter

A nineteenth-century atmosphere, redolent of Holmes and Watson,
gives these mysteries a special charm. Set in and around Victorian London, these cases star a crack team of detectives from Scotland Yard. The
lean and irrascible Detective Sergeant Cribb ferrets out the criminals,
while stoutly patient Constable Thackeray performs the dirty jobs and
gets no thanks for it. PBS's "Mystery!" aired the dramatizations imported
from Britain, to the delight of many viewers.

1. *Wobble to Death* (Dodd, 1970)
   At a six-day walking race—or *wobble* as they were called—first
   one, then another participant is murdered.
2. *The Detective Wore Silk Drawers* (Dodd, 1971)
   Clandestine boxing matches and headless corpses are the main
   ingredients in this spicy brew.
3. *Abracadaver* (Dodd, 1972)
   London's music hall performers are being sabotaged on stage,
   first by practical jokes, then by murder.
4. *Mad Hatter's Holiday* (Dodd, 1973)
   On vacation in Brighton, Albert Moscrop witnesses a gruesome
   murder through his telescope.
5. *The Tick of Death* (Dodd, 1974)
   As London is plagued with bomb threats, Cribb and Thackeray
   find themselves the unwilling accomplices of a beautiful, red-
   haired anarchist. English title: *Invitation to a Dynamite Party*.
6. *A Case of Spirits* (Dodd, 1975)
   When a medium is electrocuted during a seance, Cribb suspects
   it was murder.
7. *Swing, Swing Together* (Dodd, 1976)
   On a secret midnight swim in the Thames, young Harriet gets
   separated from her schoolgirl companions and her clothes by
   three sinister men in a boat.

8. *Waxwork* (Pantheon, 1978)
Miriam Cromer has confessed to poisoning her husband's assistant, but Sergeant Cribb smells something wrong.

Lyons, Arthur

Jacob Asch is a fairly typical Los Angeles-based hardboiled private eye, except, perhaps, for the fact that he is half-Jewish. Asch started out as a Philip Marlowe clone, but with each novel in the series his character has shown more individuality and complexity. He gets involved with a wide variety of cases—Satanist cults, motorcycle gangs, boxing, movies, meat-packing, insurance, etc.—which tend to point up the seamy underside and lunatic fringe of southern California. The novels are very good examples of the hardboiled genre with social comment.

1. *The Dead Are Discreet* (Mason, 1974)
When Sheila Warren, the young disciple of a Satanist cult, is murdered, Asch investigates.
2. *All God's Children* (Mason, 1975)
The search for eighteen-year-old Susan Gurney leads Asch to the Word of God commune and a motorcycle gang calling itself "Satan's Warriors."
3. *The Killing Floor* (Mason, 1976)
Asch goes looking for the missing partner in a meat-packing firm, a compulsive gambler.
4. *Dead Ringer* (Mason, 1977)
Asch takes on the case of a heavyweight boxer and corruption in the fight game.
5. *Castles Burning* (Holt, 1980)
A successful artist wants Asch to find the wife and son he had deserted in his less successful past.
6. *Hard Trade* (Holt, 1982)
Homely heiress Sylvia Calabrese hires Asch to find out if her fiance truly loves her.
7. *At the Hands of Another* (Holt, 1983)
Asch gets mixed up with doctors, lawyers, and the insurance business as he runs into a former lover for whom he had arranged an abortion.

8. *Three with a Bullet* (Holt, 1984)
   Rock concert promoter Freddie Segal hires Asch to find out who has been sabotaging his operation.
9. *Fast Fade* (Mysterious, 1987)
   Asch is hired to prove that movie director Walter Cairns is really William McVey, who deserted Asch's client sixteen years ago.
10. *Other People's Money* (Mysterious, 1989)
    A Turk who wants his daughter followed, a deep-sea diver involved with drug smuggling, and an attractive museum curator may be connected in some way.

McBain, Ed (pseud. of Evan Hunter, q.v.)

I. Ed McBain writes the best U.S. police procedurals. In *The Great Detectives* (Little, 1978) he explains that he conceived of the entire squad as the hero of his 87th Precinct series, but when he tried to kill off favorite Steve Carella in *The Pusher*, his editor wouldn't let him. So the staff of the eighty-seventh squadron of the Isola (Manhattan) police department has changed very little over the years. Lieutenant Peter Byrnes leads the group, and Meyer Meyer is the senior detective. Next comes Steve Carella with his young pal Bert Kling. The other detectives include Bob O'Brien, Cotton Hawes, Hal Willis, Andy Parker, and Arthur Brown. Because the multiple plots woven into police procedurals cannot be captured in a sentence or two, the books are listed without annotation in the order of their publication, which is also the correct chronological sequence.

1. *Cop Hater* (Permabooks, 1956)
2. *The Mugger* (Permabooks, 1956)
3. *The Pusher* (Permabooks, 1956)
4. *The Con Man* (Permabooks, 1957)
5. *Killer's Choice* (Simon & Schuster, 1957)
6. *Killer's Payoff* (Simon & Schuster, 1958)
7. *Lady Killer* (Simon & Schuster, 1958)
8. *Killer's Wedge* (Simon & Schuster, 1959)
9. *'Til Death* (Simon & Schuster, 1959)
10. *King's Ransom* (Simon & Schuster, 1959)
11. *Give the Boys a Great Big Hand* (Simon & Schuster, 1960)
12. *The Heckler* (Simon & Schuster, 1960)
13. *See Them Die* (Simon & Schuster, 1960)

14. *Lady, Lady, I Did It!* (Simon & Schuster, 1961)
15. *Like Love* (Simon & Schuster, 1962)
16. *The Empty Hours* (Simon & Schuster, 1962)
    A collection of short stories.
17. *Ten Plus One* (Simon & Schuster, 1963)
18. *Ax* (Simon & Schuster, 1964)
19. *He Who Hesitates* (Delacorte, 1965)
20. *Doll* (Delacorte, 1965)
21. *Eighty Million Eyes* (Delacorte, 1966)
22. *Fuzz* (Doubleday, 1968)
23. *Shotgun* (Doubleday, 1969)
24. *Jigsaw* (Doubleday, 1970)
25. *Hail, Hail, the Gang's All Here!* (Doubleday, 1971)
26. *Sadie When She Died* (Doubleday, 1972)
27. *Let's Hear It for the Deaf Man* (Doubleday, 1973)
28. *Hail to the Chief* (Random, 1973)
29. *Bread* (Random, 1974)
30. *Blood Relatives* (Random, 1975)
31. *So Long as You Both Shall Live* (Random, 1976)
32. *Long Time No See* (Random, 1977)
33. *Calypso* (Viking, 1979)
34. *Ghosts* (Viking, 1980)
35. *Heat* (Viking, 1981)
36. *Ice* (Arbor, 1983)
37. *Lightning* (Arbor, 1984)
38. *Eight Black Horses* (Arbor, 1985)
39. *Poison* (Arbor, 1986)
40. *Tricks* (Arbor, 1987)
41. *Lullaby* (Morrow, 1989)
42. *Vespers* (Morrow, 1990)

II. In addition to the 87th Precinct series, McBain has added a Florida lawyer to the ranks of amateur private eyes. Matthew Hope lives in Calusa, Florida, and gets drawn into cases by his clients, often because of his weakness for beautiful women. The plots are usually macabre variations on the fairy tales that give the titles to the novels in the series. Some readers may find an excess of violence and gore in these well-plotted, fast-moving tales.

1. *Goldilocks* (Arbor, 1978)
   Matthew Hope, who is conducting an adulterous affair, comes to

the aid of a client who is suspected of massacring his wife and family.

2. *Rumpelstiltskin* (Viking, 1981)
   Newly divorced Matt Hope has a one-night stand with singer Vicky Miller, who is found murdered the next day.

3. *Beauty and the Beast* (Holt, 1983)
   The white wife of George Harper, a gigantic black man, accuses him of wife abuse, then is murdered.

4. *Jack and the Beanstalk* (Holt, 1984)
   Jack McKinney, Hope's client, is murdered after planning to invest in a snap bean farm.

5. *Snow White and Rose Red* (Holt, 1985)
   Matt falls for Sarah Whittaker, who is confined by her mother, perhaps illegally, in a mental institution.

6. *Cinderella* (Holt, 1986)
   Private eye Otto Samalson, Hope's friend, is killed while on assignment for him. "Cinderella" is a beautiful prostitute holding on to a fortune in stolen cocaine.

7. *Puss in Boots* (Holt, 1987)
   A recently completed porno film has disappeared along with its star actress, "Puss in Boots."

8. *The House That Jack Built* (Holt, 1988)
   Midwesterner Ralph Parrish is charged with murdering his gay brother after a party in a beach house.

McCaffrey, Anne

I. The Dragonriders of Pern trilogy is enjoyed by young adults and some adult readers of science fiction. The planet of Pern is inhabited by human colonists, long out of contact with Earth, who live in Holds, or population centers. The Weyrs are the homes of the fire-breathing, winged dragons and their noble riders, who protect Pern from the deadly Threads—spores that fall at certain times from the Red Star. McCaffrey's involving and professionally crafted blends of science fiction and fantasy star young women and girls as often as men.

1. *Dragonflight* (Ballantine, 1978)
   The Dragon Weyrs have grown shabby, and the evil Lord Fax has grown very powerful, but proud young Lessa is determined to reclaim her birthright and save Pern from destruction. Original paperback edition: 1968.

2. *Dragonquest* (Ballantine, 1979)
   Lessa mediates between the land-bound people and the Dragon-riders as a new discovery threatens to change the planet radically. Original paperback edition: 1971.
3. *The White Dragon* (Ballantine, 1978)
   Young Lord Jaxon thwarts an attempt to steal a queen-dragon egg and makes a startling discovery about Pern and its history.

II. The Harper Hall trilogy, written for a younger audience, is included here because of the author's popularity and because this series, too, is set on the planet Pern. These books tell the stories of two young apprentices, the girl Menolly and the boy Piemur, who come to Harper Hall, the center where young people are trained in the use of the musical instruments used for long-distance communications on Pern.

1. *Dragonsong* (Atheneum, 1976)
   Menolly runs away from her father, who has thwarted her love of music, and finds happiness among a group of fire lizards.
2. *Dragon Singer* (Atheneum, 1977)
   After coming to Harper Hall astride a bronze dragon, young Menolly is unhappy at first, but she soon finds her rightful place.
3. *Dragondrum* (Atheneum, 1979)
   Piemur, Menolly's friend, comes of age, loses his singing voice, and must search for a new role at Harper Hall.

III. McCaffrey has written three more Pern novels; this time they cover events before the Dragonriders of Pern trilogy, including the origins of the Pern settlements.

1. *Dragon's Dawn* (Ballantine, 1988)
   Six thousand colonists escaping interstellar war and technocratic civilization settle on Pern. The colony thrives until the arrival of the Thread.
2. *Moreta: Dragon Lady of Pern* (Ballantine, 1983)
   The story of the great plague that decimates the population of Pern.
3. *Nerilka's Story* (Ballantine, 1986)
   Nerilka (a minor character in number 2), unhappy with life in the hold after the death of her mother, goes out to combat the plague devastating Pern.

IV. McCaffrey has recently added to the Pern saga with a volume that incorporates characters from both The Dragonriders of Pern trilogy and The Harper Hall trilogy. A sequel to this title, which starts chronologically during the time of *Dragonquest* and extends beyond *The White Dragon*, is to be expected. McCaffrey has collaborated with Jody Lynn Nye on *The Dragonlover's Guide to Pern* (Ballantine, 1989), an illustrated handbook to the fantastic region.

1. *The Renegades of Pern* (Ballantine, 1989)
   The trader family of Jayge Lilcamp is menaced by the Thread and renegade leader Lady Thella, while Harper Piemur has exciting adventures in the South.

Note: McCaffrey has also written a pair of paperbook novels about a planet inhabited by dinosaurs—*Dinosaur Planet* (Ballantine, 1978) and *Dinosaur Planet Survivors* (Ballantine, 1984)—and two novels about Killashandra, crystal singer of the planet Ballybran—*Crystal Singer*—(Ballantine, 1982) and *Killashandra* (Ballantine, 1985).

McClure, James

James McClure, now living in England, has written an excellent series of police procedurals set in his native South Africa. His two police detectives from Trekkersburg (based on the real city of Pietermaritzburg) are Afrikaner Lieutenant Tromp Kramer and Bantu Sergeant Mickey Zondi. The pair work closely as a successful team, though their racist society inhibits any public display of the friendship and mutual respect they feel for each other. McClure deliberately chose the detective story format as a means of reaching people who might not otherwise read much about the grim realities of apartheid. But his social comment is never heavy-handed.

1. *The Steam Pig* (Harper, 1972)
   A sharpened bicycle spoke, usually associated with "Kaffir" homicide, is used to murder a beautiful white girl.
2. *The Caterpillar Cop* (Harper, 1973)
   A twelve-year-old boy is mutilated and murdered in what appears to be a sex crime.
3. *The Gooseberry Fool* (Harper, 1974)
   When a pious hypocrite is stabbed to death with a steak knife, Zondi pursues his own investigation.

4. *Snake* (Harper, 1976)
   A stripper with a snake act is found murdered with her pet wound around her neck.
5. *The Sunday Hangman* (Harper, 1977)
   Afrikaner pathologist Dr. Strydom and Kramer suspect that some hanging suicides may actually be extra-legal executions.
6. *The Blood of an Englishman* (Harper, 1981)
   Apparently a giant has "ground the bones" of visiting former RAF airman Bonzo Hookham.
7. *The Artful Egg* (Pantheon, 1985)
   Naomi Stride, world-famous author of novels banned in South Africa, is found naked, dead, and with the tip of a sword still in her body.

McCutchan, Philip

I. This series of naval adventures, set in the 1890s, shows the British navy a century after Hornblower's time, still the mightiest of the world's fleets. The "gunboat diplomacy" of the times offers enough action to give Lieutenant St. Vincent Halfhyde plenty of adventure. True to form, Halfhyde is a brave and resourceful sailor, perhaps a shade too independent for his superior officers. This series is a little more lighthearted and humorous than other naval adventures. McCutchan, a prolific British author, has also written the Simon Shard series, and the Commander Shaw series, neither of which has been published in the United States. His Ogilvie series was written under the pseudonym Duncan MacNeil (q.v.).

1. *Beware, Beware the Bight of Benin* (St. Martin's, 1974)
   Halfhyde is sent to spy on the Russian navy off the coast of West Africa.
2. *Halfhyde's Island* (St. Martin's, 1975)
   Halfhyde races to claim a Pacific island that the Russian and Japanese navies have also set their sights on.
3. *The Guns of Arrest* (St. Martin's, 1976)
   Aboard the battleship *Prince Consort*, Halfhyde is assigned to find and capture Sir Russell Savory, who fled England with top-secret naval blueprints.
4. *Halfhyde to the Narrows* (St. Martin's, 1977)
   Halfhyde has his first command; his mission is to rescue a British merchant ship from her Russian captors in the Black Sea.

5. *Halfhyde for the Queen* (St. Martin's, 1978)
   Halfhyde's investigation into a Spanish plot to assassinate Queen Victoria ends at breakfast with Her Majesty in the royal railway car.
6. *Halfhyde Ordered South* (St. Martin's, 1980)
   Halfhyde confronts the German navy over South American trading interests.
7. *Halfhyde and the Flag Captain* (St. Martin's, 1981)
   Halfhyde must rescue the British ambassador who has been jailed during an Uruguayan revolution.
8. *Halfhyde on Zanatu* (St. Martin's, 1982)
   Halfhyde is sent to the Pacific to secure the rebellious island colony of Zanatu against possible Russian interference.
9. *Halfhyde Outward Bound* (St. Martin's, 1984)
   On the half-pay list and unhappily married, Halfhyde ships out as a seaman on a windjammer cruise to Chile and Australia.
10. *The Halfhyde Line* (St. Martin's, 1985)
    Halfhyde has dreams of starting a merchant fleet of his own, but comes to grief when his first voyage is pirated by an Irish arms smuggler.
11. *Halfhyde and the Chain Gangs* (St. Martin's, 1985)
    Back in service in the Boer War, Halfhyde is put in command of a transport of convicts bound for South Africa.
12. *Halfhyde Goes to War* (St. Martin's, 1987)
    Halfhyde is supposed to be guarding a consignment of naval gunnery and a shipment of gold bullion on the way to South Africa.
13. *Halfhyde on the Amazon* (St. Martin's, 1988)
    Halfhyde—back on his own ship, the *Taronga Park*, with Victoria, his foul-mouthed Australian mistress—is sent to spy on a German outpost on the Amazon River.

II. The prolific McCutchan has launched another naval action series. This one stars Donald Cameron, who serves in various naval capacities in World War II. Cameron is a rather phlegmatic type unlike the roguish Halfhyde, but this series is also full of naval detail, stirring action, a large cast of characters, and a little painless history. McCutchan, like Cameron, served in the Royal Naval Volunteer Reserve during World War II.

1. *Cameron: Ordinary Seaman* (Barker, London, 1980)
   Donald Cameron volunteers for the British navy and becomes an Ordinary Seaman on *HMS Carmarthen*.

2. *Cameron Comes Through* (St. Martin's, 1986)
   Brand new Sub-Lieutenant Cameron is assigned to the destroyer *Wharfedale* supplying the besieged island of Malta in 1941.

3. *Cameron of the Castle Bay* (Barker, London, 1981)
   Cameron's knowledge of the Norwegian coastline is invaluable as the *Castle Bay* is sent to destroy a secret Nazi base.

4. *Lieutenant Cameron RNVR* (St. Martin's, 1985)
   Lieutenant Cameron is second officer under old-line Captain Lees-Remington on a cruiser fighting the Germans in the South Atlantic.

5. *Cameron's Convoy* (Barker, London, 1982)
   Shipping aboard the frigate *Sprinter*, Cameron is part of a convoy on the Archangel run.

6. *Cameron in the Gap* (St. Martin's, 1983)
   Cameron, serving aboard HM Destroyer *Burnside*, is part of the naval escort protecting a convoy to Malta.

7. *Orders for Cameron* (St. Martin's, 1983)
   Serving aboard the corvette *Oleander*, Cameron takes part in Operation Torch, the 1942 Allied invasion of North Africa.

8. *Cameron in Command* (St. Martin's, 1984)
   Given his first command, the corvette *Briar*, Lieutenant Commander Cameron is sent to protect the Falklands from Japanese attack.

9. *Cameron and the Kaiserhof* (St. Martin's, 1984)
   Out of the water temporarily, Cameron is sent to neutral Spain to hijack the *Kaiserhof*, a liner being converted into a mother ship for mini-submarines.

10. *Cameron's Raid* (St. Martin's, 1985)
    Cameron is in command of one of three old P-class destroyers sent to destroy U-boat pens being built in Brest in occupied France.

11. *Cameron's Chase* (St. Martin's, 1986)
    Cameron, skipper of HMS *Glenshiel*, is part of a destroyer flotilla chasing *Attica*, the German navy's newest, most powerful battleship.

12. *Cameron's Troop Life* (St. Martin's, 1987)
    Away from the Atlantic in the Bay of Bengal, Cameron decides to intercept a Japanese liner carrying British POWs.

13. *Cameron's Commitment* (St. Martin's, 1989)
    Cameron takes on a contingent of Royal Marines to carry out a secret mission: rescuing a British leader of a Resistance group from France.

McDonald, Gregory

I. Smart-mouthed reporter-adventurer Irwin Maurice Fletcher (Fletch to his friends) is a joy to read about. Though his heart is always in the right place, his methods frequently go beyond the strictly legal—he knows how to counter-blackmail CIA agents, for instance, to his own advantage. He can tap his newspaper connections for information and is assured prominent press coverage when he wants it. Fletch likes liberalized ladies and dislikes IRS agents curious about the source of his—largely undeclared—income in Swiss bank accounts, but he remains unflappable and witty no matter what. Chevy Chase has played Fletch in two movies so far.

1. *Fletch Won* (Warner, 1985)
   When lawyer/philanthropist Donald Habek is killed, fledgling reporter Fletch sees a chance to beat out crime reporter Biff Wilson for front-page bylines.
2. *Fletch Too* (Warner, 1986)
   When Fletch marries Barbara, he receives an invitation from someone purporting to be his long-missing father to meet him in Kenya.
3. *Fletch* (Bobbs-Merrill, 1974)
   Newspaperman Fletch investigates the California beach drug scene and is offered a job of murder.
4. *Carioca Fletch* (Warner, 1984)
   Holidaying in Rio de Janeiro, Fletch turns out to be a dead ringer for a Brazilian fisherman murdered 47 years ago.
5. *Confess, Fletch* (Avon, 1976)
   Fletch finds a naked dead woman in a friend's Boston apartment, where he is staying, and becomes the prime suspect of Inspector Flynn.
6. *Fletch's Fortune* (Avon, 1978)
   The CIA persuades Fletch to do a little bedroom bugging at a journalist's convention, and the case turns into the biggest murder story of the decade.
7. *Fletch and the Widow Bradley* (Warner, 1981)
   Fletch is in trouble with his newspaper for quoting the "recent" memos of a man who has been dead for two years—or has he?
8. *Fletch's Moxie* (Warner, 1982)
   "Moxie" is Moxie Mooney, a movie star who is the prime suspect in the talk show murder of agent Steve Peterman.

9. *Fletch and the Man Who* (Warner, 1983)
   Fletch, working as press secretary for presidential candidate Caxton Wheeler, investigates the murder of three young women during the campaign.

II. Flynn, the Boston policeman, was such an engaging character in *Confess, Fletch* that McDonald has given him three books of his own to star in. In the first one, the connection to Fletch is mentioned, though he never appears in the book.

1. *Flynn* (Avon, 1977)
   A Boeing 707 carrying some very important people explodes above Boston Harbor seconds before landing, and Inspector Flynn is showered with falling human debris.
2. *The Buck Passes Flynn* (Ballantine, 1981)
   Flynn's Boston police job is just a cover for his more serious efforts as the super-agent N.N. 13 working for the mysterious "little man" on a case where sudden riches seem to be changing the lives of a lot of people.
3. *Flynn's In* (Mysterious, 1984)
   A murder at the elite Rod and Gun Club challenges Flynn to find the killer without publicizing the case.

III. Gregory McDonald also writes mainstream fiction, including this pair of novels which are part of a proposed quartet about a group of people who came together in Paris during the 1950s. The main protagonist is David MacFarlane, a jazz pianist and composer. These are thoughtful novels about complex characters in believable situations.

1. *Merely Players* (Hill, 1988)
   This tells how David MacFarlane, Janet Twombly, and other characters come together in Paris during the 1950s.
2. *A World Too Wide* (Hill, 1987)
   The upcoming marriage of children of old friends prompts David MacFarlane to propose a reunion of the group from the 1950s.

MacDonald, John D.

Not likely to be confused with Ross MacDonald's California detective, John D. MacDonald's flashy ladies' man Travis McGee lives on a houseboat in a Florida marina. He drives a vintage Rolls Royce and makes a specialty of retrieving expensive lost articles, though he occasionally takes on less lucrative assignments for his special friends. His pal Mayer, who sometimes helps out on cases, really should tell Travis that his attitude toward women is as antiquated as his car and not nearly as quaint. Originally published in paperback, then reprinted in hardcover, the Travis McGee books are listed below in order of their original publication.

1. *Deep Blue Good-By* (Lippincott, 1975)
   This book concerns a stolen sapphire and a psycho lady-killer. Paperback published by Fawcett, 1964.
2. *Nightmare in Pink* (Lippincott, 1976)
   In New York to investigate the murder of a war buddy's sister, McGee gets slipped some LSD. Paperback published by Fawcett, 1964.
3. *A Purple Place for Dying* (Lippincott, 1976)
   Mona Yeoman, a potential client, is shot, and her husband is poisoned. Paperback published by Fawcett, 1964.
4. *The Quick Red Fox* (Lippincott, 1974)
   McGee investigates the blackmailing of movie star Lysa Dean. Paperback published by Fawcett, 1966.
5. *A Deadly Shade of Gold* (Lippincott, 1974)
   The death of an old friend and the loss of a priceless Aztec gold idol are the elements of this case. Paperback published by Fawcett, 1965.
6. *Bright Orange for the Shroud* (Lippincott, 1972)
   Poor Arthur Wilkinson is tricked into marrying a nasty woman. Paperback published by Fawcett, 1965.
7. *Darker than Amber* (Lippincott, 1970)
   McGee gets involved when mobsters dump a corpse off a bridge. Paperback published by Fawcett, 1966.
8. *One Fearful Yellow Eye* (Lippincott, 1978)
   A widow finds that all her husband's money is gone and she is being accused of stealing it. Paperback published by Fawcett, 1966.
9. *Pale Gray for Guilt* (Lippincott, 1968)
   McGee encounters stock-market speculators and a new love. Paperback published by Fawcett, 1968.

10. *The Girl in the Plain Brown Wrapper* (Lippincott, 1973)
    The suicidal daughter of an old friend is McGee's concern. Paperback published by Fawcett, 1968.

11. *Dress Her in Indigo* (Lippincott, 1971)
    The investigation into the death of Bix Bowie takes McGee to a Mexican village and its sad and depraved inhabitants. Paperback published by Fawcett, 1969.

12. *The Long Lavender Look* (Lippincott, 1972)
    When McGee swerves to avoid running his Rolls Royce into a young girl, he finds himself in big trouble. Paperback published by Fawcett, 1970.

13. *A Tan and Sandy Silence* (Lippincott, 1979)
    Harry Brell, a land speculator of dubious reputation, accuses McGee of spiriting away his wife. Paperback published by Fawcett, 1972.

14. *The Scarlet Ruse* (Lippincott, 1980)
    A Miami stamp dealer's assistant is murdered. Paperback published by Fawcett, 1973.

15. *The Turquoise Lament* (Lippincott, 1973)
    A dead professor leaves McGee the problems of his lost notebook and his troubled daughter. Paperback published by Fawcett, 1972.

16. *The Dreadful Lemon Sky* (Lippincott, 1975)
    A package entrusted to McGee by an old girlfriend leads him into a case of murder and drug smuggling. Paperback published by Fawcett, 1975.

17. *The Empty Copper Sea* (Lippincott, 1978)
    A friend who has lost his skipper's license comes to McGee for help.

18. *The Green Ripper* (Lippincott, 1976)
    When girlfriend Gretel is murdered, a stunned McGee investigates.

19. *Free Fall in Crimson* (Harper, 1981)
    This installment finds McGee in a small Iowa town exposing a pornography-drug ring and escaping by balloon.

20. *Cinnamon Skin* (Harper, 1982)
    When an explosion kills two people and destroys a friend's cruiser, McGee is called in to investigate.

21. *The Lonely Silver Rain* (Knopf, 1985)
    McGee gets involved with drug dealers when he finds three mutilated corpses on board a luxury yacht stolen from financier Billy Ingraham.

McDonald, Kay L.

Oregon native Kay L. McDonald has written a trilogy of historical novels about the first permanent white settlement in Oregon in the 1840s. The protagonist is Ross Chesnut, a white man raised by Indians, who becomes a guide for explorers and settlers. This is a good adventure series with some historical characters and events woven in.

1. *Vision of the Eagle* (Crowell, 1977)
   Abigail Whitteker, traveling west from New York to St.Louis in the early 1800s, is captured by Indians. Her son is raised by Sioux Indians under the name of White Eagle.
2. *The Brightwoood Expedition* (Liveright, 1976)
   In 1842, an Indian attack on an expedition exploring mountain trails to Oregon leaves two survivors, Marlette Brightwoood and the guide, Ross Chesnut, aka White Eagle.
3. *The Vision Is Fulfilled* (Walker, 1983)
   Ross Chesnut leads a wagon train over the Oregon Trail to Oregon and tragedy strikes in the form of a smallpox epidemic.

Macdonald, Malcolm

Macdonald's smoothly crafted tale, with its lively characters and high drama, is an English family saga as easy to sink into as a comfortable old sofa. The story begins in 1839 when the young and ambitious railroad foreman John Stevenson gets his chance to make his fortune. The "canty wench" Nora joins him, and their story intertwines with that of Walter and Arabella Thornton, an unhappy upper-middle-class couple. The last volume centers on Abigail, John and Nora's daughter, and takes the family up to the 1890s.

1. *The World from Rough Stones* (Knopf, 1975)
   With Nora at his side, John Stevenson rises to a position of respect and influence as a railroad contractor.
2. *The Rich Are with You Always* (Knopf, 1976)
   Turbulent years for the railroad industry bring financial crises to the Stevensons.
3. *Sons of Fortune* (Knopf, 1978)
   John is a rich man now and determined to be accepted into society. His sons, Caspar and Boy, play a larger part in this book.

4. *Abigail* (Knopf, 1979)
   Young Abigail is followed from the age of seventeen, through her career as a writer and feminist and her love for Victor.

MacDonald, Ross (pseud. of Kenneth Millar)

Like John Le Carré, Ross MacDonald catches his characters in an authentic milieu complete with the moral ambiguities of real life. His Lew Archer is a loner who watches life from the shadows with compassion and a Freudian understanding of the tortured family tangles that his Los Angeles clients often bring him. He is an ex-policeman who was kicked out for being too honest, and an ex-husband whose wife divorced him because she couldn't stand his associates. William Goldman, in a *New York Times* review, describes the Lew Archer series as "the best detective novels ever written by an American." *Archer at Large* (Knopf, 1970) is an omnibus containing numbers 9, 12, and 14 listed below; *Archer in Hollywood* comprises numbers 1, 3, and 7; and *Archer in Jeopardy* contains numbers 8, 11, and 15.

1. *The Moving Target* (Knopf, 1949)
   A degenerate millionaire is kidnapped. The 1966 movie *Harper,* with Paul Newman, was based on this novel.
2. *The Drowning Pool* (Knopf, 1950)
   A woman is found drowned in a swimming pool. This story was also filmed with Newman as Lew Archer.
3. *The Way Some People Die* (Knopf, 1951)
   The heroin racket absorbs Archer's attention.
4. *Ivory Grin* (Knopf, 1952)
   Archer finds out what happened to spoiled young Charles Singleton. Variant title: *Marked for Murder.*
5. *Find a Victim* (Knopf, 1954)
   A problem hitchhiker intrudes into Archer's drive to Sacramento.
6. *Name Is Archer* (Bantam, 1955)
   Seven stories about Archer are collected here.
7. *Barbarous Coast* (Knopf, 1956)
   The exclusive and fashionable Channel Club is at the center of this case of a missing woman.
8. *Doomsters* (Knopf, 1958)
   This case concerns an unscrupulous doctor.

273

9. *The Galton Case* (Knopf, 1959)
   In search of a lost heir, Archer uncovers a twenty-two-year-old murder.
10. *The Wycherly Woman* (Knopf, 1961)
    Twenty-one-year-old Phoebe Wycherly is missing from her northern California college.
11. *Zebra-Striped Hearse* (Knopf, 1962)
    Archer investigates an ice-pick murder.
12. *The Chill* (Knopf, 1964)
    Beautiful young Dolly Kincaid runs away from her new husband.
13. *The Far Side of the Dollar* (Knopf, 1965)
    Archer must find a seventeen-year-old runaway from school.
14. *Black Money* (Knopf, 1966)
    The corruptions of the world intrude into a college campus.
15. *Instant Enemy* (Knopf, 1968)
    Archer tracks a high school runaway.
16. *The Goodbye Look* (Knopf, 1969)
    A theft from the Chalmers family safe leads Archer into deeper problems.
17. *Underground Man* (Knopf, 1971)
    Set amid the drama of a California forest fire, this book concerns a missing little boy and a pair of disturbed young people.
18. *Sleeping Beauty* (Knopf, 1973)
    This convoluted case centers around the kidnapped daughter of an oil millionaire.
19. *Blue Hammer* (Knopf, 1976)
    A painting is stolen and the daughter of a millionaire is missing.
20. *Lew Archer, Private Investigator* (Mysterious, 1977)
    Nine stories are collected here.

McInerny, Ralph

I. McInerny's Father Roger Dowling is a sympathetic Catholic priest whose depressing early years serving on the archdiocesan marriage court led to a bout with alcoholism. Reformed and assigned to shepherd the sleepy little parish of Fox River, Illinois, his tolerant and slightly world-weary nature win him a faithful following. His renewed acquaintance with Phil Keegan, now the town's chief of detectives, involves him in a series of mysteries. Catholic readers will find this modern successor to Father Brown a special treat. Father Dowling is featured in a network television series starring Tom Bosley that began in 1989. McInerny writes the popular Sister Mary Theresa novels under the pseudonym Monica Quill (q.v.).

1. *Her Death of Cold* (Vanguard, 1977)
   A rich and frightened widow phones Father Dowling in the middle of the night, then disappears and is feared murdered.
2. *The Seventh Station* (Vanguard, 1977)
   Father Dowling goes on a retreat and finds a corpse stabbed with an ice pick on the lawn his first morning.
3. *Bishop as Pawn* (Vanguard, 1978)
   The return of a prodigal housekeeper and the kidnapping of a bishop are Father Dowling's concerns here.
4. *Lying Three* (Vanguard, 1979)
   A young Catholic woman is involved in the murder of a Jewish fund-raiser.
5. *Second Vespers* (Vanguard, 1980)
   Phyllis O'Rourke, heiress to her writer-brother's mansion and royalties, is found murdered in her swimming pool.
6. *Thicker than Water* (Vanguard, 1981)
   A dead body is found in a truck parked in front of the rectory.
7. *A Loss of Patients* (Vanguard, 1982)
   Four apparent suicides within a few weeks in Fox River arouse the suspicions of Father Dowling and Captain Keegan.
8. *The Grass Widow* (Vanguard, 1983)
   Clare O'Leary tells Father Dowling that her radio personality husband Larry plans to have her killed.
9. *Getting a Way with Murder* (Vanguard, 1984)
   Insurance executive Howard Downs, acquitted of his wife's murder, confesses to Father Dowling that he killed his defense attorney.
10. *Rest in Pieces* (Vanguard, 1985)
    Father Dowling is asked to give asylum to a member of a political family in Costa Verde, a Central American nation gripped by revolution.
11. *The Basket Case* (St. Martin's, 1987)
    A baby is left in a basket at Father Dowling's church by a woman trying to accuse her ex-husband of plotting to kidnap it.
12. *Abracadaver* (St. Martin's, 1989)
    After a magician entertaining an elderly audience at the parish center borrows a ring from Aggie Miller for one of his tricks, Aggie is murdered.

13. *Four on the Floor* (St. Martin's, 1989)
    A collection of short stories.

II. Two earlier books by McInerny star Matthew Rogerson, a customarily mild and genial humanities professor at a provincial Ohio college, whose rebellion causes a marvelous havoc on campus.

1. *Jolly Rogerson* (Doubleday, 1967)
   After twenty years of teaching, Professor Rogerson decides he is a failure, gives up being conventional and cooperative, and winds up winning the Teacher of the Year award.
2. *Rogerson at Bay* (Harper, 1976)
   Professor Rogerson negotiates various midlife crises with irreverence and contagious good humor.

III. McInerny has started on a mystery series featuring Andrew Broom, a lawyer from Wyler, a small town in Indiana. Like the Father Dowling series, the pair of novels published so far are lively, touched with humor, and full of odd characters.

1. *Cause and Effect* (Atheneum, 1987)
   Love triangles are the basis for two nefarious plots, one of them designed to drive Andrew Broom to suicide.
2. *Body and Soil* (Atheneum, 1989)
   The family farm of Leo Barany holds a grisly secret, while Broom and his nephew Gerald Rowan are on opposite sides in a divorce case.

Mackenzie, Compton

I. Mackenzie had to resist the pull of his theatrical family in order to become a writer. His early novels won him an immediate popular audience, and *Sinister Street* (Secker, London, 1913) was a critical success as well. He received a knighthood in 1952 for his long and productive career. It should be noted that Mackenzie recycled some of his *Sinister Street* characters in novels of their own, notably in *Guy and Pauline* (Secker, London, 1915) and *Sylvia and Michael* (Secker, London, 1919). They are not real sequels, however. Edmund Wilson thought that Mackenzie was an underrated author and that the novel series The Four Winds of Love had never been given the recognition it deserved as a serious defense of oppressed people and a plea for the rights of small nations.

1. *The East Wind* (Richard Cowan, London, 1937)
   John Ogilvie is introduced as a seventeen-year-old Scottish boy at St. James School in 1900.
2. *The South Wind* (Richard Cowan, London, 1937)
   Eleven years after the first volume, John has been to Oxford and is a successful playwright.
3. *The West Wind* (Chatto, London, 1940)
   John has a romance with rich American, Athene Langridge
4. *West to North* (Chatto, London, 1940)
   John is converted to Catholicism and becomes more politically involved.
5. *The North Wind,* vols. 1 and 2 (Chatto, London, 1944 and 1945)
   The deteriorating international scene in the thirties and John's involvement with various Scottish nationalist groups are featured.

II. This early religious trilogy is of special interest because, like its protagonist, Mackenzie himself converted to Catholicism. Reviewers called these novels "beautifully serene."

1. *The Altar Steps* (Doran, 1922)
   This book tells the story of Mark Lidderdale from his infancy, c. 1880, to his ordination as an Anglican priest.
2. *The Parson's Progress* (Doran, 1923)
   Mark serves his first several curacies.
3. *The Heavenly Ladder* (Doran, 1924)
   Mark ministers in a Cornish village, is expelled from the church, and converts to Roman Catholicism.

MacLean, Alistair

Gregory Peck. David Niven, and Anthony Quinn starred in the 1961 film *Guns of Navarone,* which is hard to beat for nonstop action and excitement. The most successful novels by this popular British author are still his World War II stories. His first, *H.M.S. Ulysses,* was a naval adventure; the two listed below feature Force 10, a special British army strike team. MacLean's deft character delineation, taut story line, and convincing atmosphere are uncluttered by romantic complications; his daring commandos need all their energy for the dangers that beset their every step.

1. *Guns of Navarone* (Doubleday, 1957)
   A five-man sabotage team is assigned to destroy two powerful guns off the Turkish coast in 1943.
2. *Force 10 from Navarone* (Doubleday, 1968)
   Mallory, Miller, and Stavros take on a second wartime assignment to blow up a bridge in the mountains of Yugoslavia.

MacLeod, Charlotte

I. Peter Shandy, a professor at the Balaclava Agricultural College in Massachusetts, is a mildly eccentric fellow on a campus full of odd fish. Peter and his wife, librarian Helen Marsh, whom he meets and courts in book number 1, usually get entangled in complicated situations quite innocently, and then must call upon their amateur sleuthing powers to sort things out. This entertaining series of mysteries offers humor, clever plots, interesting characters, and happy endings. Charlotte MacLeod, who lives in a suburb of Boston, Massachusetts, worked for thirty years in a Boston advertising agency.

1. *Rest You Merry* (Doubleday, 1978)
   After temporarily abandoning his home because of its tacky Christmas decorations, Peter Shandy returns to find a corpse in his living room.
2. *The Luck Runs Out* (Doubleday, 1979)
   Peter and Helen are held hostage at a local silversmith's, a prize pig is kidnapped, and the body of a lady farrier is found in a feedbox.
3. *Wrack and Rune* (Doubleday, 1982)
   Shandy and Balaclava President Svenson deal with the death of a hired man and the discovery of a Norse rune store.
4. *Something the Cat Dragged In* (Doubleday, 1983)
   The secretive Balaclava Society gets some unwanted publicity when former Balaclava Professor Ungley is found dead behind its clubhouse.
5. *The Curse of the Giant Hogweed* (Doubleday, 1985)
   A consulting trip to Wales gets Shandy and two colleagues involved in the middle of a medieval Welsh legend complete with enchanted princes, griffins, and wyverns.

6. *The Corpse in Oozak's Pond* (Mysterious, 1987)
   A frozen corpse attired in a suit from the 1800s, and eerily resembling Balaclava Buggins, founder of the College, is found floating in Oozak's Pond.
7. *Vane Pursuit* (Mysterious, 1989)
   Helen Shandy, who has been photographing antique weather vanes created by Praxiteles Lumpkin, discovers that many of the precious vanes have been stolen.

II. Sarah Kelling, member of Boston's upper crust, finds her wealthy blueblood family of little help when she loses her first husband and most of her money. Sarah is the nicest, sanest member of a family that has more than its share of nasty, eccentric, or just plain ineffectual members. When Sarah gets mixed up with murder and other crimes, she relies on Max Bittersohn, an art detective who eventually becomes her second husband. Like the Shandy novels, this series has a good deal of humor, some romance, slightly farfetched plots, and odd characters with odd names who come to odd ends (one is soaked in honey and stung to death by bees).

1. *The Family Vault* (Doubleday, 1979)
   When the family burial vault is opened to receive another Kelling, it unexpectedly reveals the corpse of striptease artist Ruby Redd.
2. *The Withdrawing Room* (Doubleday, 1980)
   Sarah Kelling, now widowed and forced to take boarders in her heavily mortgaged Beacon Hill mansion, finds that the former "withdrawing room" is fatal to two of them.
3. *The Palace Guard* (Doubleday, 1981)
   When Sarah's lodger Max Bittersohn takes her to the latest concert of impresario Nick Fieringer, guards at Madam Wilkins's palacial museum start dying of unnatural causes.
4. *The Bilbao Looking Glass* (Doubleday, 1983)
   A series of off-season burglaries on Massachusetts' North Shore results in a valuable antique mirror turning up in the front hall of Sarah's summer home.
5. *The Convivial Codfish* (Doubleday, 1984)
   Max Bittersohn investigates the Comrades of the Convivial Codfish when Sarah's uncle Jem, Grand Exalted Chowderhead, loses the silver codfish at the Scrooge Day Dinner.
6. *The Recycled Citizen* (Mysterious, 1988)
   Sarah's Uncle Adolphus is charged with drug smuggling and mur-

der when heroin turns up in some soda cans at his recycling business.

7. *The Silver Ghost* (Mysterious, 1988)
When Bill Billingsgate misses a 1927 New Phantom Rolls Royce from his collection of antique cars, Sarah and Max come to his annual Renaissance Revel to investigate.
Note: Charlotte MacLeod also writes mysteries under the pseudonyms of Alisa Craig and Matilda Hughes.

McMurtry, Larry

I. Although he no longer wears his "Minor Regional Novelist" sweatshirt, and has written novels about other parts of the world, Larry McMurtry is indelibly associated with the state of Texas. His first six novels and the Pulitzer Prize–winning *Lonesome Dove* (1985) are all set primarily in Texas, as are the movies made from his novels: *Hud* (adapted from *Horseman, Pass By*), *The Last Picture Show*, and *Terms of Endearment*.

The north central Texas town of Archer City, where McMurtry grew up, is the model for Thalia, the fictional town that is the setting for a pair of novels written twenty years apart. *The Last Picture Show* is about growing up in a bleak small town where sports and sex are the only outlets for adolescent energies. The sequel, *Texasville*, returns to Thalia thirty years later when the town is demoralized by a sudden economic downturn. The film version of *The Last Picture Show*, which was shot in Archer City, won several Academy Awards. Thalia plays a peripheral role in McMurtry's first two novels: *Horseman, Pass By* (1961) and *Leaving Cheyenne* (1963).

1. *The Last Picture Show* (Dial, 1966)
High school student Sonny Crawford, his best buddy Duane Jackson, and Duane's girlfriend Jacy Farrow learn about life and love in 1950s Thalia, Texas.

2. *Texasville* (Simon & Schuster, 1987)
Duane Jackson, one-time oil millionaire now on the verge of bankruptcy, is jolted when his high school sweetheart Jacy, now a movie actress, returns to Thalia.

II. The novels in McMurtry's Urban trilogy also have Texas settings, primarily Houston. Just as the Thalia novels show the bleakness of small-town life, the urban novels depict the rootlessness and anomie of modern urban life. The three books have a revolving set of characters; supporting characters in one novel become the stars of another. *Terms of Endearment* is the best-known novel of the trilogy, partly because of the success of the movie version which won Academy Awards for Best Picture, Best Actress (Shirley MacLaine), and Best Supporting Actor (Jack Nicholson). In 1989, a fourth novel, set in rural north Texas and featuring Danny Deck, protagonist of *All My Friends Are Going to Be Strangers*, was added to the series.

1. *Moving On* (Simon & Schuster, 1970)
   Patsy Carpenter and her husband Jim avoid facing up to a disintegrating marriage by having a series of affairs.
2. *All My Friends Are Going to Be Strangers* (Simon & Schuster, 1972)
   Young writer Danny Deck moves back and forth between Texas and California while trying to find himself.
3. *Terms of Endearment* (Simon & Schuster, 1975)
   Wealthy Houston widow Aurora Greenway deals with a series of suitors while trying to control the life of Emma, her married daughter.
4. *Some Can Whistle* (Simon & Schuster, 1989)
   Danny Deck, producer of a successful TV sitcom, retires to a remote Texas ranch, where he is found by T.R., the daughter he hasn't seen since birth.

MacNeil, Duncan (pseud. of Philip McCutchan, q.v.)

This series about the Royal British Army in India at the turn of the century stars the dashing young James Ogilvie of the 114th Highlanders, the Queen's Own Royal Strathspeys. James's father, Sir Iain Ogilvie, is commander of the entire Northern India Army. Readers interested in the period and having a tolerance for a very British view of India will enjoy the fast-paced action and colorful setting.

1. *Drums along the Khyber* (St. Martin's, 1972)
   Young James is assigned to the 114th Highlanders; he meets and falls in love with Mrs. Archdale.
2. *Lieutenant of the Line* (St. Martin's, 1972)
   Almost twenty-one, Ogilvie meets trouble on the Afghanistan border with a resourcefulness contrary to orders, but he saves the day.
3. *Sadhu on the Mountain Peak* (St. Martin's, 1973)
   Captain Ogilvie spies on a holy man to keep him from rousing rebel forces.
4. *The Gates of Kunarja* (St. Martin's, 1974)
   Ogilvie must cross through the Khyber Pass in winter to free the regimental commander, who is being held for ransom.
5. *The Red Daniel* (St. Martin's, 1974)
   Ogilvie sees service in the Boer War.
6. *Subaltern's Choice* (St. Martin's, 1974)
   Back in India, when a foolhardy young subaltern, Hamish Dewar, loses his whole patrol, Captain Ogilvie must take over.
7. *By Command of the Viceroy* (St. Martin's, 1975)
   Ogilvie escorts a Russian mission through the Indian frontier.
8. *The Mullah from Kashmir* (St. Martin's, 1976)
   Captain Ogilvie infiltrates the mullah's secret headquarters in an effort to prevent the assassination of a young maharajah.
9. *Wolf in the Fold* (St. Martin's, 1977)
   On leave in London, Captain Ogilvie takes on a special assignment to investigate a problem of security on the North-West Frontier.
10. *Charge of Cowardice* (St. Martin's, 1978)
    Ogilvie is awaiting court martial as invaders threaten from the north.
11. *The Restless Frontier* (St. Martin's, 1980)
    Rescuing beautiful Angela, Ogilvie is captured; the enemy suspends him over a pit of vipers in an effort to get him to talk.
12. *Cunningham's Revenge* (Walker, 1985)
    The Pathans stage an uprising, and Cunningham deserts after his wife is killed during an attack.
13. *The Train at Bundarbar* (Walker, 1986)
    Captain James Ogilvie deals with floods in northern India, mutinous Pathans, and a stranded train carrying £100,000 in gold bullion and his beloved Fiona Elliott.
14. *A Matter for the Regiment* (Hodder, London, 1982)
    Not yet published in the United States.

Mann, Thomas

Mann is generally regarded as the foremost German novelist of the twentieth century. He had published *Buddenbrooks* and his masterpiece, *The Magic Mountain*, before beginning work on a novel with a biblical theme, which grew into a tetralogy. His winning the Nobel Prize in 1929 guaranteed the work an international audience, though he fled Germany in 1933 and his books were burned there. The four novels present a very detailed and leisurely recounting of the story of Joseph of the multihued coat. The tetralogy is available in an omnibus volume entitled *Joseph and His Brothers* (Knopf, 1948), translated by H. T. Lowe-Porter.

1. *Joseph and His Brothers* (Knopf, 1934)
   This book deals mostly with the story of Jacob, Joseph's father.
2. *Young Joseph* (Knopf, 1935)
   As an adolescent, Joseph is the envy of his brothers, who sell him to an Ishmaelite trader.
3. *Joseph in Egypt* (Knopf, 1938)
   Joseph becomes Potiphar's household steward but is sent to jail after refusing the advances of Potiphar's wife.
4. *Joseph the Provider* (Knopf, 1944)
   Joseph is released from prison, rises to power in the Pharoah's court, and is reunited with his brothers.

Maling, Arthur

Chicago-based Arthur Maling worked for his family retail shoe store chain until he became a successful crime novel writer. Brock Potter, his continuing character, is a securities analyst in the Wall Street brokerage firm of Price, Potter and Petacque. Potter, like Emma Lathen's John Putnam Thatcher, is drawn into investigating crimes that come to light in the course of his business. Although he is financially a solid citizen, Potter is a loner who avoids close relationships. The Potter novels are a well-plotted mix of business and crime.

1. *Ripoff* (Harper, 1976)
   Potter investigates an insurance scandal involving $23 million worth of stolen securities.

2. *Schroeder's Game* (Harper, 1977)
   A scam involving a company handling the billing for hospital medical services leads to kidnap and murder.
3. *Lucky Devil* (Harper, 1978)
   Potter investigates the murder of an investor who has acquired some rather doubtful stocks.
4. *The Koberg Link* (Harper, 1979)
   A paint company stock that suddenly rises, and the killing of the fiance of Potter's secretary's niece, are the problems here.
5. *A Taste of Treason* (Harper, 1983)
   Kevin Rand, Potter's close friend who was convicted of selling secret information to the East Germans, is murdered in prison.

Manning, Olivia

The recent PBS mini-series "Fortunes of War" kindled interest in English novelist Olivia Manning's Balkan trilogy and Levant trilogy, which form a six-part autobiographical novel set in Rumania, Greece, Egypt, Syria, and Palestine during World War II. Harriet and Guy Pringle, the two leading characters, are somewhat mismatched: Harriet is a realist; Guy is an incurable idealist who selflessly devotes his time to everyone except his wife. How Harriet comes to terms with Guy's character and her own expectations is one of the continuing threads in the series, but there are many other characters who reappear from time to time, such as the ingratiating sponger Yakimov, the callow young officer Simon Boulderstone, and the poet Castlebar. More realistic and less exotic than Durrell's Alexandria Quartet, "Fortunes of War" is about ordinary people caught up in extraordinary events. Anthony Burgess called the Balkan trilogy "probably the most important long work of fiction written by a woman since the war" (*99 Novels*, Summit, 1984). The Balkan trilogy (numbers 1, 2, and 3) and the Levant trilogy (numbers 4, 5, and 6) have been published in single paperback volumes by Penguin.

1. *The Great Fortune* (Doubleday, 1961)
   Guy Pringle, lecturer in English at the University of Bucharest, returns to Rumania with his bride Harriet just as the Germans invade Poland in September, 1939.
2. *The Spoilt City* (Doubleday, 1962)
   The German invasion and the collapse of Rumania are imminent, as the British residents of Bucharest form their various escape plans. Covers June–September, 1940.

3. *Friends and Heroes* (Doubleday, 1966)
   The Pringles and other members of the British colony in Rumania have fled to Greece, and set up temporary housekeeping in Athens, but it is only a matter of time before the invading Germans will force them to flee again.
4. *The Danger Tree* (Atheneum, 1977)
   The Pringles have escaped to Egypt. Guy gets another position as an English instructor, while Harriet makes new friends with the poet Castlebar and a young officer, Simon Boulderstone.
5. *The Battle Lost and Won* (Atheneum, 1978)
   Simon Boulderstone, mourning the loss of his brother, throws himself into the desert fighting just before the battle of Alamein, as Harriet and Guy, often separated, go through a marital crisis.
6. *The Sum of Things* (Atheneum, 1981)
   Simon is in a military hospital after being blown up by a land mine. Harriet, unbeknownst to Guy, has adventures in Syria and Palestine, while Guy, believing Harriet to be dead, tries to carry on with his teaching.

Marric, J. J. (pseud. of John Creasey, q.v.)

John Creasey wrote the Gideon police procedurals under this pseudonym. Superintendent George Gideon of New Scotland Yard is a large, handsome man with steel-gray hair, whose customary quiet manner occasionally erupts into a towering rage. Gideon was pushing fifty when he made his fictional debut in *Gideon's Day*, and though his six children are glimpsed growing up through the years, Gideon himself, his wife, Kate, and his closest associate, Chief Inspector Lemaitre, never seem to grow older. The police procedural, by its nature, has too diffuse a plot to catch in a short annotation. The last two titles in the list below were written by William Butler after John Creasey's death. *Gideon at Work* (Harper, 1957) is an omnibus containing numbers 1, 2, and 3 listed below. A series that Creasey wrote as Anthony Morton is also described under that name (q.v.).

1. *Gideon's Day* (Harper, 1955) Variant title: *Gideon of Scotland Yard*.
2. *Gideon's Week* (Harper, 1956) Variant title: *Seven Days to Death*.
3. *Gideon's Night* (Harper, 1957)
4. *Gideon's Month* (Harper, 1958)

5. *Gideon's Staff* (Harper, 1959)
6. *Gideon's Risk* (Harper, 1960)
7. *Gideon's Fire* (Harper, 1961) Edgar winner.
8. *Gideon's March* (Harper, 1962)
9. *Gideon's Ride* (Harper, 1963)
10. *Gideon's Vote* (Harper, 1964)
11. *Gideon's Lot* (Harper, 1964)
12. *Gideon's Badge* (Harper, 1965)
13. *Gideon's Wrath* (Harper, 1967)
14. *Gideon's River* (Harper, 1968)
15. *Gideon's Power* (Harper, 1969)
16. *Gideon's Sport* (Harper, 1970)
17. *Gideon's Art* (Harper, 1971)
18. *Gideon's Men* (Harper, 1972)
19. *Gideon's Press* (Harper, 1973)
20. *Gideon's Fog* (Harper, 1974)
21. *Gideon's Buy* (Harper, 1975)
22. *Gideon's Drive* (Harper, 1976)
23. *Gideon's Force* (Ulverscroft, 1978)
    Written by William Butler.
24. *Gideon's Way* (Stein & Day, 1986)
    Written by William Butler.

Marsh, Ngaio

Ngaio (pronounced NY-o) Marsh was born in New Zealand, and several of her mysteries are set there, but she writes the classic Christie type of story, and her British detective Roderick Alleyn (pronounced Allen) rivals Peter Wimsey in his culture and connections. Unlike Wimsey, Alleyn is a professional Scotland Yard detective and is frequently assisted by the stolid Inspector Fox. Marsh is vague about her detective's age but shows him first as a bachelor who meets and marries the young artist Agatha Troy; they have one son, who figures as an adult in one of the later books. *Three-Act Special* (Little, 1960) is an omnibus volume containing numbers 15, 16, and 17; *Another Three-Act Special* (Little, 1962) is an omnibus volume containing numbers 18, 20, and 21.

1. *A Man Lay Dead* (Sheridan, 1942)
   Alleyn's first appearance is a classic case of murder during a

parlor game at an English country-house weekend gathering. First published in England in 1931.

2. *Enter a Murderer* (Sheridan, 1942)
   Alleyn and his journalist friend Bathgate are in the audience when a stage gun shoots real bullets and an actor is wounded.

3. *The Nursing Home Murder* (Sheridan, 1941)
   The hospital setting makes this mystery something special.

4. *Death in Ecstasy* (Sheridan, 1941)
   Alleyn's friend Nigel Bathgate witnesses a religious cult murder.

5. *Vintage Murder* (Sheridan, 1940)
   The earliest book with a New Zealand setting concerns the murder of a stage impressario.

6. *Artists in Crime* (Furman, 1938)
   When an artist's model is murdered at Agatha Troy's art school, Alleyn investigates and falls in love with Agatha.

7. *Death in a White Tie* (Furman, 1938)
   A case of high society blackmail and murder draws Alleyn and Agatha together again, and they decide to tie the knot.

8. *Overture to Death* (Furman, 1939)
   Murder by a gun hidden in a very unlikely place disrupts life in the peaceful English village of Pen Cuckoo.

9. *Death of a Peer* (Little, 1940)
   Alleyn solves the murder of Uncle Gabriel, who held the purse strings of the delightfully irresponsible Lamprey family. English title: *Surfeit of Lampreys*.

10. *Death at the Bar* (Little, 1940)
    Death is delivered by poison dart in the private taproom of the Plume and Feathers, Devon.

11. *Death and the Dancing Footman* (Little, 1941)
    The footman figures in the alibi upon which this case of murder and suicide hinges.

12. *Colour Scheme* (Little, 1943)
    When one of the guests is murdered in a boiling mud pool at a New Zealand spa, Alleyn gets involved in some international espionage.

13. *Died in the Wool* (Little, 1945)
    Alleyn spends the war years in New Zealand and is on hand to investigate the murder of Flossie Rubrick, an M.P. who is found in an odoriferous bale of wool.

14. *Final Curtain* (Little, 1947)
    Agatha Troy had finished Sir Henry Ancred's portrait just before his suspicious sudden death.

15. *A Wreath for Rivera* (Little, 1949)

    Murder strikes the London jazz scene. Agatha is pregnant in this installment. English title: *Swing, Brother, Swing.*

16. *Night at the Vulcan* (Little, 1951)

    Marsh, who has written, acted in, and produced plays in London, uses her knowledge of the theater in this case of murder on opening night. English title: *Opening Night.*

17. *Spinsters in Jeopardy* (Little, 1953)

    The strange doings in a chateau in the Alps include the kidnapping of the Alleyn's little boy, Ricky. Variant title: *The Bride of Death.*

18. *Scales of Justice* (Little, 1955)

    Friends of Alleyn's are involved in murder in rural England.

19. *Death of a Fool* (Little, 1956)

    Murder at an annual folklorists' celebration of winter solstice. English title: *Off with His Head.*

20. *Singing in the Shrouds* (Little, 1958)

    Investigating a case of murder at sea, Alleyn follows a suspect aboard ship and sets a trap to catch him.

21. *False Scent* (Little, 1959)

    The home of a flamboyant London actress is the scene of murder.

22. *Hand in Glove* (Little, 1962)

    Superintendent Alleyn investigates a murder at a posh country house in England.

23. *Dead Water* (Little, 1963)

    This case concerns the supposedly healing waters on a Cornish island owned by Alleyn's former French teacher.

24. *Killer Dolphin* (Little, 1966)

    Playwright and director Peregrine Jay saves an old theater from destruction and opens his new play before tragedy strikes. English title: *Death at the Dolphin.*

25. *Clutch of Constables* (Little, 1969)

    Art forgery is featured in this case, as Alleyn investigates in America and his wife takes a riverboat trip through England.

26. *When in Rome* (Little, 1971)

    The Roman setting is a plus in this tale of blackmail and scandalous activities of a tour group.

27. *Tied Up in Tinsel* (Little, 1972)

    Christmas at Halberds Manor involves a missing man as well as plenty of mistletoe and holly. The Alleyns are guests.

28. *Black as He's Painted* (Little, 1974)
    A former classmate of Alleyn's, now president of an African nation, is in London on a state visit and threatened by assassins.
29. *Last Ditch* (Little, 1977)
    The Alleyns' son Ricky, now a young don spending the Easter holidays on the Channel Islands, falls in love and stumbles into a drug-smuggling gang.
30. *Grave Mistake* (Little, 1978)
    An eccentric old lady in a nursing home dies suddenly, and Alleyn suspects murder.
31. *Photo Finish* (Little, 1980)
    Alleyn visits a New Zealand paradise island estate to protect an opera star from an intrusive photographer.
32. *Light Thickens* (Little, 1982)
    A performance of *Macbeth* leads to a real severed head, instead of a prop, on MacDuff's spear as the climax to a series of odd incidents.

Marshall, William

Australian writer William Marshall writes police procedurals set in the Yellowthread Street Station in the fictional district of Hong Bay in Hong Kong. Chief Inspector Harry Feiffer and officers O'Yee, Auden, Spencer, and others deal with a variety of bizarre and often bloody crimes. The novels are a mixture of authentic Hong Kong ambience, screwball comedy, wild action, and slam-bang finales. Somehow Marshall makes this melange work in volume after volume to the delight of an increasing number of fans worldwide.

1. *Yellowthread Street* (Holt, 1976)
   A dismembered ear, a chopped-up wife, and a Mongolian giant with a knife are among the problems facing the Yellowthread Street force.
2. *The Hatchet Man* (Holt, 1977)
   A deranged killer with a four-barrel pistol must be tracked down.
3. *Gelignite* (Holt, 1977)
   A madman is sending letter bombs through the mail.

4. *Thin Air* (Holt, 1978)
   Fifty-seven dead passengers on a chartered jet and six Chinese men machine-gunned in a sewer require police attention.

5. *Skulduggery* (Holt, 1980)
   The Yellowthread Street bunch deal with a two-decade-old murder, a series of muggings, a balky radiator, and a criminal gang of deaf-and-dumb persons.

6. *Sci Fi* (Holt, 1981)
   "The Spaceman," who cremates people with a ray gun, brings unanticipated excitement to the All-Asia Science Fiction and Horror Movie Congress.

7. *Perfect End* (Holt, 1983)
   Claw-like marks on the walls of an abandoned police station, the bodies of six policemen with strange chest wounds, and the reported sighting of a huge black cat give a sinister aura to this novel.

8. *War Machine* (Mysterious, 1988)
   Amid rumors of Japanese soldiers who never surrendered after World War II lurking in a tunnel waiting to attack Hong Kong, shots ring out all over Hong Bay.

9. *The Far Away Man* (Holt, 1984)
   A pair of yellow vaccination certificates is found with each victim of a serial killer.

10. *Roadshow* (Holt, 1985)
    A series of explosions devastates Hong Kong while the police race to disarm the mechanisms setting off the bombs and find the bomber's real target.

11. *Head First* (Holt, 1986)
    Corpses from mainland China with missing or rearranged body parts are turning up, and mailcarrier's bags are apparently combusting spontaneously.

12. *Frogmouth* (Mysterious, 1987)
    Every animal in the children's zoo is found mutilated and killed, while the walls at Yellowthread Street are producing mysterious voices and dripping slime.

13. *Out of Nowhere* (Mysterious, 1988)
    A van loaded with plateglass and four passengers crashes into a truck after speeding down the wrong side of a deserted freeway.

Martin du Gard, Roger

Here is an author ripe for revival. Winner of the Nobel Prize for 1937, the Frenchman Roger Martin du Gard surely ranks among the world's most elusive writers. When accosted by Swedish journalists in the train on his way to receive his award, he pretended that they had mistaken him for someone else. Shortly before his death in 1958, he deposited all his papers at the Bibliothèque Nationale with instructions that they remain sealed for at least twenty-five years. Martin du Gard's major work was The Thibaults, a family saga published in France in eight parts and available in English translation in two omnibus volumes, listed below.

1. *The Thibaults* (Viking, 1939)
   The Catholic Thibault family is dominated by the father, an autocratic widower. Antoine, the older son, becomes a doctor, while his younger brother, the rebellious Jacques, is drawn into socialism and pacifism. The Protestant Fontanin family provides a counterpart throughout. This volume contains the first six parts, each published separately in France. All were translated by Stuart Gilbert.

   a. *Le cahier gris*
      In 1905, young Jacques and his friend Daniel Fontanin run away from home to Marseilles. First published in France in 1922.
   b. *Le pénitencier*
      Jacques spends time at a reform school as punishment for his escapade and is released through his brother's intercession. First published in France in 1922.
   c. *La belle saison*
      Four interwoven love stories are set at the family's summer home. First published in France in 1923.
   d. *La consultation*
      The action takes place during a harrowing day in the life of the young doctor Antoine Thibault. First published in France G 1928.
   e. *La sorellina*
      Antoine reads a story that Jacques has written and goes to Lausanne to find him. First published in France in 1928.

291

f. *La mort du pere*
Antoine administers a deathbed dose of morphine to relieve his father's suffering. First published in France in 1929.

2. *Summer 1914* (Viking, 1941)
The different tone of the last two parts reflects a revision of the author's plan for the series. Both were translated by Stuart Gilbert.

a. *L'eté 1914*
Jacques becomes a confirmed pacifist and dies tragically. The events add up to a powerful antiwar statement. First published in France in 1936.
b. *Epilogue*
Wounded and dying, Antoine returns home. First published in France in 1940.

Mason, Francis Van Wyck

I. Yes, the Van Wyck Mason who writes sea stories and the Francis Van Wyck Mason who writes mysteries are one and the same. The diversely talented Mason has also written war stories, flying stories, children's books, and nonfiction. In fact, he claims to have sold everything he's ever written, with the exception of two short stories. Mason conceived of the four historical melodramas listed below as a tetralogy that would "depict the maritime peoples of the American colonies during the Revolution." They do not share characters or story lines.

1. *Three Harbors* (Lippincott, 1938)
American merchant Rob Ashton stars in this romantic adventure set against the pre-Revolutionary turmoil in Boston, Norfolk, and Bermuda in 1774–75
2. *Stars on the Sea* (Lippincott, 1940)
The story of young privateer Timothy Bennett and Lucy, the girl he loves. The action takes place in Rhode Island, South Carolina, and the Bahamas of 1775–77.
3. *Rivers of Glory* (Lippincott, 1942)
Andrew Warren takes his ship to Jamaica for supplies, but pirates and the beautiful but treacherous Minga delay his return to Boston. This book covers 1778–79.

4. *Eagle in the Sky* (Lippincott, 1948)
The central figures are three colonial doctors: Asa Peabody, Peter Burnham, and Lucius Devoe. The time is 1780–81.

II. First as captain, then as major, then as colonel, Hugh North has undertaken one sensitive and dangerous assignment after another in the service of G-2, U.S. Army Intelligence. Though his six-foot frame is decorated with scars and his temples with gray, North is still as invincible and attractive to the ladies as ever. Worlds away from the subtle international intrigue of Le Carré's Smiley, North is a straight arrow who depends on quick thinking, eternal vigilance, and rugged, even merciless, methods. He never has an ambivalent moment and can always tell the good guys from the bad. The later stories are so similar that the exotic locale of the title is sufficient annotation for most. *Captain North's Three Biggest Cases* (Grosset, 1932) is an omnibus containing numbers 3, 4, and 5 listed below; *Oriental Division G-2* (Reynal, 1933) comprises numbers 2, 6, and 7; *Military Intelligence-8: Captain North's Most Celebrated Intrigues* (Stokes, 1941) includes numbers 9, 11, and 13; and *Man from G-2* (Reynal, 1942) contains numbers 3, 12, and 15.

1. *Seeds of Murder* (Doubleday, 1930)
Captain North's first perplexing case involves three seeds mysteriously placed under the bodies of two murdered men.
2. *Fort Terror Murders* (Doubleday, 1931)
Murder and hidden treasure bring North to an old Spanish fort in the Philippines.
3. *Vesper Service Murders* (Doubleday, 1931)
The small city of Deptford, Massachusetts, is the uncharacteristic setting for this study of corruption.
4. *The Yellow Arrow Murders* (Doubleday, 1932)
A laboratory in Cuba is the scene of an invention that will revolutionize naval warfare.
5. *The Branded Spy Murders* (Doubleday, 1932)
The action is set in Hawaii.
6. *Shanghai Bund Murders* (Doubleday, 1933). Variant title: *The China Sea Murders*.
7. *The Sulu Sea Murders* (Doubleday, 1933)
North returns to the Philippines.
8. *Budapest Parade Murders* (Doubleday, 1935)
9. *Washington Legation Murders* (Doubleday, 1935)
Washington is overrun with spies.

10. *Seven Seas Murders* (Doubleday, 1936)
    This is a collection of four Captain North stories: "Shanghai Sanctuary," "The Repeater," "Port of Intrigue," and "The Munitions Ship Murders."
11. *Hong Kong Airbase Murders* (Doubleday, 1937)
12. *Cairo Garter Murders* (Doubleday, 1939)
13. *Singapore Exile Murders* (Doubleday, 1939)
14. *Bucharest Ballerina Murders* (Stokes, 1940)
15. *Rio Casino Intrigue* (Reynal, 1941)
    A shipload of iron is headed for the Brazilian port.
16. *Saigon Singer* (Doubleday, 1946)
17. *Dardanelles Derelict* (Doubleday, 1949)
18. *Himalayan Assignment* (Doubleday, 1952)
19. *Two Tickets for Tangiers* (Doubleday, 1955)
    The action concerns the formula for a lethal gas that can freeze victims to death in seconds.
20. *Gracious Lily Affair* (Doubleday, 1957)
    Colonel North investigates when a Portuguese plane off Bermuda is blown up.
21. *Secret Mission to Bangkok* (Doubleday, 1960)
    North is protecting Dr. Bracht, a top U.S. scientist who is having wife troubles.
22. *Trouble in Burma* (Doubleday, 1962)
23. *Zanzibar Intrigue* (Doubleday, 1963)
24. *Maracaibo Mission* (Doubleday, 1965)
25. *Deadly Orbit Mission* (Doubleday, 1968)
    A Russian satellite with a nuclear warhead is orbiting regularly over the United States.

Masters, John

I. The Loss of Eden trilogy is a panoramic saga of World War I focusing on four families who are representative of British society: The Rowland family of auto manufacturers; the working-class Strattons; the Earl of Swanwick and his family; and Probyn Gorse, the crafty poacher and his large brood. The war's effects on this large cast of characters make engrossing and moving novels that give a composite picture of the social and economic upheaval caused by the war's trauma.

1. *Now, God Be Thanked* (McGraw-Hill, 1979)
   This account begins on July 4, 1914, at the Henley Royal Regatta and continues to Christmas, 1915, on the battlefield.
2. *Heart of War* (McGraw-Hill, 1980)
   Class distinctions begin to blur and a new society to emerge during 1916–17.
3. *By the Green of the Spring* (McGraw-Hill, 1981)
   The war ends, and in its aftermath there emerge such new problems as union struggles and flu epidemics.

II. Masters planned a series of thirty-five novels depicting the history of the British presence in India. Before his death in 1983, he had completed only ten novels about India, seven of which have one Anglo-Indian family, the Savages, as their connecting link. With the exception of *Coromandel*, which tells about Jason Savage, the first member of his family to go to India, and which is set in the 1600s, the novels deal with British India from the 1830s to the 1940s. Masters, who was the fifth generation of an Anglo-Indian family, knew India well, and his books capture the authentic flavor of India with accurate historical detail, albeit from the British point of view. *Bhowani Junction* was made into an MGM film starring Ava Gardner and Stewart Granger (1956).

1. *Coromandel* (Viking, 1955)
   Jason Savage, illiterate son of an English tenant farmer, buys a map showing buried treasure in Coromandel, India, and goes treasure-hunting. Set in the 1600s.
2. *The Deceivers* (Viking, 1952)
   William Savage, English civil servant in India, sets out to infiltrate the Thugs and destroy their murderous cult. Set in the 1830s.
3. *Nightrunners of Bengal* (Viking, 1950)
   Captain Rodney Savage has to rescue himself and his son from the horrors of the Indian mutiny of 1857.
4. *The Lotus and the Wind* (Viking, 1952)
   Robin Savage, son of Rodney, trails Muralev, a Russian agent, through the Afghan wilderness in the late 1800s.
5. *Far, Far the Mountain Peak* (Viking, 1957)
   Peter Savage, grandson of General Rodney Savage, pursues his mountain-climbing obsession in Europe and India. Covers 1902 to 1922.
6. *Bhowani Junction* (Viking, 1954)
   Victoria Jones and Patrick Taylor, young Anglo-Indians unsure of their racial status, and Colonel Rodney Savage (Peter's son) who is

in charge of guarding the trains at Bhowani Junction, are the main protagonists on the eve of Indian independence in 1946.

7. *To the Coral Strand* (Harper, 1962)
Rodney Savage, who cannot come to terms with an independent India, goes through a series of positions from big-game hunter to diplomat.

III. Another pair of novels dealing with India describe the adventures of the Bateman family.

1. *The Ravi Lancers* (Doubleday, 1972)
Captain Warren Bateman commands an Indian regiment serving in the trenches of World War I.
2. *The Himalayan Concerto* (Doubleday, 1976)
Composer Rodney Bateman, vacationing in Kashmir, is recruited by Indian intelligence to monitor Chinese activities on India's northern border.

Matthews, Greg

Australian writer Greg Matthews displayed his deep interest in American culture with *The Further Adventures of Huckleberry Finn* (Crown, 1983), a continuation of Mark Twain's classic which captured Twain's sound and style. The pair of novels featuring fifteen-year-old Burris Weems of Indiana also reveal Matthews's command of the American idiom. Burris is intelligent and articulate, but is overwhelmed by his physical, psychological, and social problems and, like most teenagers, prone to self-pity. Burris speaks for himself in these funny, touching novels.

1. *Little Red Rooster* (NAL, 1987)
Burris Weems uses a stolen tape recorder to relate his complaints about life, but finds that his life picks up somewhat when he gets a summer job stacking boxes.
2. *The Gold Flake Hydrant* (NAL, 1988)
Five months later, Burris has survived a suicide attempt, flunked out of high school, and lost his girlfriend. He befriends town character "Lennie the Loop," which leads to more trouble.

May, Julian

Julian May's four-volume Saga of Pliocene Exile is an engrossing science fiction epic spiced with plenty of action, frank sex, mythology, parapsychology, fantasy, and a host of other elements. The story begins when a group of dissidents, bored with life in the twenty-second century, travel six million years back in time to the Pliocene epoch. There they encounter two warring groups of humanoids: the beautiful, arrogant Tanu and the ugly, outcast Firvulag. In May's guide to the tetralogy, *A Pliocene Companion* (Houghton, 1984), she tells of her plans to write another related series, the Galactic Milieu Series, which will consist of three novels: *Jack the Bodiless*, *Diamond Mask*, and *Magnificat*. May is an American author who also writes nonfiction. Reading her books in the correct sequence is very important.

1. *The Many-Colored Land* (Houghton, 1981)
   A group of dissatisfied inhabitants of the twenty-second century take a one-way time trip to Pliocene Europe, where they find a world ruled by two warring groups of humanoids.
2. *The Golden Torc* (Houghton, 1981)
   The time-exiles work to overthrow the Tanu and close the time-gate.
3. *The Nonborn King* (Houghton, 1983)
   The balance of power between the time-exiles, the Tanu, and the Firvulag is upset by Aiken Drum and some new time-exiles from the Metapsychic Rebellion of 2083.
4. *The Adversary* (Houghton, 1984)
   King Aiken and the children of the time-exiles fight against Marc Remillard and his Firvulag allies.

Melville, Anne (pseud. of Margaret Potter)

This English romance and juvenile writer has produced a family saga that traces the fortunes of the Lorimer family of Bristol, England. The story begins in the 1870s when the family banking business fails due to the folly and chicanery of John Julius Lorimer, and continues into the 1970s showing how the second, third, and fourth generations of Lorimers deal with the problems of love, money, and vocation. This serviceable family chronicle is more realistic and less overheated than some of its kind.

1. *The Lorimer Line* (Doubleday, 1977)
   The failure of the family bank, which brings hardship and lost love to Margaret Lorimer, also frees her from the restricted role of an upper-middle-class Victorian woman.
2. *Alexa* (Doubleday, 1979)
   Margaret Lorimer's half-sister Alexa endures a series of calamities from unhappy love affairs to the San Francisco earthquake. Published in England as *The Lorimer Legacy*.
3. *Blaize* (Doubleday, 1981)
   The saga continues through both world wars chronicling the careers of the younger Lorimers. Blaize, the Lorimer country estate, becomes a field hospital in World War I. Published in England in two parts as *Lorimers at War* and *Lorimers in Love*.
4. *Family Fortunes* (Doubleday, 1984)
   The lives of Lady Alexa Glanville and her relatives are traced from 1946 to 1977. Published in England in two parts as *The Last of the Lorimers* and *Lorimer Loyalties*.

Melville, Herman

These two novels by Melville are sometimes classed as nonfiction since they are based on his wanderings in the South Seas. They were his first published works and won him an early reputation as a popular writer of adventure tales among readers who were dismayed at the turn his subsequent works took. While the pace of these tales slows occasionally for anthropological description, which is fascinating in itself, their main current sweeps along, as brisk and exciting as any modern thriller. Like most romantics, Melville painted his savages as much more noble than his corrupt white men.

1. *Typee: A Peep at Polynesian Life* (Wiley and Putnam, 1846)
   The author and his friend Toby jump ship in the Marquesas and are eventually taken captive by a cannibal tribe. The second edition, published in 1846, contained an addendum, "The Story of Toby," which is included in most modern editions.
2. *Omoo* (Harper, 1847)
   The author and his friend Doctor Long Ghost explore Tahiti.

Melville, James (pseud. of Peter Martin)

The Japanese city of Kobe is the setting for a series of police procedurals featuring Superintendent Tetsuo Otani and his lieutenants, the dapper Jiro Kimura and the sinister "Ninja" Noguchi. Superintendent Otani, although capable of instilling fear in the hearts of his nine-thousand-man police force, is basically a likeable man with genial good manners, humor, and an endearing tenderness for his wife Hanae. The well-plotted novels inform as well as entertain. English writer Melville, former head of the British Council in Tokyo, writes with accuracy and affection about daily life in contemporary Japan.

1. *The Wages of Zen* (Secker, London, 1979)
   A Zen community composed of foreigners and led by a money-grubbing priest gets involved in drugs and murder.
2. *The Chrysanthemum Chain* (St. Martin's, 1982)
   An English resident of Japan, an educator who has important political friends, is murdered.
3. *A Sort of Samurai* (St. Martin's, 1982)
   A German businessman is found dead at his desk after an earthquake, but Otani suspects foul play.
4. *The Ninth Netsuke* (St. Martin's, 1982)
   Otani's wife finds a netsuke hidden in the drapes of a Kobe hotel room, which may be a clue to a murder.
5. *Sayonara, Sweet Amaryllis* (St. Martin's, 1984)
   The poisoning of a prominent member of the expatriate community is linked to a drug smuggling ring.
6. *Death of a Daimyo* (St. Martin's, 1985)
   While vacationing in England, Otani witnesses a murder which may be connected to an underworld power struggle in Japan.
7. *The Death Ceremony* (St. Martin's, 1985)
   The hereditary grand master of the Southern School of the Tea Ceremony is shot through the head while ritually preparing the tea.
8. *Go Gently, Gaijin* (St. Martin's, 1986)
   Two foreigners (gaijin), Muslim members of KISS (Kinki International Students Society), die violently.
9. *Kimono for a Corpse* (St. Martin's, 1988)
   A gathering of international couturiers, invited to Japan by leading designer Madame Yashuda, is hit by murder.

10. *The Reluctant Ronin* (Scribner's, 1988)
A Dutch woman linked to Otani's son-in-law dies under mysterious circumstances during a fire.

Meredith, George

Meredith's reputation has already undergone several ups and downs. After an early success with *The Ordeal of Richard Feverel* in 1859, his subsequent novels, which were perhaps ahead of their time, failed to please either the public or the critics. By the 1880s his public had caught up with him, and his enlightened attitudes placed him among the leaders of a modernism quickly displaced after World War I. Meredith will appeal to fans of Austen and Thackeray. The pleasures of his language, his droll humor, and his feminist sympathies are evident in this pair of novels about Emilia Alessandra Belloni.

1. *Sandra Belloni* (Published under the title *Emilia in England* by Chapman, London, in 1864; the title was changed for the collected works published by Chapman and by Robert Bros. in Boston in 1885)
Emilia's innocence and honesty contrast wittily with the hypocrisy of the three social-climbing Pole sisters, who take up the young Italian girl with the remarkable singing voice.
2. *Vittoria* (Chapman, London, 1866)
Emilia, now the famous singer Vittoria Champa, travels to Italy. Less comic than the first novel, this book is more concerned with the Italian Revolution, which Vittoria symbolizes.

Merejkowski, Dmitri

Christ and Anti-Christ is the series title of this trilogy of historical novels in which Russian author Merejkowski uses three vastly different epochs to illustrate his theme of the struggle between Christian and pagan ideas. Though the translation may seem a little wooden, the books' interesting story lines can still draw readers into richly woven portraits of the fascinating periods they depict.

1. *The Death of the Gods* (Putnam, 1901)
   The central theme is the life of the Roman emperor Julian from boyhood to his death (A.D. 337–63) and the wars and controversies of his times. Variant title: *Julian the Apostate*. Translated from the Russian by Herbert Trench.
2. *The Romance of Leonardo da Vinci* (Putnam, 1902)
   Perhaps the best known of the trilogy, this volume gives special attention to da Vinci's scientific and medical researches during the period 1494–1519. Variant titles: *The Gods Reborn* and *The Forerunner*. Translated from the Russian by Herbert Trench.
3. *Peter and Alexis* (Putnam, 1905)
   Peter the Great and his imbecile son, Alexis, are featured in this concluding volume, which covers the years 1715–18 and gives a panoramic view of Russian society. Variant title: *Peter the Great*. Translated from the Russian by Herbert Trench.

Meyer, Nicholas

Meyer adroitly catches the Victorian atmosphere, language, and detail in these clever additions to the Holmes canon. The *Seven-Per-Cent Solution* was the subject of a successful 1976 movie, starring Nicol Williamson as Holmes, Robert Duvall as Watson, Alan Arkin as Freud, and Vanessa Redgrave as the mysterious lady who captures Holmes's heart.

1. *Seven-Per-Cent Solution* (Dutton, 1974)
   Dr. Watson tells how he spirited Holmes off to Vienna and turned him over to Freud for treatment of his cocaine addiction.
2. *West End Horror* (Dutton, 1976)
   George Bernard Shaw and other historical characters are featured in Dr. Watson's "posthumous memoir" about Holmes's 1895 investigation of the murder of a theater critic.

Miller, Henry

I. This controversial American author published his first novel, *Tropic of Cancer*, in France in 1934. It was promptly banned in all English-speaking countries until 1961, when Grove Press's American edition provoked a furor that eventually led to sixty lawsuits across the country. The book sold 2.5 million copies in two years, giving Miller a best-seller in his native land after many years of poverty. Miller wrote a violent stream of consciousness in which lusty incident, virtuoso prose, and lyric reminiscence churn alternately crude and exuberant. Autobiographical, like most of Miller's work, these three novels cohere as a group. A chronology would be meaningless; they are perhaps best read in the order in which they were written.

1. *Tropic of Cancer* (Grove, 1961)
   This is an account of an American in Paris in the 1930s wallowing in the lower depths. The narrator is named Henry Miller and is a writer. First published in France in 1934.
2. *Black Spring* (Grove, 1961)
   Dreams and nightmares of the artist's mind range from images of despair and horror to evocative memories of growing up in Brooklyn. First published in France in 1936.
3. *Tropic of Capricorn* (Grove, 1961)
   Before coming to Paris, the narrator, like Miller, worked as a personnel manager for a telegraph company—named the Cosmodemonic Company here. First published in France in 1939.

II. Some critics have called the Rosy Crucifixion trilogy Miller's masterpiece, though others have thought its explicit sexual content excessive. It too is a highly autobiographical work; it overlaps the period covered in *Tropic of Capricorn* and continues up to the narrator's flight to Paris. The trilogy shows the growth of the writer toward freedom and identity and the joyous acceptance of life by one who has suffered deeply.

1. *Sexus* (Grove, 1965)
   The author begins his recollections of his literary, intellectual, and amorous adventures in bohemian New York in the 1940s. First published in France in 1962.
2. *Plexus* (Grove, 1965)
   The author quits his job to write. His relationship with Mona, happy at first, becomes complicated. First published in France in 1959.
3. *Nexus* (Grove, 1965)
   Mona's crazy friend Stasia comes between her and Miller. First published in France in 1960.

Mishima, Yukio

While the scope and seriousness of Mishima's work may equal that of Proust or Sartre, and his sensibility and obsession with courage may invite comparison to Hemingway or even Mailer, the novels of this Japanese writer are quite unlike those of any Westerner. Born into a samurai family, Mishima mastered the traditional arts and became a charismatic rightist figure in Japan. He committed ritual suicide in 1970 at the age of forty-five after completing the final volume of his masterpiece, the Sea of Fertility. This tetralogy begins in 1912 and examines the social, esthetic, and moral life of Japan up to the 1960s. The character of Hondo is a continuing figure present in all four books.

1. *Spring Snow* (Knopf, 1972)
   Set in 1912, this narrative concerns the doomed affair between Ayakuras, son of a newly rich provincial family, and the beautiful Satoko, who is betrothed to a royal prince. Translated by Michael Gallagher.
2. *Runaway Horses* (Knopf, 1973)
   A conspiracy during the 1930s by a fanatical young patriot, Isao Iinuma, leads to his discovery, arrest, and trial. Translated by Michael Gallagher.
3. *Temple of Dawn* (Knopf, 1973)
   Hondo journeys to Bangkok in 1940 and becomes obsessed with a Thai princess. The second half of the story skips to the 1950s. Translated by E. Dale Saunders and Cecilia Seigle.
4. *The Decay of the Angel* (Knopf, 1974)
   In the late 1960s, Hondo, now old and rich, adopts a sixteen-year-old orphan boy as his heir. Translated by Edward Seidenstricker.

Moberg, Vilhelm

Liv Ullman and Max von Sydow starred in two riveting Swedish films—*The Emigrants* (1972) and *The New Land* (1973)—based on Moberg's trilogy about a band of Swedish farmers who emigrate to America. The story focuses on Oskar Nilsson, his wife, Kristina, their children, and his brother Robert as they leave their home in Ljuder Parish in 1850 and make the arduous Atlantic crossing. Confused but undaunted by the strangeness of the new world, they struggle west and settle in the Minnesota wilderness. This is a vivid testament to the awesome dangers of pioneer life and to the courage, fortitude, and humor of the Swedes who made the trip.

1. *The Emigrants* (Simon & Schuster, 1951)
   The Nilssons leave Sweden and cross the Atlantic in a small, cramped boat carrying freight and seventy other passengers. Translated from the Swedish by Gustaf Lannestock.
2. *Unto a Good Land* (Simon & Schuster, 1954)
   The family makes its way from the port of New York to its new home in Taylors Falls, Minnesota, in June 1851. Translated from the Swedish by Gustaf Lannestock.
3. *The Last Letter Home* (Simon & Schuster, 1961)
   The story from 1853 to Karl's death in 1890. Translated from the Swedish by Gustaf Lannestock.

Note: *The Settlers* (Popular Library, 1978) is the title given to an incomplete paperback edition of the third volume in the trilogy. It ends Karl's story in 1860. The concluding chapters are available separately in paperback under the title *Last Letter Home* (Popular Library, 1979).

Monsarrat, Nicholas

I. These two books by the author of the World War II classic *The Cruel Sea* still give a good picture of the conflicts and tensions found in developing African nations. Events as they unfold are seen mostly through the eyes of David Bracken, a novice British government official who feels a youthful rapport with Dinamaula, the Oxford-educated young chief of the Maulas. The action is set on the fictional island of Pharamaul off the southwest coast of Africa.

1. *The Tribe That Lost Its Head* (Sloane, 1956)
   A young African who has been a student in England is recalled to his native country when his father dies, to take his place as chief.
2. *Richer Than All His Tribe* (Morrow, 1969)
   Bracken is disillusioned when he sees Pharamaul's black leaders grow corrupt and tyrannical after independence.

II. The Master Mariner is the running title for a series of novels left un-finished at Monsarrat's death. His intent was to chronicle four hundred years of British naval history through the eyes of a sailor condemned to roam the seas forever because of his cowardice while serving under Drake against the Spanish Armada. The chronicle was to have been con-tinued past World War II, but it had gotten only as far as 1806 when Monsarrat died. What we have of the series are two rousing sea stories containing good, painless history.

1. *Running Proud* (Morrow, 1979)
   Matthew Lawe, doomed to wander the oceans forever, gets in-volved with several famous naval figures including Henry Hudson, Samuel Pepys, Captain Cook, and Lord Nelson.
2. *Darken Ship* (Morrow, 1981)
   In 1806, Lawe is the captain of an illegal slave trader. This novel, left unfinished at Monsarrat's death, concludes with his notes and sketches put together by his wife.

Montgomery, L. M. (Lucy Maud)

Mark Twain called Anne Shirley of Green Gables "the dearest and most lovable child in fiction since the immortal Alice." Certainly she has cap-tured the hearts of millions of American girls from 1905 onward, many of whom still come to libraries seeking Montgomery's books to renew their acquaintance. Though the books are a trifle saccharine by today's standards, their underlying theme remains fresh and relevant, especially for young people: Anne struggles against conformity and demonstrates the possibility of winning acceptance as an individual on one's own merits. Montgomery's hometown of Cavendish, on Prince Edward Island, provided the beautiful setting for the Anne books. Her house there has become a tourist attraction.

1. *Anne of Green Gables* (Page, 1908)
   Eleven-year-old Anne is sent from the orphanage to the home of an elderly brother and sister, Matthew and Marilla Cuthbert. They had requested a boy, but she soon wins their love.
2. *Anne of Avonlea* (Page, 1909)
   This account takes Anne from a winsome "half-past sixteen" to her departure for college.

3. *Chronicles of Avonlea* (Page, 1912)
   These are stories of Avonlea and Spencervale, only some of which
   include Anne.
4. *Anne of the Island* (Page, 1915)
   Anne is at Redmond College, studying to be a teacher; during her
   visits home, everything seems to be changing.
5. *Anne of Windy Poplars* (Stokes, 1936)
   During Anne's first three years of teaching at Summerside High
   School, she lives at a boarding house called Windy Poplars. English title: *Anne of Windy Willows*.
6. *Anne's House of Dreams* (Stokes, 1971)
   At last Anne marries her old sweetheart, in the orchard at
   Green Gables.
7. *Anne of Ingleside* (Stokes, 1939)
   Fifteen years have passed, and Anne is the mother of a happy
   brood.
8. *Rainbow Valley* (Stokes, 1919)
   This book centers around Anne's young children and the romance of the widowed minister.
9. *Rilla of Ingleside* (Stokes, 1921)
   Anne's youngest daughter, Rilla, is the focus of this story that
   shows how World War I affected the family.
10. *Further Chronicles of Avonlea* (Page, 1920)
    These fifteen short stories deal with Anne's friends and neighbors.

Moorcock, Michael

I. The fantasy/science fiction trilogy Dancers at the End of Time is the
best-known work by this prolific young British author. It is a space-time
travel story starring Jherek Carnelian, who, out of boredom with the
decadent hedonistic life on earth at the end of time, becomes obsessed
with nineteenth-century morality and falls in love with a reluctant time
traveler from Victorian London, Mrs. Amelia Underwood. Moorcock's
satiric touch makes these imaginative stories sparkle. Two additional
works have expanded the story, but the first three books are the best.

1. *An Alien Heat* (Harper, 1973)
   Jherek Carnelian follows Mrs. Underwood to London in 1896,
   where he gets involved in a murder trial and is sentenced to
   the gallows.

2. *The Hollow Lands* (Harper, 1974)
   After escaping death in London, Jherek seesaws through time and space in search of his beloved Mrs. Underwood.
3. *The End of All Songs* (Harper, 1976)
   Jherek and Mrs. Underwood are united at last as the end of time is threatened by final disruption.
4. *Legends from the End of Time* (Harper, 1976)
   These stories continue the adventures of Jherek Carnelian.
5. *A Messiah at the End of Time* (DAW Bks., 1978)
   Miss Mavis Ming undergoes a transformation. English title: *The Transformation of Miss Mavis Ming.*

II. For an accounting of Moorcock's early production see Peter Nicholls's *Science Fiction Encyclopedia* (Doubleday, 1979), which includes a chronology for his Elric of Melnibone series and a complete listing of his Corum and Hawkmoon series. An early precursor of Jherek Carnelian was Jerry Cornelius; he stars in the following books, which were collected in *The Cornelius Chronicles* (Avon, 1977).

1. *The Last Days of Man on Earth* (Avon, 1968)
   The swinging London of 1965 is the setting for this story about Jerry and Miss Brunner, a computer technician with enormous powers, and their extraordinary joint venture. English title: *The Final Programme.*
2. *A Cure for Cancer* (Holt, 1971)
   Several years later, Jerry, now black with white hair, runs a strange transmogrification service and visits "Amerika."
3. *The English Assassin* (Harper, 1972)
   Jerry's foulmouthed mother and the lovely Una Persson appear in this volume, set in the 1970s with Edwardian undertones.
4. *The Condition of Muzak* (Gregg, 1977)
   Jerry, as Pierrot the Weeper, confronts real death in Ladbroke Grove.

Note: *The Lives and Times of Jerry Cornelius* (Allison and Busby, London, 1976) and *The Adventures of Una Persson and Catherine Cornelius in the Twentieth Century* (Quartet, London, 1976) contain related Cornelius stories.

Moore, George

At first influenced by the naturalism of Zola, George Moore's work later became more stylized, more elaborately textured, and symbolically weightier. These two books, characteristic of his mature style, were little appreciated at the time of their publication, though modern critics have compared them to Joyce's *Ulysses* in terms of style and substance. They were written around the time of Moore's move back to his native Ireland and show his deepening involvement in Irish affairs and the influence of Yeats, George (AE) Russell, and other writers of the Celtic literary renaissance.

1. *Evelyn Innes* (Unwin, London, 1898)
   The dashing Owen Asher takes Evelyn as protégée and mistress to the Continent, where she becomes a great singer but is torn between Asher and her love for the Irish poet and mystic Ulrick Dean.
2. *Sister Teresa* (Unwin, London, 1901)
   This novel of convent life shows Evelyn's search for spiritual peace in a Catholic convent.

Morier, James

This comic masterpiece, modeled after LeSage's picaresque *Gil Blas*, has delighted generations of readers. Young Hajji Baba, the barber's son, starts off as a traveling secretary to a Baghdad merchant but is quickly involved in one harrowing adventure after another. Always living as the dervish advised, on men's weakness and credulity, the resourceful Hajji slips out of many tight spots with customary roguish charm. Morier, an Englishman, served at the British embassy in Tehran. His description of the life and manners of the Persia of his day is thought to be quite accurate. His Persians are a devious and bloody-minded lot indeed.

1. *The Adventures of Hajji Baba of Ispahan* (A. Small, London, 1824)
   Before his triumphant return home, Hajji does time as a Turcoman captive, a marriage broker, a physician, a poet's scribe, and an executioner.
2. *Hajji Baba in England* (A. Small, London, 1828)
   Hajji accompanies the Persian ambassador to London, where he is amazed at the uncouthness of British manners and customs.

Morley, Christopher

Christopher Morley was an all-around man of letters—a poet and novelist, a sparkling essayist for the *Saturday Review, New York Evening Post,* and other journals, and a witty editor of anthologies and reference books including *Bartlett's Familiar Quotations.* He was a tireless promoter of literature for Doubleday, served as a judge of the Book-of-the-Month Club for over twenty years, and found time to dabble in theater and to found the Baker Street Irregulars, the famous Sherlock Holmes fan club. Next to his popular hit *Kitty Foyle,* a novel of a young Irish-American working girl, he is best remembered for these two books, which star Helen McGill and her mentor Roger Mifflin, the lovably literate traveling bookseller.

1. *Parnassus on Wheels* (Doubleday, 1917)
   At thirty-nine, Helen McGill takes a bold step in buying the horse-drawn van of itinerant bookseller Roger Mifflin, who shows her the ropes and wins her heart. Mifflin's joy in books is still a good model for librarians.
2. *The Haunted Bookshop* (Doubleday, 1919)
   Mr. and Mrs. Roger Mifflin settle down permanently in a second-hand bookshop in Brooklyn called Parnassus at Home. Set during World War I, this novel combines a spy plot and a romance.

Morris, Wright

I. It is true that many of Morris's books have a Midwest setting, but to dismiss him as a regional writer would be to undervalue seriously this consistently original and rewarding author. His unsentimental studies of the American character often feature lonely and inarticulate people who are buffeted by circumstance in a disordered world. Morris catches their poignant and sometimes tragic moments of self-revelation in beautifully controlled prose, with the sympathy and respect that they deserve. This pair of haunting parables starring eighty-four-year-old Nebraskan Floyd Warner is a good introduction to Morris's art.

1. *Fire Sermon* (Harper, 1971)
   Old Floyd takes his orphaned young nephew to Nebraska and picks up two hippie hitchhikers on the way.

2. *A Life* (Harper, 1973)
   After leaving his nephew in Nebraska, Floyd heads south to New
   Mexico, picking up an Indian Vietnam veteran as a passenger.

II. Morris wrote several other novels with Nebraska settings, including
five novels about a town called Lone Tree, which is the fictional
equivalent of Morris's birthplace, Central City. *The Home Place* and *The
World in the Attic* are about Clyde Muncy revisiting his old haunts in
Nebraska. *The Field of Vision* and *Ceremony in Lone Tree*, two of
Morris's best novels, share several characters: lifelong failure Gordon
Boyd, his outwardly successful friend Walter McKee, and McKee's oc-
tagenarian father-in-law Tom Scanlon. All of these novels are strong on
nostalgia and realistic dialogue. They feature protagonists uncertain
about the meaning of their lives.

1. *The Man Who Was There* (Scribner, 1945)
   Agee Ward, missing in action in World War II, is remembered by
   his friends in Lone Tree.
2. *The Home Place* (Scribner, 1948)
   Clyde Muncy revisits his uncle's Nebraska farm with his wife and
   children. Real photographs of Central City and Norfolk, Nebraska, give an added dimension to the fictional text.
3. *The World in the Attic* (Scribner, 1949)
   Clyde Muncy and his family stop in Junction, Nebraska, on their
   way back east from Lone Tree.
4. *The Field of Vision* (Harcourt, 1956)
   A group of Nebraskans including Gordon Boyd, Walter McKee,
   and Tom Scanlon spend an afternoon at a Mexican bullfight.
5. *Ceremony in Lone Tree* (Atheneum, 1980)
   Family and friends prepare to assemble in Lone Tree to celebrate
   the ninetieth birthday of its last inhabitant, Tom Scanlon.

Morrow, Honoré

The last four years of Abraham Lincoln's life form the subject of this
satisfying trilogy. The books satisfy as just plain good stories, but, in addition, they also give an accurate picture of the man and his times.
Morrow claims to have used no fictitious characters and to have stepped
outside of fact for conversation and thought processes only. Mrs. Lincoln is pictured as a lovable if somewhat excitable helpmeet, not the

deranged shrew that some have painted. Figures such as Clara Barton, the photographer Matthew Brady, and the war correspondent William Russell are memorably drawn. *Great Captain* (Morrow, 1935) is a three-in-one omnibus volume.

1. *Forever Free: A Novel of Abraham Lincoln* (Morrow, 1927)
   The story begins in March, 1861, as the Lincolns move into the White House and ends with the signing of the Emancipation Proclamation in January, 1863.
2. *With Malice toward None* (Morrow, 1928)
   The Lincoln story is continued to the end of the war.
3. *The Last Full Measure* (Morrow, 1930)
   The last six months of Lincoln's life are described, ending with the gunshot in Ford's Theatre.

Morton, Antony (pseud. of John Creasey, q.v.)

The Baron is John Mannering, prosperous London art connoisseur and proprietor of Quinn's Antique Shop. He has long since given up his early shady activities but uses his special knowledge of the art underworld and his mastery of disguise for occasional private-detective jobs. Scotland Yard Chief Superintendent William Bristow has changed from adversary to friend and special employer through the years. Mannering's wife, Lorna, is a successful portrait artist. Curiously, the Baron was called the "Man in the Blue Mask" in the U.S. editions of the early books. The Baron's forty-six diverting adventures, too formula-written to annotate, are listed below chronologically as written. Creasey also wrote under the name of J. J. Marric (q.v.).

1. *The Man in the Blue Mask* (Lippincott, 1937)
   English title: *Meet the Baron.*
2. *The Return of Blue Mask* (Lippincott, 1937)
   English title: *The Baron Returns.*
3. *Blue Mask at Bay* (Lippincott, 1938)
   English title: *The Baron at Bay.*
4. *Salute Blue Mask* (Lippincott, 1938)
   English title: *The Baron Again.*
5. *Challenge Blue Mask* (Lippincott, 1939)
   English title: *The Baron at Large.*

6. *Alias Blue Mask* (Lippincott, 1939)
   English title: *Alias the Baron.*
7. *Versus Blue Mask* (Lippincott, 1939)
   English title: *Versus the Baron.*
8. *Blue Mask Strikes Again* (Lippincott, 1940)
   English title: *Call for the Baron.*
9. *The Baron Comes Back* (Low, London, 1943)
10. *A Case for the Baron* (Duell, 1949)
11. *Reward for the Baron* (Low, London, 1945)
12. *Career for the Baron* (Duell, 1950)
13. *The Baron and the Beggar* (Duell, 1950)
14. *A Rope for the Baron* (Duell, 1949)
15. *Blame the Baron* (Duell, 1951)
16. *Books for the Baron* (Duell, 1952)
17. *Cry for the Baron* (Walker, 1970)
18. *Trap the Baron* (Walker, 1971)
19. *Shadow the Baron* (Low, London, 1951)
20. *Attack the Baron* (Low, London, 1951)
21. *Warn the Baron* (Low, London, 1952)
22. *The Baron Goes East* (Low, London, 1953)
23. *Danger for the Baron* (Walker, 1974)
24. *The Baron in France* (Walker, 1973)
25. *The Baron Goes Fast* (Walker, 1972)
26. *Deaf, Dumb and Blonde* (Doubleday, 1961)
    English title: *Nest Egg for the Baron.*
27. *Help from the Baron* (Walker, 1977)
28. *Hide the Baron* (Walker, 1978)
29. *The Double Frame* (Doubleday, 1961)
    English title: *Frame the Baron.*
30. *Blood Red* (Doubleday, 1960)
    English title: *Red Eye for the Baron.*
31. *If Anything Happened to Hester* (Doubleday, 1962)
    English title: *Black for the Baron.*
32. *Salute for the Baron* (Walker, 1973)
33. *The Baron Branches Out* (Scribner, 1961)
    English title: *A Branch for the Baron.*
34. *The Baron and the Stolen Legacy* (Scribner, 1967)
    English title: *Bad for the Baron.*
35. *The Baron and the Mogul Sword* (Scribner, 1966)
    English title: *A Sword for the Baron.*
36. *The Baron on Board* (Walker, 1968)
37. *The Baron and the Chinese Puzzle* (Scribner, 1965)

38. *Sport for the Baron* (Walker, 1969)
39. *Affair for the Baron* (Walker, 1968)
40. *The Baron and the Missing Old Masters* (Walker, 1968)
41. *The Baron and the Unfinished Portrait* (Walker, 1969)
42. *Last Laugh for the Baron* (Walker, 1971)
43. *The Baron Goes A-Buying* (Walker, 1971)
44. *The Baron and the Arrogant Artist* (Walker, 1972)
45. *Burgle the Baron* (Walker, 1974)
46. *The Baron, King-Maker* (Walker, 1975)
47. *Love for the Baron* (Hodder, London, 1979)

Motley, Willard

Black novelist Willard Motley wrote two best-selling novels with Italian-American protagonists. The novels are set mostly in the Chicago slums, and depict the pervasive influence of a bad environment on its characters. *Knock on Any Door* is a grim naturalistic account of a young man's descent from altar boy to the electric chair. *Let No Man Write My Epitaph* is somewhat more optimistic. Both novels were made into Hollywood movies; *Knock on Any Door* starred John Derek and Humphrey Bogart (1949) and *Let No Man Write My Epitaph* starred Burl Ives, Shelley Winters, and James Darren (1960). A third novel was planned but never written.

1. *Knock on Any Door* (Appleton, 1947)
   Nick Romano starts off life in Denver as a good kid, but when his family loses its money during the Depression, he starts on the downward path to reform school, murder, and execution.
2. *Let No Man Write My Epitaph* (Random, 1958)
   Young Nick Romano, illegitimate son of the executed murderer Nick, Sr., and drug addict Nellie Watkins, struggles against drug addiction while his uncle Louie sinks into the criminal underworld.

Muller, Marcia

I. Sharon McCone is an investigator for the All Souls Legal Cooperative in San Francisco. She is a young, intelligent, contemporary American woman who brings to her cases a calm, reasonable style of investigation and a knack for asking the right questions. Although she likes her independence, she does get romantically involved at times with men such as Lieutenant Greg Marcus of the Homicide Division of the San Francisco Police. This is a well-plotted series with believable characters and snappy dialogue.

1. *Edwin of the Iron Shoes* (McKay, 1977)
   An antique show owner, one of McCone's law cooperative's clients, is found murdered.
2. *Ask the Cards a Question* (St. Martin's, 1982)
   An old woman in McCone's apartment building is strangled with a length of drapery cord taken from McCone's apartment.
3. *The Cheshire Cat's Eye* (St. Martin's, 1983)
   McCone finds a friend murdered in one of the "Painted Ladies," a Victorian house being renovated.
4. *Games to Keep the Dark Away* (St. Martin's, 1984)
   Jane Anthony, roommate of famous photographer Abe Snelling, is missing, and McCone is hired to find her.
5. *Leave a Message for Willie* (St. Martin's, 1984)
   Flea market king Willie Whelan is being tailed by a little man in a yarmulke.
6. *Double* (St. Martin's, 1984)
   Co-written with Bill Pronzini (q.v.), this book features Sharon McCone and Pronzini's "Nameless Detective" meeting at a private eye convention in San Diego, and teaming up to investigate the death of a hotel security officer.
7. *There's Nothing to Be Afraid Of* (St. Martin's, 1985)
   McCone investigates threats against Vietnamese refugees in San Francisco's Tenderloin.
8. *There's Something in a Sunday* (Mysterious, 1989)
   Custom shirtmaker Rudy Goldring hires McCone to tail Frank Wilkonson, manager of the Burning Oak Ranch.
9. *The Shape of Dread* (Mysterious, 1989)
   Bobby Fisher is scheduled to be executed for the murder of Tracy Kostakos, monologuist at the Club Comedie.

II. Elena Oliverez is an amateur who gets drawn into investigating crimes. She works as a curator (later director) at the Museum of Mexican Arts in Santa Barbara. In a volume co-authored with Bill Pronzini, one of his characters plays a part. Like McCone, Elena Oliverez gets romantically involved with a police lieutenant.

1. *The Tree of Death* (Walker, 1983)
   Oliverez has to clear herself of the murder of her boss Frank De Palma when he is slain shortly after she yells at him, "Somebody ought to kill you!"
2. *The Legend of the Slain Soldiers* (Walker, 1985)
   Oliverez's mother calls upon her to investigate the murder of Ciro Sisneros, who may have been killed to keep him from writing the truth about the slaying of Chicano workers in 1935.
3. *Beyond the Grave* (Walker, 1986)
   Using Quincannon's (see Pronzini) notes, Oliverez tries to solve a buried treasure mystery whose solution eluded Quincannon in 1894. Co-written with Bill Pronzini.

III. A third female detective created by Marcia Muller is recently widowed Joanna Stark, San Francisco-based security consultant to art galleries. Somewhat older and wealthier than McCone and Oliverez, she is depressed by her husband's death, and embittered by past betrayals.

1. *The Cavalier in White* (St. Martin's, 1986)
   Stark has quit the security business and moved to the town of Sonoma, but is drawn back by the news of the theft of Frans Hals's painting "The Cavalier in White."
2. *There Hangs the Knife* (St. Martin's, 1988)
   Art thief Tony Parducci is suspected of stealing several Brueghels. Joanna Stark, who was deserted two decades earlier by Tony when she became pregnant, travels to London to trap him.
3. *Dark Star* (St. Martin's, 1989)
   When Joanna discovers a painting missing from her home, she realizes that Tony Parducci is still alive.

Myers, L. H. (Leopold Hamilton)

British author, L. H. Myers is preeminently a novelist of ideas. In the series entitled The Root and the Flower, he examines the illusions of the mind as they tempt a young prince in sixteenth-century India. Not historical in any documentary sense, Myers's books have a remote setting in order to lift their central philosophical concerns out of a contemporary context; yet they reflect pointedly on the London society of his day.

Prince Jali's guru is clearly the author's spokesman, expressing Myers's own ethical preoccupations and his belief in the essential goodness of human nature. Book number 3 below was published only in both editions of the omnibus volume *The Root and the Flower* (Harcourt, 1935 and 1940). The second edition of the omnibus contains all four books.

1. *The Near and the Far* (Harcourt, 1929)
   This volume introduces Hari Khan, a tribal chieftain; Rajah Amar, a Buddhist; Sita, the Rajah's Christian wife; the Princess Lalita; and little Prince Jali, age twelve.
2. *Prince Jali* (Harcourt, 1931)
   Now almost fifteen, Prince Jali falls in love with the low-caste beauty Gunevati.
3. *Rajah Amar* (in *The Root and the Flower* [Harcourt, 1935]).
   Rajah Amar, Prince Jali's father, is the central character.
4. *The Pool of Vishnu* (Harcourt, 1940)
   Jali learns from his guru how to be a good rajah of Vidyapur.

Nabb, Magdalen

Marshal Salva Guarnaccia is a member of the carabinieri, the Italian police force, assigned to the Palazzo Pitti area of Florence. Guarnaccia, a Sicilian, is a quiet, unassuming fellow who tends to be looked down upon by his superiors, but he is a tenacious detective who always gets to the bottom of each case. The mysteries are well-plotted, with interesting characters, but the details of life in Florence and the surrounding Tuscan countryside are what make them more interesting than the average whodunit. Magdalen Nabb is a British writer living in Florence.

1. *Death of an Englishman* (Scribner, 1982) ·
   The murder of an Englishman takes Marshal Guarnaccia out of his sickbed, and keeps him away from a Christmas holiday trip to Sicily.
2. *Death of a Dutchman* (Scribner, 1983)
   Answering the summons of an elderly Florentine lady, Guarnaccia finds a Dutchman near death with slashed hands.
3. *Death in Springtime* (Scribner, 1984)
   Two teenaged girls are kidnapped during a freak snowfall.

4. *Death in Autumn* (Scribner, 1985)
   German-born Hilde Vogel is found murdered in the River
   Arno.
5. *The Marshal and the Murderer* (Scribner, 1987)
   Guarnaccia goes to a pottery factory outside of Florence to look
   for a missing Swiss student.
6. *The Marshal and the Madwoman* (Scribner, 1988)
   Marshal Guarnaccia tries to find out why an impecunious former
   mental patient is killed, and her death made to look like suicide.

Narayan, R. K.

Like Faulkner, Narayan has created a detailed fictional world. All of his
novels are set in Malgudi, a contemporary South Indian town resembling Narayan's native Mysore. Malgudi's residents come brilliantly to
life as they gossip and plot zany enterprises, fall in love, win and lose fortunes, and worry over their children. Graham Greene, in his introduction to *The Bachelor of Arts*, called Narayan's novels "comedies of sad-
ness" and compared them to the work of Chekhov. Narayan writes in
English.

1. *Swami and Friends: A Novel of Malgudi* (Michigan State College
   Pr., 1954)
   Humorous episodes in the life of ten-year-old Swami and his
   Malgudi school chums make up this novel. Originally published
   in England in 1935.
2. *Bachelor of Arts* (Michigan State College Pr., 1954)
   Young Chandran graduates from college, has an unhappy love affair, travels for a while, and then returns home. Bound with
   Swami and Friends. First published in England in 1935.
3. *The Dark Room* (Macmillan, London, 1938)
   Mrs. Ramani leaves home when her husband falls for his secretary, but she returns because she misses her children.
4. *Malgudi Days* (Viking, 1982)
   These short stories concern Malgudi residents. Originally published in India in 1943.
5. *Grateful to Life and Death* (Michigan State College Pr., 1953)
   Krishnan, a young schoolteacher, is consoled after his wife's
   death by his delightful infant daughter. First published in England in 1945 as *The English Teacher*.

6. *Waiting for the Mahatma* (Michigan State College Pr., 1955)
   Sriram, a pampered young man, falls in love with a beautiful young woman who is a protégée of Gandhi. Though written later, this novel fits chronologically about here.
7. *The Printer of Malgudi* (Michigan State College Pr., 1955)
   This novel shows the zany Indian film-making business through the involvement of a young newspaper publisher, Srinivas. Published in England in 1949 as *Mr. Sampath*.
8. *The Financial Expert* (Michigan State College Pr., 1953)
   Margayya, an entrepreneur who facilitates peasant loans, gets rich by publishing a pornographic book titled *Domestic Harmony*.
9. *The Guide* (Viking, 1958)
   Raju, a con-man who finds himself thrust into the role of a saint, stars in this novel, which some consider Narayan's best work.
10. *The Man-Eater of Malgudi* (Viking, 1961)
    Vasu, a huge taxidermist, is somewhat mad.
11. *The Vendor of Sweets* (Viking, 1967)
    Candy maker Jagan is troubled when his son Mali returns from America with a girlfriend and a story-writing machine he wants to mass produce.
12. *A Horse and Two Goats* (Viking, 1970)
    Malgudi residents star in more short stories.
13. *The Painter of Signs* (Viking, 1976)
    Raman, a college-educated sign painter, falls in love with Daisy, an itinerant family-planning advocate.
14. *A Tiger for Malgudi* (Viking, 1983)
    Raj, an eleven-foot-long tiger, relates his career as circus performer, film star, inadvertent man-eater, and disciple of a holy man.
15. *Under the Banyan Tree and Other Stories* (Viking, 1985)
    A collection of short stories.
16. *Talkative Man* (Viking, 1987)
    Journalist T. M. narrates his encounter with the mysterious Dr. Rann, philanderer and "futurologist" who dresses in three-piece suits.

Note: *An Astrologer's Day*; *Dobu*; *Cyclone*; and *Lawley Road* were short story collections published in India or England, but never in the United States. Many of the stories in these collections appear in numbers 4, 12, and 15.

Nathanson, E. M.

The extremely violent film version of *The Dirty Dozen* (1967) is probably more familiar to most people than the novel upon which it is based. Both of Nathanson's novels are set in World War II and concern difficult assignments carried out by OSS Major John Reisman. Both books are better-than-average war novels full of action, well-researched historical background, and insights into the relationships between war and politics, good and evil.

1. *The Dirty Dozen* (Random, 1965)
   OSS officer John Reisman is given the unpalatable assignment of training twelve vicious American soldier-prisoners for a mission behind German lines just before D-Day.
2. *A Dirty Distant War* (Viking, 1987)
   Reisman parachutes into Burma to try to prevent a conflict between Kachin tribesmen and the Chinese Kuomintang, both allies against the Japanese.

Nin, Anaïs

Fans of the six-volume diary by the French-American Nin (pronounced Neen) who want to sample her fiction should try this work, originally published as five separate novelettes. Their interwoven stories of several women explore the central theme, the quest for the self through the "intricate maze of modern confusion." Nin's poetic prose has always been associated with the vanguard of contemporary literature. Her psychoanalytic view, emphasizing the importance of dreams and the interior life, and her almost exclusive focus on women have won her a devoted audience. All five novelettes are published in a one-volume omnibus, *Cities of the Interior* (Swallow, 1974).

1. *Ladders to Fire* (privately published in France in 1946)
   This is the story of Lillian and Larry, an American couple living in Paris, and their friends, including Lillian's lover, Jay.
2. *Children of the Albatross* (privately published in France in 1947)
   This focuses on Djuna, a free spirit, and her friendships with Lillian, Jay, and Sabina.

319

3. *The Four-Chambered Heart* (privately published in France in 1950)
   Djuna and her lover, Rango, live in a houseboat on the Seine until Rango's deranged wife nearly wrecks their lives.
4. *A Spy in the House of Love* (privately published in France in 1954)
   The story of Sabina, now living in New York City, and her relationships with Philip, Mambo, and Jay.
5. *Seduction of the Minotaur* (privately published in France in 1961)
   This expanded version of the fifth novelette, originally titled *Solar Barque*, focuses on Lillian's search for a new life in Mexico.

Nordhoff, Charles, and Hall, James Norman

Nordhoff and Hall drew skillfully on the fascinating true story of the mutiny that took place aboard the British warship, *Bounty*, in the South Pacific in 1787. The first novel of the trilogy became an immediate best-seller, ensuring the equally good sequels an avid audience. The trilogy's high drama, tense story, and compelling characters make it a classic of popular literature that no reader should miss. It is also available in the omnibus volume *The Bounty Trilogy* (Little, 1936).

1. *Mutiny on the Bounty* (Little, 1932)
   Mate Fletcher Christian and some of the *Bounty* crew rebel against cruel Captain Bligh in 1787.
2. *Men against the Sea* (Little, 1934)
   Captain Bligh and his loyal men are set off in an open boat thirty-six hundred miles from the East Indies. These events were drawn from Bligh's own journal, and he appears more sympathetic in this book than in its predecessor.
3. *Pitcairn's Island* (Little, 1934)
   The group of *Bounty* mutineers and some Polynesians make their home on Pitcairn's Island. This violent story is also based on fact.

Norris, Frank

An early admirer of Emile Zola, Norris was the first American novelist to incorporate the new naturalism into his work with any success. *McTeague*, his masterpiece, is the grim tale of miserliness on which the silent movie *Greed* was based. Norris conceived the Epic of Wheat as a trilogy of self-contained novels that would trace the story of a crop of wheat from the time of its sowing in California to the time of its consumption as bread in a European village. His early death at the age of thirty-two left unwritten the third volume, tentatively titled *The Wolf: A Story of Europe.*

1. *The Octopus: A Story of California* (Doubleday, 1901)
   War breaks out between the railroads and the wheat growers, led by farmer Magnus Derrick.
2. *The Pit: A Story of Chicago* (Doubleday, 1903)
   The story of the wheat's sale in the Chicago market, or wheat pit, features the ruthless stock speculator Curtis Jadwin and his unhappy wife.

O'Brien, Edna

Edna O'Brien, an Irish writer living in England, established her reputation as a novelist with the Country Girls trilogy. The books feature intelligent, naive Caithleen (Kate) Brady and wise-cracking, cynical Bridget (Baba) Brennan. The girls get expelled from their rural Irish convent school; have love affairs; go to Dublin; have more love affairs; go to London; get married and have love affairs. The trilogy, while full of humor and sex, is about disillusionment with life and love, the repressiveness of Irish society, and the inadequacies of men in general and Irish men in particular. *The Lonely Girl* was filmed in 1964 as *Girl with Green Eyes* with Rita Tushingham and Lynn Redgrave playing Kate and Baba. *The Country Girls Trilogy and Epilogue* (Farrar, 1986) is an omnibus volume containing all three novels.

1. *The Country Girls* (Knopf, 1960)
   Country girls Kate and Baba go away to an Irish convent school and get expelled. Kate has an affair with rich Dublin solicitor Mr. Gentleman.
2. *The Lonely Girl* (Randon, 1962)
   Kate and Baba live and work in Dublin. Kate has an affair with documentary filmmaker Eugene Gailliard before she discovers that he is married. Variant title: *Girl with Green Eyes.*
3. *Girls in Their Married Bliss* (Simon & Schuster, 1968)
   Living in London and unhappily married—Kate with Eugene and Baba with alcoholic Frank—the girls have more love affairs.

O'Donnell, Lillian

I. Norah Mulcahaney is the likeable young New York policewoman who stars in this consistently interesting series. Her Irish father worries about the dangers his daughter faces but is understanding and supportive—though determined to find her a husband. Norah mixes professionalism and compassion, bravery and prudence in just the right proportions. As the series progresses, she marries Joe Capretto, another cop, and is eventually promoted to detective sergeant.

1. *The Phone Calls* (Putnam, 1972)
   Norah's debut case involves an anonymous phone caller and the deaths of several lonely widows.
2. *Don't Wear Your Wedding Ring* (Putnam, 1973)
   Now promoted to detective, Norah investigates the messy death of a woman found beheaded in a hotel room.
3. *Dial 577 R-A-P-E* (Putnam, 1974)
   Detective Mulcahaney helps a young neighbor girl who has been raped.
4. *The Baby Merchants* (Putnam, 1975)
   When Norah and her new husband, Lieutenant Capretto, decide to adopt a baby, they get entangled in legal troubles, blackmail, and murder.
5. *Leisure Dying* (Putnam, 1976)
   Working with her husband on a special squad covering some Central Park muggings causes Sergeant Mulcahaney some marital friction.
6. *No Business Being a Cop* (Putnam, 1979)
   A psychopath is murdering New York policewomen.
7. *The Children's Zoo* (Putnam, 1981)
   Some nasty kids are into thrill killing at the Central Park zoo.
8. *Cop without a Shield* (Putnam, 1983)
   After her husband is killed in the line of duty, Norah takes a leave of absence to a small town in Pennsylvania, but soon finds herself investigating a case of abduction and murder.
9. *Ladykiller* (Putnam, 1984)
   Back with the New York Police Department, Norah Mulcahaney investigates the murder of a young woman in Central Park.
10. *Casual Affairs* (Putnam, 1985)
    Is the drug-and-alcohol coma of a wealthy socialite attempted suicide or murder?

11. *The Other Side of the Door* (Putnam, 1988)
    Norah plays a small role, advising Gary Reissig, her partner from
    number 9, in a case involving attacks by an unknown assailant on
    young Alyssa Hanriot.
12. *A Good Night to Kill* (Putnam, 1989)
    Norah's attention is divided between two homicide cases and the
    romantic attentions of a handsome television newsman.

II. O'Donnell's second engaging woman heroine is Mici Anhalt, a
crusader for victim's rights. Her work for New York's Crime Victim's
Compensation Board has involved her in three cases so far.

1. *Aftershock* (Putnam, 1977)
   The wife of a murdered hairdresser is the police's top suspect, but
   Mici helps her.
2. *Falling Star* (Putnam, 1979)
   Julia Schuyler, a washed-up alcoholic actress, is murdered, and
   Mici was the last one to have seen her alive.
3. *Wicked Designs* (Putnam, 1980)
   When wealthy widow Blanch Landry is killed in a subway station,
   her nephew disputes the "accident" verdict.

O'Donnell, Peter

British writer Peter O'Donnell created Modesty Blaise, the woman's
equivalent to James Bond, for his comic strip, and only later fleshed out
her adventures in book form. Modesty, orphaned by World War II at a
tender age, became the tough and self-reliant leader of the "Network,"
whose lucrative smuggling and theft activities enabled her to retire from
crime a rich woman at twenty-six. With her right-hand man, Willie Gar-
vin, Modesty accepts occasional special assignments from Sir Gerald
Tarrant of the Foreign Office.

1. *Modesty Blaise* (Doubleday, 1965)
   Modesty's first case for the British Foreign Office is to ensure the
   safe delivery of a crate of diamonds to an Arab sheik.
2. *Sabre-Tooth* (Doubleday, 1966)
   Modesty and Willie fake a return to crime and infiltrate a plot to
   capture Kuwait.

3. *I, Lucifer* (Doubleday, 1967)
   Modesty and Willie are up against a fiendish group using a psychic young man's powers to predict death.
4. *A Taste for Death* (Doubleday, 1969)
   Modesty and Willie set out to rescue an archaeological expedition in the Algerian desert from the clutches of an archvillain.
5. *The Impossible Virgin* (Doubleday, 1971)
   Modesty must retrieve some stolen papers for Sir Gerald and keep a gifted and selfless African mission doctor from harm.
6. *Pieces of Modesty* (Mysterious, 1986)
   A collection of short stories originally published in England in 1972.
7. *The Silver Mistress* (Mysterious, 1986)
   Modesty and Willie must rescue Sir Gerald from his criminal tycoon captor, Colonel Jim. This title and those following were published earlier in England.
8. *Last Day in Limbo* (Mysterious, 1985)
   An attempted kidnapping leads Modesty and Willie to a slave-run coffee plantation in Central America called Limbo.
9. *Dragon's Claw* (Mysterious, 1986)
   A solo sail through the Tasman Sea leads Modesty to a kidnapped artist, murder in London, an attack in Malta, and criminal mastermind Beauregard Browne.
10. *The Xanadu Talisman* (Mysterious, 1984)
    A Frenchman mortally injured during an earthquake in Morocco gets Modesty involved in a search for a legendary "talisman."
11. *The Night of Morning Star* (Mysterious, 1987)
    A mysterious group called the Watchmen is making terrorist attacks on Eastern and Western governments.
12. *Dead Man's Handle* (Mysterious, 1986)
    Willie is kidnapped and brainwashed by mad millionaire Thaddeus Pilgrim into attempting to kill Modesty.

Ogilvie, Elisabeth

I. The Bennett Island series is composed of six novels set on a small lobstering island off the coast of Maine. Joanna Bennett, daughter of the island's leading family, is first met as a fifteen-year-old tomboy in the 1930s. The series follows her through adolescence, two marriages, and motherhood; through the World War II years; and finally as the mother of some headstrong adolescents. Ogilvie's quiet, homespun charm and picturesque setting are enjoyed by young adult and adult readers.

1. *High Tide at Noon* (Crowell, 1944)
   A slump in the lobster market causes the whole population of Bennett Island to move to the mainland, but Jo returns to start a new life.
2. *Storm Tide* (Crowell, 1945)
   Joanna has high hopes and many plans for life on the island with her new husband, Nils.
3. *Ebbing Tide* (Crowell, 1947)
   Nils sees war duty in the Pacific and returns wounded.
4. *How Wide the Heart* (McGraw-Hill, 1959)
   Ellen, Joanna's daughter, must choose between marrying her childhood sweetheart, Joey, an island fisherman, or going to art school in Boston.
5. *An Answer in the Tide* (McGraw-Hill, 1978)
   When Jamie sets up housekeeping with a married woman on the island, his parents, Joanna and Nils, disapprove.
6. *The Summer of the Osprey* (McGraw-Hill, 1987)
   The arrival of rich Felix Drake with mysterious recluse Selina Bainbridge stirs up the inhabitants of Bennett's Island.

II. Ogilvie has also produced two volumes of a projected trilogy of historical romances which begins in nineteenth-century Scotland. They tell the story of Jennie Hawthorne, an engaging but headstrong young Englishwoman.

1. *Jennie About to Be* (McGraw-Hill, 1984)
   Set in the early nineteenth century, this tells of Jennie's arrival in Scotland.
2. *The World of Jennie G.* (McGraw-Hill, 1985)
   Tragic circumstances force Jennie to leave Scotland in 1809 and settle in Maine.

Oldenbourg, Zoé

I. As a young Russian emigré, Oldenbourg began writing while supporting herself painting scarves in a Paris shop. Her fascination with the Middle Ages had led her to write several nonfiction works as well as the pair of novels listed below. Authentic, unsentimental, and solid with detail, her books have been compared to vast French tapestries showing the daily life in a medieval castle of the twelfth and thirteenth centuries.

1. *The World Is Not Enough* (Pantheon, 1948)
   The story of a petty French knight, Ansiau of Linnières, and his wife, Lady Alis, covers the second and third crusades. Translated from the French by Willard Trask.
2. *The Cornerstone* (Pantheon, 1955)
   The story of Ansiau, Alis, and their descendants continues. Translated from the French by Edward Hyams.

II. Presumably drawn somewhat from Oldenbourg's own experiences as a Russian emigré, these two novels chronicle the growing romance of two young people amid the troubles, disruptions, and disintegrating families of emigré life in Paris.

1. *The Awakened* (Pantheon, 1957)
   The story of young exiles Stéphanie and Elie in Paris extends from the late 1930s to the German occupation. Translated from the French by Edward Hyams.
2. *Chains of Love* (Pantheon, 1959)
   Set in Paris between 1947 and 1951, this book shows the star-crossed lovers Stéphanie and Elie reunited after seven years of separation during the war. Translated from the French by Michael Bullock.

Orczy, Emmuska, Baroness

Emma Orczy (pronounced ORT-zee) was the daughter of a Hungarian baron who settled his family in London in 1880. After attending art school, marrying, and first trying her pen at writing children's books, Orczy turned to the spy story. Her first book, *The Scarlet Pimpernel*, was rejected by publishers until a dramatized version became a stage hit. Thereafter her work was enormously popular, and ten sequels followed, in addition to many other works. The seemingly foppish and indolent Sir Percy Blakeney is an early Clark Kent prototype. He is really the reckless and daring secret agent known as the Scarlet Pimpernel, who rescues innocent aristocrats from the guillotine in France during the Revolution. The dashing master of disguise has been played by David Niven, James Mason, and Leslie Howard in various film versions.

1. *The Scarlet Pimpernel* (Putnam, 1905)
   Not even Lady Blakeney knows that her stupid husband is the famous Scarlet Pimpernel until she herself is rescued by him.
2. *I Will Repay* (Lippincott, 1906)
   Juliette Marny's stormy relationship with the man who killed her brother is at the center of the plot.
3. *The Elusive Pimpernel* (Dodd, 1908)
   The daring Scarlet Pimpernel continues to rescue distraught Frenchmen.
4. *The League of the Scarlet Pimpernel* (Doran, 1919)
   These short stories detail the Scarlet Pimpernel's many rescues.
5. *Lord Tony's Wife* (Doran, 1917)
   When Mademoiselle Kernogan is lured back to France and almost certain death at the hands of bloodthirsty revolutionaries, the Scarlet Pimpernel comes to her rescue.
6. *The Triumph of the Scarlet Pimpernel* (Burt, 1922)
   Robespierre, at the peak of his power, is determined to destroy the Scarlet Pimpernel, but is himself ruined.
7. *Eldorado* (Doran, 1913)
   The Dauphin is rescued from the temple.
8. *Sir Percy Hits Back* (Doran, 1927)
   The Scarlet Pimpernel rescues the daughter of his old enemy Chauvelin and emerges victorious in a final clash with her father.
9. *Adventures of the Scarlet Pimpernel* (Doubleday, 1929)
   More stories continue the Pimpernel's exploits.
10. *The Way of the Scarlet Pimpernel* (Putnam, 1934)
    The Scarlet Pimpernel outwits Chabot and saves Louise de Croissy and her little boy.
11. *Mam'zelle Guillotine: An Adventure of the Scarlet Pimpernel* (Hodder, London, 1940)
    Sir Percy saves a last victim from the guillotine.

Note: *Pimpernel and Rosemary* (Doubleday, 1924) concerns Peter Blakeney, the great-great-grandson of the original Scarlet Pimpernel. *The First Sir Percy* (Doran, 1921) is about a seventeenth-century ancestor of the Scarlet Pimpernel.

Paretsky, Sara

Paretsky has created a believable female hard-boiled detective. Her V. (for Victoria) I. Warshawski is a Chicago-based lawyer/detective who specializes in corporate crime. Of Polish and Italian descent, V. I. is attractive, tough, and independent. Her knowledge of Chicago's power structure and low opinion of businessmen and politicians usually sends her investigating in the right direction. Paretsky's fans increase with each book as readers come to rely on her likeable heroine for sure-fire action with a touch of bitter humor.

1. *Indemnity Only* (Dial, 1982)
   Warshawski's attempt to find a young woman leads her to murder, crooked unions, and an insurance scam.
2. *Deadlock* (Dial, 1984)
   When V. I.'s cousin, former hockey star Boom Boom Warshawski, is found broken to bits under a ship's propeller, she investigates the cargo shipping business.
3. *Killing Orders* (Morrow, 1985)
   V. I.'s aunt Rosa Vignelli asks her to investigate the theft of $5 million in stock certificates from a monastery.
4. *Bitter Medicine* (Morrow, 1987)
   The death in childbirth of young Consuelo Alvarado in a "model" suburban hospital leads V. I. into the world of hospital politics.
5. *Blood Shot* (Delacorte, 1988)
   A search for the father Caroline Djiak never knew brings Warshawski into contact with polluters and sleazy aldermen.

Park, Ruth

Ruth Park, a native New Zealander living in Australia, wrote two novels in the 1940s about the Darcys, a poor family of Irish descent living in the slums of Sydney. Thirty-five years later she published *Missus*, a prequel about the Darcy family at the turn of the century in the small Australian town of Trafalgar. The main characters in the trilogy are Hugh Darcy, irresponsible and irrepressible, seen in his youth in *Missus* and as "Dadda" in numbers 2 and 3, and the proud Margaret Kilker, who becomes the "Missus," then mother of daughters Roie and Dolour. The novels have their tragic moments, but are full of gentle humor, realistic pictures of urban life in Australia, and well-realized characters.

1. *Missus* (St. Martin's, 1987)
   Young Hugh Darcy and his crippled brother Jeremiah run away from a brutal father and the town of Trafalgar at the turn of the century.
2. *The Harp in the Sun* (Houghton, 1948)
   Roie Darcy, elder daughter of Hugh and Margaret, comes of age in the Sydney slums. Reissued by St. Martin's in 1987.
3. *12 1/2 Plymouth Street* (Houghton, 1951)
   Sixteen-year-old Dolour Darcy must raise Roie's motherless children. Reissued as *Poorman's Orange* by St. Martin's in 1987.

Parker, Robert B.

Spenser, Boston's own private eye, seems a shade more literate than most of Sam Spade's descendants. He leavens his wise-cracking, tough-guy brand of detection with a smattering of culture and balances his weight-lifting machismo act with a tough-minded feminist philosophy. His girlfriend Susan plays a fairly large part in some of his cases. Spenser's Boston delights locals and will disabuse outsiders' notions of the city as a quaint Puritan town. For several years *Spenser: For Hire*, a network television series starring Robert Urich, was filmed on location in Boston.

1. *The Godwulf Manuscript* (Houghton, 1974)
   Spenser's debut case involves the theft of an illuminated fourteenth-century manuscript from a college library.
2. *God Save the Child* (Houghton, 1974)
   An emotionally disturbed boy is kidnapped from his Boston suburban home.
3. *Mortal Stakes* (Houghton, 1975)
   Is Boston Red Sox pitcher Marty Raab being blackmailed into throwing games?
4. *Promised Land* (Houghton, 1976)
   Spenser must find Pam Shepard, wife of a shady real estate dealer.
5. *The Judas Goat* (Houghton, 1978)
   Spenser gets to Europe to hunt down the terrorists whose bomb killed the family of a rich American.
6. *Looking for Rachel Wallace* (Delacorte, 1980)
   Spenser is hired as a bodyguard for a lesbian-feminist-radical author.

7. *Early Autumn* (Delacorte, 1981)
   While divorced parents feud over their fifteen-year-old son, Paul, Spenser gives him a quick course in self-sufficiency in the wilds of Maine.

8. *A Savage Place* (Delacorte, 1981)
   Spenser is looking after Candy Sloan, a TV news reporter investigating movie payoffs.

9. *Ceremony* (Delacorte, 1982)
   When young April Kyle drops out of her suburban high school and disappears, Spenser tracks her down through Boston's Combat Zone.

10. *The Widening Gyre* (Delacorte, 1983)
    Spenser acts as a security officer for Meade Alexander, candidate for the U.S. Senate.

11. *Valediction* (Delacorte, 1984)
    Spenser takes on cult leader Reverend Bullard Winston, who is accused of abducting a young woman.

12. *A Catskill Eagle* (Delacorte, 1985)
    Spenser and Hawk go to California to retrieve Susan from her lover, Russell Costigan, son of a wealthy arms manufacturer who is involved in illegal arms sales.

13. *Taming a Sea-Horse* (Delacorte, 1986)
    April Kyle, the young prostitute rescued by Spenser in number 9, disappears again when a young woman and her pimp are murdered.

14. *Pale Kings and Princes* (Delacorte, 1987)
    When newspaper reporter Eric Valdez is murdered while investigating a cocaine ring, Spenser journeys to Wheaton, Massachusetts, to expose the ringleaders.

15. *Crimson Joy* (Delacorte, 1988)
    A slasher who is victimizing middle-aged black women may be one of psychologist Susan Silverman's patients.

Parkinson, C. Northcote

After paying homage to C. S. Forester (q.v.) with a fictional biography of that author's famous hero, *The Life and Times of Horatio Hornblower* (Little, 1970), Parkinson fashioned a series of naval adventures around a hero of his own creation—imitation being in this case not only the sincerest form of flattery but a boon to Forester fans and naval-adventure buffs. Parkinson's hero, Richard Delancey, a native of Guernsey, is as brave and resourceful as his fictional forebear. In setting, the books actually predate the Hornblower series, as Delancey serves in George III's navy in the last years of the eighteenth century.

1. *Devil to Pay* (Houghton, 1973)
   Delancey's ability to speak French brings him a secret assignment and a chance to restore his tarnished reputation. The story begins in June, 1794, and covers about two years.
2. *The Fireship* (Houghton, 1975)
   Posted to the *Glatton* in 1796, Delancey faces mutiny and destroys a French ship of the line by means of a delicately maneuvered fire ship.
3. *Touch and Go* (Houghton, 1977)
   In 1799, Delancey is posted to Gibraltar to command the sloop *Merlin*. He rescues a young slave girl in Africa and makes a desperate last effort to win a rich prize.
4. *So Near, So Far* (Murray, London, 1981)
   Ashore in London in 1802, Delancey falls in love with the beautiful actress Fiona Sinclair, and learns about a new French underwater vessel called *The Nautilus*.
5. *Dead Reckoning* (Houghton, 1978)
   In 1805, Delancey is promoted to post-captain and must leave his lovely young wife for the ancient frigate *Lydia*.

Peake, Mervyn

Peake's massive fantasy, the Gormenghast trilogy, has a cult following in Britain, though its American reception has been decidedly mixed. Its story follows Titus Groan, the young crown prince of Gormenghast Castle, through his childhood and youth. Grotesque characters and the baroque pseudo-medieval setting give the work a nightmarish quality quite unlike Tolkien's brand of fantasy. Peake was a true eccentric who also wrote poetry and children's books and achieved a reputation as an illustrator. Readers will have to decide for themselves whether he was a genius or a madman.

1. *The Gormenghast Trilogy: Titus Groan* (Weybright & Talley, 1967)
   This narrative covers the birth of Titus, seventy-seventh earl of

Groan, into his strange family home, Gormenghast Castle, ruled by age-old ritual and threatened by the evil Steerpike. First published in England in 1946.

2. *The Gormenghast Trilogy: Gormenghast* (Weybright & Talley, 1967)
   During Titus's childhood years, he becomes increasingly intolerant of the prescribed rituals that confine him. First published in England in 1950.

3. *The Gormenghast Trilogy: Titus Alone* (Weybright & Talley, 1967)
   Alone in the big world outside Gormenghast, Titus has misgivings, but continues to strive for understanding and maturity. First published in England in 1959.

Pearce, Mary E.

This amiable family saga was published in England in five separate volumes and issued here in three. It focuses on three working-class families living in rural England from 1886 to the 1940s. The Tewkeses are a proud and headstrong lot, from old John (who was disowned by his father when he refused to follow him in the carpentry business) to young Beth (who refuses to marry the man her grandfather has picked out). The farmers who form the Izzard family are mild mannered but no less stony in their independence. And the luckless Mercybright family rounds out the large cast of characters.

1. *Apple Tree Lean Down* (St. Martin's, 1976)
   a. Book I (originally titled *Apple Tree Lean Down*, MacDonald and Jave, London, 1976)
      The Tewkes family is followed from Beth's girlhood in 1886 to her daughter Betony's nineteenth year in 1914.
   b. Book II (originally titled *Jack Mercybright*, MacDonald and Jave, London, 1974)
      Jack comes to the Guff farm in 1891 and begins to reclaim the land.
   c. Book III (originally titled *The Sorrowing Wind*, MacDonald and Jave, London, 1975)
      Betony becomes a nurse and falls in love with Michael Andrews. The story continues through World War I.

2. *The Land Endures* (St. Martin's, 1981)
   Betony is the stern local schoolteacher as the saga goes on
   through the 1920s and newcomers bring many changes.
3. *Seedtime and Harvest* (St. Martin's, 1982)
   The deteriorating married life of Linn Mercybright and Charlie
   Truscott is the main theme of this story set in the years just before
   and during World War II.

Percy, Walker

I. *The Moviegoer*, Walker Percy's first published novel, won the National Book Award in 1962. That book and all of his subsequent novels are set in the American South and take as their theme the moral and existential problems unique to modern times. His characters feel uncomfortable in a technological world devoid of spiritual values and their search for meaning usually leads them to religion, particularly Roman Catholicism. Percy has an ability to make philosophical questions take on flesh and become real and understandable to the average reader. His inventive plots, satirical eye for current mannerisms, and accessible prose add to his appeal. Williston Bibb Barrett, protagonist of two novels by Percy, is seen at two points in his life. He is deeply unhappy in the New South, an affluent society with no spiritual roots to which he can relate.

1. *The Last Gentleman* (Farrar, 1966)
   At 25, young Will Barrett returns to the South suffering from amnesia and loss of identity.
2. *The Second Coming* (Farrar, 1980)
   Will Barrett, now middle-aged, widowed, and wealthy, suffers from attacks of heightened memory that return him to his unhappy past.

II. Percy has also written two novels starring Dr. Tom More, a descendant of the sainted Thomas. Dr. More is a psychiatrist and lapsed Catholic who fights social engineering in an America of the near future. In this pair of novels, Percy adds fantasy and suspense to his usual mix.

1. *Love in the Ruins* (Farrar, 1971)
   Subtitled *The Adventures of a Bad Catholic at a Time near the*

End of the World, this tells of Dr. Tom More's invention of a device that will measure "the perturbations of the soul."

2. *The Thanatos Syndrome* (Farrar, 1987)
Newly released from prison, Dr. Tom detects a scheme by a group of psychiatrists to eliminate anti-social behavior by putting tranquilizers in the local water supply.

Perry, Anne

The Charlotte series of mysteries is set in late Victorian London. Inspector Thomas Pitt of Scotland Yard and his wife Charlotte are the detectives, with occasional help from Charlotte's aristocratic sister, Emily Ashworth. Pitt's gentle manner and brilliant mind is complemented by his wife's quick wit and intuition. Together they solve a variety of sordid crimes. The richly evoked atmosphere of Victorian London gives the series a special distinction. *The Cater Street Hangman* was English writer Anne Perry's first novel.

1. *The Cater Street Hangman* (St. Martin's, 1979)
The conventional upper-middle-class lives of young Charlotte and Emily Ellison are disrupted when one of their servant girls becomes a victim in a series of stranglings.

2. *Callender Square* (St. Martin's, 1980)
Charlotte and Emily get involved with Inspector Pitt's investigation of infanticide in posh Callender Square.

3. *Paragon Walk* (St. Martin's, 1981)
The fashionable London neighborhood of Paragon Walk is terrorized by a rapist-killer.

4. *Resurrection Row* (St. Martin's, 1981)
Someone is digging up the corpses of recently deceased Londoners and depositing them in public places.

5. *Rutland Place* (St. Martin's, 1983)
A lost trinket at the Rutland Place home of Charlotte's parents leads to an investigation of theft, blackmail, and murder.

6. *Bluegate Fields* (St. Martin's, 1984)
A young tutor is the prime suspect in the bathtub murder of a teenager from a wealthy family.

7. *Death in the Devil's Acre* (St. Martin's, 1985)
A slum neighborhood near Westminster Abbey is the scene of a series of murders and emasculations.

8. *Cardington Crescent* (St. Martin's, 1987)
   Emily Ashworth is suspected of poisoning her philandering husband George.
9. *Silence in Hanover Close* (St. Martin's, 1988)
   Charlotte and Emily aid Inspector Pitt in the investigation of the murder of British diplomat Robert Yorke.

Peters, Elizabeth (pseud. of Barbara Mertz)

I. American author Barbara Mertz publishes popular works on Egyptology under her real name. As Barbara Michaels she writes historical gothic romances. As Elizabeth Peters, she writes lightweight detective/suspense novels with an interesting historical or archeological slant. Peters has created three female sleuths: Amelia Peabody Emerson, Vicky Bliss, and Jacqueline Kirby. Amelia Peabody Emerson is a late Victorian feminist who goes on digs with her archeologist husband Radcliffe Emerson. Their excavations are usually bedeviled by some "curse" or other which Amelia gets to the bottom of. The Emerson's exasperating precocious son Walter (nicknamed "Ramses") plays a prominent role in the later novels.

1. *Crocodile on the Sandbank* (Dodd, 1975)
   Amelia Peabody and Evelyn Barton-Forbes take a break from their voyage on the Nile, and get involved with the archeologist Emerson brothers and a wandering mummy.
2. *The Curse of the Pharoahs* (Dodd, 1978)
   Amelia and her husband Radcliffe take over the leadership of an archeological expedition excavating a "cursed" tomb.
3. *The Mummy Case* (Congdon, 1985)
   The Emerson's dig in Egypt is plagued by murder, theft, and the antics of four-year-old Ramses.
4. *Lion in the Valley* (Atheneum, 1986)
   On another Egyptian dig in 1896, Amelia has to be rescued from "a fate worse than death" by Radcliffe and eight-year-old Ramses.
5. *The Deeds of the Disturber* (Atheneum, 1988)
   At home in England, the Emersons investigate strange goings-on at the British Museum supposedly perpetrated by a supernatural Egyptian priest.

II. Another series by Elizabeth Peters stars the thoroughly modern Victoria Bliss, a tall, blonde art historian. Vicky is intelligent, strong-willed, and liberated; rather than get married, she has affairs with attractive men, including English con-man "Sir John Smythe," who has a habit of turning up frequently. Each of Vicky's cases naturally includes some element of art history or archeology.

1. *Borrower of the Night* (Dodd, 1973)
   Vicky Bliss goes in search of a medieval treasure supposedly hidden in a German castle during the Peasants' Rebellion.
2. *Street of the Five Moons* (Dodd, 1978)
   Vicky gets involved with a forgery ring, fake antique jewelry, and handsome, dishonest "Sir John Smythe."
3. *Silhouette in Scarlet* (Congdon, 1983)
   After receiving an enigmatic message from "John Smythe," Vicky journeys to Stockholm in search of archeological artifacts.
4. *Trojan Gold* (Atheneum, 1987)
   Trojan treasure buried by the Nazis after the fall of Berlin is the object of Vicky's search.

III. Peters has also written four novels starring Jacqueline Kirby, a middle-aged librarian with a Ph.D. in history and a dauntless sense of adventure who eventually becomes a romance writer. *The Murders of Richard III* provides an interesting comparison with *The Daughter of Time* by Josephine Tey (q.v.).

1. *The Seventh Sinner* (Dodd, 1972)
   Jacqueline Kirby and a Roman police official team up when someone is murdered in one of the underground passages of the Church of San Clemente.
2. *The Murders of Richard III* (Dodd, 1974)
   Someone is overdoing the reenactment of the murders alleged to have been committed by Richard III.
3. *Die for Love* (Congdon, 1984)
   While attending the Historical Romance Writers of the World Conference in New York, Jacqueline gets involved with a murder mystery.
4. *Naked Once More* (Warner, 1989)
   Jacqueline Kirby goes to the Appalachians to write a sequel to vanished author Kathleen Darcy's best-seller.

Peters, Ellis (pseud. of Edith Pargeter)

The Chronicles of Brother Cadfael are set in medieval England during the troubled reign of King Stephen (roughly the 1130s and 1140s). Brother Cadfael is a former Crusader turned monk and herbalist at the Benedictine Abbey in Shrewsbury. He has foresworn earthly vanities, but cannot resist involving himself in such profane pursuits as matchmaking and sleuthing. This is a romantic, entertaining mystery series with a very likeable protagonist and an authentic but lightly carried historical background. In addition to the Brother Cadfael series, English author Edith Pargeter has to her credit more than two dozen historical novels and a dozen translations from the Czech under her real name. As Ellis Peters she has also written fourteen mysteries featuring members of the Felse family which do not seem to be available in the United States.

1. *A Morbid Taste for Bones* (Morrow, 1978)
   Prior Robert's lust for the wonder-working relics of St. Winifred gets Brother Cadfael involved in a journey to Wales and a murder investigation.
2. *One Corpse Too Many* (Morrow, 1980)
   When Brother Cadfael gives Christian burial to 94 victims of King Stephen's "justice," he finds one corpse too many.
3. *Monks-Hood* (Morrow, 1981)
   Wealthy Gervase Bonel, potential benefactor of Cadfael's monastery, is a victim of monks-hood poisoning.
4. *Saint Peter's Fair* (Morrow, 1981)
   Brother Cadfael investigates some homicides which took place during the local St. Peter's Fair.
5. *The Leper of Saint Giles* (Morrow, 1982)
   The love affair between squire Joscelin Lucy and Iveta de Massard runs a rough course when Joscelin is dismissed by his master, who wants Iveta for himself.
6. *The Virgin in the Ice* (Morrow, 1983)
   When Brother Elyas is attacked while trying to deliver two orphans to their uncle Laurence d'Angers, Brother Cadfael intervenes.
7. *The Sanctuary Sparrow* (Morrow, 1983)
   Juggler and acrobat Liliwin of Shrewsbury is accused of stealing valuables from the town's goldsmith.

8. *The Devil's Novice* (Morrow, 1984)
   Nineteen-year-old aspirant to monkhood Meriet Aspley has such violent nightmares that he is dubbed "the devil's novice."

9. *Dead Man's Ransom* (Morrow, 1985)
   An exchange of prisoners between the Welsh and the English is thwarted by the mysterious death of the English captive Gilbert Prestcote, sheriff of Shropshire.

10. *The Pilgrim of Hate* (Morrow, 1985)
    One of the pilgrims at the celebration for wonder-working St. Winifred may be responsible for the mysterious murder of a knight in Winchester.

11. *An Excellent Mystery* (Morrow, 1985)
    The arrival at Shrewsbury of Brothers Humilis and Fidelis, refugees from the burned priory of Hyde Mead, may have some connection with the disappearance of a young girl named Julian Cruce.

12. *The Raven in the Foregate* (Morrow, 1986)
    Ailnoth, unpopular priest of the parish of Holy Cross (known as Foregate), is found murdered in a frozen pond.

13. *The Rose Rent* (Morrow, 1987)
    Brother Eluric is murdered while delivering Shrewsbury Abbey's annual rent (one rose) to the beautiful widow who owns the land the Abbey is leasing.

14. *The Hermit of Eyton Forest* (Mysterious, 1988)
    Ten-year-old heir Richard Ludel disappears from the Abbey to whose care he was entrusted, and his grandmother, Dame Dionisia, is suspected.

15. *The Confession of Brother Haluin* (Mysterious, 1989)
    Believing that he is on his deathbed, Brother Haluin confesses to an affair he had 18 years ago, and the death of his lover from abortive herbs he had supplied to the girl's mother.

Pike, Robert L. (pseud. of Robert L. Fish, q.v.)

I. The prolific Fish has written two series of police procedurals under the pseudonym of Robert L. Pike. Lieutenant Clancy of the Fifty-Second Precinct in New York City is a bit of a plodder, but his story still makes good reading, as none of Pike/Fish's characters are uninteresting.

1. *Mute Witness* (Doubleday, 1963)
   Clancy guards a West Coast mobster. The 1968 movie *Bullitt*, starring Steve McQueen, was based on this novel.
2. *The Quarry* (Doubleday, 1964)
   Clancy must find a Sing Sing escapee.
3. *Police Blotter* (Doubleday, 1965)
   A murdered recluse, a theft of sixteen dollars, and a threatened U.N. delegate make up this typical day for Lieutenant Clancy.

II. Lieutenant James Reardon is tough and aggressive, short-tempered and quick-thinking, and his cases never fail to include at least one hair-raising car chase through scenic San Francisco. Reardon is ably assisted by Sergeant Dondero in all four of his cases.

1. *Reardon* (Doubleday, 1970)
   Reardon has a hunch there is something wrong with a seemingly open-and-shut case of accidental auto death.
2. *The Gremlin's Grampa* (Doubleday, 1971)
   A prominent gangster is murdered in a waterfront bar.
3. *Bank Job* (Doubleday, 1974)
   A shipyard payroll is taken from a bank by four masked men.
4. *Deadline: 2 A.M.* (Doubleday, 1976)
   "Pop" Holland, about to retire from the force, is kidnapped.

Plagemann, Bentz

These warm and humorous novels of the tribulations of parenthood are obviously based on Plagemann's own experience. The books are narrated by Mr. Wallace, a writer who lives with his wife and son in Cliffside, a town very much like Plagemann's home, Palisades, New York. The four books trace the development of young Cameron, nicknamed Goggle, from his early boyhood scrapes to his eventual marriage.

1. *This Is Goggle* (McGraw-Hill, 1955)
   When Mr. Wallace returns home from five years in the navy, he must get reacquainted with his ten-year-old son. This humorous

account covers the next eight years in Goggle's eventful young life.

2. *Father to the Man* (Morrow, 1964)
   Mr. and Mrs. Wallace do their best to steer their son through the trials of adolescence, the disasters of Princeton, and a tour of duty in the Coast Guard.
3. *The Best Is Yet to Be* (Morrow, 1966)
   Mr. and Mrs. Wallace sail for the Mediterranean, where they find themselves acting as surrogate parents to various hometown girls in need of help.
4. *A World of Difference* (Morrow, 1969)
   The Wallaces are on the move, first to New York where Bill writes a play, then on to the big time in Hollywood.

Plaidy, Jean (pseud. of Eleanor Hibbert)

I. Hibbert writes historical novels under the Plaidy pseudonym; costume gothics under the Philippa Carr (q.v.) pseudonym; and best-seller romantic suspense novels under the Victoria Holt pseudonym. Most of the historical novels and some of the costume gothics are written as series. The historicals by Plaidy are clustered around the more interesting figures of English and European monarchy. She invests her historical characters with credible human passions and shows the conflicts, triumphs, and failures of their reigns in dramatic detail. The books are entertaining and solidly based on fact—each volume carries a brief bibliography. Many of the volumes listed below were first published in England in the fifties and sixties and are only now appearing in U.S. editions. Following Plaidy's own groupings, the books that treat the English monarchy are arranged below in rough chronological order. The four series that treat non-English figures are listed last. Plaidy is currently producing a series of novels about some of the more interesting queens of England. Since they are not really sequels, they are not listed here.

The Norman trilogy is the first set in Plaidy's chronicle of the English monarchy. It begins with the heroic figure of William the Conqueror and continues to the end of Stephen's reign in 1154.

1. *The Bastard King* (Putnam, 1979)
   William's spectacular rise from bastard to king is described.

2. *The Lion of Justice* (Putnam, 1979)
This book covers the reign of King Henry I, 1100–35.
3. *The Passionate Enemies* (Putnam, 1979)
Stephen and Matilda are lovers and rivals in their ambition to succeed Henry.

II. The Plantagenet series begins with Eleanor of Acquitaine and Henry II, those colorful and contentious figures who were the subject of James Goldman's play and movie *The Lion in Winter*. The series ends with the triumph of the Tudors under Henry VII.

1. *The Plantagenet Prelude* (Putnam, 1980)
The story of Eleanor and Henry is carried up to the death of Thomas à Becket.
2. *The Revolt of the Eaglets* (Putnam, 1980)
As Henry II grows old, his sons jockey for the succession.
3. *The Heart of the Lion* (Putnam, 1980)
Richard I, the Lion-Hearted, reigns: 1189–99.
4. *The Prince of Darkness* (Putnam, 1981)
Bad King John Lackland holds power: 1199–1216.
5. *The Battle of the Queens* (Putnam, 1981)
The feuding queens are Isabella, King John's widow, and Queen Blanche of Castille.
6. *The Queen from Provence* (Putnam, 1981)
Henry III marries Eleanor of Provence in 1236 and spends most of his long reign provoking his barons to rebellion.
7. *Hammer of the Scots* (Putnam, 1981)
The long successful reign of Edward I is chronicled: 1272–1307. English title: *Edward Longshanks*.
8. *The Follies of the King* (Putnam, 1982)
The follies of Edward II and the intrigues of his unhappy Queen Isabella bring his reign to a disastrous close. Covers 1307–27.
9. *The Vow on the Heron* (Putnam, 1982)
This volume covers the long reign of Edward III and the beginnings of the Hundred Years War.
10. *Passage to Pontefract* (Putnam, 1982)
The rivalry between Edward III's sons, Edward the Black Prince and John of Gaunt, is continued by their sons, Richard II and Henry IV.

11. *The Star of Lancaster* (Putnam, 1982)
    This chronicles the lives and loves of Henry IV, his wife Mary of
    Bohun, and their son Henry V.
12. *Epitaph for Three Women* (Putnam, 1983)
    The story of three women who made an impact on fifteenth-
    century England and France: Henry V's Queen Katherine of
    Valois; Joan of Arc; and Eleanor of Gloucester.
13. *Red Rose of Anjou* (Putnam, 1983)
    The dominant character is Margaret of Anjou, queen to the fee-
    ble Henry VI, and the real leader of the Red Roses of Lan-
    caster.
14. *The Sun in Splendour* (Putnam, 1983)
    The reign of Edward IV is troubled by the continuing rivalry be-
    tween York and Lancaster.
15. *Uneasy Lies the Head* (Putnam, 1984)
    Henry VII, victor over Richard III at the Battle of Bosworth Field,
    tries to shore up his shaky reign. This volume could also be listed
    as the first in the Tudor Series.

III. The novels in the Tudor series, some of them written as far back as
1949, don't have as tight a sequence as some of the other series. In fact,
some sources don't list it as a series at all.

1. *The Thistle and the Rose* (Putnam, 1973)
   At thirteen, Margaret Tudor, sister of Henry VIII, comes to
   Scotland to marry James IV.
2. *Mary, Queen of France* (Hale, London, 1964)
   Another sister of Henry VIII marries Louis XII of France and,
   after his death, secretly weds the Duke of Suffolk.
3. *Murder Most Royal* (Appleton, 1949)
   Anne Boleyn and Catherine Howard, two of Henry VIII's queens,
   are the central characters. Reprinted as *The King's Pleasure* (Putnam, 1972).
4. *St. Thomas's Eve* (Putnam, 1970)
   Sir Thomas More puts service to his God before service to his
   king.
5. *The Sixth Wife* (Putnam, 1969)
   Henry VIII's sixth wife, Katherine Parr, manages to escape execution and outlive him.

6. *The Spanish Bridegroom* (Macrae Smith, 1956)
   Philip II of Spain marries Mary Tudor, who tries to restore Roman Catholicism to England. Reprinted by Putnam, 1971.
7. *Gay Lord Robert* (Putnam, 1971)
   The focus here is the relationship between Queen Elizabeth and Robert Dudley, Earl of Leicester.

IV. Mary, Queen of Scots is a magnetic figure for historical novelists. Plaidy has given her a two-volume series of her own. She sees the tragic queen in terms of her passionate nature, awakened partially by Darnley and then fully by Bothwell. Plaidy has also written the nonfiction *Mary Queen of Scots: The Fair Devil of Scotland* (Putnam, 1975).

1. *Royal Road to Fotheringay* (Putnam, 1968)
   This book takes Mary from the age of five to her death. Variant title: *Mary, Queen of Scotland, The Triumphant Years.*
2. *The Captive Queen of Scots* (Putnam, 1970)
   This story backs up to give more detail of Mary's years of captivity and escape attempts.

V. James I (VI of Scotland), son of Mary, Queen of Scots, was the first Stuart king of England and the first to rule a united England and Scotland. The seven-volume Stuart Saga is set in 1603 to 1714 and covers all the Stuarts from James I to Queen Anne. Numbers 2, 3, and 4 are sometimes listed as the Charles II trilogy. Numbers 5, 6, and 7 are sometimes listed as The Last of the Stuarts trilogy.

1. *The Murder in the Tower* (Putnam, 1974)
   Conflict bubbles between poets, witches, and the king's favorite, Robert Carr.
2. *The Wandering Prince* (Putnam, 1971)
   This concerns Charles II's exile in France and Holland and the first years of his restoration as the English monarch.
3. *A Health unto His Majesty* (Putnam, 1972)
   Charles II's reign continues through the plague of 1665 and the great fire of London in 1666.
4. *Here Lies Our Sovereign Lord* (Putnam, 1973)
   The last years of Charles II's reign include his alliance with Nell Gwyn.

5. *The Three Crowns* (Putnam, 1977)
   This book covers the childhood and youth of Mary, her marriage to William of Orange, and her return to England after her father's exile.
6. *The Haunted Sisters* (Putnam, 1977)
   Anne and Mary are torn between allegiance to a Protestant England and love for their Catholic father, James, in exile in France.
7. *The Queen's Favorites* (Putnam, 1978)
   Queen Anne has two favorites, the vivacious Sarah Churchill, Duchess of Marlborough, and Abigail Hill, a devoted poor relation.

VI. The Georgian Saga, published in England from 1967 to 1971, is being published for the first time in the United States (1985–   ). It forms a link between the Stuart Saga and the Victorian Saga covering the reigns of the first four Georges of the House of Hanover, successors to the throne of Great Britain and Ireland in 1714.

1. *The Princess of Celle* (Putnam, 1985)
   The intrigues of the House of Hanover eventually lead to George I's succession to the English throne.
2. *Queen in Waiting* (Putnam, 1985)
   Intelligent and cultured Caroline must put up with a dull-witted husband to become Queen of England.
3. *Caroline the Queen* (Putnam, 1986)
   Queen Caroline must deal with her loutish, unfaithful husband and his estrangement from his eldest son, Frederick Louis, Prince of Wales.
4. *The Prince and the Quakeress* (Putnam, 1986)
   George, Prince of Wales, the future George III, falls in love with Hannah Lightfoot, a young Quaker woman.
5. *The Third George* (Putnam, 1987)
   Beset by public disasters, including the loss of the American colonies, George III tries to console himself with his wife Charlotte and large brood of children.
6. *Perdita's Prince* (Putnam, 1987)
   The Prince of Wales, the future George IV, adds to his father's woes by having an affair with an actress at Drury Lane.

7. *Sweet Lass of Richmond Hill* (Putnam, 1988)
   The liaison between George IV and Catholic commoner Mrs. Fitzherbert scandalizes his subjects.

8. *Indiscretions of the Queen* (Putnam, 1988)
   George IV's Queen Caroline gets involved in a scandal of her own.

9. *The Regent's Daughter* (Hale, London, 1971)
   Princess Charlotte, daughter of George IV and Queen Caroline, tries to live her own life, although "nobody ever had a stranger set of relations."

10. *Goddess of the Green Room* (Hale, London, 1971)
    William, Duke of Clarence, the future William IV, is smitten by Drury Lane actress Dorothy Jordan.

VII. Four volumes covering Queen Victoria's long reign bring Plaidy's chronicle up to the twentieth century.

1. *The Captive of Kensington Palace* (Putnam, 1976)
   Victoria's sheltered childhood is guarded by her mother and her faithful governess, Baroness Lehzen.

2. *The Queen and Lord M* (Putnam, 1977)
   A queen at eighteen, Victoria is still a rather silly, apolitical girl, madly in love with the aged Lord Melbourne.

3. *The Queen's Husband* (Putnam, 1978)
   Marriage to her adored Albert brings adjustments and the strain of childbearing to Victoria.

4. *The Widow of Windsor* (Putnam, 1978)
   Palmerston, Gladstone, and Disraeli figure prominently in Victoria's later years.

VIII. Lucrezia Borgia (1480–1519) is a much-maligned figure according to Plaidy, who sets out to clear her reputation in this pair of novels.

1. *Madonna of the Seven Hills* (Putnam, 1974)
   Lucrezia as a young girl is strongly influenced by her father, Pope Alexander VI, and her two brothers, Cesare and Giovanni.

345

2. *Light on Lucrezia* (Putnam, 1976)
   With one marriage annulled and her second husband murdered, Lucrezia is used by her powerful family for their own ends.

IX. Plaidy moves to sixteenth-century France for this trilogy focusing on Catherine de Medici, the daughter of Lorenzo de Medici, who married Henry of Orleans and became queen of France in 1547.

1. *Madame Serpent* (Putnam, 1975)
   At fourteen, Catherine must leave her home and friends in Florence for the unfamiliar French court.
2. *The Italian Woman* (Putnam, 1975)
   Queen regent during her son Charles's minority (1560–63), Catherine seeks revenge on those who slighted her.
3. *Queen Jezebel* (Putnam, 1976)
   Catherine's last strife-ridden years last until 1589.

X. Plaidy wrote a series of six novels, never published in the United States, about Ferdinand and Isabella of Spain and their daughter, Katherine of Aragon, who became Henry VIII's first queen. Numbers 4, 5, and 6 have an obvious tie-in with the Tudor series. The omnibus volume *Isabella and Ferdinand* (Hale, London, 1970) contains numbers 1, 2, and 3.

1. *Castile for Isabella* (Hale, London, 1960)
2. *Spain for the Sovereigns* (Hale, London, 1960)
3. *Daughters of Spain* (Hale, London, 1961)
4. *Katherine, the Virgin Widow* (Hale, London, 1961)
5. *The Shadow of the Pomegranate* (Hale, London, 1962)
6. *The King's Secret Matter* (Hale, London, 1962)

XI. The French Revolution trilogy, never published in the United States, deals with that turbulent period in French history.

1. *Flaunting Extravagant Queen (Marie Antoinette)* (Hale, London, 1957)

2. *Louis, the Well-Beloved* (Hale, London, 1959)
3. *The Road to Compiegne* (Hale, London, 1959)

Plain, Belva

Evergreen, a first novel published with little fanfare in 1978, became a word-of-mouth best-seller. The saga of Anna Friedman, which traces her life from a Polish village in the last century to affluence in 1970s New York, obviously struck a chord in millions of readers and viewers of the 1985 television mini-series based on the book. Two subsequent novels have dealt with the Werners and Roths, rich, aristocratic families living in New York, whose stories interconnect with Anna's. For the most part these novels have parallel story lines set in the early 1900s rather than succeeding each other chronologically. Belva Plain's novels are basically romantic family sagas told with restraint and without sensationalism.

1. *Evergreen* (Delacorte, 1978)
   Teenaged Anna emigrates from Poland to New York where she falls in love with wealthy Paul Werner, but marries poor, ambitious David.
2. *The Golden Cup* (Delacorte, 1986)
   This is the story of Henrietta De Rivera, who becomes Hennie Roth, suffragette, fighter for social justice, and Paul Werner's aunt.
3. *Tapestry* (Delacorte, 1988)
   Paul Werner, banker and philanthropist, unpassionately wedded, finds consolation for the loss of Anna, his first love, in an affair with his cousin Leah.

Plante, David

All of the novels in this series involve one or more members of the Francoeur family of Providence, Rhode Island. Jim and Reena Francoeur are

347

a working-class couple of French-Canadian background. Their lives are observed and chronicled by Daniel, their next-to-youngest son, who becomes an expatriate writer. Daniel takes center stage in several of the novels. Since Plante is a Providence native who has lived in London since 1966, it is reasonable to assume that the Francoeurs are based on his own family, and that Daniel is somewhat autobiographical. Although *The Woods* was published after *The Country*, Plante wrote it first, and intended it to fit between *The Family* and *The Country*, as it does in the paperback omnibus *The Francoeur Novels* (Dutton, 1983). Establishing a chronology for the novels written after 1983 is trickier. All of the novels are slim volumes, well-written and involving.

1. *The Family* (Farrar, 1978)
   Adolescent Daniel Francoeur tries to come to terms with his feelings about sex, religion, and his working-class parents.
2. *The Woods* (Atheneum, 1982)
   During two years at a Boston college and a summer on a wooded island off the Rhode Island coast, Daniel tries to discover his role in life and succeed sexually with a young woman.
3. *The Foreigner* (Atheneum, 1984)
   In 1959, Daniel, who has gone abroad to study, gets involved with Angela, a young black woman, and Vincent, her shady white boyfriend.
4. *The Country* (Atheneum, 1981)
   Now resident in London, Daniel makes several trips back to Providence to visit his aging and failing parents.
5. *The Catholic* (Atheneum, 1986)
   A one-night sexual relationship with a man named Henry takes on a great deal of significance for Daniel.
6. *The Native* (Atheneum, 1988)
   Antoinette Francoeur, daughter of Daniel's brother Philip, is torn between the wider world of her college-educated father and the "Canuck" world of her Francoeur grandmother, which Philip has tried to escape.

Plievier, Theodor

Plievier's work presents an interesting contrast to the World War II novels of Hans Helmut Kirst (q.v.) and to lighter historical novels with a wartime setting. His books give an unromanticized look at the horror and degradation of war from a soldier's point of view rather than a general's. Plievier's left-wing commitment and opposition to Nazism caused him to leave his native Germany in 1933. He settled in Russia but soon became disenchanted with that government, though not with communism per se. After the war he fled to American-occupied Bavaria; he died in Switzerland in 1955.

1. *Stalingrad* (Appleton, 1948)
   A brutally realistic account of the siege of Stalingrad shows the German army's disintegration. Translated from the German by Richard and Clara Winston.
2. *Moscow* (Doubleday, 1954)
   This grim story describes Russian attempts to halt Hitler's march on Moscow from June, 1941, to the turn in the tide of battle that winter. The author's disillusionment with the Russians is evident. Translated from the German by Stuart Hood.
3. *Berlin* (Doubleday, 1957)
   The German capital dies a slow death in 1945. Variant title: *Rape of a City*. Translated from the German by Louis Hagen and Vivian Milroy.

Pope, Dudley

Lieutenant Lord Nicholas Ramage was born to command ships for His Majesty's Royal Navy. Not only does he have the right combination of audacity, dry humor, and natural authority, but he is the son of "Old Blazeaway," an admiral before him. True to form, Ramage starts his career with an early disgrace: his leaving ship to rescue two Italian refugees—one of them a beautiful young woman—brings on court-martial proceedings. Ramage's service is roughly contemporary with that of C. S. Forester's Hornblower (q.v.), and his adventures are written with the same dash. Pope served in the merchant navy during World War II, and his lifelong fascination with the British navy has resulted in several nonfiction volumes of maritime history as well as his Ramage novels.

1. *Ramage* (Lippincott, 1965)
   Off the coast of Italy, Ramage must take command of the ship after all the senior officers are killed in battle.

2. *Drumbeat* (Doubleday, 1968)
   The year 1796 is busy for Ramage as he captures a Spanish frigate, rescues a marchioness, and is taken prisoner. English title: *Ramage and the Drum Beat.*

3. *The Triton Brig* (Doubleday, 1969)
   In 1797, Ramage takes command of the mutinous crew of the *Triton* and sails on an urgent mission to the West Indies. English title: *Ramage and the Freebooters.*

4. *Governor Ramage, R.N.* (Doubleday, 1973)
   Ramage's West Indies adventures include the discovery of buried treasure, but the vengeful Admiral Goddard raises storm clouds.

5. *Ramage's Prize* (Simon & Schuster, 1974)
   French privateers are interfering with the mail delivery to England from the West Indies, and Ramage goes to investigate.

6. *Ramage and the Guillotine* (Avon, 1981)
   Ramage is sent to infiltrate the French High Command in order to gather information about the prospective French invasion of England.

7. *Ramage's Diamond* (Avon, 1982)
   In 1804, Captain Ramage rejuvenates the crew of the frigate *Juno* and ships out to the Caribbean for the decisive battle for Diamond Head.

8. *Ramage's Mutiny* (Alison/Secker, London, 1977)
   In Antigua to fit up a French frigate he captured, Ramage is called upon to sit on a court-martial trying a bloody mutiny.

9. *Ramage and the Rebels* (Walker, 1985)
   While chasing French, Spanish, and Dutch privateers along the Spanish Main, Ramage and his men come upon a merchantman whose passengers and crew have been massacred by pirates.

10. *The Ramage Touch* (Walker, 1984)
    Captain Ramage, transferred from the West Indies to the Mediterranean, captures two French bomb ketches off Tuscany.

11. *Ramage's Signal* (Walker, 1984)
    Ramage captures a French semaphore station, and then takes off after a fifteen-member French merchant convoy.

12. *Ramage and the Renegades* (Avon, 1982)
    Ramage, sent to claim the South Atlantic island of Trinidad for the Crown, finds a pirate ship and five captured merchantmen in its harbor.

13. *Ramage's Devil* (Alison/Secker, London, 1982)
    During a temporary lull in the Napoleonic Wars, Ramage com-

bines his honeymoon in Brittany with spying on French naval preparations.

14. *Ramage's Trial* (Alison/Secker, London, 1984)
    Things look bleak for Ramage when he faces a court-martial that could lead to his execution.
15. *Ramage's Challenge* (Alison/Secker, London, 1985)
    Ramage sails the *Calypso* to Italy on a secret mission to rescue British prisoners-of-war.

Porter, Joyce

I. Porter's Inspector Wilfred Dover gives new meaning to the term *anti-hero*. The acknowledged "Shame of Scotland Yard" is enormously fat and pasty-faced, lazy, rude, and slovenly. He gobbles up everything on the tea table and then nods off while his competent assistant, Sergeant MacGregor, handles the interrogations and sorts through the clues. Watching Dover being lured and prodded and falling for every red herring is part of the fun of these lighthearted mysteries. Porter's well-sketched characters tend to be as eccentric as her detective, and her puzzles are of the classic English variety.

1. *Dover One* (Scribner, 1964)
   Dover's first case involves the disappearance of Julia Rugg, an overweight eighteen-year-old housemaid.
2. *Dover Two* (Scribner, 1965)
   Dover must travel to the town of Curdley in northern England to investigate a strange case where a young girl is murdered twice.
3. *Dover Three* (Scribner, 1966)
   Dover tackles a case of poison-pen letters that have turned into murder.
4. *Dover and the Unkindest Cut of All* (Scribner, 1967)
   Dover sets up MacGregor as an absolute patsy in this murder case.
5. *Dover Goes to Pott* (Scribner, 1968)
   The daughter of the leading citizen of Pott Winckle is murdered one evening while watching TV.

6. *It's Murder with Dover* (McKay, 1973)
   Dover hobnobs with some typically dotty and impoverished English aristocrats in this case of murder in a quiet village.
7. *Dover Strikes Again* (McKay, 1973)
   Dover must stay at a temperance hotel while he investigates a murder that was covered up in an earthquake.
8. *Dover and the Claret Tappers* (Countryman, 1989)
   The Claret Tappers gang finds that kidnapping Dover doesn't pay. Published in England in 1977.
9. *Dead Easy for Dover* (St. Martin's, 1979)
   The residents of a posh suburban enclave in the village of Frenchy Botham are suspects in the murder of a young girl who is found among some well-kept shrubberies.
10. *Dover Beats the Band* (Weidenfeld, London, 1980)
    An autopsy reveals that the stomach contents of an unidentified murdered man include a mysterious blue bead.

II. Eddie Brown is the inept and ineffective star of Porter's broadly humorous variation on the international espionage genre. Eddie would much rather crack jokes than spy rings, but he's not very good at anything but blundering into trouble.

1. *Sour Cream with Everything* (Scribner, 1966)
   Eddie's fluent Russian and resemblance to an undercover agent gets him transferred from his provincial British teaching post to a rest home in the Soviet Union.
2. *Neither a Candle nor a Pitchfork* (McCall, 1970)
   Eddie is parachuted back into the Soviet Union, where he finds that the Vavilov Collective Stud Farm has other interests besides horses.
3. *Only with a Bargepole* (McKay, 1974)
   When Miss Muriel Drom, daughter of Sir Maurice Drom, Eddie's boss at S.O.D., is kidnapped, Eddie somehow contrives to be a member of the kidnapper's gang.

III. Porter's spoof on the amateur private eye genre features the Honourable Constance Ethel Morrison-Burke, an indomitable battleship of a woman who took up detecting as a hobby because she needed another outlet for her tremendous energy. "The Hon. Con," as she is fondly known, blusters her way to, and sometimes right over, her quarry. Miss Jones is her long-suffering companion.

1. *Rather a Common Sort of Crime* (McCall, 1970)
   The first and only client of the Hon. Con's advice bureau is a distraught mother who is convinced that her son's "suicide" was really murder.
2. *A Meddler and Her Murder* (McKay, 1973)
   The murder of an Irish au pair girl on Sneddon Avenue has the Hon. Con tearing up the town of Totterbridge.
3. *The Package Included Murder* (Bobbs- Merrill, 1976)
   On a group tour to Russia, the Hon. Con and Miss Jones inevitably get involved when one of their fellow tourists suffers several violent attacks.
4. *Who the Heck Is Sylvia?* (Weidenfeld, London, 1977)
   Unavailable in the United States.
5. *The Cart Before the Crime* (Weidenfeld, London, 1979)
   In order to keep the Hon. Con from mucking up a royal visit, the townswomen of Totterbridge cook up a mystery surrounding the sale of Totterford Manor.

Potok, Chaim

Potok, a rabbi and scholar, has incorporated a good deal of talmudic argument into his novels on contemporary Jewish life in America. His fully drawn characters and interesting situations make gratifying and thoughtful reading. The story of Danny and Reuven, the two main characters, begins in their teens in the 1940s and shows the conflict between the secular and the mystical elements of the Jewish religion.

1. *The Chosen* (Simon & Schuster, 1967)
   A friendship develops between young Danny and Reuven, who meet at a baseball game between their two very different schools in Brooklyn. The 1981 film starred Rod Steiger and Robby Benson.
2. *The Promise* (Knopf, 1969)
   Now young men entering different occupations—for Reuven, the rabbinate, for Danny, clinical psychology—they offer different kinds of help to a troubled adolescent.

Powell, Anthony

Now that Anthony Powell's twelve-novel series A Dance to the Music of Time is complete, readers may want to reread the work as a whole. Narrated by Nicholas Jenkins, the books chronicle fifty years of English life from 1921 to 1971 and encompass dozens of literary, political, and social figures, both fictional and historical. It is one of the most accomplished and absorbing works of modern literature. Hilary Spurling's marvelous companion to the series, *Invitation to the Dance* (Little, 1977), contains a complete character index as well as book, painting, and place indexes and synopses. Best read in sequence, the twelve individual volumes have been consolidated into four omnibus volumes under the title *A Dance to the Music of Time: First through Fourth Movements* (Little, 1962–76). These four volumes were issued in paperback by Popular Library in 1976 under the subtitles *Spring, Summer, Autumn,* and *Winter.*

1. *A Question of Upbringing* (Little, 1951)
   The story opens in 1921, introducing Nicholas Jenkins, Widmerpool, and others at Eton. Nick goes to France for a year, then to Oxford.
2. *A Buyer's Market* (Little, 1952)
   The characters participate in the social and intellectual life of London in the late twenties.
3. *The Acceptance World* (Little, 1955)
   The climax of this book, set in the early thirties, is a dinner party given by Nick and some other "old boys" for their Eton house master Le Bas.
4. *At Lady Molly's* (Little, 1957)
   Lady Molly's 1934 New Year's Eve party begins events that lead to Nick's engagement to Isobel Tolland.
5. *Casanova's Chinese Restaurant* (Little, 1960)
   London's "smart" and "bohemian" sets contrast during 1936–37.
6. *The Kindly Ones* (Little, 1962)
   This account goes back in time to Nick's childhood in 1914, then progresses to the beginning of World War II.
7. *The Valley of Bones* (Little, 1964)
   In 1940, Nick is a second lieutenant in a backwater post of the Welsh infantry, bored and distressed with the pettiness of civilian duty.

8. *The Soldier's Art* (Little, 1966)
   Nick spends a dismal year at divisional headquarters under Widmerpool in 1941.
9. *The Military Philosophers* (Little, 1968)
   This book covers from early in 1942, when Nick is assigned to intelligence, to his demobilization in 1945.
10. *Books Do Furnish a Room* (Little, 1971)
    Nick at forty has two sons and several novels published, and his literary reputation is rising.
11. *Temporary Kings* (Little, 1973)
    Nick attends an international writers' conference in Venice in 1958 and meets old friends.
12. *Hearing Secret Harmonies* (Little, 1975)
    Now in his sixties, Nick reflects on his life and the follies of the younger generation.

Price, Eugenia

I. Eugenia Price's three novels set on St. Simon's Island, Georgia, are romantic, inspirational stories just right for readers looking for good old-fashioned, and slightly prim, stories. Her major characters are based on real people, and her scenery is painted with the appreciative and observant eye of a loving resident. Written in reverse order, they are arranged below chronologically, though each can be enjoyed separately.

1. *The Lighthouse* (Lippincott, 1971)
   Young James Gould leaves his New England home in 1791 and eventually settles with his wife and children on St. Simon's Island to build its lighthouse.
2. *New Moon Rising* (Lippincott, 1969)
   Horace Gould, James's son, is dismissed from Yale in 1830, then struggles to find himself and his place in the troubled times leading up to and through the Civil War.
3. *The Beloved Invader* (Lippincott, 1965)
   Anson Dodge, a Northerner, comes to St. Simon's Island to rebuild a church destroyed during the Civil War.

II. Price has published four novels in a completed Savannah Quartet: a series of historical romances set in antebellum Georgia. The fictional Brownings, Latimers, and Mackays interact with real people such as Robert E. Lee in a well-researched historical setting.

1. *Savannah* (Doubleday, 1983)
   Handsome Yankee Mark Browning comes to Savannah and joins Robert Mackay's mercantile firm, then finds himself falling in love with Mackay's wife.
2. *To See Your Face Again* (Doubleday, 1985)
   Romance blossoms when sixteen-year-old Natalie Browning and Burke Latimer survive the 1838 explosion of the steamship *Pulaski*.
3. *Before the Darkness Falls* (Doubleday, 1987)
   Natalie and Burke Latimer settle into married life together on the North Georgia frontier, while Natalie's brother Jonathan drops out of Yale to marry Indian Mary.
4. *Stranger in Savannah* (Doubleday, 1989)
   The Browning, Mackay, and Stiles families are all caught up in the Civil War in this volume covering 1864 to 1865 in Savannah.

Price, Reynolds

I. *A Long and Happy Life* was a highly praised first novel that won Price recognition as a talented young southern writer. Set in a small town in contemporary North Carolina, it tells the moving love story of Rosacoke Mustian, who gives herself too freely to an unworthy young man. The book's final scene, with Rosacoke playing Mary in a local Christmas pageant, gives the deceptively simple story symbolic overtones. A second novel starring Rosacoke's older brother Milo precedes the first chronologically.

After a hiatus of over twenty years, Price returned to Rosacoke and Wesley Beavers to see how they were faring after thirty years of marriage.

1. *A Generous Man* (Atheneum, 1966)
   The coming-of-age story of young Milo Mustian involves a python, a snake girl, and a desperate hunt through the woods for a possibly rabid dog.

2. *A Long and Happy Life* (Atheneum, 1962)
   Milo's sister, Rosacoke, is in love with a young man who cares more about motorcycles than the smitten young girl.
3. *Good Hearts* (Atheneum, 1988)
   Wesley Beavers, in the throes of a midlife crisis, begins an affair with a twenty-six-year-old woman.

II. Price has also written a pair of novels about a family living in rural North Carolina and Virginia. *The Surface of Earth* is a leisurely family chronicle covering the lives of three generations of the Mayfields and Kendals. *The Source of Light* concentrates on Rob Mayfield, a prominent character in the first novel, and his son Hutch.

1. *The Surface of Earth* (Atheneum, 1975)
   The elopement of sixteen-year-old Eva Kendal and thirty-two-year-old Forrest Mayfield starts a saga spanning over forty years (1903–1944).
2. *The Source of Light* (Atheneum, 1981)
   In 1955, Hutch Mayfield goes off to Oxford to study, unaware that his father Rob is dying of lung cancer.

Pronzini, Bill

I. Bill Pronzini's Nameless Detective has clearly modeled himself after the hard-boiled private eyes in the pulp magazines that he reads and collects. True to form, he hides his strong sense of justice and compassion under a tough, cynical exterior. Basically a loner, he does have a girlfriend (Kerry Wade) and a male friend in the San Francisco police department who eventually becomes his partner (Eb Eberhardt). Nameless is the hero of sixteen novels, numerous short stories, and two novelettes published in limited editions by Waves Press (*A Killing in Xanadu*, 1980 and *Cats-paw*, 1983). Two of the novels in which Nameless appears (numbers 5 and 14) were collaborations with other authors. Pronzini's detective stories are reliably taut and satisfying. The San Francisco ambience is well done.

1. *The Snatch* (Random, 1971)
   Wealthy Louis Martinetti calls in Nameless to deliver the ransom demanded for his nine-year-old son.

2. *The Vanished* (Random, 1973)
   Nameless is brought into the case of a missing soldier by the man's fiancee.
3. *Undercurrent* (Random, 1973)
   Trailing a husband suspected of infidelity, Nameless finds the man murdered in a motel room.
4. *Blowback* (Random, 1977)
   Nameless goes to a fishing camp in the Mother Lode country to help an old army buddy in trouble.
5. *Twospot* (Putnam, 1978)
   Nameless teams up with co-author Colin Wilcox's Frank Hastings to investigate a case of murder and fraud at a California winery.
6. *Labyrinth* (St. Martin's, 1980)
   The seemingly unrelated deaths of two women, one by shooting, one by car accident, may be connected.
7. *Hoodwink* (St. Martin's, 1981)
   Six members of the Pulpeteers, a mystery writers group, have received extortion threats.
8. *Scattershot* (St. Martin's, 1982)
   A philandering husband who disappears and a missing socialite who turns up dead are part of an intricate web of revenge.
9. *Dragonfire* (St. Martin's, 1982)
   Nameless, angry over the unjust revoking of his license, is further incensed when a Chinese gunman shoots him and Eberhardt.
10. *Bindlestiff* (St. Martin's, 1983)
    Charles Bradford, a government bureaucrat turned hobo, is being sought by one of his daughters.
11. *Casefile: The Best of the "Nameless Detective" Stories* (St. Martin's, 1983)
    A collection of short stories.
12. *Quicksilver* (St. Martin's, 1984)
    While investigating why someone is anonymously sending jewelry to a young Japanese-American woman, Nameless runs into murder and the dread Yakuza.
13. *Nightshades* (St. Martin's, 1984)
    Nameless goes to an old ghost town in northern California to probe the fiery death of a real estate developer.
14. *Double* (St. Martin's, 1984)
    Nameless and co-author Marcia Muller's (q.v.) Sharon McCone meet at a private eye convention in San Diego, and get involved in parallel investigations of the death of a hotel security officer.

15. *Bones* (St. Martin's, 1985)
Asked to investigate the circumstances of a 1949 suicide of a pulp detective fiction writer, Nameless stirs up some long-buried scandals and corpses.
16. *Deadfall* (St. Martin's, 1986)
After witnessing the shooting of prominent bisexual lawyer Leonard Purcell, Nameless is asked to investigate by Purcell's live-in lover.
17. *Shackles* (St. Martin's, 1988)
A masked man leaves Nameless chained in a remote mountain cabin with only enough supplies to last three or four months.

II. Secret Service agent Quincannon of 1890s San Francisco stars in *Quincannon* and co-stars posthumously in *Beyond the Grave*. The Quincannon novels are entertaining combinations of western and mystery.

1. *Quincannon* (Walker, 1985)
Quincannon is on the trail of a counterfeiting ring in San Francisco in 1893.
2. *Beyond the Grave* (Walker, 1986)
In the 1980s, co-author Marcia Muller's (q.v.) Elena Oliverez uses Quincannon's notes to find the solution to a mystery that eluded him in 1894.

Proust, Marcel

The dense and static first half of *Swann's Way* makes Proust's masterpiece Remembrance of Things Past seem more impenetrable than later parts prove to be. Time itself is the theme that the narrator Marcel explores through his reveries, which give a comprehensive view of the social, literary, and artistic life of France before World War I. Although the narrator, Marcel, resembles his creator in his sensibilities and station in life, he differs in significant respects: Marcel is heterosexual, though Proust was homosexual; Marcel is an only child, though Proust had a younger brother; and Marcel's family is not part Jewish, though Proust's mother was. Proust died in 1922 at the age of fifty-one, of stroke and complications resulting from the severe asthma that plagued him all his life—his famous cork-lined bedroom was a remedy for allergy as well as for his neurotic hypersensitivity. Though Proust is somewhat out of fashion among today's literary critics, his reputation may well rise again, especially as the newly revised translation of his works by Terence Kilmartin (Random, 1981) encourages rereading. The two-volume omnibus edition *Remembrance of Things Past* (Random, 1934) contains all seven books of the series in the Scott Moncrieff and Frederick Blossom translations. C. K. Scott Moncrieff died after completing his translation of the sixth book.

1. *Swann's Way* (Holt, 1922)
   This book covers Marcel's youth and the love story of M. Swann. Translated from the French by C. K. Scott Moncrieff. First published in France in 1913.
2. *Within a Budding Grove* (Boni, 1924)
   Marcel's boyish affair with Gilberte comes to an end, and he goes off to the seaside for his health. Translated from the French by Scott Moncrieff. First published in France in 1918.
3. *Guermantes Way* (Seltzer, 1925)
   Marcel, now a young man of fashion, moves in the Duchess de Guermantes's exclusive social circle. Translated from the French by Scott Moncrieff. First published in France in 1920–21.
4. *Cities of the Plain* (Boni, 1927)
   This volume concerns the homosexual Baron de Charlus and Marcel's growing attraction to Albertine. The Dreyfus affair is included in the background. Translated from the French by Scott Moncrieff. First published in France in 1922.
5. *The Captive* (Boni, 1929)
   Albertine now lives with Marcel, but he is tortured by jealousy of her lesbian friends. Translated from the French by Scott Moncrieff. First published in France in 1923.
6. *Sweet Cheat Gone* (Boni, 1930)
   Albertine leaves Marcel and is killed in an accident. Translated from the French by Scott Moncrieff. First published in France in 1925.
7. *Time Recaptured* (Boni, 1932)
   This book concludes the series and shows how World War I affected the lives of all the characters. Variant title: *Time Regained*. Translated from the French by Frederick Blossom. First published in France in 1927.

Puzo, Mario

The Godfather was Mario Puzo's first commercial success. It was called the best-seller of the decade by the *New York Times*. The 1972 movie version starring Marlon Brando was the sensation of the year. The God-father is Don Vito Corleone, Sicilian-American patriarch of a Mafia family determined to extend and consolidate his power in organized crime and to ensure the succession of his son Michael. *The Godfather II*, which Puzo co-authored the screenplay for, exists only in the film version. *The Sicilian* tells the story (based on fact) of Sicilian bandit and folk hero Salvatore Giuliani, with whom Michael Corleone becomes involved.

1. *The Godfather* (Putnam, 1969)
   "The Godfather" maintains order within his family while engaging in a bloody struggle for power.
2. *The Sicilian* (Simon & Schuster, 1984)
   Michael Corleone, in exile in Sicily, is asked to help the Sicilian "Robin Hood," Salvatore Guiliani, escape to America.

Queen, Ellery (pseud. of Frederick Dannay and Manfred Lee)

Ellery Queen is both the pseudonymous author and the detective who stars in the mysteries by this famous team of writing cousins. Though Ellery hasn't aged much since 1929, his style has changed to suit the times. In the early books, he is a supercilious young New Yorker given to tweeds and walking sticks and sporting a pince-nez. Later he becomes less affected, develops a sense of humor, and acquires some sex appeal. The entrée created by his father's police connections, and Ellery's own formidable deductive powers, are an unbeatable combination. As an anthologist and editor of the leading mystery magazine, Ellery Queen has had a profound influence on U.S. mystery writing. Only the novels are listed below. Any titles not included can be assumed to be anthologies or omnibus editions. See the entry under Barnaby Ross for another series written by these authors.

1. *The Greek Coffin Mystery* (Stokes, 1932)
   Though written later, this book is first chronologically. It shows young Ellery, still in college, trying to solve a case involving three sudden deaths, a missing will and a stolen painting.
2. *The Roman Hat Mystery* (Stokes, 1929)
   A missing hat is the significant clue in this famous theater murder case that first introduced young Ellery and his police inspector father, Richard.

3. *The French Powder Mystery* (Stokes, 1930)
During a window demonstration at a Fifth Avenue department store, the dead body of the store owner's wife falls from an opening wall-bed.

4. *The Dutch Shoe Mystery* (Stokes, 1931)
Two murders at the Dutch Memorial Hospital are the problem here.

5. *The Egyptian Cross Mystery* (Stokes, 1932)
This tale involves a series of bizarre murders where the victims are beheaded and fastened to crosses.

6. *The American Gun Mystery* (Stokes, 1933)
During a show with an audience of twenty thousand watching, a rodeo rider is murdered at New York's newest sports palace. Variant title: *Death at the Rodeo.*

7. *The Siamese Twin Mystery* (Stokes, 1933)
The Queens escape from a forest fire to a lonely hilltop cabin and find the corpse of Dr. Xavier clutching a torn half of the six of spades.

8. *The Chinese Orange Mystery* (Stokes, 1934)
A murdered man with his clothes on backwards is found in a locked room.

9. *The Spanish Cape Mystery* (Lippincott, 1935)
Handsome ladies' man John Marco is murdered.

10. *Halfway House* (Stokes, 1936)
Queen deals with the murder of a man who has been leading a double life.

11. *The Door Between* (Stokes, 1937)
Ellery works to clear an innocent woman accused of murdering a prize-winning woman novelist.

12. *The Devil to Pay* (Stokes, 1938)
The Hollywood murder of a crooked movie promoter is the focus here.

13. *The Four of Hearts* (Stokes, 1938)
Still in Hollywood, where he is an "idea man" for a movie company, Ellery looks into a feud between actors that has turned into murder.

14. *The Dragon's Teeth* (Stokes, 1939)
Queen and his partner, Beau Rummell, get involved in the death of eccentric millionaire Cadmus Cale. Variant title: *The Virginia Heiress.*

15. *Calamity Town* (Little, 1942)
Ellery witnesses a murder on Main Street in Wrightsville and does not solve the case until after the trial begins.

16. *There Was an Old Woman* (Little, 1943)
    A ruthless killer using Mother Goose rhymes as a pattern strikes the Potts household of New York's Riverside Drive. Variant title: *The Quick and The Dead.*

17. *The Murderer Is a Fox* (Little, 1945)
    Ellery helps a friend, Dave Fox, absolve his father of guilt in the mysterious murder of his mother.

18. *Ten Days' Wonder* (Little, 1948)
    Queen unravels an anagram that solves a case of murder, blackmail, and theft.

19. *Cat of Many Tails* (Little, 1949)
    Ellery investigates a string of murders where all the corpses have a cord tied around their necks.

20. *Double, Double* (Little, 1950)
    Set in Wrightsville, this story concerns a string of murders linked by a nursery rhyme. Variant title: *The Case of the Seven Murders.*

21. *The Origin of Evil* (Little, 1951)
    Ellery is in Hollywood to work on a book, but two beautiful women with a mystery interrupt.

22. *The King Is Dead* (Little, 1952)
    The locked-room murder of King Bendigo, a sinister munitions magnate, concerns Queen.

23. *The Scarlet Letters* (Little, 1953)
    After a friend asks Ellery to decipher some strange letters, he fears that murder is imminent.

24. *Inspector Queen's Own Case* (Simon & Schuster, 1956)
    On vacation in Connecticut, retired inspector Queen tests his detecting abilities on a case of the "accidental" death of a millionaire's adopted child.

25. *The Finishing Stroke* (Simon & Schuster, 1958)
    Reminiscing on his first solo case, in which an unidentified stranger is murdered at a house party in 1929, Ellery finally solves the mystery in 1957.

26. *The Player on the Other Side* (Random, 1963)
    Someone is methodically killing off all the York family heirs.

27. *And on the Eighth Day* (Random, 1964)
    Ellery blunders into a secluded religious community unknown to the rest of the world. The story is uncharacteristic of Queen novels.

28. *The Fourth Side of the Triangle* (Random, 1965)
    A young man falls in love with his father's mistress and is trapped in her murder.

29. *A Study in Terror* (Lancer, 1966)
    Ellery reads a lost Watson manuscript and discovers a fresh solution to the Jack the Ripper case. This is the novelization of a screenplay. English title: *Sherlock Holmes vs. Jack the Ripper.*
30. *Face to Face* (New Amer. Lib., 1967)
    The murder victim has scrawled the word *face*, the only clue Ellery has.
31. *The House of Brass* (New Amer. Lib., 1968)
    Ellery solves the investigation started by his father of the murder of a very eccentric millionaire.
32. *The Last Woman in His Life* (World, 1970)
    Ellery's old Wrightsville friend Johnny Benedict is murdered, and his three ex-wives are implicated.
33. *A Fine and Private Place* (World, 1971)
    This bizarre and confusing case starts with embezzlement and blackmail in Nino Importuna's conglomerate.

Note: *The Glass Village* and *Cop Out* are written by Ellery Queen, but do not have either of the Queens as characters.

Quill, Monica (pseud. of Ralph McInerny)

Ralph McInerny (q.v.), author of the Father Dowling mysteries, has created another clerical mystery series under the pseudonym of Monica Quill. Sister Mary Teresa, aka Emtee Dempsey, and her two companions, Sister Kim and Sister Joyce, are the last remnants of the Order of Martha and Mary. They live together in a wonderful Frank Lloyd Wright house in Chicago. Sister Mary Teresa is in her late seventies; she is short and very fat. Like Rex Stout's (q.v.) Nero Wolfe, she is a sedentary detective, solving mysteries while staying at home and working on her historical magnum opus about early monasticism in France. Sister Kim, who does the legwork, has a brother on the police force who is useful at times, but no equal to Sister Mary Teresa. The ambience of the Catholic Church adds interest to these entertaining, well-written mysteries.

1. *Not a Blessed Thing!* (Vanguard, 1981)
   When socialite Cheryl Pitman's life is threatened, Detective Moriarity brings her to the sanctuary of the nuns' home.

2. *Let Us Prey* (Vanguard, 1982)
   Sister Joyce's willingness to babysit involves the nuns with the MOMSIEs, a group of divorced women, and with murder.
3. *And Then There Was Nun* (Vanguard, 1984)
   A visit from one of Sister Mary Teresa's former students is the prelude to the deaths of two people connected with a successful women's soccer team.
4. *Nun of the Above* (Vanguard, 1985)
   Sarah Pinking, former student of Mary Teresa and presumed lover of pornography king Ernesto Flavio, is murdered.
5. *Sine Qua Nun* (Vanguard, 1986)
   Geoffrey Chaser, novelist and fellow guest of Sister Mary Teresa on a television talk show, is strangled after insulting the show's host, Basil Murphy.
6. *The Veil of Ignorance* (St. Martin's, 1988)
   Sister Mary Teresa believes that Lydia Hopkins, convicted of killing her husband and daughter, is really innocent.

Radley, Sheila (pseud. of Sheila Robinson)

Detective Chief Inspector Doug Quantrill is the star of this pleasant detective series set in Breckham Market, a country village in Suffolk, England. Chief Quantrill dislikes his assistant, Sergeant Martin Tait, who is young, ambitious, and romantically involved with Quantrill's daughter Allison. When Sergeant Hilary Lloyd, a pretty young female assistant, joins the force, Quantrill loses his heart to her. Robinson is a British author who writes historical romances under the pseudonym of Hester Rowan. Her rural English village is not a quaint and sleepy backwater, but a contemporary town with contemporary problems.

1. *Death in the Morning* (Scribner, 1979)
   Inspector Tait, newly graduated from police school, is convinced that eighteen-year-old Mary Gedge's death was not a suicide. English title: *Death and the Maiden.*
2. *The Chief Inspector's Daughter* (Scribner, 1980)
   Quantrill's daughter Allison, working as a secretary to a romance writer, finds her employer raped and murdered.
3. *A Talent for Destruction* (Scribner, 1982)
   The unearthing of a skeleton on the grounds of the rectory in Breckham Market unnerves the rector and his wife.

4. *The Quiet Road to Death* (Scribner, 1984)
   Quantrill and newcomer Hilary Lloyd investigate the case of a
   headless corpse found near a busy road. English title: *Blood on
   the Happy Highway.*
5. *Fate Worse Than Death* (Scribner, 1986)
   Quantrill and Hilary Lloyd receive little cooperation from local
   villagers when they investigate the disappearance of a young
   woman on the eve of her wedding.
6. *Who Saw Him Die?* (Scribner, 1988)
   When John Goodrum, a newcomer to Breckham Market, runs
   over the town drunk, the coroner calls it an unavoidable accident,
   but the victim's sister calls it no accident.

Rayner, Claire

The Performer series tells of the intertwined fortunes of the Lackland
and Lucas families, doctors, and actors, in nineteenth-century London.
Rayner's characters thread their fascinating way through upper-class
drawing rooms as well as the colorful theater world and the slums of the
Seven Dials criminal section, and they even range out to the Crimea in
wartime. The built-in drama of medicine and the fiery artistic tem-
peraments of the stage actors keep the action simmering along.

1. *Gower Street* (Simon & Schuster, 1973)
   Beginning around 1800, the young boy Abel Lackland is rescued
   from the slums and grows up to be an apothecary-surgeon.
2. *The Haymarket* (Simon & Schuster, 1974)
   Jonah Lackland, Abel's son, rejects his family's plans for his medical career and follows the lure of the theater instead.
3. *Paddington Green* (Simon & Schuster, 1976)
   Abel is now the patriarch running St. Eleanor's Hospital. His four
   children take center stage in this volume.
4. *Soho Square* (Putnam, 1976)
   In the 1850's, young Freddie studies medicine at his grandfather's hospital, as his cousins Phoebe and Lydia force tragic
   choices upon him.
5. *Bedford Row* (Putnam, 1977)
   Spinster Martha Lackland leaves her father's London clinic to
   care for the wounded soldiers during the Crimean war.

6. *Covent Garden* (Putnam, 1978)
   Brother and sister Amy and Fenton Lucas come to London to pursue stage careers and find themselves involved with the Lackland family. English title: *Long Acre.*
7. *Charing Cross* (Putnam, 1979)
   Set in 1870, this is the story of Sophie, Abel Lackland's granddaughter, who becomes a pioneer woman doctor. Variant title: *Trafalgar Square.*
8. *The Strand* (Putnam, 1981)
   London in 1892 is the setting for the story featuring Lewis, a young surgeon from Australia; Claudette, an aspiring actress; and Miriam, the beautiful and spoiled heiress of the Lackland family.
9. *Chelsea Reach* (Weidenfeld, London, 1982)
   Medical student Letty Lackland meets Luke O'Hare, a young actor with plans to set up a theater for poor Londoners.
10. *Shaftesbury Avenue* (Weidenfeld, London, 1983)
    Film producer Letty Lackland wants to make World War I hero Theo Caspar into her next star.
11. *Piccadilly* (Weidenfeld, London, 1984)
    Leah, Harry, Kate, and Peter are among the Lacklands doing a sixteen-week Shakespearean tour of the Continent, including Hitler's Germany.

Read, Miss (pseud. of Dora Saint)

I. Dora Saint has taken her cue from Jane Austen, who wrote that "3 or 4 families in a country village is the very thing to work on." The contemporary English village life she writes about has a quaint appeal for American readers. "Miss Read," the pseudonymous author/narrator, wrote first about her own experiences as the schoolmistress in the little brick-and-thatch village of Fairacre. The first three books have been collected in the omnibus volume *Chronicles of Fairacre* (Houghton, 1977). Saint, like her alto ego Miss Read, was a schoolteacher. She paints her south-of-England villagers with a kindly, pastoral eye just this side of sentimentality.

1. *Village School* (Houghton, 1956)
   One year in the life of Fairacre is seen through the eyes of Miss Read, the village schoolmistress.

2. *Village Diary* (Houghton, 1957)
   Will romance blossom when a male schoolteacher retires to the village?
3. *Storm in the Village* (Houghton, 1959)
   Fairacre unites in opposition to the building of a new housing development in the neighborhood.
4. *Miss Clare Remembers* (Houghton, 1963)
   Another Fairacre schoolmistress, Dolly Clare, looks back over her career, which spanned six reigns and two world wars.
5. *Over the Gate* (Houghton, 1964)
   These are episodes of Fairacre life that Miss Read has collected over the years.
6. *Village Christmas* (Houghton, 1966)
   The young couple who live across the road from the Waters sisters in Fairacre have their new baby on Christmas.
7. *The Fairacre Festival* (Houghton, 1969)
   Fairacre's villagers must raise funds to repair the roof of St. Patrick's church.
8. *Emily Davis* (Houghton, 1971)
   Retired schoolteacher Emily Davis of Fairacre loses her friend and companion.
9. *Tyler's Row* (Houghton, 1973)
   Newcomers Peter and Diana Hale take over Fairacre's ancient row house known as Tyler's Row.
10. *Farther Afield* (Houghton, 1976)
    Miss Read, recovering from a fall in which she broke her arm, accompanies her friend Amy on a holiday trip to Crete.
11. *No Holly for Miss Quinn* (Houghton, 1976)
    Miss Quinn, an efficient secretary who boards at Holly Lodge in Fairacre, must give up the quiet Christmas she had planned and, instead, tend her brother's noisy children.
12. *Village Affairs* (Houghton, 1978)
    A rumor that Fairacre school is going to close upsets the town's residents.
13. *The White Robin* (Houghton, 1980)
    Is there such a thing as a white robin? Does one live in Fairacre?
14. *Village Centenary* (Houghton, 1981)
    Fairacre has a busy year as everyone helps Miss Read celebrate the 100th anniversary of her school.
15. *Summer at Fairacre* (Houghton, 1985)
    Miss Read worries about her missing friend Amy and nurses Mrs. Pringle, the school cleaning lady, invalided with a bad leg.

II. The warm reception of her Fairacre books encouraged "Miss Read" to go on to write about the neighboring Cotswold hamlet of Thrush Green, where the houses are built of stone but the villagers are just as close-knit and amusing in their eccentricities.

1. *Thrush Green* (Houghton, 1960)
   May Day brings Curdle's gypsy caravans to Thrush Green, and the whole town turns out for the fair.
2. *Winter in Thrush Green* (Houghton, 1962)
   The arrival of elderly bachelor Harold Shoosmith brightens many an old maid's hopes.
3. *News from Thrush Green* (Houghton, 1971)
   Thrush Green's newest resident, attractive young Phil, separated from her husband, gets the village's support and help with her son.
4. *Battles at Thrush Green* (Houghton, 1976)
   The rector's innocent suggestion that the churchyard needs tidying up is the first of a series of tempests that tear through Thrush Green.
5. *Return to Thrush Green* (Houghton, 1979)
   Joan Young's ailing father returns home, and the Curdles decide to settle in Thrush Green.
6. *Gossip from Thrush Green* (Houghton, 1982)
   A fire at the rectory, a loud rock quartet, the closing of a tea shop, and a serious illness ruffle the calm of Thrush Green.
7. *Affairs at Thrush Green* (Houghton, 1984)
   Runaway wife Nelly Piggott and long absent Kit Armitage return, while the new Vicar of Lully is having problems with the officious Mrs. Thurgood.
8. *At Home in Thrush Green* (Houghton, 1985)
   Eight homes for the elderly are erected on the site of the old vicarage.
9. *The School at Thrush Green* (Houghton, 1988)
   Village primary school teachers Dorothy Watson and Agnes Fogerty decide to retire to Barton-on-Sea.

III. Caxley, the neighboring market town, is the setting for three of Miss Read's books. Unlike all her other books, which are more or less contemporary in setting, the first two Caxley volumes are historical. They chronicle two of Caxley's leading families, the Norths and the Howards, from the turn of the century onward.

1. *The Market Square* (Houghton, 1966)
   Set from 1901 to World War I, this book tells of the rise of Sep Howard's little bakery and of Sep's friendship with Bender North.
2. *The Howards of Caxley* (Houghton, 1968)
   The Caxley chronicle continues from 1939 through the war years and up to the 1950s. The story focuses on Edward Howard, grandson of Sep and Bender.
3. *The Christmas Mouse* (Houghton, 1973)
   A mouse and a bedraggled runaway boy invade the Berry house in Caxley on Christmas Eve.

Note: There is one book by "Miss Read" that is not set in any of the three towns listed above. *Fresh from the Country* (Houghton, 1961) tells the story of new teacher Anna Lacey, who comes to teach school in a burgeoning suburb, misnamed Elm Hill, from her Essex farm home.

Reeman, Douglas

Douglas Reeman, who writes the popular Richard Bolitho series (q.v.) under the pseudonym Alexander Kent, has embarked upon another series of novels, one which will cover 150 years of British Royal Marine history and the fortunes of the Blackwood family. The Blackwood tradition of serving in the Royal Marines is outlined in the first volume of the series. The Reeman novels, like the Kent novels, are full of stirring action scenes and easy-to-digest history.

1. *Badge of Glory* (Morrow, 1983)
   In 1850, twenty-six-year-old Royal Marine Captain Philip Blackwood sails off to fight the West African slave trade, then sees action in the Crimean War.
2. *The First to Land* (Morrow, 1985)
   In 1900, twenty-seven-year-old Royal Marine Captain David Blackwood, nephew of Philip, gets involved in the Boxer rebellion in China.

Remarque, Erich Maria

Since its publication in 1929, *All Quiet on the Western Front* has become one of the all-time international best-sellers and *the* anti-war novel of the period between the two world wars—it was one of the first books burned by the Nazis when they came to power. This tale of endurance, based on Remarque's own experiences, follows young Paul Baumer from his enlistment in the German army to the Armistice of November, 1918. Although he wrote several subsequent best-sellers, Remarque never quite equaled the success of *All Quite on the Western Front. The Road Back,* which contains several characters from *All Quite on the Western Front,* shows the difficulties faced by these disillusioned veterans of trench warfare when they return to civilian life in postwar Germany.

1. *All Quiet on the Western Front* (Little, 1929)
   Eighteen-year-old Paul Baumer enlists in the German army, undergoes a short, brutal basic training, and is sent to the trenches of the western front. Original German title: *Im westen nichts neues.*
2. *The Road Back* (Little, 1931)
   Ernest Birkholz and his fellow veterans of the trenches try to cope with civilian life after the 1918 Armistice. Original German title: *Der Weg zurück.*

Renault, Mary

I. Though her early works were contemporary romances, Renault was best known for her historical novels, which are masterful recreations of life in ancient Greece. The saga of Alexander the Great is a trilogy that begins in his early childhood and continues to the power struggles following his death. Renault's treatment of the sexual freedom and homosexuality characteristic of the time is frank but unsensationalized. Fans will want to look for *The Nature of Alexander* (Pantheon, 1975), a beautifully illustrated non-fiction work by Renault.

1. *Fire from Heaven* (Pantheon, 1969)
   Alexander's childhood, youth, and tutelage by Aristotle are traced up to the death of his father, Philip of Macedonia.
2. *The Persian Boy* (Pantheon, 1972)
   Alexander's expedition into Asia is seen through the eyes of his beautiful young servant-friend Bagoas.
3. *Funeral Games* (Pantheon, 1981)
   At Alexander's death, a murderous power struggle ensues as his mother and half-brother vie with the regent for the throne.

II. In an early pair of novels based on the Theseus legend, Renault demythologizes her hero, showing Theseus as a vibrant young warrior in a brilliantly imagined portrait of Greek antiquity. She succeeds in making the preclassical mind, with its superstitions and ignorance of natural law, understandable to the modern reader.

1. *The King Must Die* (Pantheon, 1958)
   At seventeen, Theseus is a wiry and quick-witted youth who volunteers to go to Crete for the bull-dances, where he kills Minotauros.
2. *The Bull from the Sea* (Pantheon, 1962)
   Theseus is king of Athens, husband to Cretan princess Phaedra, and lover of the Amazon Hippolyta.

Rendell, Ruth

Inspector Wexford gets little chance to enjoy the view of High Street that his police station office affords him. The town of Kingsmarkham and the surrounding mid-Sussex countryside provide enough crime to keep him and his handsome young assistant, Burden, fully occupied. Reg Wexford, at fifty-five is tall, heavyset, rather ugly, and devoted to his wife, Dora, and their grown children; however, he is not immune to brief encounters with attractive ladies. Like June Thomson's Inspector Rudd (q.v.) and Catherine Aird's Inspector Sloan (q.v.), Wexford solves cases cast in the classic English mold. Rendell has written numerous non-Wexford mysteries, which are quite different.

1. *From Doon with Death* (Doubleday, 1965)
   Inspector Wexford can discover no motive for the murder of an unprepossessing housewife except for a possible connection to a mysterious correspondent named Doon, who sent books and letters.
2. *A New Lease of Death* (Doubleday, 1967)
   Wexford gets involved when the Reverend Henry Archery tries to clear a young woman's father of a brutal ax murder. Variant title: *Sins of the Fathers*.
3. *Wolf to the Slaughter* (Doubleday, 1967)
   Wexford investigates a case that looks like murder in a love nest except that the victim is missing.
4. *The Best Man to Die* (Doubleday, 1969)
   A string of murders involving small-time gangsters, cheating husbands, and loose women puzzles Inspector Wexford.

5. *A Guilty Thing Surprised* (Doubleday, 1970)
   Elizabeth Nightingale is murdered on one of her nocturnal walks through the grounds at her home, Myfleet Manor.

6. *Murder Being Once Done* (Doubleday, 1972)
   A woman is strangled with her own silk scarf and left in a dusty moss-encrusted vault at a London cemetery.

7. *No More Dying Then* (Doubleday, 1972)
   With one child dead and another missing, a young mother entangled in blackmail, scandal, and murder, nears the brink of mental collapse.

8. *Some Lie and Some Die* (Doubleday, 1973)
   After a rock festival in Kingsmarkham, Wexford finds a girl dead and battered.

9. *Shake Hands Forever* (Doubleday, 1975)
   Inspector Wexford spends his vacation tracking down the murderer of Angela Hathall.

10. *A Sleeping Life* (Doubleday, 1978)
    The murderer and the victim are inexplicably confused in this case which involves a woman who had been missing for twenty years.

11. *Means of Evil* (Doubleday, 1980)
    Five Wexford stories are collected here.

12. *Death Notes* (Pantheon, 1981)
    Rich old flutist Sir Manuel Camargue drowns in his own lake just days before marrying a young woman. English title: *Put On by Cunning.*

13. *The Speaker of Mandarin* (Pantheon, 1983)
    After a trip to China, Wexford is troubled by hallucinations and paranoid fantasies.

14. *An Unkindness of Ravens* (Pantheon, 1985)
    Rodney Williams disappears, but his wife and daughter don't seem disturbed.

15. *The Veiled One* (Pantheon, 1988)
    Elderly Gwen Robson is murdered in a shopping mall garage, and Wexford's home is bombed, possibly because of his anti-nuclear arms stand.

Resnicow, Herbert

Alexander and Norma Gold are contemporary Jewish-American versions of Hammett's Nick and Nora Charles. Alex, who is a detecting genius, starts solving crimes as a diversion while recovering from a heart attack. Eventually he gives up his job as a consulting engineer, and he and Norma become full-time private investigators. Each one of the Gold mysteries involves someone in the arts: architecture, ballet, painting, opera, or a Broadway musical in the five novels published so far. These are a treat for readers who enjoy ingenious plots, witty banter, lots of New York ambience, and a wealth of information on the arts.

1. *The Gold Solution* (St. Martin's, 1983)
   Draftsman Jonathan Candell is arrested for murder after famous architect Roger Talbott is found with a knife in his back.
2. *The Gold Deadline* (St. Martin's, 1984)
   Impresario Viktor Bogulslav is stabbed to death in his curtained box during a ballet gala.
3. *The Gold Frame* (St. Martin's, 1984)
   The Golds are called in by Daniel Belmont, owner of the celebrated FAMONY Museum, to help authenticate a reputed Vermeer painting.
4. *The Gold Curse* (St. Martin's, 1986)
   Opera singer Thea Malabar is stabbed (for real) while she is performing the role of Gilda in *Rigoletto*.
5. *The Gold Gamble* (St. Martin's, 1988)
   After the Golds invest in a revival of *Guys and Dolls*, Carol Sands, Norma's choice for the role of Adelaide, becomes a prime murder suspect.

Rice, Anne

Anne Rice's bizarre fantasy series, the Vampire Chronicles, is gathering a growing cult of readers. Her vampires are creatures who look exactly like the human beings they once were, but are differentiated by their immortality and lust for blood. While most sensible vampires desire anonymity, a few individuals are so desperate for fame that they reveal themselves, and gain the wrath of the scattered community of vampires. The stories are told from the vampires' own deadpan, sometimes grisly, points of view in a wonderfully frenzied prose style. A great deal of arcane historical and religious lore is included along with the vampires' tortured philosophizing about the trials of immortality and their gradual loss of human feelings. Beware, readers might find themselves developing a taste for these spicy specialties.

1. *Interview with the Vampire* (Knopf, 1976)
   Vampire Louis tells a reporter all about his death-in-life experience and his search for the meaning of his existence.
2. *The Vampire Lestat* (Knopf, 1985)
   After centuries of wandering and uncovering lore about cults of the dead, vampire Lestat becomes a rock star in New Orleans.
3. *The Queen of the Damned* (Knopf, 1988)
   Lestat awakens the evil and destructive Queen Akasha from her six-thousand-year sleep.

Richardson, Dorothy

Dorothy Richardson was among the avant-garde writers of the early twentieth century who placed the experiencing mind at the center of the novel. Her intimate portrayal of Miriam Henderson from youth to maturity is the subject of Pilgrimage, a series published in sections beginning in 1915 and reissued in a four-volume set, called *Pilgrimage*, by Knopf in 1967. Numbers 12 and 13 below appear only in this set. Miriam develops from a bright, skeptical, and socially uncertain young girl, through crises of faith and friendship, to maturity as an assured and independent thinker with mystical religious convictions. Richardson, like Virginia Woolf, had high regard for the mystical/intuitive qualities, which both saw as essentially feminine. Richardson's stream-of-consciousness style is more accessible than Joyce's; her subjects are more interesting to women than Proust's.

1. *Pointed Roofs* (Knopf, 1915)
   Prompted by her father's financial collapse, Miriam Henderson at seventeen decides to take a teaching position at a girls' school in Germany for a year.
2. *Backwater* (Knopf, 1916)
   Miriam returns home, then spends her eighteenth year as a resi-

dent teacher at a dreary north London school, Wordsworth House.

3. *Honeycomb* (Knopf, 1917)
Miriam at nineteen is a governess for the children of the wealthy Corrie family, who live at Newlands.

4. *The Tunnel* (Knopf, 1919)
Now living by herself at a rooming house and working as a dentist's assistant, Miriam discovers London's intellectual life.

5. *Interim* (Knopf, 1919)
Miriam seems to come to terms with her feelings that religion and science include false male ideas, while she grows in intellectual sophistication.

6. *Deadlock* (Knopf, 1921)
After several increasingly self-assured and independent years, Miriam meets Michael Shatov, a new boarder at her rooming house.

7. *Revolving Lights* (Knopf, 1923)
Miriam is introduced to Quaker thought and appreciates its equal treatment of the sexes and its respect for silent meditation.

8. *The Trap* (Knopf, 1925)
Now twenty-eight, depressed and unsure of the writing career she had hoped for, Miriam debates the alternatives of marriage, celibacy, and free love.

9. *Oberland* (Knopf, 1928)
Miriam, on holiday in the Swiss Alps, regains a sense of joy and is confirmed in her new mystical orientation.

10. *Dawn's Left Hand* (Duckworth, London, 1931)
Miriam has an affair with liberal scientist Hypo Wilson, who is based on H. G. Wells.

11. *Clear Horizon* (Dent, London, 1935)
Miriam and Hypo's affair is not happy, and they finally break up.

12. *Dimple Hill* (in *Pilgrimage* [Dent, London, 1938])
Miriam takes a long prescribed rest with Quaker friends in Sussex, where her belief in the existence of God is ecstatically affirmed.

13. *March Moonlight* (in *Pilgrimage* [Knopf, 1967])
This coda rounding off the work was added to the four-volume edition of *Pilgrimage* published by Knopf in 1967.

Richardson, Henry Handel
(pseud. of Ethel Florence Lindsay Richardson)

Renewed interest in Australia may help revive the reputation of this practically forgotten author. In fact, *The Getting of Wisdom*, an early novel (1910) about a student in a young ladies' college in Melbourne, was reprinted by Dial Press in 1981 and has just been made into a charming movie with the same title. Richardson was born and raised in Australia, the daughter of an Anglo-Irish physician. After moving to Europe and marriage to German scholar John G. Robertson, she began writing fiction. The Fortunes of Richard Mahoney is a trilogy that surveys Australian history from the 1850s onward; it is a powerful and tragic work that has been compared to Mann's *Buddenbrooks* and Roland's *Jean-Christophe*.

1. *Australia Felix* (Norton, 1930)
   This shows young Richard coming from Ireland to Australia during the gold rush, marrying and keeping store for a while, then returning to his profession of medicine and building up a successful practice. Published under the title *The Fortunes of Richard Mahoney* by Holt in 1917.
2. *The Way Home* (Norton, 1930)
   Richard is increasingly dissatisfied with life in both Australia and England, even though his mining shares have made him rich and his wife and children are devoted to him. Published in England in 1925.
3. *Ultima Thule* (Norton, 1929)
   Richard suffers a financial loss, tries to take up his medical practice again, but finally descends into madness and death. This novel was popular enough in the United States to cause the reprinting of the first two volumes of the trilogy in 1930.

Richter, Conrad

I. Elizabeth Montgomery starred as Sayward in the highly praised television version of this classic American pioneer story. The Awakening Land is a trilogy of novels, also known as the American Pioneer trilogy,

that begins in the 1790s as the Luckett family leaves home in Pennsylvania and crosses the Ohio River to uncharted wilderness. Sayward,
the oldest and staunchest of the children, is fifteen at the start, and the
story, which continues to her death, is a notable portrait of an indomitable pioneer woman. The trilogy is available in an omnibus edition, *The
Awakening Land* (Knopf, 1966)

1. *The Trees* (Knopf, 1940)
   After her mother's death, it falls to Sayward to keep the family
   together and safe from danger as they put down roots in the
   new land.
2. *The Fields* (Knopf, 1946)
   Now married and with a growing family, Sayward makes a success
   of the farm and starts a school and a church in the little community.
3. *The Town* (Knopf, 1950)
   This concluding volume, which shows the thriving town and
   Sayward's move from the old cabin to a fancy new house, won a
   Pulitzer Prize.

II. Two more Richter novels are not really sequels, but they are companion volumes because they treat similar stories; young pioneer children
are raised by Indians and then returned against their wills to white
society. Both are justly popular with young adults.

1. *The Light in the Forest* (Knopf, 1953)
   At fifteen, True Son is returned from his adoptive Indian family to
   his parents, the Butlers.
2. *A Country of Strangers* (Knopf, 1966)
   Stone Girl, at fifteen, is a squaw with a little boy when she is taken
   by Black Robe back to white society.

Rikhoff, Jean

I. This popular author has two trilogies to her credit. The earlier one is a
family saga concerning the Catholic Timble family of Springfield, Illinois. Beginning at the turn of the century, the story focuses on the
marriage of Frank and Lydia Timble and continues as their five
daughters grow to maturity. These event-filled lives, realistically portrayed, are an engrossing study in love and duty.

378

1. *Dear Ones All* (Viking, 1961)
   Told mostly in flashbacks from a Thanksgiving Day family gathering in 1936, this account covers the early years of Frank and Lydia's marriage and the growth of their family.
2. *Voyage In, Voyage Out* (Viking, 1963)
   In the 1950s, the Timble family gathers for a welcome-home party for prodigal Stu and visiting cousin Lois from New York, both with problems to sort out.
3. *Rites of Passage* (Viking, 1966)
   The children of the Timble sisters are now in their middle years.

II. Part family saga, part western, this series may well grow beyond its present three volumes. It starts in 1807 as Odder Butte strikes out for the Adirondack Mountains of New York, and the narrative follows succeeding generations of the tough and isolated hard-scrabble farmers as they prosper and move further west.

1. *Buttes Landing* (Dial, 1973)
   Three generations of the Butte family are followed, from old Odder's arrival in the Adirondacks up to the Civil War.
2. *One of the Raymonds* (Dial, 1974)
   The coming-of-age story of young Mason Raymond Butte is set in the Adirondacks and in rural North Carolina during Reconstruction.
3. *Sweetwater* (Dial, 1976)
   In 1876, young cousins Mason Raymond and John Butte travel west, braving the dangers of high rivers, prairie fires, dust storms, and Indian attack.

Ripley, Alexandra

Alexandra Ripley has written a pair of historical novels about her native Charleston, South Carolina. The novels follow the fortunes of two aristocratic Charleston families, the Tradds and the Ansons, from 1863 to 1935, as they slide from prominence into decadence and penury. Inbreeding, snobbery, and obstinacy are more responsible than bad economic times for the decline of these families. The history of the city of Charleston is lovingly delineated in these readable historically accurate novels.

1. *Charleston* (Doubleday, 1981)
   Poor white Shad saves Pinckney Tradd's life in the Civil War, goes into partnership with him, but is forbidden to marry Pinckney's sister Lizzie. Covers 1863 to 1898.
2. *On Leaving Charleston* (Doubleday, 1984)
   Garden Tradd, Lizzie's niece, breaks away from her family's ruinous traditions. Covers 1900 to 1935.

Roberts, Kenneth

Roberts used his native town of Kennebunk (originally called Arundel), Maine, as the setting for four loosely connected historical novels, the Chronicles of Arundel. The Nason family and other characters from Arundel figure prominently in the dramatic stories of adventure and romance from Revolutionary times to the War of 1812. By championing Benedict Arnold in *Rabble in Arms* and a British loyalist in *Oliver Wiswell* (not one of the Arundel books), Roberts presented an unusual slant, corrective in its astringent conservative viewpoint.

1. *Arundel* (Doubleday, 1930)
   Young Steven Nason accompanies his friend Benedict Arnold on a hazardous expedition to Quebec.
2. *Rabble in Arms* (Doubleday, 1933)
   A group of men from Arundel fight under Benedict Arnold's leadership. The story ends after the battle of Saratoga.
3. *Lively Lady* (Doubleday, 1931)
   Richard Nason, son of Steven, commands the armed sloop *Lively Lady* in the War of 1812.
4. *Captain Caution* (Doubleday, 1934)
   The crew of an Arundel merchant ship is captured and detained by the English during the War of 1812.

Robertson, Don

These gently humorous and nostalgic novels star young Morris Bird III of Cleveland, Ohio, who is nine years old in 1944 when the first book takes place. Morris worries about love, bravery, and "selfrespect" as he practices his famous dropkick, tries to be nice to his little sister, Sandra, or befriends the oafish Stanley Chaloupka. Adult and young adult readers alike will enjoy Morris's adventures. A recent television drama-tization adapted the story of the third book for a black cast.

1. *The Greatest Thing since Sliced Bread* (Putnam, 1965)
   Morris and Sandra use their red wagon to rescue two victims of a gas-tank explosion.
2. *The Sum and Total of Now* (Putnam, 1966)
   Morris, now thirteen, wants to do something special for his grandmother, who is dying.
3. *The Greatest Thing That Almost Happened* (Putnam, 1970)
   Tragedy in the form of acute leukemia strikes Morris, who at seventeen, is in love and on the high school basketball team.

Rock, Phillip

The Passing Bells trilogy has dozens of major characters and a host of minor ones in its panoramic view of English society from 1914 to the 1940s. The central focus of the trilogy is the aristocratic Greville family and their servants, each coping in their various ways with the horrors of the First World War and the cataclysmic social changes that took place in the postwar years. Phillip Rock is an American novelist and screen-writer.

1. *The Passing Bells* (Seaview, 1979)
   Anthony Greville, ninth Earl of Stanmore, sees his idyllic country estate and its community of family and servants changed forever by the Great War and the years immediately following (1914–20).
2. *Circles of Time* (Seaview, 1981)
   Post–World War I England and Germany are the settings of this book and the Greville family among the protagonists observed by journalist Martin Rilke.
3. *A Future Arrived* (Seaview, 1985)
   Colin Greville, Anthony's grandson, joins the Royal Air Force rather than attend Cambridge University as England lurches toward World War II.

Rolland, Romain

Jean-Christophe Krafft, Rolland's larger-than-life hero, is a nineteenth-century musical genius obviously sprung from the same mold as Beethoven and resembling him in many of the details of his childhood—for example, his poor German origin and his drunkard father who exploits the child prodigy. Krafft is just as obviously a heroic alter ego for the sickly and neurotic Rolland, who confessed that Jean-Christophe was "the history of my soul transposed into one greater than I." In addition, Jean-Christophe symbolizes the regeneration of Europe, with the best forces of French nationalism leading the way toward defeat of the materialism and corruption rampant in pre-World War I society. It was this aspect of the work, no doubt, that won it the Nobel Prize in 1915, and which, of course, now makes the work seem very dated. The pre-Freudian analysis of character will also strike modern readers as inadequate if not bizarre. Each book was originally published separately in France between 1904 and 1912; in the United States, the books were published in three volumes in 1910-13. Later, all ten were collected in the Modern Library one-volume omnibus titled *Jean-Christophe* (Random, 1938).

1. *Jean-Christophe* (Holt, 1910)
   a. *Dawn*
      The story begins with Jean-Christophe in his cradle listening to the sounds of the river flowing through the small Rhineland town of his birth. Translated from the French by Gilbert Cannan.
   b. *Morning*
      Jean-Christophe, now almost eleven and well on his way as a prodigy, plays second violin in the local orchestra. Translated from the French by Gilbert Cannan.
   c. *Youth*
      Jean-Christophe, now living alone with his widowed mother, has a stormy adolescence. Translated from the French by Gilbert Cannan.
   d. *Revolt*
      After a scuffle with some soldiers at an inn, Jean-Christophe leaves for Paris. Translated from the French by Gilbert Cannan.
2. *Jean-Christophe in Paris* (Holt, 1911)
   a. *The Market Place*
      The cultural life of Prais is a central subject here. Translated from the French by Gilbert Cannan.

b. *Antoinette*
This volume backs up to trace the childhood of Jean-Christophe's friend Olivier Jeannin and his sister, Antoinette Jeannin, who dies young. Translated from the French by Gilbert Cannan.

c. *The House*
Jean-Christophe, now almost eleven and well on his way as a prodigy, plays second violin in the local orchestra. Translated from the French by Gilbert Cannan.

3. *Jean-Christophe: Journey's End* (Holt, 1913)

a. *Love and Friendship*
Olivier marries, and Jean-Christophe becomes famous. Translated from the French by Gilbert Cannan.

b. *The Burning Bush*
Olivier's marriage ends and the two friends become close again until their involvement in the Paris May Day riots ends in tragedy. Translated from the French by Gilbert Cannan.

c. *The New Dawn*
The aged genius is surrounded by friends and success in Paris. Translated from the French by Gilbert Cannan.

Rölvaag, Ole Edvart

Rölvaag emigrated from Norway in 1896 at the age of twenty, earned his education as a farm and factory worker, and taught for many years at St. Olaf College in Minnesota. *Giants in the Earth* was first published in two volumes in Norway in 1924 and 1925. Its U.S. publication in 1927 in the author's own translation was an immediate success: almost 80,000 copies were sold in the first year alone. The still very readable account of the hardships and isolation braved by Per Hansa and his family as they settled in Spring Creek, South Dakota, was one of the first unromanticized views of the immigrant experience.

1. *Giants in the Earth* (Harper, 1927)
Per Hansa hopes to settle his family happily in South Dakota in 1873, but his wife Beret hates the hardships and the loneliness.

2. *Peder Victorious* (Harper, 1929)
Beret rears her family and manages the large and prosperous farm as her sons, especially Peder, the youngest, lose their Nor-

wegian ways. Translated from the Norwegian by Norah O. Solon and the author.
3. *Their Father's Gold* (Harper, 1931)
   Peder's 1894 marriage to Irish Catholic Susie Doheny turns out to be unhappy. Translated from the Norwegian by Trygve M. Ager.

Romains, Jules (pseud. of Louis Farigoule)

The twenty-seven-volume novel series Men of Good Will will stand as a monument to early twentieth-century France when Romains' other novels, plays, and nonfiction are long forgotten. While his theories about "Unanimism," a sort of secular religion having to do with universal human solidarity, may have been responsible for the broad sweep of the novel series, the work is essentially the story of particular individual destinies portrayed against a collective backdrop. The novels cover twenty-five years from 1908 to 1933 and encompass many characters and events, but the heart of the story concerns the lives of two young men from their student days through World War I and into the prime of their careers. Jallez is an introspective Parisian who becomes a famous writer; Jerphanion is a practical provincial who goes into politics and eventually becomes foreign minister. Priests and poets, murderers and millionaires, and occasional historical figures like Lenin appear in the 8,000-page work, which would provide at least two years' worth of interesting episodes on "Masterpiece Theatre" if anyone were brave enough to undertake its dramatization. Appended to the last book is an index to all of the characters in the series. In the United States, the twenty-seven volumes were published as a fourteen-volume set called the Men of Good Will series.

1. *Men of Good Will*, volume 1 (Knopf, 1933)
   a. *The Sixth of October*
      The events of this single day introduce most of the characters and anchor the reader firmly in Paris of 1908. Translated from the French by Warre B. Wells.
   b. *Quinette's Crime*
      Quinette, the bookbinder, gets involved with a murderer and plans to do him in. Translated from the French by Warre B. Wells.
2. *Passion's Pilgrims: Men of Good Will*, volume 2 (Knopf, 1934)
   a. *Childhood's Loves*
      This novel covers two weeks in November, 1908. The two

friends Jallez and Jerphanion take the foreground. Translated from the French by Warre B. Wells.

b. *Eros in Paris*

Jallez reviews his tortured romance with Juliette, while Jerphanion sets out straightforwardly to find a girl. Translated from the French by Warre B. Wells.

3. *The Proud and the Meek: Men of Good Will*, volume 3 (Knopf, 1934)

a. *The Proud*

Sammécaud has an affair with Marie, and Haverkamp develops a spa in Celle. Translated from the French by Warre B. Wells.

b. *The Meek*

The story of the poor Bastide family is told through the eyes of the young boy Louis, one of Clanricard's pupils. Translated from the French by Warre B. Wells.

4. *The World from Below: Men of Good Will*, volume 4 (Knopf, 1935)

a. *The Lonely*

Jerphanion, in search of something to believe in, meets the schoolteacher Clanricard. Both are attracted to Mathilde Cazalis. Translated from the French by Gerard Hopkins.

b. *Provincial Interlude*

The time is 1910, and the main focus is on the priest Mionnet, who is investigating a delicate case of mismanagement of funds by a provincial bishop. Translated from the French by Gerard Hopkins.

5. *The Earth Trembles: Men of Good Will*, volume 5 (Knopf, 1936)

a. *Flood Warning*

This novel is set in Paris during the general strike of November, 1910. Translated from the French by Gerard Hopkins.

b. *The Powers That Be*

Gurau is prominent in this volume, which describes the Agadir incident of the summer of 1911. Translated from the French by Gerard Hopkins.

6. *The Depths and the Heights: Men of Good Will*, volume 6 (Knopf, 1937)

a. *To The Gutter*

This novel concentrates on Allory's sexual escapades. Jerphanion is still in military service; Jallez is pursuing journalism and a literary career. Translated from the French by Gerard Hopkins.

b. *To the Stars*

The question of creativity is examined as two previously un-important characters take the foreground: Viaur, a doctor at Celle, and Strigelius, a poet. Translated from the French by Gerard Hopkins.

7. *Death of a World: Men of Good Will*, volume 7 (Knopf, 1938)

a. *Mission to Rome*

Poincaré sends Mionnet on a delicate mission to the Vatican. Translated from the French by Gerard Hopkins.

b. *Black Flag*

Jerphanion marries Odette and settles in Paris; Jallez breaks with Juliette and visits England. Translated from the French by Gerard Hopkins.

8. *Verdun: Men of Good Will*, volume 8 (Knopf, 1939)

a. *The Prelude*

Jerphanion and Clanricard will see action with the infantry; Jallez, medically unfit, supervises boot repairs. Translated from the French by Gerard Hopkins.

b. *The Battle*

The vast battle of Verdun is seen through some half dozen different characters. Translated from the French by Gerard Hopkins.

9. *Aftermath: Men of Good Will*, volume 9 (Knopf, 1941)

a. *Vorge against Quinette*

With armistice and demobilization, the story takes a rather sudden turn to focus on Vorge, a Dadaist poet who makes a cult figure out of the murderer Quinette. Translated from the French by Gerard Hopkins.

b. *Sweets of Life*

Jallez spends an idyllic winter (1919–20) in Nice, has a romance, and renews acquaintance with some old friends. Translated from the French by Gerard Hopkins.

10. *The New Day: Men of Good Will*, volume 10 (Knopf, 1942)

a. *Promise of Dawn*

Jallez is now doing League of Nations work; Jerphanion is secretary to a radical leader. Various commentators have noted that the despair prevading this volume seems due more to the year in which it was written than to the year it depicts. Translated from the French by Gerard Hopkins.

b. *The World Is Your Adventure*

Jallez and Jerphanion travel to Russia and return disillusioned. Translated from the French by Gerard Hopkins.

11. *Work and Play: Men of Good Will*, volume 11 (Knopf, 1944)
   a. *Mountain Days*
      Jerphanion runs for election in 1924; Jallez is in Geneva; Doctor Viaur wins a Nobel Prize. Translated from the French by Gerard Hopkins.
   b. *Work and Play*
      Jerphanion is obsessed with the danger of a new war; Haverkamp, now very rich, tries to buy government influence. Translated from the French by Gerard Hopkins.
12. *The Wind Is Rising: Men of Good Will*, volume 12 (Knopf, 1945)
   a. *The Gathering of the Gangs*
      In 1927, two Fascist movements develop. Translated from the French by Gerard Hopkins.
   b. *Offered in Evidence*
      Jallez feels there is something missing in his life; Jerphanion is totally pessimistic about the individual's ability to influence history. The time is February, 1928. Translated from the French by Gerard Hopkins.
13. *Escape in Passion: Men of Good Will*, volume 13 (Knopf, 1946)
   a. *The Magic Carpet*
      This episode is mostly concerned with Jallez's amorous affairs. Translated from the French by Gerard Hopkins.
   b. *Francoise*
      Jallez meets his ideal love; Jerphanion resigns as foreign minister; Haverkamp loses all his money. Translated from the French by Gerard Hopkins.
14. *The Seventh of October: Men of Good Will*, volume 14 (Knopf, 1946)
   The general despair is temporarily dispelled as old friends gather. The story concludes with a last look at all the characters. Translated from the French by Gerard Hopkins.

Note: *Jerphanion fils* (published in France in 1956 and apparently never translated into English) is not part of Men of Good Will, though it does concern some of its characters, especially young Jean-Pierre, who is shown having trouble settling down after service with the Free French during World War II.

Roosevelt, Elliott

Elliott Roosevelt, son of Eleanor and Franklin, stirred up a controversy when he revealed his father's extramarital affairs and portrayed Eisenhower, Joseph Kennedy, and others in a very unflattering light in *An Untold Story* (Putnam, 1973). But his detective novels starring Eleanor as an amateur investigator are universally applauded. They are pleasant and nostalgic diversions sure to please readers who remember the era. They feature classic mystery plots, lots of period flavor, and walk-ons by J. Edgar Hoover, Winston Churchill, and other luminaries. For other detective series about this era see Max Allan Collins and Stuart Kaminsky.

1. *Murder and the First Lady* (St. Martin's, 1984)
   Eleanor Roosevelt is the only person who believes in the innocence of her secretary when she is arrested for the murder of her lover.
2. *The Hyde Park Murder* (St. Martin's, 1985)
   A Dutchess County, New York, neighbor asks the First Lady to help clear her fiance's father of an embezzlement charge.
3. *Murder at Hobcaw Barony* (St. Martin's, 1986)
   Eleanor and several Hollywood stars are fellow guests at Bernard Baruch's estate when an explosion kills a movie producer.
4. *The White House Pantry Murder* (St. Martin's, 1987)
   A corpse is found in the White House refrigerator while FDR is planning war strategy with the visiting Winston Churchill.
5. *Murder at the Palace* (St. Martin's, 1988)
   An equerry of King George VI is killed in Buckingham Palace during the First Lady's trip to England.
6. *Murder in the Oval Office* (St. Martin's, 1989)
   Congressman Colmer is found murdered in the locked Oval Office.
7. *Murder in the Rose Garden* (St. Martin's, 1989)
   Washington hostess and secret blackmailer Vivian Taliafero is strangled in the Rose Garden of the White House.

Ross, Barnaby
(pseud. of Frederic Dannay and Manfred Lee)

Under the early collaborative pseudonym of Barnaby Ross, the authors produced four mysteries starring Drury Lane, a retired Shakespearean actor and connoisseur of crime who helped the New York police. The first three listed below are collected in an omnibus entitled *The XYZ Murders* (Lippincott, 1961). See the entry under Ellery Queen for another series written by these authors.

1. *The Tragedy of X* (Viking, 1932)
   A man is murdered on a crowded crosstown trolley in New York City, and Drury Lane knows who did it but has trouble proving it.
2. *The Tragedy of Y* (Viking, 1932)
   York Hatter is dead, and someone is trying to kill his blind and deaf stepdaughter.
3. *The Tragedy of Z* (Viking, 1933)
   Drury advises Miss Patience Thumm in her investigation of a series of crimes.
4. *Drury Lane's Last Case* (Viking, 1933)
   Patience Thumm is again involved in this puzzling case involving the substitution of one rare book for another.

Ross, Dana Fuller

I. Wagons West is another series produced by Lyle Kenyon Engel, the book "packager" behind John Jakes's successful Kent Family Chronicles (q.v.). Dana Fuller Ross writes a serviceable blend of romance and adventure. The story begins in 1837 as Sam Brentwood organizes the first large-scale wagon train of settlers headed for the Oregon territory; the series goes on to chronicle the settling of the West, tracing the lives of a large cast of characters. The books are available in paperback and large-print editions.

1. *Independence!* (Bantam, 1979)
   Sam Brentwood takes the wagon train from Long Island to Independence, meeting the attractive widow Claudia Humphries along the way. The time is spring, 1837.
2. *Nebraska!* (Bantam, 1979)
   In autumn of 1837, frontiersman Mike ("Whip") Holt takes the wagon train on from Independence, and Cathy van Ayl leaves her family behind in the hope of winning Whip's heart.
3. *Wyoming!* (Bantam, 1979)
   In 1838, with the Rockies looming ahead, Whip's Indian woman La-ena joins the wagon train.

4. *Oregon!* (Bantam, 1980)
   A band of Russian settlers and the English Royal Army complicate the wagon train's arrival and settlement. Cathy is now
   married to Lee Blake.
5. *Texas!* (Bantam, 1980)
   In 1843, some of the original wagon train members join the call to
   defend Texas against the Mexican army.
6. *California!* (Bantam, 1981)
   The discovery of gold in 1848 brings a new kind of lawlessness to
   the West. This novel features Whip Holt and many new characters.
7. *Colorado!* (Bantam, 1981)
   During the Civil War, General Lee Blake fights to keep Colorado
   in the Union, and Cathy is faced with a rival.
8. *Nevada!* (Bantam, 1981)
   This book covers events in Virginia City, Nevada, during the Civil
   War.
9. *Washington!* (Bantam, 1982)
   Two Civil War veterans fight a ruthless tycoon for timber rights in
   Washington State.
10. *Montana!* (Bantam, 1983)
    In 1866, young Toby Holt, Whip's son, faces the treacherous
    outlaw Sadie "Ma" Hastings and Thunder Cloud, chief of the
    mighty Sioux.
11. *Dakota!* (Bantam, 1983)
    Toby Holt leaves his wife Clarissa at home and sets out to make
    peace with the Dakota Indians.
12. *Utah!* (Bantam, 1984)
    In 1867, Toby and his friend Rob Martin bring peace and order to
    the lawless territory of Utah.
13. *Idaho!* (Bantam, 1984)
    Toby Holt, now the new governor of the Idaho territory, must
    deal with the rowdy saloons and bordellos of Boise as well as
    marauding Indian bands.
14. *Missouri!* (Bantam, 1985)
    Toby hunts down outlaws and renegade Indians with the aid of
    young army cadet Hank Blake and the loyal Chief Running
    Bear.
15. *Mississippi!* (Bantam, 1985)
    The Mississippi River is the scene of much of the action as Toby
    Holt and his ally Domino clash with the wicked Karl Kellerman
    and Tong boss Kung Lee.

16. *Louisiana!* (Bantam, 1986)
The exotic atmosphere of New Orleans with its Creole, Cajun, and Chinese population, brings new challenges for Toby.

17. *Tennessee!* (Bantam, 1986)
Toby is sent to quash a conspiracy of outlaws and backwoods misfits in the secluded hills of Tennessee.

18. *Illinois!* (Bantam, 1986)
This is set in the 1870s in Chicago at the time of the great fire. Toby has become prosperous and his daughter Janessa feels a calling to become a doctor.

19. *Wisconsin!* (Bantam, 1987)
Toby, now widowed, watches romance bloom between his sister Cindy and friend Lt. Henry Blake.

20. *Kentucky!* (Bantam, 1987)
Toby goes to Kentucky looking for an assassin plotting to kill President Grant. Set during the panic of 1873.

21. *Arizona!* (Bantam, 1988)
The new Winchester gun is used by Cindy Holt's husband to tame the sun-scorched frontier of Arizona.

22. *New Mexico!* (Bantam, 1988)
Toby goes to New Mexico to infiltrate a band of desperadoes and bring justice to the land.

23. *Oklahoma!* (Bantam, 1989)
Range wars threaten to erupt as Oklahoma's harsh open country beckons to farmers.

24. *Celebration!* (Bantam, 1989)
A band of anarchists plans a bloody bomb to ruin the Centennial celebration of July 4, 1876.

II. The Wagons West saga is continued by The Holts: An American Dynasty series, which catches up with Toby Holt and his family in 1887. Like Wagons West, this series is published in original paperback.

1. *Oregon Legacy* (Bantam, 1989)
Toby Holt loses his fortune in a Dakota blizzard, so the Holts return to their Oregon homestead, where young Tim Holt gets a yen to go silver-mining.

Roth, Philip

Roth is best known for his satires on American Jewish middle-class life, such as *Portnoy's Complaint* and *Goodbye, Columbus*, the short novel on which the very popular movie was based. In the five books about Nathan Zuckerman, the literary life adds another dimension as Roth examines the crises, responsibilities, pretensions, and anguished loves of a writer. Zuckerman strongly resembles his creator; he has even written a novel which, like *Portnoy's Complaint*, raised controversy in many quarters.

1. *The Ghost Writer* (Farrar, 1979)
   In the 1950s Zuckerman visits the famous author E. I. Lonoff at his house in the Berkshires and meets his beautiful protégée, who has curious Anne Frank fantasies.
2. *Zuckerman Unbound* (Farrar, 1981)
   Thirteen years later, Zuckerman, now reckoning with fame and the attacks of "crazies" that it brings him, attends his father's funeral and quarrels with his brother.
3. *The Anatomy Lesson* (Farrar, 1983)
   Zuckerman, now a tormented 40-year-old, fights writer's block, baldness, and chest pains with drugs and drink until he collapses.
4. *Zuckerman Bound* (Farrar, 1985)
   An omnibus volume containing numbers 1, 2, and 3 plus "The Prague Orgy," a novella-length epilogue which takes Zuckerman to Prague in search of an unpublished manuscript.
5. *The Counterlife* (Farrar, 1987)
   A collection of four episodes in which Zuckerman undergoes traumatic experiences in England, Israel, and New Jersey.

Note: Zuckerman also appears in *My Life as a Man* (Holt, 1974) as a fictional character invented by that book's main character, Peter Tarnopol, an author who writes both his own story and that of his fictional alter ego.

Sabatier, Robert

These two books by a French novelist have something of the charm of Truffaut's movie *The 400 Blows*. They follow the life of street urchin Olivier Châteauneuf, who is only ten years old when his mother dies, leaving him the ward of some uncaring relatives. Armed with his ever-present box of safety matches—a talisman against fear—he wanders the colorful streets of Montmartre making friends with gangsters and prostitutes. Sabatier's spare, sensitive prose gives a vivid picture of Paris just before World War II.

1. *The Safety Matches* (Dutton, 1974)
   Befriended by some of Montmartre's most colorful citizens, young Olivier overcomes his grief and begins to leave childhood behind. Translated from the French by Patsy Southgate.
2. *Three Mint Lollipops* (Dutton, 1974)
   Olivier must adjust to life with his wealthy aunt and uncle and two cousins in their elegant Paris apartment. Translated from the French by Patsy Southgate.

Sabatini, Rafael

I. *Scaramouche* captured a big audience in the United States in 1921 as readers sought escape from the horrors of modern warfare in the romanticized high drama of French revolutionary times. The story features Andre-Louis Moreau, a brave, young strolling player who becomes known as the Scaramouche for his daring skirmishes in the revolutionary cause. Variously guised as politician, lawyer, swordsman, and buffoon, the hero vanquishes his enemies and wins his lady love with a flamboyance reminiscent of Orczy's Scarlet Pimpernel (q.v.). Stewart Granger starred in the rousing 1953 film *Scaramouche*. Sabatini, born in Italy of an Italian father and an English mother, settled in England and wrote his books in English.

1. *Scaramouche* (Houghton, 1921)
   Sworn to avenge the death of his friend at the hands of a rich nobleman, Andre-Louis Moreau embarks on a series of exploits in the cause of the Revolution. Set in 1788–92.
2. *Scaramouche, the Kingmaker* (Houghton, 1931)
   Scaramouche has further adventures in the days following the Revolution.

II. *Captain Blood*, the story of an English doctor forced into piracy, was an even bigger success than *Scaramouche*. The 1935 film version was Errol Flynn's first big swashbuckler. Basil Rathbone and Olivia de Havilland also starred.

1. *Captain Blood: His Odyssey* (Houghton, 1922)
   This romance of the Spanish main in the late 1600s stars Peter Blood, an English gentleman adventurer who can hold his own with bloodthirsty pirates and corrupt colonial governors alike.
2. *Captain Blood Returns* (Houghton, 1931)
   Here the author relates twelve episodes in the adventures of Captain Blood that he omitted from his previous account. English title: *Chronicles of Captain Blood.*
3. *The Fortunes of Captain Blood* (Houghton, 1936)
   Six further episodes are collected here.

Sand, George (pseud. of Amandine-Aurore Lucie Dupin, the Baronne Dudevant)

Readers whose interest in George Sand was kindled by the television series on the life of this remarkable nineteenth-century French novelist may want to try these two historical romances. Unlike her early works, which reflect the author's passionate nature and stormy affairs—*A Winter in Majorca* recounts Sand's liaison with Chopin—these novels reveal her humanitarian and socialist sympathies. They tell the story of Consuelo, a great singer, and paint a vivid picture of European life and culture from 1740 to 1786.

1. *Consuelo* (Ticknor, 1850)
   Consuelo is first seen as a child of the streets in Venice, where her striking voice brings her to the attention of a fine old maestro. First published in France in 1842.
2. *The Countess of Rudolstadt* (Ticknor, 1847)
   Consuelo, now a great singer, performs for the kings and queens of Europe but remains unspoiled by her success. First published in France in 1843.

Sanders, Lawrence

I. Sanders's suspenseful storytelling, realistic New York setting, and believable characters have created a ready audience for his Delaney books. Edward X. Delaney is first met as a precinct captain, then as a retired chief detective who takes on special cases for the New York Police Department. He is a dogged and sometimes unscrupulous investigator.

1. *The First Deadly Sin* (Putnam, 1973)
   The point of view in this novel alternates between that of Delaney, on the trail of the murderer, and that of a psychopathic killer sinking into total madness.
2. *The Second Deadly Sin* (Putnam, 1977)
   New York's art world provides the colorful background for Delaney's investigation into the murder of painter Victor Maitland.
3. *The Third Deadly Sin* (Putnam, 1981)
   Delaney is on the track of a psychopathic woman who is a mass murderer.
4. *The Fourth Deadly Sin* (Putnam, 1985)
   Eminent psychiatrist Dr. Ellerbee has been murdered, perhaps by one of his patients.

II. Sanders has also written two books featuring Peter Tangent, an American oil company official who gets involved in some fast-moving and fairly grisly cases of skullduggery in Africa.

1. *The Tangent Objective* (Putnam, 1976)
   Peter Tangent helps the ambitious and high-principled army captain Obiri Anokye plan a coup to overthrow the despotic ruler of Asante.
2. *The Tangent Factor* (Putnam, 1978)
   Tangent helps Obiri Anokye, now leader of Asante, in his plan to unite Africa under his rule.

Saroyan, William

Saroyan, Thurber, and Gerald Durrell have lightened the burden of adolescence for many young readers with their humorous and high-spirited works, often told from the point of view of young narrators. Saroyan's offbeat and spontaneous characters, and the exhilarating way they create something quite magical out of the bare threads of their often sad lives are especially appealing to young adults. The first book listed below is unusual in having a young girl as narrator; most of Saroyan's narrators are boys.

1. *Mama, I Love You* (Little, 1956)
   Nine-year-old Twinkle, who lives with her divorced mother, wins

a big part in a stage play, though she really wants to be a pitcher.
2. *Papa, You're Crazy* (Little, 1957)
   Twinkle's brother tells of his life with his father, a poor writer who lives in a beach house in Malibu.

Sartre, Jean-Paul

The Roads to Freedom (Les chemins de la liberté) is a trilogy of novels by this Nobel Prize-winning French philosopher, political activist, and author of plays, novels, biography, and other nonfiction. *The Words*, his charming autobiography of childhood, is easily his most accessible work. Next, perhaps, is *The Age of Reason*, the first volume of this series, in which the main character faces an ethical dilemma and examines the existential issues of freedom and responsibility. The second and third volumes have a broader, more documentary interest but lack the first book's narrative tension. A fourth book was planned but never completed.

1. *The Age of Reason* (Knopf, 1949)
   Philosophy teacher Mathieu Delarue faces the issues of maintaining his own personal freedom and behaving responsibly when his mistress, Marcelle, becomes pregnant. French title: *L'Âge de raison*. Translated from the French by Gerard Hopkins.
2. *The Reprieve* (Knopf, 1947)
   Sartre shows Paris during the Munich crisis of 1938 with a Dos Passos-like sweep from character to character, including some of the principal characters from *The Age of Reason*. French title: *Le sursis*. Translated from the French by Gerard Hopkins.
3. *Troubled Sleep* (Knopf, 1951)
   Familiar faces again reappear in this documentary look at World War II France after the fall of Paris. Variant title: *Iron in the Soul*. French title: *La mort dans l'âme*. Translated from the French by Gerard Hopkins.
4. *The Last Chance*
   Two extracts from this unfinished fourth volume appeared in December, 1949, in Sartre's review *Les tempes moderne* under the title "Drole d'amitie." French title: *La dernière chance*. Translated from the French by Gerard Hopkins.

Sayers, Dorothy L.

Ian Carmichael's marvelous portrayal of Lord Peter Wimsey on the Masterpiece Theatre series won a whole new generation of fans for Dorothy Sayers's monocled detective. In addition to being witty and well-written, Sayers's books have the added attraction of two very engaging supporting characters: Bunter, the perfect gentleman's gentleman, and mystery writer Harriet Vane, the woman in Lord Peter's life. Sayers has been the subject of two recent biographies: James Brabazon's *Dorothy L. Sayers* (Scribner, 1980) and Janet Hitchman's *Such a Strange Lady* (Harper, 1975). Real Wimsey fans will want to track down C. W. Scott-Giles's *The Wimsey Family* (Harper, 1977) which traces Lord Peter's ancestors and family history.

1. *Whose Body?* (Boni, 1923)
   In his first appearance, Lord Peter conducts an unofficial inquiry into a strange case involving a nude corpse found in a bathtub. Note: The 1935 Harcourt reissue of this title contains a droll biography of Lord Peter by "his uncle," who reveals that Lord Peter was a "colorless shrimp of a child" who suffered terribly from nightmares.
2. *Clouds of Witness* (Dial, 1927)
   When Lord Peter's brother, the Duke of Denver, is tried for murder before the House of Lords, Peter proves him innocent.
3. *Unnatural Death* (Dial, 1928)
   The "natural" death of an old lady turns out to be murder. Miss Climpson makes her first appearance in this book. Variant title: *The Dawson Pedigree.*
4. *Lord Peter Views the Body* (Payson, 1928)
   This is a collection of short stories.
5. *The Unpleasantness at the Bellona Club* (Payson, 1928)
   A curious will and suspicious timing raise questions when an elderly gentleman is found dead in his armchair at the club.
6. *Strong Poison* (Brewer, 1930)
   Lord Peter meets Harriet Vane in the Old Bailey, where she is on trial for poisoning her lover, and with Miss Climpson's help gets her off the hook. The escapade begins their six-year courtship.
7. *Suspicious Characters* (Brewer, 1931)
   Lord Peter's solution of this case involving the death of an artist

in a Scottish village hinges on train timetables. Variant title: *The Five Red Herrings.*

8. *Have His Carcase* (Brewer, 1932)
Harriet finds a body on the beach, and Lord Peter comes to investigate.

9. *Hangman's Holiday* (Harcourt, 1933)
Four of these short stories feature Lord Peter, and the rest star Montague Egg, Sayers's lower-middle-class salesman/detective.

10. *Murder Must Advertise* (Harcourt, 1933)
Lord Peter takes a job in an advertising agency to get to the bottom of some nasty drug-and-death business.

11. *The Nine Tailors* (Harcourt, 1934)
The art of church bell-ringing figures prominently in this investigation of an anonymous corpse in an English village.

12. *Gaudy Night* (Harcourt, 1935)
Poison-pen letters cause trouble at Oxford as Harriet returns for the Gaudy Dinner and Lord Peter comes to investigate. On the last page, Harriet accepts Peter's proposal of marriage.

13. *Busman's Honeymoon: A Love Story with Detective Interruptions* (Harcourt, 1937)
Naturally Lord Peter and Harriet encounter murder on their honeymoon.

14. *In the Teeth of the Evidence* (Harcourt, 1939)
Of these short stories, only two feature Lord Peter.

15. *Lord Peter: A Collection of All the Lord Peter Wimsey Stories* (Harper, 1972)
This collection includes "The Haunted Policeman," which mentions the birth of one Wimsey son, and "Tallboys," in which two more have arrived.

Scott, Paul

The Raj Quartet is a sweeping epic covering the last turbulent years of British rule in India, from 1942 to 1948. Scott is a superb storyteller, well able to convey the ambiguous human relationships of his large cast of British and Indian characters. The violence of the times seems to emerge all the more effectively for Scott's restrained treatment of desperate events and situations in which various characters face their doom stoically. The four volumes do not carry the story forward sequentially but rather circle certain events and characters from various points of view. The novels are also available in a one-volume omnibus entitled *The Raj Quartet* (Morrow, 1976). The recent Masterpiece Theatre presentation on PBS television has introduced this series to another generation of readers.

1. *The Jewel in the Crown* (Morrow, 1966)
   The central event in this volume, which gives a vivid picture of India before independence, concerns the rape of a young Englishwoman in the Bibighar Gardens in August, 1942. Also featured is the courageous schoolteacher Miss Crane.
2. *Day of the Scorpion* (Morrow, 1968)
   Beginning with the arrest of ex-chief minister Kasim on August 9, 1942, this account shows India engulfed in violence following the Congress party's call for nationwide insurrection. The novel also includes the stories of Sarah and Susan Layton.
3. *Towers of Silence* (Morrow, 1971)
   From the Rose Cottage in Pankot, where Mabel Layton (stepmother of Susan and Sarah's father) lives with retired mission teacher Barbie Batchelor, the upheavals tearing through India seem remote; yet they eventually have their effect.
4. A *Division of the Spoils* (Morrow, 1975)
   This concluding volume analyzes the transfer of power and the moral corruption during the pivotal years 1945–47, just prior to independence. The story focuses on army intelligence officer Guy Perron and the cruel Colonel Ronald Merrick, Susan Layton's husband.
5. *Staying On* (Morrow, 1977)
   This graceful coda to the Raj Quartet shows Colonel and Mrs. Tusker Smalley in 1972 and the life they have chosen by staying on in their Pankot home after Indian independence.

Segal, Erich

Love Story zoomed up the best-seller lists with amazing speed, and the movie starring Ryan O'Neal and Ali McGraw gave it indisputable status as a modern classic. The rich-boy-meets-poor-girl story against a Harvard-Radcliffe setting is capped with a tragic ending. But the witty dialogue, believable characters and background leaven the schmaltz. The film of the sequel starred Ryan O'Neal and Candice Bergen.

1. *Love Story* (Harper, 1970)
   Oliver Barrett IV, a rich and popular Harvard senior, falls for scholarship student Jenny Cavilleri.

2. *Oliver's Story* (Harper, 1977)
   Two years after Jenny's death, Oliver, now a lawyer in New York, takes an interest in enigmatic Marcie Nash and finally begins to shake off the guilt and grief that haunt him.

Settle, Mary Lee

Winning the National Book Award for *Blood Tie* (Houghton, 1977) has brought renewed attention to the work of this contemporary American author. Settle's Beulah series begins in seventeenth-century England, and traces the founding and development of the town of Beulah, West Virginia, through its frontier colonial days, Civil War strife, coal boom and labor confrontations and, finally, recent economic decline. While the Lacey family provides a focus throughout the series, Settle works many characters and viewpoints into her detailed tapestries.

1. *Prisons* (Putnam, 1973)
   Set in Cromwellian England, this story depicts the youth, army service, and dramatic rebellion of Jonathan Church, ancestor of the West Virginia settlers whose stories are chronicled in later volumes.
2. *O Beulah Land* (Viking, 1956)
   After the Battle of Little Meadows in 1775, young Jonathan Lacey sets out with a group of settlers for the unclaimed land of Virginia's western frontier.
3. *Know Nothing* (Viking, 1960)
   The unhappy romance of Johnny Catlett and his orphaned cousin Melinda is set on a Beulah plantation just prior to the Civil War.
4. *The Scapegoat* (Random, 1980)
   Young Lily Lacey, the Vassar-educated daughter of a mine-owner, plays a fateful role in the 1912 strike that has paralyzed the coal mines of Beulah valley. An interesting portrait of Mother Jones is included.
5. *The Killing Ground* (Farrar, 1982)
   This appears to be a reworking of an earlier novel, *Fight Night on a Sweet Saturday* (Viking, 1964). The story follows writer Hannah McKarkle as she returns to her West Virginia home and memories of the troubled and violent life of her wastrel brother Johnny. Two decades, 1960–80, are covered.

Shannon, Dell (pseud. of Elizabeth Linington)

Dell Shannon is the pseudonym Linington uses for her Luis Mendoza books, the longest running and most popular of her police procedural series. This prolific California author has earned the title "Queen of the Procedurals"; she also writes them under the Leslie Egan pseudonym and her own name (q.v.). Each novel is complete in itself, but the character development and continuing relationships from book to book add an extra interest. Lieutenant Luis Mendoza is sophisticated, well-read, and independently wealthy. His Mexican heritage serves him well in the Los Angeles Police Department. He collects sports cars and cats. Since every novel concerns multiple cases under investigation, individual annotations are not supplied.

Linington, writing as Dell Shannon, has recently returned to the historical novel-writing with which she first broke into print in the 1950s. *The Scalpel and the Sword* (Morrow, 1987) and *The Dispossessed* (Morrow, 1988) are two of these. They are not a series.

1. *Case Pending* (Harper, 1960)
2. *The Ace of Spades* (Harper, 1961)
3. *Extra Kill* (Morrow, 1962)
4. *Knave of Hearts* (Morrow, 1962)
5. *Death of a Busybody* (Morrow, 1963)
6. *Double Bluff* (Morrow, 1963)
7. *Mark of Murder* (Morrow, 1964)
8. *Root of All Evil* (Morrow, 1964)
9. *The Death-Bringers* (Morrow, 1964)
10. *Death by Inches* (Morrow, 1965)
11. *Coffin Corner* (Morrow, 1966)
12. *With a Vengeance* (Morrow, 1966)
13. *Chance to Kill* (Morrow, 1967)
14. *Rain with Violence* (Morrow, 1967)
15. *Kill with Kindness* (Morrow, 1968)
16. *Schooled to Kill* (Morrow, 1969)
17. *Crime on Their Hands* (Morrow, 1969)
18. *Unexpected Death* (Morrow, 1970)
19. *Whim to Kill* (Morrow, 1971)
20. *The Ringer* (Morrow, 1971)
21. *Murder with Love* (Morrow, 1972)
22. *With Intent to Kill* (Morrow, 1972)
23. *No Holiday for Crime* (Morrow, 1973)

24. *Spring of Violence* (Morrow, 1973)
25. *Crime File* (Morrow, 1974)
26. *Deuces Wild* (Morrow, 1975)
27. *Streets of Death* (Morrow, 1976)
28. *Appearances of Death* (Morrow, 1977)
29. *Cold Trail* (Morrow, 1978)
30. *Felony at Random* (Morrow, 1979)
31. *Felony File* (Morrow, 1980)
32. *Murder Most Strange* (Morrow, 1981)
33. *The Motive on Record* (Morrow, 1982)
34. *Exploits of Death* (Morrow, 1983)
35. *Destiny of Death* (Morrow, 1984)
36. *Chaos of Crime* (Morrow, 1985)
37. *Blood Count* (Morrow, 1986)
38. *Murder by the Tale* (Morrow, 1987)
    A collection of short stories.

Sharp, Margery

This English author is the creator of a series of children's books starring the lovable mouse Miss Bianca, including *The Rescuers*, which was made into an animated feature film by Disney Productions. Sharp's adult books are deft and ironic sketches of slightly odd characters caught amusingly in predicaments of their own making. Readers who meet Martha, the fat and inarticulate budding artist introduced in *Martha in Paris*, won't rest easy until they see how her story unfolds in the sequel. Martha's single-minded pursuit of her artistic career results in some deliciously wicked role reversals.

1. *Martha in Paris* (Little, 1962)
   At eighteen, an unprepossessing Martha is sent to Paris by her wealthy patron, and her artistic and sensual awakening has unexpected consequences.
2. *Martha, Eric and George* (Little, 1964)
   Now twenty-eight and on the verge of international acclaim, Martha returns to Paris for her first successful show and comes to terms with Eric and little George.

Note: *The Eye of Love* (Little, 1957) is related to the Martha series: it tells the story of Martha's foster parents, Harry Gibson and Delores Diver, including the events leading to their marriage.

Sharpe, Tom

I. English writer Tom Sharpe writes bawdy, hilarious, and occasionally vicious satires. Academics, the police, the military, the aristocracy, and political extremists right and left are all targets for his vitriolic pen. No single person or event in a Sharpe novel is impossible in real life, but his madcap plots are carried along by their own maniacal logic to a frenzied finish that may leave corpses and burned-out buildings in their wake.

Henry Wilt, one of Sharpe's relatively few likable characters, teaches "liberal studies" to butcher's assistants, plasterer's helpers, and the other semi-literate students who attend the Fenland College of Arts and Technology, presumably based on the Cambridgeshire College of Arts and Technology where Sharpe taught before becoming a full-time writer. Wilt is a decent, unpretentious chap and a competent teacher. His buxom wife Eva is an amiably bovine woman who is given to enthusiasms, such as compost heaping, which sorely try Wilt's nerves. Wilt is also beset by precocious quadruplet daughters (numbers 2 and 3), incompetent superiors, paranoid security officers, terrorists, sexually voracious women, and police officials who are convinced that he is a diabolically clever criminal. Fortunately, Wilt always manages to triumph over adversity in the end.

1. *Wilt* (Vintage, 1984)
   Wilt acts out his wife-killing fantasies on a life-size plastic doll liberated from a kinky American couple, only to be arrested for murder when Eva disappears. Originally published in England in 1976.
2. *The Wilt Alternative* (St. Martin's, 1980)
   Now on relatively good terms with Eva, but saddled with quadruplets, Wilt has an unsettling encounter with a rose bush, and his house and children are held hostage by terrorists.
3. *Wilt on High* (Random, 1985)
   Eva slips Wilt an aphrodisiac in his beer, producing alarming physical results, while an overzealous narcotics policeman bugs Wilt's car after one of his students ODs in the school basement.

II. Sharpe spent ten years in South Africa (1951–61) and his first two novels are set there. The Anglophile police chief of Piemburg (based on Pietermaritzburg) is the protagonist of a pair of novels that satirize the racism, paranoia, and incompetence of South African officialdom. The detective novels of James McClure (q.v.), who lived in Pietermaritzburg during the same period as Sharpe, are also set in a fictionalized version of that South African town, and make an interesting contrast with Sharpe's novels.

1. *Riotous Assembly* (Viking, 1971)
   A member of the English Hazelstone family kills the transvestite Zulu cook with whom she has been having an affair. Van Heerden's efforts to cover up the crime lead to disastrous results. Reprinted by Atlantic, 1987.
2. *Indecent Exposure* (Atlantic, 1987)
   Lieutenant Verkramp's adversion therapy program, designed to discourage his men from having sexual relations with black women, produces two hundred neurotically homosexual constables.

Shaw, Irwin

ABC's dramatization of *Rich Man, Poor Man* was one of American television's most popular mini-series. Shaw's story of the three Jordache children has all the elements guaranteed to hold a wide audience. He chronicles the rise of Thomas, Rudolph, and Gretchen from their small hometown in New York in the 1940s and continues through their various struggles with love, ambition, courage, and corruption into the 1970s with nary a dull moment. ABC commissioned the writing of a second series of *Rich Man, Poor Man* programs. Shaw, who was working on his own sequel at the time, disclaimed any responsibility for it.

1. *Rich Man, Poor Man* (Delacorte, 1970)
   The three children of Axel Jordache, a baker, grow up: Thomas becomes a prizefighter, Rudolph a successful businessman, and Gretchen a successful actress.
2. *Beggarman, Thief* (Delacorte, 1977)
   The story continues into the next generation as Wesley, Tom's son, takes center stage.

Sholokhov, Mikhail

Sholokhov is one of the few establishment Soviet writers with a reputation in the West. He was awarded the Nobel Prize in 1965. His books about the Don region of southern Russia chronicle the tumultuous years of revolution and collectivization in the arid steppe country and the feudal society of its Cossack inhabitants. Sholokhov, a native of the district himself, reveals the humanity behind the Cossack stereotype while still conveying the fierceness of the people and the primitive nature of their culture. All have been translated into English by Henry C. Stevens, who used the pseudonym Stephen Garry for the early books. *The Silent Don* (Knopf, 1941) is an omnibus containing numbers 1 and 3 listed below.

1. *And Quiet Flows the Don* (Knopf, 1934)
   The life, loves, and military adventures of a group of Cossacks living along the Don River are recounted. The story begins in 1914 and focuses on young Gregor Melekhov.
2. *Tales of the Don* (Knopf, 1962)
   Though written later, these stories also concern the revolutionary years.
3. *The Don Flows Home to the Sea* (Knopf, 1941)
   A group of Cossacks clashes with both Red and White forces during the civil war following the Revolution, 1917–21.
4. *Seeds of Tomorrow* (Knopf, 1959)
   The 1930 effort at total collectivization of farming in the Don region is directed by the gentle Davidov.
5. *Harvest on the Don* (Knopf, 1961)
   Davidov continues to meet obstacles as they arise and is increasingly drawn to Lushka. The story ends in the autumn of 1930.

Note: *Virgin Soil Upturned* is the translation of the title under which numbers 4 and 5 were published together in Russia.

Sienkiewicz, Henryk

Sienkiewicz is best known for *Quo Vadis?*, a novel about the persecution of early Christians during the reign of Emperor Nero. It was a best-seller in its day (1896) and was made into a very successful movie in 1951 starring Robert Taylor, Deborah Kerr, and Peter Ustinov. Three earlier novels, Scott-like historical romances based on Polish history, also enjoyed a huge international readership and secured Sienkiewicz's reputation as a leading Polish author. He was awarded the Nobel Prize in 1905.

1. *With Fire and Sword* (Little, 1890)
   This covers the events of 1648–49 when the Ukrainian Cossacks revolted from Poland. Fiery heroism and epic battlefield scenes alternate with quieter domestic episodes. Translated from the Polish by Jeremiah Curtin.
2. *The Deluge* (Little, 1893)
   Poland and Lithuania are invaded by Swedes under Charles Gustavus (1654–55). Translated from the Polish by Jeremiah Curtin.
3. *Pan Michael* (Little, 1893)
   In 1669–73, the Poles war with the Tartars and the Turks. *Pan* is the term of address for a gentleman, like the English *Mr.* Translated from the Polish by Jeremiah Curtin.

Silone, Ignazio

After devoting his youth to various socialist and anti-fascist activities, Silone was forced to flee Italy in 1929. During his exile in Switzerland, he turned to writing fiction and produced his best-known works, *Fontamara* and *Bread and Wine*. His novels cast a critical eye at contemporary Italian life and look with sympathy and respect at the endurance, pride, and basic goodness of the Italian peasant. Disillusioned with communism in 1930, Silone played an active role in the left wing of Italian democratic socialism from the time of his return to Italy after the war to 1950, when he retired from political life in order to devote more time to writing.

1. *Bread and Wine* (Harper, 1937)
   Pietro Spina, a young socialist disguised as a monk, tries to organize the peasants in his native village against the fascists in 1935. A revised edition was published in 1962 by Atheneum. Translated from the Italian by G. David and E. Mosbacher.
2. *The Seed beneath the Snow* (Harper, 1942)
   Pietro Spina is now in hiding in the home of his grandmother, Donna Maria Vincenza. A revised edition was published by Atheneum in 1965. Translated from the Italian by Francis Frenaye.

Silverberg, Robert

Like Isaac Asimov (q.v.) Robert Silverberg is a prolific writer of science fiction and nonfiction popularizations. He has published more than seventy volumes of fiction and dozens of nonfiction works on science, archaeology, and anthropology. He won the Nebula Award for *A Time of Changes* (Doubleday, 1971). Silverberg's Majipoor trilogy has been praised as one of the finest creations of an imaginary planet in science fiction annals. Majipoor was colonized by humans thousands of years before the action of the trilogy takes place, but it is also inhabited by other sentient beings, such as the shape-shifting Metamorphs. Numbers 1 and 3 below deal with the career of Valentine, ruler of Majipoor. Number 2 is a series of tales providing vignettes of Majipoor's past history.

    1. *Lord Valentine's Castle* (Harper, 1980)
       Valentine, a young juggler suffering from amnesia, unaware of his true identity as rightful ruler of the planet of Majipoor, wanders into a festival celebrating the visit of the false Lord Valentine.
    2. *Majipoor Chronicles* (Arbor, 1982)
       A young clerk in the Registry of Souls illegally calls up the records of the lives of famous and ordinary people from Majipoor's past.
    3. *Valentine Pontifex* (Arbor, 1983)
       Lord Valentine, facing his elevation from Coronal to Pontifex, tries to find a way to communicate with the Metamorphs, who are destroying Majipoor's food crops.

Simenon, Georges

This prolific Franco-Belgian writer belongs in a class by himself. After an early apprenticeship writing some two hundred pulp novels under a variety of pseudonyms, Simenon began to produce the Maigret mysteries in 1931. The big, patient police inspector, who solved crimes by slowly coming to understand the criminal's mind and background, was an immediate hit in France and quickly caught on in England and America as well. When first introduced, Inspector Jules Maigret is about forty-five years old. His quiet life with his wife in their Boulevard Richard-Lenoir apartment changes very little over the next four decades, though he does travel—as far afield as Tucson, Arizona—and he eventually retires at age fifty-five. Not all of Maigret's cases have been published in the United States, and apparently there is at least one title (*Maigret et l'Inspecteur Malchanceaux*, 1947) that hasn't been translated into English. For a complete listing of all of Simenon's novels, including all translations up to 1976, contents of omnibus volumes, and a cross-index to French and English titles, see Trudee Young's *Georges Simenon* (Scarecrow, 1976). The following list of all the Maigret titles that have been translated into English is as complete as possible. Titles are arranged alphabetically within the year of their publication, following Trudee Young's chronology. Some of them appear in English only in omnibus volumes as indicated.

1. *The Sailor's Rendezvous* (in *Maigret Keeps a Rendezvous* [Harcourt, 1941])
   Captain Fallut, just back from three months' codfishing in Newfoundland, is found strangled and floating near his trawler. First published in France in 1931 as *Au rendez-vous des Terre-neuves.*

2. *The Crime at Lock 14* (Covici, 1934)
   As soon as the corpse of an elegantly dressed woman is identified, another dead body turns up to keep Maigret busy. English title: *Maigret Meets a Milord.* First published in France in 1931 as *Le charretier de "La Providence."* Bound with number 16 below.

3. *A Face for a Clue* (in *The Patience of Maigret* [Harcourt, 1940])
   The Breton fishing town of Concarneau is plagued with a series of murders, poisonings, a strange menacing giant who stalks at night, and a yellow dog that appears from nowhere. First published in France in 1931 as *Le chien jaune.* Newly translated as *Maigret and the Yellow Dog* (Harcourt, 1987).

4. *A Crime in Holland* (in *Maigret Abroad* [Harcourt, 1940])
   In Holland to investigate a murder in which a French citizen is involved, Maigret manages to stay one step ahead of the local police investigation, even though he speaks no Dutch. First published in France in 1931 as *Un crime en Holland.*

5. *At the Gai-Moulin* (in *Maigret Abroad* [Harcourt, 1940])
   A dancer named Adele, a spy ring, and a corpse found in a wicker basket are elements in this case. First published in France in 1931 as *La danseuse du Gai-Moulin.*

6. *The Death of Monsieur Gallet* (Covici, 1932)
   This was actually the first Maigret case published. It concerns the corpse of M. Gallet, a commercial traveler, and the strange, sad tale that it has to tell. Variant title: *Maigret Stonewalled.* First published in France in 1931 as *M. Gallet décédé.*

7. *The Crossroad Murders* (Covici, 1933)
   Maigret ferrets out the secrets of an eccentric brother and sister who live in an old country house. Variant title: *Murders at the Crossroads.* First published in France in 1931 as *La nuit du Carrefour.*

408

8. *The Crime of Inspector Maigret* (Covici, 1933)
   On a visit to Brussels, Maigret trails a down-at-the-heels man he had seen packing money into a suitcase. Variant title: *Maigret and the Hundred Gibbets*. First published in France in 1931 as *Le pendu de Saint-Pholien*.

9. *The Strange Case of Peter the Lett* (Covici, 1933)
   Maigret must identify the body of a dead man found in the lavatory of a Paris express train. This was the first Maigret book Simenon wrote. Variant title: *Maigret and the Enigmatic Lett*. First published in France in 1931 as *Pietr-le-Letton*. English title: *The Case of Peter the Lett* (in *Inspector Maigret Investigates*).

10. *A Battle of Nerves* (in *Patience of Maigret* [Harcourt, 1940])
    The Cafe Coupole in Montparnasse is the center of the action as Maigret, who is not convinced of the guilt of a condemned man, tries to find the true murderer of a rich old woman. First published in France in 1931 as *La tete d'un homme*. Newly translated as *Maigret's War of Nerves* (Harcourt, 1986).

11. *The Saint-Fiacre Affair* (in *Maigret Keeps a Rendezvous* [Harcourt, 1941])
    Warned that a woman will be killed in his hometown of Fiacre, Maigret visits for the first time in years. Variant title: *Maigret Goes Home*. First published in France in 1932 as *L'Affaire Saint-Fiacre*. Newly translated as *Maigret Goes Home* (Harcourt, 1989).

12. *The Flemish Shop* (in *Maigret to the Rescue* [Harcourt, 1941])
    A little wineshop on the Franco-Belgian border is the setting for this case. First published in France in 1932 as *Chez les Flamands*.

13. *The Madman of Bergerac* (in *Maigret Travels South* [Harcourt, 1940])
    A psychopathic murderer has killed two women by plunging a long needle through their hearts. First published in France in 1932 as *Le fou de Bergerac*.

14. *Guinguette by the Seine* (in *Maigret to the Rescue* [Harcourt, 1941])
    The setting is a weekend resort on the banks of the Seine. First published in France in 1932 as *La Guinguette à deux sous*.

15. *Liberty Bar* (in *Maigret Travels South* [Harcourt, 1940])
    Maigret is sent to the Riviera to investigate a murder that must be handled with the utmost tact. First published in France in 1932 as *"Liberty Bar."* Newly translated as *Maigret on the Riviera* (Harcourt, 1988).

16. *The Shadow in the Courtyard* (Covici, 1934)
    M. Couchet is found shot to death in his office with 300,000

francs missing from the safe of his pharmaceutical company. Variant title: *Maigret Mystified*. First published in France in 1932 as *L'Ombre chinoise*. Bound with number 2 above.

17. *Death of a Harbor Master* (in *Maigret and M. Labbé* [Harcourt, 1942])

Maigret escorts a mute and wounded man to his home in a little harbor town and identifies him as Captain Joris, the harbor master. First published in France in 1932 as *Le port des brumes*.

18. *The Lock at Charenton* (in *Maigret Sits It Out* [Harcourt, 1941])

Maigret returns to the world of the canal boats to investigate the attempted murder of Emile Ducrau. First published in France in 1933 as *L'Ecluse no. 1*.

19. *Maigret Returns* (in *Maigret Sits It Out* [Harcourt, 1941])

Maigret's nephew, an inept detective, gets himself framed in a nightclub murder. First published in France in 1934 as *Maigret revient*.

20. *Maigret and the Hotel Majestic* (Harcourt, 1977)

Emilienne Clark is strangled, and all the residents and staff of the luxury Paris hotel are suspects. First published in France in 1942 as *Les caves du Majestic*.

21. *Maigret and the Spinster* (Harcourt, 1977)

Maigret neglects the story of a pathetic old maid only to discover her strangled in a broom closet. First published in France in 1942 as *Cécile est morte*.

22. *Maigret in Exile* (Harcourt, 1978)

Sent to the northern Provinces, Maigret is bored until a corpse is found in the home of a retired judge. First published in France in 1942 as *La maison du juge*.

23. *Maigret and the Toy Village* (Harcourt, 1979)

This concerns the murder of an old man in one of the new suburban housing developments, which remind Maigret of toy villages. First published in France in 1944 as *Félicie est là*.

24. *Maigret's Rival* (Harcourt, 1979)

Sent to a small French village to investigate the suspicious death of Genevieve Naud's secret lover, Maigret always seems to be one step behind the local policemen on the case. First published in France in 1944 as *L'Inspecteur Cadavre*.

25. *The Short Cases of Inspector Maigret* (Doubleday, 1959)

These short stories were first published in France in 1944 as *Les nouvelles enquête de Maigret*.

26. *Maigret and the Fortune Teller* (Harcourt, 1989)
The story of the odious Madame Le Cloaquen is told. First
published in France in 1944 as *Signe Picpus*. English title: *To
Any Lengths*.

27. *Maigret and the Old Lady* (in *Maigret Cinq: The Second Maigret
Omnibus* [Harcourt, 1965])
Valentine Besson is the charming old lady that Maigret tries to
help. First published in France in 1947 as *Maigret et la vieille
dame*.

28. *Maigret in New York's Underworld* (Doubleday, 1955)
A phone call across the Atlantic provides the surprising conclu-
sion to this case, which is set in New York. First published in
France in 1947 as *Maigret à New York*. Variant title: *Inspector
Maigret in New York's Underworld*.

29. *Maigret's Pipe* (Harcourt, 1978)
These seventeen short stories were first published in France in
1947 as *La pipe de Maigret*.

30. *Maigret's Dead Man* (Doubleday, 1964)
Maigret tracks down a particularly nasty and callous gang that
killed a man who had personally asked Maigret for help. Variant
title: *Maigret's Special Murder*. First published in France in 1948
as *Maigret et son mort*.

31. *No Vacation for Maigret* (Doubleday, 1953)
On vacation, Maigret's wife is hospitalized with an attack of ap-
pendicitis, and Maigret occupies himself by poking into the mys-
terious death of the girl in the next room. Variant title: *Maigret on
Holiday*. First published in France in 1948 as *Les vacances de
Maigret*.

32. *Maigret at the Coroner's* (Harcourt, 1980)
Maigret sits in on an inquest in Tucson, Arizona, and puzzles out
how and why poor Bessie Mitchell had been left dead on the
railroad tracks. First published in France in 1949 as *Maigret chez
le coroner*.

33. *The Methods of Maigret* (Doubleday, 1957)
An inspector from Scotland Yard who is studying Maigret's
methods accompanies him to the Mediterranean, where he investigates the brutal murder of a tramp. Variant title: *My Friend
Maigret*. First published in France in 1949 as *Mon ami Maigret*.

34. *Maigret's First Case* (in *Maigret Cinq: The Second Maigret Omnibus* [Harcourt, 1965])

In 1913, at the age of twenty-six, Maigret tackles his first solo case, which concerns the complicated affairs of some coffee tycoons. First published in France in 1949 as *La premièr enquête de Maigret, 1913.*

35. *Madame Maigret's Own Case* (Doubleday, 1958)
Madame Maigret must do a stint of babysitting to help her husband solve this case started by an anonymous tip. Variant title: *Madame Maigret's Friend.* First published in France in 1950 as *L'Amie de Madame Maigret.*

36. *Inspector Maigret and the Strangled Stripper* (Doubleday, 1954)
A Montmartre striptease dancer is murdered when she overhears something she shouldn't have. Variant title: *Maigret in Montmartre.* First published in France in 1951 as *Maigret au "Picratt's."*

37. *Maigret Rents a Room* (Doubleday, 1961)
Maigret moves into a rundown boarding house to keep a close watch on some suspects implicated in the shooting of his assistant, Janvier. First published in France in 1951 as *Maigret en meuble.* English title: *Maigret Takes a Room.*

38. *Inspector Maigret and the Burglar's Wife* (Doubleday, 1956)
A burglar stumbles upon a murder, and his wife passes on the information to Maigret. First published in France in 1951 as *Maigret et la grande perche.*

39. *Maigret's Memoirs* (Harcourt, 1985)
Maigret reminisces about his early years: joining the Sûreté and working his way up to the elite homicide squad. First published in France in 1951 as *Les mémoirs de Maigret.*

40. *Maigret's Christmas* (Harcourt, 1977)
These short stories were first published in France in 1951 as *Un Noël de Maigret.*

41. *Maigret and the Killers* (Doubleday, 1954)
American thugs and dead bodies dumped from cars figure in this case that Maigret helps a friend with. Variant title: *Maigret and the Gangsters.* First published in France in 1952 as *Maigret, Lognon et les gangsters.*

42. *Maigret's Revolver* (Harcourt, 1985)
While Maigret is visiting London, his revolver is stolen. First published in France in 1952 as *Le revolver de Maigret.*

43. *Maigret Afraid* (Harcourt, 1983)
On a visit to an old school friend in a small town near Poitiers, Maigret helps out on a murder case involving a grim domestic crisis complicated by class loyalties. First published in France in 1953 as *Maigret a peur.*

44. *Maigret and the Man on the Bench* (Harcourt, 1976)
A man is found dead in an alley, but Maigret does not believe he died in a drunken brawl. First published in France in 1953 as *Maigret et l'homme du banc.* English title: *Maigret and the Man on the Boulevard.*

45. *Maigret's Mistake* (in *Five Times Maigret: A Maigret Omnibus* [Harcourt, 1964])
The residents of a luxury apartment house become suspects when a woman is found murdered there. First published in France in 1953 as *Maigret se trompe.*

46. *Maigret Goes to School* (in *Five Times Maigret: A Maigret Omnibus* [Harcourt, 1964])
Maigret goes to Saint-André-sur-mer to investigate the murder of the postmistress. First published in France in 1954 as *Maigret à l'école.*

47. *Maigret and the Calame Report* (Harcourt, 1969)
Maigret reluctantly gets involved in the world of politics when he agrees to help Auguste Point, a cabinet minister, find some stolen papers. Variant title: *Maigret and the Minister.* First published in France in 1954 as *Maigret chez le ministre.*

48. *Inspector Maigret and the Dead Girl* (Doubleday, 1955)
Maigret catches a young girl's murderer by getting to know the girl's personality. Variant title: *Maigret and the Young Girl.* First published in France in 1955 as *Maigret et la jeune morte.*

49. *Maigret and the Headless Corpse* (Harcourt, 1968)
A man's body is fished out of a Paris canal limb by limb, but no head can be found. First published in France in 1955 as *Maigret et le corps sans tête.*

50. *Maigret Sets a Trap* (Harcourt, 1972)
Five women have been stabbed to death on the streets of Montmartre. First published in France in 1955 as *Maigret tend un piège.*

51. *Maigret's Failure* (in *A Maigret Trio* [Harcourt, 1973])
Maigret is reluctant to bring to justice the murderer of a thoroughly bad man, the "King of the Meat Trade." First published in France in 1956 as *Un échec de Maigret.*

52. *None of Maigret's Business* (Doubleday, 1958)
Maigret is supposed to be on vacation at the seashore, but he prefers Paris and the problem of the murder of a doctor's wife. Variant title: *Maigret's Little Joke.* First published in France as *Maigret s'amuse.*

53. *Maigret and the Millionaires* (Harcourt, 1974)

Maigret must transcend his dislike of the international set to investigate the death of Colonel David Ward, found drowned in his
bath at the posh George V Hotel. First published in France in
1958 as *Maigret voyage.*

54. *Maigret Has Scruples* (in *Versus Inspector Maigret* [Doubleday,
 1960])
 This case starts with a man's fears that his wife is trying to poison
 him. First published in France in 1958 as *Les scrupules de
 Maigret.*

55. *Maigret and the Reluctant Witnesses* (in *Versus Inspector Maigret*
 [Doubleday, 1960])
 Murder strikes a member of a family of biscuit makers. First
 published in France in 1959 as *Maigret et les témoins recal-
 citrants.*

56. *Maigret Has Doubts* (Harcourt, 1982)
 Only Maigret doubts the guilt of a man condemned for murder-
 ing his wife. This novel was first published in France in 1959 as
 Une confidence de Maigret.

57. *Maigret in Court* (Harcourt, 1983)
 In order to save an innocent man on trial for murder, Maigret
 must reveal the infidelity of the man's wife. First published in
 France in 1960 as *Maigret aux assises.*

58. *Maigret in Society* (in *A Maigret Trio* [Harcourt, 1973])
 Maigret at first feels quite out of his depth in this case of a mur-
 derous ex-ambassador. First published in France in 1960 as
 Maigret et les vieillards.

59. *Maigret and the Lazy Burglar* (in *A Maigret Trio* [Harcourt,
 1973])
 Maigret recognizes the dead body found in the Bois de Boulogne
 as a small-time burglar he has known for years—but why would
 someone murder the man? First published in France in 1961 as
 Maigret et le voleur paresseux.

60. *Maigret and the Saturday Caller* (Hamilton, London, 1964)
 A building contractor tells Maigret that he wants to kill his wife.
 First published in France in 1962 as *Maigret et le client du
 samedi.*

61. *Maigret and the Black Sheep* (Harcourt, 1976)
 Maigret can discover no motive for the shooting of a retired car-
 ton manufacturer. First published in France in 1962 as *Maigret et
 les brave gens.*

62. *Maigret and the Bum* (Harcourt, 1973)
 Maigret must discover the identity of the man who lived under a

Paris bridge and why someone murdered him. Variant title: *Maigret and the Dosser*. First published in France in 1963 as *Maigret et le clochard*.

63. *Maigret and the Apparition* (Harcourt, 1976)
Maigret discovers that a badly wounded policeman was on the trail of a major international art conspiracy. First published in France in 1964 as *Maigret et le fantôme*. English title: *Maigret and the Ghost*.

64. *Maigret on the Defensive* (Harcourt, 1981)
A bizarre plot to discredit Maigret begins when a young girl accuses him of sexually abusing her. First published in France in 1964 as *Maigret se défend*.

65. *Maigret Loses His Temper* (Harcourt, 1974)
This puzzling case concerns the murder of a hardworking family man who owns a nightclub in Montmartre. First published in France in 1965 as *La colère de Maigret*.

66. *Maigret Bides His Time* (Harcourt, 1986)
After learning of the murder of a valued informant, Maigret painstakingly investigates all major suspects in the case. English title: *The Patience of Maigret*. First published in France in 1965 as *La patience de Maigret*.

67. *Maigret and the Nahour Case* (Harcourt, 1982)
A young woman turns up with her lover at a doctor's office for treatment of a bullet wound. First published in France in 1966 as *Maigret et l'affaire Nahour*.

68. *Maigret's Pickpocket* (Harcourt, 1968)
Maigret has his wallet lifted on a Paris bus. First published in France in 1967 as *Le voleur de Maigret*.

69. *Maigret's Boyhood Friend* (Harcourt, 1970)
Leon Florentin, an old school friend of Maigret's, brings him a puzzling case of murder. First published in France in 1968 as *L'Ami d'enfance de Maigret*.

70. *Maigret in Vichy* (Harcourt, 1969)
The Maigrets are in Vichy taking the waters when a solitary spinster is murdered. Variant title: *Maigret Takes the Waters*. First published in 1968 as *Maigret à Vichy*.

71. *Maigret Hesitates* (Harcourt, 1970)
An anonymous letter warns Maigret of an imminent murder in the family of a famous Paris lawyer. First published in France in 1968 as *Maigret hésite*.

72. *Maigret and the Killer* (Harcourt, 1971)
A young man engaged in tape recording voices of poor and

working-class people is stabbed to death. First published in France in 1969 as *Maigret et le tueur.*

73. *Maigret and the Madwoman* (Harcourt, 1972)
An old woman comes to Maigret for protection when she notices little things in her apartment out of place. First published in France in 1970 as *La folle de Maigret.*

74. *Maigret and the Wine Merchant* (Harcourt, 1971)
The shooting of a rich Paris wine merchant evokes strange reactions from his family and friends. First published in France in 1970 as *Maigret et le marchand de vin.*

75. *Maigret and the Loner* (Harcourt, 1975)
Maigret shaves the beard and mustache off a dead recluse and runs a photo of him in the newspaper hoping for clues to his identity. First published in France in 1971 as *Maigret et l'homme tout seul.*

76. *Maigret and Monsieur Charles* (Hamilton, London, 1973)
Madame Sabin-Levesque becomes concerned when her solicitor husband disappears for a longer time than his usual week or two.

77. *Maigret and the Informer* (Harcourt, 1973)
Maigret rubs elbows with Parisian mobsters in this case of the murder of a well-known restaurateur with a beautiful wife. Variant title: *Maigret and the Flea.* First published in France in 1973 as *Maigret et l'indicateur.*

Simon, Roger L.

Moses Wine is cast in the Hammett/Chandler hard-boiled mold except that he is an ex-hippie who prefers marijuana to alcohol. Like most fictional private eyes he is cynical, wise-cracking, divorced, middle-aged, and impecunious. The plots of the Wine series aren't always completely convincing, but the novels are full of fast dialogue, ironic insights, sophisticated humor, and interesting West Coast backgrounds. Richard Dreyfuss played Moses Wine in the movie version of *The Big Fix* (1978).

1. *The Big Fix* (Simon & Schuster, 1973)
Moses Wine is asked by an ex-girlfriend to investigate the smear tactic sabotaging of a presidential primary campaign.

2. *Wild Turkey* (Simon & Schuster, 1975)
A writer is suspected of the murder of a prominent television personality with whom he has been feuding.

3. *Peking Duck* (Simon & Schuster, 1979)
   Moses Wine, touring the People's Republic of China with Aunt
   Sonya and other wealthy leftist Americans, is called upon to solve
   the case of a missing gold duck.
4. *California Roll* (Villard, 1985)
   After Wine becomes head of security for Tulip Computer, the
   chief engineer is murdered, and the Black Widow computer program is stolen.
5. *The Straight Man* (Villard, 1986)
   Wine takes on the investigation of the death of Mike Ptak,
   straight man for black comic Otis King.
6. *Raising the Dead* (Villard, 1988)
   In order to clear the Arabs of suspicion in the murder of Jewish
   peacemaker Joseph Damoor, Wine flies to Israel.

Simpson, Dorothy

Detective Inspector Luke Thanet is one of those gentle English
policemen who patiently untangles crimes by ferreting out subtle psychological clues and unraveling motives. Thanet is based in rural
Sturrenden, a fictional Kentish town. He is a quiet and sensitive man,
devoted to his children. His assistant, Sergeant Lineham, is dominated
by his mother and his strong-minded wife. The novels are well-crafted
and the crimes unsensationalized. For similar series see Colin Dexter's
Inspector Morse and Reginald Hill's Peter Pascoe.

1. *The Night She Died* (Scribner, 1981)
   Inspector Thanet tries to discover what forgotten event in Julie
   Holmes's past led to her death.
2. *Six Feet Under* (Scribner, 1982)
   After middle-aged spinster Carrie Birch is murdered, Luke
   Thanet finds that she was the keeper of many of her village's
   darkest secrets.
3. *Puppet for a Corpse* (Scribner, 1983)
   Respected country physician Arnold Pettifer didn't seem to have
   a motive for suicide.
4. *Close Her Eyes* (Scribner, 1984)
   Fifteen-year-old Charity Pritchard is murdered after trying to
   break her ties with her father's fanatical religion.
5. *Last Seen Alive* (Scribner, 1985)
   The woman found murdered in the Black Swan Hotel turns out to

be an old school friend Thanet hadn't seen in twenty years.
6. *Dead on Arrival* (Scribner, 1987)
   The investigation of Steven Long's murder turns up several persons who hated him, and only his twin brother, Geoffrey, has a kind word for him.
7. *Element of Doubt* (Scribner, 1988)
   There are many suspects when beautiful but unpleasant Nerine Tarrant is pushed over the balcony of her manor.
8. *Suspicious Death* (Scribner, 1988)
   The body of self-made businesswoman Marcia Salden is found in the River Sture.
9. *Dead by Morning* (Scribner, 1989)
   Leo Martindale returns to Longford Hall after more than twenty years only to be found dead in a ditch two days later.

Sinclair, Upton

Sinclair is America's best-known muckraker. His zealous attack on social and economic injustice is still unequaled, and his large contemporary following may well be envied by latter-day reformers. After a modest but commercially successful beginning writing boys' adventure stories, Sinclair in 1906 produced *The Jungle*, a novel that shocked American readers by detailing the filth and corruption of Chicago's meat-packing industry. By the time of his death in 1968 at the age of 90, he had published close to fifty novels, over thirty nonfiction works, and countless articles and editorials treating a wide variety of subjects from the horrors of venereal disease and the exploitation of coal workers to the Sacco-Vanzetti case (in *Boston*) and, regrettably, various crank causes like fasting and extrasensory perception. The Lanny Budd series of eleven historical novels covers the history of the world from 1913 to 1949. Lanny is a rich, globe-trotting American whose presence on the scene at every significant event of those years provides a useful, though admittedly not too believable, narrative device and a unifying thread.

1. *World's End* (Viking, 1940)
   Lanny is an idealistic youth of thirteen when this story begins in 1913. World War I sends him home to America, but he is back at the Versailles peace conference as a secretary to a Wilson aide.
2. *Between Two Worlds* (Viking, 1941)
   The rise of fascism is documented in this volume, which covers the 1920s.

3. *Dragon's Teeth* (Viking, 1942)
   This covers events in Germany from 1930 to 1934, ending with Hitler's Blood Purge.
4. *Wide Is the Gate* (Viking, 1943)
   This book covers the years 1935–36 and the beginnings of the Spanish Civil War.
5. *Presidential Agent* (Viking, 1945)
   Lanny serves as a special agent for President Roosevelt in Europe during 1937–38.
6. *Dragon Harvest* (Viking, 1945)
   In 1939–40, Franco wins in Spain, and France falls.
7. *A World to Win* (Viking, 1946)
   The events of 1940–42 include America's entry into the war.
8. *Presidential Mission* (Viking, 1947)
   The war continues in 1942–43.
9. *One Clear Call* (Viking, 1948)
   Fears of Germany's atomic capabilities mark 1943–44.
10. *O Shepherd, Speak* (Viking, 1949)
    Lanny uses his wealth to create the Peace Foundation in 1944–46.
11. *The Return of Lanny Budd* (Viking, 1953)
    The period is 1944–49. The cold war begins, and Lanny turns in his half-sister to the F.B.I. as a Communist agent.

Singer, Isaac Bashevis

The works of Nobel laureate (1978) Isaac Bashevis Singer are composed in Yiddish, then translated into English by Singer or by other translators. Singer is best known for his mystical short stories and novels about Jewish life in the shtetls of Eastern Europe before the Holocaust (e.g., *Gimpel the Fool* and *The Spinoza of Market Street*), but he has also published children's books, several volumes of memoirs, and family sagas that are reminiscent of the work of his elder brother I. J. Singer, author of *The Brothers Ashkenazi*. *The Manor* and *The Estate* were originally a single novel serialized in Yiddish in the *Jewish Daily Forward* (New York, 1953–55), then translated into English, amplified, and published in two volumes. It is the saga of Calman Jacoby, a wealthy Jewish grain merchant who leases the Polish estate of Count Jampolski in 1863. The assimilation into Gentile society and the loss of Calman's family's religious and social heritage are chronicled to the end of the nineteenth century. Singer is a master storyteller who catches the passion and poignance of his characters' lives.

419

1. *The Manor* (Farrar, 1967)
   Calman Jacoby becomes richer by selling the timber from the estate he has leased, but loses his four daughters to assimilation and modernization. Translated from the Yiddish by Joseph Singer and Elaine Gottlieb.
2. *The Estate* (Farrar, 1969)
   Sasha, the son of Calman's estranged wife Clara, takes over management of the estate. Translated from the Yiddish by Joseph Singer and Elaine Gottlieb.

Singer, Shelley

Jake Samson is an unlicensed private investigator living in Oakland, California. Like many of his ilk, he is a hard-boiled wisecracker who is basically sensitive and likeable. What distinguishes him from his brethren is his sidekick, lesbian carpenter Rosie Vicente. The Samson novels are well-plotted, amusing entertainments with a San Francisco Bay ambience. Author Shelley Singer, who also lives in Oakland, worked at a variety of jobs, including journalist, antique restorer, welfare worker, gardener, and carpenter before she started publishing the Jake Samson series.

1. *Samson's Deal* (St. Martin's, 1983)
   Samson is asked to find the murderer of radical professor John Harley's wife by old friend Rebecca Lilly, who is having an affair with Harley.
2. *Free Draw* (St. Martin's, 1984)
   When Jake's friend Artie Perrine is charged with murder, Jake poses as a reporter for an investigatory magazine to find the real culprit.
3. *Full House* (St. Martin's, 1986)
   Samson is hired by a band of cultists building an ark in Oakland to find cult leader and health food tycoon Noah, who has disappeared with a quarter of a million dollars.
4. *Spit in the Ocean* (St. Martin's, 1987)
   Someone has been taking the deposits from Nora Canfield's sperm bank, and tossing them into the ocean.
5. *Suicide King* (St. Martin's, 1988)
   VIVO party gubernatorial candidate Joe Richmond is found hanging naked from a tree.

Sjöwall, Maj, and Wahlöö, Per

This Swedish husband-and-wife team quickly won an enthusiastic American audience with its fast-paced and chillingly suspenseful stories about Stockholm policeman Martin Beck. The books' gritty realism, interesting Swedish atmosphere, and strong socialist orientation make them unique. Walter Matthau was a surprisingly convincing Martin Beck in the 1974 American film *The Laughing Policeman*, but the substitution of San Francisco for Stockholm was a disappointment to fans. Another crime series was written by Wahlöö alone (q.v.).

1. *Roseanna* (Pantheon, 1967)
   A naked woman is dredged up from the bottom of Sweden's beautiful Lake Vättern, and Martin Beck struggles to identify her and her murderer without any clues to go on. Translated from the Swedish by Lois Roth.
2. *The Man on the Balcony* (Pantheon, 1968)
   Beck and the large special force assigned to him race with death in the pursuit of a child murderer in Stockholm. Translated from the Swedish by Alan Blair.
3. *The Man Who Went Up in Smoke* (Pantheon, 1969)
   Beck is sent to Budapest on an exasperating search for the missing journalist Alf Matsson. Translated from the Swedish by Joan Tate.
4. *The Laughing Policeman* (Pantheon, 1970)
   When a young police colleague is one of the eight bus passengers killed by a mass murderer, Beck takes a special interest in bringing the criminal to justice. Translated from the Swedish by Alan Blair.
5. *The Fire Engine That Disappeared* (Pantheon, 1970)
   Elements in this baffling case include a cryptic suicide note and a bombed Stockholm apartment house. Translated from the Swedish by Joan Tate.
6. *Murder at the Savoy* (Pantheon, 1971)
   Victor Palmgren, a wealthy industrialist, is gunned down in the dining room of the posh Savoy Hotel in Malmö. Translated from the Swedish by Ann and Ken Knoespel.
7. *The Abominable Man* (Pantheon, 1972)
   When a police colleague is murdered in his hospital bed, Beck must dig deep into the lives of Stockholm's police to solve the crime. Translated from the Swedish by Thomas Teal.

8. *The Locked Room* (Pantheon, 1973)
   A decayed corpse with a bullet through its head is found inside a
   locked room, and the lack of a gun seems to eliminate suicide.
   Translated from the Swedish by Paul Austin.
9. *Cop Killer* (Pantheon, 1975)
   Is the dead woman found by hikers in a small Swedish town
   related to the shoot-out that left one policeman dead and two
   others wounded? Translated from the Swedish by Thomas
   Teal.
10. *The Terrorists* (Pantheon, 1976)
    Beck guards an American senator visiting Stockholm from attack
    by an international gang of terrorists. Translated from the Swed-
    ish by Joan Tate.

Skelton, C. L. (Clement Lister)

Skelton's Regimental Quartet is a cross between family saga and
regimental history: it follows the fortunes of two Scottish families, the
Maclarens and the Bruces, and the Highland Regiment in which they
serve. Skelton gives the series numerous well-drawn characters and
sweeps across class lines to show the crofters and merchants as well as
the soldiers and aristocrats who inhabit the rugged Scottish hill country
from the 1850s on. High praise met the first three volumes, and loyal
readers are waiting patiently for the concluding one.

1. *The Maclarens* (Dial, 1978)
   Beginning with the July, 1857, Indian Mutiny, this novel tells the
   story of Lieutenant Andrew Maclaren; his childhood friend, Sergeant Willie Bruce; and the beautiful woman they both love,
   Maud Westburn.
2. *The Regiment* (Dial, 1979)
   In 1883, Andrew has retired, Willie has taken over the regiment,
   and their sons, Ian and Robert Maclaren and Donald and Gordon
   Bruce, take center stage.
3. *Beloved Soldiers* (Crown, 1984)
   The men of the Maclaren and Bruce families fight the Germans in
   the first two years of World War I, as many of their women join up
   as nurses, ambulance drivers, or military recruiters.

Smith, Charles Merrill

Here is a Protestant clergyman/sleuth to keep the ranks ecumenical, along with Ralph McInerny's Father Dowling (q.v.) and Harry Kemelman's Rabbi Small (q.v.). The Reverend Cesare Paul Randollph of Chicago's Episcopal Church of the Good Shepherd is the creation of clergyman/author Smith, who injects interesting glimpses of ecclesiastical matters into his mysteries. The Reverend Randollph is a cheerfully red-blooded former pro football hero with a Ph.D. His investigative manner is thoughtful and suave but dogged. Charles Merrill Smith died in 1985. His son Terrence Lore Smith, a mystery writer in his own right, completed the sixth Reverend Randollph novel.

1. *Rev. Randollph and the Wages of Sin* (Putnam, 1974)
   The Reverend C. P. Randollph arrives at the Church of the Good Shepherd just in time to investigate a murder and some funny financial business among the trustees.
2. *Rev. Randollph and the Avenging Angel* (Putnam, 1977)
   Just minutes after the wedding ceremony, the bride is bludgeoned to death, and Randollph, an old beau, is a suspect.
3. *Rev. Randollph and the Fall from Grace, Inc.* (Putnam, 1978)
   Someone is trying to kill the TV evangelist Prince Hartman but keeps killing his aides by mistake.
4. *Rev. Randollph and the Holy Terror* (Putnam, 1980)
   Now married to the gorgeous TV star Samantha and ready to move to a posh new congregation, Rev. Randollph is threatened by a homicidal maniac who specializes in clergymen.
5. *Rev. Randollph and the Unholy Bible* (Putnam, 1983)
   A Mafia don is convinced that Randollph is a murderer and thief when the Reverend's parishioner, Johannes Humbrecht, is killed, and his Gutenberg Bible disappears.
6. *Rev. Randollph and the Splendid Samaritan* (Putnam, 1986)
   The Reverend Randollph suspects that murdered financier and philanthropist James Trent was hiding something unsavory.

Smith, Robert Kimmel

Senior citizen (70+) Sadie Shapiro, resident of Mount Eden Senior Citizens Hotel in Queens, New York, is the archetypal Jewish mother who offers sage advice in inimitable English. She is also a jogger, an irrepressible matchmaker, and a champion knitter. Sadie catapults into sudden fame with the publication of her book on knitting, and she adapts quite nicely to the life of a television talk show celebrity. The three Sadie Shapiro novels are funny, heartwarming, and enjoyable reading. Robert Kimmel Smith has written other novels, television scripts, and juveniles, including the popular *Chocolate Fever* (Coward, 1972).

1. *Sadie Shapiro's Knitting Book* (Simon & Schuster, 1973)
   Sadie sends her knitting patterns to a third-rate publishing house, and works with the firm's one female editor to produce a best-selling book.
2. *Sadie Shapiro in Miami* (Simon & Schuster, 1975)
   Sadie visits Florida to endorse a Disneyland for senior citizens, and becomes involved with a scandal and a former boyfriend.
3. *Sadie Shapiro, Matchmaker* (Simon & Schuster, 1977)
   In order to fulfill the last request of a professional matchmaker friend, Sadie takes on the task of matching six singles into three happy couples.

Smith, Thorne

Thorne Smith wrote a number of amusing novels in the twenties and thirties, several of them with elements of fantasy or the supernatural. *Topper*, partly because of its film and television incarnations, is Smith's best-known novel. The plot concerns the trials and tribulations of one Cosmo Topper, respectable middle-aged banker, who is haunted by the ghosts of George and Marion Kerby, a Jazz Age couple who are determined to show Topper how to have a good time. In 1937, *Topper* was made into a very successful motion picture starring Cary Grant. Two film sequels followed: *Topper Takes a Trip* (1939) and *Topper Returns* (1941). A network series starring Leo G. Carroll (1953–55) and a made-for-TV movie starring Kate Jackson (1979) brought Topper to television.

1. *Topper, an Improbable Adventure* (McBride, 1926)
   George and Marion Kerby, killed in a drunken automobile crash, take on the mission of helping Cosmo Topper to get more fun out of life. English title: *The Jovial Ghosts*.

2. *Topper Takes a Trip* (Doubleday, 1932)
   Cosmo Topper and the ghost of Marion Kerby go off to the French Riviera.

Smith, Wilbur

Wilbur Smith was born in Rhodesia and now lives in South Africa. Most of his books are set in the Africa that he knows so well. He has written three books that tell the story of the Ballantyne family from their departure from Scotland in the 1860s to the 1970s. Historical characters such as Cecil Rhodes and the African King Lobengula are woven into these fast-paced tales of adventure and cultural clash.

1. *Flight of the Falcon* (Doubleday, 1982)
   In 1860, idealistic Robyn and ambitious Zouga Ballantyne go to the African interior in search of their missing missionary-explorer father. English title: *A Falcon Flies.*
2. *Men of Men* (Doubleday, 1983)
   In the 1890s, the Ballantynes, now settled in Rhodesia, are drawn into the imperialistic schemes of Cecil Rhodes and the subsequent bloody rebellion of the Matabeles.
3. *The Angels Weep* (Doubleday, 1983)
   In the first part, set in 1895–96, the Ballantynes amass wealth, and face the Matabele rebellion. In the second part, set in 1977, the Ballantynes face terrorists in newly independent Zimbabwe.

Snow, C. P. (Sir Charles Percy)

C. P. Snow was trained as a physicist, taught at Cambridge, and was knighted for his government service during and after World War II. This diversity of experience gives his fiction remarkable authority and scope. In his ability to dramatize the subtle power struggles that take place among politicians, scientists, or academics, he is unrivaled. Strangers and Brothers, an eleven-volume series now complete, is the life story of narrator Lewis Eliot, a lawyer whose career follows Snow's in outline, covering the years from 1914 to the mid-1960s. Eliot is at the center of some novels and merely a peripheral observer in others. The series is available in a three-volume omnibus edition entitled *Strangers and Brothers* (Scribner, 1972). Snow was the husband of novelist Pamela Hansford Johnson (q.v.).

1. *Time of Hope* (Macmillan, 1950)
   First chronologically though written later, this book shows Lewis Eliot's childhood in a poor provincial family from 1914 to his arrival in London as a young barrister in 1933.
2. *Strangers and Brothers* (Scribner, 1960)
   George Passant, a promising provincial lawyer, is much admired by Lewis Eliot and others, but his career ends in tragedy. The time period is 1925–33. The title was changed to *George Passant* in the omnibus edition.
3. *The Conscience of the Rich* (Scribner, 1958)
   Lewis Eliot's friend Charles March, the son of a wealthy and powerful Jewish family in London, struggles to reconcile independence and family loyalty. The account covers the years 1927–36.
4. *The Light and the Dark* (Scribner, 1948)
   Roy Calvert, a brilliant Cambridge scholar, suffers and is finally destroyed by relentless personal despair in 1935–43.
5. *The Masters* (Macmillan, 1951)
   This book centers on the suspenseful struggle among the fellows of a Cambridge College over who will succeed as the new master of the college. The time is 1937.
6. *The New Men* (Scribner, 1954)
   The story of the wartime race to harness atomic fission and the moral issues involved is set in Cambridge and London from 1939 to 1946.
7. *The Homecoming* (Scribner, 1956)
   Lewis Eliot takes center stage again in this volume, which shows his first wife's deepening mental illness and suicide and his happy second marriage. The period is 1939–48.
8. *The Affair* (Scribner, 1960)
   The story returns to the setting of *The Masters* to focus on a case of scientific fraud that Lewis Eliot must reopen in 1953–54.
9. *Corridors of Power* (Scribner, 1964)
   In 1955–58, politician Roger Quaife mounts a ruthless struggle for power but suffers eventual downfall.
10. *The Sleep of Reason* (Scribner, 1968)
    Sir Lewis Eliot, now retired, is drawn by an old friend into a nasty case of a child murder. The narrative is set in his native provincial town in 1963.

11. *Last Things* (Scribner, 1970)
Lewis Eliot undergoes a harrowing eye operation, turns down a government appointment, and worries over his son, Charles. The time is the mid-sixties.

Somers, Jane (pseud. of Doris Lessing)

The author "Jane Somers" and the character Janna Somers are both creations of novelist Doris Lessing (q.v.), who wrote the two Somers novels under a pseudonym in order to draw attention to the plight of unknown writers and to receive unbiased criticism herself. After Lessing revealed her imposture, the novels were published together in paperback as *The Diary of Jane Somers* (Vintage, 1984). Janna Somers is the widowed, middle-aged editor of a London fashion magazine. Her diary records her changing feelings about love, commitment, and the decline of civility in English society. It is a moving, sometimes funny, sometimes sad depiction of the life and feelings of an outwardly successful, inwardly troubled woman.

1. *The Diary of a Good Neighbour* (Knopf, 1983)
Fashion editor Janna Somers befriends smelly, fiercely independent nonagenarian Maude.
2. *If the Old Could...* (Knopf, 1984)
When Janna's attractive niece Jill leaves her aunt's apartment, her unattractive nineteen-year-old sister Kate takes her place, while Janna gets involved in an affair with Richard, a married man.

Steen, Marguerite

The Sun Is My Undoing, by British author Steen, captured the same large popular audience that had just made *Gone with the Wind* a best-seller. Readers looking for a long and lively action-romance won't be disappointed with the adventures of its dashing and impetuous hero, Matthew Flood, an eighteenth-century Englishman who gets involved in the slave trade. The book's central theme, the evils of slavery, is continued in two sequels that tell of Matthew's descendants and heirs to his shipping business.

427

1. *The Sun Is My Undoing* (Viking, 1941)
   The beautiful English girl he loves is an ardent abolitionist, but Matthew enters the slave trade, takes a black mistress, and has many adventures on the high seas, including capture by pirates.
2. *Twilight on the Flood* (Doubleday, 1949)
   John Flood, the thoughtful great-grandson of Matthew, stars in this sequel set in Bristol, England, and Africa's Gold Coast.
3. *Jehovah Blues* (Doubleday, 1952)
   In 1931, the beautiful popular novelist Aldebaran Flood, the last of Matthew's descendants, comes to the United States in search of a lost love. English title: *Phoenix Rising.*

Steinbeck, John

This Nobel and Pulitzer Prize-winning author once lived near Cannery Row, now a tourist attraction in Monterey, California. He first wrote about the seedy residents of the rundown neighborhood behind the waterfront sardine canneries in *Tortilla Flat* (1935). Some of the same characters reappear in these two books, which focus on Doc and tell of the funny and bawdy doings of Dora, the orange-haired madam; Lee Chong and his "Old Tennis Shoe" whiskey; and the characters who frequent the Palace Flophouse and Grill.

1. *Cannery Row* (Viking, 1945)
   The motley residents of Cannery Row work together to give Doc a birthday party he won't forget.
2. *Sweet Thursday* (Viking, 1954)
   World War II has brought change to Cannery Row, and Doc's spirits are running low, but Suzy arrives and livens things up considerably.

Stevenson, D. E. (Dorothy Emily)

I. Popular Scottish author Dorothy Emily Stevenson was married to an officer in the Highland Light Infantry, and she used her own diaries as the basis for her Mrs. Tim books. These gently humorous and amiable volumes detail the life of an officer's wife in small English and Scottish garrison towns from the 1930s through the postwar period. Hester

Christie records bits of regimental and neighborhood gossip, domestic crises, and the amusing doings of her two high-spirited children, Betty and Bryan.

1. *Mrs. Tim Christie* (Farrar & Rinehart, 1940)
   Captain Christie and his family and friends in the town of West-burgh are introduced through the diary of his wife, Hester. Original title: *Mrs. Tim of the Regiment.*
2. *Mrs. Tim Carries On* (Farrar & Rinehart, 1941)
   Tim is posted to France in February, 1940, and Hester stays on in the small Scottish garrison town of Danford through the difficult war years.
3. *Mrs. Tim Gets a Job* (Rinehart, 1947)
   Suffering postwar doldrums with Tim stationed in Egypt and the children away at school, Hester takes a job at Miss Clutterbuck's guest house.
4. *Mrs. Tim Flies Home* (Rinehart, 1952)
   Hester Christie leaves Kenya—where her husband, now a colonel, is stationed—to visit with her children in England.

II. Many readers have enjoyed escaping into the happier, simpler world of Stevenson's Scottish towns and farms, where problems always work out and the basic goodness of humanity is never in doubt. These loosely related books share some of the same characters but can be read as individual volumes.

1. *Victoria Cottage* (Rinehart, 1949)
   Caroline Dering, the widowed mother of three grown children, is attracted to the village of Ashbridge's newest resident, Robert Stepperton.
2. *Music in the Hills* (Rinehart, 1950)
   Caroline's son James goes to live with his aunt and uncle, Mamie and Jock Johnstone, on their farm on the Scottish border.
3. *Shoulder the Sky: A Story of Winter in the Hills* (Rinehart, 1951)
   Rhoda, James's new bride, adjusts to life at Mureth Farm as a terrible storm hits their little community. English title: *Winter and Rough Weather.*

III. These two books featuring Gerald Brown are pleasant adventure/ romances set in London and Scotland.

1. *Gerald and Elizabeth* (Holt, 1969)
   When Gerald leaves South Africa under a cloud, he comes to stay with his beautiful half-sister Elizabeth in London.
2. *House of the Deer* (Holt, 1971)
   Gerald goes deerstalking in the Scottish Highlands, where he makes friends, falls in love, and has a close scrape with tragedy.

Stevenson, Robert Louis

Kidnapped has all the strenuous adventure, thrilling encounters, and hairbreadth escapes of *Treasure Island*, combined with the romantic scenery of the Scottish Highlands and an underlying concern with the proud and noble Highlanders, now ravaged and forced to emigrate from their ancestral home after the defeat of the last Jacobite uprising at the Battle of Culloden in 1746. Adult readers will enjoy the book's nostalgia value and find interest in comparing it to Mark Twain's *Huckleberry Finn*, which is also a tale of pursuit in which a young boy befriends an outlawed member of society and joins him in flight. Young readers will find the sequel less engaging.

1. *Kidnapped* (George Munro, 1886)
   Young David Balfour goes to the Highlands to claim his inheritance, but his evil Uncle Ebenezer has him kidnapped aboard a ship headed for the Carolinas. There he befriends Highland rebel Alan Breck and begins an eventful homeward journey.
2. *David Balfour* (Scribner, 1895)
   This sequel continues David's story to his marriage with the lovely and spirited Highlander Catriona, and recounts the story of the trial of James of the Glen. English title: *Catriona*.

Stewart, Mary

Stewart's polished contemporary gothics set in picturesque European spots won her a huge audience before she turned to the legend of King

Arthur for this tetralogy. Her skill in creating colorful characters, suspense, and a brooding atmosphere serves her well in portraying England's Dark Ages, where witches, sorcerers, and tragic kings moved heroically through an enchanted land. Though Arthur's rise to power is the subject, the true star and narrator of the tale is Merlin the magician. T. H. White has written another series based on the King Arthur legend (q.v.), and Arthur also appears in Henry Treece's Celtic series (q.v.). *Mary Stewart's Merlin Trilogy* (Morrow, 1980) is an omnibus volume containing numbers 1, 2, and 3 below.

1. *The Crystal Cave* (Morrow, 1970)
   Merlin spends his youth in the court of his grandfather, the King of Wales.
2. *The Hollow Hills* (Morrow, 1973)
   Merlin's story continues with the birth of Arthur, who has a secluded boyhood and then searches for the magical sword, Caliburn.
3. *The Last Enchantment* (Morrow, 1979)
   Merlin dies; Arthur has a turbulent early reign, marries, and fathers an illegitimate son, Mordred.
4. *The Wicked Day* (Morrow, 1983)
   Mordred, incestuous son of Arthur and his half-sister Morgause, is the unwilling agent who fulfills Merlin's prophecy of "the Wicked Day" when Arthur meets his end.

Stirling, Jessica

I. The coal-mining town of Blacklaw in 1875 is where this readable pair of novels begins, as Mirrin Stalker, a miner's daughter, is thrust rather hastily into the position of housekeeper at Strathmore, the mansion of mine-owner Houston Lamont. Some fairly predictable complications develop: Mrs. Lamont is jealous; Mirrin's loyalties are torn between Strathmore and her own humble home; and the obligatory mine disaster occurs. However, Mirrin and her brother and sisters are too engaging and credibly drawn to sink into a formula plot.

1. *Strathmore* (Delacorte, 1975)
   Spirited young Mirrin comes to Strathmore with built-in prejudices against the Lamonts, but as she begins to understand them, her heart melts. English title: *The Spoiled Earth.*

2. *Call Home the Heart* (St. Martin's, 1977)
   The story of the Stalker family continues: Drew goes to law school in Edinburgh; Kate settles into the security of marriage; and Mirrin finds success on the music hall circuit as "The Songbird of the North."

II. The Jewish Beckman family of London is the focus of three novels set in the 1920s to the 1940s. When young Holly inherits a share in an antique store, she is determined to make the most of the opportunity to pull herself out of the Lambeth slums and away from her drunkard father and crooked brother Ritchie. The vivid and convincing characters and interesting setting make very enjoyable reading.

1. *Drums of Time* (St. Martin's, 1980)
   In 1918, young Holly Beckman becomes part owner of an antique shop when the owner dies, and she is determined to make a success of it.
2. *The Blue Evening Gone* (St. Martin's, 1981)
   In 1933, love finds Holly, Leo, Maury, and Ritchie as Holly investigates some art forgeries that threaten to ruin her reputation as an art expert.
3. *The Gates of Midnight* (St. Martin's, 1983)
   World War II finds widowed Holly Beckman Deems managing an antiques business, and concerning herself about her son, her brothers, and her former lover, David Aspinwall.

III. Rural Scotland in the eighteenth and nineteenth centuries is the setting for this historical trilogy that chronicles the hardships that Gaddy Cochran bears, first as a drover (a roaming cattle seller) and then as a farmer.

1. *Treasures on Earth* (St. Martins, 1985)
   Gaddy Cochran adopts a newborn foundling and abandons her life as a drover's woman for the settled but harsh existence of tenant farmer.
2. *Creature Comforts* (St. Martin's, 1986)
   Gaddy's daughters, foundling Elspeth and Anna, are both disappointed in marriage.

3. *Hearts of Gold* (St. Martin's, 1987)
Elspeth flees her sinister spouse for an anonymous life in the
coalfields of Abbefield, while Anna is deserted by her husband.

Stockton, Frank

This nineteenth-century American author wrote what have been called
"grown-up juveniles"—i.e., whimsical and paradoxical stories full of ab-
surd characters and amusing incident. Stockton's short fable "The Lady,
or the Tiger?" won instant fame and is still anthologized and read today.
His two books featuring the unlikely adventures of Mrs. Lecks and Mrs.
Aleshine, two rather prosaic matrons, can still tickle the funny bone.
They would make good hammock reading on a warm summer afternoon.

1. *The Casting Away of Mrs. Lecks and Mrs. Aleshine* (Appleton,
   1886)
   When their cruise ship sinks and they find themselves washed
   ashore on a desert island, these two unruffled matrons set up
   house as calmly as if they were home in New England.
2. *The Dusantes* (Century, 1888)
   The Crusoe ladies have further adventures as the Dusantes, owners of the desert island, follow them home to return the money
   they paid for the use of the property.

Stout, Rex

I. Nero Wolfe fans, both old and new, were delighted to watch the fat,
orchid-loving detective come alive in a recent series of television mysteries, and many will remember the 1940s radio shows with Sydney
Greenstreet playing Wolfe. Readers will find Rex Stout's plots even
more clever and sophisticated in book form, where Archie's droll and
witty comments definitely add to the fun. Wolfe bears the mark of the
1930s' "golden age" of mystery—he is one of those eccentric private
detectives who solve relatively bloodless cases by ratiocination rather
than rough stuff. Stout is one of the few Americans to master the genre.
William Baring-Gould's lighthearted study, *Nero Wolfe of West Thirty-
Fifth Street* (Viking, 1969) is very good, though it needs updating. John
McAleer's *Rex Stout: A Biography* (Little, 1977) gives an interesting picture of the author and a complete bibliography. Many of the Nero Wolfe

books have also been published in omnibus volumes. *Full House* (Viking, 1955) contains numbers 2, 13, and 18 listed below. *All Aces* (Viking, 1958) comprises numbers 6, 12, and 15. *Five of a Kind* (Viking, 1961) includes numbers 3, 16, and 17. In *Royal Flush* (Viking, 1965) may be found numbers 1, 19, and 27 below. *Kings Full of Aces* (Viking, 1969) contains numbers 5, 21, and 32. *Three Aces* (Viking, 1971) contains numbers 26, 33, and 35; and *Triple Zack* (Viking, 1974) has numbers 13, 14, and 16. In recent years Nero Wolfe has been resurrected by Ken Darby in *The Brownstone House of Nero Wolfe* (Little, 1983) and Robert Goldsborough (q.v.).

1. *Fer-de-Lance* (Farrar & Rinehart, 1934)
   Nero Wolfe's first recorded case concerns university president Peter Oliver Barstow, who dies a strange, sudden death on the golf course. Stout teases his readers by having Wolfe and Archie refer to earlier cases.
2. *The League of Frightened Men* (Farrar & Rinehart, 1935)
   A group of old Harvard classmates are being murdered one by one.
3. *The Rubber Band* (Farrar & Rinehart, 1936)
   Anthony Perry brings Wolfe a complicated mystery that involves blackmail, a lynching, and a final shoot-out in Wolfe's office. Variant title: *To Kill Again.*
4. *The Red Box* (Farrar & Rinehart, 1937)
   Investigating a murder among the fashion models at Boyden McNair, Inc., proves very pleasant for Archie.
5. *Too Many Cooks* (Farrar & Rinehart, 1938)
   Wolfe and Archie go to a high-class cook's convention and find murder on the menu.
6. *Some Buried Caesar* (Farrar & Rinehart, 1939)
   Wolfe attends an agricultural exposition in upstate New York, where his orchids win all the prizes and he solves three murders—including one of a prizewinning bull. Variant title: *The Red Bull.*
7. *Over My Dead Body* (Farrar & Rinehart, 1940)
   The death of a fencing student, run through the heart with a strangely tipped foil, reunites Wolfe with his long lost adopted daughter, Anna.
8. *Where There's a Will* (Farrar & Rinehart, 1940)
   When eccentric millionaire Noel Hawthorne leaves a puzzling legacy to his three sisters, Wolfe must solve the riddle and investigate two murders.

9. *Black Orchids* (Farrar & Rinehart, 1942)
This volume contains two novellas, "Black Orchids" and "Cordially Invited to Meet Death."

10. *Not Quite Dead Enough* (Farrar & Rinehart, 1944)
Two novellas are included here: "Not Quite Dead Enough" and "Booby Trap."

11. *The Silent Speaker* (Viking, 1946)
Cheney Boone, director of the Bureau of Price Regulation, is killed backstage just before delivering a scheduled speech.

12. *Too Many Women* (Viking, 1947)
Archie, in disguise as a personnel expert, delves into personalities and conflicts at an engineering supply company where a murder has occurred.

13. *And Be a Villain* (Viking, 1948)
The mysterious X warns Wolfe off the investigation of horse tipster Cyril Orchad's murder. English title: *More Deaths than One.*

14. *The Second Confession* (Viking, 1949)
Archie goes off to Chappaqua to help the Sperling family solve a mystery—another case that X (Arnold Zack) doesn't like. English title: *Even in the Best Families.*

15. *Trouble in Triplicate* (Viking, 1949)
Three novellas are included here: "Help Wanted, Male," "Instead of Evidence," and "Before I Die."

16. *In the Best Families* (Viking, 1950)
The Rackham case brings about a showdown with the evil Arnold Zack, but not before Wolfe goes into hiding and emerges 117 pounds lighter.

17. *Three Doors to Death* (Viking, 1950)
This book contains three novellas: "Man Alive," "Omit Flowers," and "Door to Death."

18. *Curtains for Three* (Viking, 1950)
"Bullet for One," "The Gun with Wings," and "Disguise for Murder" are the three novellas that make up this book.

19. *Murder by the Book* (Viking, 1951)
Wolfe investigates the seemingly unrelated murders of Joan Wellman and Leonard Dykes.

20. *Triple Jeopardy* (Viking, 1952)
There are three more novellas here: "The Cop-Killer," "The Squirt and the Monkey," and "Home to Roost."

21. *Prisoner's Base* (Viking, 1952)
Archie himself becomes one of Wolfe's clients in this search for a missing woman. English title: *Out Goes She.*

22. *The Golden Spiders* (Viking, 1953)
    The case involving golden spider earrings is brought to Wolfe by a neighborhood boy, who offers a retainer of $4.30.
23. *Three Men Out* (Viking, 1954)
    Three novellas form this book: "This Won't Kill You," "Invitation to Murder," and "The Zero Clue."
24. *The Black Mountain* (Viking, 1954)
    Wolfe and Archie are off to Montenegro to investigate the apparent murder of Wolfe's oldest and best friend, Marko Vukcic.
25. *Before Midnight* (Viking, 1955)
    Louis Dahlman, the man who devised an ingenious contest, is murdered before revealing the current answers.
26. *Three Witnesses* (Viking, 1956)
    "When a Man Murders," "Die Like a Dog," and "The Next Witness" are the three novellas in this book.
27. *Might as Well Be Dead* (Viking, 1956)
    A search for a missing person leads Wolfe to the cell of an accused murderer in this surprising case.
28. *If Death Ever Slept* (Viking, 1957)
    The police suspect Archie of murder in this "distasteful" case.
29. *Three for the Chair* (Viking, 1957)
    This book contains three novellas: "Immune to Murder," "A Window for Death," and "Too Many Detectives."
30. *Champagne for One* (Viking, 1958)
    How does the one glass of poisoned champagne reach the right victim in a partyful of people?
31. *And Four to Go* (Viking, 1958)
    Four stories are collected here: "Christmas Party," "Easter Parade," "Fourth of July Picnic," and "Murder Is No Joke." English title: *Crime and Again.*
32. *Plot It Yourself* (Viking, 1959)
    Wolfe's investigation into burgeoning plagiarism in the book-publishing industry leads to murder. English title: *Murder in Style.*
33. *Too Many Clients* (Viking, 1960)
    A murder occurs in the plush love nest of a corporation executive.
34. *Three at Wolfe's Door* (Viking, 1960)
    "Poison a la Carte," "Method Three for Murder," and "The Rodeo Murder" are the three novellas collected here.

35. *The Final Deduction* (Viking, 1961)
   Mrs. Jimmy Vail comes to Wolfe when her husband is being held for $500,000 ransom.
36. *Gambit* (Viking, 1962)
   A case of arsenic poisoning develops in a Manhattan chess club.
37. *Homicide Trinity* (Viking, 1962)
   Three novellas are collected here: "Death of a Demon," "Eeny Meeny Murder Mo," and "Counterfeit for Murder."
38. *The Mother Hunt* (Viking, 1963)
   When a baby arrives on Lucy Valdon's doorstep, she turns to Wolfe for help in locating the mother.
39. *A Right to Die* (Viking, 1964)
   Paul Whipple, a black assistant professor of anthropology at Columbia, comes to Wolfe for help with a personal problem.
40. *Trio for Blunt Instruments* (Viking, 1964)
   Three novellas make up this book: "Kill Now—Pay Later," "Murder Is Corny," and "Blood Will Tell."
41. *The Doorbell Rang* (Viking, 1965)
   This very clever case involves the FBI's persecution of a woman out to cause them trouble.
42. *Death of a Doxy* (Viking, 1966)
   Wolfe's sometime assistant Orrie Cather is charged with murder, and Nero and Archie try to clear him.
43. *The Father Hunt* (Viking, 1968)
   Wolfe and Archie try to find Amy Denovo's father without a clue to start with.
44. *Death of a Dude* (Viking, 1969)
   Wolfe actually travels to Montana to retrieve Archie from a dude ranch and helps clear his friend Harvey Greve of a murder charge.
45. *Please Pass the Guilt* (Viking, 1973)
   A potential candidate for the presidency of a large corporation is killed by a bomb explosion in New York.
46. *A Family Affair* (Viking, 1975)
   Wolfe gives sanctuary to a frightened waiter and has a man killed on his doorstep in this mystifying case.

II. Rex Stout's other fictional detective is little known, perhaps because he only has three cases to his credit. Tecumseh Fox, who denies being part Indian, is a first-rate private detective who works out of his farm in Westchester, New York.

1. *Double for Death* (Farrar & Rinehart, 1939)
   A laid-off copywriter is suspected of murdering rich, old Ridley Thorpe's double.
2. *Bad for Business* (in *The Second Mystery Book,* an omnibus volume [Farrar & Rinehart])
   Uncle Arthur's horrible death and a nice lady sleuth occupy Tecumseh in this episode.
3. *The Broken Vase* (Farrar & Rinehart, 1941)
   Fox investigates the murder of a musician at New York's finest concert auditorium.

Stubbs, Jean

Four volumes of Jean Stubbs's Lancashire-based Howarth family saga have appeared so far. The story begins in 1760 with Ned Howarth, the hardworking owner of Kit's Hill, a prosperous farm, and traces the family through succeeding generations. The series documents in fascinating incident and character the social history of Stubbs's native Lancashire country. Delderfield fans should enjoy these.

1. *By Our Beginnings* (St. Martin's, 1979)
   Ned Howarth woos and weds Dorcas Wilde, an educated woman from a nearby town, who has trouble adjusting to life on the farm.
2. *An Imperfect Joy* (St. Martin's, 1981)
   The story of Ned's children continues from 1785 to 1812. Dick stays on the farm, William starts an iron works that eventually dominates the valley, and Charlotte becomes a champion of social justice.
3. *The Vivian Inheritance* (St. Martin's, 1982)
   Wealthy ironmaster William Howarth and his illegitimate son, Cornish engineer Hal Vivian, are the main characters as the railroad comes to the Valley of Wydendale.
4. *The Northern Correspondent, 1831-1851* (St. Martin's, 1984)
   Ambrose Longe, son of Charlotte Howarth Longe, joins forces with Naomi Blum to publish a newspaper, *The Northern Correspondent.*

Swinnerton, Frank

Swinnerton, who has been called one of England's most dependable storytellers, must surely rank among its most productive as well. In a literary career spanning over seventy years, he wrote more than forty novels, in addition to numerous works of biography, criticism, etc. From his first best-seller, *Nocturne* (Doran, 1917), to the tetralogy listed below, his fiction is distinguished by the solid craftsmanship with which he transforms the manners and morals of his contemporary characters into solid reading enjoyment. The books below treat four generations of the Grace family and delineate the changing relationships between men and women.

1. *The Woman from Sicily* (Doubleday, 1957)
   A mystery of hate and revenge threatens the gentle and loving Jerome Grace and his family, who live in a quiet East Anglian country town.
2. *A Tigress in the Village* (Doubleday, 1959)
   Set in 1921 in the village of Prothero, this story focuses on Mrs. Mary Grace, showing the activities of her three grown children, her husband's business failures, and her attraction to her old friend Tom Tamplin. English title: *A Tigress in Prothero.*
3. *The Grace Divorce* (Doubleday, 1960)
   In 1937, Mary, now widowed, worries over her children's marriages, which seem doomed from the start.
4. *Quadrille* (Doubleday, 1965)
   In 1960, nineteen-year-old Laura Grace, Philip's daughter, is caught in a desperate love triangle.

Tapply, William G.

Divorced, middle-aged Brady Coyne has a lucrative law practice among Boston's old rich, but his gilt-edged clients have a way of involving Brady in the seamier side of life, and bringing out the amateur sleuth in him. Beneath Brady's well-dressed and cynical facade lies a compassionate and sensitive man. A former high school teacher and housemaster, William G. Tapply is producing a series of well-written mysteries with a protagonist who becomes more interesting with each volume.

1. *Death at Charity's Point* (Scribner, 1984)
   George Gresham's mother is convinced that her son's plunge off a cliff was not a suicide.
2. *The Dutch Blue Error* (Scribner, 1985)
   Oliver Hazard Perry Weston hires Coyne to meet a man who claims to have a duplicate of Perry's unique Dutch Blue Error postage stamp.
3. *Follow the Sharks* (Scribner, 1985)
   Ex-Boston Red Sox pitcher Eddie Donagan asks Coyne to find his kidnapped ten-year-old son.
4. *The Marine Corpse* (Scribner, 1986)
   Writer Stu Carver, doing research among Boston's homeless, is stabbed to death, and sections of his journals disappear.
5. *Dead Meat* (Scribner, 1987)
   "Tiny" Wheeler turns down some interested buyers of his hunting lodge in Maine, before he discovers that the resort may be on an ancient Indian burial ground.
6. *The Vulgar Boatman* (Scribner, 1988)
   Brady's friend and client, Tom Baron, has his gubernatorial campaign rocked by the murder of a high school girl linked to Baron's ex-addict son.
7. *A Void in Hearts* (Scribner, 1988)
   After private eye Les Katz sells some incriminating photographs to a philandering husband, he has some sobering second thoughts about his actions.

Taylor, Andrew

William Dougal, English graduate student in medieval studies, is the amoral protagonist in a trilogy of thrillers by Andrew Taylor, former London librarian. More than with most series of this kind, the reader needs to read the initial volume to understand the subsequent volumes. The books are intricately plotted, suspenseful, leavened with humor, and filled with clever but nasty characters.

1. *Caroline Minuscule* (Dodd, 1983)
   The murder of William Dougal's professor, an expert on medieval scripts, leads Dougal to a search for a fortune in diamonds.
2. *Waiting for the End of the World* (Dodd, 1984)
   Dougal is forced into investigating the Sealed Servants of the Apocalypse, a survivalist group.

3. *Our Fathers' Lies* (Dodd, 1985)

When Richard Prentisse is drowned, his daughter seeks help from William Dougal and Dougal's father to unravel the mystery of his death.

Taylor, Phoebe Atwood

Many readers will remember Asey Mayo, Cape Cod's famous fictional detective—he even had a large following in England. The modus operandi of the "Codfish Sherlock" is both salty and canny as he pokes into the various misdoings of the Cape's quaint locals and uppity summer people. Most of his cases take place in the towns of Weesit and Pochet, which Taylor has adroitly tucked somewhere between the real towns of Wellfleet and Chatham. Taylor, a native of Boston, began producing these books after graduation from college and turned them out with a casual facility. Her atmosphere never fails, and sometimes her mysteries are first-rate puzzlers. She also wrote a mystery series under the pseudonym Alice Tilton (q.v.).

1. *Cape Cod Mystery* (Bobbs-Merrill, 1931)

   After a famous but much disliked novelist is murdered during an unusually warm Cape Cod weekend, Asey tracks down the guilty person.
2. *Death Lights a Candle* (Bobbs-Merrill, 1932)

   Murder by poison at a house party leaves clues and suspects aplenty.
3. *Mystery of the Cape Cod Players* (Norton, 1933)

   Asey Mayo investigates the murder of Red Gilpin, a magician with an itinerant Punch and Judy troupe.
4. *Mystery of the Cape Cod Tavern* (Norton, 1934)

   Eve Prence, the proprietor of Prence's Tavern in Weesit, is murdered, and Asey tries to clear Anne Bradford of police suspicions.
5. *Sandbar Sinister* (Norton, 1934)

   Two people are murdered—one of whom claimed to be a detective-story writer—one night in East Pochet after most of the local population had been drinking.
6. *Tinkling Symbol* (Norton, 1935)

   Was David Truman stabbed to death by someone who lost his savings when Truman's bank failed?

7. *Deathblow Hill* (Norton, 1935)
   This tricky case involves a family feud, a barbed-wire fence, and yellow handkerchiefs signaling trouble.
8. *Crimson Patch* (Norton, 1936)
   Rosalie Ray, the film star, is done in with a whale lance.
9. *Out of Order* (Norton, 1936)
   Neither bullets nor blizzard deters Asey's investigation of a puzzle that draws him away from his Cape Cod home.
10. *Figure Away* (Norton, 1937)
    A carnival of murder and mystery entangles Asey.
11. *Octagon House* (Norton, 1937)
    Murder, mayhem, and ambergris summon Asey Mayo to the mysterious Octagon House.
12. *The Annulet of Gilt* (Norton, 1938)
    Asey observes strange goings-on at Hector Colvin's house until murder gives him a more active role.
13. *Banbury Bog* (Norton, 1938)
    Asey clears a baker-benefactor at Weesit accused of distributing poisoned tarts.
14. *Spring Harrowing* (Norton, 1939)
    Murder and other strange doings—two bobcats set loose and a prisoner kept in a well—keep Asey busy.
15. *The Criminal C.O.D.* (Norton, 1940)
    Henry Slocum, an aspiring politician, seems to have vanished, but the corpse of his fiancée is left behind.
16. *The Deadly Sunshade* (Norton, 1940)
    Asey's investigation into the Cape's latest murder is not helped by the Sketicket ladies' league to "Defend America at All Costs."
17. *The Perennial Border* (Norton, 1941)
    Asey and his cousin Jennie find a corpse in a telephone booth in the Whale Inn, but it disappears mysteriously.
18. *The Six Iron Spiders* (Norton, 1942)
    Asey helps in the war effort by becoming a tank expert at Bill Porter's factory, but on a weekend visit home he gets involved in a case of a vanishing corpse.
19. *Three Plots for Asey Mayo* (Norton, 1942)
    Three short novels are collected here: "The Wander Bird Plot," "The Headacre Plot," and "The Swan-Boat Plot."
20. *Going, Going, Gone* (Norton, 1943)
    Asey's housekeeping cousin Jennie is sure there is hidden money somewhere in the Alden estate furnishings, which are being auctioned off.

21. *Proof of the Pudding* (Norton, 1945)
   A hurricane leaves Cape Cod in chaos and Asey Mayo with a compromising corpse on his hands.
22. *Asey Mayo Trio* (Messner, 1946)
   "The Third Murderer," "Murder Rides the Gale," and "The Stars Spell Death" are the three stories collected here.
23. *Punch with Care* (Farrar, 1946)
   Asey's new car figures in this case of a missing house guest and a vanishing corpse.
24. *Diplomatic Corpse* (Little, 1951)
   The production of a patriotic historical pageant has fanned so many jealousies into flames that Asey is not surprised when murder results.

Tey, Josephine (pseud. of Elizabeth MacKintosh)

Tey ended her brief teaching career at the time of her mother's death and returned to her Inverness home to look after her father. She began writing stories and verse, and in 1929 her first mystery, *The Man in the Queue*, was chosen as the winning entry in a publisher's contest. Inspector Alan Grant of Scotland Yard, her bachelor detective with a remarkable instinct for spotting criminals, stars in only six of her mysteries. He does not appear in two of her best known—*Miss Pym Disposes* (Macmillan, 1947) and *Brat Farrar* (Macmillan, 1950). *The Daughter of Time*, in which he does appear, is recognized as a masterpiece of historical detection.

1. *The Man in the Queue* (Dutton, 1927)
   Someone is stabbed while standing in one of those patient English queues waiting to buy theater tickets. Variant title: *Killer in the Crowd*.
2. *A Shilling for Candles* (Methuen, London, 1936)
   Inspired by a real crime, this book concerns the murder of Christine Clay, a famous British film star, near her seashore cottage.
3. *The Franchise Affair* (Macmillan, 1948)
   A mother and daughter are accused of imprisoning and mistreating a servant girl. The story is based on the real Elizabeth Canning—Mrs. Brownrigg case. Alan Grant has only a minor role in this one.

4. *To Love and Be Wise* (Macmillan, 1950)
   A handsome American photographer comes to an English artists' colony, launches a romance, then disappears and is feared murdered.
5. *The Daughter of Time* (Macmillan, 1952)
   This is Tey's most famous book, in which Grant, laid up in a hospital, researches one of the oldest and most controversial unsolved murder cases in history—that of the two little princes in the Tower of London.
6. *The Singing Sands* (Macmillan, 1953)
   The key to the solution of Bill Kendrick's murder is in a fragment of verse that Grant must puzzle out. This book was published posthumously.

Thackeray, William Makepeace

Vanity Fair, Thackeray's best-known novel, was an early success on "Masterpiece Theatre," and *Barry Lyndon* was revived with Stanley Kubrick's 1975 film. But many critics, including Anthony Trollope, his contemporary, regarded *The History of Henry Esmond* as Thackeray's greatest work. Its amusing story of unhappy young love and hidden true identity is capped with a surprise ending. Set during the reign of Queen Anne, it is related in the first person in the language of that time by Esmond, writing from the gentleman's estate in Virginia where he settled. The sequel concerns his two grandsons.

1. *The History of Henry Esmond* (Harper, 1879)
   The illegitimate son of the deceased old viscount, Henry Esmond, is brought up on the Castlewood estate and falls in love with the beautiful Beatrix, who rejects him for another. Some editions are titled simply *Henry Esmond*. First published in England in 1852.
2. *The Virginians* (Fields, Osgood, 1869)
   George and Harry Warrington of Virginia, the twin grandsons of Henry Esmond, fight on different sides during the American Revolution. First published in England in 1857.

Thane, Elswyth

Aeonian Press's recent reprinting of Thane's Williamsburg novels offers proof of the enduring appeal of these historical romances. The series chronicles American history from colonial times to World War II by focusing on various members of two Williamsburg, Virginia, families, the Days and the Spragues. Much of the action of the later volumes takes place in England, where the author spent part of each year and had a very large readership. Thane was married to the famous naturalist-writer William Beebe and is perversely cataloged by many libraries under her married name.

1. *Dawn's Early Light* (Duell, 1943)
   Set in Williamsburg and the Carolinas from 1774 to 1781, this story describes schoolmaster Julian Day's arrival from London, his friendship with the aristocratic St. John Sprague, and his championing of the young girl Tibby Mawes.
2. *Yankee Stranger* (Duell, 1944)
   Cabot Murray, a handsome Yankee newspaper correspondent, comes to Williamsburg in 1860, and red-haired Eden Day (Julian's great-granddaughter) falls head over heels in love with him.
3. *Ever After* (Duell, 1945)
   The story continues into the next generation: young journalist Bracken Murray is in England for Queen Victoria's Jubilee (1897), while his cousin Fitz Sprague covers the Spanish-American War in Cuba.
4. *Light Heart* (Duell, 1947)
   Phoebe Sprague, newly engaged to marry cousin Miles, travels to London for Edward VII's coronation and falls in love with another man.
5. *Kissing Kin* (Duell, 1948)
   In 1917, the young twins Camilla and Calvert set out to help with the war effort—Calvert on a gun crew and Camilla as a nurse in England.
6. *This Was Tomorrow* (Duell, 1951)
   Two dancing cousins from Williamsburg take their show to London in 1934 and meet their English counterparts.
7. *Homing* (Duell, 1957)
   Set in England during World War II, this story focuses on young Jeff Day, a foreign correspondent in London, and his English distant cousin Mab.

Thirkell, Angela

Most modern readers will find Thirkell's very British charm hard to fathom; yet her books had a large American audience well into the 1950s. Part of the appeal, no doubt, was the fun of meeting old friends and catching up on gossip offered by each new installment of her continuing chronicle of Barsetshire. Using the fictional town created by Anthony Trollope (q.v.) for his six-novel series, Thirkell follows its modern-day inhabitants through the period of rapid social change following World War I. In her later novels, plots grow very thin, tea-table chat predominates, and her conservative characters ossify into the "tweeded dummies" that eventually alienated all but a few loyal fans.

1. *High Rising* (Knopf, 1951)
   This novel introduces Mrs. Laura Morland, a fortyish writer of mystery novels, whose brusque manner and dishevelled hair betray her autobiographical origins. She is seen coping with her young son, Tony, home on school holiday, and her publisher, Adrian Coates, who proposes marriage. First published in England in 1933.
2. *Wild Strawberries* (Smith & Haas, 1934)
   Lady Emily Leslie and her family play the lead roles during the time that their home, Rushwater House, is used as a convalescent center for soldiers.
3. *The Demon in the House* (Smith & Haas, 1934)
   The first reference to Barchester is made in these short stories about young Tony Morland.
4. *Summer Half* (Knopf, 1938)
   This first novel to make deliberate use of the Barsetshire setting tells of Tony Morland, now seventeen years old and a student at a boys' public school.
5. *Pomfret Towers* (Knopf, 1938)
   Some consider this book the first real Barsetshire novel. It concerns young Alice Barton, who overcomes her shyness, accepts a weekend invitation to Pomfret Towers, and finds herself enjoying her stay.
6. *The Brandons* (Knopf, 1939)
   Mrs. Brandon, a middle-aged widow with two grown children, does her best not to be disinherited by her husband's rich old aunt.
7. *Before Lunch* (Knopf, 1940)
   John Middleton, architect and gentleman farmer, copes with the

various romantic entanglements of his sister, Lilian, and her two stepchildren.

8. *Cheerfulness Breaks In* (Knopf, 1941)
   During World War II, the headmaster of a state school and his wife evacuate their pupils to Barsetshire's Southbridge Public School.

9. *Northbridge Rectory* (Knopf, 1941)
   Barsetshire during World War II is seen through the eyes of Mrs. Villars, the vicar's wife.

10. *Marling Hall* (Knopf, 1942)
    Lady Agnes Graham and other residents of Marling Hall cope cheerfully with wartime shortages and dangers.

11. *Growing Up* (Knopf, 1943)
    Sir Harry and Lady Waring have turned most of their mansion into a soldiers' convalescent home and make the best of their life in their servants' quarters.

12. *The Headmistress* (Knopf, 1944)
    Heather Adams is the gauche and homely daughter of self-made industrialist Sam Adams.

13. *Miss Bunting* (Knopf, 1945)
    Miss Bunting, the governess who appeared in *Marling Hall,* plays a major role in this story about two middle-aged spinsters and the young girls they tutor.

14. *Peace Breaks Out* (Knopf, 1946)
    Sam Adams, the industrialist, defeats the incumbent Sir Robert Fielding in the postwar election, as the Labour party—always referred to as "Them" by Thirkell's genteel characters—comes into power.

15. *Private Enterprise* (Knopf, 1947)
    Mrs. Arbuthnot, an attractive war widow, comes to Barsetshire hoping to find a new husband.

16. *Love Among the Ruins* (Knopf, 1948)
    The romance of Susan Dean and Captain Belton is the main focus of this installment.

17. *The Old Bank* (Knopf, 1949)
    Sam Adams, M.P., buys a period house, becomes engaged to the spinster daughter of Marling Hall, and is accepted by the gentry.

18. *Country Chronicle* (Knopf, 1950)
    Isabel Dale comes into money and marries Lord Silverbridge.

19. *The Duke's Daughter* (Knopf, 1951)
    Three engagements in twenty-four hours take place in this installment, including that of Lady Cora Palliser, descendant of Trollope's Palliser family.

20. *Happy Return* (Knopf, 1952)
    The Conservative party's return to power makes Barsetshire's residents much happier. Eric Swan, the master of Priory School, plays a leading role in this novel.
21. *Jutland Cottage* (Knopf, 1953)
    Glamorous Rose Fairweather takes poor Margot Phelps under her wing, gets her some fashionable new clothes, a new corset, and a new hairdo, and finds her a husband.
22. *What Did It Mean?* (Knopf, 1954)
    All of Barsetshire's residents are affected by the coronation summer.
23. *Enter Sir Robert* (Knopf, 1955)
    This episode revolves around Lady Graham, the attractive wife of Sir Robert, and her plan to "settle things" with her husband when he comes down from London.
24. *Never Too Late* (Knopf, 1956)
    Romances blossom between the vicar and Miss Merriman, and Lord Crosse and Mrs. Morland.
25. *A Double Affair* (Knopf, 1957)
    Dean Crawley's granddaughters Grace and Jane have a double wedding.
26. *Close Quarters* (Knopf, 1958)
    Canon "Tubby" Fewling comes to the rescue of a bereaved Margot Macfadyen.
27. *Love at All Ages* (Knopf, 1959)
    Many old friends reappear in this episode, which includes a birth, a baptism, a marriage, and a generous helping of young love.
28. *Three Score and Ten* (Knopf, 1961)
    Romance for both Dr. Ford and Lord Mellings provides the focus for this last novel, finished after the author's death by C.A. Lejeune.

Thomas, Craig

Firefox and its successors are excellent examples of the thriller/espionage genre. They have plenty of action, suspense, excellent descriptions of aircraft and flying, and an interesting protagonist in Mitchell Gant, an American air ace damaged psychologically by his experiences in the Vietnam War. Part of the suspense is generated by the reader's knowledge that Gant is unstable and may crack under pressure during his missions. *Firefox* was a best-seller as a novel and a successful film starring Clint Eastwood (1982).

1. *Firefox* (Holt, 1977)
   U.S. Air Force Major Mitchell Gant is sent by the CIA and Britain's SIS to steal the new Russian warplane, codenamed *Firefox*, on its first test flight.
2. *Firefox Down!* (Bantam, 1983)
   Gant is forced to land the disabled *Firefox* on a frozen lake in Finnish Lapland, where it sinks through the ice, and Gant is captured by the Russians.
3. *Winter Hawk* (Morrow, 1987)
   Forty-eight hours is all the time Gant has to retrieve from the Soviet Union a spy who has information that could stop the signing of an arms reduction treaty.

Thompson, Flora

Critics have trouble deciding whether Thompson wrote fictionalized memoirs or autobiographical fiction, but few dispute the nostalgic appeal of Flora Thompson's picture of rural England during the 1880s and 1890s. Lark Rise and Candleford Green are tiny remote villages much like the Oxfordshire hamlet where Thompson (1876–1947) lived. She captures village life with fondness and humor, but without sentimentality. The trilogy was collected in one volume under the title *Lark Rise to Candleford* (Oxford, 1945). An abridged illustrated version, *The Illustrated Lark Rise to Candleford* (Crown, 1983), was a best-seller in England.

1. *Lark Rise* (Oxford, 1939)
   Laura, daughter of the village stonemason, grows up in tiny, remote Lark Rise in the 1880s.
2. *Over to Candleford* (Oxford, 1941)
   Miss Lane takes over her father's blacksmithing business, and becomes the village postmistress.
3. *Candleford Green* (Oxford, 1943)
   Laura moves to the market town of Candleford Green as assistant to postmistress Miss Lane.
4. *Still Glides the Stream* (Oxford, 1948)
   This posthumously published volume tells of schoolmistress Charity Finch's return to the village of her birth.

Thomson, June

Agatha Christie fans will enjoy this highly praised detective series by a British author who writes clever and bloodless mysteries in the traditional English manner. Her Inspector Rudd is a mellow, middle-aged, and middle-class chap who lives with his sister in Essex, where he is the local Criminal Investigation Department (CID) officer. His deliberately casual, gossipy method of interrogation and acute psychological assessments enable him to get to the bottom of each interesting case with a minimum of fuss but a full measure of reading pleasure. Inspector Rudd goes under the name of Inspector Finch in the English editions of this series.

1. *Not One of Us* (Harper, 1971)
   When a small-town girl is murdered, a stranger is automatically suspected of the crime.
2. *The Long Revenge* (Doubleday, 1975)
   Rudd takes on a special assignment to protect a retired British spy and finds himself in the strange, shadowy world of espionage.
3. *Case Closed* (Doubleday, 1977)
   Rudd investigates the murder of a girl four years earlier after new evidence has reopened the case.
4. *Death Cap* (Doubleday, 1977)
   Somebody has slipped Rene King a batch of deadly poisonous mushrooms.
5. *A Question of Identity* (Doubleday, 1977)
   When some archaeologists turn up a fresh corpse, Inspector Rudd must investigate.
6. *The Habit of Loving* (Doubleday, 1979)
   When a shy young man passes through a quiet village on a summer holiday, a puzzling murder results. English title: *Deadly Relations.*
7. *Alibi in Time* (Doubleday, 1980)
   When the battered body of writer Patrick Vaughan is discovered by the roadside, Rudd suspects murder.
8. *Shadow of a Doubt* (Doubleday, 1982)
   Claire Jordan, victimized wife of London psychiatrist Howard Jordan, disappears from her husband's clinic.
9. *Portrait of Lilith* (Doubleday, 1983)
   Elderly, disabled artist Max Gifford has a fixation on portraits he made of a woman called Lilith. English title: *To Make a Killing.*

10. *Sound Evidence* (Doubleday, 1985)
An old chess player may have seen the killer of a young homosexual.

Tilton, Alice (pseud. of Phoebe Atwood Taylor, q.v.)

Under the pseudonym of Alice Tilton, Taylor wrote the mysteries starring Leonidas Witherall, whose marked resemblance to Shakespeare earned him the nickname "Bill" during his teaching days at Meredith's Boy's School. In his retirement, he fills his days with travel, amateur sleuthing, and writing his Lieutenant Hazeltine mystery stories on the sly. He makes his home in Dalton, Massachusetts, which bears a distinct resemblance to Taylor's Newton home. Mystery is secondary to comedy in these books, though some readers find them arch and dated.

1. *Beginning with a Bash* (Norton, 1937)
Leonidas Witherall solves the murder of a professor in a bookstore and clears a former student of his, whose behavior is very suspicious.
2. *The Cut Direct* (Norton, 1938)
Witherall wakes up in a strange house to find himself confronted with a corpse. Witherall's inheritance comes to him in this book.
3. *Cold Steal* (Norton, 1939)
Returning from abroad to his new house in Dalton, Witherall investigates some funny doings on the train, and the mystery follows him home.
4. *The Left Leg* (Norton, 1940)
This very funny case involves a corpse minus a left leg and a woman in a scarlet wimple, who becomes known, naturally, as the scarlet wimpernel.
5. *The Hollow Chest* (Norton, 1941)
A murdered VIP and a fickle kidnapper create havoc at Meredith's Academy's Fifth Form Egg Day, when Witherall lends a hand.
6. *File for Record* (Norton, 1943)
Witherall goes in search of a lost umbrella and finds himself mixed up in car stealing and murder in wartime Dalton.
7. *Dead Ernest* (Norton, 1944)
Two drunken truckmen leave a freezer containing a leg of lamb,

some fillets of haddock, and a human corpse in Witherall's kitchen.

8. *The Iron Clew* (Farrar, 1947)

An innocent-looking package wrapped in brown paper leads Witherall to Balderston Hall, a house that resembles a wedding cake. English title: *The Iron Hand*.

Toland, John

Pulitzer Prize–winning historian John Toland (*The Rising Sun*) has had a special interest in Japan and World War II. This interest is expressed in his two volumes of fiction as well as in his nonfiction. This pair of novels tells about the fortunes of two families related by marriage, the American McGlynns and the Japanese Todas, from the period just before Pearl Harbor to the aftermath of World War II. The interest of the novels lies more with Toland's detailed and accurate rendering of historical events, especially from the Japanese point of view, rather than with the lives and loves of the fictional McGlynns and Todas.

1. *Gods of War* (Doubleday, 1985)

Members of the McGlynn and Toda families see action of various kinds on their respective sides during World War II.

2. *Occupation* (Doubleday, 1987)

The McGlynns and Todas continue their varying roles during the occupation of Japan and the war-crimes trials of Japanese leaders.

Tolkien, J. R. R. (John Ronald Reuel)

Oxford professor J. R. R. Tolkien's interest in philology led him to devise an elaborate "Elvish" language and then to create the richly imagined world of Middle Earth, where his language could be spoken. *The Hobbit* (Houghton, 1938), a fantasy for children, was the first book to be set in Middle Earth. Its story about Bilbo Baggins's adventures precedes the adult trilogy. Young Frodo Baggins, who inherits the magic ring from his uncle Bilbo, is the star of The Lord of the Rings trilogy. Frodo's struggle to prevent the powers of darkness from claiming the ring illustrates the works' central theme: the corruption of power. The posthumously published *Silmarillion* (Houghton, 1977) contains stories of Middle

Earth's First Age and two stories set in the Third Age of the Lord of the Rings trilogy. Additional poems, songs, and tales related to the trilogy are contained in *The Adventures of Tom Bombadil* (Houghton, 1962); *The Road Goes Ever On* (Houghton, 1967); *Unfinished Tales of Numenor and Middle Earth* (Houghton, 1980); and *The Book of Lost Tales*, 2 volumes (Houghton, 1984). Tolkien enthusiasts will want to check out guides to Middle Earth such as Robert Foster's *Guide to Middle Earth* (Ballantine, 1971); J. E. A. Tyler's *Tolkien Companion* (St. Martin's, 1976); and Karen Wynn Fonstad's *The Atlas of Middle Earth* (Houghton, 1981).

1. *The Fellowship of the Ring* (Houghton, 1954)
   Frodo goes on the first leg of his journey and encounters elves, dwarves, men, and other strange beings.
2. *The Two Towers* (Houghton, 1954)
   The Companions of the Ring, separated, cross the Dead Marshes and prepare for the Great War.
3. *The Return of the King* (Houghton, 1956)
   The forces of evil are defeated in the War of the Rings, and Frodo and Sam bear the Ring to Mount Doom.

Tolstoy, Leo

The 1852 publication of Tolstoy's first novel, the highly autobiographical *Childhood*, won him recognition as a promising young writer. Though he later claimed to dislike the book and its sequels, the trilogy ranks high as a sensitive portrait of childhood and a vivid picture of Russian family life. The moral and egalitarian concerns characteristic of Tolstoy's later fiction are nascent in these early works. Tolstoy never wrote the fourth book he originally projected in this series, which he planned to entitle Four Epochs of Growth. The three existing books are available in an omnibus volume, *Childhood, Boyhood and Youth* (Dutton, 1912), which was translated from the Russian by Leo Wiener.

1. *Childhood* (Crowell, 1886)
   The young narrator, Nicholas Irtenyev, tells of his life from the age of ten, when he and his older brother leave the family's estate to reside with their father in Moscow. First published in Russia in 1852.

453

2. *Boyhood* (Crowell, 1886)

After their mother's death, Nikki's sisters join the boys in Moscow, and the family group is preoccupied with young love, school, and growing self-knowledge. First published in Russia in 1854.

3. *Youth* (Crowell, 1886)

Nikki's concerns from his sixteenth year to the end of his university days include his father's remarriage and his own friendships and romances. First published in Russia in 1857.

Tranter, Nigel

This trilogy details the rise of power of Robert the Bruce, who became Scotland's King Robert I and in 1314 won the decisive Battle of Bannockburn, which rid the Scots of English kings. Tranter recreates this fascinating chapter in Scottish history with a full measure of realism— these were bloody and brutal times—but with some tender moments of romance and domesticity that usually focus on Robert's beautiful and spirited wife, Elizabeth de Burgh.

1. *Robert the Bruce: The Steps to the Empty Throne* (St. Martin's, 1969)

This account begins in 1296, when Edward I removed John Baliol as Scotland's ruler, and ends in 1306, when Robert killed John Comyn at Dumfries castle and claimed the throne.

2. *Robert the Bruce: The Path of the Hero King* (St. Martin's, 1972)

In 1306, Robert is defeated in battle after claiming the Scottish throne but recoups in the Hebrides. The story is continued to his victory at Bannockburn in 1314.

3. *Robert the Bruce: The Price of the King's Peace* (St. Martin's, 1972)

The period covered here begins in 1314, when the captive Queen returns, and ends in 1328, when the Treaty of Edinburgh is signed by a dying King Robert.

Traven, B.

This novelist's best-known work, *The Treasure of the Sierra Madre* (Knopf, 1943), was memorably filmed in 1948, with Humphrey Bogart starring as one of three greedy prospectors in search of a lost Mexican gold mine. The six Jungle novels, sometimes called the *Coaba* or Mahogany Cycle, are also set in Mexico. They show how terribly the Indians and the mahogany forests were exploited by capitalists, and the inevitable rebellion such inhumanity and greed provoked. B. Traven was deliberately mysterious about his identity. For a good summary of the problem presented by this pseudonymous author who claimed to be an American, wrote in German, and lived in Mexico, see Michael Baumann's *B. Traven: An Introduction* (Univ. of New Mexico Pr., 1967) or Will Wyatt's *The Secret of the Sierra Madre: The Man Who Was B. Traven* (Doubleday, 1980).

1. *The Caretta* (Hill & Wang, 1970)
   Set in the Chiapas region of southern Mexico in the time of Porfirio Diaz's dictatorship (before 1910), this book shows the plight of the poor peon—more slave than peasant—through the story of Andreu Ugaldo, an oxcart driver. First published in Germany in 1931.
2. *The Government* (Hill & Wang, 1971)
   The Mexican government, whose entrepreneurs like Don Gabriel Ordunez profit from mistreating poor workers, is contrasted with the more egalitarian government of an Indian tribe. First published in Germany in 1931.
3. *March to the Monteria* (Hill & Wang, 1971)
   Andreu Ugaldo journeys through the jungle to the labor camp on the mahogany plantation. First published in Germany in 1933.
4. *Die Troza* (published in Germany in 1936)
   This volume, which was apparently never translated into English, shows life on the mahogany plantation and the grueling work of cutting down the trees with axes. Trozas are mahogany logs cut to standard one-ton size.
5. *The Rebellion of the Hanged* (Hill & Wang, 1952)
   Violence breaks out among the Indian workers, and they learn to fight for their own interests, leaving the plantation. First published in Germany in 1936.
6. *General from the Jungle* (Hill & Wang, 1972)
   The little army of rebels skirmishes with the government forces, bringing up the rear guard of the revolution. First published in Germany in 1940.

Treece, Henry

Treece was an English poet and novelist with a talent for reconstructing ancient Celtic Britain and an ability to draw readers into the plausible primitive psychology of his characters. The four loosely connected novels listed below range in time from the Bronze Age to the sixth century A.D. Treece's unromanticized version of the King Arthur legend in *The Great Captains* makes an interesting contrast to the accounts of Mary Stewart (q.v.) and T. H. White (q.v.).

1. *The Golden Strangers* (Random, 1957)
   Four thousand years ago, fair-haired Aryan people armed with metal tools triumph over the dark Neanderthal tribes who live in southern England.
2. *The Dark Island* (Random, 1953)
   In the first century A.D., Roman imperial forces with their invincible elephants conquer the Celtic tribe led by Caradoc.
3. *Red Queen, White Queen* (Random, 1958)
   Boadicea's rebellion, around A.D. 60, is seen through the eyes of the Roman soldier Gemellus, who has been dispatched with his Celtic half-brother Duatha to kill the queen.
4. *The Great Captains* (Random, 1956)
   King Arthur appears as Artos the Bear, a rough figure in this history of sixth-century Britain.

Trevanian

Trevanian is the pseudonym of an American professor of English who captured an immediate following with his two books about the homicidal and amorous adventures of Dr. Jonathan Hemlock, art professor and secret assassin. Hemlock was rescued from an underprivileged childhood by a wealthy spinster, and his innate discrimination has won him professional eminence but not the wealth to support his tastes. His other inborn trait, a shocking deficiency in conscience revealed by army testing, brings him lucrative free-lance assignments from the mysterious albino Yurasis Dragon, head of CII, a counterespionage agency. A fair amount of grisly detail is sprinkled throughout these ironic and suspenseful entertainments. The film of *The Eiger Sanction* (1975) was a starring vehicle for Clint Eastwood.

1. *The Eiger Sanction* (Crown, 1972)
   Revenge prompts Hemlock to accept a hazardous sanction (assassination) assignment, which tests his mountain-climbing skills and brings him the companionship of the tantalizing Jemima Brown.

2. *The Loo Sanction* (Crown, 1973)

Amazing Grace, a black bombshell, and the green-eyed Irish beauty Maggie aid and abet Hemlock as he wrests incriminating films of high-ranking British government officials from a perverse underworld figure.

Trollope, Anthony

I. Trollope's popularity declined sharply after his death in 1882, partly because a posthumously published autobiography scandalized readers by revealing his frankly commercial attitude toward writing. Yet some of his books remained available and in high regard; in 1932, Virginia Woolf called *The Small House at Allington* one of the two perfect English novels (the other being *Pride and Prejudice*). Today, after a boost from the masterly BBC dramatization of the Pallisers in 1974, Trollope is one of the most widely read Victorian novelists, and modern readers are discovering the joys of adjusting to the leisurely style and humor of his solidly satisfying characters and stories. Even occasional Trollope readers will want to browse through Michael Hardwick's informative and entertaining *Guide to Anthony Trollope* (Scribner, 1974).

Trollope's first and best-known series, the *Chronicles of Barsetshire* grew out of its successful first novel, and was written sporadically over a period of 14 years. As was customary with novels of the day, most of these were serialized in magazines before taking book form. Dates and publishers listed below are for the first English monographs. Trollope began appearing in the United States in the 1890s. See also the entry under Angela Thirkell for stories about Barsetshire's modern-day residents.

1. *The Warden* (Longman, London, 1855)

This book concerns Eleanor Harding and her father Septimus, a gentle and innocent old cleric who is accused of profiting unduly from his sinecure as the warden of an almshouse for twelve old men. The cathedral town of Salisbury is thought to have been the model for Barchester.

2. *Barchester Towers* (Longman, London, 1857)

Thomas Proudie, an insignificant man with a domineering wife, is appointed the new bishop, and Eleanor Harding, newly widowed, is courted by several suitors.

3. *Dr. Thorne* (Chapman & Hall, London, 1858)
   Dr. Thorne faces a series of moral dilemmas as his ward Mary's love for Frank Gresham grows.
4. *Framley Parsonage* (Smith & Elder, London, 1861)
   Brother and sister Mark and Lucy Robarts both displease Lady Lufton of Framley Court, but for different reasons. Dr. Thorne appears again in this volume, as do several characters from the Palliser books, including the Duke of Omnium.
5. *The Small House at Allington* (Smith & Elder, London, 1864)
   Trollope did not consider this gem a part of the Barsetshire series, but it was included by his publishers in the 1879 omnibus edition and has been counted in the series ever since. It concerns a jilted maiden, Lily Dale, who lives with her widowed mother and sister at the Little House. Several characters from the Palliser novels make brief appearances in this volume too.
6. *The Last Chronicle of Barset* (Chapman & Hall, London, 1867)
   Mrs. Proudie persecutes the poor Reverend Josiah Crawley of Hogglestock, who is accused of theft.

II. The Palliser novels, also known as the Parliamentary novels, were conceived by Trollope as a series that would show the destinies of certain characters closely interwoven into a tapestry depicting the faults, frailties, and vices as well as the virtues, graces, and strengths of the upper classes in both the political and social spheres. A one-volume abridgement, *The Pallisers* (Coward, 1974), was issued at the time of Masterpiece Theatre's airing of the splendid BBC dramatization of the series.

1. *Can You Forgive Her?* (Chapman & Hall, London, 1864)
   Lady Glencora, a vivacious Scottish heiress married to dry and politically preoccupied Plantagenet Palliser, is tempted to run off with her first love.
2. *Phineas Finn* (James Virtue, London, 1869)
   The leading characters of this story are Phineas Finn, a young Irishman entering London society, and the women in his life: his childhood sweetheart; his first advisor, Lady Laura Standish; and the rich widow Marie Goesler.
3. *The Eustace Diamonds* (Chapman & Hall, London, 1872)
   The pretty schemer, Lizzie Greystock, who is Sir Florian's widow, plays a part in the theft of the Eustace diamonds.

4. *Phineas Redux* (Chapman & Hall, London, 1873)
   Phineas Finn, back from Ireland, raises Laura's hopes, gets entangled in a murder trial, and is saved by Marie Goesler.
5. *The Prime Minister* (Chapman & Hall, London, 1876)
   Glencora uses all her talents to help Plantagenet, now duke of Omnium, become prime minister, but she finally goes too far.
6. *The Duke's Children* (Chapman & Hall, London, 1880)
   Plantagenet copes with Silverbridge and Gerald, who misbehave at school and run up debts, while Mary seems determined to marry unsuitably.

Troyat, Henri (pseud. of Lev Tarassoff)

I. Troyat's biographies, especially his masterful *Tolstoy* (Doubleday, 1967) have overshadowed his fiction, but this five-novel series, The Seed and the Fruit, is a delightful family chronicle of French life not to be missed. Though born in Russia, Troyat spent his youth in France. He has caught the special Gallic flavor which pervades these books. The story begins with young Amelie's coming of age in 1912 and ends as her daughter Elizabeth sees France liberated in 1944.

1. *Amelie in Love* (Simon & Schuster, 1956)
   Shy and innocent at seventeen, young Amelie is courted by Jean, a local boy, until Pierre comes to capture her heart. Translated from the French by Lily Duplaix.
2. *Amelie and Pierre* (Simon & Schuster, 1957)
   Amelie runs the cafe very successfully, while Pierre serves in the army and eventually returns home injured. Translated from the French by Mary V. Dodge.
3. *Elizabeth* (Simon & Schuster, 1959)
   Elizabeth, the ten-year-old daughter of Amelie and Pierre, goes to convent school and stays with cousins in the country. Translated from the French by Nicholas Monjo.
4. *Tender and Violent Elizabeth* (Simon & Schuster, 1960)
   At nineteen, Elizabeth is torn between the sensual and violent Christian and the gentle and loving Patrice. Translated from the French by Mildred Marmur.

5. *The Encounter* (Simon & Schuster, 1962)
   Elizabeth runs her shop alone in German-occupied Paris, and she meets the widowed Boris, a character who also appears in *Strangers on Earth*, listed below. Translated from the French by Gerard Hopkins.

II. Troyat's understanding of Russian character is shown in this trilogy entitled While the Earth Endures, which depicts the effects of the Russian Revolution on an upper-class family, presumably like his own, who became exiles in Paris.

1. *My Father's House* (Duell, 1951)
   The story of a love triangle between Tania and Michael Danov and their best friend, Volodia, covers the years from 1888 to 1914. Translated from the Russian by David Hapgood.
2. *The Red and the White* (Crowell, 1957)
   The Revolution affects the Danov family in various ways; their responses range from idealistic support to ardent Czarist loyalties. Variant title: *Sackcloth and Ashes*. Translated from the Russian by Anthony Hinton.
3. *Strangers on Earth* (Crowell, 1958)
   The Danov family, exiled in Paris during the 1920s and 1930s, adjust and become reconciled to their new circumstances. Translated from the Russian by Anthony Hinton.

Twain, Mark (pseud. of Samuel Clemens)

As Twain's preface to *The Adventures of Tom Sawyer* made clear, he intended the book for adult readers as well as for youngsters, in the hope that it would remind them of how they once felt and thought and of what "queer enterprises" they sometimes engaged in. The book's insight into the young mind is still as valid as its humor and adventure are fresh and exciting, though the two Sawyer sequels are disappointing addenda. All four titles listed below are included in the two-volume *Complete Novels of Mark Twain* (Doubleday, 1962).

1. *The Adventures of Tom Sawyer* (American, 1876)
   The adventures of the two friends Tom Sawyer and Huck Finn begin when they witness a murder late one night in the cemetery, and the story concludes with their discovery of hidden treasure.

2. *The Adventures of Huckleberry Finn* (Webster, 1885)
   Tom plays a role in this companion piece in which Huck decides to run away from his drunken father, and meets up with the runaway slave Jim, after which the two of them float down the Mississippi on a raft.
3. *Tom Sawyer Abroad* (Webster, 1894)
   This short novel narrated by Huck shows Tom, Jim, and Huck traveling by balloon to Egypt and fantastical adventures.
4. *Tom Sawyer, Detective* (Harper, 1896)
   Another short sequel narrated by Huck has Tom solving a case of mixed-up brothers and diamond theft.

Uhnak, Dorothy

New York City police detective Christie Opara, a slender, twenty-six-year-old blond, lives with her son Mickey and her mother-in-law in a quiet Queens neighborhood. Her husband, a policeman, was killed in the line of duty. The occasional hint of romance between Christie and her boss, Casey Reardon, has never developed into anything more. Uhnak, herself a policewoman for many years, writes with authority. She has not used Christie in her most recent novels.

1. *The Bait* (Simon & Schuster, 1968)
   Christie plays a dangerous game when she sets herself up as the next victim in order to catch a mad killer who preys on young women.
2. *The Witness* (Simon & Schuster, 1969)
   Christie is the only witness to the murder of a young, black civil rights leader, and only she can clear the policeman wrongly accused of the crime.
3. *The Ledger* (Simon & Schuster, 1970)
   Christie must gain the confidence of the beautiful mistress of a drug-ring leader in order to locate his secret ledger.

Undset, Sigrid

I. Winner of the Nobel Prize in 1928, Sigrid Undset produced epics of medieval Norway that show a primitive and feudal society only partially restrained by church and civil law. Her books offer an intimate picture of fourteenth-century family life and culture and breathtaking glimpses of Norway's natural beauty. Undset's strong Catholic and moral views are expressed through her characters' religious conflicts and the anguish they suffer for their sexual transgressions. The universality of her themes of loyalty, responsibility, and faith give her books a timeless quality and continuing appeal, especially for Catholic readers. Available in an omnibus, *Kristin Lavransdatter* (Knopf, 1929), the work was originally published in three separate volumes.

1. *The Bridal Wreath* (Knopf, 1923)
   This introduces the headstrong young Kristin, oldest daughter of Lavrans Björgulfssön, a prosperous landowner of the Gudbrandsdal region. Kristin dishonors her family when she spurns her betrothed for her true love Erlend. English title: *The Garland*. Translated from the Norwegian by Charles Archer and J. S. Scott.
2. *The Mistress of Husaby* (Knopf, 1925)
   A repentant Kristin proves a good manager of Erlend's family estate at Husaby, and eventually they have seven sons, but Erlend gets involved in a treasonous plot. Translated from the Norwegian by Charles Archer and J. S. Scott.
3. *The Cross* (Knopf, 1927)
   With Erlend's lands forfeited, the family moves to the home Kristin inherited at her parents' death, but unhappiness and eventual tragedy follow them. Translated from the Norwegian by Charles Archer and J. S. Scott.

II. Those who enjoyed *Kristin Lavransdatter* will want to go on to read Undset's second medieval Norwegian saga, about the ill-starred lovers Olav and Ingunn. Originally published in Norway in two volumes (*Olav Audunssön I Hestviken* and *Olav Audunssön og Hans Börn*) and in the United States in the four volumes listed below, the complete work is also available in an omnibus edition under the title *The Master of Hestviken* (Knopf, 1942)

1. *The Ax* (Knopf, 1928)
   Olav and Ingunn, raised together as children, are torn apart by violent and tragic events. Translated from the Norwegian by Arthur G. Chater.
2. *The Snake Pit* (Knopf, 1929)
   The couple are reunited at Olav's family estate in Hestviken, but

462

true happiness still eludes them. Translated from the Norwegian by Arthur G. Chater.

3. *In the Wilderness* (Knopf, 1929)

    After Ingunn's death, Olav raises little Eirik and Cecelia and travels to England. Translated from the Norwegian by Arthur G. Chater.

4. *The Son Avenger* (Knopf, 1930)

    Cecelia marries, and Eirik seems destined for the church. Translated from the Norwegian by Arthur G. Chater.

Updike, John

One of the most highly regarded contemporary American novelists, Updike attempts to catch the quintessential American male in his portrait of Harry "Rabbit" Angstrom. After the glory of his high school days as a basketball hero in a small town in Pennsylvania, Rabbit seems unable to find satisfaction in the responsibilities of the adult world. Lacking the self-knowledge to understand his feelings of meaninglessness, Rabbit's sporadic attempts to escape only make matters worse. In the two sequels, Updike shows Rabbit growing older if not wiser.

1. *Rabbit, Run* (Knopf, 1960)

    At twenty-six, Rabbit leaves his pregnant wife, lives for a while with a prostitute, then returns after tragedy strikes.

2. *Rabbit Redux* (Knopf, 1971)

    Ten years later, Rabbit is a conservative suburbanite, abandoned by his wife and confronting drugs and black power in the radical sixties.

3. *Rabbit Is Rich* (Knopf, 1981)

    Rabbit, now forty-six and paunchy, runs the Toyota dealership he inherited from his wife's family, fights with his son Nelson, and searches for his illegitimate daughter.

Upfield, Arthur

The immense and primitive Australian outback pervades these detective stories starring Inspector Napoleon Bonaparte of the Queensland Police. Rescued from the bush, where he lay beside his dead mother, "Bony" was raised at a mission school and went on to Brisbane University. His uncanny ability to track miscreants through the rough outback country may be attributed to his part-aborigine heritage, but his ego and deductive powers come straight from Sherlock Holmes. Fans of *The Thorn Birds* who like mysteries might give these a try.

1. *Lure of the Bush* (Doubleday, 1965)
   Trouble for prosperous New South Wales landowner John Thornton begins when King Henry, an aborigine chief, is found murdered on his land. First published in England in 1928 as *The Barakee Mystery.*
2. *Sands of Windee* (Hutchinson, London, 1931)
   Bony proves that a murder took place at a bush station in New South Wales when others see no evidence of crime. This book became an exhibit and Upfield a witness in the trial of a man who patterned a real murder on it after reading Upfield's manuscript.
3. *Wings above the Claypan* (Doubleday, 1943)
   Bony gets help from an ancient tribal chieftain to solve this case of a drugged and paralyzed young girl found in a stolen airplane. Variant titles: *The Winged Mystery* and *Wings above the Diamantina.*
4. *Mr. Jelly's Business* (Doubleday, 1943)
   In this case, which introduced Upfield to U.S. readers, Bony helps a policeman friend solve a missing-person case and runs across another mystery as well. Variant title: *Murder Down Under.*
5. *Winds of Evil* (Doubleday, 1944)
   A sandstorm has obliterated all clues to the two murders Bony must solve.
6. *Bone Is Pointed* (Doubleday, 1947)
   Black magic almost does Bony in as he investigates the disappearance and probable death of a white man hated by the local aborigines.
7. *Mystery of Swordfish Reef* (Doubleday, 1943)
   Bony learns the fine arts of swordfishing as he investigates the disappearance of a fishing party.
8. *No Footprints in the Bush* (Doubleday, 1944)
   One policeman has already lost his life while investigating two murdered stockmen on Donald MacPherson's cattle station, and Bony himself narrowly escapes. Variant title: *Bushranger of the Skies.*
9. *Death of a Swagman* (Doubleday, 1945)
   Bony reopens a two-year-old case of the murder of an itinerant worker, called a swagman in Australia.
10. *Devil's Steps* (Doubleday, 1946)

An army intelligence assignment for Bony gets him involved in secret documents and sudden death in Melbourne.

11. *An Author Bites the Dust* (Doubleday, 1948)
Bony's jaundiced view of the Melbourne literary crowd shows as he investigates the death of writer Merwyn Blake.

12. *The Mountains Have a Secret* (Doubleday, 1948)
Two missing hitchhikers and a dead detective lead Bony to the closely guarded sheep ranch of Carl Benson.

13. *The Bachelors of Broken Hill* (Doubleday, 1950)
Someone has been dropping cyanide into the drinks of aging bachelors in the mining town of Broken Hill.

14. *The Widows of Broome* (Doubleday, 1950)
Two rich widows are strangled in a lonely town on the tropical northwest coast of Australia.

15. *The New Shoe* (Doubleday, 1952)
Bony investigates a corpse found entombed in the walls of a lighthouse. Variant title: *The Clue of the New Shoe.*

16. *Venom House* (Doubleday, 1952)
The two hateful Ainsworth sisters and their lunatic brother are the central figures of this case.

17. *Murder Must Wait* (Doubleday, 1953)
Bony helps the local police in Mitford, New South Wales, solve a puzzling case of the apparent theft of five babies.

18. *Death of a Lake* (Doubleday, 1954)
As the water of Lake Otway recedes during a severe drought, tensions mount among the local residents who expect a dead body to surface.

19. *Sinister Stones* (Doubleday, 1954)
Aborigine justice clashes with the law in this case of the murder of Constable Stenhouse. English title: *Cake in the Hatbox.*

20. *Battling Prophet* (Heineman, London, 1956)
Bony is called in to investigate the mysterious death of a weather prophet.

21. *Man of Two Tribes* (Doubleday, 1956)
A little dog and two wily camels help Bony search for an acquitted murderess involved in some atomic-secret business.

22. *The Bushman Who Came Back* (Doubleday, 1957)
Only Bony can save the kidnapped child of a murdered woman. Variant title: *Bony Buys a Woman.*

23. *Bony and the Black Virgin* (Heineman, London, 1959)
Very similar in plot to *The Lure of the Bush,* this novel has a theme of miscegenation and a setting in a remote outpost in New South Wales.

24. *Journey to the Hangman* (Doubleday, 1959)
    Three brutal murders in the remote west Australian village of Daybreak challenge Bony's detective skills as relations grow tense between the white and aborigine populations. English title: *Bony and the Mouse.*

25. *Valley of Smugglers* (Doubleday, 1960)
    Bony poses as a horse thief in order to investigate an Irish enclave in New South Wales. English title: *Bony and the Kelly Gang.*

26. *The White Savage* (Doubleday, 1961)
    Bony poses as stationmaster Nat Bonner as he patiently sniffs out a rapist-murderer being protected by his family. English title: *Bony and the White Savage.*

27. *The Will of the Tribe* (Doubleday, 1962)
    Inspector Bonaparte finds both whites and aborigines strangely unhelpful while he investigates a body found in a desert meteor crater.

28. *The Body at Madman's Bend* (Doubleday, 1963)
    Anybody might have murdered the drunk and violent William Lush, but suspicion falls on his pretty stepdaughter, Jill Madden. English title: *Madman's Bend.*

29. *Lake Frome Monster* (Heineman, London, 1966)
    This last episode was completed by Mrs. Upfield after the author's death. It concerns the sudden death of a roving photographer and something in the lake that frightens the natives.

Valin, Jonathan

Harry Stoner is a decidedly hard-boiled private eye who practices in Cincinnati. His investigations take place among middle-class middle Americans rather than the upper and lower extremes of West Coast society. True to type, Stoner's compassion for the underdog sometimes gets him in trouble. The novels are fast-paced and well-plotted, and at times, very grim and violent. Valin, a native of Cincinnati, does his hometown justice.

1. *The Lime Pit* (Dodd, 1980)
   Harry Stoner gets involved with the child pornography racket when an old man asks him to find his "little girl."

2. *Final Notice* (Dodd, 1980)
   The vandal who is mutilating books in the Cincinnati library may also be murdering young women.

3. *Dead Letter* (Dodd, 1981)
   Physics professor Daryl Lovingwell suspects his radical daughter of stealing secret documents from him.
4. *Day of Wrath* (Congdon, 1982)
   A fourteen-year-old girl disappears, and her boyfriend is the victim of a torture slaying.
5. *Natural Causes* (Congdon, 1983)
   A writer for a daytime soap opera sponsored by a Cincinnati businessman's firm dies suddenly and suspiciously in Hollywood.
6. *Life's Work* (Delacorte, 1986)
   Bill Parks, player for the Cincinnati Cougars football team, disappears after signing a lucrative contract.
7. *Fire Lake* (Delacorte, 1987)
   Old friend Lonnie Jackowsi signs into a Cincinnati motel under Harry Stoner's name, and attempts suicide.
8. *Extenuating Circumstances* (Delacorte, 1989)
   Stoner is skeptical when teenager Terry Carnova confesses to the murder of businessman Ira Lessing.

Van de Wettering, Janwillem

Van de Wettering's Amsterdam police novels are based on first-hand knowledge—the author has been a member of the Amsterdam Reserve Police since 1965. His continuing cast includes the stolid, hen-pecked Adjutant Grijpstra, the affable but dreamy and sensitive Sergeant de Gier, and the aged, arthritic, wise "Commissaria." Van de Wettering's unique injection of Zen Buddhist ideas and perspective into his mysteries gives them a special distinction. Van de Wettering spent a year in a Japanese monastery and five years with a Buddhist group in Maine, experiences which he describes in two autobiographical volumes, *The Empty Mirror* (Houghton, 1974) and *A Glimpse of Nothingness* (Houghton, 1975). For police novels about Amsterdam from a different perspective see Nicholas Freeling's Van der Valk series (q.v.).

1. *Outsider in Amsterdam* (Houghton, 1975)
   The suspects include narcotics pushers, the victim's insane mother, and his exotic Papuan wife, when the owner of a commune restaurant is left hanging.
2. *Tumbleweed* (Houghton, 1976)
   Witchcraft may be involved in the murder of a young woman from Curaçao.

3. *The Corpse on the Dike* (Houghton, 1976)
   Their investigation of the murder of Tom Wernekink leads de Gier and Grijpstra to Cat in Boots, leader of a band of thieves.
4. *Death of a Hawker* (Houghton, 1977)
   A street market vendor is found murdered in a locked room while Amsterdam is being torn by riots.
5. *The Japanese Corpse* (Houghton, 1977)
   The Japanese criminal organization, the Yakusa, may be responsible for murder, art theft, and heroin smuggling into Amsterdam.
6. *The Blond Baboon* (Houghton, 1978)
   A fatal tumble by Elaine Carnet, retired cabaret singer, may have been no accident.
7. *The Maine Massacre* (Houghton, 1979)
   The Commissaria and de Gier travel to Maine to help the former's sister, who has been widowed by a suspicious accident.
8. *The Mind-Murders* (Houghton, 1981)
   Grijpstra and de Gier have dark suspicions about a publisher's missing wife and a corpse that the coroner says died of natural causes.
9. *The Streetbird* (Putnam, 1983)
   De Gier sees a vulture, an unusual sight in Amsterdam's red light district, near the scene of a pimp's murder.
10. *The Rattle-Rat* (Pantheon, 1985)
    The murder of a sheep farmer from Friesland brings Grijpstra and de Gier to that Dutch province.
11. *Hard Rain* (Putnam, 1986)
    The police trio suspect that the sniper killing of banker Martin Ijsbreker and the heroin overdose deaths of three drug addicts are linked.

Van Dine, S. S. (pseud. of Willard Huntington Wright)

Like the early Ellery Queen, Philo Vance is an uppity young man whose languid erudition and aristocratic tastes make him a distant American cousin to Albert Campion and Peter Wimsey. Readers of the 1920s took to him immediately, and his successful translation into films starring William Powell and Basil Rathbone gave him enormous popularity. Van Dine/Wright, an editor at *Smart Set* before he turned to the detective story, was a bit of a poseur himself. His theory that any detective writer

had about "six good ideas in his system" was proved by his own work—
the later volumes show a decided falling off.

1. *The Benson Murder Case* (Scribner, 1926)
   Vance spots the murderer of wealthy Wall Street broker Alvin
   Benson quickly, but the New York district attorney and police
   force flounder badly.
2. *The Canary Murder Case* (Scribner, 1927)
   The "canary" is famous Broadway nightclub singer Margaret
   Odell, found strangled to death.
3. *The Greene Murder Case* (Scribner, 1928)
   The Greene family is being murdered one by one, and Vance uses
   all his knowledge of criminal psychology to solve this sinister
   case.
4. *The Bishop Murder Case* (Scribner, 1929)
   Mother Goose nursery rhymes seem to be inspiring a madman
   to murder.
5. *The Scarab Murder Case* (Scribner, 1930)
   An ancient Egyptian mystery gives Vance a clue to the murder of
   philanthropist Benjamin Kyle.
6. *The Kennel Murder Case* (Scribner, 1933)
   Archer Coe is found stabbed, shot, and battered, and Vance uses
   a scale model of his house to solve the crime.
7. *The Dragon Pool Murder* (Scribner, 1933)
   A man drowns in Mrs. Stamm's pond, called the Dragon Pool
   because of old Indian legends about lake monsters, and his body
   is never found.
8. *The Casino Murder Case* (Scribner, 1934)
   This story, which begins and ends in a gambling casino, is about
   the poisoning of three members of the Llewellyn family.
9. *The Kidnap Murder Case* (Scribner, 1936)
   Vance gets a chance to show his sharpshooting skill in the case of
   the kidnap and murder of Kaspar Kenting.
10. *The Garden Murder Case* (Scribner, 1938)
    The tension between Professor Garden and his nephew Woody,
    who bet the last of his fortune on a horse called Equanimity, turns
    into murder.
11. *The Gracie Allen Murder Case* (Scribner, 1938)
    Philo is assisted by George Burns's wife, the fey and funny radio
    comedienne Gracie Allen, in this case which brings Philo and
    friends the acquaintance of a highly cultured underworld charac-
    ter. Variant title: *The Smell of Murder.*

12. *The Winter Murder Case* (Scribner, 1939)
This spare last case was left in draft form at the author's death; some critics think it shows Philo to best advantage. The plot concerns a jewel theft at the Berkshire home of millionaire Tarrington Rexton.

Van Dyke, Henry

Not to be confused with an earlier Henry Van Dyke (1852–1933) who wrote popular inspirational books, this Henry Van Dyke, born in Michigan in 1928, is a talented black writer whose books have been widely praised. The two novels listed below are narrated by Oliver, a young black boy who sees through the pretensions and defenses of the adults around him.

1. *Ladies of the Rachmaninoff Eyes* (Farrar, 1965)
Etta Klein and her longtime Negro companion, Harriet Gibbs, bicker and fuss amusingly throughout the story, which focuses on Etta's attempts to contact her dead son through séances.
2. *Blood of Strawberries* (Farrar, 1969)
Now a debonair college student, Oliver spends a summer in New York City with his well-heeled bohemian friends Max and Tanja Rhodes, who are producing a Gertrude Stein play.

Varley, John

The Gaea trilogy is about mankind's first contact with intelligent extraterrestrial beings. Gaea, a wheel-shaped planetoid in orbit around Saturn, not only has sentient life forms, it *is* a sentient life form. The trilogy traces the changing relationship between Cirocco Jones, the earthwoman who commands the expedition to Gaea and Gaea herself, an immense fickle goddess. Varley's highly inventive plot and characters, and his feminist point of view give the books a special slant. Varley is an American science fiction writer who has won Hugo and Nebula awards for his shorter fiction.

1. *Titan* (Berkley, 1979)
An expedition from Earth is stranded on a three-million-year-old

world populated by singing centaurs, and ruled by the goddess Gaea.
2. *Wizard* (Berkley, 1980)
Twenty years later, two humans are sent on a quest through Gaea in order to receive the "miracles" promised by the goddess.
3. *Demon* (Putnam, 1984)
Cirocco Jones and her human and non-human allies battle the insane goddess for control of Gaea.

Verne, Jules

I. Jules Verne is often called one of the fathers of science fiction, especially of the "nuts and bolts" variety, with its emphasis on the machinery of the future. In this early pair of novels, Verne's unqualified enthusiasm for technological progress and his faith in its benevolence reflect the optimism characteristic of the nineteenth century.

1. *From the Earth to the Moon* (Newark Printing, 1869)
Michel Ardan, a Frenchman, joins two Americans on the first moon launch of a satellite named *Columbiad* that is shot from a huge gun. First published in France in 1863.
2. *Around the Moon* (George Munro, 1879)
The three astronauts, who were left stranded in moon orbit at the end of the last book, make a perilous return to earth. First published in France in 1869.

II. There is a good deal of Verne in the character of the megalomaniacal Captain Nemo, who steers his submarine *Nautilus* on its 20,000-league (about 60,000 miles) underwater journey. The memorable 1954 Disney film starred Kirk Douglas, James Mason, Peter Lorre, and others.

1. *Twenty Thousand Leagues under the Sea* (G. M. Smith, 1874)
The inscrutable Captain Nemo battles monsters of the deep and braves other perils of the undersea world. First published in France in 1870.
2. *The Mysterious Island* (Lovell, 1883)
Captain Nemo reappears in this story, a new twist on the Crusoe theme in which five men and a dog land mysteriously on an island. First published in France in 1874.

Veryan, Patricia (pseud. of Patricia V. Bannister)

I. Acknowledging Jeffrey Farnol and Georgette Heyer as her models, Patricia Veryan has written a series of Georgian novels of consistently high quality. The years 1811–1820, when the future George IV was still Prince Regent, have been called the "Age of Elegance" and have attracted many chroniclers. While Veryan aims for historical accuracy and period ambience, it is her well-told love stories that carry readers through each installment. Many continuing characters are sprinkled throughout the series, including a villainous French family, the Sanguinets, who plot to assassinate the Prince Regent and take over Britain.

1. *The Lord and the Gypsy* (Walker, 1978)
   Lucian St. Clair is too enamoured of a beautiful gypsy to settle down in a prearranged marriage after he returns from the Napoleonic Wars.
2. *Love's Duet* (Walker, 1979)
   Young Sophia Drayton is surprised to find that Camille, Marquis of Damon, whom she blames for the loss of her brother's arm, is very handsome, and seems to be hiding something behind his cold facade.
3. *Nanette* (Walker, 1981)
   Nanette escapes from her wealthy, wicked stepfather by disguising herself as her maid, and meets aristocratic Harry Redmond.
4. *Feather Castles* (St. Martin's, 1982)
   After Waterloo, Rachel Strand helps a handsome amnesiac to escape to England.
5. *Married Past Redemption* (St. Martin's, 1983)
   Rachel Strand's brother Justin marries Lisette Van Lindsay, who really loves Rachel's husband, Tristram Leith.
6. *The Noblest Frailty* (St. Martin's, 1983)
   Yolande Drummond has been promised to her handsome cousin Alain Devenish, but is strongly attracted to Craig Tyndale, newly arrived from Canada.
7. *Sanguinet's Crown* (St. Martin's, 1985)
   Rakish Mitchell Redmond and his lover are the only ones who can save the Prince Regent from the poisoned crown that Claude Sanguinet has sent to him.
8. *Give All to Love* (St. Martin's, 1987)
   Young Josie Storm tries to arouse the romantic interest of her guardian, Alain Devenish, as the Sanguinets plot to poison the Prince Regent.

II. For her next series, Veryan has chosen to re-create another dramatic period in the history of England and Scotland. The six Golden Chronicles are set in the period immediately following the Battle of Culloden (1746), when the forces of Bonnie Prince Charlie received a crushing defeat, and the Jacobite cause was lost. The plot of each novel revolves around a cipher that is the key to a treasure that the defeated Jacobites hope to smuggle to France. Each novel also contains a satisfying love story amid the intrigues of the Jacobites and their enemies.

1. *Practice to Deceive* (St. Martin's, 1985)
   Penelope Montgomery joins the Jacobite cause of Quentin Chandler, a fugitive after the Battle of Culloden.
2. *Journey to Enchantment* (St. Martin's, 1986)
   Prudence MacTavish joins forces with the mysterious Ligun Doone to help the Jacobite cause.
3. *The Tyrant* (St. Martin's, 1987)
   Wealthy bachelor Meredith Carruthers unwillingly aids his Jacobite friends by pretending to be betrothed to Phoebe Ramsay.
4. *Love Alters Not* (St. Martin's, 1988)
   Horatio Glendenning passes the treasure cipher to Miss Dimity Cranford, who gets involved in some adventures of her own.
5. *Cherished Enemy* (St. Martin's, 1988)
   Embittered against the Jacobites by her fiance's death at Culloden, Rosamund joins forces with the mysterious Dr. Robert Victor.
6. *The Dedicated Villain* (St. Martin's, 1989)
   Opportunistic Roland Mathieson loses his heart to Miss Fiona Bradford in the conclusion to the chronicles.

Vidal, Gore

Vidal has woven American history, politics, and journalism into a rich and satisfying tapestry in this series of five novels. Both fictional and historical characters move convincingly through his books as he shows the human motives, maneuvers, and failings behind historical events. Vidal's wit, polished prose, and suspenseful plotting have made these books popular with a wide audience. Vidal also has written detective stories under the pseudonym Edgar Box (q.v.).

1. *Burr* (Random, 1973)
   Charles Schuyler, a young law clerk and aspiring journalist in the 1830s, tells of his friendship with the aging Aaron Burr. The account is interspersed with sections purporting to be Burr's own early journals.
2. *Lincoln* (Random, 1984)
   The newly elected President Lincoln is held in light regard by Washington insiders, including William H. Seward, his Secretary of State.
3. *1876* (Random, 1976)
   Now a respected journalist in his sixties, Charlie Schuyler returns from Europe to America in its centennial year and is drawn into the politics of a presidential election.
4. *Empire* (Random, 1987)
   Young Blaise Stanford learns about journalism from William Randolph Hearst during the presidencies of William McKinley and Theodore Roosevelt.
5. *Washington, D.C.* (Random, 1967)
   Blaise Stanford, a ruthless newspaper tycoon, and his son Peter, a liberal editor, star in this volume set from the New Deal to the McCarthy years.

Vinge, Joan D.

American writer Vinge came to science fiction via anthropology, and her novels and stories show a concern with the cultures, both human and non-human, of the worlds she has created. Two such worlds are Tiamat, where Summer and Winter alternate every 150 years, and World's End, a harsh frontier with a Fire Lake that seems to produce madness in those who approach it. A firm scientific basis underlies Vinge's worlds, but it is the characterization and portrayal of alien cultures which sets her work apart. *The Snow Queen* won the 1981 Hugo Award, one of science fiction's highest honors.

1. *The Snow Queen* (Dial, 1980)
   The reign of Arienrhod, the Snow Queen of Tiamat's 150-year Winter, is nearing its end, but she hopes to extend her life through other Winters by cloning.
2. *World's End* (Bluejay, 1984)
   BZ Gundhalinu, having failed to win the love of Tiamat's prospec-

tive Summer Queen, finds himself on World's End, a harsh, barely inhabitable planet, searching for his treasure-hunting older brothers.

Wahlöö, Per

Per Wahlöö was half of the Swedish collaborative team that produced the Martin Beck series of detective stories, listed here under Sjöwall and Wahlöö. Working independently, he wrote two detective novels starring Chief Inspector Peter Jensen. They are dark, symbol-laden explorations of society and the nature of crime.

1. *The Thirty-First Floor* (Knopf, 1966)
   Though a bomb placed in the offices of a large publishing concern fails to go off, Chief Inspector Jensen is directed to catch the culprit in a week's time. Variant title: *Murder on the 31st Floor.* Translated from the Swedish by Joan Tate.
2. *The Steel Spring* (Delacorte, 1970)
   In this futuristic novel, Peter Jensen, who left his country under the rule of benevolent despots, returns to find corpses littering the streets and all services and communication cut off. Translated from the Swedish by Joan Tate.

Walker, David

The charming 1955 British movie *Wee Geordie* was based on Walker's first book about George MacTaggart of the Scottish village of Drumfechan. Embarrassed when his sweetheart, Jean, calls him "Wee Geordie," young George, at fourteen, embarks on a body-building program. After reaching a height of six feet, five inches and winning the shot-put event at the Boston Olympics, George returns to his Highland home to claim Jean's love. This is a good-humored *Rocky* story, set in a gentler time and place.

1. *Geordie* (Houghton, 1950)
   Young Geordie MacTaggart, ashamed of being shorter than his girlfriend Jean, trains and exercises his way to success.

2. *Come Back, Geordie* (Houghton, 1966)
   Geordie and his wife, Jean, worry about their son, Charlie, who seems to be turning into a discontented and aimless teenager.

Walpole, Hugh

Fans of Winston Graham's Poldark Saga (q.v.) should also enjoy Walpole's engaging adventures of the Herries family. Set in the picturesque lake country, these novels chronicle English history from Elizabethan times to the 1930s. *Rogue Herries*, the first of the series to be published, was a best-seller on both sides of the Atlantic and shows Walpole at the peak of his storytelling powers. Somerset Maugham's nasty caricature of Walpole as Alroy Kear in *Cakes and Ale* (1930) hurt Walpole personally and may have seriously damaged his reputation. Certainly his popularity has dropped sharply since his death in 1941. Perhaps it is time for a revival of these eminently readable novels.

1. *Bright Pavilions* (Doubleday, 1940)
   Set in Elizabethan England, this book tells the story of two Herries brothers: Robin, a dreamer, and Nicholas, a doer. This story was to have begun a second Herries tetralogy (the first consisting of numbers 2 to 5 below), but the next book, *Katherine Christian*, was left unfinished at this author's death.
2. *Rogue Herries* (Doubleday, 1930)
   The story of Francis "Rogue" Herries, an eighteenth-century gentleman, from his arrival in Cumberland in 1740 with wife, children, and mistress to his death in old age as his second gypsy wife bears him a child.
3. *Judith Paris* (Doubleday, 1931)
   This book traces the turbulent life and loves of Judith, the daughter of Francis Herries and his gypsy wife, from her birth in 1774.
4. *The Fortress* (Doubleday, 1932)
   Judith vies with Walter Herries and young Adam reaches manhood during the period 1822–74.
5. *Vanessa* (Doubleday, 1933)
   Vanessa, Judith's granddaughter, is a dreamer who makes a disastrous marriage. This account—and the tetralogy—ends in 1932.

Waltari, Mika

Finnish author Mika Waltari's epic historical novel, *The Egyptian* (Putnam, 1949) was an instant best-seller that Hollywood made into a successful film spectacular in 1954 starring Victor Mature, Peter Ustinov, and a host of other big names. Waltari next turned his talents to these two picaresque novels about the adventures of a young Finn in sixteenth-century Europe.

1. *The Adventurer* (Putnam, 1950)
   Michael the Finn is raised by a witch woman and educated by priests before he takes off for adventure in foreign lands. Translated from the Finnish by Naomi Walford.
2. *The Wanderer* (Putnam, 1951)
   Michael and his companion, Andy, are captured by Arab pirates and see North Africa and the Ottoman Empire in the days of Suleiman the Magnificent. Translated from the Finnish by Naomi Walford.

Warner, Rex

These two volumes of Julius Caesar's fictional memoirs will interest readers who enjoyed Masterpiece Theatre's production of "I, Claudius," which was based on the Robert Graves book (q.v.). British author Rex Warner has combined his skill as a poet with his scholar's knowledge of classical history to produce these solid and authentic documentary fictions.

1. *The Young Caesar* (Little, 1958)
   Caesar reminisces on his youth and rise to power.
2. *Imperial Caesar* (Little, 1960)
   Subjects covered include Caesar's military conquests, his affair with Cleopatra, and other activities of his last fifteen years.

Waugh, Evelyn

Readers whose interest in Waugh was reawakened by the airing of "Brideshead Revisited" on Masterpiece Theatre will find his World War

II trilogy similar in tone and appeal. Its central figure is thirty-five-year-old Guy Crouchback, an English Catholic of comfortable means, whose wife's desertion and lack of strong family ties has left him a lonely and rather cold person. Stirred by patriotism and a desire to participate meaningfully in a worthy cause, Guy enlists and eventually sees action with the Halberdier Regiment abroad. The one-volume omnibus edition entitled *Sword of Honor* (Little, 1966) incorporates some revisions.

1. *Men at Arms* (Little, 1952)
   After the boredom of training camp and duty in the English countryside, Guy's regiment is shipped to Dakar, where he finds himself leading an unauthorized night raid.
2. *Officers and Gentlemen* (Little, 1955)
   Guy is in London during the worst of the German bombing, then sees action in Crete, where his disillusionment and feelings of betrayal are complete.
3. *The End of the Battle* (Little, 1961)
   Amid the otherwise inane last years of Crouchback's military career, he aids a group of Jewish refugees and comes to his ex-wife's rescue. English title: *Unconditional Surrender*.

Webster, Jan

Glasgow and the nearby mining towns provide a solid background to this three-volume saga that follows the Balfour, Kilgour, and Fleming families from 1840 to the present day. Star-crossed lovers, philandering mine owners, passionate union organizers, and some extraordinarily feisty women figure in the interrelated plots that keep the reader moving right along.

1. *Colliers Row* (Lippincott, 1977)
   The story begins in 1840 as young Kate, pregnant and in disgrace, is dismissed from her job as housekeeper to the mine-owning Balfour family.
2. *Saturday City* (St. Martin's, 1979)
   This account follows the fortunes of Kate's children from 1880 to 1918 as Sandia opens a shop in Glasgow and Duncan fights to unionize the miners.
3. *Beggerman's Country* (St. Martin's, 1980)
   Wealthy Mairi Fleming marries a communist while her brother

Patie marries a beautiful aristocrat with Scots Nationalist sympathies.

Webster, Jean

Daddy-Long-Legs, a Cinderella story about a young orphan girl, has proven its perennial appeal. At least four film versions have been made of the book: Mary Pickford starred in the 1919 film; Janet Gaynor starred in the 1931 version: Shirley Temple starred in the 1935 adaptation titled *Curly Top;* and Fred Astaire and Leslie Caron starred in the 1955 musical version. The novels were written in a sprightly, epistolary style by an American author who died young.

1. *Daddy-Long-Legs* (Century, 1912)
   Judy Abbott, the oldest orphan at the John Grier Home, is sent to college by a mysterious benefactor to whom she writes entertainingly of her student days.
2. *Dear Enemy* (Century, 1915)
   Sallie MacBride, the new superintendent of the John Grier Home, writes of her work with the orphans to her friends, including Judy and Jervis Pendelton, and to the dour Scottish doctor who is the "Dear Enemy" of the title.

Weidman, Jerome

Less acerbic than Weidman's early works, such as *I Can Get It for You Wholesale* (Simon & Schuster, 1937), the Benny Kramer books are warm and humorous recollections of growing up Jewish on the Lower East Side in the 1920s and of the depression years spent "uptown" in the Bronx. These sharp and entertaining tales and portraits are thought to be highly autobiographical.

1. *Fourth Street East* (Random, 1970)
   Young Benny, innocent of the dangerous lowlife all around him, wends his way through the neighborhood and meets success at school.
2. *Last Respects* (Random, 1972)
   Benny at fourteen helps in his mother's bootlegging business.

479

3. *Tiffany Street* (Random, 1974)
   Benny, now a successful attorney, is plagued by feelings of inade-
   quacy; his reaction to his son's decision to become a conscientious objector is a central concern.

Wellman, Paul

All the conflicts of passion and ambition that keep TV viewers watching
"Dallas" are included in full measure in these readable novels set in
Jericho, Kansas. Wellman first described his fictional small midwestern
city in an earlier novel, *Bowl of Brass* (Lippincott, 1944). The Wedge
family, owner of Jericho's newspaper, the *Daily Clarion*, provides the
unifying focus for the trilogy listed below. Wellman draws effectively on
his own experience as a midwestern newspaperman.

1. *Walls of Jericho* (Doubleday, 1947)
   Tucker Wedge's new wife stirs up trouble when she comes to
   Jericho, and the friendship between Tucker and aspiring young
   politician Dave Constable is endangered.
2. *The Chain* (Doubleday, 1949)
   The Reverend John Carlisle, a man of conscience, brings social
   reform and hope to Jericho and finds some bitter resistance.
3. *Jericho's Daughter* (Doubleday, 1956)
   Murder and blackmail are elements in this story about Mary
   Agnes Wedge and her unfaithful husband.

West, Rebecca (pseud. of Cicily Isabel Fairfield)

Dame Rebecca West is perhaps best known as a literary critic and political journalist, but she also wrote fiction, including a three-volume family
saga tracing the fortunes of the Aubrey family from Edwardian times to
the years immediately following World War I. The Aubrey family is
based on West's family. Rose Aubrey, the books' narrator and central
character, is thought to be the autobiographical figure. The works are
conventional in form, strong on characterization and period flavor. The
last two volumes were published posthumously nearly thirty years after
the appearance of *The Fountain Overflows*. *Cousin Rosamund* was not

finished by West, but was fully outlined in the manuscripts she left. Much of West's earlier fiction has been reprinted by Virago Press.

1. *The Fountain Overflows* (Viking, 1956)
   The Aubrey family migrates from Edinburgh to London in the early 1900s, and is kept together by their strong-minded mother, Clare.
2. *This Real Night* (Viking, 1984)
   The Aubrey family has been abandoned by their father, but the children reach adolescence strongly motivated to pursue musical careers.
3. *Cousin Rosamund* (Viking, 1986)
   The Aubrey children have reached adulthood after World War I. Rose pursues a career as a professional pianist, and falls in love with a young composer.

Westlake, Donald

Westlake is a master of the funny "big caper" novel. His effervescence, humor, and unflagging inventiveness have drawn comparison to P. G. Wodehouse (q.v.). The six novels below star Westlake's most lovable criminal mastermind, John Dortmunder, and his band of inept heist men. The film of *The Hot Rock* (1972) starred George Segal and Robert Redford, while *Bank Shot* (1974) was filmed with George C. Scott in a starring role.

1. *The Hot Rock* (Simon & Schuster, 1970)
   The extraordinary John Dortmunder masterminds the theft of the Balambo emerald from an exhibit at New York's Coliseum.
2. *Bank Shot* (Simon & Schuster, 1972)
   Dortmunder returns with plans to steal a Long Island suburban bank—lock, stock, and barrel.
3. *Jimmy the Kid* (Lippincott, 1974)
   Using a tough, no-nonsense paperback thriller about a kidnapping as their guide, Dortmunder and his gang kidnap twelve-year-old Jimmy Harrington, and the fun begins.
4. *Nobody's Perfect* (Evans, 1977)
   Stolen paintings, a missing old master, and a hired assassin on Dortmunder's trail keep this installment lively.

5. *Why Me?* (Viking, 1983)

Dortmunder inadvertently comes into possession of a ring with a very large ruby hotly desired by numerous law enforcement officials, criminals, and terrorists.

6. *Good Behavior* (Mysterious, 1986)

Dortmunder drops in (through a skylight) on a group of nuns, and finds that they regard him as a godsend.

Wharton, Edith

I. The assignment of *Ethan Frome* to generations of high school English classes seems to have given American readers a permanent distaste for the fiction of Edith Wharton, not unreasonably. Readers willing to give her a second chance might find they enjoy these ironic vignettes of four decades of New York society collected under the title *Old New York*, originally published in four separate volumes, then in an omnibus edition by Scribner in 1952.

1. *False Dawn* (Appleton, 1924)

In the 1840s, New York art collector Lewis Raycie buys Giottos and Mantegnas and other unfashionable Italian primitives on his visits abroad.

2. *The Old Maid* (Appleton, 1924)

The story of Charlotte Lovell, an old maid with a secret, is set in the "complacent '50s."

3. *The Spark* (Appleton, 1924)

The story of Hayley Delane, a young soldier wounded at the battle of Bull Run, has several ironic twists.

4. *New Year's Day* (Appleton, 1924)

Hidden under the conventions of the 1870s lies the tragic heroism of Lizzie Hazeldean.

II. Reputed to be among Wharton's own favorites, these two later novels focus on Vance Weston, a young midwesterner who becomes a writer. Central to his artistic development is his relationship to young Halo Spear and "The Willows," her family home. Vance expresses many of Wharton's own ideas about the art of fiction.

1. *Hudson River Bracketed* (Appleton, 1929)

New worlds of culture open to Vance when he comes to visit his eastern relatives, meets Halo and Laura Lou, and marries the wrong one.

2. *The Gods Arrive* (Appleton, 1932)
   After his wife's death, Vance and Halo leave for Spain, where they both undergo artistic and emotional crises.

White, Antonia

Dial Press has performed a service in republishing this brilliant quartet of autobiographical novels by an English author who deserves to be better known. After the publication of *Frost in May* in 1933, Antonia White worked in advertising, as a free-lance journalist, and as a translator (of Colette, primarily), though plagued by bouts of mental illness. Then in 1950 she began writing fiction again, continuing the story of young Nanda—though changing her name—through a trilogy of novels. Together they form a vivid account of a young Catholic girl growing up amid complicated family relations.

1. *Frost in May* (Viking, 1934)
   In 1908, nine-year-old Nanda Grey's convert father takes her to the Lippington convent school; she stays until she is thirteen.
2. *The Lost Traveller* (Viking, 1950)
   Clara Batchelor (the same character as Nanda in all respects except name) attends a London school in 1914 as this book begins. The story continues through her disastrous short stint as a governess.
3. *The Sugar House* (Dial, 1981)
   Clara, now working as an actress in a small touring company, has her first love and a doomed first marriage. First published in England in 1952.
4. *Beyond the Glass* (Regnery, 1955)
   Clara has an intense new love affair, endures a harrowing descent into madness, and begins to recover.

White, Edmund

White has written a pair of autobiographical novels about an American boy growing up in the 1950s and 1960s. Although the theme of these novels is the gradual awareness and acceptance of the narrator's homosexuality, they also deal movingly with the universal themes of growing up, dealing with adults, being loved, being popular, and finding one's way in the world. White is also the author of the guide *States of Desire: Travels in Gay America* (Dutton, 1980).

1. *A Boy's Own Story* (Dutton, 1982)
   The nameless narrator reminisces about his childhood and adolescence during the 1950s and his conflicting emotions about his homosexuality.
2. *The Beautiful Room Is Empty* (Knopf, 1988)
   The narrator comes of age at the University of Michigan and in New York during the late 1950s and early 1960s.

White, T. H. (Terence Hanbury)

The Once and Future King, White's tetralogy of novels on the King Arthur legend, was the source for the play and movie *Camelot*. Bending both legend and history to his needs, this English author has fashioned a humorous, inventive, and compelling story that thoroughly debunks the inflated chivalric myths and shows a fascinatingly detailed picture of medieval English life and manners. The one-volume omnibus, *The Once and Future King* (Putnam, 1958) shows considerable revision, especially of *The Witch in the Wood*. Mary Stewart has also written a series about King Arthur (q.v.) and one volume of Henry Treece's Celtic series (q.v.) also features him.

1. *The Sword in the Stone* (Putnam, 1939)
   Two boys, Kay and Wart (who turns out to be King Arthur), learn the gentlemanly arts of jousting, hunting, hawking, and swordsmanship. A Disney film cartoon version of this book was made in 1963.
2. *The Witch in the Wood* (Putnam, 1939)
   This volume tells the story of Queen Morgause (the witch in the wood) and her four sons. Arthur, now the young king, battles with other kings and debates might versus right with Merlin. The account was titled *The Queen of Air and Darkness* in the omnibus volume.
3. *The Ill-Made Knight* (Putnam, 1940)
   The conflict between Lancelot, Guenever, and Arthur forms this book's central focus.

4. *The Candle in the Wind* (published with the three earlier books in the omnibus entitled *The Once and Future King* [Putnam, 1958])
Evil Mordred brings disaster to Camelot; Arthur dies.
5. *The Book of Merlin* (Univ. of Texas Pr., 1977)
This posthumously published volume is made up of sections removed from earlier volumes and reintegrated. It consists mostly of dialogue between Merlin and the defeated King Arthur, and of animal fables illustrating an antiwar theme.

Whittle, Tyler

Though this British author takes pains to stick to the known facts about Queen Victoria and the events of her long reign, his trilogy of novels shows the human and family side of the formidable monarch, making her seem much less stuffy and narrow-minded than she is usually portrayed. Those who enjoy this trilogy will want to read Whittle's equally interesting and well-written novel about Victoria's son, *Bertie, Albert Edward, Prince of Wales* (St. Martin's, 1974).

1. *The Young Victoria* (St. Martin's, 1972)
Victoria, portrayed from the age of seven until her marriage to Albert, is seen as a self-possessed and energetic young woman determined to have her own way.
2. *Albert's Victoria* (St. Martin's, 1972)
Between their wedding and Albert's death twenty-one years later, the couple worked well together, complementing each other's talents, always with much affection.
3. *The Widow of Windsor* (St. Martin's, 1973)
Family and public service help the queen conquer her grief in part, and Disraeli's help becomes indispensable.

Wibberley, Leonard

This prolific Irish author of children's books and light adult fiction is best known for *The Mouse That Roared*, a delightful satire on cold-war power struggles. Moviegoers will remember Peter Sellers's hilarious performance of multiple roles in the 1958 film of that book. Wibberley has set four equally amusing sequels in the Duchy of Grand Fenwick, the tiny European principality of six thousand citizens whose leading product is the fine wine Pinot Grand Fenwick.

1. *Beware of the Mouse* (Putnam, 1958)
   Though written second, this book is first chronologically, as it concerns the great crisis of 1450 when Sir Roger Fenwick and an Irish knight, Sir Dermot of Ballycastle, unite and prove victorious over the new French invention, the cannon. Despite the chronology, this book is perhaps best read after *The Mouse That Roared*.
2. *The Mouse That Roared* (Little, 1955)
   In 1956, Tully Bascomb leads the Duchy of Grand Fenwick's army of twenty-three longbowmen to war against the United States in order to win the generous economic aid usually allowed defeated enemies.
3. *The Mouse on the Moon* (Morrow, 1962)
   After Duchess Gloriana buys her sable coat and has plumbing installed in the castle, there are still enough U.S. dollars left over to allow Grand Fenwick to enter the space race.
4. *The Mouse on Wall St.* (Morrow, 1969)
   Grand Fenwick invests its chewing gum profit in the U.S. stock market, expecting to lose it all and thus spare the country runaway affluence.
5. *The Mouse That Saved the West* (Morrow, 1981)
   Grand Fenwick solves the world oil crisis by discovering "bird water," an alternative energy source.

Williams, Ben Ames

House Divided, a best-seller in its day, was frequently compared to *Gone with the Wind*. Its Civil War setting is quite authentic, though Williams never lets his thorough research intrude into the book's swing of action and romance. Though written from the aristocratic Currain family's southern point of view, the series portrays historical figures realistically or with a light revisionist touch—Jefferson Davis, for instance, is seen as a fool and a bit of a rogue.

1. *House Divided* (Houghton, 1947)
   The Civil War is seen through the eyes of the Currain family of Virginia, loyal friends of James Longstreet and the Confederacy.

2. *The Unconquered* (Houghton, 1953)
   The narrative continues through the Reconstruction years of 1865–74, focusing on the New Orleans branch of the Currain family.

Williams, David

English author David Williams came to mystery writing in his fifties after a successful career in advertising. His novels are in the classic British mystery tradition: intricately plotted intellectual diversions starring an amateur sleuth. Mark Treasure is a British merchant banker and sometime detective. He is a civilized, unflappable fellow, fond of golf and old buildings. He and his actress wife Molly live at a fashionable London address. The Treasure novels are an urbane mix of comedy and detection, a delight for fans of the well-made mystery.

1. *Unholy Writ* (St. Martin's, 1977)
   The alleged discovery of the manuscript of Shakespeare's *As You Like It* involves a cast of characters including Mark Treasure and a vicar who knows karate.
2. *Treasure by Degrees* (St. Martin's, 1977)
   A nearly bankrupt British agricultural school must accept financial aid from Funny Farms, Inc., of Pennsylvania.
3. *Treasure Up in Smoke* (St. Martin's, 1978)
   When the leading citizen of the West Indian island of King Charles is murdered, Treasure is on the spot to investigate.
4. *Murder for Treasure* (St. Martin's, 1981)
   A body located by a self-proclaimed psychic in a Welsh fishing village may have a connection with the competition between two foot deodorant manufacturers.
5. *Copper, Gold and Treasure* (St. Martin's, 1982)
   A schoolboy works with his elderly kidnappers to secure funds for a destitute old age home, but things go awry.
6. *Treasure Preserved* (St. Martin's, 1983)
   Lady Louella Brasset dies in an explosion after she opposes a redevelopment scheme in the Sussex town of Tophaven.
7. *Advertise for Treasure* (St. Martin's, 1984)
   After Rorch of the London advertising firm of Rorch, Timms and Bander opposes its takeover by an American ad agency, he has a fatal "fall."

8. *Wedding Treasure* (St. Martin's, 1985)

   After Mark and Molly's journey to a wedding in a village near Wales, the father of the bride is killed by a golf ball.

9. *Murder in Advent* (St. Martin's, 1986)

   The argument over the disposition of a copy of the Magna Carta dating from 1225 may have led to arson and murder in Litchester Cathedral Close.

10. *Treasure in Roubles* (St. Martin's, 1987)

    When Mark joins Molly in a weekend tour of Leningrad, one of the tourist group is murdered at the Kirov Opera.

11. *Divided Treasure* (St. Martin's, 1988)

    Hundreds of workers may lose their jobs when a candy manufacturing firm in North Wales is sold.

12. *Treasure in Oxford* (St. Martin's, 1989)

    The discovery of some rare architectural sketches leads to hot debate, behind-the-scenes maneuvering, and murder at the annual meeting of the Moneybuckle Architectural Endowment.

13. *Holy Treasure!* (St. Martin's, 1989)

    The campaign of Angela Culdlum, wife of the vicar of St. Martin's, to save the church is ended by a suspicious fall of roof slates.

Williamson, Jack

The Humanoids is a classic dystopia (the opposite of utopia) and one of the best "robot" novels outside of Asimov's Robot series (q.v.). It is a parable of how mankind, in trying to create a universe without risk, produces a universe without freedom. *The Humanoid Touch*, written thirty years later, pursues the same theme. Veteran science fiction writer Williamson has had a career spanning sixty years—he published his first story in 1928.

1. *The Humanoids* (Simon & Schuster, 1949)

   "The Humanoids," robots designed "to serve and obey, and guard men from harm," have carried this injunction to its logical extreme of now allowing humans to do anything that might conceivably harm them.

2. *The Humanoid Touch* (Holt, 1980)

   The Humanoids are only a legend to most of the inhabitants of a two-planet system populated by descendants of refugees from their benevolent despotism.

Wilson, Sloan

The Man in the Gray Flannel Suit added a phrase to the English language and, along with William H. Whyte's *The Organization Man*, epitomized the American 1950s. It portrayed the daily life of Tom Rath, middle-class, middle-aged corporate executive. Tom's ordinariness was well portrayed by Gregory Peck in the 1958 movie version. Wilson brought Tom in all his grayness into the 1960s in *The Man in the Gray Flannel Suit II*, where he goes through a midlife crisis of sorts.

1. *The Man in the Gray Flannel Suit* (Simon & Schuster, 1955)
   Thomas Rath works in a New York office, lives in Connecticut with his wife and children, and has memories of the War and a romance in Italy.
2. *The Man in the Gray Flannel Suit II* (Arbor, 1984)
   The 1960s find Tom working for a broadcasting company, divorcing his wife Betsy, and marrying his young assistant.

Wodehouse, P. G. (Pelham Grenville)

I. P. G. Wodehouse's special brand of inspired zaniness and verbal sparkle has entertained generations of readers and kept the belly laugh in English humor for over seventy years. Perhaps the best known of all Wodehouse's characters is Jeeves, the perfect gentleman's gentleman, who came to life in September, 1915, in the short story "Extricating Young Gussie," published first on this side of the Atlantic in the *Saturday Evening Post*. Jeeves's employer, the irresponsible young man about town Bertie Wooster, also made his debut in that story, and the pair quickly became favorites. Their adventures are always enjoyable, and the play between Bertie's irrepressible good humor and Jeeves's unflappable ingenuity is a delight in itself. David Jasen's *Bibliography and Reader's Guide to the First Editions of P. G. Wodehouse* (Archon Books, 1970) contains a complete bibliography and descriptions of Wodehouse's characters, including coverage of his many nonseries books and of his Mulliner and Drones Club books, which are all collections of short stories. Many of the Jeeves books are collections of short stories, too, but, for convenience, they are all listed below in chronological order as written. There are also two omnibus volumes of Jeeves narratives: *The World of Jeeves* (Jenkins, London, 1971) and *Much Obliged, Jeeves* (Jenkins, London, 1971). Northcote Parkinson's *Jeeves: A Gentleman's Personal*

Gentleman (St. Martin's, 1981) is a "biography" of Jeeves that will delight fans. Actor Edward Duke has been convulsing audiences since 1980 with his one-man show *Jeeves Takes Charge.*

1. *The Man with Two Left Feet* (Burt, 1933)
   This short-story collection includes the first Jeeves story, originally published in 1915.
2. *My Man Jeeves* (Newnes, London, 1919)
   More short stories are collected here.
3. *Jeeves* (Doran, 1923)
   These short stories had the English title *The Inimitable Jeeves.*
4. *Carry On, Jeeves* (Doran, 1927)
   Revised versions of stories in number 2 above are included here along with five new stories.
5. *Very Good, Jeeves* (Doubleday, 1930)
   This is another book of short stories.
6. *Thank You, Jeeves* (Little, 1934)
   His banjolele having alienated Jeeves, Bertie finds himself defenseless at a country house party with Pauline Washburn, to whom he was once engaged.
7. *Brinkley Manor* (Little, 1934)
   Jeeves does his best to patch up two broken romances, but Bertie manages to get engaged accidentally to Madeline Bassett. English title: *Right-Ho Jeeves.*
8. *The Code of the Woosters* (Doubleday, 1938)
   Jeeves eventually sets things right in this sinister affair involving an eighteenth-century cow creamer.
9. *Joy in the Morning* (Doubleday, 1946)
   Bertie and Boko Fittleworth stage a fake burglary in the hope of winning over Uncle Perry and getting his consent for Boko's marriage to his young ward, Zenobia Hopwood. Variant title: *Jeeves in the Morning.*
10. *The Mating Season* (Didier, 1949)
    The romantically inclined party at Deverill Hall includes Corky and Catsmeat Pirbright, Gussie Fink-Nottle, and Esmond Haddock and his five aunts.
11. *The Return of Jeeves* (Simon & Schuster, 1954)
    While Bertie is off at a school that teaches impoverished gentlemen how to take care of themselves, Jeeves aids his new employer, the ninth Earl of Towcester, in his amorous pursuits. English title: *Ring for Jeeves.*

12. *Bertie Wooster Sees It Through* (Simon & Schuster, 1955)
    Bertie's newly acquired mustache gets mixed reviews, but his attentions to a young girl bring him swift retribution from her fiery-tempered fiance. English title: *Jeeves and the Feudal Spirit.*
13. *How Right You Are, Jeeves* (Simon & Schuster, 1960)
    While Jeeves is off on a holiday, Bertie gets himself into big trouble over some old silver at his Aunt Dahlia's. English title: *Jeeves in the Offing.*
14. *Stiff Upper Lip, Jeeves* (Simon & Schuster, 1963)
    Bertie relays a friend's marriage proposal to Madeline Bassett.
15. *Plum Pie* (Simon & Schuster, 1967)
    This collection of short stories includes one about Jeeves.
16. *Jeeves and the Tie That Binds* (Simon & Schuster, 1971)
    Bertie's light fingers are exercised in aid of an old pal who is standing for Parliament in Market Snodsbury.
17. *The Cat-Nappers* (Simon & Schuster, 1974)
    A racehorse named Potato Chip has fallen in love with a cat.

II. Blandings Castle in Shropshire is the stately home of Clarence, the ninth Earl of Emsworth, and his pride and joy, the prize-winning pig Empress of Blandings. Other Blandings residents include Beach, the butler, and Lord Emsworth's son, the Honorable Freddie Threepwood, a young chap sprung from the same mold as Bertie Wooster. The Honorable Galahad Threepwood, Lord Emsworth's younger brother, also makes occasional appearances, as do his formidable sisters, Dora, Constance, and Hermione.

1. *Something New* (Appleton, 1915)
   A young American in London answers a newspaper ad for a young man to undertake a "delicate and dangerous enterprise," which takes him to Blandings Castle. English title: *Something Fresh.*
2. *Leave It to Psmith* (Doran, 1923)
   Lady Constance's necklace is stolen, and Freddie loses his girl, Eve Halliday, to Psmith.
3. *Blandings Castle* (Doubleday, 1935)
   Though published later, the Blandings stories in this collection belong here chronologically.
4. *Fish Preferred* (Doubleday, 1929)
   Lady Constance objects to the wedding plans of both her niece Millicent and her nephew Ronnie Fish, but Blandings Castle has its usual effect. English title: *Summer Lightning.*

5. *Heavy Weather* (Little, 1933)
   This book continues the saga of Ronnie Fish's determination to marry his chorus girl.
6. *Crime Wave at Blandings* (Doubleday, 1937)
   One Blandings story is in this collection. English title: *Lord Emsworth and Others*.
7. *Uncle Fred in the Springtime* (Doubleday, 1939)
   Uncle Fred, the fifth Earl of Ickenham, saves the Empress of Blandings from the clutches of the duke of Dunstable and sets a romance to rights for Polly Potts.
8. *Full Moon* (Doubleday, 1947)
   Colonel and Lady Hermione Wedge hope that a rich American bachelor will fall for their daughter Veronica.
9. *Pigs Have Wings* (Doubleday, 1952)
   The Empress faces some stiff competition when Lord Emsworth's neighbor buys a new pig, the Queen of Matchingham.
10. *Service with a Smile* (Simon & Schuster, 1962)
    Some consider this novel about Uncle Fred's return visit to Blandings one of Wodehouse's masterpieces.
11. *The Brinkmanship of Galahad Threepwood* (Simon & Schuster, 1965)
    Galahad has his hands full as one Blandings romance after another seems to require his attention.
12. *Plum Pie* (Simon & Schuster, 1967)
    This story collection includes one set at Blandings Castle.
13. *No Nudes Is Good Nudes* (Simon & Schuster, 1970)
    A nude painting owned by the duke of Dunstable is coveted by Lord Emsworth, who thinks it resembles his Empress. Variant title: *A Pelican at Blandings*.
14. *Sunset at Blandings* (Simon & Schuster, 1977)
    Left unfinished at Wodehouse's death, this novel concerns Galahad's efforts to straighten out his niece's love life. In a concluding note, Richard Usborne speculates on how Wodehouse might have finished the book.

Woiwode, Larry

Beyond the Bedroom Wall was a popular and critical success, being nominated for the National Book Award and the National Book Critics Circle Award. It is a saga covering several generations of the Neumiller family of North Dakota and Illinois. Its sequel, *Born Brothers*, concentrates on two members of the younger generation of the Neumillers who appeared as characters in the earlier volume. Taken together the two novels are a haunting portrait of the farms and small towns of America's heartland.

1. *Beyond the Bedroom Wall* (Farrar, 1975)
   The history of the Neumiller family is chronicled from the death of Otto, its patriarch, in 1935 to the late 1960s when the younger generation is growing up and moving away.
2. *Born Brothers* (DiCapua, 1988)
   The stories of Jerome Neumiller, successful physician, and his brother Charles, who has failed in his career and is failing in life, are told by Charles.

Wolfe, Gene

The Book of the New Sun has already become a science fiction classic. Originally planned as a tetralogy, but now up to five volumes, the series depicts an Earth (Urth) of the far future—a depleted planet revolving around a dying sun. Its humanity is so far past its great accomplishments that it has almost forgotten them. The protagonist of the series is Severian, who progresses from torturer's apprentice to potential savior of Urth over the course of five novels. Although the plot summaries of the novels may give the impression that The Book of the New Sun is a fantasy "quest" series, it is mainline science fiction. The technology, natural history, and anthropology of Wolfe's future world is painstakingly done, and his evocation of the far future is entirely convincing.

1. *The Shadow of the Torturer* (Simon & Schuster, 1980)
   Severian, apprentice to the Seekers for Truth and Penitence, is expelled from the Citadel when he allows a "client" to commit suicide.
2. *The Claw of the Conciliator* (Timescape, 1981)
   On his journey to distant Thrax to take up his new position of executioner, Severian inadvertently comes into possession of the Claw of the Conciliator, a gem with seemingly miraculous healing powers.
3. *The Sword of the Lictor* (Timescape, 1982)
   Severian retreats to the mountains after failing as an executioner,

and encounters the Alzabo, a creature that can reproduce the voices of those whom it has eaten.
4. *The Citadel of the Autarch* (Timescape, 1983)
   Arriving at the battlefield where his Commonwealth is fighting the Ascians, Severian renews old acquaintances, and realizes the destiny which had been awaiting him.
5. *The Urth of the New Sun* (Tor/St. Martin's, 1987)
   Autarch Severian embarks on a spaceship journey to a distant star in the hope of finding the "new sun" that will rejuvenate Urth.

Wolfe, Thomas

I. Wolfe's lyrical novels memorializing his large and quarrelsome family and the provincial atmosphere of his hometown of Asheville, North Carolina, occupy a unique place in American letters. Criticized for their formlessness, the books are nonetheless a moving portrait of a sensitive young man's coming of age. The well-known editor Maxwell Perkins recognized genius in the manuscript Wolfe submitted to him at Scribner and helped the author fashion these first two books into their final form.

1. *Look Homeward, Angel* (Scribner, 1929)
   Eugene, youngest son of the large and somewhat eccentric Gant family of Altamont (read Asheville), grows up, attends the local university, and leaves for Harvard.
2. *Of Time and the River* (Scribner, 1935)
   During Eugene's Harvard years, he strives for success as a playwright, accepts a teaching post at a New York university, and travels abroad.

II. When disagreements about his novel in progress caused Wolfe to break with Maxwell Perkins, he switched to Harper. But his untimely death of tuberculosis at the age of thirty-eight prevented the completion of the sprawling manuscript on which he had been working. Perkins and Harper's Edward Aswell both worked to shape these books into their final form.

1. *The Web and the Rock* (Harper, 1939)
   George Webber is followed from his childhood in a small southern town through college and his early years in New York, including an affair with a married woman.

2. *You Can't Go Home Again* (Harper, 1940)
   George breaks with Esther, meets a helpful editor who shepherds
   his book to successful publication, and travels through Europe as
   Nazi power rises.

Woods, Sara (pseud. of Sara Hutton Bowen-Judd)

Sara Woods put her firsthand knowledge of law office work to good use
in this engaging series starring English barrister/detective Antony
Maitland. With occasional assists from his famous uncle, Sir Nicholas
Harding, Q.C., and the loving support of his pretty young wife, Jenny
Maitland, Tony sorts out one complicated puzzle after another. His solid
deduction and skill at cross-examining witnesses enable him to prove his
clients' innocence and reveal the real culprits with style and plenty of
courtroom suspense. All Woods's titles are Shakespeare quotations.

1. *They Love Not Poison* (Holt, 1972)
   In 1947, Antony is just out of the service and taking up his law
   studies again when he and Jenny get caught up in a web of black
   magic and black marketeers.
2. *Bloody Instructions* (Harper, 1961)
   After a long day interviewing clients in his law office, elderly
   senior partner James Winter is found stabbed to death.
3. *Malice Domestic* (Cassell, London, 1962)
   Apparently this book was never published in the United
   States.
4. *The Third Encounter* (Harper, 1963)
   Old grudges and betrayals of former members of the French
   Resistance figure in this case. English title: *The Taste of Fear.*
5. *Error of the Moon* (Collins, London, 1963)
   Maitland and his uncle get mixed up in some secret missile
   research out in the moors.
6. *Trusted like the Fox* (Harper, 1964)
   This treason case with several surprise twists shows Maitland at
   his finest.
7. *This Little Measure* (Collins, London, 1964)
   This book, too, was apparently never published in the United
   States.
8. *The Windy Side of the Law* (Harper, 1965)
   A boyhood friend of Antony's needs help with his amnesia and his
   apparent involvement in drugs and murder.

9. *Though I Know She Lies* (Holt, 1965)
A young woman who admits to disliking her sister is accused of her murder.

10. *Enter Certain Murderers* (Harper, 1966)
Maitland defends a young man accused of murdering the black-mailer who drove his mother to suicide.

11. *Let's Choose Executors* (Harper, 1965)
A young woman is accused of poisoning her godmother, wealthy old Mrs. Randall, in order to speed up her inheritance.

12. *The Case Is Altered* (Harper, 1967)
A young French girl forced into a loveless marriage starts the trouble here.

13. *And Shame the Devil* (Holt, 1972)
When two Pakistanis sue the local Yorkshire police for false arrest, Maitland is retained to defend the police.

14. *Knives Have Edges* (Holt, 1970)
Tony risks disbarment and a murder charge in this case.

15. *Past Praying For* (Harper, 1968)
Camilla Barnard is twice tried for murder in this unusual case.

16. *Tarry and Be Hanged* (Holt, 1969)
Dr. Henry Langton, family physician and avid gardener, who has just been cleared of his wife's murder, is accused of a second crime, and Tony's successful defense seems unlikely.

17. *An Improbable Fiction* (Holt, 1971)
Tony defends Lynn Edison, a TV columnist, against charges of slander and murder in the death of her sister.

18. *Serpent's Tooth* (Holt, 1971)
In a bleak industrial town in Yorkshire, Maitland defends a seventeen-year-old boy accused of murdering his foster father.

19. *The Knavish Crows* (Collins, London, 1971)
While touring the United States by car, Tony and Jenny solve a mystery involving an inheritance.

20. *Yet She Must Die* (Holt, 1973)
Jeremy Skelton, a writer doing research on the famous Wallace murder, is accused of using that same method to kill his wife.

21. *Enter the Corpse* (Holt, 1973)
Maitland helps his friends, Roger and Meg Farrell, whose ex-con uncle's arrival coincides with the mysterious appearance of a corpse.

22. *Done to Death* (Holt, 1974)
Poison-pen letters in a peaceful English village touch off a lot of trouble for Jenny and Antony to solve.

23. *A Show of Violence* (McKay, 1975)
A Yorkshire boy of thirteen who seems to have appeared from nowhere is charged with murder.

24. *My Life Is Done* (St. Martin's, 1976)
Maitland and Jenny travel to the Northumbrian home of politician Graham Chadwick to investigate a blackmail attempt.

25. *The Law's Delay* (St. Martin's, 1977)
The outcome of Ellen Gray's murder trial hinges on a bizarre double murder that took place twenty years before.

26. *A Thief or Two* (St. Martin's, 1977)
Posh jeweler George DeLisle has been murdered, and the firm's costliest jewels have disappeared.

27. *Exit Murderer* (St. Martin's, 1978)
Tony defends a policeman accused of wrongfully arresting some smugglers who hide their diamonds in pots of cheese.

28. *This Fatal Writ* (St. Martin's, 1979)
Maitland's client is investigative reporter Harry Charlton, on trial for treason and suspected of murder.

29. *Proceed to Judgement* (St. Martin's, 1979)
A diabetic receives a fatal dose of morphine with his insulin shot.

30. *They Stay for Death* (St. Martin's, 1980)
Nasty gossip turns into a murder charge after four recent deaths at a nursing home.

31. *Weep for Her* (St. Martin's, 1980)
Was Emily Walpole encouraged to commit suicide during the séances she was attending?

32. *Cry Guilty* (St. Martin's, 1981)
A stolen Rubens painting leads to the murder of Maitland's client, young Alan Kirby.

33. *Dearest Enemy* (St. Martin's, 1981)
When his wife is murdered onstage, famous actor Leonard Buckley is charged with the crime.

34. *Enter a Gentlewoman* (St. Martin's, 1982)
Maitland finds himself pitted against his uncle in this scandalous case of divorce and murder.

35. *Most Grievous Murder* (St. Martin's, 1982)
While on holiday in New York, Maitland is asked by the British Ambassador to the United States to investigate the murder of a young African dignitary.

36. *Villains by Necessity* (St. Martin's, 1982)
Jim Arnold, a supposedly reformed thief, is caught committing a burglary.

37. *Call Back Yesterday* (St. Martin's, 1983)
Harriet Carr is convinced that Peter Wallace is her husband, although he is married to someone else.

38. *The Lie Direct* (St. Martin's, 1983)
Maitland defends John Ryder, on trial for treason after Soviet defector Boris Gollnow fingers him as a spy.

39. *Where Should He Die?* (St. Martin's, 1983)
Two poisonings, a contested will, and beautiful twin sisters engage Maitland's attention.

40. *The Bloody Book of Law* (St. Martin's, 1984)
When he defends a young man accused of jewel theft, Maitland finds himself on the defensive.

41. *Murder's Out of Tune* (St. Martin's, 1984)
Actor Richard Willard is charged with hiring a hitman to kill his estranged wife.

42. *Defy the Devil* (St. Martin's, 1985)
Simon Winthrop, accused of killing his grandfather, seems to be a split personality.

43. *Away with Them to Prison* (St. Martin's, 1985)
Two policemen are suspected of involvement with a protection racket linked to organized crime.

44. *An Obscure Grave* (St. Martin's, 1985)
Oliver Linwood has been arrested for the murder of his two-week-old nephew.

45. *Put Out the Light* (St. Martin's, 1985)
A dramatic production is plagued by what seems to be supernatural malevolence.

46. *Most Deadly Hate* (St. Martin's, 1986)
A custody fight may have led to the strangulation murder of Philippa Osmond.

47. *Nor Live So Long* (St. Martin's, 1986)
A Yorkshire village has been rocked by the murders of three young women.

48. *Naked Villainy* (St. Martin's, 1987)
Was Emile Letendre's father murdered by his own son or by a coven of witches?

Wouk, Herman

Wouk is best known for his Pulitzer Prize–winning novel, *The Caine Mutiny* (Doubleday, 1951), though all of his other novels have been popular successes as well. The two volumes listed below represent an ambitious attempt to capture an American era by examining the lives of Commander "Pug" Henry and his family. None of Wouk's readability has been sacrificed to the works' near monumental length and scope. Robert Mitchum played "Pug" in the recent television dramatizations of the two books.

1. *Winds of War* (Little, 1971)
   In his prewar progress toward a command of his own, "Pug" Henry runs special missions for President Roosevelt, including one dramatic encounter with Hitler.
2. *War and Remembrance* (Little, 1978)
   This sequel describes "Pug" Henry's successful naval career in 1941–45, the fortunes of his two sons, and his relationships with his two wives.

Wren, P. C. (Percival Christopher)

P. C. Wren was an adventuresome, Oxford-educated Englishman who worked his way around the world as a schoolmaster, journalist, soldier, etc., serving in both the British army and the French Foreign Legion. He spent ten years as a British government official in India and led Indian forces in east Africa during World War I. *Beau Geste*, the first of his romantic adventures about the French Foreign Legion, was a big success and was made into a silent film starring Ronald Colman. The 1939 movie version starred Gary Cooper, Ray Milland, and Robert Preston.

1. *Beau Geste* (Stokes, 1924)
   The three valiant Geste brothers—Michael ("Beau"), Digby, and John—star in this still very readable and suspenseful tale about the strange and desperate events at a Saharan outpost threatened by Arabs from without and mutiny from within, and the mystery of Lady Brandon's stolen sapphire.
2. *Beau Sabreur* (Stokes, 1926)
   Major Henri de Beaujolais, the French soldier who played a significant minor role in *Beau Geste*, returns as the sword-wielding hero who aids a beautiful American girl.
3. *Beau Ideal* (Stokes, 1928)
   Otis Vanburgh, an American, goes out to North Africa to search for John Geste, who is being held captive by an Arab tribe.

4. *Good Gestes* (Stokes, 1929)
   These stories detail the early exploits of Beau Geste and his brothers and comrades in the French Foreign Legion. Chronologically this book is the first in the series, but *Beau Geste* is the best book to begin with.
5. *Desert Heritage* (Houghton, 1935)
   This complicated tale of love and scandal features John Geste, the last of the famous brothers, and Consuela Vanburgh, an American with a secret past. English title: *Spanish Main.*

Zelazny, Roger

The versatile Zelazny has mastered several science fiction subgenres. His award-winning early novels, *This Immortal* and *The Dream Master*, are "new wave" psychological stories. His *Damnation Alley* is a post-Holocaust tour through a vicious America. And in the Amber series he created the imaginary world of Amber as the setting for his chronicle of fantasy and adventure starring Prince Corwin. Corwin's adventures apparently ended with *The Courts of Chaos*, but the Amber series has been revived with the adventures of Corwin's son Merlin.

1. *Nine Princes in Amber* (Doubleday, 1970)
   In this first volume, Corwin has an attack of amnesia and realizes that he is one of nine princes of the kingdom of Amber, each of whom wants to claim the throne.
2. *The Guns of Avalon* (Doubleday, 1972)
   Corwin labors under an evil curse as dreadful forces impede his search for his stolen birthright.
3. *The Sign of the Unicorn* (Doubleday, 1975)
   This episode shows the princes and princesses of Amber temporarily united to rescue one of their number held captive by evil beings.
4. *The Hand of Oberon* (Doubleday, 1976)
   When King Oberon is found missing, Corwin leads a group of his brothers in the search to set things right, while others work against him.
5. *The Courts of Chaos* (Doubleday, 1978)
   This satisfying conclusion explains many secrets of the world of Amber and clears up the mystery of Oberon's disappearance.
6. *Trumps of Doom* (Arbor, 1985)
   The focus is on Corwin's son Merlin, who follows his father to Earth, one of Amber's many alternative worlds.

7. *Blood of Amber* (Arbor, 1986)
   Merle Corey of San Francisco, a.k.a. Merlin, learns the identity of two would-be assassins.
8. *Sign of Chaos* (Arbor, 1987)
   Merlin discovers that he has a guardian angel in the form of a noble lady.
9. *Knight of Shadows* (Morrow, 1989)
   When he escapes from the Citadel of the Four Worlds, Merlin becomes involved in a series of new adventures.

Zola, Emile

I. Perhaps the showing of "Thérèse Raquin" on Masterpiece Theatre will spark a revival of interest in Zola. While his realistic portraits of alcoholics and prostitutes shocked the gentler sensibilities of the 1870s, modern readers will find his dark explorations on the themes of greed, obsession, and lust to be fascinating and powerful works. The twenty-volume Rougon-Macquart series is an extended family chronicle tracing certain hereditary traits through several generations. The series is also a detailed social history of France during the Second Empire (1852–70). Early English translations, including those by E. A. Vizetelly (who translated all titles here except *Nana*), for the authorized Chatto editions below were much bowdlerized, but for many titles there is no other translation available. Modern translations of several titles (numbers 7, 9, 13, 17, and 19) are available in the Penguin Classics series. J. G. Patterson's *A Zola Dictionary* (Dutton, 1912) is a helpful reader's companion to the series.

1. *The Fortune of the Rougons* (Chatto, London, 1898)
   This volume introduces the widow Adelaide, who takes the drunken Macquart as a lover, then follows the stories of her children, Pierre Rougon and the illegitimate Antoine and Ursule Macquart. The narrative shows the effects of the coup d'etat of 1851 on the small Provençal town of Plassans. First published in France in 1871 as *La fortune des Rougons*.
2. *The Rush for the Spoils* (Chatto, London, 1885)
   Rich builder Aristide Saccard enters extravagant Parisian society. Variant titles: *In the Swim* and *The Kill*. First published in France in 1871 as *La curée*.
3. *The Fat and the Thin* (Chatto, London, 1895)

The great Paris market Les Halles and its contrasts between rich and poor are seen through the life of Lisa Macquart in 1857–60. First published in France in 1873 as *Le ventre de Paris.* Variant titles: *La belle Lisa; The Paris Market Girls; Savage Paris.*

4. *The Conquest of Plassans* (Chatto, London, 1900)
The story returns to the town of Plassans and focuses on the granddaughter of Adelaide, Marthe Mouret, a weak-willed heroine who destroys herself and her husband. First published in France in 1874 as *La conquête de Plassans.* Variant title: *A Priest in the House.*

5. *Abbé Mouret's Transgression* (Chatto, London, 1900)
The evils of celibacy are the subject of this story which focuses on Marthe Mouret's son, a village priest. First published in France in 1875 as *La faute de L'Abbé Mouret.* Variant title: *The Sin of the Abbé Mouret.*

6. *His Excellency* (Chatto, London, 1897)
Eugene Rougon, a powerful and complex character, becomes prime minister under Napoleon III. First published in France in 1876 as *Son excellence Eugène Rougon.* Variant titles: *Clorinda; His Excellence, Eugene Rougon.*

7. *The Dram Shop* (Chatto, London, 1897)
This treatise on the evils of alcohol, focusing on the pathetic heroine Gervaise, was the book that brought Zola fame. First published in France in 1877 as *L'Assommoir.* Variant titles: *Gervaise; Drink; The Gin Palace.*

8. *A Love Episode* (Chatto, London, 1895)
This is a touching story about a Parisian widow, mother of a consumptive little girl, who falls in love with a doctor. First published in France in 1878 as *Une page d'amour.* Variant titles: *Helène: A Love Episode; A Page of Love; A Love Affair.*

9. *Nana* (Peterson, 1880)
Nana, a beautiful Parisian actress and courtesan, brings ruin to her lover and dies a miserable death. First published in France in 1880. Translated from the French by J. Sterling.

10. *Piping Hot* (Chatto, London, 1886)
The home life of the French bourgeoisie is revealed to be a mass of obscene secrets and private vices. First published in France in 1882 as *Pot-bouille.* Variant titles: *Lesson in Love; Restless House.*

11. *The Ladies' Paradise* (Chatto, London, 1896)
This book deals with life in a big department store. First pub-

lished in France in 1883 as *Au bonheur des dames*. Variant titles: *Shop Girls of Paris; Ladies' Delight*.

12. *How Jolly Life Is!* (Chatto, London, 1886)
    Set in a seaside town in Normandy, this story contrasts the self-sacrificing Pauline and the miserable hypochondriac Lazare. Variant title: *Zest for Life*. First published in France in 1884 as *La joie de vivre*. Variant title: *The Joy of Life*.

13. *Germinal* (Chatto, London, 1885)
    Etienne Lantier leads his fellow coal miners to strike against cruel and greedy capitalists. This book is regarded by most as Zola's masterpiece. First published in France in 1885.

14. *His Masterpiece* (Chatto, London, 1886)
    Claude Lantier, an artist modeled after Manet and Cezanne, struggles unhappily to express his genius. Variant title: *The Masterpiece*. French title: *L'Oeuvre*.

15. *The Soil* (Chatto, London, 1888)
    Zola's portrait of the French peasantry shows them to be a greedy and unprincipled lot who will do anything to acquire more land. Variant title: *The Earth*. First published in France in 1887 as *La terre*.

16. *The Dream* (Chatto, London, 1893)
    Zola tells the idyllic story of Angelique, a foundling raised by an old married couple who tend a cathedral. First published in France in 1888 as *Le rêve*.

17. *The Human Beast* (Chatto, London, 1901)
    Jacques Lantier is just one of the evil fellows who work for the railroad. Variant title: *The Monomaniac*. First published in France in 1890 as *Le bête humaine*. Variant title: *The Beast in Man*.

18. *Money* (Chatto, London, 1894)
    The world of high finance and the evils of speculation are the subject here as Saccard again takes center stage. First published in France in 1891 as *L'Argent*.

19. *The Downfall* (Chatto, London, 1892)
    The brutality of modern warfare is seen through the eyes of two young soldiers. Variant title: *The Debacle*. First published in France under the title *La débâcle*.

20. *Doctor Pascal* (Chatto, London, 1893)
    Pascal, a student of heredity based on the real-life figure of Claude Bernard, draws up a Rougon-Macquart genealogy, an apt conclusion to the series. First published in France under the title *Le docteur Pascal*.

II. The Three Cities series follows Pierre Froment, a skeptical priest, as he seeks to regain his faith. The books are more successful as documentaries than as artistic works.

1. *Lourdes* (Chatto, London, 1894)
   Pierre accompanies the crippled Marie de Guersaint, an old friend and sweetheart, to Lourdes, where she is cured. Translated from the French by E. A. Vizetelly.
2. *Rome* (Chatto, London, 1896)
   Pierre goes to Rome to protest papal condemnation of a book he has written. Translated from the French by E. A. Vizetelly.
3. *Paris* (Chatto, London, 1898)
   Pierre finally leaves the church, falls in love, and marries. Translated from the French by E. A. Vizetelly.

III. The Four Gospels series was left unfinished at the author's death. A fourth book, entitled *Justice*, was to have completed the set, which aimed to capture modern French life (at the turn of the century) and to demonstrate Zola's standards of morality and social progress. Each book in the series concerns one of the sons of Pierre Froment, chief protagonist of the Three Cities series listed above.

1. *Fruitfulness* (Chatto, London, 1900)
   Mathieu and Marianne are prolific parents in this anti–birth control tract. First published in France under the title *Fécondité*. Translated from the French by E. A. Vizetelly.
2. *Work* (Chatto, London, 1901)
   Luc Froment founds a utopian community. First published in France under the title *Travail*. Translated from the French by E. A. Vizetelly. Variant title: *Labor*.
3. *Truth* (Chatto, London, 1903)
   Marc Froment defends a Jewish schoolteacher accused of murder. The story is modeled on the Dreyfus case. First published in France under the title *Vérité*. Translated from the French by E. A. Vizetelly.

TITLE INDEX

SUBJECT INDEX

561

Janet Husband is the director of the Rockland Memorial Library in Rockland, Massachusetts. She previously served as an acquisitions librarian at the Thomas Crane Public Library in Quincy, Massachusetts. An active member of the Massachusetts Library Association, she served as editor of MLA's *Bay State Letter.* Janet Husband received her MLS from Rutgers University.

Jonathan F. Husband is the reader services librarian and program chair of the library at Framingham State College. Previously, he served as a chief bibliographer and serials librarian for Boston State College, and as a librarian at the Free Library of Philadelphia. He is also a reviewer for *Library Journal.* Jonathan Husband received his MLS from the Drexel Institute of Technology; he also holds a master's in English from the University of Pennsylvania.